FITBA DAFT

FITBA DAFT

◆

A story of total soccer addiction in Scotland and America

James Meikle

iUniverse, Inc.
New York Bloomington Shanghai

FITBA DAFT

A story of total soccer addiction in Scotland and America

Copyright © 2008 by James Meikle

All rights reserved. No part of this book may be used or reproduced by any means, graphic, electronic, or mechanical, including photocopying, recording, taping or by any information storage retrieval system without the written permission of the publisher except in the case of brief quotations embodied in critical articles and reviews.

iUniverse books may be ordered through booksellers or by contacting:

iUniverse
1663 Liberty Drive
Bloomington, IN 47403
www.iuniverse.com
1-800-Authors (1-800-288-4677)

Because of the dynamic nature of the Internet, any Web addresses or links contained in this book may have changed since publication and may no longer be valid.

The views expressed in this work are solely those of the author and do not necessarily reflect the views of the publisher, and the publisher hereby disclaims any responsibility for them.

ISBN: 978-0-595-49612-9 (pbk)
ISBN: 978-0-595-61175-1 (ebk)

Printed in the United States of America

For my love; Bunty forever.

For Dale.

For Kyle.

For Brooke.

For Mongo (John Mungo Wilson).

"MEIKLE
To John Kelly and Margaret Jane(Nee Miller) of 7 Albert Street, a boy; James, 8lb 2oz at Seafield Hospital on September 10th …

… (son kicking like crazy)

Edinburgh Evening News—1957 …

Contents

ACKNOWLEDGEMENTS.................................. xiii
PREFACE.. xv
FOREWORD... xvii
PRELUDE—1965... 1
PRELUDE—1992... 2
PRELUDE—CURRENT.................................... 3

Chapter 1	A FIELD'S WHAT YOU MAKE IT............... 5
Chapter 2	THE STREET, THE CIRCUS AND TAM'S RED BLOUSE.............................. 13
Chapter 3	A SMELL TO REMEMBER................... 24
Chapter 4	THE QUEST FOR SILVER.................... 31
Chapter 5	BIG ARCHIE, MR DEVLIN AND THE JANNIE TROOSERS........................ 36
Chapter 6	VALUE FOR MONEY....................... 43
Chapter 7	THE BEST TEAM ON THE PLANET.......... 52
Chapter 8	READING PRACTICE...................... 56
Chapter 9	SUMMER IN THE CITY.................... 65
Chapter 10	LEARNING TO SWIM IN THE BIG POND.... 71
Chapter 11	MOVIN' ON UP........................... 78
Chapter 12	A NEW CREW AND A HISTORY LESSON..... 86

Chapter 13	WHO SAYS HOSPITALS ARE GLUM?	91
Chapter 14	CATCH A FALLEN STAR	105
Chapter 15	A PURPLE PATCH FOR HIBS	110
Chapter 16	S..A … TUR..DAY NIGHT	118
Chapter 17	CLOUDS OF GLORY	127
Chapter 18	GIMME THAT OLD TIME RELIGION	131
Chapter 19	A TEMPORARY LULL IN THE FORCE	136
Chapter 20	SCRATCH THE ITCH	144
Chapter 21	SOAP POWDER ON THE PITCH	147
Chapter 22	QUE SERA, SERA	153
Chapter 23	GOING TO THE CHAPEL	161
Chapter 24	A HOUSE, TRANSPORT AND SEEKING MESSIAHS	167
Chapter 25	ON THE MARCH WITH ALLY	175
Chapter 26	BILLY'S BOOTS	183
Chapter 27	HEIGHWAY HOPE AND A TOUCH OF THE BEST	196
Chapter 28	A TASTE OF THE BIG TIME	204
Chapter 29	COMING TO AMERICA	211
Chapter 30	DIXIE LIQUER AND TURKEY RUN	240
Chapter 31	A GRAND HOUSE AND … A BOAT	249
Chapter 32	MEIKLE AGAINST CRUYFF … NOT QUITE	258
Chapter 33	THE STUFF OF DREAMS	264
Chapter 34	THE OLD GUY WITH HIS NOTE PAD	273
Chapter 35	A TRIP TO THE BEACH	279

Chapter 36	IN SEARCH OF A GOOD SIGNAL. 285
Chapter 37	YET ANOTHER GALLANT FAILURE 293
Chapter 38	JINGLE BELLS, JINGLE BELLS … 296
Chapter 39	FINDING GED. 301
Chapter 40	CARPENTER UNDERCOVER 308
Chapter 41	A GAME OF DIPLOMACY 315
Chapter 42	SEIZE THE PEN AND THE MOMENT. 318
Chapter 43	A SPARTAN EXISTENCE 323
Chapter 44	NEGATIVE JOLLIES AND THE MISSING MVP TROPHY 332
Chapter 45	GOING DUTCH & TAKING OVER THE TOLLIE 339
Chapter 46	MAMMY'S AWAY & THE YANKS ARE COMING. 347
Chapter 47	KICKIN' AROUND 358
Chapter 48	THROUGH KALIEDISCOPE EYES 370
Chapter 49	BACK IN THE LIMELIGHT 382
Chapter 50	A LEAGUE OF THEIR OWN 388
Chapter 51	A JAMBO-ROBBO DILEMMA 399
Chapter 52	CRAZY BUS. 404
Chapter 53	HIBS WIN THE LEAGUE 409
Chapter 54	SUNSHINE ON LEITH 414
Chapter 55	VIVA LAS VEGAS 427
Chapter 56	FROM HELL TO HEAVEN 438
POSTSCRIPT 2008. 453	

ACKNOWLEDGEMENTS

I need to thank Tim Mulligan, Roy (coach) Forey, Ged Corrigan and my Dale for test reading early segments and giving me enough encouragement to keep going.

I need to thank big George (Dode) Hunter and brother John for scouring Edinburgh pubs to confirm many names and places which were stuck on the tip of my tongue!

I need to thank my parents and grandparents for a consistent, well balanced upbringing. They taught me faith, good manners, an appreciation of basic work ethics and self discipline which ultimately shaped me to put family and community first.

I need to thank my Dale for writing a foreword most elegant and poignant.

I need to thank my Bunts for her patience throughout my fitba addiction and most recently on this book project.

Last but not least I thank God for the many blessings bestowed upon me and mine.

PREFACE

I love Scotland. I love America and Virginia in particular. I love Arlington. I love fitba—football-soccer.

A few years ago I set out to explain to my kids how I became the soccer addict they have known all of their lives. I also wanted to give them a feel for the environment in which I loved growing up. It was so different to theirs yet both had many great merits. As the project evolved it struck me that I might attempt to explain to American soccer fans how the soccer "passion" is born, nurtured and sustained. I also became anxious to illustrate to Scots how our sport has thrived here even through long periods without a major professional domestic soccer league; the traditional central driver for the beautiful game in all other parts of the world.

It also became important to me to articulate how a guy who "didn't make it" might ultimately still draw as much or perhaps more pleasure and joy from the game than the most successful professional ever could.

As I proceeded further I realized it might also be fun to explore how the Scots and Americans are both united and divided by a common language and how that principal also cascades through many regions within each country. A little social history and pop culture are natural by products of how the story unfolds but it always drifts back to its football roots. I think it's clear from the foreword that my kids got from it what I hoped they would. I really hope the sum of the above can also evoke some nostalgic pauses and a few laughs from readers on both sides of the Atlantic, especially those who share my love of fitba.

I also want to apologize in advance for the odd inaccuracy which results from me writing the great majority of this direct from my aging memory.

FOREWORD

I know what the streets of Paris must have looked like during the French Revolution. I know this because, by coincidence, I happened to be in Paris when France beat Portugal in the semi-finals of the World Cup in 2006 (*malhereusement* for them, they would shortly fall to the Italians). What I saw that evening, from the safe distance of my hotel balcony, was total pandemonium; streets overflowing with people, home-made fireworks displays being set off, strangers embracing and dancing (often wearing nothing but a French flag, tied toga-style around their body), deadlocked traffic as far as the eye could see, car-horns blaring in melodious rhythm, scooter horns sounding—the Parisians were even ringing their bicycle bells that night, if they had one to ring. And of course the echoing cries of *Vive la France!* It was truly epic in proportion and the uniformed *gendarmes* looked on at the revellers with sly smiles as they casually smoked their cigarettes without the least intention of intervening. Okay, so it had been an exciting match, with Zidane scoring the only goal from a penalty kick—but come on—this wasn't even the final.

I mention this because the precise place and time in which I first read the draft of this, my father's book, was very fortuitous. The particular environment in which I perused the early pages became significant to the insight I was about to gain into fanaticism. I had moved to Europe, a place, as I was to learn, that takes soccer—or football (that's *foot* in French, *fussball* in German, *futbol* in Spanish) quite seriously. I was to learn, in fact, that the Europeans rank football in importance just one notch above, say, God, and just one below their annual holidays.

I learned, situated as I was, just a few miles from Germany, who was hosting the World Cup that particular year, how to predict whether or not the Portuguese had won their game on any given night. Now, you should know first that there are vast numbers of Portuguese living in Luxembourg, and second that Portugal, though beaten by France in the previously-mentioned game, had quite a strong team that particular year. And so, there would be the tell-tale warnings of inhuman screams coming from the balconies of our apartment complex, reverberating against the trees. Next, the skies would erupt into a cacophony of car horns, the likes in sound and duration as we had never heard before. "I guess Portugal won again," I would say to my husband, dumfounded that it was still going on when we woke up (though, I have to admit, that next morning on my drive to work, passing through streets so full of Portuguese flags that you felt you were in Lisbon, rather than Luxembourg, it was hard not to get caught up in the enthusiasm. More than once, I found myself grinning and giving the "thumbs-up" to the many cars passing by in a flurry of cries and a blur of red and green.)

Then, there was the business dinner that I attended in Marseille. My colleagues and I were sitting in an elegant banquet hall in a five-star hotel eating fine French cuisine, everyone dressed to the nines, regarding power-point slides on an enormous screen. I admit, I had sensed a little bit of tension in the room, but what happened next still surprised me. Suddenly, a rotund Frenchman took the podium. "*Excusez-moi,*" he said, speaking into the microphone. He wiped the sweat off his forehead with a handkerchief pulled from the pocket of his immaculate suit. He explained in rapid French to the audience that the presentation had to be put on hold for a little while … and suddenly—*voila!*—a football game was being broadcast on the huge screen. Marseille was playing Paris and it appeared that the intense rivalry between these two teams warranted cancelling the business presentation. More amazing was that no one blinked an eye, although there were some relieved murmurs from the men in the room. Again I was baffled. (As Marseille won that night, the ill-fated presentation never did appear again.)

When I finished reading a later draft of this book, I was living in Paris during qualifying rounds of what will be the next Euro Championship. My apartment happened to be in the relatively lively area of Montmartre, and I bore witness to the spectacle that is the Tartan Army, as Scotland was slated to play France in Paris (and respectably enough, would beat France, although their ultimate end would not be a happy one). The French have something fairly important in common with the Scots: A deep-rooted dislike of the English. When the English (rugby) team had been in town, the streets were quiet and local pubs closed. When the Scots came to town it was a different story entirely, both, I suspect due to the more convivial nature of the Scots and to France's apparent affection for them. I watched in awe as the notoriously aloof Parisians warmly welcomed the kilt-clad, bagpipe-playing Tartan Army to their city. The French like a good show after all, and they were delighted by the theatrical die-hard nature of the Scots. The newspaper headline the next day read: *Les Ecosaais ont atterri sur le Champ-de-Mars!* (the Scots have landed on the Champ-de-Mars!) The story was accompanied by a picture of the Tartan Army marching beneath the Eiffel tower.

Now, don't get me wrong—I had lived in Washington through a few Redskin Super Bowl victories—I thought I knew a pretty hearty celebration when I saw one. But the intensity and passion that appeared to accompany these football games were unprecedented in my own American upbringing. It was something that I simply had never seen before and clearly something that I did not understand. But my father understood it—this I knew for sure. I could see a clear connection between these experiences of football in Europe and my father's own love of the game; he was, is, and always will be … fitba' daft. Reading this book in the particular context of football madness in Europe gave me some real-life traction with the phenomena that he attempts to explain (quite well, in my opinion) to the lay-person in this memoir.

I happened to be in Ireland when George Best tragically passed away and couldn't get over the 24-hour news coverage of the sad event. "They're like, obsessed with it over here," I told my father over the phone, utterly confounded. "What's the big deal?"

"You're joking, right?" was his reply. I could practically hear him shaking his head on the other end of the phone, thousands of miles away. He then sighed with the incredulity of someone who knows not how such apparent strong football genes on both sides of the family could have possibly evaded so completely each of his three children.

I knew that when I was growing up, I would hear my dad get up at some un-Godly hour to attend his weekend football matches. I knew that he was pretty good at football; he couldn't resist mentioning over breakfast later that morning—at a more reasonable hour—that he had scored one—or all—of the goals. I knew that I had once been made to drag an enormous, glass-encased framed Hibernian Football Club jersey thousands of miles on a transatlantic flight so that it could be displayed in his office; I knew at various points in time, our basements (location tastefully selected by my mother—conveniently hidden from company) had been nothing less than shrines to football—full of trophies, medals, team pictures, scarves and flags in green and white, and an array of newspaper clippings and other tattered memorabilia. I knew, even at that young age in our first house, that it was strange for a grown man to have what appeared to be a children's game with a miniature pitch laid out on the pool table and players set up (ready: in formation—eternally anticipating their match). And I knew we couldn't drive around Arlington, VA and pass any organized or pick-up game of football without a wistful glance in its direction from my father (depending on how long we were sitting at the traffic light, he might also immediately point out the best player or players with his discerning eye). So, in short, I knew there was a connection between the over-the-top behaviour I'd seen in relation to football during my time in Europe and my father's own love of this game.

But this was also a story about where my father had come from—of his own family and the era in which he came of age. As a child, it's difficult to imagine a world before you were born. It's always a revelation when later in life you wake up and realize that—*parents are people too! They have had the audacity to have whole lives and experiences before you came along to irrevocably change everything!*

What I learned in reading this book, is that it's a special sort of gift to discover the roundabout story of how your mother's wedding ring was purchased, or that your father almost—almost—had an alternate career as a singer in a famous band (but, for football, of course). I learned about the family dynamic of my grandfather, my grandmother and my aunts and uncles, and in fact that my father had had the same excruciating—and sometimes triumphant—school experiences as me. As I read this story, there were so many personal surprises or reminders about my father's or my own childhood: Granny was a 'Proddie'?; mom, the proverbial good-girl went clubbing at the age of 16!?; *We shall not be moved* is not a spiritual hymn (or perhaps it is depending on who you ask)?; "Frenchie" wasn't really the surname of the (French) people that lived next door to us when we first moved to America? And incidentally that large stag lying motionless in the trunk of their SUV had not actually been "sleeping," as I had mercifully been told at the time ...

It's interesting to see the very particular path that your heritage took; how but for certain events—some small, some more significant (taking an unfortunate tumble one day, moving to one neighbourhood rather than the other, taking one job rather than the next, being posted to one country instead of another) one's life may have turned out quite differently. Certainly, if my father had reached super-football-stardom at the age desired, he would not have subsequently met my mother ... and so on, and so forth.

Apart from my obvious interest in the familial history aspect of this story, I also got swept up in the nostalgia of a past era. It's fascinating to see—particularly now with my own expat experience—what Washington D.C. looked like, through my father's eyes in 1980. And more interesting, still, to go back further than that, to the world that was 1960's Edinburgh and to see what that world looked like to a mischievous, football-obsessed boy.

There's no doubt that this is a story about football. But it's also the story of a world in which you could still run onto the field of a professional football game and slap your favourite hero on the back; a world where pretty much the most sinister thing going on in the neighbourhood consisted of a black market for irons and hairdryers. It affirms the undeniable ties we have to our childhood and how those childhoods consist of elements that aren't as different as we might think: In fact, a Jewish kid from Brooklyn obsessed with the Dodgers looks a lot like a homesick Hi-Bee Scot from Drylaw, it turns out. It reminds us of that singular joy of a crisp unworn jersey, of a shiny new ball and an unoccupied field, imperfect and slanted as it might be; or the resourcefulness and courage children can exhibit when they want something badly enough—like making it to a football match.

This story was also a reminder to me and a testament to the fact that truth is stranger than fiction. What else could account for the incredible coincidences, the eerie connections between people and places over continents and time? I've always been an avid reader and lover of great epic tales, and so the anecdotes in this particular story, the lore and legends of both family, country and yes—football teams—appealed to me in that respect. And that's not even to mention the rich cast of characters itself—from Mrs. Boyle to "Bogie" and "Mongo" to Miguel-the-driving-instructor—that you couldn't make up if you tried.

The rich anecdotes of a time past were compelling and satisfying even for the non-fanatic football fan, it turned out for me. Among other things, it contained a surprising amount of hospital intrigue, some very odd nicknames, the meaning of the ominous-sounding "long-banging," some lessons in slang, a pink blouse-wearing football player, the appearance in multiple unexpected locations by the Duke of Sutherland, the "janny-troosers" incident of the 1960's, a short history of the English-Scottish rivalry (as if I didn't already know …), some fairly die-hard football fans on various continents, a little bit of unsuccessful thievery, a foul-mouthed parrot, some small moments of glory, and quite a few comebacks.

I also learned that I will probably never really know certain things in this life, at least as they pertain to football. Much like a great master painting is rendered meaningless by a viewer with no experience in painting or art history I will never be able to appreciate, as my father can, the difference between a football player with world-class technical skill and one that plays more like a dancer than an athlete. But I now know that that kind of complexity and artistry really does exist in the sport. And I can recognize that appreciation and commitment in my own love of, say, literature.

I will close with a small anecdote of my own. It's 1995 and I've just had dinner at the local *Chili's* with my future college roommate, who just happens to live a few towns away, in Great Falls. She walks me to my car and as we're saying our goodbyes, her jaw drops. "That is your car?!" she asks, looking at the not-so-subtle electric blue Ford Festiva.

"My dad's" I reply. She starts laughing and then explains. "I can't believe this! My friends and I have *seen* this car before, driving around McLean. We've been dying to find out what the license plate means! We've even placed bets!"

The licence plate reads: HIBS FC (that's Hibernian Football Club, and if you don't already know what that is, you will, very shortly). I don't know whether to be pleased or mortified that this car is in itself a local celebrity, but since I'm still seventeen at the time, I lean towards the latter.

"So," she says "you're about to put a year-long debate to rest. Please dispel the mystery. What *is* Hibs F-i-c?" (she says it phonetically) "And why is it on your dad's license plate?"

I sigh. I sigh very heavily. "Well," I reply, "it's a long story ..."

Dale Meikle
February, 2008

PRELUDE—1965

(Age about 9)

You know you shouldn't be doing this. You know it. You have other things to do. You have responsibilities. Important stuff. Likesay (my own spelling of my favorite slang word; the likes of) Geography lesson. It's involuntary compulsive body movement—up goes your hand; "Please Miss Westlake?" Instant response; "NO, too soon James!"

But you know you're going anyway, and with the older boys.

Not fair really. You getting off and leaving the rest of them in the stale, stuffy, smelly classroom trying to find the capital of some poor African country which won't even exist when they grow up. Desperate for the bathroom on account of stomach nerves but I daren't ask to go there right now.

Hand not even up this time but you're twitching and she's reading your eyes. She knows you well. "NO James, it's still not time." The class clock seems in ultra slow motion; agony.

Paul to my right, Stewart to my left. Pleased for me but resentful at the same time.

Adrenalin … mild fleeting guilt … Adrenalin … mild guilt … "OK TIME JAMES."

ADRENALIN … whoosh. I'm on my way.

PRELUDE—1992

(Age 35)

You know you shouldn't be doing this. You know it. You have other things to do. You have responsibilities. Important stuff. Likesay kids to drop off and pick up at their activities. Your garden is a mess, your car is filthy and you haven't been to church.

But you know you're going anyway, and with the younger men.

No problem. You'll catch up with all the chores later so it won't matter. Except you know it does; there won't be enough time and you'll be too tired and even the late mass will be well over.

But its never in doubt.

Adrenalin … mild, fleeting guilt … Adrenalin … mild guilt … "IS THAT YOU AWAY THEN?" I reply; "AYE, BY HON, WON"T BE LONG."

She says nothing but I know she's thinking; aye, sure.

ADRENALIN … whoosh. I'm on my way.

PRELUDE—CURRENT

Arlington, Virginia, USA
Spring 2003
(PRE-MATCH PREP)

It's 7:20 on a quiet Sunday morning. Spring is here and the weather is mostly good now. Cherry blossoms are out in vibrant Pinks. Azaleas and Dogwoods are about to follow in a mass of White. However this morning's a bit bleak with grey skies and a hint of rain. There was a lot of rain yesterday too. This means the ground is wet and your "Fix" could be in jeopardy. Butterflies churning. Dial the "Montgomery County Sports and Recreation Department Inclement Weather Line" So far so good; "All mens soccer on today" just another ten minutes without a change to that recorded message and I'm probably safe.

I'm in the smallest room in the house now. The doubt really is playing havoc with my stomach. This is ridiculous eh? I'm a forty-five year old Scotsman living in America. Been here a while now. Came for three years stayed for twenty three so far. Nothing changed about this ritual though just a bit more intense today because of the element of doubt. Much the same as that wee laddie in the primary school classroom back in Pilton. Seems like that was just yesterday. Doesn't time fly? Yet another cliché from the parents proving to be spot on. Don't you just hate that? But it is indeed thirty six years later and the feelings haven't changed a bit. Funny, eh?

Didn't pay enough attention to Chemistry and Biology to understand how all the stomach nerves thing works. I just know that excitement and anticipation send me here before a game of football (they call it soccer here in the US so as not to confuse it with their own Gridiron version). I've always just put it down to Adrenalin and maybe it is. It's one of those things you've explained to yourself. You're comfortable with the theory so you adopt it and never discuss it with anyone in case they complicate things with a logical contradiction.

To use a "Kornheiser" (my favorite Washington Post newspaper columnist,) a woman whom I live with and to whom I'm related by marriage, has observed and tolerated this ritual since we were sixteen years old. She often teases me about it;

"Is that you away for your pre-matcher son?" But I think she's both disgusted and impressed at the same time. I can just tell. Though its caused her many lonely days and nights she understands that if your still as excited about something (besides the obvious) at forty five as you were as a little boy there has to be something wholesome, maybe even magical about it. As always, she's right. To me, football has been and still is all of the above. The following story may at least explain some of the why.

1

A FIELD'S WHAT YOU MAKE IT

There was a sudden thud, thud, thud from below. I recognized this as the sound of Mrs Boyle's broom handle being applied to her ceiling with some force. Mrs Boyle had the misfortune to occupy the flat underneath ours in a typical three-storey council block in West Pilton, Edinburgh, Scotland; mid 1960's.

The area was the product of the baby boom era built quickly to cope with the overspill from the traditional inner city neighborhoods. It could just as easily be Glasgow or Dundee. The accent and slang varied a bit but the vast majority of men and boys of these areas had a couple of very basic things in common. Working class roots and an absolute passion for football. We were indeed "Fitba Daft".

The ultimate dream of almost every young lad was simply to one day pull on *the* dark Blue jersey of Scotland. With the rampant Lion badge stitched over a pounding heart the dream would always climax with a victory over the English at their hallowed Wembley stadium. Popular theory would paint the poor youth playing his way out of poverty to great fame and fortune. However any thought of financial rewards paled into the background versus the potential glory and national pride.

Only a tiny fraction of the dreamers would actually make the grade but the rest of us could still extract incredible satisfaction from playing, watching, talking and even writing about the worlds greatest game. With the right motivation and a little imagination a football pitch could be created just about anywhere but finding a ball was not always so easy. You could judge your true popularity by how many pals still wanted to play with you after your ball got burst. Anyway talking of innovation and making do brings me back to Mrs Boyle's place in the immediate plot.

My brother David, four years my senior, had challenged me to a one against one on the tarmac (blacktop) of the local school playground. His physical edge against my better skills could make for quite a competitive game.

My Dad's income as a grinder at Ferranti Electronics factory and my Mum's early morning cleaning job at the same firm combined to keep us fairly well off by average West Pilton standards. We were always well fed and cleaned with a treat thrown in on paydays. Because of this relative affluence I actually had a fairly new ball at the time. It was a "Wembley World Cup" quite glamorous looking with its large black and white dots with stars' autographs. Not authentic signatures of course but what can you expect for eleven pence ha'penny! The reason it was so affordable of course was that it was a very thin plastic job with a low life expectancy in an environment filled with broken glass and hungry dogs. Because it was so light, this ball would swerve suddenly and violently. Kind of like the Brazilians could do with a real ball except with no control whatsoever!

With no wristwatch between us we agreed upon the 5-half time 11-the winner format. No idea why the extra goal in the second half that's just how it always was. Within seconds of us starting the rain came pouring down in typical cold, swirling Edinburgh torrents forcing us to retreat indoors. With no let up in sight we decided to continue the game indoors. You entered our flat into a long narrow hallway (the "Lobby") which led off to the various rooms. The doorframes at either end would do nicely as goalposts and the well worn linoleum was a slick but acceptable playing surface. Refereeing was on the honor system which is where each player promises to be honest then proceeds to cheat like mad. We survived a gradually increasing volume of warnings from the living room where my Mum was trying to watch the TV (telly to us). We were tied at 8-8 when she finally emerged and announced the game was over. There was no whistle but the signs were absolutely clear. The only thing worse than no football at all is being prevented from bringing an exciting game to its conclusion. We decided to negotiate a compromise and knew we had a chance with my Dad out and my Mum clearly tired and vulnerable. After several minutes of orchestrated whimpering and pleading we wore her down and struck a deal. We could finish the game if we could find a smaller, quieter ball! No problem. Three pairs of thick woolly football socks wrapped tightly together approximately round and not a sound when dropped on the slick linoleum floor! The new ball was inspected and approved and the game was back on. The only flaw was that whilst the ball was silent we had to jump around much more vigorously to maneuver it and the overall racket was worse than before.

The score progressed to 10-10 as Mrs Boyle's broom handle signaled that she'd had enough. Just as my Mum appeared to abandon play I managed to toe-poke a winner in off the skirting board. David protested that the ball had actually unraveled before it crossed the line but our argument was halted with a wrap on the front door. Mum appeared and commanded, "Well ... open it then." I obeyed. On the other side stood the short stout frame of Mrs Boyle in her faded pinafore and cord slippers with the dirty white furry trim. She had a swarthy complexion under a dark mop of hair with one curler on each side. She had a forehead full of worry lines and deep smile dimples either side of her mouth. Teeth were sparse. She tried to put on her angry expression but could never really lose the kindly sparkle in her eyes. She clarified that, once again her peace had been shattered by "They bloody laddies Margaret; can yae no dae somethin' aboot them". Then she turned and ambled back down the stairs.

Her complaints were always tempered by the knowledge that her own boy (of forty—something!) Frank would return the favor on the next Saturday night. There was no resemblance physically or vocally but several pints at the "Doocot" or "Ferry Boat" convinced him that his surname was Sinatra. You'd hear him in the distance then clamor to the window to see him swaying down the street. Arms spread-eagled with open palms towards the heavens, head tipped back dramatically and at the very top of his powerful lungs; "Hi ... d..hid it ... M..Hi ... W..hay."

In predictably, unpredictable Edinburgh fashion, the rain stopped as abruptly as it started, the sky changed from grey to blue and the sun was suddenly beaming. Mum hurriedly encouraged us outdoors again and decided to do laundry. We chose a game of headers in the backgreen but were soon chased from there as she followed us out to hang her washing. Unfortunately the poles she needed to string her washing line were our goalposts! That done, she left to do some shopping and we were well warned, "One ball mark on those clothes and your both for it." Though "For it" was very non-specific it was a threat to be taken seriously. As we sat around pondering our next move we could see Mrs Boyle leaning out her kitchen window scanning the skies. Despite the recent exchange we all knew that if the rain threatened mum's washing before she got back, Mrs Boil would be out in a flash to save it. She would even iron it and fold it all before she passed it back upstairs. The word grudge was not in her vocabulary.

We decided to head for the "Big Field" (details on this venue later) where we were at least likely to be able to play uninterrupted for a while. We picked up a few fellow die-hards on the way and found a patch which was reasonably clear of doggie do. The ground was now really soggy so we decided we could re-enact a recent Scotland match which was still fresh in our minds. It had been against Wales at Ninian Park in Cardiff and played on a heavy, quagmired surface. The highlight for us was Denis Law (of Manchester United) sliding several yards through a mud puddle to force home a late winner.

We always adopted the identities of our heroes for our own games and Law and Baxter (Glasgow Rangers) were two of the most popular at the time. These were players who possessed great skill and balance. However it was something about their demeanor which pushed them a notch above the rest. Hard to quantify exactly but they had a certain swagger, a defiance, mixed in with a rye humor all clearly evident in their body language. This just fit perfectly with the role of Scottish underdog. It served as a coping mechanism for the many disappointments and enhanced the sweetness of victory when it came our way. Law and Baxter had their (and our) ultimate international success in a 3-2 victory at Wembley in 1967 over England, then reigning World champions. It wasn't the score itself which mattered as much as the domineering style of that victory. It *was* our dream. It was "Braveheart" magic long before Mel Gibson even met his long lost cousins.

Beating Wales was still good though so back to our game. A lad turned up with a "Filly", a proper leather ball which would add glamour and realism. The Filly was a brown leather skin filled with an inflated rubber bladder. The bladder was stuffed in through a small opening in the skin, inflated with a pump and sealed shut. The opening was then tied with a bright yellow lace in the same manner as a shoe. Waterproofing wasn't what it is now (just a rub with Dubbin leather cream) so the Filly would take on water like a sponge and between that and the large exposed double knot it could leave a serious dent in your forehead if caught at the wrong angle. We all had several attempts at emulating the Law goal and ended up plastered in thick mud from head to toe. As we trekked home my thoughts turned from the fun of what had just been to what would follow.

One of my least favourite rituals was the strip off in the draughty stair. No way would my mum let me in the house like this though. My fears were well founded as my mum, using a radar system which I have yet to detect, spied us from the window and warned us not to spread mud on other peoples landings on the way up(we lived on the top level of three). She was in position guarding the door when we got there and gave clear and concise direction, "Everything off, straight in the bath and make sure you clean it after you." Ah well, not a bad price for a pretty full day of fitba.

My Dad had been an orthodox left winger and played senior (professional) with Dunfermline and Leith Athletic and Junior (semi-pro) with a number of local teams. He was fairly useful and well addicted. During his national service he even once managed to persuade guards at the military jail in Perth to give him a Saturday pass to turn out for their local favourites; Jeanfield Swifts. He never did tell me why he was "In" but most likely some kind of football related distraction or for going AWOL for a date with my mum.

My older brothers John and David (the one I just cuffed in the lobby) both inherited the football bug but perhaps not quite to the extreme I did. I was, am and ever shall be a helpless addict and football is my drug. I'm convinced the cravings are just as strong as those of a smoker, alcoholic or junkie. For me, being aware that a game is available but not being able to participate is absolute agony. This is no different at 45 than it was at 7.

As a kid, every toy or game I ever got was somehow converted into a form of football. I started with my Lego builder block set. Three "Eights" topped with a "Four" for a head constituted a player. Different colored block combinations allowed for a great variety of strips (uniforms). The goalposts were a bit chunky and I used cuts from the orange stringy bags in which onions were supplied to create nets. The ball was borrowed from a blow football set. This was a really basic game where two opponents blew through straws to force forward a small plastic ball up or down any flat surface. The ball was a bit out of proportion with the lego players being up to their shoulders. We had a green tight piled carpet in a bedroom on which I would chalk the pitch lines. I spent thousand of hours playing everything from the local derby to the world cup final in this format. As well as operating both teams I was the referee, commentator and provided all the crowd noise.

One of the more interesting matches I ever had was when the three inch plastic figures from my "Battle of the Little Big Horn" game took up football. Custer lost the toss to Sitting Bull and it was all downhill from there for the US Cavalry. Without the boring limitations of reality, John Wayne and Roy Rogers played for the Cavalry and Geronimo scored a cracker from well outside the box for the Indians. I even had a World Cup for miniature (Airfix I think) soldiers. Romans, Commandos, Highlanders and Confederates all kicking around a dried pea!

As well as the basic addiction I was fortunate enough to inherit a decent amount of natural skill and instinct. This was the essential foundation for a budding pro but taking this to its full potential required constant practice and repetition. As you couldn't always raise enough people for a game all sorts of mini games and drills were developed so that there was always a way to hone skills, even on your own. The names and specifics of these would vary greatly from one area to another but almost everywhere in the world you would find some version of; Keepy-Uppy, Long Banging, Seven Byes, Tippy Tappy, Pairs, Barrie, Shapes and Curbie to name just a few. I offer my own description of these which will hopefully stir some fond memories or at least a knowing nod and grin.

KEEPY-UPPY was exactly as it suggests; keeping the ball in motion and never letting it touch the ground. Of course, no use of the hands was allowed. We would spend hours practicing this, mainly with the "strong" foot—right in my case. Most players seemed to accept that their "weak" foot was merely for standing on but I always made a conscious effort to develop a basic competence with my left. The knee, thigh, head and chest were also gradually introduced as the skill level improved. We would set ourselves targets and many of us could go into the hundreds before the age of ten. The ultimate goal was catching the ball and holding it still on the foot then flicking it up high and catching it on the back of the neck. America's latest soccer phenomenon, a naturalized Ghanaian-born kid called Freddy Adu, can do this and remove his shirt without dropping the ball!

LONG BANGING was probably the most common drill for us. Two players would set up goal posts (as always, using whatever we could lay our hands on) about twenty yards apart and take shots on each others goal with the emphasis on power rather than finesse. The toe-bashers dominated this but the players with a more subtle touch got their own back at TIPPY-TAPPY. This was the same basic idea except the pitch was usually a bit shorter and only one touch of the ball was allowed. This meant that save, control and shot all had to be combined into that single touch and there was usually a "No blootering" rule. This was a really effective control skill development method.

SEVEN BYES was also very popular. It required a minimum of three players consisting a goalie, (aka "Keeper") a crosser (winger) and a centre forward (the term striker hadn't yet surfaced). The basic idea was that the crosser would chip balls across the front of goal for the centre forward to attempt to score. The key rule was that you could only score with a "First Timer" which meant making contact with the cross before it hit the ground. This made for some spectacular volleys and dramatic diving headers with arms fully extended for maximum patter. The ultimate was a perfectly timed overhead (aka bicycle or scissors) kick into the postage stamp corner. A failed attempt which passed either side of goal or over the imaginary crossbar counted as a "bye" for the goalie. The objective then was to get seven goals before the keeper got seven byes. When one or the other was achieved we would start over after rotating positions. All sort of tricks were employed to avoid a turn in goal. Sudden hand injuries and the more desperate, "Oh I think I hear my ma callin' me in fir dinner" were very common.

No matter what type game we played, getting a genuine voluntary goalkeeper was a tall order. We often would simply bully (harsh but true) the meekest characters to go in goal. We even created a position called "Goalie-and (or "Backie-and") which meant you could be regular defender but revert to goalie when inside your penalty box! Over the years I played in Scotland even the best of the goalies I played with were all closet centre forwards desperate to show off their outfield skills in training matches. Scotland's traditional goalkeeping problem was no mystery then, simply the law of percentages at work. By contrast, although the USA is still in its infancy in soccer terms, because of its plethora of tradition in hand/eye co-coordinated sports, it has already produced a stream of world class goalkeepers (I'm thinking Keller, Friedel, Howard for starters).

PAIRS was yet another small game we often played. It required five people with two teams of two (hence the name) playing into one goal against a neutral keeper. The only rule was that both players had to touch the ball at least once before attempting a shot on goal. This was a very serious problem if your partner happened to be rubbish. The usual Goalkeeping problem also occurred in pairs. The way around it was for the volunteer to turn his back whilst someone allocated numbers. The volunteer would then choose up pairs and the keeper via these random numbers. The flaw was that the volunteer would almost always end up in goal. His subsequent dedication to his job was somewhat questionable.

CURBIE was a rather unusual one in which the non-football addict could participate. We used it to practice throw-ins (which we also called a shy ... don't know why.) Two players would stand at either side of the street, Shy the ball and try to make it rebound off the opposite curbstone and bounce all the way back across the street. I was never very keen on this one although I suppose it did develop the art of the long throw which in turn found its place in the game. There were likely earlier versions but I recall the first real proponent of this as Ian Hutchinson of Chelsea in the late 60's. He could have played Curbie on the M1 motorway!

SHAPES may have just been an Edinburgh thing as I have drawn blank stares on this one from people from other major cities. It was basically a rebounding game. Find a solid upright surface like a wall or a fence with some open and reasonably flat ground in front of it. Pick a small target area and start kicking the ball against it as many times as you could manage using only one touch of the ball each time. Start straight on with gentle inside foot taps then gradually move further back from the target and increase the force used. The name shapes is derived from the angles that start to develop essentially creating triangles between one kick, the rebound and you moving into position for the next kick. With a little practice this became a tremendous control and fitness drill forcing use of both feet instep and outside and keeping you on the move constantly. When you mastered the basics you could then introduce some chipping which would add a little more unpredictability to the bounce increasing the level of speed and challenge. This did much more for my left foot than reasonably regular attendance at church.

BARRIE entailed two players standing either side of a set of proper goalposts trying to deliberately hit the crossbar. A point was scored for a success and of course an extra turn earned as the ball rebounded back to your side. I became very good at this and carried it into many real games where my team would have preferred the ball under the crossbar. Seriously though this was a great drill for developing an essential component to the school of Scottish football superstar wanabees, the cheeky and arrogant deft touch. The ultimate example of this would be a flick from a standing start and with no back leg swing which dropped the ball perfectly over a defender into the stride of a teammate. Alex Edwards (Hibs) did this best in a famous New Years' derby against city rivals Hearts which we'll get to later. Pele wasn't bad at it either.

Again, there were no doubt a million variations of and names for these type drills but I bet they were more or less the same in Scotland as they were in mainland Europe, South America or North Africa (tell me Zidane didn't play all of these). These were vital ingredients in the making of likesay Georgie Best, Jimmy Johnstone, Charlie Cooke and Jim Baxter. The environment itself was also a crucial part of the deal. Maybe the kids now just get on real fields too soon or maybe video games are too affordable. With "better" organization these drills have now mostly been sanitized and put in pretty little instruction books and even on videos. They've been given boring formal names and are carried out in better organized, sometimes even custom designed, settings. However I loved them in their purest forms and remain convinced that is where they had the most profound impact.

2

THE STREET, THE CIRCUS AND TAM'S RED BLOUSE

An extension of this type of challenging practice were street pick-up games. Small standard metal corporation gates would be jammed open to create goals and after dark, lampposts would provide a glamorous "European" atmosphere (night professional games at the time were fairly rare, mostly European competition games or cup replays). To the uninformed eye the pitch would seem totally absurd. The goals might be approximately opposite each other but they might just as easily be several buildings apart or even around a corner from each other. They would be perceived to be full of dangerous obstacles like the lampposts, curbs, drains (which we called Sivers) and parked and moving cars. With some imagination these could all be converted into assets. Many a perfect one-two was worked with the curb and what better way to shield the ball than behind a moving vehicle. The ability to swerve the ball was vital as most shots were taken from ridiculous angles.

The biggest problem with street football was the amount of times the ball would find its way into the surrounding gardens. For the most part it was just a case of hopping over the small wire mesh fence to retrieve the ball. Pilton will never be famous for its gardens although there were a few tenants who managed to maintain nice lawns and flower beds. A few even tried vegetable patches but being edible in a poor neighborhood resulted in very few crops making it to harvest!

There were also a few "Territorial" gardens with tenants who protected them like their lives depended on it. A consistent feature of these was a deliberately overgrown thick hedge permanently swarmed by a second line of defence; midgie flies (gnats). We had one particular such garden on the corner of our block. Mr MacHolmsie was an elderly man with a bitter manner. He may have been a widower and had other reasons behind his demeanor—we didn't know. What we were all sure about was that he terrified us. His war cry which will be familiar to all street footballers "If it comes in here again I'll be putting a knife through it!" I only remember one time when he actually carried out his threat and I was just relieved that I neither owned the ball in question or had "the last touch". The last touch was the accepted method of selecting who should go in to get the ball back.

    I recall one lad, Andy Mac, being smacked between the eyes by a serious blooter (more power, less control) from big Tam Finlay. Big Tam was inept in most football skills but could put his toe through a ball with incredible force. If we managed to line him up properly he could get the ball the full length of a small pitch. He took penalties in the style of Tommy Gemmel (Celtic 1967) and rare was the keeper who wanted any part of them. Anyway from poor Andy's forehead the ball deflected about fifty feet in the air and eventually landed in MacHolmsie's garden. Andy was flat out on the pavement and concern and sympathy abounded but only to a point. As soon as he showed positive signs of life he was lifted up and tossed over the hedge on the basis of the last touch rule. Although it was only a couple of yards away there was a tremendous feeling of isolation on the other side. It reminded me of that feeling you might get when diving under the water at the beach; very close to the real world but definitely separated from it. It was a great relief to get back out without a verbal assault, grimacing look and shaking right fist.

    Initially there were very few cars in our streets, it was a predominantly walking or "Public transport" (Buses) environment. The main traffic was a steady stream of vans selling Ice Cream, Groceries, Meat, Coal, Milk and even the Ragman who would take our old clothes in return for a cheap plastic whistle or a balloon. Fish was on sale too but that came on a large wooden cart which a sixty something year old woman pushed all the way from Granton—a serious uphill trek. Some colour was added by our "Onion Johnnie" a genuine Frenchman in a loose hanging trench coat and beret, who hauled his fresh onions around on a shiny black bicycle with large mudguards. He took merciless stick from all directions and just kept smiling and reciting the merits of his produce. As people started to acquire cars it didn't take too long for the relatively narrow streets to fill up forcing us to seek other venues. As in my opening story, we often ended up in the Backgreen.

    To paint the picture, the "Tenements" which we more commonly called "Stairs" in Edinburgh, they consisted of six flats each. You entered the stair through a common door then there was one flat to either side. This repeated for three floors. These stairs were organized in a large rectangle with fronts facing the surrounding four streets. The resulting enclosed area, to the back of all the houses, was known as the Backgreen; "Backie" to us. The area immediately behind each stair was allocated to that particular stair and some iron clothes poles were dotted around for stringing laundry. Washing machines were pretty rare and dryers non-existent. Most washing was done in a large sink and put through a hand ringer—mangle—then strung outside to dry or draped on a "pulley" suspended from the kitchen ceiling. The alternative was a trip to the local launderette which we called the "Bendix" after the machine manufacturer I think—with a pocketful of small coins. A large patch was left in the centre of the Backie for communal use. I suppose the theory was that everyone would pitch in to keep this area tidy. However the reality was that it was mostly unclaimed, neglected and overgrown with a variety of weeds, including such staples as jaggy nettles, thistles and dockin leafs. The latter with their large, relatively soft leaves often provided the answer to a number two bathroom emergency for those too lazy or just too desperate to wait. This space had two large pluses. It was clear of all the washing poles and lines and a safe distance (less Big Tam perhaps) from all the back windows of the houses.

You tended to take on the collective name of your streets. We were the "Avenue" lads and we had a "Take-On" (challenge match) due against the "Drive". It was summer and so we had lots of time on our hands and with cash in constant short supply we were always looking for new and creative cost neutral pastimes. We decided to attempt to recover our wilderness area and create a little home field advantage for our take-on with the Drive. We all got caught up in it and set about our task with a great sense of pride and purpose. With no tools to speak of, weeds and tuffets were pulled by bare unprotected hands until, after a couple of hours' effort, the area was approximately clear. It was much more dirt than grass but reasonably even. Big tam produced a few planks of wood and ordered us not to ask where he got them. We then sifted through our regular Bonfire site which was always good for a few bent and rusty but salvageable nails. Using a half—brick as a hammer we formed scaled down goalposts. Wee Bobby (the majority of boys had either wee or big prefixes to their names) kept rabbits and guinea pigs so always had bags of sawdust on hand. We used this very sparingly to mark the lines. The result was hardly regulation but it was a great testimony to the power of fitba to inspire a bunch of enthusiastic youngsters. The site of our own little pitch in our own Backie with its enclosed stadia like feel, had the adrenaline pumping; "Bring on the Drive".

We won the match handily despite the absence of our stalwart goalie Lochie Brown aka "Lucky" Broon, at his grannie's funeral (I guess he was *lucky* to be one of the few not to be big or wee something). The goalposts did collapse several times during the match but never on anyone's head so all in all it was a pretty wonderful day.

At this stage (mostly very colloquial 7-10 year olds) take-ons were the nearest thing we got to an organized match and they subsequently offered a little more glamour than playing amongst ourselves or even playing with ourselves. (Which we all did with great regularity with or without the ball … Enough so to conclusively disprove the "Going blind" threats we all heard about). If that theory was true we would have all had white sticks by age ten. Any opportunity to play with or against new or fresh opposition offered a little extra spice and excitement.

I got one such opportunity to do so whilst visiting with a school pal; Alan Borthwick; Wee Borrie. We were pals all the way through primary and secondary. He lived in a very special place which at the time I thought of as far away. It was probably less than a mile from my "Bit" (our term for ones immediate neighborhood). He eventually ended up in a lot of bother for petty crime. Strange when I think back on how just a kind or cruel bounce of the ball here and there can contributes to our ultimate destiny. For example:

CRIME A—GRAND LARCENY CAR THEFT—I was caught stealing a Matchbox miniature car off a floor sample set in the toy department at Woolworths in Princess street. Mongo's wee brother Alex had been playing with it and was crying when we tried to leave as he had taken a real shine to a little red truck. So I pocketed it and we headed out. I was nabbed at the door by a store detective and hauled up to the "Woolies" office. They took my name and address and told me the police would be around to press charges. My stomach churned every time I came home for a month or so but they obviously only wanted to give me a fright. (Didn't they just!) This will be news to my dad but I have to assume the statute of limitations is up on it. Lucky me.

CRIME B—WANTON VANDALISM—Me and another pal Sorley got bored during the Summer holidays and broke several small windows at the Pennywell School. Someone saw and reported us and we could easily have been charged. However the decision was left to Mr Boyle, the School Deputy Head who I knew well through the fitba and he decided to defer formal action and let us off with a very stern warning and some school community service. Lucky me.

CRIME C—SMASH AND GRAB—I held Borrie by the ankles as he leaned through the St Oggies school office window (over a wide counter) and chibbed the drawer on the opposite side with a penknife to snag a full roll of lunch tickets. We came within a hair of getting caught cold as the Secretary came back from lunch a little earlier than during our recce of the previous few days. The tickets fetched a good price and we were on the decent fags and favored large Crusty (subs) lunches for several days! Nine times out of ten somebody would shop you for something like that at school. Amazingly nobody did. Lucky me.

CRIME D—THE GREAT SHOE ROBBERY—From the top deck of our school bus, Veitchy, Borrie, Paul and I plotted a robbery of the shoe shop next to Ye Auld Inn Pub in Davidson Mains. We passed it every day and decided it would be an easy in via the vulnerable looking skylight on the flat roof. We could haul out dozens of pairs of "Clerks" and "Doc Martens" and make a small fortune. Paul and I crapped out at the last minute. Borrie got nabbed and charged. Lucky me.

Point is; he got caught early and was prosecuted and never really got back off that track. With a fair amount of luck I never got on it before I was sensible enough to make better decisions. My parents have to also get some credit for sewing enough doubts in my conscience via constant reinforcement to keep me out of the great shoe robbery.

Anyway here we are at Borries bit in earlier, more innocent times. We mostly had very predictable street names as you just read. Ferry Road Avenue, Drive, Place, Grove … and then there was … West Pilton Circus! Yes, Circus! No doubt named by some sage and benevolent urban planning committee all of whom lived in mansions in Ravelston and none of whom ever visited the place or met the eventual occupants, except perhaps for a fake handshake on polling days. Maybe they were just trying to give Pilton a "Georgian" feel. Some hope. They probably genuinely thought they were being brilliantly creative. Anyway, the Circus was a great circular grassed park of about 200 metres diameter surrounded by dozens of stairs. It even had its own play park, tennis courts and bowling green.

My Mum was neurotically over-protective and rarely let me (Knowingly at least) venture far. On this occasion I had assured her it was just around the corner (Lie #1) a very clean house (Lie #2) and very religious people (Lie #3) and in a weak moment she relented on the clear understanding that I would be "Home in time for tea" which was code for, before my dad got home from work. The amusing part is none of us had wristwatches but we all managed to know and keep time just fine when it suited us. Back to the Circus then, a magical place in every sense. No lions or elephants but lots of clowns! The main hazards of the Circus park were broken glass and dogs' dirt. A lot of the occupants of the Circus owned dogs but, much like some of the children, they had to get by on their own wits. Male dogs roamed in packs and any Bitch in heat would be heavily serviced on the spot causing many an awkward question for the young mums patrolling the park with their freshly filled prams and straggling toddlers. On Borrie's strong recommendation I was quickly drafted into his team at the expense of a very frail looking lad with those dreadful pink national health spectacles and a faceful of freckles. The lad seemed greatly relieved to be dropped.

The opposition Captain was Brady, a short squat guy who turned out to be much more mobile and skillful than seemed possible at first glance. This was a common trait. We had so many gifted players who were out of shape but could compensate with great ball skills and balance, at least until they reached the professional ranks. A few even managed to get by there in what was clearly less than peak condition, something I just can't see happening now with such great emphasis on the technical aspects and physical fitness. Brady quickly recognized me as a "Ringer" and protested my inclusion. He explained that he would have no objection for a regular take-on but since this was for "The Cup" guest players were taboo. I soon learned that the cup was a small trophy no more than four inches tall. It was silver coloured metal on a tiny black plastic square. Not much to look at but clearly held in very high esteem based on the lengthy argument which ensued over participation by yours truly! The Cup was put up for grabs approximately monthly at the discretion of the holders and Borries team had been dominated by Brady's for several months. I was eventually declared ineligible but the decision was subject to review at half time.

Brady's team strolled to a large half time lead of 10-2. The other outstanding player they had was a stocky lad called Lex who was deadly despite having only one eye. Between them they dominated play and Borrie was his own side's strongest player but his main talent lay in the art of thievery where his small stature and subsequent ability to fit through small spaces was a great asset! Brady sauntered over to where I was huddled with Borrie and his mates. With a very smug grin he said "You can bring him on now … and Denis Law as well if he's handy". I did help make the second half a little more respectable but still ended up on the wrong end of 21-12. My first shot at a trophy blown and my first taste of the substitute's bench. Thirty some years later I still hate the bench as much as I did that day. To rub salt in I was late home for tea and got a sharp clip 'round the ear.

Back in the comfort of my own bit the quest for playing venues was never ending. We would occasionally try to play on the field bordering the very busy main Ferry Road. It had really good grass and a handy "NO BALL GAMES" sign which made a great goalpost. It had a line of small trees along the centre but we just got used to playing around them. It sloped away from the main road which helped keep the ball in play most of the time but it would still occasionally roll out over that road creating a danger for cars and pedestrians alike. As a result, these games usually were cut short by the arrival of the local cops in their Panda car—Volkswagen Beetles or Morris Minors painted Black and white and with the first American style "Nee-Naw" siren lights on top. "Now move along boys" was the standard instruction. At the time we thought they were just being mean but with 20/20 hindsight they probably saved a few lives as some of our lot were daft enough to think they could outrun or outmuscle a number 1 double decker bus.

The other regular location and the one we should have really used all the time was the centerpiece of the neighborhood and aptly known as "The Big Field". It was a vast open grassy area dissected by a concrete footpath with a small steep slope running alongside it to the lower half. This served as our sledding hill in Winter. The top half had two proper fields though you could barely make out the lines and the goalposts were kept in the "Auld Kirk" hall and only brought out for matches. The genius urban planners even decided to add a large square swing park in the middle. They started out with good intent but still managed to screw it up. They certainly showed some creativity as it had an old Royal mail van cemented in place as well as the more conventional swings, slide (Chute) and Monkey bars. But these were all set on a tarmac base and where there was tarmac there was always a ton of broken glass. There was also a lack of forethought in leaving a lot of sharp metal edges exposed ultimately causing cuts galore. Then we come to the most absurd feature of all—an eight foot high dark Green spiked fence with a large, padlocked double gate. Why on earth would you build an exciting new park in a neighborhood with thousands of not so well off kids and then turn it into Fort Knox? There was a Park attendant (Parkie to us) with a key and I guess he was supposed to unlock it at certain times. However he was usually half-guttered in the Doocot, Ferry Boat or Gunner. So we were left to stare at this very inviting new toy but could not touch it. Not acceptable! Inevitably we began scaling the ramparts but the spikes were large and deadly and a few serious injuries occurred in the first few days before we managed to borrow some tools and dislodge a selected spar and create our own permanent easy access. We had great fun there though the mailvan occasionally got stunk out by some kid who was too lazy to go home for a number two. On a recent visit I saw a new swing park in Sighthill. I was delighted to see it had a mulch/woodchip base, no sharp exposed edges and a small fence to keep toddlers safely in and even a couple of comfy benches for mum or dad—finally a designer with some common sense made it onto the Council planning committee.

I can't really explain why we didn't just use the Big Field all the time. It was a few hundred yards away, even less if we short cut across Pennywell School which I recall as the Holy Cross Primary (Elementary) until they got a new building at Trinity. It then served as an overflow annex for both Craigmuir and St Davids primaries the latter of which I eventually attended.

My mum even liked the big field as you could see most of it from our front windows and she could shout on us and just about be heard. Our hearing was selective depending on what stage the game was at—"Deafies" were common. She was always obsessed about us being where she could see us and would get seriously wound up if we were longer or later than expected. Then as soon as she was sure we were safe she would go ballistic in the other direction. I can't remember it clearly but my brothers always laugh about the time she got so mad at us she pretended to run away from home. "That's it I'm finished with the lot o' ye" she screamed, slamming the front door behind her. As we all stood bawlin' our eyes out "Mamie's gone—she's left us—wawawa …" she was actually hiding in a cupboard off the lobby. And my kids think I'm neurotic? Wonder where I got it?

On Sundays the Big Field hosted the mother and father of all pick-up games. Simply called the Sunday Game it would start around ten in the morning and go on through most of the afternoon with people coming and going throughout. There was no specific age parameters but it was unusual for anyone under sixteen to get in the game unless there was a really "Slow" spell. Even then a "Kid" in the game might barely get a touch of the ball. The starting teams were picked via what we called tic-tac method. Two self appointed captains would start about ten or twelve feet apart and advance towards each other via tightrope (i.e. heel to toe) steps. Whichever ended up with his foot overlapping the other would have first pick of whoever was there. The system was very primal. There was a real reluctance to pass over the known "Hardmen" as they might get upset and throw a punch so it wasn't just a skill based selection process. It usually ended up with remarks like "I suppose I'll have to take that useless c*nt as he's the only one left". If this was directed at you you're strength likely lay outside the realms of fighting and fitba and you probably had a "Wee", "Fat" or "Fairy" prefix to your given name! You were probably also in danger of developing severe self-esteem issues. But that was just tough.

The length of the pitch was adjusted as the numbers grew and shrunk but always on the fly; the play never even stopped for that. Width was virtually unlimited though it was bad patter to go ultra wide just to avoid a challenge. New arrivals would join in pairs using the "Cock'n'Hen" method. The players would stand behind a goal and secretly agree to be either Cock or Hen. The goalie would select one or other and the players would simply run into the game and letting everyone know "Am shootin' that way and he's shootin' the other way". It was amazing how you could have forty or more people running around in no particular style or colors with constant subtractions and additions and yet everyone managed to keep track. There was certainly no upper age limit and loads of old farts would come out to show they still had a wee bit o' the magic in them. Some played in shorts, some in jeans, some in sweatshirts, work shirts, T shirts and even one in string vest, regardless of weather. There were some really talented lads out there most of whom couldn't leave the fags and/or beer alone. I remember one guy, Paddy Bowen who had brilliant skills yet never played on any serious organized team. I'm sure you've heard the term a million times regardless of what sport you follow. "He was wasted" (This before the term became associated with overindulgence in drink or drugs!) Eddie Robertson was the string vest man. He had one move and would dribble round in circles until he tripped over his own feet. Not much laughing though as Eddie was just a wee bit unsteady and might pat your back one minute and kick your nuts the next! There was a wide cast of characters one of my favorites being Lucky's big brother; Tam Broon. We had several injury prone "Oscar merchants" as we called them but Tam was the best. After anything resembling a serious tackle he would do a full somersault and a couple of "Henners" (regular tumbles) before landing and announcing the latest tragedy; "Ahhhhh … ya bastard, it's really f***in broken this time, am no f***in jokin', it's a gonner". The thing is, it never actually was so the game would roll on merrily with Tam writhing and squealing in the background until he got fed up.

The only thing that could stop the Sunday game was the arrival of the Milk van. On Sundays it would stop by the big field loaded with a mixture of orange diluted juice and milk and do brisk business with the Sunday game participants. We young lads would become runners for the players getting their refreshments and getting to keep a few pennies of their change for our efforts.

I wonder if any kind of Sunday game has survived the Sunday opening of the pubs? I highly doubt it. In those days everything was shut on Sunday except the churches. No bad thing as many very heavy and regular drinkers gave their livers an enforced rest. A few hotels had Sunday booze licenses but the pricing was mostly out of reach of the Pilton clientele.

To make a transition from street to my early memories of organized football I'd like to recount my first (sort of) organized club match. I can still see and hear it vividly.

We were asked if we could put up a team against a newly formed boys' club; Granton Emit 10 (Years old) and under. I'm pretty sure the name was a revival from some years before. The man behind the team was Hugh McGauran whom I came to know and admire greatly. He was a true gentleman as well as a genuine enthusiast for youth football—obviously motivated by a love of the art of the game. He also had that special knack for getting the best out of a group of generally tough, cheeky and very street wise youngsters without having to scream constantly. His own son Shug (Hugo) junior was a decent player who had a good run with Meadowbank Thistle (Formerly Ferranti Thistle and now Livingston in the Scottish Premier League) including one cup match against Hibs where he came very close to pulling off a major upset. It was played at Tyncastle (Hearts FC ground) as Meadowbank's stadium was too small but they didn't want to give up home advantage to Hibs. The game ended up close but Shug had a half chance near the end which might have bounced a different way. It didn't and Hibs ultimately beat them but I imagine his dad was bursting with pride that day at Tynecastle. Shug followed his dad's example in coaching and eventually started Celtic Boys Club East based in Edinburgh (the existence of such a club in the mid 60's might have had a major impact for me but I'll get to that later). Anyway, Hugh senior had decided to start his own club and had already combed his immediate Granton/Royston territory and gathered up the best local players. He was arranging a few matches in the surrounding areas to complete his squad knowing that the obvious proper organization, training and real gear would be a magnet for those still just playing amongst themselves. He had his players sell "Pontoon" (Blackjack) tickets and had raised enough money to buy a full set of sky Blue Coventry City strips which was considered one of the smarter ones out at that time. This was before every team brought out new jerseys every year to maximize income!

We happened upon Emit playing at Pilton Park and got talking to Mr McGauran who quickly offered us a challenge. We acted like we were also sort of an organized team and told him that we played in Red and our home park was at Craigroyston School (a small white lie). Our quickly nominated player/coach was my pal John Mungo Wilson nicknamed "Mongo" after his middle name. I would be his assistant. We shared a passion for fitba and Hibs in particular. He wasn't the best player but held his own considering he had a serious heart condition resulting in what was called a pigeon chest. He had to go through several operations at a very young age. He always said he would have his own ice cream van and he did just that. However I was saddened to hear that he still died around thirty years of age. My favorite memory of him was when he commissioned the TV lounge at the Western General Hospital Heart Specialist wing so that our gang could come and watch the European Cup final on the color TV. This was amazing for us as the only place we'd seen color TV's to that point were in very posh shop windows. So even as he recovered from open heart surgery he was thinking of fitba and his pals. A good man; gone far too early.

Committing ourselves to Red wasn't too bad as a few of us had Man Utd or Aberdeen shirts so we were off to a good start. The balance scrounged what they could and apart from the Deek (Derek) Weir and Tam's; Broon and Big, we looked pretty respectable. Deek had a thing that looked like a tie-dye before they'd even been invented it was more towards purple than red. Tam Broon had a mostly red T shirt but it had something likesay "Campbell's Soup" in big letters on the back. Isn't it ironic that nowadays every shirt is plastered with sponsors' marks but at that time it was really uncool to have anything more than a badge and a number! A man ahead of his time. Big Tam's situation was even more desperate. He came from a large, mostly skint (Poor) family and the best he could do was borrow his sisters red blouse which, to make matters worse, was shiny silky material and had a bit of a frilly collar and cuffs which he'd unsuccessfully tried to tuck under. By now his face was red too. "What the hell's that supposed tae be?" shouted Mongo. "Look" says Tam "It's the only f**kin red 'hing a cood git 'n if any o yae say the word Poof ye'll be gittin belted one ... am no missin our first real match". Nobody was going to argue with that besides, Mongo knew we needed Tam for taking goal kicks.

We started with a slight setback as, on our arrival at Craigroyston School the goalposts had been taken down. This was a frequent occurrence to stop the likes of us wearing out the goalmouth areas with our various mini games. However they hadn't moved the field hockey goals and that slightly smaller scale field was a good fit for us. They had even left the nets on which was pure and rare nectar to us. Mr McGauran was the ref and we agreed upon 30 minutes each way and no "Offsides" rule. We put up a very respectable show, losing 6-4 and immediately after the game, Mr McGauran asked Alex Sim (Simmy) and I if we would like to join his team. He clearly had Simmy tagged for a defender as he was tall, strong and fast and stubborn as a mule; very hard to get past him. I was tagged as a playmaker in midfield. We both accepted on the spot and were given a full kit each. It is hard to express the level of excitement and elation I got from this. I took it home laid it out on my bed; Beautiful brand new crisp shirt, shorts and socks. I stared myself into a daydream. This was just the inevitable first step towards the number 10 jersey at Easter Road (Home ground of my beloved Hibernian FC—Hibs for short) or maybe even a Dark Blue one!

3

A SMELL TO REMEMBER

I was at last part of organized football matches with real strips, marked pitches, full size goalposts and proper referees. About the same time I joined Granton Emit I made my debut for St Davids Primary school "Wee" team. Instead of first and second teams we of course used our favorite "Big" and "Wee" terms. The Big (ie First) team was generally drawn from the oldest grade (Primary VII) boys who were mostly 11-12 years old. The Wee team from Primary VI; ages 10-11 and there was a little cross over between the two. It was a very rare exception for a 9 year old primary V boy to make it into a team. This was part of Primary school folklore and I was lucky enough to become one such exception. I can only recall two others in my era at St Davids, both a few years ahead of me. One was Stevie Hancock who went on to become a Celtic player at a time when they had one of the strongest squads of players in the world. The other was Willie Murray who had a good run with Hibs as part of one of their strongest ever squads.

Primary school matches were usually played on Wednesday afternoons with the exception of the annual knockout competitions which were played Saturday mornings. The team was managed by one of the male teachers who would do most of his "Scouting" around the playground (I don't recall any try outs). He'd post the line-up on the school notice board the day before a match. This preceded all the tactical overload we now have and so *the only* formation was a 2-3-5. The numbers and positions were consistent and a couple of generations of players were identified by these:

1. Goalkeeper

2. Right Back   3. Left Back

4. Right Half   5. Centre Half   6. Left Half

7. Right Wing   8. Inside Right   9. Centre Forward   10. Inside Left   11. Left Wing

Those selected would then go to the school office and pick up a jersey (you had to find your own shorts and socks). I had often fantasized about my name being on the list and when it happened I went a little queasy! Again, not yet really expecting to be under consideration I was having a kick around (just for a change) with my pals at "Play time" (our term for recess) and had made no effort to visit the notice board. A buzz started around that I was on the Wee team for the next days' game against Royston. I sprinted to the main hallway where the notice board was located and there it was; 10. Inside Left James Meikle. I proudly collected my jersey from the school Secretary. It was well worn with quite a few old tears and repairs evident. Repairs were made with only approximately matched threads. Material was very thick cotton with light and dark blue hoops and badly "Yellowed" white button down collar and cuffs. It looked more like what we'd have called a Rugby shirt but that's because these were so old! When I showed my dad he confirmed that they were the exact same jerseys which were in use when he and my Uncle Charlie played for St Davids 30 years earlier! Nevertheless it was perfect and had a great starchy smell which I can relive at will. It turned out that the set had been supplemented a little over the years and as a result some had slightly broader scaled stripes than others. It didn't matter a toss. I was now a real St David's player on the eve of the most important match on the planet.

Neither St David's nor Royston had our own proper pitch so we played all our matches at the nearest High School; Ainslie Park. The Big team played on the perfect flat pitch which ran alongside the railway line and the Wee team played on what we affectionately called the "Seagull's Hill". The hill part is self explanatory it was on quite a steep slope. It was also fairly close to the Firth of Forth. Perhaps the Seagulls congregated there because it was one of the first large open spaces near the water? Regardless of why, they did so in abundance and it was always odd to find a football pitch covered with feathers. The grass was exceptionally lush, probably with all of the natural fertilization the Seagulls provided. Nets were also a great rarity in those days but Seagulls Hill had some of the best ever. They were very deep and secured to green poles at the rear corners. As a result they hung loose but straight with plenty spare gathered on the ground. When hit by the ball they would ripple for several seconds. To pure and true fitba addicts this ripple was the ultimate thrill; way beyond anything which might be achieved with the right (or left) hand.

I slept very little that night. I was nervous but also sweating like a pig on account of wearing the St David's shirt underneath my cotton pajamas! I also kept it on under my school clothes when I got ready the next morning. With laces tied together my boots were slung around my neck, a gesture to signify to the whole street that I had a serious game today. Conceited I admit but irresistible at that age. My teacher Miss Westlake was not a sports fan and hated the idea of me getting out of class early to play football, especially as I was the only one. It didn't seem like nearly such a big issue the following year when a few more of my classmates were involved. You might recall from the prelude that she made me wait a while but had to let me go eventually as her boss, Mr Caden our Headmaster was also fitba daft and wanted a result! After my very rushed compulsory trip to the loo, I joined the rest of the team at the school gym and we started the fairly brief walk to Ainslie Park. We didn't mix much with the class above us and in their eyes I was a little upstart keeping one of their mates off the team. As a result, by the time we crossed the "Ghostie Valley" path—over an old abandoned air raid shelter which inspired many a tall tale in this part of Edinburgh—I was lagging behind on my own having given up trying to spark a conversation with a very reluctant audience. This didn't concern me too much as I felt confident that I could win them over once we got on the field.

We made it to the Ainslie dressing room where we picked a peg each and hung up our school uniforms. This typically was Grey flannel shorts and a white shirt with a sweater over it in Winter. Socks were grey wool and laced black shoes. The identifying items were a "Snake" belt (stretchable with an S clip fastener), a school tie and a blazer. These were all in school colors. Even although lots of the kids were poor everybody had a school uniform. There was no excuse not to as we were very much a welfare state at the time and those whose families couldn't afford to buy the uniform were given special vouchers to obtain it from a place called Clarence House.

Early in the game I won over my teammates when I got a corner all the way into the goalmouth. Not a great feat you might think unless you're familiar with the "Mouldmaster" ball used in these games. This was the thickest, heaviest, hardest plastic ball you can ever imagine. A thwack on the thigh with a mouldmaster could make even the proudest boy cry openly and leave a large dimpled strawberry for several hours. God forbid you take one full force in the crown jewels! Royston beat us 4-2 but it was still a brilliant high to take part. I was allowed to join the group on the walk home.

I was starting to develop a reputation for being one of the better young players in the area and unfortunately my head was growing along with the recognition. At such a young age with so much ambition it was difficult to keep a balance between confidence (which you most definitely needed) and conceitedness (which you did not). Fascinating and perhaps unique to Sports that arrogance on the field was so admired but arrogance off the field abhorred. Anyway I was about to be put in my place by a very humbling experience which proved the theory that just when you think you're the cat's meow somebody better comes along. Our second last match of the season was against Silverknowes and they also had a player who was starting to get some attention. He was tiny and had closely cropped red hair which was emphasized by the all white Silverknowes jersey. He looked like a cross between Jimmy Johnstone and Billy Bremner. However they were clearly Wing and midfield respectably whereas he was truly both combined. He was all over the place with the finest display of precision dribbling and shooting I had seen to that point. He destroyed us and we ended up on the wrong end of a 7-0 thrashing. You've probably heard of him. His name was Gordon Strachan and he ultimately fulfilled one of all of our very popular fantasies of the time ending up playing for Manchester United. Earlier he helped Aberdeen to great success (also with Alex Ferguson at the coaching helm) and he even managed to extend his career well past the average age by virtue of a very strict diet and training regime. He helped Leeds to a title then went on to a successful coaching career at Coventry, Southampton and most recently Celtic. Before all that materialized our paths would cross again and I'm pleased to say that this time we would both be on the same side.

We were part of the Leith District Schools and they held their annual knockout tournament towards the end of the school year. The Big teams played for the Leith Schools Cup and the Wee teams played for the Mackie Shield. To us at the time, these were no less important than the Scottish Cup and we had our own version of Hampden Park (Scotland's national football stadium) at a place called Warriston. The pitches there were kept for special occasions and were immaculate with very lush green turf even in the goalmouths. Lines were always freshly painted and they had smart orange nets and matching corner flags. They even had individual team changing rooms.

The two finals would be staged there on an early Summer evening with a few hundred paying spectators (and even more fence jumpers) looking on. Relatively speaking it was a very glamorous setting and along with the prospect of a very smart medal, it provided great incentive to all participants in the tournies. I remember my Mackie Shield debut not so much for the match itself but for the strips we wore! You will recall the old, tatty (but still wonderful) jerseys I described earlier. When I went on Friday afternoon to pick up my jersey for our Saturday morning game the janitor said "No jersey son, the teacher's bringing the kit the morn". I was a little concerned but on checking with a few of my teammates they had all got the same story and were just as mystified. On arriving at the match Saturday we were all shocked, confused and delighted to find a full set of relatively modern strips awaiting us! What we knew as "Sheffield Wednesday" at the time—Royal Blue with white cuffs and Vee neck, solid Blue Shorts and Blue socks with two white bands near the top. They even had numbers. The Teacher explained that these were kept for cup and shield matches only and as we had barely progressed in either tourney for several years the kit was in very good shape. Unfortunately in my three years of primary school football we only advanced once past the first round. Even that took a replay (7-2 after a 2-2 draw) against Leith Victoria, a tiny school located right on the water at Newhaven. In that match I encountered the only primary age player who could kick a mouldmaster the full length of the field. He did so whilst scoring against us from a goal kick. It was at Wardie school down the hill of the smallish field in the quadrangle and ably assisted by our fumbling goalie but still quite an achievement.

I was subsequently a very jealous onlooker at many Warriston finals but there were other ways to reach the hallowed turf. One was via the annual Primary schools athletics contest; the grandly named "INTER SCHOLASTICS". I made it there once and only as a last minute stand in for Jimmy Watt who got sick or went on holiday (can't recall which) the week of the competition. He was all about speed and I am not. I was left embarrassingly in the wake of a pair of Whippits from Davidsons Mains and Hermitage. Anyway I didn't want to run around the track there I wanted to play fitba.

Leith was originally a town in its own right and many Leithers still consider it so. Probably evolving from that it was still a separate school district from the rest of Edinburgh. I didn't know much about the Edinburgh Primarly schools set up though I recall reading in the "Pink" (Saturday sports edition of the Edinburgh Evening News—printed on Pink rather than White paper—I never knew why) about their annual tourney; the "Inspectors Cup".

Every year, towards the end of the season, each primary school district in Scotland would have to select a team to compete in the national championship; the Wilson Cup. Most readers can probably recall their local representatives in this as it was always well publicized. For us this would mean a mention and maybe even a photo in the "Craigie Veitch" (Schools football) section of the "News" as well as coverage in Leith's own weekly "Gazette". The quest to make Leith Select was quite arduous. First you had to be nominated for the initial trials with each school typically sending one to three players. Again it was big news around the playground when I was nominated to go the trials which were also held at Warriston but without the nets and corner flags up. I was very excited but also quite nervous knowing how steep the competition would be. My angst was well founded as there were absolutely no passengers at this level.

It was really tough going with about fifty very competent players on hand. Being shunted in and out at a variety of positions made it difficult to impress. I managed a decent short dribble down the right wing and delivered a couple of well placed long passes. It seemed harsh to be judged on such brief snapshots but I was one of the lucky ones invited back later for a second session. This time there were only about half as many and we all got more or less a full game. I felt I did really well but knew it would be a very fine line between making and not making the final squad. At that time you didn't have the size of squad you commonly have now, just your starting eleven and maybe two or three reserves.

The following days were very tense as there was no announcement made on the spot. On leaving we were just told to "Watch the paper the next few nights." The tension turned to joy when, on the Wednesday, squashed between the Racing form and a speedway report "Final Pool—Leith Schools Select" was listed and the last name was "J Meikle—St David's." Gordon Strachan was the one who went on to most fame but several others made their mark playing or coaching at various levels. Right off hand I can remember Davie Trotter (Goalie) and "Bin" Anderson of Clermiston, Ian (Rammo) Randal of Groathill, Neil Forbes of Wardie, Stevie Torrance of Holy Cross, Brian Weddle of Hermitage, Davie Rodgers of Bonnington and Gordon Smith—can't remember his school but would never forget his smile full of teeth and skills galore. The Manager was Mr Duncan, Headmaster of Craigmuir Primary who probably had no formal coaching badges but seemed to know the game at this level as well as anyone.

We were brought together for a couple of practice sessions and the final warm up for both sides prior to Wilson Cup play, was an annual challenge match against the Edinburgh Schools. The Edinburgh team came from a much larger catchment area of schools and had traditionally dominated the fixture. It was played at Warriston in front of a decent sized crowd and we won a thrilling 6-5 victory. We were drawn against Midlothian away in the first round and went out 2-0 to two goals by a lightning fast shocking blond haired centre forward. My disappointment was doubled as I was a reserve for the match and only made a fleeting and fruitless appearance near the end. However the overall experience was still fantastic at such a young age. We all met in Leith Saturday morning and were driven through town in a luxury coach. The venue was Victoria Park, home of the famous local Junior (Semi-Pro) side; Newtongrange (Nittin) Star. The dressing rooms seemed very grand and the kit was already laid out. (White Shirt, Black shorts, White Socks) It looked as if it had just come straight out the packet!

The roar as we entered from the tunnel under the stand seemed deafening to our little ears. The pitch seemed massive. Afterwards we made full use of the grand facilities and then both teams attended a banquet with hot pies, sandwiches and piping hot tea (with a ton of sugar in my case) and as many chocolate biscuits as you cared to have. Several of these were pocketed for the journey home. We were then coached back to town. I remember thinking if this was how great the Junior Pro's had it, how brilliant would it be at the top level? As if any of us needed it our appetite for the big time had been whetted some more. I did have one regret from the whole experience—I don't have a copy of the team photo. At that time there were tracksuit tops for the reserves and so I appeared in the team photo in the paper with mines on. I deservedly took some stick from my mates who were getting a bit fed up with my growing conceit at the time. Subsequent silly pride meant I didn't send a copy to my Grannie Miller in Wick which would have been the most reliable way of preserving it for the future. I only recently learned via a chance meeting with big Pilton Hibee; Johnnie Ramsay (now of the Swedish houses) that my dad also played for Leith and once roasted future superstar Davie MacKay.

4

THE QUEST FOR SILVER

Okay. I'm in organized football now both school and club and I've earned it but do I fully appreciate just how lucky I am? I think back … For Mongo, Big Tam, Wee Bobby and most of the Ferry Road Avenue gang, our semi-organized take-on on the hockey field at Craigroyston was probably as near as they would ever get to playing in proper games. Yet they all loved the game passionately and they were not bad players. Only a guess but I bet less than one in fifty fervently enthusiastic boys made it on to any kind of proper teams at that time.

In contrast … I have three kids. They have grown up in America in the 80's/90's. They're great kids (who's aren't?) and politely supportive of my playing habit as well as my Hibs and Scotland addictions. They've been to quite a few DC United games and had a good time. Eventually it all has to rub off, right? Read on.

Whilst visiting Scotland, my eldest daughter went to Easter Road with her granddad to a Hibs versus St Johnstone game in the middle of November. This was bound to be the final conversion. When she got back I said "Well?" She said she thought the terracing banter was very "Creative and colorful and the language was terrible but at the same time hilarious". Funny how the circumstance and delivery of a swear word can make its offensive value vary so much. Her clearest memory though was of how cold she was and that when she was handed what she thought was a cup of hot chocolate it tasted disgusting   like mince! She'd never heard of Bovril. Can you believe that? Such neglect on my part. So I pressed her; "But how was the game?" "Pretty good, they really go after each other, don't they? It's all very fast and intense". I'm getting desperate now. "So what was the score?" "They won, eh Hibs, I think. 1 or 2 something. Well there was certainly lots of singing at the end so they must have won, eh, yes. I got a bit squashed coming over a funny little bridge on the way out". One down. (To her credit she went back much later to do "Study Abroad"—ironic as she was actually born at Simpsons in Edinburgh—at St Andrews and even learned the Highland Fling)

My son got to see DC United win the Major League Soccer (MLS) final amid 53,000 in driving rain at Robert F Kennedy stadium in Washington. He got to feel the electricity of an Italy versus Mexico World Cup match at the same stadium with flags, horns, war paint and all! For goodness sake he even got his photo taken with a life-sized cardboard cut-out of Pele. Converted, right? I asked him recently where his souvenirs were. (Posters, pennants et al) "In the basement in a box somewhere" and as if not to hurt my feelings "But I'm keeping them really safe, dad". Meanwhile Stanley Kubrik and Weezer are plastered all over his walls and to make matters worse my brother John took him to a Pearl Jam concert and recently sent him an electric guitar! A potential football addict. Not. (To his credit he does wear a Scotland jersey quite frequently, loved Trainspotting and has all the Rebus novels!)

So, for soccer at least, it's down to my youngest; another girl. A promising start. She's quite aggressive, a big asset in the very early stages. She makes it onto a "Select" level team and wins the Most Valuable Player Award. She's also at the DCU championship game. She even criticizes substitutions made by her coach in a couple of games and explains her reasoning to me in the car on the way home. Her arguments are crisp and logical. She's there, right? Oh but wait. It's Junior year in High School with a ton of homework every night. It's the busiest and most critical year for college preparation. She's also a Captain on the school dance team. She wants to sing in a band that she and her friends are forming. There's a boyfriend on the scene. Something's got to give. What will it be? Ah well, came pretty close on that one! (To her credit, at the school concert, she sung "A love a lassie" and "A wee doch'n doras" in front of several hundred people wearing her granny's tartan shawl).

So overall they are fairly lukewarm about the game amidst a variety of other activities and priorities. Maybe that's the key? They have so many more options than we did. Is it possible to become fully hooked to sport as a player, fan or both without focused weekly exposure and heroes to adore and aspire to? I have my doubts. Point is, despite their relative apathy my three all got to play in organized teams with the best of kit, on good pitches with referees, linesmen and the lot. Does this seem fair to Mongo and big Tam? Who can say? Different times in different places.

Anyway back in mid-sixties Pilton, I'm in the mix and on my way. Having made the first steps the next is obvious and mandatory for an aspiring superstar. The Holy Grail—a winners' medal. Groathill won the Mackie Shield so I knew a few boys who had them. I was pure rotten with jealousy. It wasn't fair (poor me) but with St Davids' futility in the Mackie Shield/Leith Schools Cup and Leith

District Select being unable to progress in the Wilson(Scottish) Cup I was stumped. There was one other chance. I grant you, not as glamorous as those mentioned but nonetheless a football tournament with shiny Silver medals for the winning team. The Boy Scouts summer six-a-side tournament. And I did it but never got the medal yet! Here's how and how not.

In our neighborhood two things were sure to get you a merciless slagging. Joining:

a. The Boy Scouts.

b. The Boys Brigade.

Let's take b first. Affectionately known as the "BB's" and cruelly referred to as the "Bum Boys" I don't know much about them to be honest but that didn't matter. I do know that they wore outfits which included mega flairs and a funny hat. They looked like midget sized sailors and when spotted in this uniform they were immediately barraged with the following ditty:

"Gonna join up, gonna join up, gonna join up the Boys Brigade
Two bob (Shillings) a week, *uck all to eat and a pair o' baggy troosers
To wear in the street"

The Scouts got it just as bad. There wasn't a set song but rather an assortment of expletive filled insults about ones manhood focusing mainly on the shorts, the neck scarf and the toggle.

The crowd at number five the Grove were the worst. They would just hang around the stair door waiting to spot and exploit a weakness in any passer by. Most Scouts and BB's took whatever detour was necessary to avoid them but God help them if they didn't. Despite the high risk factor the possibility of a medal or a camping trip often persuaded us to swallow our pride, if only temporarily.

Truth be known the Scoutmaster should have chased us as it was very obvious that we'd join about the same time each year but never last very long. He knew the score but that's the irony. He was willing to compromise his own principals and "Bench" his regular Dib-dib-dobs in favor of our motley crew. Why? Because he knew we were good at fitba and he wanted a trophy and some glory for his troop by fair means or foul. A devil's bargain then. A win-win situation if only we could win the "Annual six-a-side Boy Scouts Tournament—Edinburgh North".

This was staged at Inverleith Park, a fairly typical sprawling municipal inner city park with the maximum possible volume of minimum-sized football pitches squashed into the available space at a variety of angles and grades. There was one large communal changing pavilion with zero security so it was just as well none of us had any tangible valuables to worry about. It did have one big communal shower but it wasn't used much by our age group as we were still at the "Scared of Willie scrutiny and comparison" stage. Over the years a couple of these pitches (Numbers five and six I think) had become infamous for their ridiculous slopes which made even the Seagull's Hill appear flat. They were so bad that if you took a bye kick from the "High" end and started it on a straight trajectory, it would get airborne by the edge of the penalty area and, with sufficient velocity, go well over the crossbar at the other end. That was quite possible with a direct tailwind. Conversely, if you were facing directly into the wind from the "Low" end you could easily put a bye kick over your own crossbar. The ensuing corner kick could be a serious threat for a goal if aimed at the center spot (talk about an inswinger)! But hey, the pitches had lines and goalposts and they would certainly do for the Scout tourney in search of silver.

No surprise. We romped through it as most of the other teams were not filled with "Ringers" like us. In fact I got the clear impression that most of the players would have been much more comfy in a Rugby scrum. Not least because of the Cramond troop who had to be told to stop picking up the ball and running with it! I remember Wee John Calvie just destroying them—scoring about six unassisted goals in that game. Davidson Mains gave us a decent game in the final but it was never in doubt.

Mission accomplished then. Job done. However the scoutmaster wasn't quite as daft as we thought. He got the cup presented to him but told us the individual medals would be kept for presentation at the end-of-year Troop party and that good attendance until then would be a requisite. The party wasn't until December which meant six more months of trying to sneak past the Grove crowd et al to the Friday night sessions. Don't get me wrong some of the activities were really great fun but it was just bad patter to admit that at the time. We resolved to grind it out and we got to go on the troop camping trip to the Pentland Hills. That's a story in itself but nothing to do with this fitba theme. We finally conceded defeat when "Bob-a-job-week" (Annual fund raiser) started to seriously encroach on our free time. I just wonder what that bastard done with our medals? Probably sitting in the drawer of some boy who never kicked a ball in his life and could care less. So I would have to wait a while longer. Still, as a dedicated Hibbie and a Scotland diehard I had learned great patience. I was used to the concept that success would taste all the sweeter after a very long wait.

5

BIG ARCHIE, MR DEVLIN AND THE JANNIE TROOSERS

I emerged from the changing rooms at Ainslie after a midweek primary schools match and was approached by the man I recognized as the local schools Skipping (Truant) Officer. At this stage I had never skipped school but I was still a bit panicked trying to work out why he wanted to see me. Maybe he'd want me to shop (clipe, grass, tattle on) one of my pals, some of whom were known to miss the odd day without proper explanation. That would be awkward. He was a tall, strong upright man with a couple of strands of jet Black, glistening brylcreamed hair dangling over his small dark piercing eyes. He wore a long grey overcoat, unbuttoned and swinging around the hem as he moved. He looked just like I imagined a hardened detective would.

He gave me a serious stare; "What you been up tae then son, eh?"

"Nothin' Sir, honest—you sure its me you want?"

He cracked a sly devilish smile then said "Oh its you awright but dinnae worry its for fitba, no for "kippin" (skipping school—truant).

What a relief. "How'd ye mean Sir?"

It was big Archie Buchanan one of the stalwart supporting cast in the Hibs famous five (Smith, Johnston, Reilly, Turnbull, Ormond) team of the late 40's, early 1950's. I knew his name well and had probably seen him in a few photos but I'd never made the connection. I'd heard him mentioned in football talk amongst my dad and uncles "Aye, big Buchanan was some player, unsung hero in that team." Even though I'd never seen him play I'd nod knowingly.

He explained that he combined his Truant Officer duties with the Leadership of the Edinburgh Thistle Boys Club which we all recognized as a feeder for Hibs' farm system at the time. He'd watched me in the playground and at a few school games and thought I had what it takes. I was delighted and very excited. There was a drawback as I was only ten and the youngest team they had was under thirteen. He suggested I would get great experience training along with the cities finest youth prospects even if I might have to wait a year or two to be playing very much. Archie had plenty school and local authority connections so we were well looked after. I agreed to give it a go.

We trained in the Norton Park gymnasium which literally backed onto the main stand at Easter Road stadium home of my beloved Hibs. The whole set up seemed very professional to me with a club leader, a fitness trainer and individual Managers and assistants at each age group. There was some circuit training, lots of exercises with the ball and some indoor football to round off the session. Benches on end were the goals in a very tight space where close control was vital. "Nutmegs" (putting the ball clean through opponents' legs) was the ultimate achievement. Through Archie's connections we also got an hour of swimming at Abbeyhill baths just a few minutes walk away. Then a bag of piping hot chips (Fries!) smothered in brown sauce for the number one bus journey home. Absolute luxury. I slept without rocking on training nights.

I played in the odd friendly but with three years' worth of very good players ahead of me games were scarce and my feet were very itchy. Various other clubs were beckoning with under eleven and twelve sides and the promise of immediate playing time. I had to play and so it was time to move on. Not sure why but shortly thereafter Edinburgh Thistle went through a re-organization and were scaled down considerably without any teams below the age of fifteen so just as well. There was a revival ahead for Thistle in the not too distant future and I would be back.

About this time the biggest moment of my developing football career occurred. It was incredibly exciting in the moment. However in the long run, it was probably the worst thing that could have happened to me!

The Granton trawler (Commercial fishing boat) owner Mr Devlin (Tom I think but I'm really not certain) was a Director of Celtic Football Club who were dominant not only in Scotland at the time but Champions of all Europe. He came to visit our school and brought the Scottish Cup with him. The janitor (Jannie—Custodian) came around gathering up members of the "Big" team and we were taken to the Headmaster's office. Our Headie, Mr Caden and Mr Devlin were obviously old pals. We were introduced to Mr Devlin and taken outside to the playground where we were allowed to peruse and handle the famous old trophy. It was amazing. I only had it for a few seconds but I was gone in my own little fantasy world thinking of all the great names and games associated with it. I did one quick raise above my head with both hands on it—a practice for later in life. Something a Hibs player has not done for 100 years! It was thrilling, exhilarating. By no coincidence photographers from the (Edinburgh Evening) News and the (Leith) Gazette showed up and took our photo. I still have that one!

We were dispersed back to our classrooms but then the Jannie asked me to hold back. I did and when everyone was gone he walked me back over to the school office where Messrs Caden and Devlin waited. They explained that Celtic already had me "On their books" and that I would be formally signed as soon as I was old enough to do so, probably by means of an "S" (Schoolboy) form when I went to Secondary (High) school. This would never actually come to fruition but the ecstasy of that moment is mines to cherish for ever. I floated home on cloud nine; desperate to shout the news to everyone I passed on the street. As much as it hurts to admit it now, my head instantly grew several sizes and I must have been a total pain in the backside.

It suddenly strikes me that it's been an awful lot of St Davids, Hibs and Celtic. To re-emphasize my lack of bigotry let me just say that I would have been just as elated had it been Hearts or Rangers or even Brechin City (well perhaps more chuffed than elated with Brechin). Anyway, predictably, my pals were skeptical of the news but the Jannie kept them all straight and I was put on a pedestal for a few days. The Jannie was soon to switch roles from good guy to bad.

The Jannie was a central character in Primary School life being involved in every aspect of School business and often in lots of the after school activities too. Even the word "Jannie" is very special. It is one of very few words on which Edinburgers and Glaswegians concur. Billy Connolly fans will certainly know the term well and I can confirm to any skeptics that "Jannie troosers" really do exist. In our school there were two visual signals which were unmistakable. If you were handed a brown envelope on the day your hair had been inspected by the school nurse with her bone comb—you had "Nits". (Hair Lice eggs) It was not subtle or gentle. Somebody marched into the class and shouted out a few people and gave them the dreaded envelope. It was like a death sentence and there were a thousand cruel songs at the ready which would be unleashed on you the second school ended. Even worse than this were the Jannie troosers; a pair of large baggy Green pants which were issued to anybody who lost bladder control (or worse) during the school day. Everyone knew these pants. There was no escape. If you had them on everyone knew what it meant and you better brace yourself for the worst slagging imaginable. No doubt quite a few Psychiatrists heard about all this stuff from patients on their couches many years later. Thank God I never got to try on the troosers or take a brown envelope home.

It was the baby boomer era and this was even more pronounced in a neighborhood sprinkled with staunch Catholic (i.e. Non-contraception oriented) families. For example my pal; yet another Tam (Ward) was one of thirteen bairns. St Davids again burst at the seams and this time it was solved by using the aforementioned Pennywell School as an Annex. My class was sent to the Annex which suited me just fine as it was directly opposite my stair. In fact it was so close that I could go home for lunch and be back in time to sneak into school dinners for dessert. This was easy as the girls in my class were the monitors and servers. From this "Split" a new tradition evolved which was an annual challenge match between the "Main school" and the "Annex". The match was held at the main school on the playing field, not a proper pitch but made serviceable by a combination of cones and poles. The big thing was that the entire school got out early to watch so it had a bit of rivalry and atmosphere. In what was supposed to provide a lighter touch, the Jannie from each location would guest for their respective teams.

Our Annex Jannie, Mr Smith, was an older, graciously graying gent with a warm, crease filled smile and rosy cheeks. As I recall he wasn't a big football fan. He was very popular with us as he made sure we all got a fair chance at early morning milk duty. This entailed delivering crates of half-pint bottles of milk to all the classrooms before school started. At mid-morning we'd all be given one and for some of my pals this was probably the most guaranteed nutrition they would get all day. Maggie "The Milk Snatcher" Thatcher earned yet another black mark in Scotland when she was reputed to be responsible for the demise of that programme. However that is politics and this is football eh? The reward for the boys who helped with the morning milk delivery was "All you can eat" of the previous days' school dinner dessert just before it was dumped in the "Pigswill" bin. There was always fierce competition for milk duty on the days following Bakewell tart and Caramel Cake.

The Jannie Smith went through the motions with token participation in our match. However the main school Jannie (Wilson) was a different Kettle of Fish. (Yet another oft-used Scottish metaphor which I like but can't fully explain to you). He was much younger and brasher. He had a stocky build, a mop of Black hair and a large square chin which gave him a street-tough look in the "Desperate Dan" comic mould. We often debated with him about football issues and he could get a bit intense for an adult dealing with kids but he could also be good fun. He had always told us how good a player he had been and warned us that he wasn't going to miss this chance to prove it. We just didn't realize he wasn't joking! Reading their faces, several of the teachers were clearly surprised as he went bombing around at full speed applying his clear physical advantage without hesitation. We were both intimidated and amused at the same time. Overall, we had a stronger side and that about evened things out. In the dying minutes (When else?) with the score tied at five, I broke clear with only the goalie to beat. As I steadied myself to shoot I felt a great rumbling and snorting behind me. It was honestly like that noise you hear on the nature telly programmes with the Buffalo on the move. The most basic advice in football is to keep your eye on the ball but I was compelled to glance over my shoulder. A large dark blur was sliding towards me at great speed and just before impact I recall his grimacing scowl and menacing smile both somehow combined into one facial expression. He was out of control. Crrrrunch. I landed in a heap and must have been hurting badly as I cried openly with the entire school looking on.

I was quickly surrounded by anxious teachers who wanted to make sure the damage wasn't serious or permanent. As they tended to me they were also firing puzzled looks at Jannie Wilson who was still close by on the ground. His own expression had quickly changed to one of remorse, guilt and embarrassment. He blurted out an apology and a pathetic attempt at an excuse of having slipped but nobody was buying it. The game was not re-started.

I was bruised but not broken with only my pride badly dented by the open tears. A couple of my pals helped me limp home. There was one plus as a few days later I was voted the schools' best player. I might not have won the annual vote (by peers) but for the sympathy I got from the Jannie incident. Quite a few of my pals might have otherwise voted against me just to shut me up as they thought I'd been unbearably big headed since the Celtic incident. I can admit now; they were right.

When he got home from work that night my dad asked me how the game went. Before I could respond my Mom intervened and relayed the full story which she had got in dramatic fashion from one of my pals. He went wild. My brothers and I had the odd serious skelping and clips around the ear. He could moan with the best of them but the strongest word out of his mouth was "Bloody" and we'd certainly never seen any violence from him … until now. He insisted I accompany him to the school as he sought out Jannie Wilson to "Sort out that loony". By now I was over it and not keen on the idea but I was not getting any choice. We were hardly out the door of our stair when my pals sniffed what was happening and started to trail a few yards behind us. We picked up a few more en-route and had a small crowd by the time we reached the school. I was hoping that we wouldn't be able to find him and my dad would cool down and give up. No such luck; there he was working on the gate as we reached it.

There was no hesitation as he immediately grabbed Jannie Wilson around the throat and thrust him against the fence. "What kind of nutter are you, kicking wee laddies?" He choked out an apology saying he got carried away but my dad was not impressed. He was going to write to the School board questioning their screening policy (I highly doubt that letter ever got written). My pals were all impressed and I was sort of proud but also a wee bit embarrassed. Weird as it is, I ended up feeling a bit sorry for the guy. I recall that Jannie Wilson did eventually lose his job in very unsavory circumstances. It was something to do with school funds and extortion and "Beheading" death threats. Highly colorful and publicized accordingly by all the local media. It was a pity in some ways as I guess there was just an immature streak in the man. He was a big factor in the Pilton Sporting Club, a five-a-side league which brought a degree of organized football to lots of boys who wouldn't have otherwise participated. He also did a lot for the scouts and various other groups which used the school. Whatever the outcome, he's apparently over it all now and so is my dad. He surprised me in a recent phone call when he said, without any reference to the original incident; "Met Alan Wilson, mind, your auld Jannie? He was at the British Legion Club and doing away fine" All's well that ends well.

It was soon time for the "Eleven Plus"; the big exam which would determine which secondary (High) school we would attend. I fancied St Anthony's (Tony's) because they always had the best football teams but that wasn't to be (more on which later). The final event of Primary school life was the "Quallie" (Qualifying Dance—sort of Prom) Other than family funerals and weddings this would be the only formal social event for most of us to this point in our lives. The Quallie was mostly a hated event as our last two months of Gym Class (PE) was taken up by learning and practicing the Scottish Country dances we would have to do. If you wonder why every Scottish person you ever meet knows how to do the "Gay Gordons" thank the Quallie. The worst part of the Quallie though was that you had to have a partner. You could pick your own but if you didn't you were paired up with somebody, like it or not. The process was just as cruel as how we picked fitba teams with the perceived ugly/gawky/smelly kids left to each other at the end! Funnily enough ugly at eleven can be quite different by sixteen. I dreaded getting a girl forced upon me and vice-versa so was very pleased to get a date with Olga, the only Black girl at our school. She was very pretty and pretty nice.

Anyway, after a Dashing White Sergeant, an Eight some Reel and several Gay Gordons I treated her to a bag of chips, a bottle of cream soda and a Mars bar. She seemed to enjoy them and I even got a couple of snogs on the way home but failed to make progress beyond that. I clearly made no lasting impression as that was our only date and I believe she ended up married to one of my classmates. A bit much as the boy in question; Peter Greenan and I had just teamed up to sort out an older bully (Fin) who had been terrorizing everyone leaving through the main school gate in Troll-like fashion. That fight included the first serious kick to the face I remember which, sadly, became fairly standard thereafter. After several minutes of circling each other I jumped on Fins back, clinging for dear life and forcing enough weight (the extra school dinners had made their mark) to bend him forward. I was terrified that Peter might bottle it and run and I would be mauled. But he steamed in right on cue and applied the decisive kick with his Beatle style side zip pointer boot. In a ten second blur Fin's reign was over. We were both heroes but apparently Peter got the girl!

Never mind. Time to move on to the big school with some serious new challenges ahead, both on and off the field.

But first we need to visit the foundation roots of the supporting elements of my disease.

6

VALUE FOR MONEY

As was fairly typical, the Hibs supporting side of my addiction started even earlier than the playing part. Most of us just adopted our fathers' teams but to get to the diehard level the relationship between team and boy had to be carefully nurtured through being there in person to see, hear and smell the various elements and, most importantly, to feel the emotional ups and downs. Once this all penetrated your nostrils, lungs, heart and gut you were helpless—you had the disease and there was no known cure. It was there to stay—for better or worse, for richer or for poorer, in victory and defeat, 'til death us do part! How many genuine fanatical fans do you know who ever divorced their football clubs?

I have no memory of my first game (I wish I did) but apparently my Uncle James took me to see Hibs play Barcelona before I even turned six years old. It was one of the biggest ever crowds at Easter Road; somewhere around 63,000 I think. Amazing how they get chuffed now with 20,000. I know from the record book that we beat Barcelona 3-2 to go through after drawing with them in Spain 4-4. Even with no recall my totally romantic view is that something got deep into my soul that night and its still there! And for anyone who's been there, romanticism is a perfectly reasonable part of football addiction. I do have some vague mental traces of my next big European Match; a 2-0 win against the cream of all Europe; Real Madrid. (Puskas, Ghento, Di Stefano) Talk about heady days!

We had a great Fairs (now the EUFA Cup, started as the "Fair Cities") Cup run in 1967. It started with a comprehensive 3-0 defeat of Porto and we survived the away leg 1-3 with a vital away goal from a Joe Davis penalty. We overcame a 4-1 defeat in Italy with a 5-0 thrashing of Napoli in the return leg. Mongo and I were exhausted as we sat on a wall at the highest part of the main terracing to get a better view and jumped off to celebrate each goal. We were also voiceless but still ecstatic by the time we got home. We then met the Don Revie Leeds team which was about to start dominating the English scene and we got a respectable 0-1 away from home. At Easter Road Colin Stein got us level on aggregate and we had a lot of great chances to go ahead. Then, with just a few minutes left the gangly Jack Charlton stretched his giraffe-like neck to get on the end of a free kick and steal the away goal which burst our bubble. No time to recover. Game over. A similar run the following year saw us exit at the same third round stage against Hamburg on away goals with the famous Uwe Seeler (West Germany) getting the goal which killed us. There was always great excitement to see these teams packed with internationals in glamorous strips and under the lights. There would often be a new twist, a new move or a flick or set piece that we hadn't seen before.

Just as vital to the process of supporter addiction were the freezing mid-winter early round cup treks to small, raw and basic grounds (Stadium would be a misnomer for most of them) to play unglamorous teams like Third Lanark and A.S. Clydebank. In England this would send a Man United or Chelsea to places like Yeovil and Kettering. What's amazing is that all of those "Little" teams had die hard fans too who would endure an entire lifetime of relative futility for one magic moment. For example, when Hereford knocked Newcastle out of the FA Cup long before the former were a league team. Any true football fan, even the vanquished Magpies, could see and feel the pure electricity of that moment for a few thousand long suffering Herefordders. Just like real life, some pain and suffering was an essential part of the process for the ultimate joy to be properly savored.

For aspiring players like me all of this supporting stuff *had* to come really early on because as soon as you made it into organized football, chances are you were playing at the same time as your adopted Pro team on Saturday. So from around the age of seven I was there every other week and by nine, the odd away game figured in too. Soon thereafter however my regular Saturday attendance tailed-off as playing took precedence but the beautiful damage had been done!

Though my dad was always playing himself and therefore rarely able to take me to a Saturday Hibs game I benefited from chumming him to his own games. His serious professional days were past by then but he was still playing in the "East of Scotland" league for Ferranti Thistle and being in and around the dressing rooms, playing ballboy and getting a kick around with the "Reserves" at half time of these games also made it's mark on me.

I also had two uncles (both my Mom's brothers) living with us off and on and this before they were married and had kids of their own. Both tried to exert influence on my affiliations. James the elder of them was a good Hibee and took me to some matches and bought me a team scarf and various football books with a focus on Hibs. David was the younger and he had somehow become a Rangers' fan. He was quite well off as an Officer in the merchant navy (Blue Funnel line) and tried a more mercenary approach. He offered me two shillings to swear my allegiance to Rangers and forsake Hibs. That was a small fortune for me at the time (I'm guessing I was about six or seven) and I had the traitor money in my hands for about half an hour. I said the words he insisted upon "I love Rangers, I hate Hibs" and felt really guilty but never had any intention of switching. I kind of hoped he'd laugh it off and tell me he knew I wasn't a turncoat and let me just keep the money. No chance. He took it back—he would always make us stick to our word—not a bad lesson as it transpired. So I was skint again but with my loyalty intact.

This was the era before we all felt we had to get very cool and creative with Christian names and most kids were named after their relatives. However with my eldest brother named John after my dad, my other brother David named for the uncle who just finished tormenting me and I named after my uncle James, it got complicated—especially when we were all in the house at one time! For basic distinction we used the same system as with our pals on the street; adults were "Big" and kids "Wee". This led to some absurd conversations around the house. An example. A voice from the kitchen whilst all six said males are sat in the living room watching a football game;

"John, can you help me lift this up on the table please?"

Response in deep voice "Wee John or Big John? How heavy is it?"

"Not very, pretty light, just a washing"

Wee John says "Dad, surely David or James could dae it"

Wee David says "I washed the dishes surely James should dae it"

Wee James says "Always the wee-est eh?"

Big James and Big David in unison; "James, help yer ma".

Angry reply from kitchen; "Aw forget it, I've already done it maself … and stop picking on wee Chames!"

Primitive male delaying tactics work out again.

(Incidentally my mom was from Wick in the far North East of Scotland and she still retained parts of her very heavy highland accent. "Ch" for "J" was a staple—hence Chames and Chon)

Just this week in the Edinburgh Evening News (which I still read daily on line from Virginia) I see Hibs and Hearts talking about ways of making matches more "Family affordable". For the few times I've been to a match in the last few seasons I can't imagine how a working class family can afford to go regularly to games nowadays. Tickets ten to twenty pounds each, a couple of pounds for a programme, snacks and drinks costing an arm and a leg and forty pounds for a team jersey!

By contrast let me describe a typical Saturday home game for my generation. I'm not sure if it was great long term marketing strategy but I doubt it. I think it was just our luck but the bottom line for the club was a guarantee of the next generation of ardent fans.

You didn't wear team kit in those days. You might get a strip for Christmas or birthday but you'd wear it to play in, not to watch your team in. A scarf was the most prevalent display of team colors and there would also be a few caps and bobble hats. For cup ties a few "Rosettes" would also appear but that was about it. Some of the older, posher men might even wear a team blazer and/or tie.

A standard home league game day for us (i.e. versus anybody except, Hearts, Rangers or Celtic—separate coverage later) would start around noon with us watching the weekly pre-game show on national television. There were two main stations at the time; British Broadcasting Corporation (BBC) and Independent Television Network (ITN). The former was funded via an annual license fee from every honest TV owner. The latter was a "Commercial" station funded by advertising revenues and it had a series of regional affiliates, ours being Scottish Television (STV). Each would feature a variety of sports all through Saturday afternoon, including football preview, Horse racing and Wrestling mixed in with whatever else might be current that particular week.

The name and formats were ever evolving but I mostly remember "Grandstand" which I think was the BBC version and "World of Sports" on ITV (STV) One was hosted by the very cheery Dickie Davies who looked more Italian than English! Each included a fairly comprehensive football preview looking at that days' fixtures and goals and other highlights from previous meetings of the teams involved. At the end of the afternoon there'd be a camera fixed on a typewriter (The forerunner of teletype I guess) which would clatter out results letter by letter and number by number. Then at the very end there would be the "Classified results". These would be read by a guy whose voice gave away the results before he finished announcing them. If he went higher in tone when saying the away team name that usually meant they won. If he went lower on the away team name; home win. If he kept them both right about the same tone, it was probably a draw.

After a general introduction to what lay ahead that afternoon the football previews would get started so that fans could watch them before heading out to their own various games. The stations even co-operated in staggering them so you could see both consecutively. The result was a full hour of great viewing to get you in the mood to see or play some live stuff. These preview shows also changed formats and hosts constantly over the years but I remember "Football Focus" lasting longest. It was hosted by Bob Wilson an Arsenal goalie who played for Scotland despite his English accent! Des Lyneham also had a good run. Much later, Ian St John (Liverpool and Scotland) and Jimmy Greaves (Tottenham and England) had the best run of all with the "Saint and Greavsie" show. This capitalized on the Scotland/England banter in a fun and positive way.

One of those special "Warm and comfy" memories is sitting watching these shows with the "Quickie" Saturday lunch on my knee. We were, exceptionally, allowed to eat in the living room. Sat by a blazing coal fire with a hot pie, sausage roll or bridie, with a blob of brown sauce, a slice of generously buttered plain bread and a cup of steaming hot, sweet tea. For dessert; a shortcake caramel slice with chocolate topping or a coconut snowball or maybe even a Vanilla cake. Mmmmmmmmmm … If you've ever had anything like this your mouth is watering right now. All this and one hour of football—what could be better? Why, a real match of course.

Right. On with the anorak. Scarf around the neck—mines is a classic (Circa 1964) the silky emerald green one with the original club badge repeating between white stripes and white fringe on either end. I'm good to go—all I need is money. How much?

"Ma, any chance of a wee bit extra for a sweetie?"

"Sorry pal, your dad had a flat pay this week"

"A tanner then?"

"A tanner"

A flat pay for the uninitiated meant no OVERTIME. As most of our parents were "Blue Collar" factory workers and tradesmen, overtime was the great double-edged sword. Good whilst you got it but a real miss when it suddenly dried up. For us kids a good run of overtime by our dads always turned into a few extra treats, an extra few days on our summer holidays, bigger better birthday or Christmas presents or some new clothes. We all could care less about the clothes at this stage! Anyway I've got my tanner (Sixpence) which covered my bus fare of three pence each-way. So how am I going to get to see the game? No problem.

Whoosh down the stair. Deek (Who lived opposite Mrs Boyle) hears my door slam and appears on cue on the middle landing. He has no scarf. He doesn't even have his bus fare but he's coming anyway. Out to the front of number 27 we go. Magically, Mongo appears out of number 29 right at the same time. He's got the darker green scarf with the thin diagonal white stripes and the tailored pointed end. He has an exact matching bunnet (Flatcap) which he pulls down tight over his eyes. It has a little metal stud to keep the peak neatly in place. We get to the corner and Andy Mac is there with Big Tam. Andy has a thick woolen scarf with alternating green and white panels. It's obviously a home knitting job. You can tell because the panels are very irregular and the thing is a mile long. It's around his neck and both end still almost brush the ground. His ma obviously made sure she used up all her wool. Big Tam has no scarf and no hat but he does have his pride and joy; a big green and white rattle which he ratchets around and around constantly deafening everything within ten yards. It leaves that residual ringing in your ears, even when he stops. Tam and Lucky Broon are going straight from their grannies and Simmy's not coming as he's the odd Jambo (Hearts fan) in our crew. As we head up the Grove to the number one bus stop on the main Ferry Road Mongo gets the singing started; "Oh, oh, oh Ha-a-ibees, na, na, na, na, na …". Rattle, rattle, rattle!

The bus stop is busy so we know a bus is due and sure enough within a few minutes along rolls the number one double decker. It's already jam packed which is exactly what we hoped for. We pile on and wriggle upstairs almost all the way to the back and try to work our way under the bench seats. This is before the one-man bus where you pay as you get on. It has an old fashioned conductor who works his way around collecting fares and issuing tickets. Here's how it works. The trip takes about twenty minutes. If we're lucky the conductor won't reach us or find us in time to collect our fares. If he does, it's a little embarrassing but we just go red and hand over our money. However it's well worth the try to save our three pence for something else. Deek is out on a limb though. If he gets caught he's off. He has no fear. He figures he'll survive at least ten minutes plus a few more dragging out the "Chuck off" process. Then he can run the rest of the way and catch up to us later! We're in luck. It's a young Pakistani conductor and he's having nothing to do with the back half of the upper deck which has broken out in loud aggressive chanting.

We make it to Great Junction Street and decide to make our move. The trick is to wait until the last possible minute and dash for the door to avoid any chance of a final fare confrontation. It's smooth sailing and were all safely in Leith, three pence each to the good. This still leaves us a fair walk but we can spend some of our loot in the "Toffee doddle shop" a home made sweetie specialist with brilliant tablet. I go for tuppence worth of "Pineapple chunks" and give my spare penny to Deek for a couple of "Whoppas". Mongo gets a poke of the trademark toffee doddles and Andy gets a bar of Butterscotch tablet. We can hear Big Tam's saliva sloshing but he's holding his cash for chips on the way home. We cross the road at the brand new "Pelican" crossing which neither driver nor pedestrian understand but we somehow make it safely to the other side. We spend a while "Bagsin" stuff from Thomson's Sports Shop window. We basically take turns of claiming stuff which we can't afford but would buy if we ever come into any money. I "Bags" a spanking new "Dundee United" jersey. A really bright Tangerine with Black trim and very different from anything we'd seen previously. Big Tam gets slagged rotten for "Bagsin" a pump even though he's not got a ball or a bike. We go about three rounds of "Bagsin" before we get fed up with it.

We head up Leith Walk to Albert Street and turn left towards the hallowed ground. Our route is calculated, we'll pass several pubs. Of course we're far too young to drink but we watch for men emerging from the pubs and heading for the grounds and we're especially interested in men without children! We make it all the way to Easter Road without any serious candidates. It's still early though. We head to Tamson's; a bar that rarely lets us down. Sure enough, three middle age guys come waddling out all flush with a few pints in very happy mood. We go for it.

"Any chance fir a lift-over Mister?"

"Awright, c'moan then son—we can take three—you, you 'n you he points."

No surprise. Me, Mongo and Deek are picked. Tam's size always puts them off and Andy's pretty well built too.

"See ye at the back ae the goals at kick-off, awright."

"Nae bother" says Tam.

We march up the road taking two steps to each one of the men's just to keep up with them. Past the graveyard up the hill and we're at the gate. They mostly ignore us as they debate the day's team selection and tactics. We look at each other thinking what a load of rubbish they're talking but we're saying nothing as they are our way in. Here's how this part works. The man pays cash and the steward releases the waist-high turnstile for one click. At the same time as he pushes through, the man lifts you up and over so your entry isn't recorded. I don't think there were any formal policies or rules on it. There were a couple of grumpy old stewards who would moan and occasionally reject us but most of them simply turned a blind eye and "Presto" were safely inside.

I'm our spokesman; "Thanks very much mister, mibbe see ye's ootside Tamson's again some time"

'No problem boys enjoy the game" and they immediately head off to the toilets to start emptying out all that beer to make room for tea or Bovril at half time. We climb the long steep stairs and emerge onto the terracing.

The pitch at Easter Road has its famous slope (recently removed to meet European rules—alas!) and so we know if we win the coin toss we always shoot uphill first half. We decide to be optimistic and make our way to the top (Dunbar) end and stake out a spot at the low wall immediately behind the goal. We're playing Motherwell and they're on a decent run so the place is filling up nicely and there are a few pockets of Yellow and Maroon sprinkled around. It's cold but not freezing and its dry so even the fair weather brigade are out in force. This is also before any segregation of fans so you stand anywhere you like and move around as much as you want. Despite this you see familiar groups in the same spots week in and week out, except perhaps when the Western invaders hit town. (Celtic and Rangers) I should explain for our American friends that the majority of the stadium (three sides) has no seats and is totally open to the elements. Just concrete steps with the odd staunch on (Bar for leaning against) dotted around. Just to confuse everyone there is enclosed and roofed seating along one side. This is called the "Stand" (with Grandstand as the origin I assume) where the directors and posh folks (or at least we thought they all were at the time) sit and under which the changing rooms are situated. Big Tam and Andy finally managed to find a couple of guys big and drunk enough to heave them in and so they join us behind the goals.

We were doing okay in the mid-sixties. We'd always finish in the top ten in what was then a 22 team league and we still played regularly in Europe. We had a decent Manager in Bob Shankly (Brother of "The" Shank—Bill of Liverpool) but we were slow getting over our beloved Joe Baker's departure to Torino in Italy. We tried his brother Gerry but he just wasn't in the same league. The rock on which to build the next great team was there in Pat Stanton but it would be a few years before we could retain enough top talent around him to get us back into the trophies. Rangers, Celtic and the big boys from England constantly picked off our best with offers Hibs just couldn't afford to refuse (i.e. Peter Cormack to Liverpool, Colin Stein to Rangers, Peter Marinello to Arsenal). Even during that transition phase we had many good players to entertain us and several great characters to amuse us. Just in this one game against Motherwell we had our two big Johns; McNamee and Baxter—a scarier pair you'll never meet—crush a Motherwell forward, Wee Paddy Quinn grab a linesman and Joe Davis make a terrible hash of a direct free kick. We sometimes even loved to hate certain players.

A lot of the spontaneity has been lost with segregation, fences and increased police presence. At that time when Hibs scored we could actually dash onto the pitch briefly, congratulate the scorer and dash off again with only a token pursuit by the police. Mongo even managed to get to the ball once and blast it into the net. We talked about it for weeks.

We had picked right. Hibs shot uphill first but without any threat of a goal. We moved around to the other goal at half time and had better luck with Hibs netting twice for the win. I confess to not remembering if it was 2-0 or 2-1 or even who scored though I think Eric Stevenson got one. About twenty minutes from the end, all the gates would be opened so we would exit the terracing and sneak into the stand. There we would always find discarded programmes (which contributed to our all-rich theory) and claim one each. After the game we went to the back of the stand and patiently waited for the players to emerge. Access was great. We'd get a few words with each of them and get our programmes autographed by our personal favorites. Very few of them were getting into fancy cars. Some were getting taxis but others were just walking or getting a bus. Pat Stanton once tussled my hair and I didn't want it washed. Truth is I never wanted it washed anyway! A few years later John Blackley gave my wee sister Sheona a kiss and won a fan for life.

The one drawback of hanging around was with the dispersal of the big crowds already over we couldn't play the crowded bus fare skipping con. Still, Big Tam had his bag of chips, lathered in Brown sauce and despite his grunting we all managed to nick a couple. Deek pulled the petted lip "Lost my fare" routine and the conductor cracked up laughing and said "Your on your own if an Inspector gets on". What a civilized world it was.

So a great day was had by all and let me just recount the costs:

TRANSPORT TO GAME	Free
SWEETIES (ME 'N DEEK)	3d (Pre-decimal; 12d = 1shilling, 20 Shillings = 1 Pound)
ENTRY TO GAME	Free
PROGRAMME	Free
MEET PLAYERS	Free
2 x BIG TAM'S CHIPS	Free (Including sauce)
TRANSPORT HOME	3d (d was the symbol for old pennies)
GRAND TOTAL	6d = 2 ½ new pence = less than 5 cents!

Now that's what I call value for money!

7

THE BEST TEAM ON THE PLANET.

Picking up the national supporting habit came as second nature from whenever you were old enough to comprehend speech and interpret body language. Scotland would have three annual fixtures spanning one week in late May each year at the end of the domestic club season. It was known as the Home International Championship, a round-robin tournament between Scotland, England, Wales and Northern Ireland. There would be games on Saturday, Midweek, Saturday with two points for a win and one for a draw. The order of the games would switch around except that Scotland would always play England in the last game and more often than not for the title. The venue also rotated annually.

At one time the "Home Championship" even dictated progress into later stages of the European Nations Cup or World Cup but by the mid sixties these tournaments had progressed to having regionalized group qualification systems. So the other international fixtures were typically a series of qualifying group matches for either the European Championships or the World Cup Finals. These two tournaments rotated so that every second year there was a "Finals" to look forward to. Same as it is now except that the numbers of qualifiers were much smaller and getting to the finals accordingly difficult.

My first live Scotland game was against Germany at Hampden. I went through on a Ferranti works bus with my dad. I'm guessing it was 1965 and we drew with a late goal by Bobby Murdoch for one each. We almost missed the goal trying to get an early start to the exit. Many others did. It was exciting but unusually for me I haven't retained much detail. Probably because at that time everything paled in comparison to our annual match with the "Auld Enemy". Scotland versus England is by far the longest running international football fixture at well over a hundred years.

There was a raw fervent passion for this fixture which came from deep within. Some of it can be explained and rationalized but not it all. There was an element that was purely guttural which had to be blood borne. Growing up and listening to our parents, grandparents, uncles and aunts definitely sewed some of the seeds. Through a thousand small remarks we grew up perceiving England, our much larger neighbor, as a bully. Arrogant, overconfident, snobby even. We had been at war with them for hundreds of years until they somehow beat us by cheating. Don't sweat the detail that's how we wanted it, needed it. Yet there were contradictions. Lots of the same relatives fought alongside Englishmen in the second (even a few in the first) World War and talked well of them. We watched Coronation Street on TV every week and the people on that didn't seem too much different from our own neighbors. We met Geordies and Scousers who seemed much more like us than what we expected "English" to be. Even the Cockneys had some traits and characteristics very much like ours. I'm sure the English wanted to beat us but never, it seemed at least, as badly as we wanted to beat them. We needed to dislike them, love to hate them, especially on this particular day each year.

If there was ever any chance that this collective resolve would soften it was blown away by one Englishman who rapidly became our poster boy for hatred. One, who looked, talked and acted *exactly* as we expected. He was tall and thin, pointy chinned, squinty eyed, bowl cutted, tash and bearded, sarcastic smiling, smarmy, patronizing, condescending bastard. He was perfect. He was … JIMMY HILL. Put him in a pair of tights and tunic and give him a badge and he'd pass as the Sheriff of Nottingham—no make up required. He was the first of the modern TV "Football pundits" and he made no effort to hide his disdain for the Scots. He reveled in insulting and tormenting us and we lived for the day we could prove his predictions wrong.

At eight years old, if you asked me what day of the year did I look forward to most? My Birthday—third place. Christmas—fantastic but only runner-up. Scotland versus England—Adrenalin beyond description. In fact England versus Scotland would be the right way around. A victory for us on their turf was somehow much more desirable. So to the ultimate international experience as a Scotland fan. *The one* for the ages. Wembley 1967.

England had just conquered the footballing world winning the 1966 World Cup. They had a great team, a dominant team and of course playing all their games at home didn't hurt. They had a tactical technician of a Manager in Sir Alf Ramsey who, love him or hate him, had delivered the goods. We still had something to cling to though. Even in all his great success we could still criticize him for leaving arguably the most talented English striker of his generation, Jimmy Greaves, sitting on the bench.

In May of 1967 we went to Wembley as a heavy underdog. Our mortal "Auld" enemy sitting on the throne sneering at all below. It set up like the perfect movie script—the result a foregone conclusion. Big bad guy beats up on small good guy. Still, the blindly loyal, fatally optimistic hordes rolled south to London following the same established routes like migrating cattle—creatures of habit. They stopped at the same watering holes—The Greyhound pub—to name but one which suddenly became tartan for a day once every other year. My own first trip on this pilgrimage was still several years away but like almost every household in our nation we were glued to our TV set soaking up whatever we could from that distance. We only had a Black and White TV but we could still see how Green and lush the grass was and how Yellow and Red the constantly waving Rampant Lion flags were on the terracing. Most of all we could see how beautifully dark Blue the jerseys were.

We had two debutants at either end of the age spectrum. Jim McCalliog at nineteen years old and Ronnie Simpson in Goal winning his first international cap at age thirty six. We had mostly reliable, steady seasoned club campaigners including one William Wallace! (How appropriate was that?) We had Denis Law in the prime of his career. He was the Laughing Cavalier and the genius of the guy who painted him all rolled in together. With Law in your team, you always had a chance. And then there was Jim Baxter. This was and ever shall be his game. In a lifetime of sports, if you're lucky, you'll see a couple of great performers give their best ever display in the ideal circumstances. This was one. Baxter controlled the game but not just with his skill. He dominated with his grace, his body language and even his facial expressions which said unequivocally "Just give me that ball".

With Baxter orchestrating, Scotland dominated in a way we'd never seen before. Their football was fluent and the goals came. England rallied towards the end to make the final score line a respectable looking three-two but nobody who saw the game would pretend it was ever close.

Our ecstatic fans invaded the pitch to celebrate taking large chunks of the turf home for souvenirs. It sticks in my mind that, to there credit, the police just watched in mild amusement, a nice contrast to some of the overreactions I've seen over the years. So the sacred turf was scarred but it could easily be mended and considering what was pumped into the London economy over the weekend it was probably a fair trade. All the famous London landmarks were taken over by joyous Scots for the night. Best of all, despite the massive size of the crowds it was mostly good natured. This was the start of the "Tartan Army" developing their reputation as a loud and colorful but mainly peaceful fun loving support.

You didn't get long winded post mortems and a zillion replays then so within a few minutes all the local fields around Pilton were filled with groups of boys imitating Baxter's moves, Law's headers and Wallace's charges (If you'll pardon the pun) Mongo and I were no exceptions. We were out there sharp and quickly joined by the usual suspects. After playing for a good couple of hours we flopped in the grass and contemplated what the day meant.

Big Tam; "So England were the world champions right?"
Mongo; "Aye"
Big Tam; "'n likesay, we jist beat them right?"
Mongo; "Aye Tam"
Big Tam; "So we're now the best team in the world right?"
Mongo; "Canny argue wi' that Tam"

So there we were, all just looking at each other smiling and shaking our heads. A bunch of the happiest boys you'll ever meet sat in a muddy corner of the big field as the light started to dim. Proud supporters of Scotland; unofficial champions of the entire planet!

8

READING PRACTICE

Yet another element to the consolidation process for football fandom was collecting memorabilia and programmes. Almost all of us at least dabbled in it. Many sustained it for a season or two and for a few it became a serious lifetime pursuit.

Prior to football programmes the collection bug was generally introduced to us early via bubble gum cards and comics. I was one of the few kids you'd meet who did not like bubble gum (I'm cringing a bit even writing the words—weird eh?) Still, it could have been worse as our parents got a lot of their early collections out of cigarette packets!

I don't recall sustained interest in the football player cards in fact the card series I remember most vividly had nothing to do with football. It was a set of Beatles cards. If you got an entire set and reversed them all and set them out in the right pattern you got a giant Beatle's face.

Comics were more widespread. They would offer an assortment of collections of cards and toys as enticement to get you started, especially in the summer when your Mom might be tempted to throw you the few pennies required just to get you out of her hair for a little while. Of course what they really wanted was you on a subscription basis but there weren't so many of those in Pilton. Years later when I delivered on a paper round in the much more affluent Blackhall area every other house seemed to have subscriptions. I admit that the odd free gift "Fell out" of the comics on the way around! We were more the buy as you go crowd. Besides the cards I remember liking two particular toys which came with comics. The first was a set of little plastic "Rockets"—they may have called them "Bombers". They had a little steel nose cone into which you inserted a small "Kep". A kep was a tiny circle of explosive stuck on paper. You launched this thing in the air as high as possible and when it hit the ground the nose cone was forced shut and caused a small clap of explosion including a dramatic puff of smoke! My other favorite was a little plastic "Glider" that you set off with a rubber band. The girls got similar cheap things in their comics.

There was a central core of "Funnies" which boys and girls shared; The Beano, The Dandy, The Beezer and the Topper. The rest were very much geared towards boys or girls specifically. The girls' main ones were the Bunty, the Judy and the Mandy. We boys would never be seen dead near these, at least in public but Mongo managed to corner me once in a game of "Truth or Dare" and I had to admit to liking a story called "The Four Mary's". Redder. For Boys there were The Lion, The Tiger, The Hotspur, The Valiant. In the end it got silly with demand shrinking the makers started to join the most popular comics just to survive. The last and most absurd one I remember was called "The Whizzer and Chips!"

For us though, everything leads back to fitba. The shop where we got our comics was "Barrs" and the owner, Colin Barr was quite a big shot in the Hibs supporters club. The boys' comics were also sprinkled with sports stories including quite a few football specific ones. We all loved "Tough of the Track" which was about Alf Tupper. A gritty English distance runner who trained on Fish and Chips and still won the Olympics. However the main man of comic football was undoubtedly "Roy of the Rovers". Although he was an Englishman we never held it against him; Roy Race of Melchester Rovers and his mate Blackie in their distinct Yellow and Red strips supported by their goalie Tubby in his baggy Green shirt were the world's team long before Real Madrid! I also loved "Billy's Boots" about a pair of magic football boots which enabled an otherwise ordinary skinny kid to rescue big games in the dying seconds. "Raven on the Wing" was also cool.

The comics each produced book versions called Annuals at Christmas time. There were also a series of Football books produced at the same time. Our main one was the Scottish Football Book which recounted the previous season in detail. It was always great fun whizzing through looking for Hibs bits. Even in years when they won nothing (which were plentiful!) you always found a reference and photo or two. I also loved a book called the Topical Times. Although it was heavily English based there were tons of Scottish, Irish and Welsh players, Managers and coaches involved in the English game at that time.

Getting back to programmes—it started simply with your own team's home game programmes. Then you'd pick up a few from away games. You could also get someone you knew to bring you an international one now and again. Then began the quest for some from South of the border. You could buy them from dealers but my gang was not going to make much progress that way. As always we found a seam. I'm not sure where we got it from but someone came up with a standard begging letter. I can remember the exact wording:

"Everton Football Club
Goodison Park …
Liverpool …
England

Dear Sir,

I would be grateful for any of your new or used programmes.

A stamped addressed return envelope is enclosed

Yours Faithfully,

J Meikle
Age 9"

We always put the age as we were told they found it hard to ignore such pleas from really young fans. Any time I knew my Mom had stamps I'd try a couple of these and they were incredibly successful, although they often took a while. The great thing is you'd have forgotten all about it and then come home from school. Mum would say "Oh there's one of those envelopes for you son—from England I think". It was very exciting ripping open the flap and seeing the glossy programmes emerge. They would usually send you a couple so you could then swap one for a team you didn't have. I clearly remember Wolves, Everton, Sheffield Wednesday and Newcastle as the most generous and reliable respondents.

Another collection we were all keen on but a bit wary to admit at the time was the "World Cup Coins" leading up to 1970. England was in as holders and we were not and ESSO petrol came out with a collection of coins of the players in the England Squad. There was even a special presentation board that you fit them into. We'd hang around the garage at Crewe Toll asking everyone who filled up if they "Needed their football coins?" Many just flipped them at us. I was able to build up the entire set that way.

My Mom's pal Sally King had a boy Billy who died very young. One day he was fine and the next he was going to die and there was nothing could be done. Billy was mad keen on all things football. A lot of my stuff went to him during his sickness. I can't pretend that I didn't make mild selfish protest on a couple items at the time but I'm so glad now that my Mom imposed the much greater good on me! Hopefully these things gave Billy a wee break from his troubles at a terrible frightening time. Years later I played alongside his brother John (Kingie) for Groathill.

I'm finally at the point where I understand that collections and souvenirs are fine but it's the fond memories which really matter most. The only things I have left nowadays are my Scottish Football Annuals, my Hibs books and of course, my original scarf. My favorite Hibs book is "100 Years of Hibs" by Gerry Docherty and Phil Thomson (John Donald Publishers) Inside the front cover was taped a white card with:

"To James
Best Wishes
Pat Stanton
Hibs FC"

The tape has deteriorated so the card is loose now. On the reverse is a (Carbon copy) typed menu so I guess either my dad (Playing a gig with his band) or my uncle James (A great "Scottish" singer in the Kenneth McKellar, Heid-a-rum-ho genre) were at some function Pat attended around 1975 and got it done for me. Incidentally, Scotch Broth was .17p, Gammon Steak Grilled Hawaiian Style (A Scottish favorite!) .94p, Choice of sweet from the Trolley .23p. You could have a glass of Burgundy for .27p or a coffee for .12p. No mention of Beer or Tea so it must have been a relatively posh place! Once in while I'll open this book and an hour or so later I come back around so thanks Gerry and Phil (and Joe McMurray) for persisting with it. I now know it's not easy. I scribbled the concept and the first two chapters for this book fifteen years ago!

In 1968 I collected a cup final programme in person for the first time. In those days the League Cup started the season off in August. Teams were drawn in sections of four and played a round robin with the top team going to the quarter finals. We won our section which I believe included St Johnstone, Partick Thistle and Raith Rovers. We drew East Fife in the quarters and hammered them with a six-two aggregate over two legs. The Semi's were always on a neutral field although this often still meant playing Celtic at Ibrox or Rangers at Celtic Park or either at Hampden which never seemed that neutral to me! In the '68 semi we got a bit lucky with a taste of this "Neutral" advantage ourselves. We drew Dundee and the powers that be decided it would be played at Tynecastle (Hearts ground) in Edinburgh. The more obvious venue would have been St Johnstone's Muirton Park in Perth. It was the largest playing surface in Britain at the time and fairly placed between Edinburgh and Dundee. I guess the ground capacity was just too small. We—Mongo and the gang—had no routine set for Tynecastle so my oldest brother John took me. As good Hibees we were always looking for faults with anything Hearts and Tyncastle related and we found plenty that night.

As John tried to lift me over the Steward exclaimed; "Sorry, no lift-overs tonight son".

John explained and appealed. "I'm looking after him pal he has to stay with me!"

The steward's getting a bit stroppy now; "This is a bloody adult gate and its full price for everybody passing through it, regardless of size"

John pulls out another pound note and throws it through the little opening "Greedy Jambo bastards" he says.

The steward clicks the turnstile twice and replies; "Aye, f**k you too pal".

John's ranting about it. "No the money, it's the principal" (He's sincere about this—he's making good money at the "Gas conversion" whatever that is) I'm nodding and pursing my lips in serious agreement but truth be known I don't give a toss how I got in. I'm in and that's all that matters. The place is packed and the atmosphere is great and we undoubtedly have a large crowd advantage because of the location. It's mostly a pleasant blur. The only detail I clearly remember was Alan McGraw being carted off and bandaged up before coming back on to score a late winner. As we spill out into Gorgie Road it is a sea of green instead of the usual Maroon and the high tightly enclosed tenements cause the sounds to reverberate like a canyon;

"We're on our way to Hampden, we shall not be moved … not by the Hearts, the Rangers or the Ce-el-tic, we shall not be moved"

Funny we should mention Ce-el-tic because that's exactly who's waiting for us in the final at the ever neutral Hampden!

Neither John nor David volunteers to take me to the final. I'm guessing they're making a day of it with their mates. Up town for a few pints (John legally, David not!) and then onto another pub in the Hampden area before the game. Same after. Pubs were much less accepting of kids then so I'd be a handicap. My Dad's working so he can't take me and he isn't keen for me to go through anyway. He thinks I'm still a bit young for it. My mum explains this all to me. She can see how devastated I am. It's not like the game is live on telly even. She's got the guilts and gives me a little extra pocket money and tells me to go enjoy myself. Oh I will!

Late morning Mongo and I are sitting at his stair door. He's got his cap and scarf on. I've got my scarf on too but we're both glum. "They'll no let me go through on my own" I say. "I'm allowed bit am short on dosh" he says. The cheapest way through is the "Excursion" buses which are just some of the normal city buses used for extra duty on Saturday. They always leave in a convoy from St Andrews Square (The Square) in the town centre. Even if I give him what I've got its not enough to get him through. Anyway we know that just wouldn't be the same. We see quite a few people streaming up the street towards the main roads heading up town to the square or to the train station, the quicker but even pricier option. Mongo sees a couple of guys he knows pass by. He shouts "On yer way tae Hampden Bogie?" Bogie used to be in his class at primary. He replies "Aye, there's a special bus picking us up at Crewe Toll at half-twelve. You?". "A bit skint like bit mibbe we'll come 'n wave ye's off". "Nae bother says Bogie". So we tag along with them to Crewe Toll. The pick up point is in front of the new fire station. There are four other older boys there from Telford.

Bang on time the bus pulls in. More a "Coach" than the buses we were used to. A private hire. Very smart. The singing is already in full flow. A man with a giant green and white rosette on his lapel steps off with a clipboard. His cheeks and nose are beaming red and eyes squinting. He's had a few nippie sweeties and is clearly feeling no pain. I get close enough to peek at his sheet. He's just got "CREWE TOLL—8" at the bottom of his list—no names. He shouts; "Hibees fans only … all aboard. You're the last eight". Mongo and I immediately make eye contact. We're doing our sums. Bogie's reading us too. All eyes no words. We look in all directions not a soul headed this way. Bogie says to the guy; "We're all squared in advance here right pal?" "Aye it was sorted at work" says the man and he's got his pencil with the wee rubber on the end and he's started counting heads. Bogie eyes Mongo and I and gives the shrug with the open hands and wide eyes. The man even taps me and Mongo on the head "Seven, eight—right let's go. Next stop Hampden Park". I take a deep breath and climb the steps. Mongo and I slide into the last vacant double seat. Bogie and his mate are killing themselves laughing. I'm terrified that two people are going to come rushing up at the last second and bubble us but it's worth the risk. All along Ferry Road and through Davidson Mains my stomach's churning. Besides cheating our way on to the bus I'm on my way to Glasgow without permission!

We climb over the Drumbrae through Clerry and onto St John's Road. Then we wend slowly through the build up of traffic at the Maybury. It's becoming clear that this bus is an ad-hoc for the final rather than a regular supporters group. As we lug the confab there are small groups from all different parts of the town. They are all firmly united in Hibs but other than that mostly unconnected. By the time we get to Ingleston I know were safe and I can tell Mongo does too. I have a few flutters about the trouble I'll be in when I get home but then I'll worry about that later! I also have the guilts about the boys whose seats we have but then I rationalize it. They weren't there and the seats were paid for anyway so we're actually helping prevent waste. Something we're encouraged to do every night at teatime ("David, your not going to leave that bit spam are you? That could feed a whole family in Africa!") I always wondered what my mum would do—stick it in an envelope and send it. Wouldn't it be a bit rancid by the time it got there? That's it then. We were actually doing something really good. Mongo looks at me with the broadest of grins; he slings one arm around my shoulder and gives me a big nougie (friendly twisting knuckles) to the side of the head. "We're really gaun James—we really are on our way tae Hampden" Indeed we were!

Edinburgh had some plant and factories but traveling through the outskirts of Glasgow reminded us of their much heavier industrial roots. Lots of warehouses and hard to tell which are derelict and which are still in use. Tall smoke stacks all over the place. Finally we park, conveniently outside a pub and most of the men pile in. We can't even see the ground but it's obvious from the stream of people which direction it's in. With the similar colors its a bit tricky telling Hibees and Celtic fans apart at least until they start talking. There's no confusing Glasgow and Edinburgh accents though! Even then there are tons of Celtic from Edinburgh. Few are likely to bother laddies our age but you just never know. We take a landmark of where the bus is and join in the flow. After a couple of turns we see the towering stands and floodlights not too far away.

I honestly can't remember if we were able to get a lift over. I'm sure we would have tried but there would be a boy's gate at a relatively cheap price and having been provided free transport we were in good shape. We even bought a programme and a Macaroon bar (A Glasgow street vendor staple) each. Most finals then were not all ticket as Hampden could still take one hundred and thirty four thousand. The game itself was what we always expected from Celtic at that time; a thrashing. We expected it whilst always hoping this would be the exception and once in a while it would be but not this day. Celtic led by six until Jimmy O'Rourke replied. Eric Stevenson scored a late free kick from a weird angle to make the final score line two-six. That's all I remember about the game besides some spirited singing for the first little while until Celtic took control. Still we were definitely edging a bit closer to Celtic and Rangers and in the not to distant future we would find a man who could get us over the hump against them both.

As we made our way back to the bus I hear a voice shouting "James, James!" Across the street is my brother David and he says

"What the hell are you doin' here? I thought Dad said you wirnie allowed?"

I'm nabbed but stay cool "No, eh, he changed his mind efter you left this morning".

"Did you get the Excursion or the train?"

"No. Mongo's pal Bogie had a couple of spare seats on the 'Crewe Toll' bus"

"That right Mongo?"

"Aye, bit ae luck Davie, ken"

I ask "Where's our John?"

"Don't know if he even came through in the end" says Davie "Cannie say av ever heard ae the Crewe Toll bus bit fair enough. Watch yersels on the way back"

So any thoughts I've had of pretending to have had a lovely afternoon at the Museum or the Pictures are blown. I could ask Davie not to tell but I've lost faith in him ever since he shopped me for feeling Lanie's bum behind the stair door. The journey home is much cheerier than you would imagine for a team so badly beaten. There's plenty defiant singing. We'll be back. I also decide that I'll come clean with the bus organizer just before we get off but when I approach him he's so guttered it would be a waste of time. We ask the driver if he can stop before Crewe Toll to save us having to walk back along and it's no problem. Bogie and his mate also jump off at the same spot and we say our goodbyes and thank him for staying mum.

As we walk down the street Mongo and I make enough noise so that anyone listening might realize we were at the game. As we reach my stair Mongo asks "So what's your story in case your Ma or Dad corner me?" I thank him for the thought but tell him I'm coming clean as soon as I get in and I do. I've beat David home as he's got to make his way back from up town so at least my Dad's not standing at the door waiting to clip my ear! They are both in the living room having a cup of tea.

"See the result then son. Pity but you usually have to get to a couple finals before you win one. Experience is a big part of it"

Deep breath, exhale; "Well Dad, to be honest a was actually there"

He stares hard at me and my Mom does too. "You were whaaaaat?"

"Well it wasn't planned. See, Mongo and I went to wave off a supporters bus at Crewe Toll and it turns out his uncle is on the bus and they had spare seats for free and the next thing is we're on our way to Glasgow. There wasn't any time to come and ask but I thought it'd be OK since there was an adult we knew with us" I've done it again despite promising myself not to; I've added a softening lie to the plot which always backfires.

I wait for the shouting but it doesn't come. They look at each other and smile which is agreement that there won't even be a suspended sentence.

It's weird because I know it would be so different if my Mom had found out earlier and had time to start worrying herself sick and winding up my dad in the process! In that case he would have been waiting at the bottom of the stair for me. But because I'm here and obviously safe with not a bad explanation they're pretty calm. I've also lucked out with the timing. They're in relaxed mode as they're about to get ready for their Saturday night out at the "Social" at the Ferranti Hall at Crewe Toll. As soon as they leave I'll nip down and brief Mongo about his Uncle's presence and of course I'll have to tell David I forgot that bit in our brief exchange in Glasgow!

Home free with just a little white lie to feel guilty about and I can square that in my prayers later. So I've felt the joy of seeing Hibs in a final and felt the pain of them losing it. Another vital step completed in the process of preparing for the ultimate joy when they actually win something.

Likesay; heartfelt thanks to whoever paid our way to Hampden.

9

SUMMER IN THE CITY

The eleven-plus scores were in and I was near the top. This should mean Holy Cross Grammar and some bragging rights for my delighted Mum who could tell relatives and neighbors about her "Clever laddie". Of course some parents took this more serious than others. Pat, who I met and worked for later in life in the States, told me the most extreme such story. He was from Leith and his mum set her heart on him going to Holy Cross. She was so obsessed with it she advance bragged to everyone in their stair and even bought the uniform. It was never in doubt. Except that Pat fell a few points short and was designated for Saint Anthony's (aka Tony's). He ended up at neither opting instead for Broughton. However his mum just couldn't face Mrs Friel on whom she'd turned the bragging screw so hard and who would surely reciprocate with a vengeance when the truth came out. For several months he left the stair wearing a green Holy Cross Blazer and changed into his proper one when he was a safe distance away. He reversed the process on the way home. How mental is that? I'm glad to say that Pat survived this without therapy and did very well for himself.

Pardon the pun but for me it turned out to be all academic. They were building a brand new school at Broomhouse to be called St Augustines and it was to be a model for the new "Comprehensive" system. This would mean a merger of the Holy Cross grammar and the more technical/trade focused St Andrews. Part of the concept was that we would all have a couple more years before being channeled so that late bloomers or exam-phobics would have a fairer chance at academic success. The eleven plus still would play a role in our initial class placements but failure in it would not necessarily bring a life sentence. It probably did rescue a few kids as planned but it also had a down side keeping many others in school long after their interest expired. A National Insurance Number was mandatory to enter the workplace proper but within the new system this was not available until the end of term in which your sixteenth birthday fell. Lame Duck student equals boredom equals disruption. Like all building projects, the new school was running late so we (The first year—freshman) class would be temporarily housed in Dumbryden primary school in the heart of the developing concrete jungle which would become the infamous Wester Hailes. Fortunately, we had our long summer holidays to enjoy before we had to deal with all that …

Summer at that time brought a slight lull in all things football. The professional stuff finished in May with the Cup Final and Home Championships and that was it until late August. Changed days from current players who seem to barely get a month off. Mind you, with the money involved now they can hardly complain. All the amateur and youth stuff followed the same pattern. We would always go to my Grannies in Wick for two weeks but that left about six weeks of school-fewer days to fill. We still played some football but the abundance of free time and mostly suitable weather allowed us to seek greater adventure at places like the beach, the Zoo, the Museum, Edinburgh Castle and Cramond Island to name but a few. These all had the attraction of requiring little or no cash! Hormones were also hard at work and the pursuit of the opposite sex was taking on a bit more urgency.

Absurd as it may sound, the Royal Scottish Museum during summer was one of the hottest spots for the ten to twelve year old dating scene. They had fantastic collections of stuffed birds, fish, animals and even insects. They had coins, pottery and stamps. They had a Roman section, a Greek section, an Egyptian section. They also had an extensive "Hands On" section long before the concept was cool and trendy. By pressing buttons on the sides of large glass cases you could see a variety of electrical and mechanical devices operating. They would have cut-away sections so you could see all the inner workings—it was fascinating and great fun and all within our normal price range—free. My favorite was a full size lighthouse lamp which we could switch off and on and rotate.

As well as providing all of this gratis interest, fun and potential for a "Bag off" (our term for a date which resulted in at least a planting of the lips) the museum had the bonus of a live fish pond which offered "Gold" as well as Goldfish! Visitors were in the habit of throwing coins (mostly pennies) into the large ponds in the main entry/reception atrium area which had seats all around the perimeter. With luck you might reach back far enough to snag a penny without being too obvious. Three successful dips could send you scurrying off to the well stocked cafeteria for a cake or a scone.

The Edinburgh Zoo will be familiar to most people who have visited the City as its large façade and entrance area is located on the main road in from the Airport and it would be listed high on most tourist hit lists. The zoo was essentially built into the South side of Corstorphine Hill with fairly steep paths winding upwards through the various enclosures. The Lions and Tigers and Bears were quite near the top which was probably good strategy as many people, especially those with little kids, may have otherwise never made it more than half way up! There were a few sparsely populated field enclosures right at the top containing relatively boring things like deer, Llamas and some kind of weird hogs. A small path between these led to an old exit turnstile. No idea why it even existed but it served admirably as the unofficial entrance for a generation of kids from the schemes. It wasn't completely free as it was a fairly taxing hike up the North side of Corstorphine Hill and through the Clerry (Clermiston) woods just to reach it. The turnstile only moved in an exit direction but a selection of spars had been skillfully loosened so that you could pick your way through. Like most such things a much easier proposition for us than for Big Tam who we somehow managed to squash through, though he changed shape several times during the process.

We would then work our way down and typically head for two spots to cause mischief. First, in the large birdhouse there was a Mina bird which was a fantastic talker. We would spend ages carefully trying to teach it swear words in the hope that it would repeat these at inopportune moments. Occasionally it worked as planned. For example when a nice American family approached with big wide smiles and eyes saying "Preddy Pally, Preddy Pally" and were told categorically "F*ck Off, F*ck off". Simple minds easily amused I know. I feel bad when I think about it now but at the time it seemed perfect.

Next stop was the Monkey House. There was one called George and we loved to pick on him. Not sure exactly what type he was but he was a bit like a chimp and even for a monkey, he definitely wasn't quite the full shilling. It was well known that he hated being stared at and it was rumored that he could sense insults and be wound up. We would patiently wait for a gap in the crowds and surround him with hard stares from three or four of us from different angles. You could see the agitation as he wanted to stare all of us out. Then we'd start saying things in monotone like "George is a radge", "George is ugly", "and George stinks badly". You could see it taking effect. His teeth would start to show and he'd have a low growl more like you'd expect from a dog. His eyes would get wide and then he'd suddenly just lose the plot and launch himself at us screaming in a high pitched whine and with no regard for his own safety as he cracked against the bars of his cage. Mission accomplished the satisfied horrible, evil little men would move on.

Edinburgh Zoo's trademark attraction was something called the Penguin Parade. At the same appointed time each day a selection of the Penguins would be let out of their enclosure and go for a march around the small grassy picnic area with their keeper. Families would enthusiastically circle the route forming a narrow gauntlet. The penguins and the little kids seemed to thrive upon this very close contact without doing one another any serious damage that I can remember. Sea Lion feeding time was also a great laugh.

There was a little kiosk selling Walls vanilla ice cream blocks in square cones. This was and is one of those childhood tastes which can still make my mouth water right now just thinking about it. As always our problem was lack of cash but even at the zoo there were ways of getting some. The first was a scour of the grassy areas immediately after the Penguin parade. With so much jockeying for position there was often loose change dropped from shallow pockets and we only needed to raise three pence.

Failing this there was the aquarium. There was an extra fee to get in there but we had also perfected a system for working backwards through the exit turnstile there. It took much more patience with lots of people around and occasionally caused a serious embarrassment when paying customers emerged halfway through the process! However with a Walls' cone at stake it was well worth the risk. Once in we had to work against the flow of patrons back to the entrance hallway where there were a couple of large open ponds filled with very small sharks and the likes. These had also been adopted as wishing ponds with lots of pennies, some three penny bits and even the odd silver coin tossed in. The distance to the water was much further than at the museum. So it took two of us working in unison and with a lot of trust with one holding the others legs. Deek and I had this down to a fine art. We were helped a bit by the very dark "Mood" lighting as there was always an attendant on the prowl. For the most part we'd manage a few pennies and occasionally get really lucky with a shilling which meant cones all round.

The tourists were awed by Edinburgh Castle but we came to see it as one great big adventure playground. There was no general admission at the time but there was a fee to get into certain "Special" exhibits including the Scottish Crown Jewels. Though there was no financial incentive we took it as a personal mission to get into all these restricted areas without paying. It was all part of the game. I could also take my pals into the memorial hall and proudly show off my Uncle Andrew Meikles' name listed in the Black Watch—Second World War dead log book. He died in France but my aunt eventually got his remains back to join my grandparents in Seafield cemetery at the end of Leith Links. My Mum's there too now. The castle is also where, besides television, our early stereotypical view of Americans was formed. They seemed loud, demanding and well off. I've now lived here long enough to appreciate that many of these Yanks we encountered were in fact middle class families who had saved their meager annual leave allowance (many of them even today get just a week's paid leave per year) and holiday funds for several years to make the trip. If we only had one decent holiday every four or five years we might be just as demanding and brash!

Cramond Island was another favorite spot. It was in the middle of the Firth of Forth and a long, narrow causeway allowed access when the tide was fully out. However the access window was only a couple of hours and if you weren't careful you could get stuck there for twelve hours waiting for the tide to turn again. It was full of old abandoned gun enclosures from WWII and a great place for a full scale game of "Japs and Commandoes" our favorite war game.

The highlight of the summer for me was always the annual family trek to the far North to my Mom's hometown of Wick. That is the subject of a whole book in its own right though it's worth mentioning that Football was just as big all the way up there. They had three local teams; The Groats, The Rovers and The Academy. For years they weren't even allowed in the semi-pro Highland League. The existing teams wouldn't vote them in because they were so much farther North than the rest of the teams! Ironically the same economic (distant travel) logic kept the Highland Leagues strongest teams (Inverness, Elgin, Ross) out of Senior Scottish Football for far too long!

For example in 1974, when for the first time in many years, the Scottish League was re-aligning and had room for one extra club. The other relatively poor and mainly lowland based lower division teams rejected by far the most qualified candidate, Inverness (they actually had three well qualified individual teams—Thistle, Clachnacuddin and Caley and were willing to merge resources and potential) in favor of the Ferranti works team who were conveniently based in Edinburgh. Ferranti's ground; City Park, couldn't even meet minimum standard so they had to move to Meadowbank stadium and the name change to Meadowbank Thistle became part of the deal. They eventually took a sweet offer to move to Livingstone under a hungry chairman (Dominic Keane) and have never looked back playing in the UEFA Cup last year!

But don't be fooled. Look closely. Their roots, colors and badges are still all based on the original Ferranti Thistle designs most of which were hatched on the drawing board of Alan Hartman who still runs a trophy engraving business out of Drylaw. I actually have a founder members tie (Also designed by Alan) as my dad was heavily involved at the time they were accepted into the league. The only reason he didn't become the first Manager of the league team was he already committed to his drummer/singer role in the band; Town n' Country. (Not quite top of the pops material but well known and loved around the Edinburgh bowling clubs!) Even the old Ferranti Thistle Leader; Johnny Bain, is a lifetime board member with Livingstone. Quite a stretch from the old wooden hall at Crewe Toll to the Directors Box at Almondvale for games against Celtic, Rangers and Europe's best! My dad just loaned me his personally signed copy of Johnny's recent book "Public Parks to Premier League"; a good read, especially for Edinburgh area fans.

Anyway when the best Highland league teams eventually got their deserved spots in the Scottish league, the impact cascaded North with Wick finally getting into the highland league proper. In reality the new motorways probably played a crucial role in the process!

Constrained to mainly local Caithness (Thurso, Halkirk) competition for so many years the turnout at the Harmsworth Park was fairly small. My dad even guested for the Academy well into his thirties. So which pro teams did they all support? Celtic or Rangers. They were divided about evenly from what I can remember. There were thriving supporters clubs and they ran regular buses to Glasgow. Not every game but at least a couple of times each month. There was also a great rivalry between the supporters clubs teams partly as they only had each other to play! My uncle Robbie ran the Rangers' boys so I guested for them many times scoring several goals. My Uncle David was very proud of me but it didn't persuade me to give up my Hibs' scarf!

On a recent whistle-stop visit to show my youngest two the merits of Wick it seemed not much has changed. I was standing in a line and the two kids in front of me were wearing football shirts, one Celtic and one Rangers. Not that unusual except that the line was for communion at the local Catholic Church! Now if that doesn't kill bigotry for good nothing will!

10

LEARNING TO SWIM IN THE BIG POND

Summer's done and it's time to get back to school and on with the story. Starting secondary school was quite a traumatic experience even for us Pilton hardened boys. Most of my street pals were off to either Ainslie Park or Craigroyston but I was headed up to the Ferry Road where we would catch a "Special" school bus headed for Wester Hailes. At least I'd have a few familiar faces with me. Wee Borrie and Veitchy (Michael) are at the bus stop when I get there. The bus comes and we jump on. Paul (Ferguson—another "Best" pal from our primary class—actually my second cousin—his mother was a Meikle) is already on. The other guy I recognize (from playing football for Leith) is Stevie Torrance and he quickly joins our crowd. We're upstairs at the backseat and have one John Players Special tipped cigarette making its way slowly around the five of us. On the outside we are all cool about this new adventure but I suspect we are all inwardly a bit nervous. In primary we were all big fish in our own little pond. Now we have to get ready to encounter lots of people who are bigger, stronger, better, brighter, tougher and worst of all just as good at fitba!

   I end up in fairly good level classes with a sprinkling of familiar faces in most of them. It's not a bad little school, quite new with good facilities. Boy's and girls roam around the playground, mostly with primary school buddies, sizing each other up. There are a few early brief fights as a few potential hardnuts try to establish themselves. All I really care about is when, where, how do they run the football team trials? I quickly learn that they have two teams for first year boys. Just to confuse matters the first team is called the B's. This bothers me. My first thought is egotistical and selfish pride! I'm already worried that even if I make this team people won't believe that the B's is the top team! I mean if you buy a single record the B side's inferior right? And everyone knows what a B movie is. Within the first couple of days there's a notice posted. "Football trials will be held immediately after school at St Joseph's school field next Tuesday, Wednesday—all welcome—any questions to Mr MacDonald, English Department or Mr Harvey, Geography Department". That's it. There are also rugby trials which seemed to be drawing interest. Good, it might cut down the fitba attendees! There's field hockey for girls.

St Josephs is nearby at Sighthill, quite walk able from where we are. The following Tuesday after school gets out I hook up with Stevie Torrance and we head for St Josephs. We're already convinced that it's unfair. The guys who went to St Josephs have the edge. They'll be comfortable. Amazingly, quite a few of my pals who are not bad players are just too intimidated to try out. We get there and find Mr MacDonald (who will later become one of our favorite teachers) He adds our name to what looks like a very long list on a clipboard. In theory he has no preconceptions or prior knowledge of players. In reality he obviously knows us both. "Ah. Torrance, popped in quite a few for Holy Cross" and "Meikle, St David's—I'm told Celtic's looking. You boys both represented Leith last season right?" This was great news. The pecking order even carries forward to secondary. We have the inside track. It's ours to blow or consolidate. The confidence soars.

Mind you there is a fair size crowd. I'm guessing forty or more even with the intimidation factor drop-off. I can't remember much about the first day. I had a few nice runs, done okay and was told to come back. Stevie too. We were happy campers.

Next day we repeat the drill and I've also got talking to Tony Marinello (Cousin of Peter) and we get on good. Just like his cousin he's a dramatic winger with slanting eyes (Nicknamed "Tojo") and arms all over the place but he is a player. No doubt about it. Another obvious stand-out is Sam Lynch. Word is Celtic are also watching him close. Larger than life "Cubby" Cuthbertson also shows well, magic left peg. By the last session on the second day they have us just about where they want us. Goalie is obvious—Stewart Blaikie—Tall, vocal and confident. In the last couple minutes Tojo sends over a perfect cross to me I do a falling backwards overhead kick into the corner and I know I'm home and dry. I can just feel it. Stevie says he feels pretty good about his chances too.

About a week later the results are posted on the notice board. A new 4-4-2 formation is gaining popularity now but we're still in our traditional 2-3-5 as follows:

1 Stewart Blaikie

2 Charlie Donaldson   3 Ged Corrigan

4 Sam Lynch   5 Gordon Gow   6 Kevin McCall

7 Tony Marinello   8 Stevie Torrance   9 Tony Perry   10 Ian Cuthbertson   11 James Meikle

Being listed in the number eleven spot was unusual for me. Tojo and Cubby had my favorite numbers seven and ten but I could have no argument with either. Our shirts were one of my least favorites, white with navy blue bands around the middle and less special as everyone in the school had to buy their own. For some reason the first game was in midweek which was unusual for secondary school where the vast majority of games were Saturday morning. We were to play Norton Park and I remember they wore Hibs strips except they were Yellow where the white bits should be! The other unusual thing which I don't recall happening any other time was that we were taken in a minibus from our school across town to Duddingston playing fields. These would eventually become the home of Holyrood School but that wasn't even built at the time. We were taken to a changing pavilion that looked much more rugby oriented than football. This made sense as we learned that it was mainly the home field for Portobello High which was just in the process of introducing football as a competitive sport. There was one football pitch marked out amongst several rugby fields. It was positioned in a way that made the howling wind a major factor in the game. We won comfortably (Four or five—two I think) and I played okay but it would take some time to get used to being just one of many very good players all of whom liked lots of the ball!

What we all really looked forward to was our first home game. The home field for both Holy Cross (now St Augustines—Oggies) and our major rival, St Anthony's (Tony's) was a place called Arboretum. It was on Ferry Road at the end of a long strip of playing fields belonging to posh private schools (Fettes, John Watson's, Stewarts Melville etc) most of which were for rugby, cricket and field hockey as these schools did not play football. We just accepted it at the time but I wonder now why they didn't play football? Later in life I met lots of guys from these type schools many of whom were as fitba daft as me but never had the opportunity to play at school! Unfortunately my best guess would be that there was a "Snob" factor in this. We even had one very old fashioned PE teacher; Donald Corr, who would constantly tell us the real mans game was "Rrrrugby boys, Rrrugby, football's for nancy boys". So rugby and cricket had the perception of being more "Gentlemanly" and football was for the other half. Sport was no doubt the loser in all of this as good athletes given the opportunity to try all three might have produced a few more gems in each. Proof of this potential were Donald Ford (My all time favorite Hearts player—yes, I admit I really liked a Hearts player) who also played cricket for Scotland and David Johnston who was a Winger for Hearts football team as well as a Scottish International rugby player!

We were willing participants in this stereotyping as, until we broadened through direct life experience our view was that "Rugby's fir poofs". Then we got to know a few Guys who played and learned better. For three of us we had an even more acute rude awakening. We just finished a football game at a place called Meggetland which was one of these massive multi-field complexes for just about every sport you could imagine. Mr Hamilton, another of our PE teachers who doubled as the rugby coach, caught three of us as we were leaving the pavilion and commissioned us for his team. He gave us no choice. Just grabbed us and explained that he was three players short and we were now on the team! We were playing Boroughmuir and they were supposed to be really good. However they didn't look very intimidating. I wasn't even sure of the rules or where to line up but I could pick it up as we went along. Didn't look like a difficult game to me. In fact this would be an ideal chance to show once and for all that football players were tougher, fitter, stronger and more flexible. We got our backsides handed to us in a basket something like twenty eight to nothing! Boys about half my weight and size ran past me like I wasn't there and for the few times I managed to make contact I was still left in their wake covered in welts from long studs and sharp elbows. That was my entire rugby career and I was glad it was over. In case I entertained thoughts of having another go at proving myself Mr Hamilton thanked me for "Volunteering" and advised me "Stick to the round ball, Meikle". I did leave with a slightly better understanding of and respect for Rugby and quite enjoyed the next "Calcutta Cup" match between Scotland and England beyond the pure raw patriotism. I recall at that time Wales were usually the team to beat and even us football riff-raff knew Barry John and John Williams of Wales and Willie John McBride of Ireland! Of course though our rugby interest was only fleeting we all knew that the best rugby commentator in the entire world was our own Bill McLaren.

Back then to our first game at Arboretum. The place was a legend with two of the best pitches in Edinburgh. The surface was like a bowling green and the deep nets were Seagull's Hill quality. It had a single rugby pitch squashed on the end but Arboretum was unequivocally a schools football Mecca. There were always decent crowds for the games there and adding to the lore was the fact that Pat

Stanton and Jimmy O'Rourke were just two of the many famous names to have preceded us there both having attended Holy Cross. We called the changing room there the "Magic Pavilion" as it could make good clothing, watches and cash disappear! There were no individual changing rooms, just one large space with pegs and seating around the edges and constant to-ing and fro-ing by dozens of boys. Those familiar would know that you wore as little as you could get away with and certainly leave anything with a "Designer" label at home. The most desirable item was a pair of Levi jeans. You'd see many a boy leaving there in shorts with a dropped bottom lip. For once, my anonymous WWW denims and canvass casual pumps put me at a clothing advantage! The other hot items were decent training shoes with Addidas Samba at the top of the list. Interesting that here in America almost forty years later the most popular "Soccer" training shoe is … Addidas Samba. Now that's longevity for you. If you watched carefully you could see boys hovering around the door weighing up those entering and selecting their new wardrobe!

Our first game there was against Forrester. They would become a new main rival when we moved to the new Oggies School as Forrester was right next door. They had one player; Arthur Albiston, who had already made his mark on the boys club scene. He ended up as a regular full back in the Manchester United team of the 1970's. It didn't help them that day as we won three-two in a pulsating game on what was recognized as the prime (slightly larger) pitch. Arboretum was everything it was cracked up to be. I left with a glowing inner satisfaction and my entire non-designer "Provy" (Leith Provident Store credit account) outfit intact.

Our first big clash with Tony's at Arboretum also lived up to the build-up with the added spice of Mike Stanton (younger brother of Pat) in the Tony's line up. We ended up in a two-two draw and this was the first time I was in a game where someone broke a leg. I think the boys name was something like Rose or Rosie and he just seemed to land a bit awkwardly after a fairly innocuous challenge for a bouncing ball. I was close enough to hear the "Snap" and it was quite frightening and sickening to see a bone protruding from his shin. An ambulance from the nearby Western general was there within minutes so there must have been a phone somewhere in the magic pavilion (no cell phones in those days) though I can't ever remember seeing one. It took a little bit of the sparkle off the game momentarily but it's always amazed me (I've seen many such injuries over the years) how quickly everyone just gets on with it as soon as the victim has been removed from view.

That first secondary school team was stuffed with potential professionals and yet nobody on it ended up truly making the big time. Sam Lynch duly signed an S form with Celtic and seemed like a sure thing. Next I met him was in a Junior (Semi-pro) match many years later at Burngrange Park in west Calder when we would both be early twenties. He was easily recognizable with his distinct stooped stance, curling locks, bright eyes and a warm grin tilted to the right side of his mouth. I was playing in midfield for the home side; West Calder United and he was sweeper for our opponents that day; Arniston Rangers. He was still solid. We had a cup of tea and sandwich together in the pavilion afterwards and caught up. He was obviously a bit disappointed at not going farther but I will say his personality hadn't changed a bit. Despite his hard edge on the field he was always a gentle, mellow and genuinely nice guy off it (unlike most of us at school age). Reading the evening news regularly I see he's a relatively successful coach/Manager in the East of Scotland League—no surprise.

Tojo was in the same category. He and I were quite friendly for a while and regularly visited each others houses after school. We were all a wee bit jealous that maybe the Marinello name helped his cause a little. Maybe so but there was no doubt he was fast, explosive and extremely talented. He went off to Burnley on a football apprenticeship at a time when Burnley were famous for their youth development system but didn't complete it. Again, next time I encountered Tony was several years later in an under twenty-one Juvenile match against BMC Thistle at Saughton Park. I was playing for Cavalry Park. We had a great laugh afterwards. He hadn't changed either. He had been and still was larger than life mental—but funny mental as opposed to nasty mental. He could always make anybody laugh even when they desperately tried not to. Hopefully he still can.

Kevin McCall was a hard, steady reliable player who flirted with the senior ranks. Before the internet I used to get a "Pink" sent regularly so that I could keep up with everyone's progress. Through this I tracked Kevin having a long and successful career in the juniors mainly with Dalkeith though I think he also had a decent run with Bonnyrigg or Newtongrange.

Stevie Torrance was another player with obvious star potential but who never hit the big time. What was a little different about Stevie was that although he made his name initially (Holy Cross Primary, Leith Schools) as an out and out Striker, he always seemed much more set on making a perfect assist via a pass. This hadn't changed when we ended up back on the same dominant under twenty-one Cavalry Park team. He was also a Manager in the East of Scotland league last I looked.

Cubby was probably the most pure football talented of the bunch but he never seemed that motivated in pursuing it. Last I knew of him he was an established regular at Stratties Pub on Gorgie Road. He was a die-hard Jambo so maybe that had an impact on him! Thing is, Cubby excepted perhaps, there was still a ton of healthy recreation and pleasure extracted by all of these guys and it still continues for many of them today in some shape or form. Besides what I've been able to pick-up through the pinks and more recently the internet I bet by now there will be a few budding stars amongst their offspring. Of course making the school team kept me right on track for stardom regardless of what happened to the rest of them!

11

MOVIN' ON UP

Following the temporary demise of Edinburgh Thistle it was time for me to settle on a new club team. Granton Emmitt had sort of been subsumed into Royston Boys Club and Mr McGauran was there so that was a strong possibility. A pal of my dad's; Jacky Landells was heavily involved with Salvesen Boys Club. They were always one of the best youth clubs and a steady supplier to the Pro's so that was tempting too. I also had a visit from a coach from "Crossroads" who were planning a big move on the teenage football scene. Tynecastle boys club showed interest but there was just something about the name which didn't appeal to me! Edina Hibs wore Hibs strips, had their own facilities. It was a park and clubhouse at Newcraighall named for the original mining pit "The Jewel" I assume, after its abundant yield of coal. Two of their prospects had recently progressed onto the bigger Hibs. (Alex Cropley and John Brownlie) This I really fancied but it was so far way from Pilton.

There was also talk at Colin Barr's shop of formation of a new Pilton Sporting Club, our very own neighborhood team with Colin leading and Blair Welsh, Rab Lettuce and Jannie Wilson running things. They would start with an organized outdoor five-a-side league with proper strips for all and include anyone who wanted to play. They would spread out the strongest players to encourage parity in competition. Ultimately they would form the strongest players from each five into one full size team. Doesn't sound much now but at the time this was a very novel and innovative concept with organized playing potential for many that wouldn't otherwise have the chance. However timing was still a bit vague.

Amidst all this I had a visit from "Wee" Peter O'Neil and his assistant Graham Warren who had started up Restalrig Boys Club based in a little clubhouse in an old railway building at the end of Leith Links. I visited and was swept away by the hard sell. They had pennants from all the major teams in England and Scotland. Plans to play in tournaments down South and abroad, maybe even in America. They also had the best of kits (Aston Villa) and were willing to help fund better boots if anybody needed them. It felt like a real football club. I trained with them a couple of times and they even provided diluted orange and digestive biscuits afterwards. They had a great collection of players, though with nobody from my side of town amongst them. I enthusiastically signed but quickly got fed up traveling back and forth on my own. I met and spoke to Mr McGauran one night and just like that I was back nearer home with a bunch of familiar Pilton, Granton and Royston faces at Royston Boys Club. We trained hard in a tiny Hall on Boswell Parkway and had great indoor fitba afterwards despite the very tight confines. Ironically our main rivals were all the aforementioned clubs and I admit I was a bit embarrassed facing the people I'd rejected the first time we played against each of them.

Back at school Oggies B's were having a respectable season winning more than we were losing and I finally got on the score sheet at Wardie against David Kilpatrick's. A few months later than planned we moved down to the new school on Broomhouse road. It was spectacular with state of the art Science, Art and technical blocks. A full size theatre, a lecture theatre and a PE block which was bigger and better than anything we could imagine. It included a massive main gymnasium with a small sub-gym off to one side and a full size swimming pool. It even had a Rock Climbing room with a variety of grips and surfaces on which to practice. It had the first "All weather" pitch. There were dining halls for each year of students with multiple choice menus and even a sweet shop which was open during breaks and lunchtime. The classes were all well equipped as was a substantial library.

Shortly after we settled in I got summoned to the main office. I was convinced someone had seen me smoking behind the Gym or under the stairs and that I was in trouble. However when I got there the Secretary told me to sit at her desk. She dialed a number, waited a few seconds and handed me the phone. "Hello James" I recognized it but before I could register who it was he continued;

"Listen son, its Mr Duncan here from Craigmuir."

I'm now totally confused thinking why would he be after me?

"James, I'm running the Leith Primary Schools select again this year and want you to play."

"But sir, I'm at my secondary school now."

"Aye, I know son but there's been a rule change and eligibility is based purely on age now. You're birthdays September tenth, right?"

"Yes sir"

"Well technically you're still actually primary school age" Then he joked "Your mother must have started you really early to get some peace at home"

He's joking but I'm thinking. Ironically though my mom loved me plenty I knew this to be actually true! As it transpired I benefited all the way through my career getting an extra year at each age group because my birthday was after first September.

"James you still there son? You do want to play for Leith again right?"

I snap to "Yes sir, sorry sir, of course sir. What do I need to do?"

I didn't even have to go through trials. Just show up at Warriston for the final practice session and I was straight in at inside left. This time I knew a few of the players in fact a couple were also at Royston Boys Club with me. And of course no tracksuit top for me this time so I do have that photo. It doesn't have the names listed but as I look at it now I remember most of them, some by nickname only! Alan Tennant (Goalie), Lex Shields and Brian Carnie from Groathill. "Winker" Watson and "Dodser" from Royston. Nicky Marino from Silverknowes. Big Tom Carter I think from Muirhouse or Craigmuir. Eric Alison was from one of the old Leith schools, maybe Hermitage and David Rodgers was a returnee like me.

Our main tune up was again a challenge match against Edinburgh at Warriston. Tojo also had a September birthday and was recalled by Edinburgh so we got to play against each other. This time we were badly thumped mainly because of a superb five goal performance by their fast, burly, powerful centre forward; Chris Robertson. Chris played for Salvesen and he and I clashed many times over the years. He was the best purely instinctive scorer I ever saw. He ended up having a respectable pro career and came within a crossbar of a cup final headed goal for Rangers which might have set him off to greater stardom. He played at Hearts too and ended up as the lovable "Rocky" at Meadowbank Thistle until his knees forced the issue. His younger bother John didn't do badly either but we'll get back to him later. Although we had a mutual football based respect I can't say Chris and I knew each other well until much later when I married his cousin! I saw him quite recently at my father-in-law's funeral. We had a good blether over a pint in the room above the Tolbooth Bar and caught up. He and Ronnie Tolmie (another Celtic S form) were coaching in the Juniors. There was an older brother George who was quite a player too but like many of that generation he preferred a pint at the Queens Arms!

This time we drew East Lothian in the first round of the Scottish (Wilson) Cup. We played them in a cold driving rain and hailstorm at Prestonpans and I got a metal stud in the knee causing a nasty gash. Not enough to stop me carry on playing though. We came out with a two-one win with Lex and I netting a goal each and we even got a match report in the pink by Craigie Veitch. I did my best to make sure the blood was showing in the photo which was taken at the end of the game! This earned us a return trip to Victoria Park in Newtongrange to face Midlothian in round two. The experience of the bus trip, changing rooms, strips and refreshments was no less great the second time around. In fact I probably enjoyed it even more knowing that I would be playing the whole game barring injury. Unfortunately the result was even worse this time—we ended up on the wrong end of a seven-two thrashing.

As projected Pilton Sporting Club (PSC) managed to get their 5-a-side league underway and they made a great job of it. They started with three small pitches running sideways across the St David's main school field. They had crisply marked lines, scaled down goals with nets and little corner flags. Age range was about ten to thirteen. The rules were modified with no offside and corner kicks accumulating where three got you a penalty kick. This was effective in keeping the fairly short games (something like five minutes each way) moving along. The most exciting thing was they had spanking new strips, including shorts and socks for every team. They used animal and insect names which generally related to the colors. For example the "Wasps" wore Yellow and Black hoops and the "Lions" All Yellow with Black cuffs. I was on the "Buffaloes" and we wore Black and White (Newcastle) stripes. They also did a good job of distributing the more experienced talent fairly evenly. The formula was basically two well established players per team and the rest made up with relative newcomers. I had Kevin Thomson with me as our other seeded player. He was yet another very goad goalie who always wanted to play centre forward! It really was a very creative concept and did have the entire neighborhood bubbling with enthusiasm.

Just as PSC got going my parents got a letter from the local council (nicknamed Corpie for Corporation; local authority) with the news that a "Main Door" house was available in Drylaw. A "Main Door" meant a street level house with its own direct entrance and no significant steps or stairs involved. My Mum had a heart condition and so, with her Doctor's written support, she had been on the waiting list for one for years. I guess we were vaguely aware of the list but never really expected anything to come of it as good "Main Door" rentals rarely became available. Most people once in them stayed for life. I should explain that although many of the people in the working class areas now own their houses the overwhelming majority were rented from the Corpie at that time. My dad went and picked up the keys and we had a family outing to give the place a look. It was in Wester Drylaw Drive only about a mile from where we were in Pilton but it seemed like worlds away at the time.

It was mostly four-to-a-block houses with centered main entrances to the lower two houses in front and small stairs up each side to the two houses on the upper level. All of them had individual gardens in front with little latticed thin wire fences and they were generally very nicely kept. There were a few "Stairs" a little farther up the street but even these looked in pretty nice shape compared to the average Pilton ones. Around Edinburgh, Drylaw's reputation was, inaccurately as it transpired, stereotyped by the up and coming gang "Young Mental Drylaw" (YMD) which brought images of the Wild West. However, anyone who spent enough time to get a proper look around the place would see that it was actually a fairly respectable area with some really nice stretches of houses.

We were being offered the bottom right as you looked at the block from the street. As it transpired this block was actually about three feet above grade so there were four small steps at the start of the path. As we browsed outside and prepared to enter, a few kids quickly accumulated on the street to give their prospective incoming the once over. I also noticed a couple of curtain turners having a peak from across the street. Inside we found three bedrooms, kitchen, bathroom and reasonably sized Living Room with two large windows looking out to an individual rear garden. We would have the approximate half immediately outside the house (around 15' x 30') and the upstairs had a narrow path up the side to the other half. All neatly divided with low, wooden, slatted fencing. There's a tall solid wooden fence along the back of their bit which we found out later separated us from the old railway line. This was no longer in operation but like most of the old lines which were very straight, direct routes it had been converted into a useful footpath.

I could tell my Mom was very enthused despite her trying hard to play it cool until she could get our vibes. She also told us that the Corpie had explained that there were a lot of Policemen living in this stretch which she liked but I saw as a possible double-edged sword! My guess is that my Dad was also very keen but he would stay non-committal and concur with her wishes regardless. We had moved from Leith proper (Albert Street) to Pilton with the rest of the baby-boomers when I was an infant so "Flitting" (as we called it) would be quite a big deal to me. We opened the back door and went outside to have a look and for me it was over in seconds! The upstairs garden had two half size football goals at either end complete with nets. I had also been promised that if we ever had a house with a garden like this I could keep pets. On double-checking my Mom said that offer still stood.

Mind you her "Pet Ban" in our flat hadn't prevented me keeping several Hamsters. This until "Goldie the third" (It seemed that ninety percent of hamsters were named Goldie or Hammy) escaped into the back of our small upright piano and started running up and down the keys causing an eerie Phantom of the Opera effect. It took us about two days and lots of smelly cheese to tempt him out by which time his fate was well sealed. Fortunately the school adopted him, cage, little exercise wheel and all. This is a football story so I don't want to digress too much on a Hamster theme but I must mention that Miss Yandros (spelling a guestimate) a very lovable but somewhat eccentric female teacher of Polish extraction who was at St David's, actually walked about all day with a Hamster on her person! Honestly, it sat on her shoulder most of the time but disappeared under her clothing for long periods causing very disturbing moving bulges, especially to the uninitiated. It made it even harder for us recent puberty boys to keep our eyes of her firm point chats (breasts).

My Mom declared her hand and we all fell like dominoes. Truth was we all loved it. It was a done deal then. That night my gut swirled as I argued the pros and cons inside my head. In theory I would still come back regularly to play with Mongo and the rest of my crew but I was old enough to know that in reality that just wouldn't happen. My other dread fear was that we might have to flit on the cheap. Several of my pals had moved within Pilton and many of them couldn't afford to hire a proper truck. Some of them even done what was called "Moonlighting" which was swapping houses with another renter without prior permission. The Corpie were often left with a fait a complit and just seemed to accept it as such. I volunteered to help one family with their move and was mortified when I was stuck guiding one corner of an old metal double bed on castors down the middle of the street. They even left the old granddad in it in his nightshirt and stacked various other pieces of junk on top of him! We had to go all the way from Ferry Road Avenue to West Pilton Circus and almost lost control on a steep section of the Drive. This was the ultimate "Redder" (Red face) as I passed many people who knew me en-route. Fortunately my Dad would have enough contacts to raise a couple of pick-up trucks … Whew! So I shut my eyes tight and just kept thinking about that fabulous little pitch in the neighbor's garden.

As we gathered up our belongings before heading to Drylaw we reflected. We'd all miss Mrs Boyle and hoped we could find a new neighbor as genuine. Maybe she'd even get lucky and get someone less noisy above her. My Mom would miss Mrs Weir as they'd become quite good pals. My Dad would miss walking to and from work with the Dode (George) Burnett an old football pal of his. My dad didn't throw football compliments around lightly but he always said Dode Burnet, in his prime, was "One of the best full backs ever". Maybe he'd even drive to work now in his recently acquired shiny black "Rover 10" complete with running boards and sunroof—bought from Crewe Toll garage for twenty five pounds with the proceeds of him stopping smoking! If only we'd had the foresight to stick it in mothballs somewhere—it'd be worth a fortune now! Anyway Ferranti employed half the men in this part of Edinburgh so there'd be a few in Drylaw too. My eldest brother John had completed his apprenticeship with the Gas Board and headed off to make his fortune in Australia so he had no say. At that time any qualified tradesmen could get a free passage there as they were desperately short of skilled workers. David had finished at Tony's and started his apprenticeship as a Shop fitter/Joiner with R.L. Rae. He seemed fairly indifferent about the move. I guess he'd already started to develop a wider circle of pals beyond Pilton via his work. My wee sister Sheona was keen. She already knew a couple of girls from school who lived at our new bit and a couple more who were in her highland dancing troupe.

Me? I'd miss a lot.

I'd have to give up my recently acquired job on Willie Dobie's Ice Cream van. I was proud of that job. Willie gave me it because, he said, "I can tell your honest son, I can trust you" He was right. Though it would have been a synch, I never did him out of a penny. I sold the Ice cream cones, juice, sweeties and of course our number one sales item; fags. (Our term for cigarettes which my kids quickly check me on every time it slips out! Not a PC expression Stateside). A lot of people couldn't afford a whole pack of fags which came in tens or twenties. There was one really cheap brand (Park Drive I think they were called) which came in a five pack. We happily broke them open and sold "Singles". The profit margin in this was phenomenal. Whilst I was busy with this part of the business Willie would slip into the driver's seat and chat through the window with a string of adults peddling an assortment of goods. I was never to notice this but I did. I was never to ask about it and I did not. This was before the nasty scepter of drugs appeared seriously on the scene so it was only things like Irons and Hair dryers and Electric Fires some of which were likely "Hot" without even being switched on.

I'd miss Barr's and the Chippie and the Butcher and the Dry-salter's and the Co-operative Store, where you gave your magic number for discount. David and John still know it. I don't as I was a deliberate failure at going for messages on the basis this would get me out of it. My strategy was to get it badly wrong; "Oops sorry Ma, I thought you said a tin o' Pears, no Peas" It worked a treat. I'd miss the old Fishwife with her hand cart and Onion Johnnie; they'd never make it all the way up to Drylaw. I'd miss the ragman I bet he didn't come to Drylaw. I'd miss the roll man and the coal man and the juice lorry.

I'd miss the unique sound of a hundred kids at playtime at the school opposite our stair on days when I was off sick from school. That was a really great sound. A sort of busy contentment and innocent joy sandwiched between two rings of a school bell. It was almost like white noise but with a distinct Scottish accent and there was just something very happy, comforting and re-assuring about it. My son made me a CD with a contemporary mix of Scottish bands recently and there was a couple songs on there by "Sebastian and Belle" (or vice versa?) whom I'd never heard of to that point. On one track they had the sound of kids playing in the background and it reminded me precisely of that great noise.

I'd miss looking out of our window for hours across the school and over the big field awaiting the return of my Uncle David from one of his Merchant Navy trips, knowing he would come laden with exotic gifts from Hong Kong or Singapore. I know now that he never even came from that direction but it doesn't matter. It was a bit like staring out into the sky for Santa—you could see whatever you wanted. Of course I had outgrown that by now but I had to keep it up for my wee sisters' sake! I'd miss inventing a million different ways to climb up and down the stair banisters. I'd miss the classic Backgreen concerts (Written, produced and directed by ourselves!) in the summer. I'd miss "Kick the can" and "Kissy Chasey" where I would always try for Lanie or Liz Taylor (Another Liz Taylor) and neither of them seemed to try too hard to escape!

Funnily enough I'd even miss some of the "Bad" stuff. Likesay, my ongoing feud with the Kane brothers, Alex and Billy, (I once tied the latter to a backgreen pole for two hours) which was occasionally a little violent but never dangerously so. I'd miss Mr Casey a diehard "Bluenose" on the bottom flat blasting "The Sash" at top volume on his record player every time Rangers had a good result. Fortunately this was before sub-woofers and in fact Rangers didn't win as often as you might think in the late 1960's. I'd miss the diminutive Mrs Miller with the mostly pure white but occasionally pink or blue hair. She would moan in her strangely deep excorcistic voice every time I trailed mud into the stair. I'd also miss the dulcet tones of Frankie Boil-Sinatra on a Saturday night and I'd even miss the threat of old MacHolmsie putting a knife in my ball. I didn't see many hedges or midges in Drylaw—did they even play street football there? I'd miss volunteering to climb 50 feet up the drainpipe and squeeze in through a small window when Mrs Fraser locked herself out the house.

Most of all I'd miss my pals especially Mongo and Deek.

But life moves on.

12

A NEW CREW AND A HISTORY LESSON

So we get settled in our new house and it's out the door to see who's who in that part of Drylaw. The news is positive—there's football everywhere you look. Upstairs are the Mansons including three fitba daft laddies approximately ages with our three boys and with the older two even having the same names! Johnnie their oldest is already playing for Falkirk. Davie is keen but headed towards a refereeing career. Kenny is ages with me and already a fast powerful winger with a really hard shot—a mini Peter Lorimer and he even looked a bit like him. Through the wall are the Bains; "Dubb" and "Egg" no idea of their proper names even now. They're a bit older than us but seem keen enough on football. Either their sister or one of the girls from the house above them is dating Kevin Hegarty who is about to sign for Hearts so he's around a fair bit. Not a bad start and that's just my immediate block of four.

Across the street is big Gordon (Gogsie) Black he's probably a year or two older than me. His dad's one of the cops and they're good Hibees who, I understand, both ended up as Stewards at Easter Road. Gogsie is not a great player and has the disadvantage of trying to play with his specs on and he's always pushing them back up his nose with his right index finger (no contact lenses then). His size compensates some and he's keen as mustard. Next door is John Percival. (Percy) I think his dad was a cop too but they seem quite posh. Percy plays the bagpipes. He's quite a gentle soul and always strikes me as someone who should be across the old railway track in Blackhall. He can take or leave the fitba but participates most of the time. A couple more doors down is Tommy Duff. He's not a bad player with breakaway speed—he's a diehard jambo. A little further down there's a half circle of grass with neat houses around the perimeter. This produces two more players. "Skin" Wright who is more game than skilled and Keith Mulligan with the mop of black hair and long eyelashes who is clearly already much more interested in girls than the ball! That constitutes our immediate crowd. They do indeed play street football from gate to gate as well as in a corner of Groathill primary school where lampposts from the street are close enough to allow nighttime play.

A couple hundred yards in the other direction there's a row of shops including a Newsagent, Bakery, Grocer and Bookie! There are a few more players dotted around this part. Ian and Ross Jack who's dad Sandy, as well as being a top cop, is a bigwig in the East of Scotland League. There's also Roy, who is surprisingly skilful and mobile for his short tubby build. Harry O lives above the shops and Ronnie Hogg and Davie Cooper on the cul-de-sac opposite. These two groups form the nucleus of a regular pick up game which is played on a sloped field behind the few stairs. On high days and holidays Kenny Manson was allowed to bring the goals up from his garden to this field which usually guaranteed a really good turnout. People gain the respect of others through many conduits but, fairly or otherwise, if you are particularly good at something it often speeds up the process. Football was always like that for me. Hopefully I would be able to retain credibility through more important means like just being a decent person but football would always get me in the door. This made the transition to my new patch quick and easy. I played. They saw. I was one of the boys.

Stairs backed on to three sides of the field we used and the other had a high wall with some glass embedded in the top. I quickly learned this was a section of the perimeter wall for an estate called "Dockies" which covered several acres stretching all the way down to the main Groathill Road on which there was a grand entrance with crests fashioned into the wall. At the time none of us knew or cared very much about it. Details were sparse and unconfirmed. Dockies was occupied by a "Weird" obviously very wealthy family. They never mixed with the locals and there were signs all over the place telling us to "Keep Out" and "Beware of the Dogs". I was told that the latter sign was definitely no empty threat. There were at least two bulldogs which "patrolled" the grounds and attacked anything that moved. Several of the boys had encountered these dogs on trips over the wall to retrieve a ball or steal some apples. The biggest, meanest and most notorious of these dogs was a legend in his own right. He was called "Titus Oats" and the name alone generated fear amongst the Drylaw children. Rumor was that he had chewed the foot off one boy and the owner had somehow won the battle to keep him from being put to sleep on some ancient Scottish trespassing law.

It was a bit like our MacHolmsie syndrome but even more scary. There were enough footholds on our side to make getting to the top of the wall quite easy and with care you could avoid the glass shards which had long since lost their sharpness. It was even a fairly easy jump down on the other side. The problem was getting back up. There were virtually no footholds on the inside so you had to use a couple of apple trees with a few limbs which were fairly close to the wall. It was tough to get out quickly. The same "Last touch" rule applied in Drylaw as in Pilton. This again caused problems getting goalies at that end of the field as a great save would sometimes mean tipping the ball above the bar but it would carry all the way over the wall. People were also a bit more selective with their shooting at that end cautious not to blooter one high over the wall! When it did happen there was no mercy. We'd all scramble up the wall and keep watch as the poor victim went in. There would always be cruel shouts of "Titus". He was real and did appear a couple of times and he was every bit as evil looking as advertised. His scowl and growl were indeed terrifying. Fortunately his jumping ability was zero and there were tons of trees so worse case scenario is you could scramble onto a branch and wait him out. I'm glad I never got to see him get his teeth on anyone. I imagine he would not let go easily. A couple of us did get the courage once to make our way up the long driveway to go "Guising" (Our version of Trick or Treating) We did not encounter Titus and got to stand just inside the door for a few seconds whilst a very guarded, reserved lady found a few pennies for us. She said almost nothing. With hindsight it looked a bit creepy and jaded but must have been a relatively grand place in its prime. We sprinted back down the driveway at top speed feeling very brave and pleased with ourselves.

Years later when I got fed up meeting Americans who knew more about our rich Scottish history than I did I made the effort to do some catching up. Thinking back we had very limited coverage of our own history in my time at school and I'm not sure why? On the advice of my good friend here Tim Mulligan, a war Historian (and author) at the US National Archives, I started with John Prebble's "Culloden", "Glencoe" and "The Highland Clearances' (all Penguin Books). If you ever have a notion to get a feel for the roots of Scottish character, feelings and emotions, whether you've experienced them first hand or just observed them, reading and absorbing these three books will provide great perspective and context. They should certainly be compulsory reading in Scottish High Schools!

We're always talking about what a small world it is and how we often find unexpected connections in the oddest ways. This is exactly what happened when I read The Highland Clearances. On page sixty nine in a chapter called "Year of the Burnings" I was taken aback by the following:

"Loch was at this time only thirty-three, a broad shouldered, fair haired young man with the type of resolute head that strikes well in profile on coin. His home at Drylaw, a house and acreage near Edinburgh, had been bought by a Seventeenth-century ancestor …"

I did a double take. They were referring to James Loch descended from Norman de loch or de lacus though the authenticity of their "Gentry" status was never really proven. In short, James Loch was a Lawyer who in 1813 became the main architect of the plan to replace the common people with more profitable sheep in the Duke of Sutherland's (Stafford) vast highland territories. He met with Stafford at his house in London and occasionally at Dunrobin Castle in Sutherland. He even met regularly with his main henchmen Young and Sellar at the small manse on the corner of the estate at Drylaw. The Manse is still there right at Groathill roundabout. It's converted into a small house and one of our crew; Henry used to live there and I'd been in it with him. I suspect his family had no clue about the historic significance. I'm not sure if the main house is still there. It is clear that large chunks of the former estate have been sold off to make way for dozens of "Barrett" type homes.

I researched through some old ordnance survey maps just to be sure and confirmed that, yes; Dockies and Drylaw House were indeed one in the same! I have yet to meet any of my old Drylaw pals who even had an inkling of this connection despite many of them staying there their entire lives. Always wanting to put two and two together and get four I theorized that the current occupants were descendants of Loch who assumed that all the locals would know the facts and hate them for it, hence their great efforts to remain aloof, distant and mysterious.

This also dotted another "I" for me. When we traveled to Wick there was only one main road North to Caithness. This went through Sutherland and passed Dunrobin Castle and a statue of the Duke perched high on a hilltop. My Mom would always make a point of rolling down the window and spitting in the direction of the statue. This was very out of character for her but apparently a custom she had picked up from the previous generation of Highlanders. If she explained it to us at the time I certainly never took it in but now I finally understood her inherent hatred of a man who, through Loch's hand, starved the local people and burned their "Trees". Trees were the wooden supports which were essential to them forming roofs on their houses. Hence they ended up on ships bound for the mid-Atlantic US seaboard and Nova Scotia. Ultimately Scotland's loss was North America's gain with tremendous positive Scottish influence still clearly evident on all aspects of present day Canada and the USA. In fact if this particular subject line tickles your fancy I would also recommend "How the Scots invented the modern world" by Arthur Herman. (Three Rivers Press)

Finally, a few years ago, my government work took me to a place called Lancaster House in London for a few days. I learned that this in fact was originally Stafford House the London home of the Duke of Sutherland. This means by four completely unconnected co-incidences I had been in all the locations where the Highland clearances were planned and plotted and executed. This gave me a very eerie shiver yet I was still glad it had all been joined up for me.

See how distracted I can get when the ball goes out of play?

In one of our many games on this little field I got yet another stud in my upper right thigh. Oddly, it didn't bleed much though it appeared quite a deep puncture to my skin. It seemed to close up quickly and felt fine. I didn't even mention it to my folks.

13

WHO SAYS HOSPITALS ARE GLUM?

A few days later I had a continuous nagging ache in that area of my leg. Eventually it got so painful that I was in tears and could not sleep. I wasn't (and still am not) a good patient even with a minor ailment and was heavy on the whining anyway but this definitely felt more serious than anything I'd ever experienced. I'm sure my dad initially thought I was angling for a day off school (which I was known to do once in a while) but when I also developed a temperature he knew there was more to it. Late on Wednesday night he carted me up to the Western General Hospital Emergency Unit. The duty doctor was at a loss but decided to keep me in for observation. By the next day they concluded I had some kind of infection but they weren't exactly sure what. They gave me some tablets and it seemed to settle the pain down and my fever subsided. I was to be transferred to another hospital.

There was a roster system in place where, once the immediate emergency was in hand, you would be transferred to the duty hospital for that day. In my case this meant a trip to Longmore, a small, mainly geriatric hospital on the Southside of town near the Commonwealth Swimming Pool (The Commie) originally built for the 1970 games but now a public facility. This would be my home for the next two weeks. Once I stopped feeling sorry for myself it was quite fascinating to be the only patient under the age of sixty in the entire place. I was totally spoiled by the nurses who no doubt found me a refreshing change from the grind of having to look after a bunch of old, seriously ill biddies with generally very poor bladder and bowel control. You'd think even the most dedicated of nurses would eventually get a little worn down by it all but if they did they certainly kept it to themselves.

Surprisingly, in amongst all the perceived depression there was a fair amount of humor. I was both amused and terrified at different points. A few examples from Longmore:

BENNY—Was suffering from Parkinson's disease or something similar. He was in the occupational therapy class making Basket trays and, for reasons unknown, he was dressed in a lovely light gray suit. These were the trays built up on a "Horse and hounds" baseboard picture with a few colored beads built into the handle area at either end. I became quite expert at these in a very short time. The process started with getting a few thin canes and soaking them in a large jar of water to make them pliable. Unfortunately Benny picked up his canes and got them in the jar but on his way back to the table took a shaking fit. To me it seemed terrible. He was shaking water all over his lovely suit and could do nothing to stop it. But he had a rye smile on his face and the nurses were in hysterics. "Bad timing again Benny" one said. It subsided and they all had a laugh and poor Benny just sat down and got on with his tray. The human spirit is quite something!

ANDY, TOMMY AND HAMISH—These guys are ancient to me. Probably all in their 80's and the only three, besides me, who are allowed out of their beds. They get to eat lunch and dinner at a table in the middle of the ward and I get to join them. They mostly act like I don't exist. They have very few teeth between them so it's a noisy experience. At first it puts me off my food but I get used to it to the point where I don't notice any more except when a bit of mince or semolina comes flying directly at my face! Every day they have great debates about the war. Almost exclusively the First World War from what I can gather. They were obviously around for the second one too but perhaps already too old to go fighting. In fact they're very like the characters in "Dad's Army"; a popular telly comedy series about the "Home Guard". Strange but they seem to almost have a contempt for the second war like it was some kind of inferior cousin. The Matron stops by periodically to remind them that if they get too wound up they will lose their table privileges. They take the threat seriously as they obviously treasure this perk. They wave off frequent attempts by the bed-ridden men to get in on the discussion. They seem to have no sympathy for their less fortunate colleagues. It's almost like they should be ashamed of being too sick to get up. Only the strong survive. Though it's measured not to be too insulting, the nurses tease them about them still having all this machismo even at their ripe old ages. They always complain that the bed bottles for peeing in are too small for their privates! They're also in competition for the bed nearest the door as there is an old dear in a nightie constantly shuffling up and down the corridor on a Zimmer frame.

Hamish had been a Sergeant the other two Corporals so even fifty-odd years later rank counts and he's the designated spokesman for the group. His standard reply to the nurses "So where um I takin' ye the night doll?" Imagine what they'd be like nowadays on two Viagra a day? Mind you the barter seemed to help both nurse and patient. Likesay; a kind of therapy.

BOB—Is never supposed to get up out of his bed but frequently does. He's got some tubes and stuff but he just pulls them off! He was actually the nicest to me but also scary at times. He would say "How are you, son?" with a big smile. He never used my name and I got the impression he may have been talking to somebody else, maybe a son he'd once had? He clearly disliked the table crowd who brutally referred to him as "The Loony". I helped the nurses collect the trays from the bed-ridden guys and one time I caught Bob putting a knife under his pillow. I said "Oh … eh, where's your knife Bob?" He slid his tray towards me, winked and beckoned me closer with a scrawny, liver spotted index finger. He whispered in my ear; "I'm keeping it for the night son, I'll get them all later." I gave him a nervous smile whilst sliding the knife out from its hiding place. He saw what I did but there was no reaction. I told the nurse but she just laughed and told me not to worry about it. Her explanation was that his thought process just wasn't properly joined up anymore. Hadn't heard of it then but I guess it was Alzheimer's though he obviously had some physical ailments too. One night I woke up to him cursing and swearing to himself on the chair by my bed. I peaked over my covers and saw the source of his frustration. He was trying to get my new slippers on and they were about four sizes too small! Like magic (as always) the night nurse appeared and gently escorted him back to his bed and re-attached him to his tubes.

MR MONTCRIEF—He was in the bed next to me. He told me in a very thin raspy voice that he was a soldier in the "first war" and a miner the rest of his days. He had an awful cough. I went to sleep one night and when I woke up in the morning his bed was empty and freshly made. When I asked the nurse where he was she just said; "He's moved on James". I thought I knew what she meant but was afraid to ask for confirmation. The nurses all seemed numb to it. Not another word was said about it. It didn't even get acknowledged at the lunch table. By dinner time there was a new man in the bed. He got some coverage with Andy and Tommy already agreeing he was a "Funny bugger" even though he hadn't said a word yet. "Aye" said Hamish, "Probably didnae even make lance Corporal". Goodbye Mr Montcrief, it was nice to almost know you. We owe that generation so much.

YOURS TRULY—For the first couple of days I got a wheelchair. Again, after I stopped feeling sorry for myself I had some fun with it and being the only youngster seemed to allow me to get away with murder. I zoomed along the corridors much faster than I should have taking bends on two wheels! At Longmore they had a "Sun Room" (all glass) overlooking the garden. It must have been like gold to some of these people who could not get outside. It was approached via a long wheelchair ramp and had a large clear notice "ALL WHEELCHAIRS MUST BE PUSHED UP THIS RAMP BY A STAFF MEMBER". Being exempt from all the old folks' rules I took this as a challenge. I got to within a few feet of the top and lost control. I immediately rolled backwards, gathering great speed and crashing into a startled porter and his laundry basket at the bottom of the ramp. I only got a small cut on my head but my pride was severely dented. The Matron informed me in no uncertain terms that my special liberal treatment in respect of the rules was over. The nurses were all falling about laughing in the background. So hospitals are not all gloom and doom but for me there was no longer room for zoom. Boom, boom. (Sorry, I just watched Cat in the Hat movie!)

They had finally got a handle on my problem and thought that penicillin could keep it under control. I have never liked needles but with so many blood tests I had now gotten used to them. However they decided to give me my medicine directly with injections in the rear end every six hours rather than via pills. I hated these jags (shots) and sweated over them an hour or more before each one. Some nurses were more gentle than others and I remember one very large Irish lady who would just give me a shake and shout "Bums up James me boy, let's get it over with darlin'". Without hesitation she'd pop in the syringe and I could feel the stuff pumping into my thigh area. It would tighten up and pulsate with pain for several minutes then gradually subside over the next half hour or so.

They thought I had something called "Osteo mylitas" which was a poisoning of the marrow of the bone. They guessed it may have started with the stud in my leg but they couldn't be sure. Sometimes they could solve it with medicine and in other cases it might need an operation. They decided I was in the former category and so I could go home. and continue my medication for a while—pills by mouth thank goodness. The nurses at Longmore were pleased for me but seemed genuinely touched to see me go. They had enjoyed our little interlude. I think the table crowd could care less but they had kind of got used to me sitting there listening in to their confab. Hamish did make eye contact once as I was leaving the ward and I felt he was going to say something but a leader couldn't afford to let sappy emotion show in front of his men, right? I tried to say goodbye to Bob but

I knew it didn't register. I had very strict instructions to do nothing beyond walking for at least a month.

I got home on a Wednesday and by the Saturday I was stir-crazy. I took a very slow walk down to Craigroyston School. PSC had grown so rapidly that St David's' small field couldn't cope so the five-a-side league had expanded onto Craigroyston's massive field where several additional mini-pitches had been laid out. By co-incidence the Buffaloes had a game and were short a player and Kevin was relieved to see me. I should have immediately explained the situation but the urge was uncontrollable—addiction is the correct term for it. I said I'd had a sore leg but would probably be okay for such a short game (twelve minutes in all) on a small field. As soon as I tried to make a full out run I collapsed in a heap and the pain came surging back into my leg and it was much worse than before. Rab Lettuce, with help from Kevin Thomson, shuffled me into the back of his small van and I was on my way to the Western General Emergency Unit for the second time in a month. I assume they called my Dad who met us there and gave me a serious ear bending for being daft enough to try to play. They again held me overnight for observation and obtained the rest of the story from Longmore. The next day I was seen by an apparently much esteemed surgeon, a bone specialist called Dr Soutter. He had several young Doctors trailing alongside him and hanging onto his every word. He determined that I would need to go to the Royal Infirmary for an operation and then onto Princess Margaret Rose (PMR) for a lengthy convalescence. If I understood it correctly what they did is extracted the infected fluid from the marrow of my right thigh bone. I was then taken to the PMR and put in a massive children's ward. I was to continue with antibiotics (pills again, phew!) and was also to be on traction for a few weeks. This involved a bunch of weights being attached to my right leg. It felt weird and I had a moan at my Mom and Dad but they assured me it would speed the recovery process.

At PMR I didn't feel sorry for myself too long. It was the absolute opposite of Longmore in that I was surrounded by boys mostly younger than myself. Many of them clearly had much more serious conditions than I was dealing with. Despite all the pain and suffering it was a mostly happy place. More so for me because it transpired that the beds to either side of me were occupied by equally keen football fans.

To my left was Archie. He had something very seriously wrong with his head. It was disproportionately large because of some kind of fluid retention and apparently they couldn't do much about it. I'm guessing he was nine or ten years old. He slept a lot but whilst awake his constant pre-occupation was Falkirk Football Club known affectionately by their fans as "The Bairns". He was impressed when

I told him my neighbor was an actual Falkirk player. Falkirk's not far from Edinburgh but the accent is much thicker. He was "Pure Falkirk" (A phrase coined by John Blackley of Hibs to describe his not so smooth appearance in a TV interview with Archie MacPherson following the 1972 League Cup final) and wanted to just double check my story first.

"Whit's aes name?"

"Johnnie Manson"

"Aye, ken um. Mind you mair in the reserves the noo bit aes had a couple ae runs wi' the big team. So aes yer neighbor, eh?"

"Aye, lives right above me, a play fitba wi' his wee brother Kenny. Johnnie joins in once in a while. They've got actual nets in their gairden"

"Nah, yer kiddin' me oan"

"Honest, likesay wee scaled doon ones, they're barry" (very good).

"Awright fir some, eh? Bet ye've niver been tae Brockville though?" (Falkirks' home ground—sadly dilapidated to where it just prevented them taking promotion to the Premier League—Being demolished and replaced)

"Aye Archie, couple ae times"

"James—is it? Your awright"

So I'm quickly established with one neighbor, now for the other.

Brian is thalidomide. He has no arms. Just a couple of fingers growing out of one shoulder. He's ten going on thirty and has a broad Irish brogue. He's up and about as much as he wants. He catches the end of my exchange with Archie and is quickly over and sits on my bed. I have never been this close to somebody with no arms and I'm quite intimidated by it. The harder I try not to stare at his shoulder the more difficult it becomes. He senses it and tries to put me at ease.

"Oim Brian and don't ye worry 'bout tha' "He nods and eyes towards the left shoulder which has the fingers. "Oim fine. It don't hurt and ye'll see it don't hold me back from nuttin'—ye like futbal den?"

"Aye, love it"

"Erchie told ye al about his beloved Bairns den?"

"Aye"

"So what's yer own team?"

"Am a Hibbie"

"Hibernian's a good team Oi loik der shirts and Oi like Pat Stanton"

"Aye, we all love Pat. So what team do you follow Brian?"

"Oi like Celtic and Rangers and Manchester United" Not often you met a Celtic/Rangers fan in fact this was my first but I could tell he was sincere.

"So what about when they play each other"

"Oi go for de draw. Do ye play futbal den?"

"Aye"

"Any good?"

I know I should be modest but the ego takes over and I blurt out; "Well I play for the School and for a Club team and Celtic have taken an interest"

"Cheez, ye must be vary, vary good den"

"Well I was but we'll have to see what happens with this" I point to my leg.

"Ye. What's up wit'dat?"

"Some kind of poison in my bone. They've got it out and it should be okay after a while"

"Dose weights look like a pain in de arse—are de tryin' to stretch you or sumtin'?"

"I guess its something like that"

A staff nurse shouts over from her station at the door of the ward and beckons to Brian.

"'Scoose me James, one of moi birds needs to see me"

It's a massive ward and has an assortment of noises, cry's and moans to get used to. There's always movement as many of these boys have medicine every couple of hours even during the night. Brian doesn't warn me that Archie always sings his song just before he goes to sleep for the night so I get a bit of a start when out of the blue I hear

"Falkirk Bai..airns, Falkirk Bai..airns, we'll support you evermore …" He gets in a couple of repeats before the staff nurse comes and calms him down and tucks him in.

From the other side I hear "Noit Hibs". I reply "Night, Celtic, Rangers and Man U!" took me a while but I must have eventually nodded off. When I awake, Brian's already sat on my bed! "Mornin' Hibs. Taut oid help ye wit' de routine you bein' new 'n al" He hands me a damp cloth and a small towel. "Pretend to woip yer face wit' de cloth den wit' de towel. Bein' mobile Oi help de nurses and dats why der al moi birds"

Between his chin and his two little fingers he carries a tray of food to me. Then he brings his own plate and sits himself on my bed with it. He grabs a fork with his right foot and gets stuck into a plate of sausage and egg. He is smooth as clockwork and has no problem reaching his foot all the way up to his mouth. I'm amazed and at first a little disgusted but it seems so natural to him I get over it quickly. Archie's awake and grunting about the cloths which, I have to agree have a funny smell to them! He looks over and says "I see wee Irish is huvin aes breakfast wi yae. He's better wi aes feet thin most are wi thir hauns. Pity ae disnae even ken whit team ae supports".

On reflection I'm pretty lucky. If you've got to be in hospital you may as well be stuck with a fitba' daft crowd. The banter goes on all day and even the nurses and doctors get in on the act. I have a birthday whilst I'm in the hospital, must be my thirteenth. My Mom asks me what I'd like. She's never done that before, she always just new and always got it just right. I think she's wary to get me a ball or a strip as it might depress me thinking that I won't be using either for a while. There's a new football game out—something called "Subbuteo". Brian and Archie and I have been talking about it a lot—it's supposed to be the most realistic football game ever but it's quite expensive. I tell my Mom about it and she says she'll have a look. The sympathy factor is at work and I can tell she'll probably get me it, even if she can't afford it! On my birthday her and my Dad come in with a large package with a ribbon around it. I quickly rip off the wrapping and reveal a large lime green box marked "Subbuteo Table Soccer—Starter Set". There are a couple of plastic windows in the lid through which you can see the players and the Goalposts complete with nets. My parents are a little puzzled to hear Brian shout "Boi gash, we got it James" and Archie chimes in "Ya beauty". As it transpired it did become something for the entire ward to share.

A subbuteo pitch was a piece of emerald Green cloth about 4' x 6' and was neatly marked with a pitch. You could tape it onto a table top or spread it out on a tight piled carpet or any other reasonably flat surface. It had one additional line what would be about twenty five yards from each goal and you were only allowed to take shots inside that line. The players were tiny detailed figures (About half an inch high) and were mounted on a heavier round base shaped and curved underneath so it almost always sprung back to an upright position when moved. The ball was very light and disproportionately large compared to the players though you progressed to a much smaller ball as your skill level improved. The goalies were on a long stem which you fed through the net. You then could hold the stem behind the net and maneuver the goalie in all directions making him dive and jump and charge out. You "Flicked" the players to make them "Kick" the ball. There were deluxe sets and all sorts of accessories like corner flags, a perimeter fence, referees and linesmen and even floodlights which worked with batteries or an AC adapter. stands and spectators. There was a scoreboard like the "Half-Time" ones they had at most grounds a well as, stands and fans, a TV Tower with cameras and even photographers for behind the goals. The possibilities were endless but the basic set was plenty for us right now.

We approached the staff nurse with the suggestion that we set it up on a table at the end of the ward. He was agreeable as long as it was to be shared by all those interested. A deal. The nurses, as usual with Brian's help, found a table big enough and set out the pitch. The table was an old wooden one so they actually tacked it on at each corner with a drawing pin which prevented any creasing. The goals were set up and Goalies threaded through, one in a Yellow shirt the other in Green. The teams were set out in 2-3-5 formation which was now under heavy threat by 4-2-4 and 4-3-3 at the professional level. The teams which came with the starter set were Red tops, White Shorts, Red Socks and Blue Tops, White Shorts, Blue Socks. "Two of moi three teams" says Brian thinking Man U and Rangers. "Falkirk and Hearts" says Archie. But as it was my present I got to choose who would be in the inaugural game. It was never in doubt. Although the Blue wasn't quite dark enough and England usually only wore Red tops against other white top teams (i.e. the unmentionable game in 1966) it was all close enough. The hospital table would be Wembley for this one.

I got my traction off and was put in a wheelchair which was quite a suitable height to reach across the table from. About a dozen of us showed up to play and we all had a little fiddle around to get the idea of how to do it. It was very difficult but you did kind of develop a knack. It would take too long to get everyone an individual game so we decided that we would have three people on each team, one boy as team Manager, one to operate the goalie and one to do the outfield play. The Manager thing was a good idea as Archie couldn't get out of bed that day but they wheeled his bed over beside us and he became Scotland Manager, a job which he took very seriously. This would be the biggest representation Falkirk would ever have on a Scotland team and Johnnie Manson's one and only appearance at Wembley. Brian would be the Goalie and persuaded Archie to put Ronnie Simpson in over Peter McCloy and the Falkirk goalie. I was our outfield and as long as Archie put Pat Stanton in the team I could care less about the rest.

Having watched the warm ups carefully we looked to make sure England were at as much of a disadvantage as possible. There was a boy called Mario (also in a wheelchair just for this event) who had came all the way from Malta for a treatment of some kind of blood disorder. He had pallor white skin which made his lips seem too red and his eyes too blue. A mop of reddish/Brown hair emphasized his skin tone even more. He was actually a bit doll-like. He did have a bit of presence about him. He would be England Manager. He'd have Thomas (back problems) as his goalie which was good news as if you knocked over your own goals it was a penalty against you and Thomas had looked very heavy handed in practice. Their outfielder would be Graham (Foot problems—wore special shoes) who coming from the borders (Hawick) so was as near to a real Englishman as we could find. He liked all sport but suggested he cared more about rugby which would be about par for a borders boy. A male nurse called Jimmy volunteers to be referee and does a quick skip-read of the rules which are printed on the inside of the box. He even borrows a whistle from somewhere and puts it round his neck on a string.

We're all set to go. The rest will get to play in a second game later but for this one they are to be supporters and its clear Scotland, just as in the real thing, will have more fans at Wembley than the home team! Even quite a few who have shown no previous interest are perked up in their beds now looking over in our direction. The word is getting around PMR. Two doctors, a few nurses, a cleaner and a porter also stop by and take an interest so it's a big time atmosphere. Jimmy lifts his whistle to get things started but before he can blow it a loud familiar voice interjects. "Eh excuse me ref but could ye haud on fir jist a minute, please" Its Archie. "A hauv a few words fir ma team". So here you have it. A wee boy with a grossly enlarged head but an even bigger heart and a satisfied grin barely showing behind a business like expression. He's dying and truth be told he knows it. For now though via the magic of his fitba' daftness, he's completely forgotten his woes. He's on a mission, a very serious one. He claps his hands together once, then rubs them back and forth several times before ending with them out in front of him in a clasp almost like he's going to say a prayer. "Now then boys, a jist want ye tae go oot thair 'n enjoy yersels, awright". That's it. The perfect pep talk, perfectly delivered from the perfect manager. To keep things even Jimmy asks Mario, the England Manager if he's got anything to say. "Come on Jimmy let's just get on with the game" he responds with a bit of an attitude. Actually there is a trace of upper crust English within his mixed accent, he's perfect too.

It,s hard for the game to live up to the build up and its really difficult to get much flow as we're such novices for now but there are a few exciting moments. As predicted, Thomas helps us out with three penalties in the first half. Bobby Murdoch played by middle finger fluffs the first two so I switch to Stanton, my index finger, on the third and of course he puts it away. Mario brings himself on at Goalie in the second half and he's very competent and saves the few respectable chances we make. Graham generates little threat at the other end and Brian who has the goalie stem tucked between his chin and shoulder is on top of anything which comes his way. Brian and I swap for the last few minutes and he does some amazing play with his chin and his nose! We hold out for the 1-0 win and the crowd goes wild. Only Mario seems not to have appreciated it. I don't think he likes me. That night our Manager varies his bedtime song; "Bo … nnie

Sco..otland, Bo … nnie Sco..otland, we'll support you evermore …" Brian shouts over; "James, tell Jock Stein to settle daan" A great footballing day in the boys' ward at the PMR hospital.

I'm guessing I spent somewhere between two and three months at the PMR. There was never a dull moment and here are a few selected high and lowlights:

THE FIGHT—Mario and I were three beds apart. He had been a kind of leading light before I arrived and seemed to resent how Brian and Archie and I had become so tight. We both got good at Subbuteo and we had a couple of respectable games, winning one each so we had quite a rivalry developing. He was apparently from quite a well to do family in Malta and he did have a little bit of a superior attitude though it may have just been a Maltese thing. I could tell even the nurses were cool to the tone he sometimes used towards them. One evening he and I got into a slanging match from our beds. I called him a Peely Wally (pale, ashen) Malteser (A popular sweetie/candy of the time) and he responded by calling me a Wee Scottie dog. I warned him that was too near the bone (no pun intended) but he just waved me off saying "Like you can do anything about it". "Is that right" I replied in a developing temper. I leaned into my cage (A frame which kept the weight of the covers off my legs) and started working my traction off. I had become quite expert at this though officially only a nurse could do it. The next time the nurse left the ward I slid out my bed onto the floor. I still couldn't walk yet and there was no wheelchair in reach. I climbed onto Brian's bed and he was doing nothing to discourage me. I slid off the other side and back onto the floor. I repeated the process two more times getting some stick off Kevin in the last bed because I squashed his sore foot. Mario saw me coming but couldn't make a move. I grabbed his covers, pulled myself up and landed one fairly pathetic punch to his face. The nurse came in just I did this and she came bounding over in a panic. "Do you know what you've done?" Mario was flat on his back and the area around his eye where I'd made contact was going a weird color. A side effect of the problem he had was that he bled profusely and bruised terribly (hemo-something was the proper term). He was out of the game for two days and I was in serious trouble. My parents were called and had to go through big meetings with his parents and the staff nurse and the Matron. If I hadn't been so sick my dad would have killed me! I got off with a severe warning. The guilt and shame I felt inside was actually a sort of punishment in itself. Especially as I knew I'd given my folks a serious Redder. It was several days before the butterflies in my stomach settled properly again. I was so relieved when they confirmed that Mario had suffered no serious permanent damage. I apologized to him but that was the last direct contact we had. I hope they were able to get him sorted.

THE BATH—After a couple of weeks of "Bed baths" with those awful smelly cloths they finally decided I could get a proper bath. They had a couple of rooms off the ward with generous sized tubs. For the first time in my life I was genuinely excited about getting a bath! Then Jimmy showed up with a wheelchair and said "Right James, its time". Jimmy was a great guy and all that but I knew from the "Pilton encyclopedia of Stereotyping" that all male nurses had to be poofs.

"Eh, Jimmy. Hope you don't mind but I really wanted one of the women to give me my bath"

"Aye, don't we all son but you're stuck with me this time"

"No, sorry Jimmy—I'll just leave it then"

"James, you're windin' me up son, right?"

"No I'm dead serious" and I've locked both hand onto my cage ready to put up a struggle if necessary.

He's frustrated but also a bit amused and he wanders off shaking his head and muttering. I see him and Nurse Liz having a confab at the ward door but they're too far away for me to hear anything. Next thing Nurse Liz comes over and says;

"I understand I've to get the pleasure of bathing your Lordship tonight?"

"If you don't mind Nurse Liz, likesay nothing against Jimmy but I'm just a bit feared of being naked in front of a man"

"But you don't mind baring it all for me?"

"No, not at all. You look a bit like my Ma anyway"

She just laughed and said sarcastically "C'mon then. I can't wait to see what all the fuss is about!"

As she wheeled me away Brian chirped in "Now moind 'n behave in der wit' me bird James"

Jimmy tried to shrug it off but he was definitely never quite the same with me after that. And who can blame him?

The bath was barry and I confess that later that night, in the privacy under my cage I played a little game with Nurse Liz though my eyes were tight shut through most of it! Maybe that's where the saying "Rattling your cage" comes from?

THE SWIM—PMR had a little swimming pool. There were lots of people there who couldn't walk but who were comfortable and confident in the pool. It was great exercise and a critical part of therapy for many of us on the road back to normality. My Mom brought in my swimming trunks. They wheeled me to the pool in a slightly different type chair (I guess it was rustproof). There was a ramp so you could be wheeled all the way into the water. As soon as I got in deep enough I was off. It was amazing how I could be so suddenly mobile. It was much more arms than legs but I was able to swim around for about five minutes before suddenly feeling knackered. I floated back to the ramp and eased back into the wheelchair. This became a daily event which I really looked forward to. The other bonus was you might encounter a girl or two from their separate ward along the corridor en-route or even better, in the pool. Mind you with the wee tight trunks it was a bit "Hard" getting out of the water sometimes!

FATE—You know already how I'm obsessed with small world connections right? There was a girl in PMR at exactly the same time as me. She was the same age as me (within a month) She had exactly the same condition as me. (Osteo Myilitas). By co-incidence her elder sister was a nurse at PMR and she had told her all the ridiculous tales of the boys ward. I never met that girl at the time. So how do I know all this? Well I met her about three years later. Her name is Bunty. She's my wife and has been for over thirty years now! She even remembered Brian who had managed to make a few unapproved trips into the girls ward. Now if that doesn't give you Goose bumps—what will? I know she now regrets telling me this part but her sister also told her at the time that "The one at the centre of all the trouble in the boys ward is a lovely looking wee chap". I still remind her of this once in a while.

A BLACK DAY—For some reason Archie was being "Moved to a private ward". I was pretty sure I knew what was going on, I just wouldn't say it. The body language of his parents the last few days was quite telling even if you were only half watching. They didn't even take him out of his bed. They wheeled the whole thing away. He was struggling a bit, his voice not nearly as forceful as usual. "Bye James, Bye Bri, um gittin' a special ward tae masel bit al see ye's later" and he was on his way. Brian had a keen eye and ear and picked up all sorts of snippets from staff conversations. He was also much braver and more direct than me but still had a tear welling up in the corner of his eye. "Oi heard dem talkin' we won't be seein' him again James, it's his toim". Mr Montcrief, in his eighties was sad enough but Archie was just a wee laddie. Even the nurses struggled to hide their true feelings on this one. Football fans will know this thing where if you only meet one big fan of a certain team you always associate that person with that team for life. I bet I'm that person for a few people in respect of Hibs, especially here in America where Hibs supporters are hardly abundant and my Virginia license plate is "HIBS FC". Every time I see a Falkirk reference I think of Archie, always will. Bye Archie. Really glad I knew you pal.

MORE TROUBLE—There was a lady who came around with a trolley laden with comics and juice and sweeties. We had become partial to something called "Pippin" which was a kind of apple flavored soft sparkling soft drink. There was another lady who was a cleaner. She looked a bit witchy with long straw like grey hair and a pointed nose. She scowled and moaned at us constantly while she was doing her work. Who knows what problems she had in her own life but she was certainly not the right person to be around young kids in any capacity. One day she had a nasty go at Brian and me for the volume of crumbs around our beds so we resolved to get our own back. We got a bottle of Pippen and put a tiny hole in the lid. When you shook it up the gas would make it squirt out in a powerful jet stream. It was ultra-sticky. We hid out in my bed cage which I didn't really need anymore but it still had its uses! When she got within reach and turned her back I did the shake and spray routine then we quickly dipped back under the cage. We got about three or four shots in before she sussed (discovered) us and she came at us with a brush! The nurse had to intervene quickly to save us but we were back in the mire again. With a long lecture from the Matron and trolley privileges withdrawn indefinitely. She didn't want to hear our apology but rather wanted us over someone's knee. Again my Dad would have been happy to oblige if I wasn't so sick.

My traction came off. I went from a wheelchair to a frame to a stick to nothing in fairly quick time and after one last visit from Soutter and his fawning entourage I was getting to go home. My folks were over the moon and I told them I was too but I actually had strangely mixed emotions about it. Brian was pretty upset. He was putting on a brave face but I knew him well now. He'd miss our banter as most of the remaining kids were that bit younger. We resolved to stay in touch but of course we didn't. I've no idea what became of him. I saw something recently about all the fantastic prosthetics they have now and thought of him. With his very sharp mind and ingenuity and a couple of new "Arms" he could be a success at most anything he chose. Hopefully he is. Bye Brian. We had a blast.

14

CATCH A FALLEN STAR

So I'm home. My first thoughts are that the house smells strange and that it's the size of a shoebox! The ward at PMR was so massive and open with glass on three sides. I've never been the claustrophobic type but that's kind of how it felt the first few days back at home, especially in the bedroom. The smell is not what I'd call bad or dirty. My Mom is a clean freak so dust doesn't get much time to settle. Ultimately the house will smell much better than the hospital but my nose just has to get reacquainted with it. I'm spoiled the first few days. If I want something I mostly get it. I'm also bored out of my mind. Funny how at the hospital there was always something going on. It'll be another couple weeks before I can go back to school and the days are just too long. I'm allowed to go for walks. A big outing is a trip up to the shops. It's a couple of hundred yards at most yet it takes me ages to get there and I have to stop for rests on the way. It takes me about an hour to do the round trip which I used to make in ten minutes. A very humbling experience.

Having been the self-absorbed, arrogant type its no surprise that there is now a bit of reciprocation from many of my former foils. "How's it gaun, hop-along" says one boy and "Dragging a bit are we?" says another. They're full of it and they are fully confident there is no chance I can get after them. I'm relieved to get back to the relative safety of the house. I think to myself—what's it going to be like at school where loads of people owe me one? I have a slight limp which is very slagable. Even my closer pals have sarcastically called me "Gimpy" and "Gammy" already! The slightest exertion and I can feel a very mild version of how my leg felt at its worst. It scares me so I don't push it. I try to stay upbeat and I keep reminding myself that despite my injury I'm still being courted by a few teams. Mr McGauran had visited me in hospital and told me there would be a place for me at Royston whenever I was ready. PSC had their under fourteen team off the ground and I had also got word that there was a place for me there. There are even rumors of a serious Edinburgh Thistle revival. But I need to walk before I can run.

I go back to school and it's odd not to be able to even participate in the tennis ball football match which takes place daily in front of the science block. It's no surprise that a lot of old scores are indeed being settled. School is no less cruel—I'm taking some stick for my limp. I focus on less healthy playground activities like Pitch-and-Toss and cards, mainly Pontoon (Blackjack). I become very competent at both to the point where I earn yet another nickname; "Fagan" to recognize my ability for separating gambling fools from their lunch money. Though justifiable, I hate this nickname and am relieved it does not stick long term! I struggle to recover from the months of missed classes, especially in Math and French where I have missed vital segments of fundamentals. In those days they didn't make any special allowances for such circumstances. There was no offer of individual make-up tutoring. I lighten my load by switching to a couple of "Softer" classes including "Food and Nutrition". This was another "poofs only" listing in the "Pilton Book of Stereotypes" but several of us straight boys signed up for it anyway. Safety in numbers you see. Part of this class was cooking/baking. We would make a batch of cakes and occasionally they would turn out half decent. The challenge was getting cakes home safely. Even if you managed to get through the whole day with your cakes intact the journey home was perilous. Stevie Torrance was a particularly good agitator in this respect. He'd rarely get caught doing anything himself but he was skilled at providing bullets for others to fire. I remember several times when, on the bus home, he'd start a "Cakes, cakes, cakes" chant and before you knew it, the rock buns which you thought you'd be proudly showing your Mum, were being consumed by everyone on the top deck of the bus!

After a few weeks I began to join in casual kickabouts again in the street, at the "Dockies" field and at the top corner of Groathill school field under the lamp-posts. I wasn't doing much running and my touches were few and far between but it was a start. It also gave me an appreciation of how the boys who were lesser players tolerated this marginal participation all the time and in fact were happy to just be included. I gradually increased my fitness and stamina to where, at least at street level, I was back to a fairly dominant role. Back at school Mr MacDonald, who was now affectionately known as "Ted" by all of us, stopped me on the stairs and asked; "Meikle—how's your leg son? Ready to get back out there yet?"

"No really sir, I'm kicking about with the lads but I don't have any stamina back, widnae last long". I replied.

What pride prevented me from admitting was that my confidence was not back. Although it's been sport-clichéd to death, I found it to be absolutely true that inner confidence is critical regardless of a person's skill level.

Perhaps he sensed this as he continued; "Maybe you should have a run out with the 'Seconds', I could have a word with Mr Mackie". In second year (sophomore) the team names were much more logical with the first team being the "Firsts" and the second the "Seconds". Mr Mackie, a Technical/Metalwork teacher, runs the Seconds.

"That would be great" I said and part of me meant it. However another part of me was embarrassed by the prospect of being in what I perceived as the reserves!

He obviously followed through and Mr Mackie sought me out and offered me a game against Firhill the following Saturday. It was at a field in Oxgangs but I don't recall the name of it. Just that it was on the number twenty seven bus route and had big orange nets the likes of which I hadn't seen since Warriston. I was just relieved that the Firsts would be playing at Arboretum and not right alongside us. Most of the B's from first year had progressed into the Firsts but there were a few on this team who had played the odd B game. I remember in particular Ronan O'Carroll, a hard name to forget, Charlie Donaldson a hard personality to forget and George Meehan a hard voice to forget—the deepest you could ever imagine on a schoolboy. I also remember Mike Gizoldo because his dad ran the Wimpey in Castle Street and if you went there with him you got a free feed. There was also a Ricky Marzcek who ended up pursuing refereeing and was doing very well by the time I left Scotland already refereeing the under 21's when he was the same age as most of the players. Mackie told me I'd be playing up front and to "Pick my runs" until I got some fitness back. It worked out well. Though playing within myself, I scored two very nice goals in a good win. I was immediately accepted by the team and felt a little confidence flowing back. The pattern continued over several more games and it was a good feeling to get back into a leading role, albeit on the Seconds.

Word was out that I was back on the field and Royston and PSC came calling again. I was mulling between the two when I had a surprise visit from Dave Clark. Dave was better known as "Biffo" after the cartoon bear character from the Beano comic. He had an abundance of dark hair, eyebrows, beard and moustache surrounding a mildly upturned nose and sharp eye teeth. Biffo explained to me that the Edinburgh Thistle revival was definitely on and that he'd be running the under fourteen team. There would also be under thirteen, under sixteen and under eighteen teams. They would have permanent training and playing rights at

St Marks Park. He was from Telford and his aim was to get all the best "Local" talent (Telford, Drylaw, Groathill, Muirhouse) on one team together. Perhaps in response to the Pilton Sporting Club approach? He also acknowledged that it may be a while before I was at full speed but thought I could still be an important part of his team even as I worked my way back. If this was just polite PR it felt good. In the neighborhood he already had Alan Tennant, Dougie Clouston, Lex Shields, Stevie Lodge, Graham Woodward and Nicky Marino signed up, a pretty strong nucleus. From further afield he had Jocky Slater (Penicuik) Eamon Bannon from Liberton, Brian Lee (Portobello) and Michael Sidonia (Known as "Sid") all the way from Lauder in the borders. I was definitely in.

St Mark's Park was squeezed in between Warriston Cemetery, Chancelot Flour Mill and Powderhall greyhound racing stadium. It had two fields. They were flat if not very large but had no nets. On Wednesday nights this became Edinburgh Thistle central with around fifty boys aged from twelve to eighteen training. There was even a little crossover training/interplay between the age groups giving us direct exposure to some of the older lads many of whom were about to go pro. Scouts were around all the time and I'm still not sure what the Hibs and Hearts guys were doing when Strachan went very early to Dundee? Some others which come to mind are Gerry Adair(Hibs bound), Les Thompson (Hibs bound then on to Australia) Brendan MacKelvie (Man Utd bound) Alan Holt (Falkirk bound) and Ambrose Hunter who somehow ended up at Hong Kong Rangers before returning to sell me life insurance when I got married! Even in the youngest group they had Billy Kirkwood who would go on to a very good career, mostly with Dundee United. They had brand new strips for all teams and they were custom designed. The top was white with a broad navy blue vertical band down the middle. On the front there was a Thistle in the centre. Shorts and socks were white and the socks had some navy trim. When they arrived we got to display them for the photographers and a photo of the entire club appeared in that Saturdays Pink newspaper. Another one which I still have—no names listed but a real fun browse.

I recall our major rivals being Links boys club which was basically Restalrig renamed. They had a great side led by John Young one of the most skilled and tireless midfield players I ever saw. I can't imagine any reason why John would not make the pro ranks but if he did it wasn't at the very top echelon. Years later via my imported "Pinks" I did see "J Young" listed in lower division and East of Scotland League teams and even as a manager (Craigroyston) but I'm not sure if it was the same guy? Ronnie Tolmie was their goalie. I was playing wide left as part of my gradual rehabilitation process and because we played them so often I developed a great rivalry with their right back, Walter Kidd. ("Kiddo") He had a wide (Not fat) body and was stubborn as a mule. A very hard man to get past but I always relished the challenge. There was an unspoken mutual respect. He went on to a long steady career with Hearts and was a natural fan favorite. I always wished we could have renewed our rivalry with me in a green and white strip! Salvesen continued to be up there too with Chris Robertson still scoring freely and the effervescent Brian Ross driving them from midfield. I don't recall any of the individual players but we also had some real ding-dong matches with North Merchiston Boys Club at Harrison Park in Slateford. If you were protecting a narrow lead there near the end you could waste precious seconds by simply booting the ball into the canal on one side or over the high Dairy fence on the other. Harrison Park had one other oddity. There was a well established diagonal footpath shortcut right across one half of the field. Of course the intent was that this wasn't really for use during games. However many young mums with prams and toddlers in tow or old dears with their message bags just ignored this making for some interesting stoppages in games!

So I'm back playing for the school and for a very respectable boy's club side, yet there's something missing. When I train really hard or push myself a little extra in a game I still get these little twinges reminding me of my injury. It is definitely mainly physical but when it starts the psychology plays into it too, I'm sure. I should be really chuffed just to be back on the field but I'm greedy, I want to be a star again right now! Let's say I'm a car. I'm a Rover 2000. If I'd always been a Rover 2000 I'd be happy as a lark but I used to be a Mercedes. I'm welcome and wanted on my teams but I don't make or break them. I don't just want to be wanted. I want to be *needed*. I *need* to be *needed*.

15

A PURPLE PATCH FOR HIBS

Whilst, at least by my own ridiculous standards, I'm struggling on the field, Hibs are about to offer a great deal of solace on the supporting front. Rangers have nicked Colin Stein for one hundred thousand pounds but there is other great talent coming through and suddenly the key ingredient arrives at Easter Road. He's very familiar with the surroundings having been part of the "Famous Five" team which dominated Scotland in the late forties and early fifties. He used to be number ten in your programme. He's Eddie Turnbull. But first let me back up a little and get the credit chain correct.

In 1970, Tom Hart; a lifelong Hibs fan who made his fortune in the building trade, took over as Managing Director. After a few months of a man called Dave Ewing (From Man City I think) and a brief nostalgic but not really effective second coming of an aging Joe Baker he turned his sights on Eddie Turnbull. Turnbull was at Aberdeen and had them seriously challenging Rangers and Celtics dominance of the Scottish football scene. In the end it's the players who have to play but it seems that every great team you think of had a truly outstanding Manager at the helm. Celtic—Jock Stein, (Also stolen from Hibs by the way—along with our goalie Ronnie Simpson) Rangers—Jock Wallace, Dundee United—Jim McLean, Ipswich Town—Bobby Robson, Leeds—Don Revie, Manchester United—Sir Matt Busby (Who some might be surprised to learn played for Hibs during the war years) and more recently Sir Alex Ferguson. Fergie also did the same for St Mirren and for Aberdeen. And of course "The Shank"; Bill Shankly at Liverpool. At Hibs we got the other Shankly brother; Bob, but it wasn't quite the same. Right about this time we actually met Liverpool in the third round of the Fairs cup and gave a decent account before eventually yielding to the Toshack-Keegan led side.

So, get the right people running the clubs then appoint the right Manager and you're off. Of course every week someone thinks they've discovered the latest Shank but most don't pan out that way. The determined Hart landed Turnbull.

He seemed a good bet. Besides being Hibs through and through you could see and feel the attitude of his team at Aberdeen. He had shed them of the inferiority complex which had become a staple for all Scottish clubs when they faced the "Old firm". (Celtic and Rangers) Could he do the same for Hibs?

Besides Stanton he inherited a good squad including some younger players (Schaedler, Brownlie, Blackley, Duncan, Cropley) who were just reaching maturation point. He wasn't fully comfortable with the goalies so quickly rescued Jim Herriot (Ex Dunfermline and Scotland) from the relative obscurity of South Africa. He wanted a certain type of forward and always liked Alan Gordon; a former Jambo who was now with Dundee United. He also loved the skills of Alex Edwards a superb long passer of the ball with a sometimes problematic temperament and questionable wasteline. He figured him worth the risk. He got them both for bargain prices—thirteen thousand pounds apiece! As he confirmed so vividly in the recent video "Turnbull's Tornadoes" he saw his biggest challenge as convincing his team they were "Just as good, if not better" than Rangers and Celtic. In this respect he had a great advantage over most. When he was in his prime Celtic and Rangers were not nearly as dominant. The money aspect was a much lesser factor and transfers were much less frequent. He played in a team which was completely confident of its collective capability. He also reveled in explaining how he loved to beat the Old firm both as a player and as a Manager. He even had a little jibe for Jock Stein who, he said, "Thought he could dominate everybody … ahhhhh … but he'd never dominate me … phuph". A Hibs Manager with a superiority complex—wow!

Though he came quite late in the off-season (July) Turnbull set to work and had immediate impact. They had a good strong showing in the League Cup and were mid-table in the league. They went all the way to the Scottish Cup Final eliminating his still strong former Aberdeen in the quarter finals. He quickly got them over the Rangers hump defeating them after a replay in the semis. Celtic awaited in the final. They would take a bit more work. They destroyed Hibs 6-1 after a couple of early bounces might have taken the game in another direction. Turnbull said afterwards that he could feel that one coming. He could sense the intimidation and nerves which still sometimes gripped his players in clashes with the old firm were especially strong that day. But he also knew this factor was gradually diminishing and his own supreme self confidence was starting to seep deep into the players' "Brain boxes" to use his own signature term which was always accompanied by his index fingers pointing direct at either temple. Long before Arnold Schwartzeneger could even speak English, Turnbull's finishing line to the press pundits after that Scottish Cup final defeat was; "Ahhhhhhh … we'll be back". It was just a matter of time.

Having got to know his players well now and with a full pre-season to prepare, Turnbull had Hibs flying out of the gate the next season. There was a new pre-season tournament; the Drybrough Cup. The criterion for qualifying was simply the highest scoring teams from the previous season. The sponsors wanted lots of goals and even modified the offsides rule to only apply within twenty five yards of goal. Boy did they get their wish! There were four teams the first year. We comfortably beat Rangers (3-0) in the semi and ended up in the final, against … you've guessed it … Celtic. I'll never forget it. It was so early in August that I was still on holiday in Wick. I'd been allowed to take a pal with me and chose my schoolmate and second cousin Paul Ferguson. We had gone through St David's together and were always great pals despite fighting each other in a "Square go" (Fair fight—pre-arranged!) on a fairly regularly basis. These were always about even up but I knew if I could hang in long enough Paul's asthma would play up and he'd have to stop for a shot of his puffer. It was too hard to get re-started after that so we'd just shake hands and resolve to fight again another day. He was a stubborn, proud bugger! We went to Oggies together too and I can still remember the day he got a call at school to say his dad (A strapping great docker) had suddenly died. We rode the school bus home like any other day and he maintained a brave face all the way. I've only seen him twice in the last twenty years yet still consider him one of my closest friends.

Anyway we were sat in my grannies living room at Ackergill Crescent, Wick, with my dad and my Uncle Robbie (The Rangers man) at about ten o'clock that night for the highlights of the game on TV. Again, no live coverage then and in Wick it was possible to avoid the score which Paul and I did by spending it isolated up the Wick River. There was no sporting Pink in Wick. The Sunday papers (The Post and the Mail) didn't even reach Caithness until well into Sunday afternoon!

Both BBC and STV (Grampian was the Wick affiliate) had their football highlight shows on Saturday nights then. We would get about half an hour of the Scottish "Game of the day" and about fifteen minutes of an English game. This was a special as neither the Scottish nor the English season was properly underway yet. I'm pretty sure this one was on BBC because Archie MacPherson was commentating. Scotland had three classic football commentators, Archie on BBC, Arthur Montford and Bob Crampsey on STV. Archie had a large swirl of frizzy ginger hair which he'd curl on the top of his head like a bird's nest. His oversized headphones always looked like they held it all in place. Bob was rumored to have once been the "Brain of Britain" and was very cerebral in his comments, out of sync with much of his clientele. Arthur also loved to weave his extensive vocabulary into his description of the action. His trademark phrase, instantly recognizable to any Scottish football fan of the era; "What a stramash!" Perhaps he was the inspiration for the example on a tea towel we just received from home called "A celebration of the Scots language". The word stramash is on it and the explanation in context is football related.

So it was Archie making the call on this one. There was a new tune used to start the show. Would it ring in a changing of the guard? There was also some new intro film to accompany the new tune. It featured a close up of the Celtic fans waving one of those little inflatable players in the hoops with the big ears and the ginger hair—a reminder of who stood in our way once again. Paul and I were in ecstasy as Hibs took a three goal lead in the first half with Alan Gordon popping up in all the right spots at the right moments. However Celtic just wouldn't go away and they came storming back with three goals of their own. Our stomachs churned as the game went into extra time. In all sports, the best teams have to reach the point where they can instinctively finish off teams "On the ropes". This would be the final lesson in the Turnbull School of football. Whatever he said to them in the short break preceding extra time made its mark. They came out suddenly calm and back in control. Jimmy O'Rourke picked up the ball around halfway and ambled forward unchallenged. About thirty yards out he suddenly let fly and the ball took an unusual upward and outward trajectory then rocketed in off the underside of the crossbar. Arthur Duncan added an almost surreal insurance goal when he looked to just be trying to run out the clock and we finally had a trophy. It was only the Drybrough Cup but we had finally crossed the considerable hurdle of Jock Stein, Celtic and inflatable Jimmy Johnstone's to get our hands on it. We were also getting vital seasoning playing regularly at Hampden. Robbie and my dad were both smirking as Paul and I savored the moment. It transpired that they had bumped into a Celtic fan drowning his sorrows at the Back Bridge Street Club so whilst not knowing the actual score they knew who had won. Avoiding scores was a big deal which is why Mongo and I had often got abuse for singing our way down Ferry Road Grove after midweek games making a Hibs win obvious before the highlights were shown! The TV stations were even used to this and would often warn us to "Turn away now if you don't want to know the score of the game which follows this newscast".

It was a great feeling to have won a cup. Any Cup. We had won something called the Summer Cup in 1964 but I didn't really remember it. We had won the

East of Scotland Shield a few times but that was really just a challenge match with Hearts until Meadowbank Thistle provided a third serious contender.

We carried this momentum into the season proper and again dispatched Rangers in the semi-final of the League Cup at Hampden. As always Celtic awaited in the final. The Drybrough Cup was one thing but this was another. Though the least prestigious of Scotland's trophies it was still a genuine "Major" and a passage to European football. I made the trip through by special train with another pal from school; Paul Rooney, better known as "Prune". It was a cold December day and it was the first time we were headed to Hampden with real hope. We still weren't a bookie's favorite at 3-1 but we genuinely felt if things went well the game was winnable. I've heard the game described many different ways and times but I saw it clearly as THE PAT STANTON GAME. He dominated the field from start to finish and he looked as if he was never in doubt about the outcome. I've never been keen on the popular American term AWESOME as its way overused but Stanton was truly awesome in this game. Turnbull's had finally got his wish. His defiance was now truly installed in his Captain's mind and it spread through the entire team. Stanton scored the first goal himself and had a hand in the second which was scored by his pal Jimmy O'Rourke. We had to endure a bit of nail biting as a youngster called Kenny Dalglish pulled one back for Celtic with about 15 minutes left. He turned out to be not a bad player! If Pat was the physical heart of Hibs, Jimmy was the emotional heart. A lifetime fan who still comes over as exactly that. His own description (In a fairly recent interview on the Turnbull's Tornadoes video) of the experience of this final and its aftermath is way better than anything anybody could ever write. I admit it had me crying. Just as I had when Pat raised the Scottish League Cup high above his head.

I ended up back at the West End in Edinburgh awaiting Hibs slow ride through town on an open top double decker bus. I was detached from Prune as the crowds were so immense with scarfs, banners and flags waving furiously. A fantastic day but one that was definitely enhanced greatly by the long and arduous wait. I sometimes wonder if Rangers and Celtic fans can truly feel that depth of satisfaction when they're winning ten titles in a row. They would probably all say they do but how do you compare the inner feelings of one person against the next?

That same team provided one of the all time great performances later in the season in a European Cup Winners Cup tie against Sporting Lisbon. Down 1-2 from the first leg, Hibs, again driven on by Stanton, devastated the Portuguese side (Considered amongst Europe's' best at the time) 6-1 overrunning them down our famous slope in the second half. Jimmy O'Rourke had a hat-trick. He had another hat-trick in the next round against FC Besa in a 7-1 win and Hibs were being considered as serious contenders to go all the way. They got a bit careless in the home leg against Hajduk Split conceding two sucker punch counter-attack goals in a 4-2 win. The away leg took them to one of the most hostile environments with deliberate disruptions to their travel and a noise vigil at their hotel. It appeared to work and they lost 3-0 to a team which was clearly their inferior. A great pity.

Rangers got a little revenge, eliminating Hibs in the second round of the Scottish Cup in yet another tie which needed a replay. We moved up to fourth in the league but should've been higher. We sometimes let our guard down against lesser rated teams. The killer instinct still needed work. In Turnbull's tenure we kept moving up the league from 4th to 3rd to 2nd but never did manage the ultimate goal of a Championship. We continued our Cup runs and repeated in the Drybrough with another extra time win over Celtic; 1-0 on an Alan Gordon goal. Celtic got us back in a Scottish Cup final 6-3 despite a hat-trick by Joe Harper. Most of us identify Harper, signed from Everton for a fat sum, with the beginning of the end of the Turnbull era but that's probably a bit unfair. He was an excellent striker.

Another historic Hibs moment occurred on New Years Day of 1973. Local derby matches were typically arranged for New Years. That year was the first time I was allowed to go out all night on Hogmany with my pals rather than with my parents. I somehow ended up with wee Borrie somewhere down Newhaven way and vaguely remember getting a New Years kiss from some old toothless auntie of his in heavy make-up who tried to slip me the tongue. As my kids would now say; "Gross dad"! We had a few drinks of something they called "Scotsmac" which I'm now told was a mixture of sherry and whisky. It was cheap enough for us to afford a half bottle between us and the off-license was desperate enough for business to sell it to us even though we were clearly well underage. I awoke on the floor of Borrie's house in the Circus with a slightly sore head but not too bad. Fortunately for me, he had the much bigger share of the Scotsmac. I couldn't get him awake so I slipped out quietly and headed direct to Gorgie. Kick off was three O'clock. We now had a phone. I called home, reversing the charges from a Circus telephone box which was actually working. (A rarity) My mum appreciated confirmation that I was safe and well after my first solo Hogmany but I left the "Tongue" part out of the description of my lovely evening. She told me that my dad would be in the Ferranti social club after the game so I should meet him there. By now the old Crewe Toll Social Hall (The Bon Amie) had given way to

Telford College and the new club was at Robertson Avenue just a couple of minutes from the Hearts ground. I was in the Gorgie road end for what proved to be the most lopsided Edinburgh derby ever. Hearts missed a couple of good early chances and Jimmy O'Rourke scored, then the floodgates just opened. It ended up 7-0 and could have been a lot worse as Hibs, by now complacent forwards, missed a few sitters (A sitter means a really easy chance—from the expression Sitting Duck I believe) towards the end. I felt really bad for one Hearts player that day; Jim Brown. Jim was also a hairdressing student at Telford College and had been cutting my hair regularly. The cost was minimal as it was a way for the students to practice. He was a really nice guy. I was much happier when he later saw the light and got himself a transfer to Hibs!

The Ferranti club was buzzing with a dangerous amount of drink flowing all around. Hibs fans celebrating and Jambos drowning their sorrows. I found my dad in the snooker room and he bought me a Coca-cola and a packet of Smokey Bacon crisps. Some things just go together perfectly and I always enjoyed that combination. I did have a notion to ask for a half-pint but thought better of it. Not sure why but I remember there was a very serious game at the next table with a pile of money at stake. It was sitting right on the edge and might have been fifty pounds or more. A very drunk depressed Hearts supporter, a middle aged man, seemed to be trying to exact some revenge via this game. My dad explained that his opponent was a guy called Stan Vincent who was a youth coach at Hibs. I guess the man was just desperate to beat someone who had anything at all to do with Hibs. Most of the other banter seemed much less intense which was much more typical for the New Year game. Mind you, scores this lopsided were also very rare. Draws were much more common, a result especially popular with the Edinburgh constabulary. My favorite New Year day game incident was when a drunken fan managed to elude several sober policemen to reach Willie Hamilton. He was on Hibs at the time but had also played for Hearts. Willie graciously accepted the man's scarf and tied it onto the goalpost. Many thought that Willie might have had a couple of nips himself before the game.

There was one other big European series in this span. We got Leeds again in a EUFA second round after beating Keflavik of Iceland. The first leg was to be at Elland Road and we heard "Ted" who was now our school Housemaster, was going down. Prune and Stevie Torrance and I approached him and asked if there was any chance of a lift down. He said it would be fine as long as we got permission from our parents. We did. It was during the autumn school break we had (October I think) so Hibs took down a big support. Ted was staying at the "Station" hotel for the night. He parked there and gave us a spare car door key and told us we could sleep in the car if we wanted. The free transport and accommodation made the trip affordable. The Leeds police had experienced earlier trouble either when Celtic or Rangers came down and they seemed to be way over the top in their preparation for us. They had tons of mounted police and used the horses to herd us to the ground. I'm loath to criticize police but I witnessed some really heavy handed overly-aggressive tactics that night. A few Hibs fans took exception and before you knew it there were a number of arrests even before the game. Leeds were past their "Revie" prime and had been badly hit by injuries but they were still among the top English teams.

Hibs played a surprisingly attacking away leg and were unlucky not to come out ahead. It ended nil-nil after Tony Higgins missed what seemed like a sure goal. Still, we were delighted with the result. The herding back to the station area was just as bad with a few more arrests en-route. Stevie reckoned he knew a guy (Ramie somebody) who put a brick through a store window in full view of the cops. Scotsmac talking I suspect. He would be staying in Leeds for a few days! We got back to the car around midnight, locked ourselves in and managed a little bit of sleep. Ted had thoughtfully left a few blankets in the car and as it was an inside car park it really wasn't too uncomfortable. Ted showed up very early in the morning and we were on our way home. He dropped us near his local in the Tolcross area by mid-morning. His sexual orientation was always a subject of great speculation at school but he was nothing but a model of courtesy on that trip.

The return leg had us feeling pretty confident and a great crowd turned out. Leeds had piled up even more injuries so they adjusted their strategy accordingly, playing Billy Bremner in an extra deep defensive roll. It was like they were deliberately playing for stalemate and that's exactly what we got. Bremner was boring but brilliant. Another full game and extra time without a goal being scored despite sustained pressure by Hibs. Penalty tie breakers had only just been introduced. This was the first major one we'd see. The conversion rate was almost perfect. The only miss was by our hero; Pat Stanton, who hit the post and Leeds, escaped with a 5-4 margin. I still see this as the biggest smash and grab job I've ever witnessed over two legs. Interesting also that one of the biggest stars missed the vital kick. That would become quite a recurring theme as penalty shoot-outs became a regular feature of cup games.

16

S..A … TUR..DAY NIGHT

Our Edinburgh Thistle side progressed to Under 16 more or less intact. Big Alan Tennant's interest waned a bit and he was replaced in goal by another Penacook lad, Brian McLeish. We also picked up Kenny McCallum (From Crossroads) but other than that we had the same group Biffo had skillfully put together. He had passed us on to a new coaching staff with Ian Grassick in charge, ably assisted by Adie Jackson. (His son Darren ended up a decent player with Meadow bank, Newcastle, Hibs and Hearts and Scotland) and Jimmy Fetes (Who's son Mike played for the under 18's). They complimented each other well which only made a great side even better. We won several cups. I was commanding a regular spot wide on the left with good success but my heart still wanted to be back in a central midfield role. However we were loaded at every position with several guys being invited to trials by top clubs all over Britain. Kenny MacCallum and Eamon Bannon both went on trial to Derby County.

The first to stick was Eamon who signed locally for Hearts. Shortly thereafter Danny Blanchflower thought enough of Eamon's talent to take him to Chelsea for a hundred and sixty five thousand pounds. The Jambos simply couldn't afford to turn down that kind of money. Eamon, Woody (Graham Woodward—His dad Charlie scouted for Hearts) and I were quite pally as we were three of the quieter souls on a team as loaded with strong vocal personality as it was with talent. A few years later whilst Eamon was still a Jambo I met him in Marks and Spencer's in Princess Street. I was with a pal from work who was a big Jambo and he was really chuffed with the personal contact with one of his team's stars. It was fascinating to see such hero worship towards one of my own contemporaries. Part of me was very jealous but overall I was pleased for Eamon who was one of the nicest guys you could meet. He went on to a tremendous career with the brilliant Dundee United team which actually got past the Old firm to win the premier league one year—a truly magnificent achievement for a team with relatively limited resources. He also got to play in the world cup finals as did Strachan. Eamon was quite a brainy type and I believe he went on to do some writing for the evening news as well as coaching at Hibs.

We dominated at the Edinburgh under 16 scene winning several Juvenile cups with odd sounding names like "Baillie Theurer". We even progressed to the semi-finals of the Scottish Cup where we drew the Ayr United youth team who had some very large and hairy looking 16 year olds! The first leg was played at Groathill School a hard fought 1-1 draw. We had a horrendously long journey in a convoy of cars for the return leg which was played on a shale field in dreadful weather conditions. We never got in it and went down something like 6-1. It was really our only major disappointment with that team. It just seemed a shame that they didn't play both games at much more worthy venues. Several of us on that team went on to play for Semi-pro teams but many knowledgeable football pundits at the time would have put money on it producing a couple more major stars.

At the same time I had got back to where the school wanted me in the top team again and because of my September birthday I could play for the year below my own in regional and national competition. That team had some stand-outs too with Derek Rodier eventually joining Hibs. Peter Finn and Billy MacLelland also come to mind and I'd play on another team with both of them again later.

So I was part of success again and collected a drawer full of medals but was I content? Mostly but not completely.

I still had an occasional twinge restricting me getting my fitness and confidence back to full peak. I was still a quality Rover instead of a loaded Merc! The basic addiction was still intact though because I remember being really sick about missing an important Thistle match because of my Uncle David's wedding. Now I love my Uncle David but it was doubly frustrating because the wedding was at the white church on Groathill Road and the game was just up the road at Groathill School. I was an Usher and as I stood at the door waiting to show people to their seats I could hear some of the shouting from the game! The pangs were strong as ever. To rub in salt they had me dressed in a Penguin suit for the first time.

Celtic and the promised "S" form had gone AWOL. At a match at Saughton Park I met a little red headed man called Bobby Johnston with stumpy legs who I identified with Tynecastle Boys Club as well as pro-scouting. He was always around youth football and had watched me over the years. He made an effort to catch me after the game. "How ye doin' James?' he asked. "Aye, awright Mr Johnston, thanks". He gave me a friendly but serious stare and said "Look son your doin' okay but I know there's much more in ye. Ye've had an auld heid since ye were ten. Bit ye winnie fully enjoy yer game until you get yourself that last bit fitness" An Auld heid was the term for a youngster who read the field really well. It was the most flattering thing you could hear from a scout. "Aye, thanks Mr Johnston". It was a double edged sword though. The worst thing you could hear from a scout is that you weren't quite as fit as you should be. To this day I know he was dead right on both counts. Something did stick with me. The fact that he said get fit to *enjoy your game* No mention of fame or fortune. Mmm?

Maybe I needed to starting to think seriously about other career opportunities and then, out of the blue, along came a really strange one. I had auditioned for a school performance of Gilbert and Sullivans' "Pirates of Penzance" and landed the leading male role of Frederick. I wish I could say it was for my great singing voice but I know it was more my "Acceptable and loud' voice coupled with my boldness. I gave it laldy (a big effort!) at the audition, which three of us took as a bet, and Ms Caden, daughter of my primary school headmaster, loved it! I would never play the role as when they got to making costumes they tried to put me in Green silk tights, a cape and furry boots. This was undoubtedly in the Poof category in the Pilton Book of Stereotypes. After great debates with Ms Caden over how silly I was being I ceded to my understudy and moved into the chorus of pirates, the costumes for which were a bit manlier. My understudy was a girl (Ann McBain) but it wasn't uncommon for girls to play leading boys in these type plays. As a token of my appreciation I took her on a date to Port Seaton sands and paid her on the trampolines.

One of my classmates, card school participants and occasional smoking under the stairs buddy was Stuart Wood, also nicknamed Woody. He had observed the pirates process and asked me if I'd ever thought of singing in a band? He was a guitarist in a band and was never done telling us how they were headed for the top. We didn't take it too seriously but he was always in absolute earnest. I said it sounded interesting but I was honest enough to again raise the limitations of my voice. I was kind of shocked when he said "Your voice is good enough. Anyway, how you look is more important. You'd be a great fit for the image we're developing". And here's me thinking they were musicians. Next day he came back very enthused. He'd had a word with the manager and he was very interested and wanted me to go practice with the band for a week's trial. This would mean every single night and all other activities would have to be dropped. "I know you play fitba James but that would have to go. The Manager wants everyone involved to be one hundred percent dedicated, no distractions; we're not even allowed to have birds!"

My right hand was still my steady lover at this time so giving up birds would be doable but fitba? Despite the niggling dissatisfaction of not being the main man every game I didn't think I was quite ready to give it up completely. I was also much less confident in my pop stardom potential than Woody. "C'mon James its set up for tonight, he's expecting you". I said I would go but stood them up. By now you may have worked out that the manager was Tam Paton and the band was the Bay City Rollers. There had been several versions of the band over the years but this time Tam Paton had a specific marketing plan. They cultivated a teeny bopper image with boyish faces, feathered and spike haircuts and tartan patched "Cowboy" shirts. They'd revive a few popular lovey-dovey teenage standards and jazz them up a bit then add a few new ones of their own. Tam's plan worked brilliantly.

The Rollers became huge and Woody did indeed become a superstar as he had always confidently predicted. People still love celebrity. Many who had scoffed him were suddenly his long lost best pals from school. I was honestly delighted for him and I had a great coulda-woulda story to tell for life. A boy called Les McEwen ended up in the spot Woody tried so hard to get me in. Les seemed to go a bit off the rails when their star fell. I saw Woody in a recent documentary and he seemed much the same as ever. The same programme explained how they had ended up with much less money than they should've had and that Tam Paton was being investigated for somehow salting it all away for himself. There were also some accusations of sexual misconduct. Mind you there were always rumors about Tam but as far as I know nothing stuck. Maybe that's why they weren't allowed to have birds! I still love the Rollers' version of "Saturday Night" having been re-united with it in America via the Mike Myers' movie; "So I married an axe murderer". This was long before his Austin Powers and Shrek induced super stardom but if you are Scottish and haven't seen this film, you must. Myers lived around Scottish immigrants in Canada and was obviously paying close attention to the fine detail of their mannerisms! I admit that I have done S-A-TUR-D-A-Y … on the Karaoke a few times. Just for a laugh of course! And by the way, I never owned a Cowboy shirt.

So having possibly missed my football star calling and definitely missed my pop star calling I thought I'd better buckle down for my "O" levels to try to create some normal gainful employment alternatives. I did okay getting respectable passes in English, History and Geography. I should have also strolled Art (I was always a fairly decent drawer/painter) but I missed the school buses and ended up with about a half hour to do two hours worth of exam stuff. Likewise for arithmetic. All my own fault. After I started work I ended up retaking these via day release classes and had no problem getting them both which helped me clinch my first promotion!

I was never scared of hard work. You couldn't really call it a job but message running for house bound old dears with no relatives was my first sort of paid assignment. I had one regular back in Pilton in the early days; Mrs Rae, who would be constantly leaning out of her second floor flat at the corner of the big field, arms folded and resting on the sill. "C'mere up son" she'd summon me. "Nip roond tae Barr's and get me fags. Ten Embassy". These were the most popular cigarettes at the time and there was just the red and white pack. (No Regal or lite or double decaf). Payment on return was a piece of bread with thick butter and sprinkled with sugar. It was tasty right enough and great for the Cholesterol but offered no potential for starting a bank book.

My next job at around age seven I'd guess, was supposedly helping my brother John on his morning milk delivery out of the St Cuthbert's' store at the corner of Crewe Road and Boswell Parkway. This meant getting up at 5am and walking a mile or so including through the Ghostie Valley in pitch darkness. The job entailed loading several crates of milk onto a large wooden cart then pushing it around the neighborhood leaving a pint or two or more at each subscribing house. Why did he need me? There were a few fairly posh houses on the route and whilst he was delivering the milk, I was in their back gardens choring (stealing) apples. The milk came in pint bottles. There was always about an inch of cream gathered just under the silver or gold paper top. Mmmmm, delicious. If you weren't too greedy about it you could sneak a little taste of this from any bottle and carefully replace the lid undetected. I would occasionally get a tiny cut of John's pay but had to mostly settle for cream and apples.

For proper cash based jobs, besides the Ice Cream van, I'd done strawberry picking in the summer. I'd delivered newspapers, in Pilton for Barr's and later on for RS McCall in Davidson Mains and Blackhall. I also delivered the Catholic Newspapers around Pilton, Muirhouse and West Granton. I'm sure that many people took these out of guilt based obligation as some of the families appeared to have more pressing needs evident as we waited at their doors for payment. I say this as we'd often see the previous weeks' editions still sitting untouched where they'd been dumped on the lobby floor a week earlier. An interesting observation which I found to be very consistent in the Newspaper delivery business. The poorer the family the better the tip for the delivery boy. I hear another oft' used family cliché coming on; "Thaim thits goat it ken how tae keep it".

My most lucrative schoolboy job came after we moved to Drylaw. Tommy Duff's mum worked at the petrol station on the main Queensferry Road. It was part of the Esso hotel complex. Mrs Duff got Tommy a job washing dishes in the hotel kitchen. Tommy got Kenny Manson, Gogsie and I in on the act. It was hard graft but well paid at 30p an hour cash in hand each night. They had a large busy restaurant and although we had commercial level dishwashing gear all the pots (And there were plenty) had to be cleaned the old fashioned way. I came to despise beef strogonov which stuck to the bottom of the enormous pot like glue. You did a four hour stint (Approx 7-11pm) and left with one pound twenty cash in your pocket. This is also where I first learned properly about "Pockle" the Scottish term for unapproved bonuses. As well as washing dishes we had to put out the rubbish (trash). There was often a nice steak or Trout or the likes very well wrapped and "accidentally" dumped near the top of the bucket (trashcan). After saying goodnight and leaving out of the staff entrance we'd be round the back to collect our bonus. Word was that the Head Chef (Ian) knew this went on but would turn a blind eye as long as we didn't "Kick the arse out of it". Another test for a Pilton book of stereotypes entry; Chefs and Waiters at posh hotels—all poofs. Didn't see too much to contradict that one!

What was fascinating to me was how much people were willing to pay for a nice meal in a nice atmosphere. (Something I have come to appreciate greatly now—as my waistline will attest) Must all be *rich Americans* I thought at the time. Ian ran a fairly tight ship with strict rules on hygiene but there was the occasional shortcut taken. I remember "Nicky" and "Doug" waiters who made no attempt to disguise their sexual orientation. They'd come poncing into the kitchen and, in put on posh accents, scream "Where is my f**king order of sautéed mushrooms darlings? My f**king tip is in jeopardy here". There had been a missed communication but rather than wait they'd come over and do a survey of our slop area where all the "Finished" meals would be dumped. "This'll do me nicely dear" and they'd spoon a batch of leftover mushrooms on to a sparkling clean plate. After you'd worked there a while you were elevated to the position of "Still room". This entailed making pots of tea and coffee and rounds of toast for room service, a breeze versus scrubbing Strogonov! There would also be the odd half-drunk glass returned with Whisky, Brandy, Wine, beer et al but supping even posh person's slops did not appeal to me!

In fact at this stage I had no serious interest in drink. Even the time when there was a ton of beer discarded at the old Granton dump down the "Diverno's" path (Now approx B&Q DIY etc) I didn't go down as the word spread through the entire neighborhood that it was all-you-can-drink-for-free! I recall Snap MacGregor and Wobo Meldrum coming stoating up the street in very good form. It turned out the beer was off and quite a few people ended up at the emergency unit at the Western General. However despite not really caring for beer, the challenge of trying to get served in a Pub was still somehow irresistible. There was talk that the Junction Bar, on the corner of the very end of Ferry Road where it met Great Junction Street, was fairly liberal in its serving policy at the time. Several mates had bragged about getting served there and I felt a little macho/inferiority pang. I decided to give it a go. Most such ventures would be undertaken with a mate but word was that this drastically reduced the chances. When I had enough cash one night I got the number one bus and jumped of at Leith Town Hall. I crossed the road took a deep breath and parted the saloon doors into the Junction. They flapped behind me then went through that gradually diminishing rattle until still again. I suddenly felt like Gary Cooper though I was even shorter and had no ten gallon hat to help my confidence. It did have similarities to a Western Movie scene. Time frozen for a split second whilst the sprinkling of regulars all stop what they are doing and turn heads to eye the stranger in their midst. I obviously posed no threat and most of them quickly went back about their business of second guessing every decision made by a politician or football manager that week. As in almost every local, a few old men played dominoes in one corner. I have this absurd thought that a set of pub dominoes comes complete with four old men. Two younger guys resume their darts match. Only one man maintains an interest in me. He's the one that the other locals never start a conversation with because they know it'll go on indefinitely. He perches on the corner barstool just waiting for someone to give him enough eye contact to provoke an opening line. I'm blinkered now and headed straight to the bar taps. I've been practicing my serious face and gruffer voice in the bathroom mirror.

I'm also carrying a well turned newspaper as part of my disguise. I take it with my right hand from under my left arm and wave it nonchalantly at a SKOL tap. "Half ae Lager please pal". This is risky as I've been advised a full pint is a much better order to place but I don't have quite enough money for that. He smiles at me and I think he's going to slag me and chase me out. I can't help turning to see the reaction of "Naebody Likes me" at the end of the bar and his pupils lock on me like lasers, his head starts to move, his lips are about to move too when I turn my face back to the barman. I've already pictured my own puzzled look and tone should he challenge me. But he doesn't. He lifts the glass, flips the tap and my first self-purchased draught beer is on the way. I drop the exact money on the bar. Pick up my Half. "Cheers pal" I say then head in the opposite direction of "Naebody". I can feel his eyes burning holes in my back—a missed opportunity for him to corner a naïve sucker and talk the ears off him. I find a small table close to the door and sit down doing a good impersonation of my dad engrossed in the evening news. My mind is racing. I sup down my beer rapidly. I'm not actually that fussed about drinking it but feel I'd better. After no more than five minutes I'm up and out the door and, to use a baseball expression; "He'ssssss Safe!"

Of course I could have done as we all did many times and pretend I'd actually done something I hadn't. Likesay, when your dad wouldn't let you watch something risqué on telly but for the sake of pride you'd have to pretend to your pals you'd seen it. You'd cobble together enough second hand information about it to participate in the post mortem at school next day. "Aye, a loved the bit whair … blah, blah, blah" Once in a while you'd get caught out with a crossed wire and that really was a redder. But the beer buying thing was too important for that. It had to be done. It was.

Buoyed by the experience of the Junction, Prune and I brassed out a trip into Clark's Bar preceding Saturday night forage at "Clouds" disco in Tollcross. A local in Leith in midweek is one thing but this was another—the town is always crawling with Pubtecs! (Searchers of under-aged drinkers) I buy two half pints and am immediately captured and booked! I had to go to court and was fined five pounds. Not having that sort of money I went straight from the court to the new Ravel shoe store in Princess Street where my brother David was doing shop fitting for R L Rae. He loaned me the money and I went back up to the court and paid my fine. I had to work at the Esso for four extra nights to pay him back. That's a lot of dishes for bugger all! The only break I got was that in the evening news list of underage drinkers in court that day I was only listed anonymously at the end; "… and one minor—all fined five pounds".

I mentioned earlier we were the first lot to go through the comprehensive system at school. My birthday which had served me so well on the football playing front was now back to haunt me on the job front. I hadn't paid proper attention to the leaving constraints and merrily applied to join the government; The Ministry of Defense no less, as a Clerical assistant; whatever that was. You needed at least two "O" Levels to be considered and one of them had to be English. I got an interview and it seemed to go quite well. A couple of weeks later I got a letter informing that I had the job and was to start in October. However when I went to get my insurance cards (Work permit) at the City Chambers they said I couldn't leave school until Christmas (i.e. the end of the term in which my sixteenth birthday fell). It seemed absurd and I was devastated. My dad was anxious for me not to lose what he saw as a great opportunity; "The Civil Service. Cushey number that. Steady pay. Good Pension. Jobs for life". He took me back to visit the Army Headquarters Personnel Office where I was to actually work and explained the odd circumstances on my behalf. A friendly, helpful man called Mr Hill said they were fine with it and that they had another opening in January. They'd simply slot me into that one. Phew!

As it transpired my first day of work was originally to be the third of January. I got a letter saying that it had been made an extra civil service holiday so I needn't come in until the fourth. So my first day of paid work was a holiday. Some might say nothing's changed in the thirty odd years since!

17

CLOUDS OF GLORY

In the same week as my government career was rescued Scotland poured on some fabulous gravy. As if the Hibs run didn't have me giddy enough, Scotland were knitting into a very well rounded team. Another member of the Hibs famous five side was responsible for this great success. Willie Ormond had been number 11 to Eddie Turnbull's 10 and had also shown some good promise as a club Manager to where Scotland handed him the reigns for the qualifying campaign for the 1974 world cup finals which would be held in Germany. Ormond subdued Scotland's traditional cavalier approach to where they were still quite creative but had much more sensible "Holding" capability through which they started to pick up vital away points which may have previously been lost. Ormond and his strategy should certainly get credit for this but I think it was made possible because of the collective experience his players had gathered from regular European club matches.

Scotland had played a few great games since *the game* in 1967 but they hadn't qualified for any of the major tournaments in my conscious fandom. Pulling against England was a poor second to being able to support Scotland. Anyway this was as much tinged with jealousy as guttural historical bigotry. Scotland always played better as an underdog. The more impossible the task the more inspired they were. However send them to get a routine win against a minnow like Cyprus, Iceland, Estonia or Faroe Islands and they seemed to struggle to get a hard-on! They couldn't get going until you gobbed (spat) in their faces and insulted them. Ormond changed this. He was workmanlike and managed to make sure they didn't get too far up or too far down. For the most part he also kept a good balance between focus and relaxation. The exception of course was when half his team got pissed at Largs and wee Jinky Johnstone ended up having to be rescued from an out-of-control rowboat by the coastguard.

So, after eighteen months of qualifying matches, here was the simple scenario. Beat Czechoslovakia at Hampden and you can go to Germany to play in the world cup finals next summer! The Czechs were hardly a patsy at the time. In fact, soon thereafter in the European nations championship, they would destroy a very decent German team in the final. For me it's hard to describe how exciting this was to likesay a Brazil or Germany or Italy or (swallow hard) England fan. They expected to and played in almost every major tourney. The fact that they expected to (Besides some pretty decent players) was probably always a big part of it. CONFIDENCE begets success.

So it will be on the telly but that just won't do. If we are making history I must be there. I must. By now Harry O has become my closest pal. We've developed a mutual love for the horses and Percy the bookie is willing to take our cash. We even lay bets for the cravat wearing Board marker Jack. C'mon a cravat in a bookies in Drylaw—has to be a poof. We're also both George Harrison daft and sing along with his records competing to sound most like him. Harry lives above the shops. He comes from a gambling family. They all like a flutter on the Geegees too and they also love the "cairds". I play with them and learn some of the intricacies of dealing from his mum who is a pro-dealer at an Edinburgh casino. She is a Magician with the pack and can do things I cannot work out, even after watching up close and trying to catch her out. The whole family plays something called "Chilookay". (Spelling a guess) It's a sophisticated version of "Rummy" with two full packs and can keep a big group amused for ages. Harry's family plays this for a small wager. His mum usually wins and slips me back my stake when I'm leaving! Harry and I set out by train for Glasgow and make our way to Hampden. We're in the covered "Rangers end" but it really is all Scotland tonight.

The Czechs score quite early with a speculative twenty yarder which we think the goalie should've had. Is this a bad thing? Not necessarily. We are now firmly behind the eight ball where we love it best. The charge begins and eventually pays off when big Jim Holton nods home from close range. We're a goal away from the first world cup finals for my entire generation. Scotland players are flowing forward in waves. The singing is intense and really does make the hairs on my neck brim to attention. The pressure is also intense and sustained. Tommy Hutchinson constantly probes from the left and even the dogged, experienced Czechs are feeling it. Chances are coming. Then Willie Morgan has it on the right and flights an inviting cross somewhere between the penalty spot and the six yard box. Several players are looking at it but one is in total attack mode. He's our sub. He has no top teeth except on the ends. He's fanged with big furry eyebrows. He has an enormous Scottish heart and this is his moment, our moment. He's Joe (Jordan). He launches himself like a human missile and meets the ball with full force of his head. It's like the one in a million perfect successes from our earliest games of seven-bys. It's there … but there's a weird pause. Probably only a split second but it feels like much longer. Everything goes into a warped slo-mo and voices become inaudible. I'm looking at Harry. He's looking at me. Everybody is looking at everybody. It's like we expect to wake up and find it was a great dream ruined. We're conditioned to something going wrong at this point. But no, we've checked each other and we're all agreed it's real so we focus on the referee. He could still spoil it. A push we didn't see. An offside. An over-zealous linesman who spotted something off the ball. But no, the linesmen are sprinting to halfway and the referee is blowing and pointing to the centre spot. It really is there. "SSSSSER" …

When the sound kicks back in it's suddenly deafening. It's a complete frenzy. Harry and I are locked in embrace pogoing in unison just screaming violently and incoherently right into each others faces. A lot of the Hampden terracing is still just hard caked dirt packed between wooden supports and it's relatively dry. All I remember after that is the clouds. Dust clouds rose and never subsided. Long after the final whistle after several laps of honor by the players the sky still looked like a civil war battlefield. It was one of the greatest feelings. Scotland. My Scotland were going to be in the world cup finals. Really. Finally. Fantastically. So excitingly. Even George Harrison got a rest as Harry and I sang ourselves all the way back to Edinburgh with any and every Scottish nationalistic song we could think of. For many of them we only knew a line or two but so what.

"On our way to Germany, we shall not be moved …"

To make it even sweeter, the Polish goalkeeper Tomachevski, labeled a clown by then English football guru Brian Clough, had a miraculous performance to knock them out. That night I dreamt I was interviewing a certain bearded Englishman about the situation;

"Well Mr Hill what do you make of this? Scotland in, England out. Still at least it will give all of Britain an interest right?"

There was no clear answer. Just a Braveheartesque-Longshanks-choking-on-his-spit sound with swollen frustrated bloodshot poppy eyes … which was exactly the response I wanted.

We put up a very respectable show in Germany and even the practical Mr Ormond allowed himself a little Scottish romanticism when he included Denis Law in the final squad. I, and many others, have always thought this was more a lifetime achievement award than a current form selection but it didn't matter a toss. We all loved the Lawman and we loved Ormond for taking him. He'd been the bridesmaid too often watching inferior players out there on the world stage while he watched from a studio. He was due.

Our fate was really sealed more by the order of play than the opposition. We got Brazil, Yugoslavia and Zaire. (Used to be the Congo—remember the prelude?) We had to play Zaire first and really had absolutely no clue what to expect. We subsequently started very cautiously. We ended up 3-0 victors but clearly would have had more if we'd charged right out of the gate. With the benefit of watching them against us, Yugoslavia came out all guns blazing and scored nine against them. We played well against Brazil, though to be fair this was as mediocre a Brazil team as we'd ever seen. We were unlucky not to get a win, Billy Bremner scrambling one off the side of the post when it might have been easier to score. Yugoslavia and Brazil also drew so it was down to the last two games. We drew 1-1 with Yugoslavia and Brazil did just enough in a 4-0 win over Zaire to push us out on goal difference.

It was disappointing but respectable enough even to keep the smirk off the bearded ones' face! The spectacle of Scottish fans in assorted kilts and Brazilian samba dancers in bright yellow tops is about as spectacular a mix as you could get. They had friendly banter before, during and after the Scotland versus Brazil game and the world media soaked it up. There was a collective pride in being voted "Best behaved supporters" which appeared to inspire more of the same. This at a time when our auld enemies' fans were taking their own reputation in the polar opposite direction and earning the nickname; lager louts. It got to the point where host nations were keen to have Scotland in and hopeful that England didn't make it. This gave our fans even more incentive to sustain this great reputation something they've managed to do all the way to present day.

18

GIMME THAT OLD TIME RELIGION

Religion is so simple. Religion is so complex.

My favorite religious line comes from an okay movie called *Keeping the Faith* where a Rabbi and a Priest are best pals fighting over the same bird in New York City. Ben Stiller is the Rabbi, Ed Norton; the priest. Norton is depressed when he find out his girl (Jenna Elfman) is chasing Stiller so he punches him out at the Synagogue and retires to an Irish bar (an easy thing to find in NYC) and drowns his sorrows with an old, wise barman (Brian George). The older guy explains how someone is always worse off and describes his own heritage which leads to Norton's question;

"So you're a Sikh, Catholic, Muslim with Jewish in-laws?"

All we've got is Catholics and Proddies and some don't even really know which is which. As far as I know I've never even met a real Jew at this point.

Our own Edinburgh rivalry with Hearts was always intense, especially for the few days either side of a derby match. However it never seemed quite as acidic and bitter as that of our Glasgow counterparts; Celtic and Rangers. That old time religious bigotry (Catholic/Protestant) always seemed much more prevalent in the West of Scotland. Speaking in depth with many Glaswegians (whom we liked to torment with the term "Weedgies") over the years has done nothing to dispel that view. In fact I was quite shocked at some of the stories they told me about being passed over for jobs because they had attended a certain school or lived on a certain street. That seemed absurd but contemporaries of mine who grew up in the Glasgow of the early sixties assured me that it was not uncommon. Most of the stories I heard cited Catholics being disadvantaged but I was also assured there was equally voracious reciprocation whenever the opportunity presented itself.

Not that we didn't have Hibs and Hearts bigots in Edinburgh but the real diehard religion-in-football zealots on both sides were relatively scarce. I try to have respect for all religions and admire people who stick to their beliefs without trying to ram them down everyone else's throat. I also admire the basic self discipline of regular attendance at Kirk or Chapel or Synagogue or Mosque for that matter. What has always tickled me though is that many of the worst religious bigots I ever encountered appear to have never been near a place of worship or service for years, if ever at all. What I've also found within the religious aspect are countless anomalies and inconsistencies.

What is unequivocally clear to me is that wherever I encountered strong bigotry, religious or racial, it was perpetuated by either or both parents and/or other close and influential older relatives. As a result I genuinely believe it is being diluted with each new generation. It'll never go completely but its definitely on the right track. That's yet another thing I love about football. Good football can transcend such problems.

Rangers appeared, at least to those of us with only general knowledge (as opposed to the inside scoop), the team most guilty of perpetuating the religious thing. However someone in their organisation eventually deserved serious kudos for breaking both religious and racial barriers. They signed Maurice Johnson (MoJo) and broke their stupid, self constraining, unwritten non-Catholic rule. They also signed Mark Walters and although there had been previous black players in Scottish football he was high profile on a leading team. Kudos to whoever made that decision at that particular time. The poor guy got some dreadful stick on his first go around but he can now consider himself a sort of pioneer, paving the way for those who followed. So many in fact that skin colour seems to have faded to a non factor save for a few nutters (idiots).

So I say I'm not and have never been bigoted but let's review. When I was about eight its clear in my memory that I went through a brief period where I had a theory in my head that Catholics made better footballers. This certainly didn't come from my family where there was a mixture of Hibs, Hearts, Rangers and Celtic Supporters, even on my Dad's (Catholic) side. It was just something I developed myself. I had it in my head that catholic schools were heavily outnumbered by protestant ones yet produced loads more great players. There was no scientific base to this rather just a daft little kid counting around primary schools in his head. For example I knew of three Catholic Schools on the North (Leith) side of town; St David's, Holy Cross and St Mary's York Lane. The rest I knew of which I assumed were all Protestant (But didn't really know for sure) were Craigmuir, West Pilton (Later Muirhouse) Royston, Granton, Wardie, Hermitage, Silverknowes, Davidson Mains, Cramond, Pilrig, Newhaven, Clermiston.

Not sure where it stands now but about mid 20th century Catholics were estimated to represent about ten percent of the Scottish population. So my rudimentary sums were probably in the ballpark!

Even at that young age you new the basic history and key statistics of your favourite team pretty well. You had to to be prepared for constant arguments with Jambos, Bluenoses and Celtic fans. So I knew Hibs had religious roots. They were founded by the Catholic Young Mens Society in the late 1860's attached to St Patrick's Church in the Cowgate and based at a hall in St Mary's Street. The Scottish Football Association (SFA) didn't want them at first as they thought they represented Irish rather than Scottish interests with so many poor immigrants pouring in from post-potato famine Ireland.

In 1875 they evolved to become Hibernian Football Club and were admitted into the Edinburgh Football Association. Even this had a hiccup as they were supposed to be SFA members first but the local association sensibly waived this requirement as they were keen on building up new teams. The SFA did eventually let Hibs in but they were not allowed to play in the Scottish Cup (run by the SFA) that first year. In 1878 the intense rivalry with Hearts was cemented for ever with an Edinburgh Cup Final which went five very controversial games! Yes—four replays.

The first game was a goalless draw but according to the Docherty & Thomson version we wuz robbed! A Hibs goal being disallowed without clear explanation. Number two—we wuz robbed again. With Hibs pushing hard for victory the Hearts Captain refused to play extra time which he apparently had the option to do! Amazingly they played to a third then a fourth draw before Hearts finally got their hands on the cup with a 1-0 win on a disputed goal at a place called Powburn. I have no idea where this is if in fact it still exists?

I guess its safe to assume that Hibs players remained predominantly Catholic and Hearts predominantly Presbyterian for several years thereafter so this would certainly lay the foundation for the religious rivalry aspect which survives to present day Edinburgh but again not to a very significant extent from what I can glean from a great distance at least.

Ignorance has also always been a critical factor in perpetuating bigotry and there was certainly plenty of that around Pilton in my day. I had many Catholic pals who would unhesitatingly use the "Fenian Bastard" epithet and Protestant pals who would use the "Orange bastard" version respectively against their

"Own" in football arguments! All of us too young to really fully care about or comprehend the implications.

At Hibs games we'd sing songs with warm references to the Irish Republican Army (IRA) something I really didn't get at the time but am not too proud of now. Though I'm hardly a loyalist or Royalist neither am I proud of spouting lines like "**ck King Billy and the Queen" albeit in youthful ignorance. This always provoked an equally offensive response about the Pope's latest exploits. The hilarious (well, in a way) part is that I'd often spot pals of mine in a Rangers group spouting all this poison about the Pope then I'd be in the communion line with the same boys at Catholic mass on Sunday and at Catholic school with them on Monday! For most though I think it was genuinely just a sidebar to the football rivalry which didn't carry too deep (again—you might still get quite a different view from the Weedgies on this).

So back to my original question. At the tender age of eight was I a bigot? Well I've admitted to doing the Catholic/Protestant school ratio and thought I was quite good at arithmetic. I deduced that based on the schools data Hibs should have a couple of Catholics on the team on average. I was pretty sure they had at least five or six in the first team squad alone. So my simplified and short lived conclusion was that papes were generally better fitba players than proddies! No other comparisons because frankly, I didn't really know of any other religions at that point.

Now that I think about it there was other evidence that I was a little tainted at eight. I did go to church regularly and most of my Protestant pals did not. A few went to Sunday School and when I occasionally went with them I always seemed to know more bible stuff than them. I gave up stuff during Lent, they did not. Surely all of this made me a morally superior kid in the eyes of God, right?

Still some doubt but then came the clincher. In our Pilton stair underneath Mrs Boyle on the ground floor were the Casey's. I knew Mr Casey was a keen Rangers fan. I'd seen him and his son all decked out in their Blue scarves and hats many times but Mr Casey was generally quite quiet. Then one day we all heard "The Sash" blasting on a record player. It was reverberating around the stair and I said to my dad "That's an anti-Catholic thing, right dad?" He said it was indeed a Protestant song but just to ignore it. I couldn't. Next day I say to Casey junior;

"Could your dad keep the music down a bit please—we don't all want to hear your Rangers songs."

I didn't realize that this was like a red rag to a bull and Caseys junior and senior started blasting away even louder. My dad said to just ignore him and he'd get fed up. Poor Mrs Boyle must have been demented with it and I'm surprised

Frankie boy didn't go down and threaten Casey as it was undoubtedly disturbing his recovery naps.

I had gotten money from a few relatives for a recent birthday and accumulated ten shillings. I was contemplating what new football strip to buy. Thomsons in Junction Street had a few nice ones on show. Then I was in the Drylaw Post Office on Ferry Road and saw that they were selling LP records. On sale for nine shillings and sixpence was one called "Irish Rebel Songs" with a green, white and gold flag on the front. I browse and see that it has something called "The Merry Ploughboy" which I recognize as one of the Hibs (and Celtic) chants used at games in response to "The Sash" from the Rangers fans. Instinctively I buy it and take it home. I get out our very basic turntable and stick it on at full pelt. Its just a childish reaction but it's a strong one. Its not so much against Protestants in general but more my competitive instincts coming out against the Casey's. I wish I had a dramatic conclusion to give you on this one but I don't. My Mom and Dad seemed to like my assertiveness knowing I'd need it to thrive in 60's Pilton. On the other hand I'm sure they would have preferred it on something other than a religion based squabble. I don't know if my dad spoke to Casey or not but the whole thing faded quickly and I was told I could play any music I like but to consider the neighbours! Having paid nine and six I was determined to get my moneys worth and so played my record many times over. To this day I know all the words to some very controversial songs.

So was I a bigot? No. Why? Simple. Whilst there was enough seed via what I just described for an eight year old to be quickly and easily swayed I got no signs or encouragement from either parent to be that way. This meant that I stayed mostly neutral until old enough to reach my own conclusions and that right there is the key. What you see and hear is mostly what you become.

Blissfully, Ireland, whilst still problematic, has paled into the background of the Balkans and more recently Afghanistan and Iraq. I even just saw a TV report with the Reverend Ian Paisley (mega proddie) and Martin McGuinness (ex IRA) joking around like old buddies. Amazing.

Me. I'm not a bigot and I doubt that any of my kids will be one. According to my kids though I'm still a racist for using the terms "Chinky" and "Paki" quite freely in conversation. I argue that I never use it to an actual person so don't see the harm in it but they assure me that's no excuse. It's simply unacceptable as is my perceived homophobia with all the Pilton stereotyping syndrome. So they are working on me and I'm getting better but still have a ways to go. A few more generations and maybe we'll do more than "Imagine" John Lennon's lofty goals.

Amen.

19

A TEMPORARY LULL IN THE FORCE

Despite continued success in the Juvenile ranks, in my own eyes and heart, my comeback had fallen short. It had topped off with me in a solid supporting role wide on the left when where I wanted, no *needed* to be, was in the central midfield role pointing and barking instructions and dictating the flow of the game.

There was no under-17 age group in Juvenile football. You moved from U16 to U18 and from there to U21. I did start the pre-season training for the Edinburgh Thistle U18's but my heart was just not in it. I walked away. Packed it in. At the ripe old age of sixteen I was retired. Now established in my real job and earning a few pounds and having the start of a social life was probably softening the impact of not being on a fitba team. I filled some of the void by picking up the golf clubs. Good fun but a bit like an alchie having a lite beer when he really fancies a double Grouse whisky. I also got back into the habit of attending Saturday Hibs' home game and the occasional away match with a new pal I made at work called John Jameson ; "JJ". He even satisfies my small world/connections obsession by explaining that his cousin knows me. His name was Graham Lowe and he was a Goalie on the next age group up from me at Edinburgh Thistle. He ended up having a good junior (Semi-pro) career and was a stalwart at Haddington for a while. I wasn't really much of a drinker yet but a couple of pints followed by the match followed by another pint then a pie supper wasn't a bad way to kill a Saturday afternoon. Then it's home, shower, change and borrow from my mum and back out on the town again. I borrow the "Perpetual Fiver." This is a floating five pounds note which never really hits the ground. I borrow it. I pay it back. I borrow it. I pay it back. It never even gets to dry. I borrow it again. I found out later in life that this activity, which I fear at the time is totally dysfunctional, is actually completely normal behaviour.

"Clouds" was the main destination for me on Saturday night because it's the only place I could get in. Where I really wanted to go was Flanagans (Flannies) or Mr Bojangles but, with a face covered in nothing but white bumfluff, pimples galore and a barely tenor voice to match, I have no chance of getting past the bouncers in these places. Some cool clothes might improve my chances but my wardrobe is pretty limited. Our David's a bit of a poser and he has all the gear but he won't let you near it. Of course I borrow stuff on the fly but it's a bit dodgy as he would notice if a fly farted on one of his precious shirts or jackets! So its Clouds or nothing; three floors of sweaty under-agers flailing around in a blurr of noise and flashing lights. When we compare notes on Monday morning I'm frustrated and embarrassed that Bunty (the girl in the next door office) and her pal Linda, have been able to go to both Flannies and Mr B's with no problem. They even get served for fancy cocktails; ordering the likesay Moscow Mules and Blue Lagoons!

(Pause and morph to real time—Its Friday and I've got the day off work. I'm collecting my son who's coming home for the weekend. He's a sophomore (Second year) at the College of William and Mary in Williamsburg, Virginia. I know his last class is in the English department at Tucker Hall. I find it and it's a little chilly on the bench outside. So I sneak in behind a group of students. I find myself a nice unclaimed desk in the corner of the large foyer area and set up my laptop. I spread around a few notes and my cell phone and Gregory pecs—Scottish Ryhming slang for specs = spectacles = glasses—and I act like I belong. Lots of official people come and go and all of them just nod and smile as they pass. Kyle arrives with a few friends and is both embarrassed and amused that I am managing to pass myself off as a very mature student whilst waiting on him. No danger that I'll be mistaken for a Professor though. I'm wearing my brand new Scotand away strip—the Diadora with the small central badge. Point is; I can at least say that I wrote a little bit of this book when I was at the university, right?) Back to work ...

"So, where'd'you go at the weekend Jim?" asks Bunty as we pretend to re-organise the archives. The Archives is a great number by the way. It's a regular assignment; weeding of old files for an hour each morning in a storeroom well away from any serious supervision. There are thousands of files and nobody is really measuring our progress so it becomes more of a social hour with a little weeding thrown in to ease our consciences. There's Bunty and I and another young guy called Robin who looks a bit like a stout version of Mick Jagger (especially the lips) with thick tousled ginger hair. I create a makeshift billiards game on our worktable with typewriter ribbon cans and the broom handle as a cue! We put some cardboard boxes on chairs at the four corners for some very generously sized pockets. Robin's well up for it. This is also where we have a daily visit from "Elvis". One of the Labourers, Billy S, stops in daily to take away archive rubbish. He's an Elvis fanatic and gives us daily updates on all things Elvis related. He is in a very serious fan club and makes regular visits to Memphis, Tennessee. He even wears the white cat suits with the braid and all (not to work of course). He explains how he's often mistaken for "The man" around Edinburgh. This is hard to reconcile as although he has the dark hair and features, he's about one third the size of Elvis by now! Once in a while he gives a rendition of "Poke, salad, Annie". It's something to behold. Your tax money hard at work, eh? Anyway, back to Bunts' question.

"Oh, Clouds again. Fancied Flannies but my pal wis a bit worried he'd get bumped by the bouncers". I can tell Bunty's thinking "Yeh, sure" and Robin's smirking away as he lines up a shiny silver Olivetti can for the top left cardboard box.

Did you notice the "Jim" thing by the way? It's always been James or Meikle, at least to family and teachers. As I explained before, we Scots are nickname mad so there's been a slew of those too. Meeks or Meeksie or Jamsie boy all of which I quite liked. Meikle-Treacle which I hated and for which my old pal Stu Manson got several bloody noses! The most absurd one was Jeek. This was the brainchild of Tojo (remember Tony Marinello) who appointed himself nickname maestro at secondary school and had this thing for combining bits of first and last names into one. My least favourite nickname ever was Fagan after the miserly Dickensian villain. Unfortunately a childhood pal of Bunty's called Billy Pike was one of my regular card victims and years later he shared this information with her. It is still referenced quite frequently to torment! Anyway, its been mostly James all the way then suddenly … its Jim. Well, it's a work thing.

On my very first day at work I'm assigned a desk in a big open-plan office. I'm chuffed to bits. A proper desk with dark grey metal frame and an inset light grey vinyl top on two pedestals with drawers. There's also a phone (now classic—black rotary dial) with my own extension 6510, a stapler, a single hole punch and two very faux mahogany letter trays. I've arrived. We have about ten staff in the office. The boss man is a Mr Hadwin. He has a slightly bigger desk as you enter the office with a big clock on the wall behind him. He looks at it a lot even though he seems to have a decent wrist watch. He's an executive so no matter how well you get to know him, he'll be *Mister* Hadwin (but I soon learn that even civil servants use nicknames so its Wee Haddy out of earshot). Mr Hill, the Personnel man, who I'm already allowed to call Alec, has brought me in for introductions. I'm stood at Wee Haddy's desk and he's peering over his half glasses and waving in his staff with the full hand circling the way the policeman directs traffic when the lights break down. They gather around me and suddenly I know how poor old George the Monkey felt at the zoo. They're weighing me up, sniggering, and whispering to each other, getting ready to meet the new office boy. Wee Haddy says; "Well, what do you go by then lad?" (using the term lad in this context is an immediate indication of at least some degree of anglification and/or poshness!) I freeze with nerves. All my life I've been James but I somehow think that they'll think that's stiff. No idea why but regardless, suddenly and involuntarily from my mouth emerge the words; "Eh, Jim. Jim's just fine". I'll never really know where it came from but that was it. For the rest of my working life I'll be Jim. How am I going to explain this to my family?

I meet Jimmy Gray and Chris(tine) McAllister and Rena McIntosh and Tom Connolly and Maureen Wilson. The rest are off that day. Maureen is the only one remotely near my generation but they are all really nice to me and do make me very welcome. I'm lucky. My predecessor, Angus, was apparently a bit unconventional so even if I just do average I'm going to seem impressive to them. This logic has proven true throughout my career and I've got lucky with it a few times. Follow a loony and it makes you look damn good. Of course it works fine in the Civil Service but not in fitba!

Immediately sorting stuff into order of importance I learn that working at the Army Headquarters compound means that Wednesday afternoons are for sports. Any soldier who has nothing particular scheduled for Wednesday afternoon has to do some form of sports activity. Many choose individual activities like track and field but there are a few teams too. They play in local leagues as well as in challenge matches against other military installations in the area. They have a cricket team in Summer and field hockey and of course a fitba team in season. The fitba team plays in the Edinburgh Midweek Amateur Footbvall Association (EMAFA). The league is made up mostly with Police and Fire Brigade teams.

They play as "HQ SCOTLAND" and have a great field on the camp at Craigiehall, right outside our office block. It's on a slight slope but its long and wide with good grass and nets and corner flags. It's always freshly lined and, like all things military, well maintained. On a visit to Transport Section, which has windows facing that way I see some movement. There's a game on and I must have a little look. I find an excuse to go to the NAFFI (on camp Military discount store) for a packet of McVities Digestives. Civil Servants like their tea but they can't possibly have it without a biscuit. I'm learning my trade fast, eh? I stop by the pitch for a few minutes. A widely varied age range. A good if not great standard with a couple of obviously talented guys in the mix. I notice that the HQ team is not exclusively military. Interesting. A couple of "Civies" are playing and neither that great. I watch and listen to work out who the Coach is; a Warrant Officer Johnson apparently. I file this away. I've become super at filing stuff—as office dogsbody I get to do tons of it. I'm already a whiz with the double hole punch.

Next day I find an excuse to pass by WO II Johnson's office in "G" branch and say hello. As it transpires; a lovely guy. He's neat as a pin, spotless starched uniform and perfectly combed dark hair. Easy going, friendly and sports mad. He tells me he's even a Steward at Wimbledon tournament in London every year. Filed. That might come in handy later but tennis can wait for now. I'm there to take the lead but he pre-empts me; "So old Eddie from the 'Victuals' (food Supplies) section tells me you were a player."

Were a player ... were a f**kin player? I think to myself. *I'm only sixteen.*

But rather than offend me or hurt me this confirms my own theory. In fact it justifies the logic behind my decision to retire. Someone who knew me and saw me at eleven, then knew me and saw me again at fifteen would think. "He *used to be* a player". That's the whole reason I'm retired. Anyway who the hell is old Eddie? Someone who obviously knows football and specifically the area youth scene pretty well but we'll get back to him in a while. WO II Johnson is Dennis and were already on first name terms!

"Fancy a wee run out with us then?" He asks.

"Thanks, but not right now. I'm trying to give it up. Besides I don't think Wee Haddy would be over the moon about me taking a half-day off work to play football"

"Ah well Jim, just give me a shout when you're ready. Football's a wee bit like the church, you'll need it before it needs you (another of my dad's favourites). And don't worry about wee Haddy, his boss is quite the football fan too you know".

Part of me (ego) is pleased just to learn that somebody out there still knows my name and has interest but I am resolved to take a break and get established as a good Civil Servant—including gallons of tea per day and regular trips to the NAFFI for biscuits and fags of course.

My desk is opposite Tom Connolly. Tom's in his fifties he has a drawn, worn look about him (yet with rosie cheeks) with just a few thins strands of hair left which he regularly re-organises with his left palm in a wide sweeping motion. He has an unusual voice which is both gruff and soft at the same time. We become great pals despite the large age gap. We are bound initially by the fact that we both struggle to afford enough fags to keep our nicotine cravings satisfied. He's got a much better excuse than I have for being skint. He's a Catholic and apparently very devout at least in respect of the rules on contraception. He's married to Mary and has nine bairns! A Clerical Officer is a respectable steady job but its clearly a challenge for Tom to keep a family that size housed, fed and clothed on his basic salary. He grows his own vegetables and does anything else he can to help make ends meet. They live in Broxburn. He likes the football and supports Celtic. He's mildly bigoted because, as he explains, Rangers were very keen on his eldest son Kevin until they found out his religion. He also suggests there's a lot of "Masonic stuff" in little mining towns like his but at this stage I'm not clear what he means by that.

We often combine our small change to get a five pack of the cheapest fags available at the NAFFI. They're Park Drive brand and they're awful. Our last resort is for him to take advantage of his good relationship with Father Kennedy, the camp Chaplain who always seems to have plenty fags. Father K also plays on the football team which seems really strange to me. I guess this at least confirms that fitba's not a sin? Tom calls him by his first name; John, and I get to too. I think this is very cool as its something we would never have been allowed to do (though its quite common nowadays). Tom has a lot of knowledge about a lot of stuff and he's a very accomplished musician. He plays the coronet in a well rated brass band. The only downside is, having had to struggle to get by, he doesn't waste anything. I hadn't long started and one morning said that I really fancied a Hamburger roll from the canteen but had already spent my lunch money on ten Embassy Regal tipped.

"No problem" says Tom, "You've got the fags and I've got plenty sandwiches, here you go son" and he quickly thrusts two thick slices of white bread in my direction. They are bulging out with filling but I can't quite see what with.

I notice Rena and Maureen making big eyes at each other across the office. Chris is staring hard down at her desk, old Jimmy's in his own world, humming away to himself.

"That's really nice of you, thanks Tom" I say in earnest.

Its food, I'm hungry so I take a large bite. There's meat, mince I think … yep, and … peas and … carrots and … tatties and of course its all cold. Now, don't get me wrong; I love my mince and tatties but I'm used to them piping hot and fresh and served on a plate! But I don't want to seem ungrateful so I keep on chewing politely and trying to smile. I swallow the first lump after labouring a bit with it. Tom's watching and smiling so I'm committed.

"Aye" says Tom. "Can you believe my wee Mary (His daughter of about five at that time) refused to finish that last night. Says she wasn't feelin' well. Honest, these bairns just don't know they're living. Mind you, poor wee thing wis sick this morning right enough."

Suddenly I'm feeling a bit queasy. I'm eating a sickly five year olds stone cold left over mince and tatties. For all I know she might have even spat back out a couple of bits! I fumble in my jacket pocket, awkwardly extracting a ciggie from the pack with one hand.

"Mm, oh, eh, here's a fag Tom"

He grabs it between his thumb and forefinger and slides it behind his right ear and I get exactly the reaction I hope for.

"Thanks Jim, I'll just fill the kettle then" and he's up and away to the tea point.

As soon as he clears earshot the ladies erupt with laughter and start shredding me.

"How's yer Mince and slaver sannie, Jim?" says Maureen with a cackle.

"Could you spare a wee bite for us"? says Rena, then she shrieks like a hyena!

Chris' lips are tight but she's smiling and shaking her head—she's just too nice too slag anybody.

I think even wee Haddy might be chuckling to himself in the corner.

I get a couple of napkins and fill them with everything except a couple of crusty edges. I bury it all deep in my rubbish bin. When Tom comes back he's oblivious to all the banter.

"Was that alright Jim"?

"Aye, lovely, thanks Tom"

"Want another?"

Serious sneaky grins from the ladies.

"No, hit the spot Tom. I'm fine now"

In future I'd be finding out what was lurking in Tom's drawer and pockets before I declared my hunger! That said—I can't say I've met anyone more gentle, generous, genuine and loyal in my over thirty years of employment so far.

We got the work done and had a good laugh in the process. There was a good core group of youngsters and we socialized fairly regularly. I felt from the first day that Bunty and I had a strong and immediate connection beyond the "just good pals" syndrome. She had an equally fascinating group of characters in her office (next door to mine) and we shared tons of laughs about their idiosyncrasies(school of life observation—laughing together will always be absolutely critical to any long term successful romantic relationship). I had a steady girlfriend which was a double-edged sword. I could impress Bunty with how nice and considerate a guy I was towards my girlfriend. On the other hand she wasn't the type to encourage interest from someone who was already spoken for! Development beyond pally would therefore have to wait for the right opening. I was very sure about my vibes but less so hers. I was also still intimidated by the fact that she could get into pubs and clubs where I'd be laughed off. I was always delighted if I caught the same bus as her in the morning but I was at a disadvantage as there were other suitors who got on several stops before me. So life was moving along fine even without the ball at my feet.

20

SCRATCH THE ITCH

So what more could one want? Well. As predicted by WO II Johnson the church of football was nibbling away at me. Every other Wednesday I'm watching bits of the game at Craigiehall. Its like a finger nail down a chalkboard. Each time I watch its getting harder to bear.

My fitness is poor but I keep thinking I could survive okay at the pace and level of this stuff. Towards the end of the season I bump into Dennis on a Monday morning in the corridor.

"You still retired Jim? I'm really struggling for numbers for Wednesday. We've got Leith Police here at three o'clock."

I knew it was time to take the plunge. "Thanks Dennis, maybe you could put me on the bench and give me a half hour?"

"Aye, we'll see son."

Only obstacle was Haddy. I didn't have the nerve to ask him and thought I'll leave it until the Tuesday. Mid-morning Tuesday I work up the nerve and approach Haddy's desk.

I blurt it out nervously "Excuse me Mr Hadwin, eh, I've been asked to play for the HQ football team tomorrow and, eh, wondered if it would be okay with you". I exhale hard.

"Yes lad, Mr Johnson had a word earlier. Make sure you leave a clear desk and if it becomes regular I may have to charge your annual leave."

I'm nodding furiously and turning away in relief. As I sit back at my desk Tom gives me a wink and a thumbs up.

I wake up on Wednesday morning and my stomach and legs are full of nervous excitement and energy. I'm about to make my debut in the EMAFA league and you'd think it was the World Cup final. This is the longest I've gone without kicking a ball in earnest (I'm guessing around six months). I already have regrets about that "Bench" remark I made to Dennis. Who was I kidding? If he puts me on the bench my bottom lip might reach my knees!

The experience was eerily similar to my old primary school routine. I just wanted the morning to fly by and the best way to make that happen would be to work really hard. Yet I wasn't really interested. Even the archives hour seemed to drag. Lunch was a hot bridie and game of snooker in the Junior Ranks club. I had thought of playing the martyr and suggesting to Haddy that I skip my lunch in part exchange but I didn't as I was pretty sure he'd accept.

That got me to one thirty. Now it really was like the bad old days with Haddy playing the role of Miss Westlake and me looking at my watch constantly during the last hour of waiting. I'm really surprised when about two thirty Haddy shouts; "Right lad, you better be off".

Tom purses his lips, makes big eyes and nods to the door. I know he'll be having several smoke breaks by the field today! Whoosh … I'm on my way. Haddy surprises me as I pass his desk; "Nice day for some exercise, enjoy it lad". I don't think he cared for football but neither did he seem to grudge me it. This erased the last remote pangs of guilt I had for getting off and leaving my colleagues working.

There is a proper "Pavilion" for changing but its opposite the Cricket pitch at the rear of the camp (can't have the officers walking too far). There are well equipped separate rooms for both teams which is much better than the typical municipal park set up. I am introduced to my teammates. I know a couple already and recognize other faces from around camp. There are also some complete strangers and it transpires these are soldiers from other Army locations in the area which aren't big enough to raise their own team. There's even a GD (General Duty) man; posh term for Labourer. Obvioulsy a civilian employee (i.e. not a soldier) judging by his long light brown locks which flop over his face in one big curly wave. He's from Edinburgh Castle. He's wee Alan Greenan, one of those very slight, very tricky players you can barely see when he turns sideways. The army is never short of sports gear and we play in various strips. Today its Yellow shirts, Black shorts and Yellow socks all in very good nick.

Dennis announces the team and I'm in at right midfield (Phew). Leith Police look a very tough crew (I guess they'd have to be) as we all walk up to the pitch together. I find out through time that they're not all necessarily policemen. That's the basis of the team but, like most EMAFA teams, they are topped up with guys who are simply able to get Wednesday afternoons off work or some who just don't work period. Old Eddie's out to have a look. As I pass him he gives me an up and down look with his good eye—the other is either damaged or glass. He says nothing. Yet, of all the people there, somehow its him I want to impress.

My legs feel like lead for the first five or ten minutes until I get one of those special touches. Its funny how people who know football well, recognize these touches and grant instant credibility with them. We have a guy called John O'Rourke (no relation to the Hibees' strain). Its only taken a few minutes of action for me to conclude that he's by far the best player on the team. Though well into his thirties he's still got great strength and balance and shields the ball wonderfully. He's still fit as a fiddle and has apparently played at very decent (Full Army team/English non-league semi pro) levels. He gives me a short sharp inside footed pass and makes a run into space. I give him a perfectly weighted instinctive no look return and he doesn't have to break stride. He shoots and scores. He raises a fist very briefly and turns to shake my hand and he gives me that *look*. A look that says **I** can play and **you** can play and **we** both know it. Though nothing is said, the entire team sees and senses this bonding and John's respect for me instantly cascades to the rest of them. This fills me with confidence and I start to demand the ball. I face the back four and goalie, I open my palms and with fingers tightly together, point both arms directly down and inwards towards my own feet; "Feet, feet" I shout with authoritative tone and look and, courtesy of John O'Rourke's unspoken blessing, it starts to come my way.

The flip side to this is that the opposition sense it too and start to give me a little extra attention. I'm taking some serious stick on the back of my calves. It hurts but absurd as it may sound, its very welcome because its also a sign of respect. I own the first half and we're up by three. Wee Alan got a great goal. He's got legs like a starving chicken yet he's blasted it in from twenty five yards; a sound argument for good technique over power. I've added one myself though a much less spectacular tap in after a random deflection fell right to me at a corner kick. As we come off Dennis hands me half an orange and gives me a smile; "Eddie was right then". Tom joins us and with fag in one hand and half an orange in the other says "No bad Jim, no bad at all". Eddie's is the opinion I covet the most but he's gone. My long lay-off and the heavy ground start to take their toll early in the second half. I feel a cramp developing and let Dennis know before I embarrass myself. I'm subbed out but still feel great to have been back in a "Needed" role in a real game of fitba. We run it out 3-1 and everbody's happy. I shower and leave with sore calves and that very warm cosy satisfying tiredness which I haven't felt in a long, long time. It's a promising start to my latest comeback.

21

SOAP POWDER ON THE PITCH

I play the last few games of the season with similar results and enjoy a brief spell of being able to play real games without any pressure to practice or train. I know in my heart there's no serious footballing future with this approach but for now it suits me just fine.

The new season picks up around August and HQ are starting with a friendly match (Exhibition in American terms) against a newly formed British Rail (Waverley Station) team who were contemplating joining either EMAFA or the "Edinburgh Sunday Churches League".

Their Player/Manager/Organiser/Come everything is a guy called Mark Curtis. He is stocky built with a mass of Black hair resembling a Lions' mane and a thick moustache to match. You might guess him to be Mexican or Mongolian rather than Scottish but only until he opens his mouth and you hear his broad Edinburgh brogue! He's a Muirhouse boy. Muirhouse is the younger cousin of West Pilton. Yet another baby boomer housing estate, slightly more modern than the Pilton version and built on what used to be a massive estate of single level "Prefabs". These were small "Kit" houses thrown up as a post (Second World) war housing stop gap measure. I guess they stayed around much longer than anticipated. I had a couple of pals who lived in them and I always thought they were very cool because they came in a great a variety of pastel colors and all had their own main doors.

The new Muirhouse was mostly stairs like our old one in Pilton except they were coated with a much lighter pebble finish giving a fresher look, at least in the beginning. There were also large stretches of main door houses and a few high rise tower blocks, including the later infamous Martello Court. This had twenty three stories which was double or more anything we'd seen previously. Mark stayed in a similar block to the Pilton ones except his only had three sides with a common green space leading to the street in front. The other difference was he had upstairs and downstairs even though you entered on the second floor!

Mark worked as a Steward on the Edinburgh—London train route from a base at Waverly Station; just off the East end of Princes Street in the shadows of the Royal mile and the Castle. His team has a core of players who work in the railway system but its supplemented by a lot of his old mates from "Jims' Boys Club" a Leith (Kirkgate) based youth team. Mark visited the USA a couple of times when Jim's Boys came over to play in youth soccer tournaments held in the Kearney, New Jersey area in the late sixties/early seventies. That area of New Jersey had a strong Scottish connection (Kearney still has traditional Scottish bakeries and butchers and a real fish and chip shop along its main street. You could see live Celtic and Rangers games at the working Men's clubs there long before it became commonplace elsewhere in America). It was a hot bed of kids' soccer long before it spread across the entire country.

It was interesting to hear Mark say, as far back as the mid-seveties;

"You ought to have seen some of these Yankee boys Jimmy, they really could play and they are super fit and practice like crazy. They're just as fitba daft as us—just wait until they all grow up. They even took us to games at Meadowlands with bigger crowds than we get at home. We got to see Pele play for a team called the Cosmos. There were dancing girls with pom poms, fireworks and everything"

I was very cynical at that time but have to say now; "Spot on, Mark".

Look at what happened in the World Cups from the nineties onwards. Here's a pretty decent foursome which quickly spring to mind. John Harkes, the first American to have a significant impact in the modern English Football leagues. Tony Meola still one of Americas favourite goalies. Tab Ramos a forward thrusting midfielder with an incredible work rate and Claudio Reyna a thoughtful prober most recently of Manchester City. And those are just a few of the Jersey boys.

Whilst there, Mark stayed with American families and also got a feel for the lifestyle. Years later when I was posted to the States, at our farewell party in the Junior Ranks Club at Craigiehall, he predicted confidently;

"Well Jimmy a' the best—you won't be back"

It sounded totally absurd at the time but here I still am.

I digress but yet again a little connection. From Muirhouse to America and back in a heartbeat, with Football as the conduit.

We creamed Mark's team in their inaugural game 8-3 but agreed to a rematch a week later. This time he spread his search for players a bit broader and came with a stronger team re-named British Rail Edinburgh. We won again but by a much narrower margin. Over the course of the two games he and I quickly became good pals. He decided to put his team in the Sunday Churches rather than the midweek league and a deal was struck. He and two or three of his best players became regulars for HQ when they needed extra bodies on Wednesday and a couple from the HQ joined his new Sunday team under its third and final name in ten days; Waverly Star Football Club. He asked me to join too so I said I'd give it a run.

Besides the fitba' bond Mark and I hit the social trail together too. He is a Clouds guy so we get into the habit of going there together on Saturday nights. He's also a bit of a Bay City Rollers Fan and likes my near miss story on that too. Just like Harry O he has a large and very colourful family. His mother, known simply as "The Ma" is a total gem and still spoils him. For example we get back from the dancing to his house in the wee hours after splitting a few cans of lager which is more than enough to put us in tipsy mode. We have a fitba discussion disagreement en-route home and decide to settle it through a game of subbuteo! He has the full kit. We set it up on the floor, fences, scoreboard, floodlights and all, but decide we still need a bit extra atmosphere. We somehow come up with the idea of making it snow and manufacture the effect by sprinkling Daz washing powder all over the green baize pitch as well as the living room carpet. It becomes a carry-on and I start stealing his players one-by-one to see how long it takes him to notice. I've got him down to six men when he suddenly clicks as to why I'm dominating the game. He spots his kidnapped players under the corner of the coffee table.

"Ya cheatin' bastard ye" He says but can't stop his lager induced giggling.

The Ma has heard the kafuffle (which I have just discovered via the wonders of computer *really is* a word—all these years I thought it was an Arthur Montford invention. She appears in her lime green candlewick housecoat and fumbles on her thick black rimmed specs to check on her golden boy. Her hair is very similar to his.

"Ye awright son? Hi Jimmy hen"

Another charm of Mrs Curtis is that she randomly swaps word use. "Hen" is typically a female address yet she uses it for almost everyone. We're used to it and its no big deal. Mark throws in that were fine but adds;

"Hud a wee bevy Ma. Bit hungry, likesay widnae mind a bite ai sumpin".

Without another word she disappears into the kitchen and just a few minutes later we are served with a large plate of Bacon and Egg rolls and mugs of tea. Don't forget she's been awoken from her sleep at 2 a.m. by a couple of loonies spreading soap powder on her living room floor and her response is to make us some grub! The Ma is happy now. Her boy's home he's been fed and soon he'll be fast asleep. She's back to her bed with a;

"Right Mark, dinnae be styin' up too long. Night Jimmy hen" and she's off.

Soon I'm off too on the fifteen minute walk home to Drylaw, just long enough for the brisk, cold night air to fully sober me up. Its close to 3am but there is no possibility of undetected entry to my house. All passing pedestrian footsteps are carefully monitored from a half asleep mode in my parents' room. There's no doubt disappointment when several earlier approaches carry-on up the street. Then, eventually, there's me. Clip, clop, clip, clop, clip, clop … stop. Now, no matter how gently you pull it, our corporation standard metal garden gate has got a unique little squeak in the spring. Next are approximately twelve padded footsteps. The first three slightly heavier because they are upwards and require more purchase. There's one more heavy one at the end, a plant more than a step taking position at the door. Then its the telling turn of the handle instantly followed by the "Click" of the nylon roller on the inner glass door which the sudden rush of air always forces open. One hollow echoing step on the small parquet entrance between doors with the always-empty plastic Virgin Mary holy water container on the wall. A second click/ching releasing the Chubb "Snib" lock which has been deliberately left off. Then lastly, re-close the glass door and proceed. Your on pile carpet now so no sound at all but it doesn't matter. You know the entire process has been monitored, indeed welcomed, by a tilted ear on a face with one eye closed. Mostly Mammy, sometimes Dad, sometimes both. Doesn't matter its an interchangeable role. As you pass the inevitably slightly ajar bedroom door the predictable script is completed. You stop in half stride to respond to a low whisper;

"That you Chames? D'ye put the snib back on? ("Chames" tells me who's on vigil tonight)

"Aye Ma"

"Where d'ye go? Were ye drinkin?"

"Couple ae cans—Clouds then back to Marks—I'm fine"

"Ye should sty away fae the beer and yer no feird walkin' through **that** Muirhouse yersel at this time"

(In Edinburgh-speak an emphasized "That" before a name or place almost always indicates a negative context. For example used before a place name it usually indicates general disapproval. Its also commonly used to confirm non-intimacy with a person—especially the opposite sex—when relaying a story)

"I'm fine Ma"

"Night son"

"Night Ma"

See. My Ma loves me just as much as The Ma loves Mark. Mind you, I wonder what she'd say if I asked her to jump up and make me some Bacon and Eggs right now? Nah.

Sunday I'm back down to Muirhouse by 9:30am for mass at St Pauls. Not bad considering the late night I had. My Dad's system is that once you start working its basically your own decision whether you go to mass or not. Not sure how David handled this I think he still went whilst he was living at home at least. John (lifelong Church passer-ooter; fainter) had no problem quitting. I'm somewhere in the middle. Both parents are good at laying on the catholic guilts even though my Mom's a proddie! I'm a little intimidated so I mostly still go. Father McAllister is on good form and I actually stay awake through the entire sermon and even get his general point about envy and pride. He's a bit more upbeat than most of our childhood priests many of who were basic fire and brimstone. As mentioned in an earlier chapter, he's done a good job establishing the new Parish. On the way out I get a "Hi James, how's it going" from Willie Murray who's there with his dad. Even at sixteen its still pretty cool being treated like an equal by a real Hibs player. A few other boys look a bit jealous and at first I'm glad but then I think of the sermon and get the catholic guilts back!

It's home to a superb smell of Bacon, Egg, Sausage, Black Pudding, fried tatties, fried tomatoes and crispy rolls slightly burnt on top. However I can smell but not touch! Why? Waverly Star has a game at three o'clock at Gypsy Brae and I still can't eat within several hours of a game. Gypsy Brae is located in the shadows of the enormous blue/green Gasworks' tanks (which can be seen from just about anywhere around Edinburgh) It's on a brief grassy plateau between the Granton "Dump" (Landfill) and the Silverknowes beach. This is the North side of Edinburgh which is actually the South shore of the Firth of Forth. Its right on the water and an Eastward wind just howls along the miles wide channel. You can see the spectacular Forth Rail and Road Bridges silhouettes overlapping in the distance. The rail bridge is like one we'd build with our meccano set, the road one is the new suspension style with sleek curving lines.

The pitches run on an almost exact East-West plain and being elevated well above all of the surrounding ground, most Gypsy Brae games are of two distinct halves. A ton of time is wasted simply retrieving the ball, occasionally from the ocean but if the tide's going out the ball is gone! Marks put together a nice set of Manchester United strips, they even have the thin red stripes on the white collar. Its as cold and windswept as ever and we score three with the wind at our back and lose three with it in our face. Can't remember much else about it except that

Ronnie Paterson scored a cracker and Big Rab Henderson and I were daft enough to go in the water for a brief swim afterwards. The tide had turned so this meant trekking out through about a hundred yards of oily silt just to reach a place where the water is actually deep enough to swim. We emerge freezing and with dyed black feet!

We dry off and head up to the Marina Hotel opposite the short fifteenth hole of the Silverknowes (public) Golf Course. Its one of the few places with a bar open on Sunday at the time. Rab Hendo looks old enough to get served easy so he buys a round and brings it to a well concealed table where we can safely have a swig.

So it's Waverley Star on Sundays and HQ Scotland Wednesdays. Not quite the acme of the soccer world but it's a couple of small steps back towards glory.

In fact I'm doing well enough to attract a rather obscure Pro offer though I suspect this one's more on reputation than current form. We have a distant relative (my Grannie's cousin I think) visiting all the way from Australia. The game there is still mainly part-time but serious money is starting to creep into a few of the top clubs. He's involved with a team called Keilor City (Perth area I think), and he's doing some recruiting whilst in Scotland. They're in one of the higher divisions. I've seen their name on the Vernons and Littlewoods Football Pool coupons as they both used the Australian leagues to keep the national gambling habit going during our summer. He knows I was a hot prospect but I doubt he ever saw me play. Nevertheless he makes me a sincere offer to go to Australia and sign for Keilor City and he'll also get me an office job in local government. He assures me I can make a decent living off the two combined. I'm flattered but haven't completely given up on my dream of a bigger stage yet. I politely decline and he says if I change my mind to just get in touch. I never do. Wullie Murray ends up heading "Down under" along with Les Thomson, another local Drylaw/Edinburgh Thistle boy who was on Hibs books. They seem to make ends meet at it for a while.

22

QUE SERA, SERA

Hibs had finished a very respectable second in the league for the 1973/74 season but the first signs of the break up of *THE* Hibs team of my generation also emerged. Joe Harper's arrival from Everton was always seen as the catalyst for this which eventually saw the exodus of our beloved Stanton, Cropley, Blackley, Brownlie, Edwards, O'Rourke and Gordon. As covered earlier, Scotland had a very respectable showing in the World Cup Finals that Summer and I was back playing on not one but two teams. So there was a lot to be optimistic about as the new season (1974/75) got underway around the end of August. Of course with no proper pre-season training I got off to a slow start but by the time Christmas rolled around I had regained a little fitness and was showing quite well on both the HQ team and for Waverley Star, despite my smoking. I could make this perverse argument that smoking made me fitter as I walked a lot to save bus fares to buy fags but you wouldn't buy that I'm sure! From very early on Star were in a two-horse race with a team called Carricknowe for the Sunday Churches League title. It was the start of a brief but very intense rivalry in all things Sunday Churches football.

That Christmas was also when I finally planted the seed which would determine my romantic destiny. It was delivered on the back of a number 81 double-decker corporation bus somewhere along the Queensferry Road. The young crowd from work ended up having Christmas drinks in the Barnton Hotel. Not by co-incidence I decided to leave at the same time as Bunty hoping to get her on her own. Unfortunately, another of our pals; a soldier called Manus, trailed out with us. We all boarded the 81 at the Barnton roundabout but within a few minutes Manus was snoring loudly courtesy of several pints. I tried to find a natural lead in but couldn't. We were fast approaching my stop so I just went for it. I looked Bunty in the eye and blurted out how I felt and attempted to put the lips on her. Predictably, she eased me back and politely reminded me that I already had a girlfriend. However even in her rebuff there was something in her eyes and voice which told me there might be at least a degree of reciprocal feeling. I ended up getting off two stops past my normal one and having a long walk home!

My girlfriend and I had been dabbling in a series of side relationships for a while, both pretending we didn't know. So it was hardly a shock when we parted company. I experimented with my free agency very briefly but still was limited to what was available at the local pubs or Clouds on a Saturday night! Bunty still mostly went to places I couldn't get into so manipulating a "Co-incidental" meeting was a problem. Fortunately we had another "Works" do—a Jacobean banquet at a place called Dalhousie Castle somewhere on the outskirts of Edinburgh. I guess it was a way of keeping one of Scotlands Stately Homes afloat. As I look back I imagine its something the American tourists would love. It was surreal to see our diverse cast of characters, including Old Haddy, dressed in bibs and swigging back the Mead. My objective was clear from the very start. To end the night alone with Bunty. To avoid any danger of drinking and driving a coach had been part of the deal. It dropped us all back at the Waverely Bridge just off Princess Street somewhere around 11pm. My plan was to get sat beside her on the bus back but that was thwarted as she got sat beside another girl; Alma who had supped enough Mead to be oblivious to my blatant hints to shove her out of the way.

I was determined though so I asked her straight out if I could walk her home. She agreed. I finally thought I had it cracked but hadn't legislated for JJ. As we got off the bus and headed up Market Street, JJ trailed along with us! He and I had arrived together but I thought he would take my wink and nod as a sign to split. However the Lager and Mead had also got the better of his thinking pattern and before I knew it he was hanging on Bunty's other arm, grinning like a Chesire cat and slurring nothing in particular as we passed the already bustling Scotsman newspaper loading bays. He was always great to me so I just didn't have the heart to tell him to **ck off. As luck would have it he had to break off for a call of nature just before we reached Bunty's stair which was right opposite the "Tempting Tattie" baked potato shop on Jeffrey Street. This was one of the first (and by far the best in my opinion) of a whole new generation of alternative carry-out foods which were starting to dent the long held monopoly of Chippies (Fish and Chip shop) and Chinese (my kids of course continue to keep reminding me that the term "Chinkie" makes me a racist). Anyway, JJ's disappearance into a doorway to empty his lager/mead shandy finally gave me my chance as I escorted her into the stair passageway of number twenty nine. I emerged after a few minutes with a proper date secured and found JJ fighting with his zipper and a little befuddled by Bunty's sudden disappearance. With arms draped around each others necks we headed round to the High Street in search of any form of alcohol.

Back to the passion at hand. I really was starting to "Feel the pleasure" of playing again. The nearest I ever heard to an explanation which did any justice to my depth of feeling was by Ian Charleston playing Eric Liddel in the brilliant movie; "Chariots of Fire". In trying to explain how he might help the world via running, winning and preaching rather than just straight preaching. He explained that he could feel "God's pleasure" in exploiting his natural ability to the full. The inference was that, what on the surface seems a clearly self satisfying, egotistical activity could somehow be felt and have collective benefit for others. It just felt right. I love to draw and paint a little too and I've also had a similar feeling (not very frequently unfortunately) when a finished drawing or painting just feels right. I'm finding this more elusive in trying to write this story as it takes me several reviews and rewrites until I'm happy with how a sentence feels. Yet, instinctively without forethought I can stand in a field, redirect a little round ball with a deft flick of my foot and immediately feel a wave of inner satisfaction.

Waverly Star are tearing up the Sunday Churches league and HQ Scotland (Army) are holding their own and I'm a part of both and content with that. Then, out of the blue my professional fitba taste buds are tickled again by a confluence of circumstances.

The British Army football team has come on a short tour of Scotland and they are headquartered at Craigiehall. Now consider that they can choose from all soldiers based in UK at the time and think how fit they keep themselves and that makes for a very high quality team. On their second day at HQ Scotland there's a big social night at the Junior Ranks Club and there is a major punch-up involving several of the squad members. This results in six of them facing minor disciplinary action and being sent home to their various bases. Next day W.O. Johnson comes into my office and tells me that their coach is struggling with their training/practice routine and wants a few "local" players to fill the void. He suggests that I would fit the bill if Wee Haddy will agree to release me for two or three days. As usual Denis has it all fixed in advance and I'm about to get three days off work to train full time! So here we go again. Just when I accept that my life career path is outside football I'm thrown a morsel.

I turn up at the pavilion at eight thirty the next morning and I'm relieved to see that John O'Rourke has been drafted in too so I've got a buddy who can bridge the gap between serious soldiers and a wee civvy. The players are generally older than me and pretty conceited from what I observe. The coach explains that they have a game Thursday night at Redford Barracks Field (a neat little army stadium with a sparingly used pitch—Edinburgh pro teams sometimes trained there) against the Scotland under-18 team which is preparing for an international tournament—serious stuff. They talk and act as I imagine they would at Easter Road, Ibrox or Parkhead on a daily basis. Football, football football with a little bit of sexual innuendo thrown in.

The training is hard but manageable and the "Mess" (Soldiers' canteen) lays on special meals to the Coaches specifications. In the afternoon we finally get on to some ball work and a full field practice match. And I'm holding my own. The coach likes my attitude which contradicts all the stereotypes of soft civvies being less committed! By Thursday I'm pretty wound up. It's clear that the place will be buzzing with pro scouts but I'll only be there filling space and unlikely to even get off the bench. I start to think about how great an opportunity this might be. Technically, I'm still under 18 qualified. Hmmmm.

In the end the coach plays his own players but he does give me the last half hour as thanks for my helping out his squad numbers. I'm up front rather than in my natural midfield but that's okay because the youngsters are working hard to impress their coaches and the pace is really fast even in the late stages. They have obviously been told to "Knock it about" as they make a ton of short crisp passes. I think they beat us 4-2. There was no doubt a few future stars in that side but as it was really just a practice match there weren't any programmes or other written records to check. I had a few nice touches and one half chance comfortably gathered by their goalie but apparently didn't do enough to be invited to change teams! I thought seriously about offering to swap shirts at the end just to get my hands on one of their beautiful dark blue jerseys but it was hardly that type of situation.

The good news is that I felt quite satisfied at just having been involved rather than any sense of envy, injustice or bitterness which would certainly have been the case a couple of years earlier. So at least I've now played in a Scotland match albeit on the wrong side. The culmination of my comeback would surely be a "Cap" of my own. In those days they really did get Caps for international appearances. They were in national colors with tassels and embroidered details of the game. I remember eventually seeing one close up at Chris Robertson's house in Meadowfield. They had a nice trophy cabinet which was stacked full courtesy Chris and George long before young John (JR) even started his long successful pro career. The cap (A schoolboy's version I think) looked very "Cool" but I can't imagine anyone actually wearing one, except to pose for a photograph. Though I recall from my "Pictorial History of Soccer" (Dennis Signy/Paul Hamblyn; another great fitba book from my Uncle James) that very early players did indeed wear caps as part of their uniforms which looked more like baggy pajamas. This couldn't have done much for their mobility or heading ability.

The first proper date I had with Bunty was a trip to the pictures (our term for Movies) to see Dr Zhivago at the Ritz in Rodney Street. Even this had a football connection being immediately in front of the site of "The Gymnasium" home of the long since defunct professional team; St Bernard's (though, at least until I left Scotland, the club name was sustained via the amateur ranks). Years later, in the States, I became friends with one of St Bernard's stalwart players from that era; Jock Russell who's daughter Rose worked with Bunty. Well into his seventies, Jock was still a mind of fascinating football knowledge and he told great stories of an era when few of the top level footballers made a living wage on the field. Most had other full time jobs. For example, whilst participating in the Scottish Cup semi-final (against East Fife I think) in 1935 Jock's day job was as a Keeper at Edinburgh zoo! It was very exciting when reading Bob Crampsey's fairly recent "First one hundred years of Scottish football" one of the photographs was an action shot from that match. There in the foreground was the imposing figure of Jock Russell in his prime. I really enjoyed sharing that discovery with Rose. Jock also followed the modern game closely and was still well connected at the professional levels. One of his best pals was Tommy Walker of Hearts from when they were next door neighbors at Livingstone Station. He also followed Whitburn juniors through some great success. ("Juniors" in this respect does not mean kids/youth but rather a second tier of professionals on which I will expand in detail in a later chapter).

So back to my date. For reasons which I can't rightly remember (Nerves perhaps) Bunty and I giggled our way through all the wrong parts of Dr Z to the point where we got some tuts, shss and dirty looks. We eventually retired to the Ritz's famous "Chummy" seats and the relationship was finally cooking with gas (Scottish for damn good).

That summer we were pretty inseparable except when I took the annual pilgrimage to "WEM-BAL-EE" for our match against England. I went down with a large group of Drylaw boys on a "Football Special" British rail train. This went down overnight Friday/Saturday and returned overnight Saturday/Sunday and the price was right. It was pretty wild despite having a large contingent of Edinburgh's finest constables aboard. As we pulled out of Waverly Station flanked by Calton Hill on one side and the dark silhouette of the back of the Royal Mile on the other, Saltires (St Andrews cross) Rampant Lions, Tartan scarves and "Bannockburn" banners waved furiously from every door and window and the entire train erupted in a chorus of;

"Que sera, sera,
Whatever will be, will be,
We're going to Wem—balee,
Que sera, sera"

With his regular trips to London Mark had managed to get quite a few tickets but not enough for all of us so there were four traveling down in hope of buying at the stadium. A couple of them (Henry Hoskins and Joe Brady) couldn't afford the touts' asking prices and couldn't get into the pubs so ended up watching it on telly through a Rediffusion (TV store) window. This inspired a new mercenary chant which we sang to them on the return trip and for several months' afterwards;

"Henry went tae Wem-bly,
Tae watch it on the tel-ly,
Na, na, na, na,
Na, na, na, na"

"Ya rotten bastards" says Henry over and over until he flakes out on his large bottle of Woodpecker Cider.

There were a couple of eerie similarities between this and my first big game outing to the '68 League Cup final. We had heard that lots of Scots always gathered at a pub called "The Greyhound" and it was large and had outside seats so there was a good chance for underagers to get beer. We found it without having any real clue where we were. This is another football oddity. No Mapquest needed. You never looked up directions to a ground—just follow the crowd and you must be headed the right way! My brothers David and John were living in Jersey (Channel Islands) by now and it wasn't like we had regular contact (they probably called my Mom about once a month to say they were still alive) and I had no idea they would be going to the game. So who do I literally "Bump" into as I try to get in the door to scope out our buying strategy. David it is and in Kilt and full regalia and clearly well oiled with the deadly Guinness and straight Bacardi mix (a scary thought nowadays).

"Jamesy boy, wha' you daein here ya wee shite ye, dis mammy ken yer here?" he grins widely with one eye squinting shut (it's so like my granddad Miller after a few nips) and gives my hair a major ruffle the way happy drunks always do to little kids, then shuts his eyes and shakes his head slowly.

I reply; "Don't forget I'm a working Civil Servant now pal and yes I told her I was coming down"

Next thing John appears too with a whole bunch of Jersey Scots most of whom I've never met. They're all well full of booze and joyful optimism and for five minutes I'm a novelty;

"Look" Says John, "It's the wee bra'ar, how's it gon weedo?" (Weed/The weed/Weedo were common affectionate terms used for the youngest male of the brood)

Before I get a chance to speak a very large, bearded hairy man in a kilt and tee-shirt shouts at the top of his lungs;

"Zat the yin that wiped aes erse wi the bry-nylon shirt at Galashiels?"

Nice to know they've been sharing my most embarrassing moments with a bunch of relative strangers. Hopefully this writing thing will take-off and I'll have the chance for some payback.

"Aye, Z'him—wee shite" and they all erupt in drunken laughter.

Still, the upside is that they're all falling over each other to buy a Lager for the "Wee Shite". Yet another kilted man I don't recognize hands me a pint and puts the arm on my shoulder to impart worldly advice;

"Wadge yerzel zon, loat ae bampots doon here" and I'm thinking. Yep am lookin' at one!

As fast and suddenly as they appeared I lose them as the hoards suddenly decide its time to march on Wembley. We strike up the traditional rendition of "Bonnie Scotland" and it starts with the special slow hold on the first O;

"BO … nnie Sco—ot—land,
Bonnie Sco—ot—land,
We'll support you evermore,
We'll suppo—ort you, e—ver—more"

It's incredibly loud and really does raise the hairs on the back of your neck. When we get inside the stadium it's even more tremendous and as usual we out-sing our English counterparts by a million decibels in their hallowed home. Unfortunately, the actual football match itself goes in somewhat the opposite direction. The other similarity to my first big outing is that my team ends up going down by four goals. Final score; England 5 Scotland 1. Without looking it up I couldn't even tell you who scored our goal. My everlasting memory from that day (albeit Lager clouded) is of the less than handsome, chicken-legged Scottish keeper; Kennedy of Rangers, throwing himself around his goalmouth missing everything that came his way! This included one extremely ugly moment when he almost brained himself on the post whilst "Whiffing" on a fairly speculative long range shot from Beattie or Francis or one of the other many instant English stars that game created!

The other fascinating thing was how all these English supporters just appeared from nowhere when they scored and by the end they summoned enough courage to unify in their very boring;

"Ing—glan" clap, clap, clap. (Mega yawn).

Mark and I ended up sat on the terraces in tears before the final whistle was anywhere in sight. On the bright side the aftermath saw a great deal of drunken revelry, including the standard sieges at Trafalgar Square and Piccadilly Circus but not a lot in the way of serious trouble. The only fight I saw was between two Scottish supporters over who had done the best dive into one of the fountains! The journey home started out with defiant loyal singing but by the time we reached York the collective snoring was louder than the train engines.

So instead of Bannockburn we got Culloden but never mind; you can't win 'em all.

23

GOING TO THE CHAPEL

That summer Bunty and I went to Northern Ireland to visit her sister who was married to a Military Policeman serving at Aldergrove; a military camp near Belfast. We had a fabulous time and when we got back we were pretty much set on getting engaged and married in the fairly near future. Though young by today's standards we were both working and ready to fly the parents' nest. Only problem was I'd have to save up for the ring first and that might take a while. We agreed that Bunty would wear a ring she had (With a little red stone) on her engagement finger as a temporary measure to show our intent!

We told her Mum and they started looking at dates in the autumn. They managed to book a lovely place called "The Mansion House" for Saturday October 4th, 1975 and so we had our date set. It was just as it sounded; a large light stone mansion located up a long driveway off the Milton Road on the grounds of Duddingston Golf course.

Now we had to do the church bit. I just assumed that we'd get married in my Church and Bunty didn't seem to have any strong feelings against it. So off we go to St Paul's but Father McAllister was on a sabbatical of some kind. We were sent to St Margaret's, Davidson Mains to see Father Donoghue. We got the date fixed up okay but then were told that as Bunty was non-Catholic we would have to come to six weeks of classes before the wedding! Father Donoghue was a very old fashioned priest and our weekly sessions were full of single minded bigotry and male chauvinism. I confess (a very appropriate term I suppose) that I saw this as the price of a church wedding and so didn't pay much attention to what he was saying. I just agreed and nodded my way through to try to keep the discussion short as possible. These sessions would justify a whole book in their own right but in short they invariably ended with us coming out fighting as we waited in line for a supper at the Corbie Chip shop. Besides being bombarded with all this instant Catholicism Bunty was regularly sniffed and accosted by Father D's slobbering, panting Red Setter which liked to try to mount our knees! We pull our chairs in tight to the table leaving him as little room as possible for approach.

In stark contrast, we meet a couple of times for a courtesy chat with Bunty's Episcopalian minister; Father Holloway (Old St Paul's, Jeffrey St) and I have to admit he seems to have a much calmer, balanced view of the world than Father D.

On Thursday nights the Edinburgh shops stayed open late. Common now but rather unusual then when everything generally closed sharp at 5 p.m. on weekdays. I was walking along Princess Street with JJ and saw a nice little diamond ring in H.R. Samuels' window for sixty pounds. I mentioned that I'd love to buy it and wondered aloud if they'd do some kind of hire/purchase (We didn't use the term credit then!) Right out of the blue JJ said;

"I'll lend you the cash if you want?"

"Jokin' right?" I laugh.

But his face is dead straight, wide eyes, protruding lower lip. "No. I'm saving up for my car but won't be getting it for a while so as long as you square me in the next two or three months it's really not a problem"

JJ was car daft. It was ironic that at the time I had a car and he didn't. He had his license and I didn't and of course, he had cash in the bank and I didn't. David had left his two—tone (Burgundy body/Powder Blue roof) Ford Anglia to me when he took off for Jersey. It was left registered to him with me named as an eligible "Learner" driver. All I had to do was pay the insurance premiums and this kept continuity for his "No claims bonus" something which had a significant impact on rates.

JJ lived not too far from me in the lovely Belford bungalows. He was public school and his family was pretty well doing but with no airs about them. As a learner I needed a licensed driver in the car with me. We set up an arrangement where he would get the bus a couple of stops then walk through Blackhall to meet up with me at the end of my street in Drylaw in the mornings for the drive to work. We'd reverse that process at nights.

In practice this lasted only a few days and our pick up/drop off points got gradually nearer and nearer his house until eventually I just picked him up and dropped him right there. So there I was gallivanting about Edinburgh in my Anglia with no license and mostly without the requisite co-driver! I had taken lessons with Mr Waldie (everyone in Drylaw did) in his famous little shiny metallic Blue Volkswagen bug with the dual controls. You know how some people look like their dogs? Well Mr Waldie looked like his car—he had the same chubby round shaped body and head and the thickest ears I ever saw. I was always getting caught staring at the one nearest me. "Eyes on the road son" he'd scream at me.

I was more than ready to sit my test. However I whizzed by Mr Waldie one day in the Anglia and he waved and smiled. A couple days later I see him at the Chip shop and he says;

"Well James—wondered where you went? Passed yer test without me, eh son?"

He was quite an intimidating presence and there are lots of people looking and listening so I blurt out;

"Oh, eh … aye, Mr Waldie. Likesay sat it in my uncle's car to save a few quid. Sorry"

"No apology needed son. Happens a lot with the prices we charge you nowadays. I'm just delighted you got through".

"Aye, well thanks very much" and I make a quick exit without even buying anything. Of course I'll apologize and come clean with him later, right. But I can't. So that's me stuck. I need him to take my test but I just can't face him with the truth.

So we'll worry about a license later. My dad does confiscate the keys to the car and ban me several times for driving without a "Co" but I know all his secret hiding places well and I'll never do it again right? I'm not proud of it now but I do it all the time. My night usually finishes with me dropping Bunty at her house which means I come back across Princess Street and down through the West End towards Dean Bridge. The area is crawling with cops, especially Charlotte Square where I pass a few of them sitting on the bonnets (hoods) of their patrol cars almost every time. Fortunately they seem much more interested in their coffee and fags than in me.

I have just one slip-up with this system. One night I stop to "say goodnight" to Bunty. As is customary we park about thirty yards short of her stair. When I start to pull forward to finally drop her off I don't switch my lights back on and attract the attention of a very young cop who's routinely checking the storefronts to Bert's the Hairdressers, Cannongate Publishers and the likes. He waves me over and asks;

"Something wrong with your lights, son?" Son! He looks about ages with us more like a cadet than a real cop. Still, I recall some old advice that when your caught red handed, flattery and courtesy are at least worth a shot.

I'm thinking ahead and attempt to lay some cover; "Sorry Officer just dropped our pal and was pulling forward to park"

"Can I see your license and registration please?"

"Sure, eh here's my license and I'll just …" I fumble around the glove compartment but the registration slip isn't there. I remember. It's in a drawer at home.

"Actually the registration's at home sir"

"Don't you know it's supposed to be kept in the car?"

"Yes, sorry sir, my dad (always the parents' fault) likes to keep all that legal stuff in a specific drawer at home"

"We'll come back to that. I notice that this is just a learner's permit. Can I see your license please" He points to Bunty.

She immediately goes bright red and responds; "I don't have a license."

I intervene. "Well, y'see Officer, the boy I just dropped off was my co-driver, he has the license".

With clearly sarcastic tone; "Oh, and does this mystery co-driver have a name and address?"

"Jameson sir, John Jameson, 2 Belford Avenue"

"And you decided to drop him in Jeffrey Street and now he's disappeared, eh? Could you both step out the car please?" We oblige and sit against the bonnet. He squares up to us.

"Now sir this is your vehicle, right?'

"Well it's actually my brother's but I'm a named driver on it"

"But with a co-driver of course"

"Course, your right sir" Grovel, scrape, grovel.

"Could anyone verify all this?"

I point to Bunty. "Her parents could. They live right here" I flip my hand the other way and point to number twenty nine.

He marches us up three flights. Bunty's dad opens the door and must have wondered what the hell's going on here. He stays calm though and invites us all into the living room. Her mom joins us from the kitchen. The officer explains what's transpired and at least seems to quickly realize we're not car thieves! Bunty's folks duly vouch for me and her dad says he'll be happy to sit as my co-driver on the ride home. The cop clearly knows that JJ was never in the frame but all the groveling has paid off and he's decided to just give me a stiff lecture. He recites the trouble I can get in for driving without a license and taps his pencil on my head in rhythm with his closing phrase.

"So … don't … do … it … a … gain"

I'm maintaining a forced smile. I'm thinking. I know what I'd like do with that pencil pal but better judgment prevails and my mouth keeps saying; "Yes sir, no sir, three bags full sir."

I'm instructed to take a copy of the registration to my local (Drylaw) police station within seven days to avoid a fine. I'm very embarrassed as Bunty and her dad follow me down the stairs for the ride home with the prospect of having to get a bus back! In the event I drop them at the bus stop opposite the Esso hotel where they have plenty choices and sneak through the last little bit of the journey solo. Next day I pop into Drylaw Station with the registration and I've avoided prison once again. Lucky me.

Back to Princess Street then and JJ is genuinely keen to help me despite me abusing his name with the cops! He's geared up to give the right answers if they get in touch but of course they never do. He knows I can be a bit of a show-off and mouthy about the football sometimes but there's a solid level of trust between us. He goes to his bank the next day and withdraws the sixty nicker. (Yet another name we used for cash pounds which I can't explain the logic behind) Without fuss or fanfare or an IOU or even a handshake he just hands it over.

Me. "How will I square you then John?"

JJ. "Fiver a week sound alright to you?"

Me. "Sounds great but what about the interest you're losing?"

JJ. "Not worried about that pal"

And that was it. So each Thursday for the next twelve weeks I open my pay packet which by now has grown to a whopping twelve pounds sixty two pence after tax. A fiver to JJ, the "Revolving" fiver to my ma and two pounds sixty two to yours truly! And I smoke, drink and have a fiancée and we're getting married in October! Still it's something I never regretted and though it was hardly Hollywood, Bunty had a nice wee proper engagement ring. Thanks JJ! Anyway, the fitba comeback's well underway so I'll get her the big fancy ring later with my signing bonus from Manchester United or Chelsea.

I've told Bunty's dad and my ma how I got the ring so they're both very good with the hand-outs over the ensuing few weeks when they know I'm pretty skint. Bunty's dad's a brewery man so he slips me the odd few cans and my ma suddenly has the odd spare packet of Embassy Regal available.

In the meantime Hibs have let Jimmy O'Rourke go to St Johnstone. Ironically, on his first visit back he's scored the only goal of the game to beat us but I just know he takes no great pleasure in it. He's been a fixture since Hibs got into my blood and he just doesn't look right in Blue. Talking of colors, this is confirmation to me that the Purple patch is definitely over.

Before you know it 4th October's here. There's a high wind but we're blessed with bright sunshine. We had a great wedding day despite Father D keeping us in a brief panic as he returned slightly late from a walk on Silverknowes beach with the randy red setter. One of Scotland's best pipers (John; the Pipe Major from Edinburgh Castle's famous piping school) ushers the newest Mr and Mrs Meikle out onto Davidson's Mains High Street as the majority of the guests get in the fag they have been craving since half way through the service. The reception is a hoot with the bar doing great business and neither family short of volunteers for a go on the mike or the dance floor! We even have Sheona doing a sword dance. By tradition we cut out around 9 p.m. and leave them to sup and sing and dance the night away. We had thought about the Caribbean or Hawaii but on checking our Building Society statement we settled for a rented caravan at the "Pantiles" Hotel in West Linton all of forty five minutes South of the city.

If your over forty and "Embra" you must have heard of the Pantiles, eh? Sunday night, third rate cabaret, Chicken-in-a-basket and grab-a-granny combo all yours for a mere one pound sixty. Though we had only paid for a caravan, on noticing the confetti stuck in my hair, the receptionist upgraded us to a real hotel room for the first night explaining:

"A bit dark trying to find your way around the woods tonight—we'll sort you out in the morning."

I did not play or watch football during our honeymoon. I didn't even take my subutteo with me.

I did have one game of golf for which my new bride helped carry a borrowed half-set of clubs and watched me hack my way around the West Linton course. This has never happened again since.

We did spend several afternoons in the West Linton high street tea room talking to the locals who seemed very impressed that you could now make over fifty pence an hour clear money in the big city nearby.

I also decided to show-off to Bunty by pouring myself a "Free" half pint in the Pantiles lounge whilst the barmaid took a break. Problem was I couldn't get the tap switched off again so we had to do a runner with the place flooding rapidly with Tennent's Lager.

Of course being such a tight knit family, Bunty's Mum and Dad joined us for the Pantiles' midweek special; a comedian called Pancho Villa who I suspect had never seen Mexico.

Say what you want about Bermuda, Barbados and the Bahamas. How could you beat the Honeymoon we just had?

24

A HOUSE, TRANSPORT AND SEEKING MESSIAHS

So we're married and all we need now is somewhere to live. A minor technicality. Almost all of our relatives have always lived in rented Council/Corporation property. Leith, Granton, Royston, Pilton and Drylaw on my side. Lochend, Craigentinny and the Cannongate on Bunty's. This is the norm for post-war working class but a few are starting to break the mold. My generation seems much more inclined to try to buy rather than rent. This is certainly what we fancy doing but there's the question of raising the deposit and I'm only just done clearing the engagement ring mortgage! We have our joint account with the Nationwide Building Society in George Street but it is likely to grow very slowly on Clerical wages, especially as we are both partial to a decent social life and Bunty likes to get her hair cut at Bryan Drum.

The Council housing estate is also in the process of being drastically diluted by Maggie Thatcher's latest brainchild which is to sell off the rental housing stock to long standing tenants at bargain prices. (I think her intent is to create more homeowners who will, in due course, in overly simplistic theory, become good Tories). For the working class as a whole this is a double edged sword. The upside is that this allows many families to escape the cycle by which their rent payments prevent them ever saving a deposit to buy a place of their own. The downside is that all the best council houses are being snapped-up fast. In many cases younger relatives are putting up the money to buy their parents/aunties/grannies places for future use and/or sale at a profit. Although the government has created rules to prevent this happening, as usual, these rules are no match for the ingenuity of the natives! The result is a very limited choice of locations for those newcomers not yet in the system.

Our likely council options are subsequently West Pilton or Niddrie. Whilst I loved growing up in Pilton in the 1960's it has changed a lot. Drugs are starting to creep into the story and as always they are accompanied by much more serious crime. Niddrie's much the same from what I hear (with apologies to the many very nice people who are indeed still stuck in the rental cycle in both areas or just too old and set in their ways to make a move). A lot of young couples, not yet ready to buy, are looking to private housing associations for a better choice of properties/locations to rent. Father Holloway is on the board of "The Castle Rock Association" and suggests we put our name in with them. (I suspect he also put in a good word for us). We register at their office in Albany Street and the lady at the desk sounds encouragingly optimistic about a fairly early result. They've recently taken over quite a few inner city flats and are restoring and modifying them prior to rental to young couples, single parents, widows/widowers and the likes and all at generally affordable rates. They're able to do this because they're a "Not for profit" outfit on generous tax breaks.

At a push my parents could squeeze us into my old room temporarily but we all know this would be far from ideal for us and them alike.

Fortunately we get a great "Holding" arrangement. I write off to my Uncle David. He was way ahead of the curve in bucking the council housing trend, buying a semi-detached in Silverknowes when they developed the new part in the early 1960's. He's still in the merchant Navy (Benline having now replaced Blue Funnel) and on long term travel accompanied by his wife. He had been renting to a cousin from Wick (small world syndrome again—Bill Miller aka "The Wicker" who, it transpired, worked beside Bunty's dad at Scottish and Newcastle Brewery in Fountainbridge) but they had found a place in East Calder, formerly a separate town but fast becoming part of Edinburgh sprawling outer-layer of suburbs! They quickly give us their blessing to use the house for a couple of months whilst we await allocation from Castle Rock. It is spacious and well furnished and has all the mod cons of the time. It will definitely be "Downsizing" wherever we end up next! I'll also miss my Uncle David's superb radiogram and his comprehensive Sinatra record collection.

As promised within a few weeks Castle Rock comes through and we get the keys to a one bedroom flat in Smithfield Street at twenty six pounds a month. It's small enough where we can scrape together enough furniture to fill it. It's very cozy and we're especially proud of our little dining nook which features a trendy pine table and benches on rush matting with a bunch of elephant grass in an earthenware jug in the corner and a framed Ha van Vong print (The Banana sellers) on the "Woodchip" papered back wall.

This is also where I have my first couple of attempts at DIY. I "Build" a little stand at the fireplace. Two bits of wood as runners with three small planks nailed across them. Slap on some thick chocolate Brown paint and; Voila. I think it's very cool. Every visitor politely admires it ("Aye, that's barry James") but years later they all admit to actually peeing themselves whenever I turned my back! Having almost no tools and having never been introduced to rawl plugs ("Anchors" to the yanks) my attempts at mounting bathroom fixtures in the old plaster walls are pretty futile. Of course instead of admitting any fault I explain to Bunty that she pulls far too hard on the toilet paper and that's why the holder keeps falling off the wall! We have a Grocery store right opposite our stair and Newsagent, Baker, Butcher, Pub (Stratty's) and Bookie at the corner. We are also very handy for the new Ferranti Club in Robertson Avenue and our close pals; Helen and John, have a flat just up the road at Slateford.

Despite all this there's a problem. We are smack bang in the middle of Gorgie which is Jamboland. We can see Hearts' ground; Tynecastle Park (Wheatfield Street gates) from our stair door and we have to constantly pass the monster maroon "Heart of Midlothian" sign entrance on Gorgie Road itself.

Bunty's mum treats us to a fitted carpet and I'm delighted because it has tight pile which means my subbuteo pitch will sit very smoothly on it. I'm back to playing with myself again … at subbuteo I mean. I have not managed to persuade Bunty to participate. I set myself up behind the sofa. The games flow back and forward with Hibs and Scotland winning most of the time. I'm doing my usual running commentary. Bunty can't get peace to watch our 12" Black and White Portable telly which sits on the little Yellow/Green braided stool sent from the "Blind" factory in Wick via my Grannie. Bunty's concerned because we haven't bought our TV license yet. I'm trying to put it off as long as possible. You had to pay an annual fee to legally receive the BBC. It was mostly an honor system but there were rumors of a little "Detector" van which came around and caught cheaters for whom jail was inevitable. Of course I never got caught. Lucky me.

Now I'm Bob Crampsey with a sprinkling of Arthur Montford and a hint of Archie MacPherson (but not the hair),

"Edwards … he swings it out to Duncan … he whips over a hard low cross to MEIKLE and … s'c … !" I exclaim with the protracted exhale to simulate the crowd reaction to my wonderful strike.

"Off your head" she says and I know she's shaking hers even though I can't see here from behind the sofa. No doubt wondering to herself what kind of loony she's married. I confess that although she knew I was a football addict, I hadn't really got around to fully explaining the subbuteo and Lego football stuff. I imagine the conversation at her work next day;

"So, what d'the newlyweds get up to last night then Bunts?"

"Oh I just watched the telly 'cause Jimmy was busy playing football."

"Bit dark for night games—was he at the indoor five-a-sides at Meadowbank?"

"No—he had the world cup final on the carpet behind the sofa in our living room!"

C'mon. Be fair. I'm only eighteen and hanging on to one sort of childish thing in marriage isn't so bad is it? Well, that and the fact that I insist on keeping Brian the decrepit teddy bear in our bedroom! Oh, and I don't like sleeping at the side of the bed by the door and, eh, I still like to keep the lobby light on at night with the door cracked open. But, apart from all that I'm a real caveman.

David's Anglia has finally died and been towed to its grave in a lock-up in Dalkeith where "Big Alex" Alexander (My uncle James' pal—who also ends up later working in the Brewery with Bunty's dad) will salvage it for parts. I have no interest in inheriting David's subsequent vehicle. It's another two-tone. Again, Burgundy (can't bring myself to say Maroon) and Blue. Austin Cambridge or maybe a Morris Oxford I could never really tell those apart. He's added a personal touch with two foot high Disney stickers on each of the front doors; Mickey Mouse on the drivers side and Goofy on the passengers'. My dad's embarrassed as the car is sarcastically "Admired" by friends and neighbors. He won't take a ride in it.

"Ph … no danger ye'll get me in that"

My mum just giggles every time she looks at it.

For travel to work I have two choices. First I can get almost any bus which comes along Gorgie Road to the West End then pick up an "Eastern Scottish" to Craigiehall. The ES buses mostly go to the destinations beyond the city limits—all the little surrounding towns and villages. I like them better than the corporation buses simply because they are painted green and white. I get these at the stop in Charlotte Square. This has an added potential benefit as several co-workers who have their own cars drive past this bus stop each morning. I thrust myself on the very edge of the kerb in my easily recognizable flowing sage green trench coat. I pretend to read my Scotsman but am scanning carefully for passing Craigiehallers. When they feel obliged to stop I always act surprised but they know I'm not. Pat McDonald's mini is my most frequent success. She's my boss so at least she can make sure I'm on time this way. I'm a little embarrassed but its well worth it as this means cash on my tail for fags or maybe even a hamburger roll at the canteen.

We go through a spell where a regular "Lift" (which the yanks call a ride; a term which has much different connotations in Scotland) is arranged. One of our young crew, "Bob T" (Towler) gets his license and he drives his dad to his work at St Andrews Square from their home in Mussleburgh. He then continues on to Craigiehall. He's not supposed to give anyone else a lift but cheats on this by picking up Manus in George Street and myself and John Falconer at the Charlotte Square. For this we agree to give him a set amount which is much less than our cumulative bus fares. It only lasts a few weeks and very little cash actually changes hands as quick Friday exits are accompanied by "Oh, I'll need to square you for petrol on Monday Bob". Bob T is always a bit distracted by us and trying far too hard to impress us with his smooth, fast driving. He even has these oversized humpty (uncool) leather driving gloves which seem to hinder rather than help his grip on the steering wheel. One morning this culminates in him crossing the median and completely taking out a give way sign on the old Linlithgow Road (the back entrance to the camp). Fortunately there are no other cars around and as we swerve back to the correct side he is grinning and assuring us it's all part of the act. But we know its not and decide to revert mainly to use of public transport (i.e. except when absolutely desperate).

My other option is to get a Jambo maroon and white corpie bus through Saughton, Carricknowe and Clermiston and pick up an ES at the foot of Drumbrae on Queensferry Road. However even if someone from Craigiehall sees you there it's almost impossible for them to stop in rush hour so I rarely use this route. Bunts has been transferred to Edinburgh Castle so it's an easy commute for her with lots of choices of buses.

One of her co-workers there is a lady called Blanche who is married to George Stewart and he's just been brought to Hibs from Dundee. He must be doing okay because he's taken over the Chesser Inn, a fairly thriving pub. He's a solid big defender but his and the earlier arrival of the likes of Roy Barry (Ex jambo) from Crystal Palace, are just two more moves which confirm the demise of "The Hibs team" of my lifetime. Both Roy Barry and big George give their lot every week and the fans appreciate them. Ally MacLeod (Not *THE* Ally MacLeod who I'm just about to get to, but a different, younger one) also shows some dazzling skills and scores consistently (Including a New Years' day winner against the Jambos at Tyncastle) Jackie MacNamara's adored and revered and still is today. But … the fans knew the bottom line; whilst our grit and heart was still intact and there was still the occasional brilliant flash, our overall class and standing had declined considerably.

The 1976/77 season brings modest expectations for Hibs and the first sponsored (BUKTA) shirts in Scotland. We all have pretty mixed feelings about this knowing that they need the money it brings in but sensing that it's the end of a certain valued traditional era and that perhaps the start of money taking over the game completely. This instinct has certainly proven accurate with some strips now plastered in logos and greedy commercialism meaning teams appearing in colors very much at odds with their roots. Liverpool in Aqua just looks wrong as do Manchester United (Red Devils) and Chelsea ("Blue is the Color") in Black. Rangers in Red or the Jambos in Grey is also absurd to me and I've never really felt comfortable with Hibs in Purple though I confess to having the shirt! Interesting that in the last year a few teams started selling throwback shirts sans sponsors crap and they've been selling well. When you look at them they confirm that less can indeed be more.

Anyway it's clear to us that "Turnbull's Tornadoes" have been and gone and it's doubtful we'll see their likes for a while, if ever again. The cash rolls in with Cropley headed to Arsenal, Brownlie and Blackley to Newcastle and the ultimate hurt; Pat Stanton to Celtic! This is the hardest to swallow. Years removed from the event though I am willing to admit something which I never could or would have at the time. By now I was sure that Hibs chances of a league title had realistically gone. By going to Celtic there was a very strong chance that my favorite player of all time would get a league winners medal. He was brilliant and he deserved one and he got it. So there was a tiny part of me that approved the move in the circumstances. Anyway I knew that you could take Stanton out of Hibs but you'd never take Hibs out of Stanton. Ultimately most fitba people are nostalgic and sentimental to a fault so it was inevitable that somewhere down the road he'd be back for better or for worse.

With commercialism starting to dominate it's inevitable that Rangers and Celtic will ultimately pull away from the rest of the pack. It's to their tremendous credit that Aberdeen and Dundee United manage to breach Old Firm dominance a couple more times before it reaches today's point of no return where the economic gap means that third place is the realistic goal for all the other clubs.

You often hear it said that there's not much a Manager can do once the players are out there on the pitch but if you look at the real success stories of the last fifty years there's always a special Manager at the root of it. Someone who knew how to get the blend right and someone with enough presence to hold on to his "Core" players in spite of fat foreign gentlemen with equally portly check books. A quick look.

Think about it. Busby, Shankly, Stein, Revie, Clough, Turnbull (It's my book and I can include who I want with the elite!) Clutching at straws as a typically biased homer you can always find connections to your own club. Did you know that Matt Busby played for Hibs? Did you know that Jock Stein was Hibs manager just before he took Celtic to the moon? Do you recall that the other (Bob)

Shankly managed Hibs. Revie got one of his key early European results at Easter Road and Cloughie's connection? Well I know it's a stretch but he was a staunch Labor man just like most Hibs fans!

More recently take the two who managed to get passed the old firm and win the Scottish Premier League title—a truly remarkable feat. Aberdeen in the hands of (Now Sir) Alex Ferguson with Strachan, Miller and McLeish on board. This was no surprise for those who tracked Fergie's revival of St Mirren just prior. He brought together the likes of McGarvey, Stark and Fitzpatrick and refused to sell them until his mission was accomplished. Even before they came up to the Premier anyone who knew the game could see there was something special, fresh and exciting about this team. Can you imagine what Fergie said to the Directors the first time the big boys came chasing the McGarvey signature? Recognizing the ultimate limitations of Love Street he moved on to Aberdeen and sustained his success on the bigger stage, including beating Real Madrid in the European Cup Winners Cup Final, using his same special blend. Ultimately he moves onto Manchester United and with almost no financial limitations there he blends his magic again, then keeps stirring it and refreshing it (an even greater challenge) periodically for unprecedented long term success. He is the maestro of motivation and timely substitutions and this ultimately gets him the European Champions Cup in the last few minutes against Bayern Munich in Barcelona, Spain.

Jim McLean's achievements at Dundee United might be even greater in a one-off snapshot sense. He put together Hegarty, Narey, Sturrock and Bannon and chased the poachers several times including when they came after McLean himself. He brought a league title and European success to a team with a tiny fraction of the resources of the old firm and the English giants. Unlike Aberdeen he had to share the support of the town with another full time club, Dundee FC, literally just across the street at Dens Park. (Trivia—The two closest located professional stadiums in Britain—and probably the world for that matter)

Of course Fergie is still at it but he's been joined by Wenger now as Arsenal sustain incredible form for the third consecutive season. And the owners get greedier. Poor Ranieri of Chelsea got the boot for reaching a European Cup semi and finishing second in the Premiership! Mind you Chelsea ends up with Jose Mourihno who turns out to be a very special one.

I recall one notable exception to the "Supercoach" theory. Tottenham Hotspur had a quick short passing game which I think started with Bill Nicholson in the sixties and they seemed to keep this very attractive style going for over twenty years transcending several managerial changes. Of course bringing in players like Perryman, Ardiles, Villa, Hoddle, Waddle and Gascoigne might have helped but that pure footballing reputation probably attracted some of them to White Hart Lane in the first place. It brought some modest success with cup runs but nothing like that of the Leeds, Man U, Liverpool and now Chelsea and Arsenal.

So here's the simple formula. A really hungry ambitious chairman goes and finds a Manager with that special ability to *blend*. In most cases a few of the pieces (Players) are already in place and the Manager makes just a few hand picked additions to complete his vision. The players sense it and buy into it. You're off to the races. Quite a few Managers have this gift but cannot sustain its effect. However even one good run buys long lasting credibility. For example take Souness. He goes somewhere now and there is a quick boost but it always seems to fade back to mediocrity. Regardless there will always be a long line of desperate Chairmen who think the "Failures" are an aberration and he will immediately turn their team into the Rangers of nine-in-a-row fame! He did well with that run but he had a massive economical edge over every team except Celtic and the good fortune to catch them on their back foot organization wise. Ironically it was only when Celtic found their latest savior (Martin O'Neil) that the fortunes have been completely reversed again. Newcastle is the latest to give Souness a whirl. We'll see. True saviors are so rare. In fact if you can get a Strachan or an O'Leary take 'em and enjoy sustained respectability from whatever resources you can give them to work with.

To emphasize my point it's now almost thirty years since Turnbull and guess what? Hibs are still waiting for his next coming. Alex McLeish might have fit the bill but Rangers snatched him before he even got his arse warm on the Hibs bench. (Rangers are hardly known for their patience so he'll likely be on the move again by the time this book makes it to print). Hibs didn't have the sense and patience to hold on to Frank Sauzee a bright soccer mind with broad European credibility critical for persuading the right players to brave the Edinburgh climate. Not letting him mature into his post may be our biggest blunder in fifty years—we'll see.

The other team close to my heart nowadays are the one which plays in the USA's National Football League in helmets and pads with a rugby shaped ball; the Washington Redskins. They just took this whole savior theory to a new level. They got so fed up waiting for a second coming of their "Turnbull"—a guy called Joe Gibbs, they brought the original back out of retirement after twelve years! Likesay, we'll see.

25

ON THE MARCH WITH ALLY

That season did end with a very uplifting highlight for all of us from our national team. It wasn't quite the upset of ten years earlier because we were arguably the better constructed side now but a win over England at Wembley still had some very special magic to it. Which brings me to the other great Manager of my lifetime; the one I didn't mention above because he needs some ink to himself. The one who took us on a wild exciting "Magic carpet" ride.

Following great success at Ayr United and Aberdeen Ally MacLeod had taken over as Scotland manager. He was fiercely nationalistic and didn't hide it one little bit. He was also a happy, smiling, clearly confident optimist—a refreshing change from his solid but rather stoic, cautious predecessors. He allowed sentiment into the frame. He even encouraged it. He reminded me of ten years back when my runny-nosed gang of ten year olds sitting in the big field concluded that Scotland was the best team in the world. Now here's a fully grown man in a key position who agrees that our boyhood dream of winning the World Cup is entirely possible. He tells us so, frequently.

Talk about deep fitba roots. As a boy he supported Third Lanark a team which no longer exists but which is burned into Scottish football folklore for ever. Like most of my generation I was never near it but I know the name of the ground; Cathkin Park. I feel sure that it was a special fitba place—I can just feel it. Ally played for Third Lanark at eighteen years old. At the other end of his life, at sixty one years old he scored a goal in a reserve match for Queen of the South, a record in a British professional match. In between was a lot more fitba, fitba and fitba. This included a great run in the Blackburn Rovers team which reached the FA cup final in 1960 (Lost to Wolves) as well as a brief twilight spell with my own beloved Hibees. All of this blended and simmered to create one of the brightest, bubbly, positive football personalities we've ever had.

But there was a hell of a lot more than bravado and effervescence to this man. A shrewd judge of talent. A clearly inspirational motivator and above all that special vision to "Blend". And that is exactly what he did with his teams. No question of simply putting his eleven "Best" players out there, he carefully mixed strength and speed and vision. What was most impressive was when he got to the international level he went even further seeking out players who specifically matched the sometimes slightly different requirements to compete at that level. The greatest international teams to that point had lots of cavalier in them but they could also catch their breath and with great patience and discipline, hold possession for long periods of time to defuse any momentum the opposition might try to muster. Then strike like a scorpion. He achieved exactly that with Scotland. With the likes of (Willie) Johnston, Dalglish, McGrain and Jordan the full charge could be summoned at will but we'd had that before. What was new was the deep group of ball "Winners" and "Holders" including Hartford, Rioch, Masson, Souness, Gemmill and Hutcheson. Think how you could dominate a midfield with that group of calm, crisp short passers and, at the time, this formula was the true route to international success.

The May 1977 England game was part of Ally's building process but you just felt on that day he took the brakes off a little with a bit more "Charge" than "Hold". He knew deep in his soul what this fixture meant to us. How? Because he *was* one of us. All I can remember is Willie Johnston charging up and down that left wing roasting whichever poor English defender had to attempt to cover him. Final score England 1 Scotland 2 but again, the style of the victory was much more important than the score line itself. So formed "Ally's Tartan Army". They took the turf, they took the goalposts, and they took the nets. A small price again for the boost they gave the London pub economy! Scotland's fitba managing messiah had finally arrived.

Despite our imminent greatness by the autumn we were locked in a battle with Wales to get a spot in the 1978 world cup finals which were to be held in the Argentine. The game was held at Anfield and the place was packed to the gills. It was a very tight tense affair until Scotland was given a questionable penalty. Welsh defender Joey Jones and Joe Jordan both jumped high after a cross and their outstretched arms became entangled. The ball certainly hit a hand but it seemed more likely to have been Jordan's! Nevertheless the referee pointed to the spot and Masson did the business; 1-0. A few minutes later a classic arms-all-over-the place flashing Kenny Dalglish header put it beyond doubt and Ally's army was on the march to South America.

Right about the same time Bunty and I became the very proud parents of a bouncing baby girl; Dale Elizabeth. She still laughs at how her "Baby book" which contains here precious little pink hospital wristbands and cot sign and details of all her baby gifts also has the full Scotland football squad listed amongst her visitors? (No, of course they didn't)

Sorry, darlin'—it was the Grouse Whisky that done it.

With Ally on the Baton, the months leading up to the cup were a hoot. He was the first Manager I can remember to take a little share for himself as he became spokesman for a Scottish carpet maker hence so many references to "Magic" and "Flying" carpets. The adverts were cheap and tacky and great fun to watch.

We even had a gala send off from Hampden with pipes and drums and saltires and rampant lions and fireworks, helicopters, the lot. If you doubt that we were all buying into his optimism explain why tens of thousands turned up for the send off which didn't even include a football match.

And, of course, we had a record. I don't have a copy but let's have a go at the main verse right off the top of my head;

"We're on the March with Ally's ar ... my,
We're going to the Argentine,
And we'll really shake them up,
When we win the world cup,
'Cause Scotland is the greatest football team"

We sang it and we started to believe it and what's wrong with that?

By now Bunty and I had moved to a slightly larger flat in Dalry Road just about fifty yards up from the Haymarket clock. This was again courtesy of Castle Rock. With a baby in tow our down payment savings account was seeing very little progress. We were on the top (Fourth) floor front windows to the main Dalry Road. Buildings on the opposite side were lower so we had a panoramic view of the city centre. A great location. Everything you could want in reach. We had Bakeries, Butchers, Fruiters, and Fishmongers, several Chinese, Pubs galore and a corner store. We were two minutes from Brattisani's, one of Edinburgh's best fish and chip shops which is right next door to the famous "Spiders Web" pub and of course the Torphicen Street cop shop. We were a five minute walk from the West End and had a magnificent choice of buses. We could even get a train as our back windows overlooked Haymarket Station. Yet I can't ever remember being bothered by the noise. On the contrary being on one of the main thoroughfares heading west provided great entertainment when there was nothing decent on the telly, especially on SA-TUR-DAY night.

We'd lean on the windows watching the late party crowds meandering home to Gorgie, Saughton, Broomhouse and beyond. These were mostly people who had favored a final pint or nip over holding onto their taxicab fare. Many clearly needed the walk anyway. Besides the usual Frank Sinatra's and Dean Martin's there were always plenty rowing couples. It's terrible really that we all hate having a fight with our own spouse in public but watching others do so is irresistible. They'd walk twenty feet apart or on opposite sides of the street hurling abuse at each other and always blissfully unaware of the rapt audience. A typical conversation would go something likesay;

HERS—"No gittin ye another Bacardi, No gittin ye another Bacardi. Hud enough, aye, what a cheek you've got"

HIS—"Aye well ye'd hud plenty doll 'n a wis tryin tae save the taxi money"

HERS—"Oh aye, a seen how hard ye wir tryin to save money buying yersel doubles aw night"

HIS—"Aw c'mon hen, dinnae be like that now"

HERS—"Aye, well yer savin' never helped did it 'cause wer huvin tae walk efter aw"

HIS—"Aye, sorry aboot that hen bit we'll soon be hame"

HERS—"Aye. Ye'll be sorry awright 'n a hope ye'll be comfy on the couch. Oh aye 'n I'll try savin on the bacon 'n eggs the morn"

They'd fade around the bend at the top of the hill and become inaudible except for the muffled echoes which confirmed the conversation was continuing in the same vein.

Right underneath us was the big MFI furniture shop and fortunately most of the stuff in their window was far too big even for an optimistic drunk to think about lifting. So their windows mostly done okay. The opposite side of the road was a different story. A Granada shop with Televisions and other electronic devices in the front window—deadly temptation for thieves with alcohol clouded judgment. The scariest thing we saw was a Chinese waiter in a red jacket and black bow tie storming up Dalry Road waving a serious sized meat cleaver after a bunch of youths. When it became clear he wasn't bluffing a couple of them stopped and dropped a pile of crumpled notes in his direction before taking off again at great speed. The assumption was that they had tried to do a runner without paying their bill (not an uncommon occurrence). He chuntered (talked inaudibly) away to himself on his way back down the street. Raising a few eyebrows of those who'd missed the main show. Cleaver nonchalantly under his armpit as he carefully unfolded and counted the belated take. Judging by the ultimate satisfied murmurs he seemed content with the tip!

The most absurd incident we watched was the fleecing (sorry) of the wool shop. An elderly gent approached from Morrison Street with all the tell-tale signs.

Hands tight in trouser pockets, head hung forward, pointy triangle of shirt hanging out at front and always leaning right. Rock back, pause then several quick short shuffling steps forward. Repeat several times. The head would occasionally lift to see what he was passing but it always seemed just to heavy for him to keep up for more than a second. Passed the TV shop, passed the Leather Handbag shop, passed the wool shop ... stop. Turn. Now as he couldn't get his head up he maneuvered his body backwards, defying all the laws of gravity getting his eyes to where he could do a double take on the wool shop. A discernible nod. Yep, he seemed to have the one he wanted. Right hand comes out of his trouser pocket and into his jacket from where he pulls a large portion of a brick. Perhaps the reason for his leaning right.

Without hesitation. Aim. Fire. Smash. No alarm that we could hear. The brick is through the wool shop window and the effort has put him on his backside. With a struggle he hauls himself up rocks to and fro a few times then steadies, symbolically brushes his hands as he admires his work. He smiles and stoats away. No attempt to take anything. No apparent motive. Maybe just hated the stuff his wife knitted for him? We'll never know. What we do know is that people cannot resist something that's free, regardless of what it is. Next passed is a similar looking man. Well under the influence though a bit steadier on his feet. He's noticed the window is mostly gone. Checks up and down the street. People in both directions but none in wooly suits and chequered caps. He quickly starts grabbing balls of wool and stuffing them into every pocket and eventually down his shirt. Didn't seem selective, any color will do. Then he's off at a fairly clipped pace. How do you explain it in the morning when you find balls of wool stuffed in all of your pockets? The absurd part was the number of people and not all of them drunk who had a quick grab in the wool shop window on the way past! Despite it being so near a major police station it was ages before the uniforms appeared. Missing wool rather low on the Saturday night priority list I guess.

In the meantime some noisy inebriated youths extracted an oversized ball of wool from the central display and started up a game of football with it. See, I always get back to the subject eventually. They're crunching clumsily over shards of broken glass and getting serious toots from the odd passing car.

The TV shops were pushing special rental deals on Color TV's for the world cup. Three months at a ridiculously low rate with no long term obligations. Obviously banking on plenty customers getting the taste and keeping them. Americans reading this might be amused and surprised to think that in 1978 a Color TV was still not a household product in Scotland. (or most of Western Europe for that matter) We still had our 12" Black and White portable now with paid up license as I'm scared that the detector van can get us easily on the main drag. We love that little TV but it just won't do for something as massive as the World Cup. So it was that we took the Granada special and became proud renters of a huge (Its all relative) 19" color set. It even came with fake veneer trim and a tacky rack underneath for magazines.

So instead of gathering elsewhere for the big group opener against Peru it was party time at Jimnbunts! My father-in-law gave me a few cans from his monthly brewery ration and we bought in a few large packs of crisps. We had a small crowd from Craigiehall but the only ones I remember for sure were JJ and RR. (Ronnie Ritchie) Ronnie was from Dunfermline; a big "Pars" (Dunfermline Athletic Football Club) fan. We supped our beers and soaked in the build-up. It wasn't quite so over-hyped then but they had a small panel for about an hour or so prior to kick-off. Can't remember who the talking heads were that day. Of course with England eliminated in qualifying the only thing Jimmy Hill could do was cast his evil beardy spells on us. Always smiling and saying I hope the Scots do well but we all knew what he was really thinking; "Beat those Jock bastards"

We had very limited exposure to the South American game. Like everyone, we feared Brazil but had held our own against them (1-1) in the last World Cup. Argentina was finally escaping from the "Animals" tag gained through their performance at the 1966 World Cup in England. Though clearly skilled, they had kicked lumps out of everyone there especially the hosts (which I don't recall minding too much at the time)and their Captain; Rattin, seemed to revel in it. This nasty reputation was cemented and (Unfairly perhaps) spread to South America generally as Racing Club against Celtic and then Estudiantes against Manchester United played similarly rough games in consecutive world club championships.

From a fans standpoint we underestimated anybody outside the big three (Brazil, Argentine, Uruguay) and that should be understandable as we rarely encountered anyone else from that region. Chile was usually next on our uninformed, unscientific pecking order and we had handled them easily (6-2) in a friendly. So we (the fans at least) certainly took Peru too lightly and it's likely the Manager and team did too. That said it all started great. We went 1-0 up and then got a penalty kick which Don Masson missed. I've learned over many years of playing against South Americans that momentum plays such a big part in their game (much more so than elsewhere in my opinion). Had Masson scored I feel sure Peru would have imploded and we would have got more goals. However the missed penalty (As often happens) had exactly the reverse effect. With Cubillas, who we all eventually got to know and admire greatly, taking command with a couple of wonderful strikes on the very hard, fast surface. End result 3-1 Peru.

We also had a "Scandal" setback with Willie Johnston banned from the tournament for taken an off-the-shelf cold medication and failing a routine drug test.

Despite the poor start and negative publicity we couldn't be kept down long with Ally at the helm. He knew how good his team was and we had Iran on the slate which would give us a chance to recover our goal differential, right? We scraped a 1-1 draw and I don't blame Ally a bit for this one. He put the right players out there. They had an off day, Iran had an on day and so it was that we end up in the crazy position of having to beat Holland by three clear goals to qualify for the quarter finals.

True to our national character there's nothing we respond more to than being in a deep dark hopeless hole! We finally play to this teams' true potential and, for a fleeting moment, on the strength of wee Archie Gemmil's amazing solo goal, come within a sniff of the impossible. We're up 3-1 and flowing until Han or Rep or Rip Van F***ing Winkle scores a surreal rocket shot from about forty yards out. Final score Scotland 3 Holland 2. A well deserved win but not quite enough. Pack your bags boys, time to go home. And yet it could've, should've, would've been so different. Holland went on to lose a very close world cup final to what transpired to be a brilliant Argentine side in extra time. I've just watched the Boston Red Sox win the World Series of baseball; something perceived as impossible for the past eighty some years due to various curses and planet alignments, so I should never say never … but I will. Scotland will never have a more realistic chance of winning the World Cup than they did in 1978.

Of course everyone developed twenty-twenty hindsight and Ally, having worn his heart on his sleeve (Something else I loved about him) on global TV at the frustration of watching his underachieving squad, predictably and bravely made himself the scapegoat.

By sheer co-incidence (through Alex McAdam; Ayr United's *fan* in the USA) almost thirty years later and three thousand miles removed, I end up in the same BBC Fantasy football division as one Andy MacLeod, son of *the* man. As a few Scots in a mostly English filled division we take great delight in sharing the season's spoils and supporting each other against constant Anglo banter.

Ally died recently and although I only knew Andy via our harmless fantasy league E-banter, I felt compelled to open up to him about my feelings towards his dad. I then had the privilege of getting a copy of the eulogy he delivered. One line towards the end particularly caught my eye and I'm sure Andy won't mind a direct quote.

"Ally's enthusiasm, his humor, kindness, loyalty, generosity and inspirational qualities ... When will we see his likes again?"

He even joked that Ally's favorite song was "Don't cry for me Argentina" This is the epitome of self effacing Scottishism. Just what you'd expect from Ally.

Why would we cry? You had it right Ally. So from one ordinary punter; Thanks so much for the magic carpet ride—it was a blast.

26

BILLY'S BOOTS

I can summarize Hibs mediocrity through this period by telling you that they were in the "Anglo-Scottish Cup". Understand? This translates into "Not good enough for European football". It reminds me of the old Texaco Cup where the Jambos and Motherwell used to play every year when we were a cut above them (though I admit I saw a pretty decent Wolves team at Tyncastle in the Texaco). We scrape past Ayr United 4-3 on aggregate. Then beat Blackburn Rovers 2-1 at home and 1-0 away but this is not to be confused with the Blackburn post arrival of millionaire owner and King Kenny. That was the thing. Many qualifying English teams passed on playing in this tournament out of contempt for it. I guess we weren't in a position to turn down the extra income. We got Bristol City in the Semi's. To be fair unlike most of the participants they were on a bit of an upsurge at the time. We drew 1-1 at home and lost 3-5 away. No surprise.

I've also found an actual Subbuteo opponent in Bunty's young cousin John. He's a few years younger than me but visits our flat once in a while to provide me with live opposition. He's a pretty accomplished Subbuteo player though a bit of a "Shovalino" our Russian/Brazilian nickname for questionable flicking style. We have fairly competitive matches. He's also doing very well at the real game and starting to get some early attention from pro scouts. Did I mention his surname; Robertson, Chris' younger brother? Yes, that "Robbo" aka "JR"; the one who ended up as Hearts all-time leading scorer against us; a constant thorn in the side of Hibernian football club.

Last time I saw him was when we held a party in the room above the Tolbooth Bar in the Cannongate (more on which later). Bunty's folks now lived in the stair directly opposite, above Scotland's most comprehensive Malt Whisky shop and Benny's Chippie. Location, location, location! Even one time visitors to Edinburgh might remember this pub with the small Victorian bay window—right under the protruding clock, next door to the famous Cannongate Kirk where The Reverend Selby Wright christened, married and buried generations of Dolbears and Robertsons. Besides Bunty's relatives, the regular cliental essentially consisted the occupants of nearby Whitefoord House, an early version of "Assisted Living" before it was called that. It was for army veterans and the occupants were elderly single/widowed men. The Royal Scots of course dominated the crowd in "The Tollie" with (Uncle) Jimmy Dolbear as the ringleader. In the summer months the veterans would filter out onto the benches in front of the Kirk and offer free history lessons to the (mainly American) tourists. Amazingly old Tam could do this after downing a crate of bottled export. Their depth of local knowledge and insight was far richer than anything that could be gained from a guidebook and the American's "Jast lavd" their accents. When Jimmy passed on, one of the benches was actually named for him (check it out next time you pass).

The reason for our "Do" was simple. Trying to drag kids around dozens of relatives' during family visits back from the states was always a challenge but the Ma's tended to get a bit edgy if you didn't do the rounds. We found this pub gathering a great way of seeing a lot of pals and relatives in one fell swoop. Anyway they all seemed to like it too as by now it seemed family gatherings were mostly reduced to weddings and funerals with the latter starting to outnumber the former. I recall it being a great night with a good old fashioned sing song. You know. Round the room no excuses, no exceptions. Then all roll across to Benny's for a white puddin' supper. Mind you I don't recall John singing though we did get a respectable country number out of Paul Ferguson. John was at Newcastle at the time and personalized a note for a Geordie mate of mine who was fair chuffed. Unfortunately Newcastle didn't work out for him which was a great pity as he just came back to punish Hibs for several more years.

More recently he played a coaching role in the great Livingstone story and is now managing just as successfully with Inverness Caley Thistle in the Scottish Premier League. I suspect he'll be back at Tynecastle in due course. If Craig Levein delivers anything short of sustained success or catches attention elsewhere; watch that space.

However despite all his fame and fortune he has failed to return my personally customised (stripes on shorts, badges, numbers) Chelsea Subbuteo team which he borrowed approximately twenty eight years ago!

Did I mention how we dealt with Subbuteo injuries? You often had a player "Snap" from his base under a wayward knee and this was before the emergence of Super and Krazy glues. Dr Meikle's repair surgery entailed lighting a match to the plastic legs until they liquefied, pressing the player back on his "Base" then quickly running him under the cold tap so he stuck and hardened! These players usually ended up as "Wee" wingers in the traditional Scottish fashion.

Reverting to the main story yours truly is yet another year into the comeback trail and it's all starting to get serious again. A regular on HQ Scotland on Wednesdays and for Waverly Star on Sunday's and I'm starting to hit some consistent form again. I always scored plenty goals even playing from midfield but I get on one of those runs where I just can't miss. In a really absurd game I score four against our arch rival Carricknowe yet Waverly still go down 5-4 in the Churches Cup semi. I score lots in the league too but miss a penalty in the waning moments of the final game of the season at Sighthill park which costs us the title.

To balance this I collect two medals with HQ Scotland. The first is in the "Minor Units Scottish Cup" which is strictly for military players. However I agree to a suitable crop at the camp barber and someone takes care of the "Paperwork". "Corporal" Meikle scores two in a 4-2 win over one of the Force Field Units at the Scottish Infantry Depot at Glencorse Barracks near Penicuik. Corporals Meikle, (Jimmy) Kelly and (Paddy) O'Connor enjoy a rather lively celebration at the Other Ranks' mess in Edinburgh Castle that night. It's the nearest I come to joining up though I have the good sense to resist participation in the obligatory "Zulu warrior" dance. It's a severely sorry heid in the morning.

The midweek team also make a final (EMAFA Trophy) at Saughton Enclosure against our old rivals; Leith Police. I recognize their goalie; Ronnie Dignan. Not sure if he's a cop or just plays one on the football field? I get a very odd hatrick against him in our 3-2 win; two penalties (both taken identically) and one direct from a driven inswinging corner—deliberate I might add, taking full advantage of the strong wind. This time a quick pint at the "Wheatsheef" is a more sensible toast. I kept records for that particular season. (77/78) I got sixty two goals from a central midfield spot—my best ever production by far. My confidence is back full pelt and people are starting to take notice again.

A new teammate in the HQ side is a guy called John Hoban. He's a sound centre half/sweeper but is already talking more about the coaching side of things. He is heavily involved with the Cavalry Park Boys Club. He's the clubs General Manager and helps with the Under18's. The club operates out of Holyrood High school in Duddingston. John asks why I'm not playing at a more serious level and I give the very short version of what you've just read. He suggests I have a trial for the Cavalry Park Under21 squad which has become one of the top outfits on the Edinburgh Juveniles scene of late. They've also had great runs in the nationals

(Scottish) developing a strong rivalry with Campsie Black Watch (isn't that a fabulous name for a football team?) in the process.

The team is coached by George Brough. "Broughie" is well known to a generation of St Anthonys/(later became) Holyrood students as a demanding PE teacher. He's also been a decent player, a regular for Hawick Royal Albert (another great team name, even if English flavoured) in the East of Scotland league. The club leader is Sid Bryden who wanders around with a mostly unlit fat cigar between his right thumb and forefinger.

I turn up cold for a pre-season game at Duddingston. The team have already been training for a few weeks and most are in their second year together so once again I'm the new boy. However there are a few familiar faces from the past. Stevie Torrance from the Leith Primary Select and later my pal and teammate at St Augustines. Peter Finn and Billy MacLelland both from the year below us at "Oggie's". Norrie Chalmers who I recognized from a different type of "Team" altogether; Young Leith Team—YLT, a gang rival of Young Mental Drylaw—YMD. Funny that I recall some of the stalwart members of both gangs being a bit questionable to fit the term "Young"! Norrie and I got on fine as we were the only regular smokers on the team. Brian Holmes ("Holmsie") a Muirhouse boy had once been at Royston Boys with me. Jim McGaff (a Porty Thistle boy) and John Dignan (Diggie, they were cousins I think) both of whom I'd played against many times. Other faces I recognized without a name immediately springing to mind. The obvious star was a guy called Danny Ferry whom I hadn't come across before. He looked as if he should have made the grade but no idea if he did. Mike Fettes was a familiar smiling face from the old Edinburgh Thistle days.

Despite knowing a few people, I'm a little nervous and failing to completely disguise the fact. Stevie sees this and makes an effort to put me at ease. Broughie tells me to get changed and indicates I'll get a run at some point—he seems a pretty serious coach;

"Mr Hoban tells me you can play a bit—we'll see"

I can't remember much about the game other than I got on with about half an hour left. I had a few okay touches but not much opportunity to shine. The opposition were playing a very disciplined and well rehearsed offside trap and we'd been pulled up several times. I see them very square near halfway and advancing forward to leave Diggie in an obvious offside position so I decide to have a go. I chip the lot of them and take off on a straight sprint catching them all off guard. They're beat but unfortunately for me the Goalies been well positioned at the edge of his own box and is out early and gets his chest on my attempt to chip him. Its enough to get Sid and Broughie's attention and I'm signed before I leave.

This is good and bad. Good in that, other than being in the pro's I'm back at the top level for my age group. Bad in that it adds Monday and Thursday training and Saturday games to my Wednesday and Sunday games encroaching heavily on family time. As usual my addiction selfishly outdoes my mild guilty feelings and I press on with it. Broughie's training is tough but great, especially early in the season. We typically jog over to the "Queens" park and work our way up Arthur's Seat the extinct volcano which forms a spectacular centre to the East side of the city. We start via the (Several hundred!) steps opposite Duddingston Loch sprinting up and down. After various demanding stages we end up in the meadow under the summit where we get to play a game for a while. We work our way back in similar demanding fashion finishing with a sprint through old Duddingston village back to the ecstasy of the steaming hot showers. I rarely have the cash at this stage but I occasionally join the lads for a pint in the Sheeps' Heid; the fabulous (Hundreds of years) old pub in the village. For American readers; you might not find it in the tourist brochures but if you visit Edinburgh and can spare an hour or two—find this place and have a pub lunch—you'll see what I mean.

If I do have a pint it's often funded by the "Pontoon" money which should be going to the club coffers. A few of us always end up in Pontoon arrears, Stevie Torrance especially (He's addicted to the things) with Broughies sidekick wee Davie chasing us for weeks for the cash. Unfortunately all our old tricks of "Splicing" together fake winners have been overtaken by the latest cheatproof versions of the cards. Holmsie also kindly helps me out once in a while. I can't say he's a typical Muirhouse boy. Though aggressive on the field he's very calm and gentle off it and just genuinely helpful. He's is in the food sales business and slips me the odd "Damaged"case of Gerber baby foods for Dale—a significant savings as those little jars are very pricey. I offer him a token payment but he mostly waves it off. The lads are always amused to see a case of "Mushed peas and carrots" with a big smiling baby face on the side tucked under my spot in the dressing room.

Time Out—I've just had a message from the computer to say there are too many spelling and grammatical errors for the machine to continue displaying them! Hopefully by the time you read this I'll have tidied things up a bit. Though I confess to a perverse degree of satisfaction at being able to piss-off a Pentium 4. It's usually the other way around.

Both Broughie and Sid are very well connected and we get a friendly match against Stirling Albion (second division at that time) on their new "Synthetic" home field. This is an obvious chance to make an impression at Pro level but I end up just warming the bench. I so wanted to be able to say I'd played at "Anfield" once (the ground had the same name as its more famous counterpart down South). Alas, I cannot tell a lie. I soothe my ego by telling myself that Broughie reckoned my fitness wasn't quite ready for this yet. He can see I'm sick and just says; "Your turn'll come". I am delighted for (and jealous of) Diggie as he has a blinder and gets some follow-up attention from Stirling Albion though I don't think they signed him.

Anyway once I get my fitness back properly I manage to break into the regular line-up but it's a really first class squad of twenty players and not easy to keep a place. Especially as Broughie is a strict disciplinarian. Miss training without a very solid excuse and you're back on the bench. I suffer this a couple times due to lack of bus fares but of course I'm far too proud to admit that's the reason. I know Bunty's occasionally given me her lunch cash for my fares and as a helpless addict I've taken it shamelessly. Lateness is also a complete no-no. If you're not in the dressing room thirty minutes prior to kick-off you can forget it. This is also a problem for me as I am bussing it from the other side of town through the centre and all the constantly growing Saturday traffic. Even then I have a good half mile from the bus stop to the school. I often end up having to sprint the whole way and even then don't always make it. I recall one time getting in there at three thirty one—I know because Broughie showed me his watch! Despite having been central to several set pieces we had been working on at the Thursday night training, there was no compromise. Not even on the bench with sixteen players getting dressed that day. But that is why he was such a great coach—absolute consistency.

Even when we trained on the school grounds in near darkness (winter nights—no lights) he put us through tremendous physical work before retreating for a game of fives in the lovely big Gym. This was another place I regularly encountered young Robbo as he and his mates from nearby Meadowfield often hung around our practices. I have to say that a couple years later when I was playing "Junior" (Chapter to follow) the training was never any more taxing or preparation more thorough than what we had with Broughie.

Edinburgh under 21 football has more cups than you can imagine. Not sure why I guess they honored lots of their previous organizers with competitions named after them. For example a couple of names immediately come into my head. "Bob Tait". Now this one must have gone back a while because my dad and I both have a winners' medals for it. Another was the "Oliver Hemming".

Again I don't know who Oliver Hemming is/was but thanks for the many extra games you got us Mr Hemming.

So what happened in early Summer for the more successful teams was a glut of fixtures and with most of them being semi's and finals they were at the decent grounds; Patties Road, Saughton Enclosure and my favorite, just because of the history associated with it; City Park. They were also usually quite well attended, including plenty scouts. This is when the depth and fitness created by Broughie always paid large dividends. Our main rivals in my time at Cavalry Park were a revived Salvesen, (Salvie) Whitehill Welfare and BMC Thistle. This also afforded some great battles against old friends and foes. I had several ding-dongs with Dex Triplet who went all the way back to my Granton/Royston days and was now Salvesen's midfield enforcer. Dex could run forever. We always ended with a hug and a smile, regardless of result. Tony (Tojo) Marinello had gone off to Burnley at sixteen but it hadn't worked out for him so he was back as the flying winger with BMC. He hadn't changed a bit—switching rapidly between ultra serious and fun loving modes all through the game. As he was right wing and I was left midfield we encountered each other plenty and he still talked a lot:

"Come 'n take it oaf me, Jeek, c'moan" with his smiling slanted eyes and giggling.

He still dribbled with the aero plane arms and multiple crossover steps just like cousin Peter Marinello did so beautifully at Easter Road and Highbury. They both make this new Ronaldo of Portugal seem pretty ordinary (P.S. Okay, I'll take that back now). We had BMC's number so I always enjoyed seeing him again though he was too quick to use a "Glasgow Kiss" and took quite a few early baths. I also recall traveling down to Port Seaton where we played a cup tie against Cockenzie Star at their neat little ground a few blocks from the paddling pools, trampolines and putting green (another fond childhood memory). Another two familiar faces; Stevie Lodge was their captain and Brian, their pixie-faced goalie of the tipped blonde flowing locks. We beat them fairly comfortably despite Brian having a blinder which led to him joining us for the following season. He was always Mr Cool and drank regularly at the trendy Mad Hatters bar in George Street where one cocktail would kill my entire pocket money for a week.

Broughie also displayed some real loyalty that day. With HQ winning the midweek Cup the Edinburgh Evening News reporter/photographer had snapped us after the game. We had heard that the photo would likely be in that nights sporting Pink and there was every indication I'd get a special mention for scoring all three goals in the final. Problem was, though quite a few did it, it was technically illegal to play in the amateur and the Juvenile ranks simultaneously. He was clearly planning to start me so I came clean with Broughie in the changing rooms at Port Seaton.

"George, eh, the last thing I want is to lose my place again but … well you see I play midweek amateur as well. John Hoban probably mentioned it".

"So?" he says.

"Well there's a good chance there'll be a photo and mention of it in the Pink tonight".

He rubs his hand across his chin and purses his lips; "Which makes you a potential PROTEST today, correct?" This means that we would forfeit the game if Cockenzie appealed and we're certainly favored to beat them with or without me.

"Hmm. You sure it'll be in?"

"Pretty sure, th guy at the Scotsman tipped off the publicity Officer at the HQ".

"I'm glad you were honest about it Jim. Putting team first. You know how I feel about that"

"Aye, sorry George".

He gives me a very serious stare then does this kind of half smile he had. It looked like a smile but you could never be quite sure.

"Get your strip on. You're playing. I'll take my chances".

Not a peep from a single player all of whom had picked up on the exchange.

I'm surprised and delighted and inspired.

I play my backside off and score a pretty decent half-volley into the roof of the net in a fairly comfortable win for us. Goals are much harder to come by here than on Wednesdays and Sundays.

Broughie pulls me off with twenty minutes to go and congratulates me on a good performance. He doesn't mention the protest angle again at all—ever. I adore the loyalty and commitment he showed that day.

Norrie and I are out the shower sharp and having a fag at the gate. Broughie has instructed us that we can't smoke around the changing rooms and we mostly honor that though we might cheat the odd time Davie's in charge.

Norrie looks at me. Knows I'm still a bit worried. He takes a deep draw and through streams of smoke from his nose and mouth says;

"Dinnae f**kin worry aboot it Jimmy, these posh Port Seaton c**ts dinnae even read the Pink," and we both burst into laughter.

The picture was indeed in that night though I'm mildly huffed that my hatrick gets no mention. No protest lodged and we move safely on to the next round.

Back to Broughie's general fitness, preparation and organization. We won a ton of these games in the last fifteen minutes or in extra time when we could simply out-physical opponents with superior stamina and the confidence and will which come along with it. We saw Rangers do this in the first Jock Wallace phase. His Gullane Sands were Broughie's Arthur's Seat and they both worked a treat. I had many memorable games with that Cavalry Park squad but I guess my personal favorite was my very own "Billy's boots" game!

Remember Billy's Boots, the comic strip mentioned earlier. This otherwise ordinary player would put on a magical pair of lumpy old fitba boots and suddenly become unstoppable.

We had reached yet another cup final (Arnott-McLeod Trophy; my dad had two tarnished old winner's medals for this one too so it had obviously been around a long time) and the opposition was once again Salvie. I guess we played them in six or eight finals in a two year period. This game is on a warm summer Friday evening at City Park around 7 p.m. Kick-off so will draw a fairly decent crowd.

On Friday's we usually go to my Mum's for dinner so I head straight to Drylaw after work. I run into my old pal Harry O as we cut through Blackhall and over the abandoned railway line into the (Wester Drylaw) Drive. Harry's brother's working in Manchester and he's thinking of joining him there. He peels off into Percy's bookie shop wishing me luck. Bunty and Dale bus it down from town to meet me at my mum's. Amazing how Bunts can juggle a bairn, a buggy and a big blue bag full of laundry off and on a corpie bus. I eat very little and can't join my mum in the cocktail which I normally would on a Friday. The game'll go on too late for Dale so Bunty will be taking her home and I'll be headed along the Ferry Road to the park. As I get ready to go it suddenly hits me—where's my fitba bag?

Bunty assures me I took it with me in the morning and I remember it sitting by my desk at work but I don't remember having it on the bus back and no, I didn't have it when I was talking to Harry. It's still in my office and it's far too late to get it now. This is unheard of. My memories not great but I always remember anything to do with fitba. In those days shin guards were not compulsory and Cavalry had full kit (Yellow top and socks, Blue Shorts—Everton away) so the only issue really was my boots. Very few of us had multiple pairs and it was terrible form to cadge (borrow) boots from a mate who wasn't in the squad for a final. Even then you'd have to be lucky enough to find someone with the right size.

The squeaky turn of the handle and the customary snap of the glass door indicated my dad was home from Ferranti's. He quickly sees I'm in a panic and asks what it's about.

"Left my boots at work and I have to be at City Park in half an hour"

"Tut, what a stumour. How d'you manage that?"

"Disnae really matter Dad—does it?"

"Well. You can borrow mines if you want, they're in the washing machine cupboard—size 8 I think" The washing machine cupboard is off the small kitchen. Surprisingly we keep the washing machine in it as well as the shoe polish box, washing lines and pegs, the gas meter in there too and other assorted junk which never moves. I open the large sliding door which swings freely at the bottom as our family joiner (Brother David) has never quite got around to finishing it. It smells like the Dry-salter's shop. I find a Marks and Spencer carrier bag near the back and extract it. It's silver with green writing which is badly faded and it has a draw string. It appears to contain my dad's (very) old fitba boots. I forgot he still had them. He's fifty now so doesn't play regularly but keeps them handy "Jist in case, ye never know".

I take the bag through to the living room and open it. My mum and Bunty erupt in laughter. The boots are ancient and look like something out of an antique shop. They're crude and clumpy looking and have large yellow (fortunately mostly faded to beige) toe caps which looks like they could be wood. The studs are definitely wood and of course, for real emphasis; fairly new bright Yellow laces! I give my dad a quizzed look and get a predictable response;

"Phi, nowt wrong wi thaim, try them oan".

Not having any other option I do just that. They're a bit tight but I can get them on and they're not nearly as uncomfortable as they look on the outside.

"No bad" he says.

"Look at thum dad—I feel like Stanley Matthews".

"Phi, bet you wish you could play like um, eh?" and snickers "Beggars can't be choosers"

"S'pose not"

Bunty's containing her laughter but it's threatening to burst out anytime. My mum is on her second vodka/lemonade and is giggling uncontrollably. Dale is mystified as to what all the hilarity is about.

So it's "Billy's Boots" or nothing. No choice. I'll take 'em.

I can't say I've ever been terribly wedded to a particular pair of boots. Like most of my pals I more often had "Hand-me-down" pairs and so was never obsessed with the "Latest" craze in football style. I do remember most of us around ten year old craving a pair of Addidas Santiago but they were relatively pricey at the time. The first brand new pair I recall getting were Mitre Milan and the publicity suggested Denis Law wore them so that was pretty exciting. I do remember the Georgie Best boots with laces up the side and some very daring trim color; Purple or Burgundy I think. They certainly looked very snappy but couldn't have been very practical. My one boot indulgence was with an innovation to the stud system. Can't remember who the manufacturer was or if they used a particular pro to promote them but they brought out a white boot with a special new twist (I will always identify White boots with Alan Hinton of Derby County—Don't recall seeing them before him). These had a "Swiveling" circle of studs towards the front. So if you put all your weight forward on one foot you could spin like a prima Ballerina! The idea was to stop the twisting of ankles in hard ground but I found they caused more tweaks than they prevented and so the experiment was short and sweet. I did manage an "Unconditional" swap with an unsuspecting pal who was taken with the swivel concept. I think I came off best by far scoring a reliable pair of Golas.

I dash down through Dockies field and over the big grass circle to the main Ferry Road and a number one bus comes almost right away. Five minutes later I'm at City Park. There's a small entrance fee so you have to identify yourself as a player as you come in to avoid paying. I open the Marks' bag and flash my boots and see the gateman's eyebrows lift but he shrugs and waves me on through.

Of course I know much worse is to come when I start getting changed.

Diggie and Stevie have laser like senses for anything slaggable and the second the boots come out it starts. Broughie's got his game face on but even he allows himself a wee laugh. I know he could care less what you have on your feet as long as you do the business. Anyway, I'm on the bench having missed training on Monday following a mediocre outing the previous Saturday.

Diggie's first; "New boots Jimmy? Very smart—snigger, snigger. Will you need a pair of extra long shorts and some newspaper shin guards?"

Stevie barely let's the laughing subside; "Pass the 'ovis Jimmy lad" (cruel but right on the mark; a reference to the classic Hovis brown bread advert where a Yorkshire lad is running around in hobnail boots). More laughter all around and my face is beaming red.

Davie's smiling "So Jim is your old man coming to see how his boots perform?" I smile too;

"Canny come Davie, he's got a band job, but your right; they are actually my dad's boots, they might have even been here thirty years ago with Leith Athletic".

Then Jim McGaff creates the inspiration for my theme here;

"Mind Jim, Billy'll be wantin' them back for the morn," a reference to the comic which came out on Saturday mornings.

And so I face the prospect of having to chase Dex Triplett around City Park wearing Billy's Boots. Hopefully Maxi Davitt, who's starting ahead of me, will wear him down before I get on. It's a tight scrappy defensive game and Broughie throws me in at half time hoping I can find a tiny seam for our front runners. Always a man of few words, first time I close up on Dex at a throw in he nods;

"James" (Because we'd met when I was still James he always called me that)

I nod back;

"Dex"

Then I see him do a double take at my feet.

"Some boots thaim, James" Then he's quickly back to business.

No breakthrough in normal time so it's two 15 minute halves of extra time. Still no goals so it's on to the dreaded penalties. There were just so many fixtures that replays became impractical as happened a little later at all levels, including the Pro's and even the World Cup.

Broughie had all of us practice penalties regularly and he had a simple system in place. He gathered the eleven players on the field at the end and simply said;

"Right, who really wants one?"

First five to respond were on his list in whatever order he wrote them down. He always displayed total confidence in us. I'm in and I'm fourth. This was one of the few teams in my life where I wasn't the regular penalty taker. I did so for both HQ and Waverly so was well used to it. I always (still do) took them the same way.

Starting position four yards back from the ball and about a yard offset to my left. Slow run with a stutter step in the middle, eyes fixed on goalies lower right corner, hips open leaning left. Right side footed (but with some force) into the opposite corner. It's almost impossible for the goalie not to react to the body language and he almost always goes the wrong way. Estimated success rate in the high nineties percentile (notwithstanding one recent critical failure).

Two goals and one miss each through the first three rounds then the Salvie guy before me balloons one a mile over the bar. It's easy to do that as we're taking them at the top (Ferry Road) end of City Park which has a fairly acute slope so it only takes the slightest lean backwards to launch the ball high. I have a chance to put us in front but I'm concerned about my how the boots will impact my normal form. They've mostly been okay during the game save a couple of Ally Brazil type banana shots! I remind myself never to second guess at this point so line up as usual and go through my normal routine. Whoosh—a spectacular success and the crowd acknowledge it with polite applause. I trot back to halfway and accept the kudos from my teammates. One kick later Peter Finn calmly slots away the fifth to preserve our lead and the Cup is ours.

We have a raucous celebration under the lovely, creaky old City Park stand. Dancing around in the ancient bath slurping champagne (it's legal to drink in Britain over 18) and belting out the song of the moment extra loud so the Salvie boys can hear us through the wall:

"We're go-nna cel-e-brate,
We're gonna cel-ebrate,
We're gonna cel,
We're gonna celebrate" … repeat over and over.

What I didn't bother to mention was that my penalty streaked into the postage stamp corner like a rocket despite my intent to put it low in the opposite side. Neither did I share this fact with anyone until years later.

Maybe they were indeed magic boots. They certainly worked that one time though I wasn't inclined to test them again.

They're probably still sitting somewhere in the back of that cupboard in the same plastic bag. Likesay, just in case.

27

HEIGHWAY HOPE AND A TOUCH OF THE BEST

My Civil Service career has moved on steadily if not spectacularly. Having learned soon after starting that I can escape the Dogsbody/Teaboy role by adding just a couple more O'levels to my resume. I've got myself day release at Telford College and done the minimum to pick up the soft touches of art and arithmetic. When I think how easy I could have picked these up at school with just the slightest effort I start hearing those standard parental clichés all over again (stick in at school son). So I'm now a Clerical Officer which is hardly flying but it certainly makes for slightly more interesting and responsible daily work. Besides this I've made the effort to move around, Personnel, Policy and Finance sections gathering broader marketable experience. I volunteer to run the CISCO (Civil Service Catering Organization) Canteen and do the books with the help of the stalwart canteen ladies; Molly and Vera. I always make sure they're well looked after and in return my meal portions are pretty generous (the only corruption of my career to date). I've even been allowed formal "Substitution" for Executive Officer (EO) a few times so I'm knocking on the door for the next promotion.

I can get my E.O. immediately on "Temporary and Geographical" grounds if I'm willing to move to central London (they're always desperately short of experienced Civil Service staff there) but this just doesn't appeal to me as I still see it as enemy territory. I've been down on several training courses and whilst it's fine to visit neither Bunty nor I have the inclination to move there. We've both been keen to taste life abroad and at the same time hopefully finally accumulate a down payment for a house. Consistent advice from returning colleagues is that overseas postings are the real ticket to serious financial progress and career advancement. A boy from Transport section; Ian Wither, who also plays on the football team (not a bad full back, hell of a darts player) has done his three years in Germany and seems comparatively well off on his return. My boss Pat Mc

Donald has done two overseas postings and now has a lovely house in Liberton and her brand new yellow mini. Big Ian Dobie, a real character is so keen to get back to Germany he's thinking of joining the NAAFI (PX in US terms) as a store Manager! There must be something to it.

I'm trying a two-pronged approach. I've gone through the MOD qualifying process and made it on to the "Eligible for Overseas Postings" list. You then simply wait for someone to decide you're a good fit for a particular place and circumstance. Most of the overseas opportunities for us at the time related to British Army on the Rhine (BAOR) so to try to enhance our chances JJ and I enroll in night school for Conversational German.

I've also responded to a member nations' government trawl for volunteers to join the rapidly growing European Community Administration (EEC) in Brussels, Luxembourg or Strasbourg. Fluent French is a requisite and I boldly claim to have it. In fact the only practice I've had since school is when my brother John trades a hitched lift to Edinburgh (from Jersey via London I'm guessing) for a bed for the night from a random Frenchman called Gilbert. He seems a nice enough man and we guide him around Edinburgh in his old style Renault 5. Bunty does better than I do with the French but it's not critical as Gilbert's English is sound. I fill out some forms and take an "Aptitude" test and am subsequently invited to London to sit the EEC exam proper. I must have done well because I'm then invited to Brussels (all expenses paid) for a final interview. I turn up at "Rue de La Loi" in Brussels fully expecting to come a bit unstuck on the language front. Just before I go into the interview a young English guy comes up to me. He's shuffling my paperwork;

"How's you're French, really?"

"Tres rusty, I'm afraid"

He smiles and winks; "Just be straight with them. As long as you've got a decent grounding you can pick it up when you get here, most people do".

"Ca va bien, merci".

He leads me into a large timber paneled room and seats me at a grand, highly polished wood conference table opposite a three person panel with little national flags and name tags in front of them. High back black leather chairs all around. There is a booth along one side where people are busily fussing with earphones and microphones on little wire stems—Translators. I'm thinking cheez, I'm just looking for an office job, and I don't expect to run all of Europe. The Chairman is an Englishman. He introduces himself and tries to put me at ease with some small talk. He introduces his colleagues, tall serious looking French lady to his right. To his other side is a small portly Italian gentleman. He's has a couple of small beads of sweat on his brow and has slightly loosened his collar and tie. He's smiling and nodding real friendly so that helps me relax a little.

The Chairman does most of the initial talking with the Italian clearly getting some help understanding my responses from the booth. I mention football as my main hobby and can immediately tell I'm on a winner with Luigi. He's clearly a fanatic so I throw in the Celtic connection and I can tell he thinks I'm exactly what they need to keep the EEC running smoothly! Then comes the crunch.

The French lady takes over. She slides a local Newspaper across the table and asks me to read the article marked "X" in my best French accent. I do okay with this but then I'm asked to explain what the hell I just read? I've only got the broadest gist of it; something about a wedding which finished with a great ado. She laughs and tells me that I'm in the ballpark. It transpires that the bride is actually a man and this comes as a genuine surprise to the groom. I'm mildly embarrassed and follow the advice given by splurting out;

"Yes. I'm sorry I haven't really had a chance to use my French since school but I'm keen to refresh it"

I depart to satisfied looking nods, especially from Luigi.

A few weeks later I get an information package from the EEC with a covering letter informing me that I've made the top list of candidates and should expect to get a posting to Brussels within a year. It also politely reminds me to brush up my French in the meantime.

Though still mediocre overall, Hibs have a great Scottish Cup run and end up taking Rangers to a second replay in the final before going down to a bullet header own goal from our beloved Arthur Duncan ; final score 2-3. Of course it's only going to be a matter of time before we get our hands back on the trophy which we last won in 1902. *(Morph to real time—we have now surpassed one hundred years without winning it!)*

Age catches up with me and its time to leave the juveniles. My time with Cavalry Park has really been a great success by most standards. We're always in the thick of things and I'm playing pretty well but it's still not quite enough to get me to the next level. Although I have the odd day here and there where I shine above the crowd, I can't dominate a Saturday game the way that I can on a Wednesday or a Sunday. The reality is this is down to the level, speed and fitness of the competition. The Wednesday league is respectable and there are some brilliant individual players in the Sunday leagues but there's always that extra yard of space or half second which allows you to do much more.

I should say now that Broughie was as good a coach as I've ever had. I was really sad to hear that he ended up going through a terrible spell a few years later with some kind of scandal which resulted in serious charges and prison. I hear more recently he's reconciled with his family (six or seven kids as I recall). Not to condone whatever he did but hopefully he's paid his dues and his life's back on track.

At one point, if you hadn't made the senior professional ranks by the time you were twenty one; your chances were more or less gone. However a new thread of hope arrived with one Steve Heighway. He is like thousands before him. Very talented but perhaps more interested in booze or fags or birds or dancing or music or telly or church or all of the above. But … at the ripe old age of twenty four he has been plucked from the obscurity of the Sunday leagues almost directly into the Liverpool first team. It's a wonderful story and more importantly, it revives and extends the hopes of a generation of previously "Over-the-hill" twenty to twenty five year old dreamers; one of whom you now know quite well. Heighway is a dashing (looks and speed wise), charging, strutting winger who is often on the start of one of the most memorable triple plays in the game.

John Motson; "Heighway … Toshack … Keegan … one-nil"

So although I leave Cavalry Park with no offers from the big leagues it isn't time to give up. I do get several approaches from well respected Edinburgh amateur teams. My Uncle Charlie knows the amateurs well. He's played for loads of different teams as a rambunctious centre forward lastly that I can remember for Muirhouse Violet (his wife's name, my favorite auntie as when I was younger she'd slip me the odd Kensitas Club ciggie on the fly). I think he usually ends up in the Wardie (Shore) or Whitson's in Leith after the game. Yet another Davie (whose surname I can't recall) sells me on a team called Telman Star. I ask Uncle Charlie. He's heard of them so that's a good sign. I've seen the name in the pink and associate the club with some success. Home games at Letham Park a very nice venue with decent nets. The only bit Davie leaves out is that he and his mate Arthur actually run the second team; Telman Star "A" which is in a middling Edinburgh amateur division as opposed to the first team which was in the top (wider catchment) Lothians Division.

I work this out after the first couple nights training and Davie explains how everybody starts in the "A" team but somebody like me will move up rapidly to the main team. That's the theory but as it transpires it's only a theory. In the few months I play with Telman "A" I see zero movement up our down. Not that the "A" team was bad but there was a much better chance of the Liverpool scouts finding me in the Lothian Premiership than in Edinburgh Division three! I also get a bit complacent about training just to play in a "Second" team and so Davie benches me in what transpires to be my last game for him at Peffermil. He eventually puts me on whilst down by three and I have one of those special games inspiring us to a draw but that's it.

Perhaps it's time to take another break from Saturday games. Not bad timing in a way as there will be something worth seeing. Hibs have had a dreadful start to the 1979/80 season and are early candidates for relegation for the first time in my lifetime. In November they go in search of salvation and end up at Craven Cottage, London where Georgie Best and Rodney Marsh have been doing a "born again" thing with Fulham. It's been great entertainment but unfortunately this has been true both on and off the field and Fulham are ready to cut their losses. Rodney heads off to America. Though it's supposed to be hush-hush George is clearly fighting the demon drink which is going to be a very tough task in Edinburgh; a town with more pubs per-capita than anywhere else in the world. Of course Weedgies might dispute this. Regardless, we are all ecstatic when Hibs fork out just fifty thousand pounds for one of the all time greats.

At 33 years old it's hardly as if he's ancient. Not quite as trim as in his prime but still fantastic to see him in a Hibs strip. He scores in his first game; a 2-1 win at St Mirren and boys who saw it are raving about some of his deft touches. For reasons I can't recall I miss his home debut at Easter Road; another 2-1 win this time against Partick Thistle. Surely with Georgie in the team we will be safe from the drop.

I'm finally getting to see him live against Celtic at Easter Road and I'll never forget it. JJ has something on so can't meet up for a pint before the game. Instead he just says he'll meet me at the "Usual" spot. I know what this means, main terracing, about halfway line, two thirds up the lower segment. It sounds very informal but it worked just fine for all except Rangers and Celtic matches. This still preceded the "all seater" era and groups of fans tended to claim regular territory in the ground. For example when my brother John first came back from Australia, he and his Scottish Gas Board cronies (Pat and Jim Kearney, Kenny Clark, Brian "Mutley" Whatley) used to stand in the exact same spot in the "Enclosure" every week. This is the standing bit traditionally placed along the front of the main stand where you actually sit. Clear? Anyway their "Bit" is just a few feet from the left touchline when Hibs are firing down the slope and they are able to develop a fairly regular banter with Arthur Duncan during games!

"Awright lads" smiling, says Arthur as he reaches in to retrieve the ball for a throw.

"Gaun yersel Arthur" is the response from nobody in particular.

Mind you a smile from Arthur Duncan was pretty normal. He always seemed like he got great joy from the game. I especially liked him because the one time I persuaded Bunty to go to Easter Road with me, Arthur totally destroyed the Jambos in a 3-0 onslaught down our famous slope. Though she was hardly a fan and most of her family were die hard Jambo she leaned towards Hibs because of her dad and hopefully I consolidated that lean. She only came the once mind.

So I've had a quick pint in Robertson's Bar on Leith Walk and am headed to the main terracing gates opposite the old Strangs School. As always with the old firm everywhere is mobbed. It's especially hard against Celtic because with so much Green and White you can't be sure who's who. Of course it becomes clear quickly when the Weedgies start to talk but even then there are lots of native Edinburgh Celtic fans.

I suspect Georgie has drawn even more Celtic than usual too. The games well underway but there are still thousands milling around the place, jockeying for position. I go with the flow of human traffic (no choice really) and make it to our approximate meeting place but no sign of JJ. Suddenly there's an anticipatory roar from the stand. Despite losing dominance of the ground sometimes against Old Firm Hibs always command the stand (more "Season" ticket holders I guess). Georgie's got the ball on the left corner of the Celtic box, he advances forward wrong footing the defense; shimmie left, right, left, right again, he shoots, he sco … res. The place goes wild and I am no exception. It's one of those totally uncontrolled, unabashed jumping, scarf waving fits accompanied by primal, guttural screaming. A greatly extrapolated "Ye … e … e … e … s" perhaps the only discernible sound. Then, after two or three seconds, I snap back to consciousness and realize that a small gap has evolved and I'm in it. The fifteen to twenty hairy gentlemen immediately around me clearly do not share my enthusiasm for Georgie's gem! Oops. The "Yes" tails off abruptly and I start smiling and nodding as I do a sort of backwards crab walk through the mob until I reach the safety of a pocket of cabbage (Cabbage and ribs; the rhyming slang nickname for Hibs). I think it ended 1-1 but the main attraction was clear to all.

The other "Best" Hibs match I remember most was at Christmas time against Rangers with snow on the field. We always seemed to play them around Boxing Day. I'd seen flashes of it before but this time Georgie played a withdrawn central midfield role and sprayed passes all over the place, perfectly adjusted to the conditions and with pinpoint accuracy. He'll certainly always be remembered most clearly for his brilliant running and shooting in Manchester United red and Northern Ireland green. His tireless running in the 1968 European Final against Benfica. His impertinent "Steal" of the ball from behind Gordon Banks in a home International tie against England. How many thousand Goalies have checked over their shoulder since that one? But nobody can ever take away the brief spell where he was a Hibee.

Alas, even the genius that was Georgie Best couldn't prevent Hibs from slipping out of the top flight. The demon was obviously still nipping away at him and there were a couple of times where he didn't make it to the games after adoring fans insisted on buying him a lunchtime pint which turned into many. He was soon headed to America for yet another "Fresh" start. He even brought his Yank team; San Jose Earthquakes of the old North American Soccer League (NASL) back to Easter Road for a friendly the next year (3-1 Hibs).

Not sure how old it was (fairly current I think) but BBC America just showed a re-run of a "Parkinson" interview with him. He looked thin and his face showed the tell-tale signs of tough times but he still had a lot of humor about him and that bright sparkle in his eye. He spoke very frankly about his addiction and resulting struggles and seemed committed to continuing recovery. They always do. Fingers crossed and thanks, Georgie, for some really special memories.

On the Sunday scene, Mark's got too busy to keep things going so I've moved on with several other Waverly players to a revived neighborhood side; Groathill Thistle. It really is local with a core of myself, Fred Hastings (the best of the bunch by far), wee Brother Charlie Hastings, Nora (Ian Macleod), Joe Brady and Gogs Gray all from the immediate area. We're playing in the top Edinburgh Sunday Amateurs division so the level is a few steps up from the churches league. We develop a hot rivalry with Liberton Cropley who I greatly admire and not just because they play in Hibs strips. They are loaded with talent. They have some of Edinburgh's best players who have chosen ale over football fame much earlier in their lives than Georgie. Some of them are deceptively mobile despite carrying serious extra weight (curly blonde Peter Wardlaw comes to mind—a superb controlling midfield player). They play some of the sweetest football you'll see anywhere. We get close to them a couple of times at the Jack Kane Centre pitches but never quite manage to beat them.

The EMAFA still beats work on Wednesday afternoons and I get a surprise when about halfway through the season old Eddie approaches me after a game at Craigiehall. I've scored a couple and know I've played well.

"How ye doin' son" says Eddie.

"Aye, awright Eddie".

"Played some game the day".

"Aye enjoyed it. Felt good, thanks".

"Tam Connolly tells me yer no playin wi embdy Saturdays?"

"That's right".

"Ever thought aboot the Juniors?"

"Sure but no bites unfortunately".

"We'll yer aboot tae be bitten—Neil Morton wants you to hae a run oot wi' Cauder next week if that disnae work oot my man wants tae gie ye a run at Livvy".

In Scotland there is a whole other tier of professional football called "The Juniors". In England they call it "Non-league", in America; "Semi Pro" or "Minors" and there are likely versions all over the world.

"Cauder" was West Calder United and sure enough I got a call from Neil Morton, their Manager to join them at training the following week.

"Livvy" was Livingston United and this was long before the Livingstone we know now even existed.

So suddenly two bites at the juniors awaited me and don't forget, there was still plenty of movement between the juniors and the big leagues (Hibs got John Brownlie via Pumpherston).

Hope springs eternal.

28

A TASTE OF THE BIG TIME

Remember how impressed I was with Victoria Park, the ground of the junior team Newtongrange Star at ten years old? Well now I would finally get a chance to see the glamour of junior football first hand.

I had been to watch quite a few junior games with my dad when I was a kid. He had also played Junior for several teams, including, as it transpired; West Calder. The Scottish Junior Cup was a massive deal to all the small Scottish towns and their teams. These were predominantly mining towns in the industrial central belt. They would mostly play in front of sparse crowds but the "Bigger" clubs could pull in a few thousand for Scottish cup ties and the final was played at Hampden and televised live nationally. A good cup run was worth significant money to these clubs.

I remember dad taking me to the Kings Park in Dalkeith where the local team; Dalkeith Thistle (yet another of his ex-teams) had a Scottish tie against one of the decent Ayrshire junior teams. (Darvel I think they were called) The ground was really just a fenced-off area within a larger municipal park. I just remember it being crammed full and very intense that day with lots of men making what seemed like serious wagers on the outcome.

I also watched the spectacularly named; Kirkintilloch Rob Roy quite a few times. My Uncle Malcolm (Meikle) lived in nearby Lenzie so we would sometimes fit a Rob Roy game in with a family visit. Their ground was much better than some of the lower division "Senior" professional clubs I followed Hibs to in cup ties. This was true too of teams like Kilsyth Rangers, (if you sat on the correct side, you got a peak at this very trim looking ground as you passed on the train) Cambuslang Rangers, Linlithgow Rose (Named for Mary Queen of Scots who's palace is there) and Irvine Meadow.

Junior football has its own personality and tradition but is most generally seen as raw, hard, and tough. The best and most amusing account of junior football I ever read was in the John Fairgrieve (late of the Scottish Sunday Mail) book;

"Away wi' the Goalie" which was a compilation of some of his own favorite stories. His "Junior" tale culminated with half the population of a small mining town chasing the villain of the day, a prototype junior hard man; Hamilton (Hammie) Ferris, down the local high street with his strip and boots still on. As I recall Hammie had basically assaulted the home team's star player, the referee and a couple of supporters prior to making his dash for it. It was rich, descriptive and absolutely hilarious but a fair reflection of the junior scene in my view. Although Fairgrieve tweaked the team names a little they sounded suspiciously similar to Whitburn and Bonnyrigg!

So I accept the West Calder invite and turn up at the Wester Hailes Community Centre on the South West corner of Edinburgh on a cold, wet Monday night. Training is scheduled at the all weather pitch there. First I meet the Manager; Neil Morton and he explains the set up. Why Wester Hailes? The players come from a very wide geographical area from Mussleburgh in the East to Cumbernauld in the West so they have one nights' training here and the other at our home field in West Calder which spreads the travel load a bit more evenly. Thanks to Broughie's regimen I find the training comfortably manageable and hold my own in some ball drills and a game of two-touch.

Neil tells me to come out to West Calder Thursday and introduces me to Andy Reid who has a car pool which will pick me up in Gorgie en-route. Another passenger is Dorrie Boyle who I recognize vaguely from earlier days though he's now got a thick beard. I never liked beards on fitba players, not even Georgie Best! The last member of the car pool is Jimmy Anthony, a big centre half. I'm impressed when they explain that as we're junior pro's we either get our bus fares refunded or the carpool driver gets his petrol money paid! It takes around half an hour to wend through Sighthill and a series of tiny villages to West Calder. I get my first look at Burngrange Park.

Though it's dark I can see right away that its not quite Newtongrange standard. It does have the customary coal bins surrounding it but it's missing a stand? There is a nice pavilion behind the goal though and decent dressing rooms besides. I'll have to wait for a daylight visit to see it properly. There are a few more new faces which weren't around at the Monday session.

We train on the narrow grass strip alongside the main road where we can exploit the light from the lampposts. It's a slightly harder work-out this time on the wet mushie turf but again, Broughie's got me well prepared. I've also finally managed to stop smoking at my umpteenth attempt and this is a big help. Having tried everything you can imagine to stop previously, I've gone cold turkey and it's held now for several months. As always fitba plays a role as I quickly find some extra stamina on the field which gives me even more incentive (besides for Dale) to stay off the fags. The financial difference is obvious too. You don't realize just how much is being puffed away until you stop. I already eat like a horse so I don't expect weight gain to be a side effect.

I enjoy my training and get in some good touches in our drills and pick-up game at the end. We're playing Broxburn away on Saturday in the Johnie Walker (Of Red/Blue/Black label fame) League division "B". Andy tells me we occasionally make a run at the top "A" division where likesay; Newtongrange star, Bonnyrigg Rose, Boness United and Dalkeith Thistle hang out, but we mostly hover in division "B". Neil explains I'll get a run out at some point by way of a trial. He likes what he's seen of me in training and certainly wants me signed but the "Committee" needs to see me in a game first.

At work I seek out Eddie and thank him for the opportunity and I mention to Tom Connolly that I'll be playing against his local side on Saturday.

"I'll try and stop by Jim" says Tom.

Andy picks me up at the old railway bridge at Robertson Ave/Gorgie Road and we're in Broxburn nice and early. Albyn Park looks pretty good to me. It has a bit more proper shed and terrace than Burngrange. The dressing rooms are larger but much older. They have the big ancient baths in which there are two large dead rats but nobody seems much concerned about it. I'm a little nervous and trying to keep a low profile. The squad is big and competition for places keen so any newcomer is a threat to the incumbents. As expected, I'm on the bench. The uniforms are AC Milan or Manchester City away; Red and Black Stripes, Black shorts, Black Socks. Broxburn wear Red tops, white shorts, Red socks. I'm guessing the crowd is about two or three hundred sprinkled sparsely along either side of the field. The pitch is in pretty good shape and after a kick around warm up I take my place in the semi-sunken dug outs with the other subs next to the Manager.

The pace is fast and it's extremely physical with midfield enforcers on both sides. Nobody jumps out at me in the first half. We have a boy called Robyn Hendrie who curls some lovely crosses from either side, especially well on in swinging corners from the left. We have another boy Neil Gibson, whose brother (Ian I think) is playing for Kilmarnock at the time—he's pretty useful too. Our elder statesmen and Captain is another Jimmy—Walker, this one with ginger curls and beard, a bustling centre forward. The goalie is Gordon Cramb; a policeman from Cumbernauld. He's very solid and gets plenty of work. I couldn't name a single Broxburn player though I would say they were the slightly better side.

Just after half time I see the familiar figure of Tom Connoly headed towards the dugout, fag in corner of mouth. Neil looks a bit mystified as Tom bends down in his face filling the dug out with smoke and asks;

"Jim Meikle no playin?"

"He's here on the bench "says Neil starting to get perturbed as Tom blocks his view of the game.

Then tom notices me; "How ye doin Jim, Broxburn are poor eh?" oblivious to his role as an obstruction and distraction.

Neil's now staring at me as are the other subs; "Eh, mibbe catch ye at the end then Tom?"

"Oh aye, nae bother Jim—Ye'll git on soon" and wanders back to the shed, puffing happily.

Neil cracks a rye smile and tells me to get warmed up. He quips perhaps also for the benefit of the other subs;

"This is what I planned Jim—dinnae want yer pal thinking' he can tell me how tae run ma team".

I'm quickly out of my track suit top, skipping up the touchline, arms swinging full circles forwards. I'm trying but failing to tone out the abuse coming from the shed. With the smallish crowd you can hear the insults echoing around the place. I remember one which was pretty direct and stinging. He was only a few yards from me and I was naïve enough to make eye contact; a burly, pocky faced boy in a grubby parka with the dirty, furry hood pulled tight around his face. Cupping hands around his mouth, interlocked thumbs under chin, steering maximum volume directly towards me and revealing serious gums but few teeth;

"Canny be up tae puckin much if ye a thub it Cauther pal". Welcome to the Juniors James.

I get on and play okay. I err on the side of caution going against my natural attacking instincts to make sure I stay deep enough to take care of my basic defensive responsibilities first. Doing so definitely cramps my creativity. The pace is indeed furious and despite the large pitch it's a problem just getting enough time and space to get the ball under control. They take no prisoners. (Fitba speak for follow through on tackles!) I only manage complete control a couple of times and thread decent long diagonal balls which create a half-chance each for our wingers. We draw 1-1; a better result for us than them.

Neil gives me an encouraging word and customary pat on the arse on the way to the pavilion. Apparently I've done enough. I'm fairly content and have a quick dip in the bath after the rats have been discarded and the bottom disinfected and rinsed! Neil collars me as I'm getting dried and tells me to get ready quickly and go speak to the team owner outside. The main man is "Tam the Builder". I step outside. It's drizzling cold rain and he's not in immediate view? I check around the corner and see him huddled there with another committee member, some papers creasing between his left thumb and forefingers. He gives me the beckoning right index finger;

"C'mere son"

I obey.

He checks around for eavesdroppers as if he's about to reveal some great national secret to me (I learn later this is just part of the junior culture).

"Right, we want tae sign ye for whit's left ae the season. Uv goat a fiver for your signature and a couple ae quid fer yer efforts the day—happy wi' that, eh?"

I guess this is what you call negotiation. Hey I'm delighted to just get in the squad and though hardly a fortune, seven pounds is not to be sneezed at in my financial situation.

"Great. Aye. Thanks. Delighted."

I'm a pushover and he knows it. Probably just realized he could have got me for three pounds fifty!

"Jist sign here then son" and he points to the bottom line on a form which already has all my vital statistics written (i.e. not typed) in. The raindrops are starting to make the ink run in places. He hands me a yellow bic biro from behind his ear and I put my squiggle on the form.

"He goes into his pocket and pulls out a thick wad of notes, peels off one fiver and two singles. He thrusts them into my right hand and shakes it heartily at the same time.

"Welcome tae the club son."

"Thanks very much."

They both depart hurriedly, checking once again for spies as they go!

So it's official. I'm a professional footballer at last. Not rich, not famous but that's bound to follow in due course. Then I'll be able to laugh at this and recount how it all began behind the changing room in the rain at Albyn Park, Broxburn.

I go back into the dressing to get my bag and Neil adds his congratulations and tells me to buy a decent new pair of boots and bring him the receipt and he'll take care of that too. Wow. Andy adds a sincere "Well done Jim" as we head to his car. Dorrie's congrats are a bit more subdued as it's him I replaced in the game.

A few kids are hanging around at the car park but none ask for my autograph.

I'm listed in the match report in the sporting pink as "Newman" which is a blanket alias used for players on trial. They also use "Trialist" sometimes.

My first home game is a couple weeks hence. It's against Arniston Rangers. Andy has us there nice and sharp. Burngrange looks a little better in daylight. No ambiguity. Neil tells me I'm in the team, right midfield and he wants me pushing forward more. We come out to a very sparse crowd (less than two hundred I'd guess). The field is heavy with rain all week but at least it's stopped today and the sun has peaked through the clouds.

The opposition is in Blue and white. I recognize the other teams centre half; Sam Lynch from school who signed "S" forms with Celtic. The games about five minutes old when Sam acknowledges me as we get close up at a corner.

"James Meikle, right?"

"Aye, Hi Sam"

But we're cut short as Sam's got a defense to organize. He's quickly pointing and barking instructions—same old Sam. He's still got that distinct longish wavy hair which looks a bit "Colonial" now that I know what that is. Can't remember the score but we did get a good catch-up blether over lovely tea and sandwiches afterwards in the pavilion.

Next, to old Eddie's chagrin, we dump division "A" Livingstone United out of the Dryburgh Cup and get a home tie against Armadale Thistle.

We fall behind 2-0 early before I drag us back into the match with my first goal at this level. We force a corner. Robyn's in swinger is too low and tight but has some force so the man on the front post toes it to safety for another corner. As he steps backwards to take the second one, Robyn's waving us all out and clearly intending to do a better job this time. I walk away from the goal out to the eighteen yard line but have Robyn in the corner of my right eye. As he steps forward to strike the ball I suddenly reverse my direction and lose my marker. I get lucky. Robyn's cross is low again but powerful and curling hard. The tall men have all neutralized each other and I meet the ball in full stride at the penalty spot with my right instep and it somehow finds a seam through the mass of bodies and hits the back of the net with some authority. One nil and I've scored my first junior goal (little did I know then it would be my only one). We hold it like that until the half.

After the break their striker; a boy called Feeney destroys us with some clinical finishing and we eventually go down 1-5.

This time I get a cup of tea with Billy Ritchie, the old Rangers' goalie whom I've screamed abuse at many times from the back of the goals at Easter Road.

He's come along to "Assist" Neil but even to a fairly green observer like me it looks like an audition for a take-over next season. Neil's obviously on the bubble.

In the few remaining games I'm mostly starting or at least playing a half off the bench. My last game is against Bathgate at Creamery Park. This is a classic old junior ground where the changing rooms are behind the shed and you jog down the steps through the middle of the shed to get on the field taking serious abuse en-route of course. As it's the last game of the season (we're out all the cups early) "Tam-the-Builder" decides to incentivise it a bit for us.

"Right, listen laddies"

But we're all still milling around. Neil intervenes on the owners' behalf with a few sharp claps of the hands;

"Hey, hey, hey, listen up boys".

Tam continues; "Right. Lit's finish strong. Three pounds a man fir the win plus fifty pee (Pence) a goal"

We are inspired and run out a 4-3 victory which nets us a fiver each—a very good pay day for us. Bunty and I have a good night out at the White Hart in the Grassmarket listening to the blind folksinger doing his standard Jacobite set, throwing in a few funnies (i.e. "The Sunday Driver") and finishing with a powerful "Flower o' Scotland" to which the whole pub joins in. John and Helen and Bunty and I make the trek back to Dalry in fine spirits.

29

COMING TO AMERICA

It's more than six months since my qualifying for the EEC when I get a follow-up letter with the distinctive foreign postmarks. I rip it open with great excitement but it's just a routine renewal thing. It looks like a fairly stock proforma which I have to sign and return to confirm our continuing interest in a posting to Europe. Why wouldn't we be? The money is about four times what I currently make and with all sorts of clothing, housing and travel allowances thrown in on top! I sign and post it immediately. Hopefully it means an offer is imminent.

Meantime overseas postings within my contemporaries at the HQ have started becoming a reality and I'm pleased for them but gutted with jealousy. JJ's headed to Rheindalen, so is Ronnie. John and Derek (Munro) decide to take a year's detachment down South with the Army Pensions Office which comes with a promotion (E.O.) and promise of a return to Scotland as part of planned northwards Civil Service devolution. In the end most of the job migration doesn't materialize but they both ultimately find their way back.

Watching all this movement makes me very restless but I'll just have to be patient. I know I done well on my London interview as I had a long chat with the two guys from the postings section afterwards. They're both fitba' daft too. The EO is a guy called Roy Forey. He bleeds Chelsea blue and knows everything about them. We explore all their Scottish connections and he's especially impressed that I played with Eamon Bannon who he really liked during Eamon's brief spell at Stamford Bridge. Like me he adores Charlie Cooke. We even both love Frank Sinatra. We definitely hit it off. Likewise his assistant Les Green and I. Les plays "Non-league" so we swap some funny semi-pro stories. I leave out the Brussels stuff in case this works against me.

I'm always desperate to contact them and just ask straight out when it'll be my turn for a posting but Pat advises me that's just not the done thing. So I wait impatiently for a call.

I get really wound up when a week or so later I hear what I recognize as Roy's warm cockney twang on the other end of my line. He explains that I'll be receiving a wad of forms shortly and that I need to fill them in quickly, carefully and totally honestly! I will of course. I immediately worry what impact my underage drinking charge might have because I know what these forms are of course (Vetting) but I act the daft laddie anyway in the hope of drawing a hint about my posting;

"What's this for Roy, movement on a posting?" He's well used to this type probing.

"Possible Jim but we can never guarantee anything. Just be patient and things will work out, I'm sure."

And I'm thinking; 'Easy for you to say, Roy' but I finish off with a polite;

"Sure. Thanks Roy and tell Les I was asking for him"

"Will do, cheers Jim" and I hear the hang-up tones.

Pat sits directly facing me so she's picked up the gist and I fill in the blanks. She's genuinely excited for me.

"Sounds promising Jim, fingers crossed."

We're now at the summer of 1980 and we're about to have a new Scottish sports hero via Alan Wells' defeat of Valeri Bortzof in the 100 meters at the Moscow Olympics. (Sans boycotting Americans of course but still our biggest track coup since Eric Liddell).

I get a letter from West Calder United FC informing me that they wish to retain my services for the 1980/81. It's a standard Scottish Junior Football Association form which contains my "Qualifying" offer for the coming season. This is a compulsory part of the SJFA red tape. Some of their rules and by-laws are long outdated and one of the stipulations is that the minimum offer of a signing bonus and weekly wage must be made in the amounts of Five pounds and Seven Shillings-sixpence respectively.

Further down the page is a part for a set appointment with the Club management. So then you take your letter and negotiate with the committee on an actual signing fee and weekly wage. My appointment has two dates listed 17th/18th July so it looks they'll be rolling us through on the first couple of days of pre-season training. Andy kind of explains the process to me and suggests I should be pushing for Fifty pounds to sign and three pounds a week plus expenses. He reckons they'll counter with Forty pounds signing and two pounds a week. All sounds fine to me.

The hilarious thing is that although the rule book still stipulates "Seven Shillings and Sixpence" which in its day, was quite respectable but we're on decimal currency now. The conversion equals "Thirty seven and a half pence per week" and that is exactly what it says on my offer sheet!

I still have the original. I treasure it now as it's such a fun talking point. To put this in perspective for any American readers 37 ½ p equals about 50 cents! And it's not as if we're in Victorian times. It's likesay; Nineteen hundred and eighty.

Hey I'm not proud. As far as I'm concerned it's enough to justify me listing my occupation as "Civil Servant and part-time professional footballer!" Great for the ego!

As it turns out I don't get my big meeting with "Tam the Builder" after all. In early July I get another call from Roy in Postings section.

"How are you Jim?"

"I'm fine, yourself?"

"Great. Right, it's your turn. Ever thought of going to America?"

"Can't say I have, Roy" is my honest response. Never given it a thought—been so locked into Germany or Brussels for so long.

"Well Jim—I have a job for you at the British Embassy, Washington DC if you want it. Three year tour."

"Wow … eh … don't get me wrong Roy, I'm extremely excited but eh, well …"

He cuts in "Look Jim we don't force you to decide within five minutes. Go home tonight, talk it over with your wife and give me a call tomorrow. What I will tell you is this. I was posted there myself with my wife and young kid a few years back. It's a fabulous area with tons to do and I've thought for a long time you'd be a great fit there. Allowances are very generous and your pound's will get you stacks of dollars at the moment" (about $2.70 per pound then and we think $1.80 is great nowadays).

One question slips out without me even thinking;

"Any fitba there Roy?"

"Course there is mate. You'll be amazed how much though they call it soccer of course. Tons of other great sports too".

"So I can let you know in the morning then?"

"Absolutely. Just write down any other questions you think of and fire them at me tomorrow. Hopefully we can get this ball rolling quickly".

I'm totally wound up and dying to tell Bunty. We don't have a phone in the flat (yes American readers, even in 1980 there are many Scottish people who still don't yet have a phone in the house). We mostly use public call boxes although finding one which works properly can sometimes be a challenge. Mind you, once in a great while the fault is in favor of the patrons. An example. Years later I'm in America and right out of the blue, I get a call from my old pal Mark Curtis who now lives in Drylaw in some new Barrett homes which have been built on a parcel of former "Dockies" land. There's a call box at the roundabout at the corner of Groathill Road and he tells me that's where he's calling from. After the usual niceties I ask;

"So anyway Mark, why are you callin' me?"

"Jist because a kin Jimmy, jist because a kin" comes his reply and he's snickering away to himself.

"Howd'ye mean?"

"Um callin ye fae f**kin freephone Drylaw, Jimmy. It's magic."

He goes on to explain that by some fluke this payphone is working without you having to deposit any coins! Now remember this is Drylaw and word of something so lucrative has spread like wildfire.

"Should see the queue Jimmy. Ye'd piss yersel. Thirs auld dears (Mothers) lined up half wey up the street waitin tae phone their relatives in America, Australia, New Zealand, South Africa, you name it. Price is the same fir everywhere—nowt! Thir gittin a bit restless now so a better gie sumbdy else a shot bit barry tae talk tae ye"

"Aye great tae talk tae you tae Mark, take it easy pal"

And so it was apparently for about ten days the GPO or British Telecom or whoever was running the show at that time inadvertently re-united Drylaw with long lost family and friends all around the world. I'd love to have seen that bill!

It's Wednesday which is usually dinner at Bunty's folks and I meet her there straight from work. I call and Tommy picks up. He's usually there days as he works shifts at the brewery. Mainly "Backshift" (2-10pm) or "Continentals" (8pm–8am) 4 days on, 3days off. Sounds a bit much but it suits him fine as he's a passionate golfer and this gives him lots of opportunity to play when the courses are least busy. Amazing how many guys like the shiftwork because it accommodates their golfing addiction. I love the golf myself but it will never be on a par with the fitba pangs. Bunty's not there so I just ask him to get her to call if he sees or hears from her.

Pat sees how excited and distracted I am and so suggests I just take off early. Whoosh, I'm on my way, jogging the long camp driveway and breaking a sweat as I do so all the way up to the Barnton roundabout to broaden my choice of buses. I'm in the town by late afternoon and headed along Princess Street, across the Waverly Bridge passed the station entrance which is clogged with Taxis. Two empty tour buses opposite, one with an open top. Then it's along Market Street onto Jeffrey Street and I'm pulling on the bell at number 29. As I push the door open I hear Dale's voice echoing around the stair "Ga, Ga … Ga, Ga" identifying the bell with the arrival of her "Gags". Her pet name for Bunty's mum. She gets a surprise when the response comes up the stairwell;

"Day-al, hi-ya" She recognizes my voice and quickly switches her shout to;

"Dad? Dad?" She says in a surprised, questioning tone.

"Hiya Hickey" I reply to torment her, doing a poor impersonation of what my father-in-law always shouts to her when he comes up the stairs. This is his nickname for Dale because of her frequent bouts with hiccups as a baby. Tommy loves giving out nicknames, everybody gets one. In fact I pass the woman he's dubbed "Wee Arthur Askey" on the way up the stairs. She nods and smiles as usual. She's a lovely old lady (Chrissie) and her constantly smiling face, big specs and very short stature are indeed a bit reminiscent of the old comedian. She saves pennies in a jar for Dale.

As I round the last flight of stairs Dale's stood at the door with Tommy holding her back from the banister, the corner of her tiny cardigan folded tight between his huge thumb and forefinger. She looks really cute in her little sage green "French" outfit and she's excited to see me and does a few rapid knee buckles, nodding in rhythm with them.

Tommy let's her loose and "Wham"; I get the big running, arms spread, unconditional loving welcome. I scoop her up and join Bunty and Tommy in the kitchen.

I can't contain myself any longer and blurt it out;

"Roy Forey called today and offered us a posting"

"Well … where about?" says Bunty impatiently.

"America! Washington DC. British Embassy"

"Very good' says Tommy with more "fff" than "vvv" on the very and protraction on the "oo" in good.

"America?" says Bunty "America. Wow. Didn't expect that. What d'you think?"

"Roy did three years there. Says he loved it. Money sounds pretty good too. Wants me to let him know in the morning if we want it. What d'you think?"

"America. Just never thought about America. When would we go?"

"They want me there by mid-August; so about six weeks time".

"Wow, that's quick".

Tommy weighs in positively as always; "Great opportunity mind".

As the family file in; Gags from her work at the Castle, Lorraine from School, Carol from her new Window-dressing apprenticeship at Patrick Thompson's, the talk is all about America. How little we all really know about it other than what we've seen on telly and most of that is cowboys and Indians, detectives (i.e. Kojak, Rockford, Ironside) sitcoms (Lucy, Bewitched, Rowan and Martin) and of course now classic serials (Peyton Place, Dallas, Roots, Rich man—poor man).

I phone my folks and let them know. They're also very surprised to hear America rather than Germany.

So we're very excited about it all but at the same time a little nervous about having to suddenly make a decision. By the time we leave to head back along Princess Street towards Dalry it's in the bag. We are going to America! We tell Dale over and over and she senses it's something we're pretty enthused over without really understanding what. It's a dry night so we just walk all the way.

As soon as we get in our flat door I've dug out the big maroon hardback "Colliers World Atlas" (stolen from my Mum's, much to Brother John's chagrin—and I've still got it). This a fantastic old fashioned "Gazetteer". As well as maps of the entire world it has comprehensive data about all of the major cities.

I find the main map of America and identify the location of Washington DC. I confess I knew it was East Coast somewhere about halfway down but I really did not know much US geography. Which brings me to an interesting aside.

Having lived here (USA) for almost twenty five years now lots of my initial impressions and ideas about America have been changed drastically by the reality. For example; when I was first here I used to be amazed at how, even some highly educated Americans had very scant knowledge of European geography. I even used to be very offended by this "Ignorance". People with a vested interest such as second, third, fourth generation Scots typically knew how Britain was set up. Beyond that though, it might as well have been attached to mainland Europe. Most of them had heard of England and many clearly saw England and Britain as one in the same. Being a diehard I was always most upset when some innocent Southern Virginian would ask me;

"Whar d'ya'll kam fram?"

"Scotland"

"Ah, Scatlan bat y'all speak English?"

Or even worse.

"Ah, Scatlan—is that in Inglan?"

Ouch.

Then I thought back to me. Excited about my posting. Looking at a map of America and having at least completed my high school education I could pick out New York, Florida and California. Beyond that I'd start to struggle. So here's the bottom line. America is massive and students have plenty of their own geography to learn so they typically barely touch the fringes of elsewhere. Not so different then to us. At eighteen I knew Europe well. Name the capital, pick the flag—I'm your man. Of course, as always there's an odd anomaly. For reasons I can't explain I could also do a pretty good job on Africa and come out respectable on most parts of the world except America; the big blob to the left of your world map. The bit with Canada above it (Canada was always pink for some reason). So why should I hold it against Americans if they didn't know that Scotland, Ireland and Wales were proud nations in their own rights.

And that's the key. They concentrated on their own part like most people do. Let's reverse roles for a second. I arrive in America. I meet a guy. He says he comes from the southern part of Kansas and asks me to point it out on an unmarked map. I'm stumped (all I know is Dorothy comes from there but Wizard of Oz never showed me where it actually is) Ces't la vie.

Sorry. In the words of a famous actor turned U.S. President (recently deceased);

"There you go again, Jim. This is supposed to be a Saccer book"

So Bunty and I have studied the map of Washington DC and even located the British Embassy and a whole bunch of malls. Except that by the time we get here malls are becoming much more a retail attraction than a tourist trap!

I call Roy in the morning and tell him we're keen to go. He congratulates me and tells me that I'll be getting a letter shortly with all the details of what I have to do and how I go about it. In the words of the band who will become my serious favorite in part II of this story; "A'm on ma way".

The next six weeks are a whirlwind of running around making arrangements to prepare for our move. This includes several "Farewell" do's. A good night at the junior ranks' club at Craigiehall. I get to wear my white jacket, brown pinstripe trousers and smoke a cigar for the last time. We even have an "Alternative" sports farewell which is a bowling night at the Carousel in Ferry Road. Again, a good time had by all. Most of all we'll miss our mad Saturday nights with Helen and John at the White Hart—they'll always be a special memory.

Before departing I do have just a little more fitba business. Of course I inform West Calder United that they will have to manage without me regardless of whether the Manager is Neil or Billy Ritchie.

Then. One night. Just a few days before we're due to go. A knock on the door to our Dalry flat. I open the door and who is there? Fat Eddie Campbell and his Assistant. They have come to ask me if I'd like to sign for Liberton Cropley for the coming season. They're exploring a merger with Links FC, a top Saturday team. Regardless, this is the most flattering offer I've had since Mr Devlin visited

St David's primary all those years ago. This is a team I admire. In any other circumstances I'd consider going through the bureaucratic "Amateur re-instatement" process to play for them. I explain;

"Thanks for asking boys. I love your team, I love your strips but I'm going to America."

"Oh, very good Jim; who ye gonnae play fir there?"

"No its no for fitba. I actually work for the government and they're sending me"

"Oh well then a' the best. When you come back, gees a shout"

And so I was ready to leave for America. My confidence at its highest ebb for many years. Playing junior and being offered a chance to join the cream of the amateur teams.

But I'm still younger than Steve Heighway when he was discovered so there's plenty of time. Maybe I can get on the same team as Georgie Best or even Johan Cruyff who is moving to play in Washington.

Once again, hope springs eternal.

If you want a pee or a pie and Bovril now's the time. The first half just ended. You can even browse some photos if you like.

PHOTO INDEX

1. First Communion. Mrs Boyle with Uncle James. Primary Class. Nothing stops him playing fitba.

2. Leith Schools second time around at Prestonpans.

3. Edinburgh Thistle U16 graduates in 1974.

4. Edinburgh Thistle revival U14's—U18's. Taken at St Mark's park.

5. Waverley Star 1976 at The Gyle, Edinburgh.

6. Waverley Star; Sunday Churches Cup Winners at Leith Links.

7. My best match ever.

8. Big-time Professional contract with West Calder United.

9. British Lions at Turkey Run, Virginia; NVSL Champions 1980.

10. Typical player pass. British Lions 1981. Lions article from magazine when Pan Am sponsored the team in 1981. Bulldogs versus Soccer Supplies at Turkey run mid 1980's.

11. Lions celebrate NVSL cup win at RFK stadium, Washington; June 1981 (Mascot is Crossan junior).

12. NVSL select team for game versus Royal Air Force touring team at 23rd/M street, Washington DC (mid 1980's).

13. Official Program for NVSL versus U.S. National team at Annandale High School, Virginia, June 1983.

14. British Bulldogs at School field behind Dairy Queen on Route 1 near Fort Belvoir. Ged and Alex still discussing defensive stuff!

15. Program for New Year Derby match in Subbuteo.

16. Ged, JimmyDolbear, Tommy Barnes and I at Walter Johnson High School in Maryland following Scotland's second consecutive victory over the auld enemy. Scott and I try a change of sport and both make the Embassy finals. JJ (#3 Mosely) and I (#7 Theisman) dress to go to the Chesterbrook pub (shooters for touchdowns) to watch the Redskins; early 1980's. Embassy fives team at Corner Kick with my dad guesting in goal around age 60.

17. Dad takes Dale to Easter Road in 1998. The famous Rubik's Cube costume which deserved a better reward. Spartans mid-eighties at Mason District Park, Columbia Pike, Virginia.

18. Brooke sneaks in to Easter Road. Brooke in Potomac Kiwanis colors. Arlington Tsunami of Old Dominion Soccer League.

19. World Cup comes to RFK in Washington in 1994.

20. The Proclaimer triplets. Danny Brogan's weirdest soccer shirts ever.

21. Ian Smith waxes lyrical in Vegas 2006.

22. Priceless moment with Uncle James after Hibs' CIS Insurance cup win in 2007.

23. Eddie and I; team mates for almost thirty years (at Winding Creek Park, Maryland in 2006.

24. Rangers' celebrate championship at Germantown (Maryland) Sportsplex in 2007.

COMING TO AMERICA 221

222 FITBA DAFT

The Leith Danriot Primary School team who beat East Lothian Select XI by two goals to one at Prestonpans on Saturday. The team will back row, left to right: E. Allison, T. Carter, D. Davis, A. Tennant, D. Davis, A. Tennant, D. Rodgers, R. Watson, A. [illegible]. left to right: N. Marino, B. Carnie, J. Meikle, H. Thomson and J. McVicar.

Leith Schools — James.

Leith Schools players' pool

A trim turn-out as the Edinburgh Thistle Juveniles line up in readiness for a new season in the Under-18 League. Thistle won the Bailie Thearer and Wilson trophies as an Under-16 outfit and are hoping to extend their victory run this year. Kenneth McCallum and Eamonn Bannon were on trial with Derby County recently and club officials are confident that a few more Senior clubs will be taking note of their young campaigners. Thistle line-up, back row, left to right: Jimmy Fettes (secretary), Graeme Woodward, Steven Lodge, David Torrance, Brian McLeish, Brian Lee (captain), Micahel Sidonis and Adam Jackson (trainer). In front, Ian Craswick (trainer), Stuart Johnson, Kenneth McCallum, John Sclater, Jim Meikle, Alex Shields and Eamonn Bannon.

COMING TO AMERICA 223

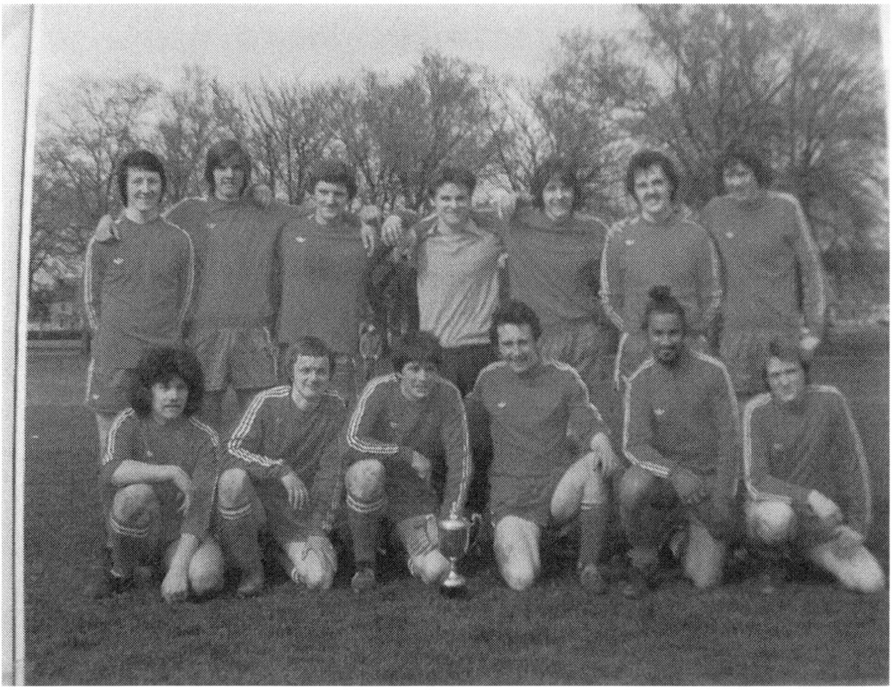

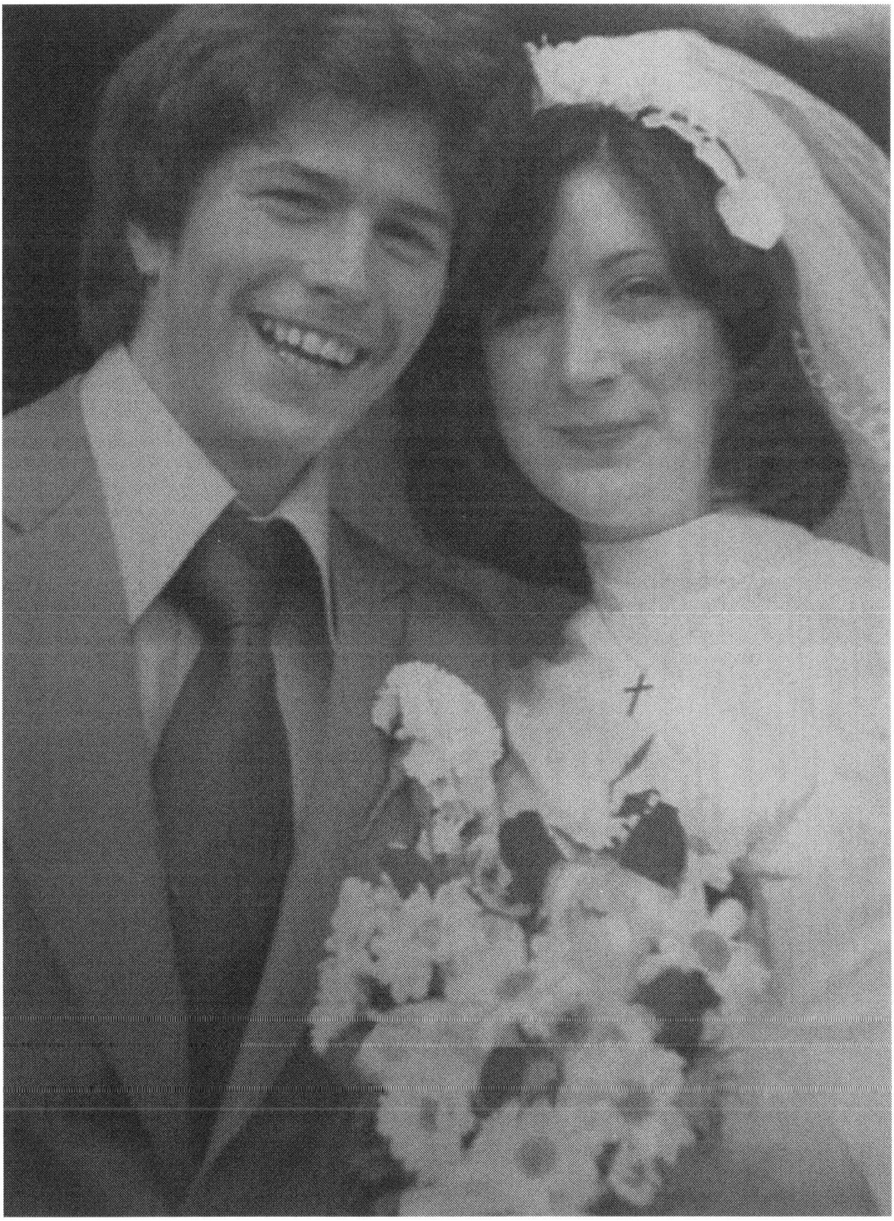

226 FITBA DAFT

Scottish Junior Football Association

WEST CALDER UNITED Football Club
(Member of the Scottish Junior F.A.)

DAVID CAMPBELL
16 Manryck
EAST CALDER

Mr James Moore
53 Dalry Road
EDINBURGH

Dear Sir,

This club for whom you are a *registered* / *desired* player for Season 79/80 is desirous of your services for Season 80/81.

(*Delete as applicable)

I am, therefore, directed to offer you the following terms to sign Registration Form and be registered for the club for Season 80/81:

£5 signing on fee, £30 a match for a win, etc.

The officials of the club will meet you on 18th/19th June at Logans at Ramoyle Flat, what time that you have been offered terms to sign for this club for Season 80/81 and in virtue of this, they have bound themselves in accordance with Rule 40(a) of the Association to refrain from approaching, offering to sign, sign or play you without the consent of this club.

Should you consider you have cause or reason as to why this club should not seek to secure your services as player for Season 80/81 and that all other clubs in membership of the Scottish Junior F.A. should not be so advised, you may make representation in writing showing such cause or reason to the Secretary of the Scottish Junior F.A., Wm. Glancy, Ishabad Gourn, Inchinnan, Renfrew. Each representation must be accompanied by a fee of £3.00 which will be returnable if the case presented by you is considered by the Committee of the Association to be justified.

Such representation must be lodged not later than the first Saturday in August.

Yours faithfully,
Secretary

BRITISH LIONS - N.V.S.L. CHAMPIONS
FALL SEASON 1980

228 FITBA DAFT

BRITISH EMBASSY SOCCER TEAM

The British Embassy Soccer Team won the Northern Virginia Soccer League cup finals at RFK stadium on June 24. Pan American World Airways sponsored the team this year with new uniforms and kit bags.

Jim Meikle, clerical officer in the scientific division at the British Embassy is the team captain. Meikle, who played professionally for Edinburg in Scotland, has made the British team the number one amateur club in the Washington area.

Sporting the jersey donated by Pan Am, team manager Tom Kauffman shows the winning trophy to their sponsor, Dolores Welting from Pan Am.

Jim Meikle

COMING TO AMERICA   229

ANNANDALE BOYS CLUB
PRESENTS

Team America Soccer

VERSUS

The Northern Virginia Soccer League Select

WEDNESDAY, 29 JUNE, 1983. KICKOFF 7.30p.m.
AT ANNANDALE HIGH SCHOOL, ANNANDALE, VIRGINIA

OFFICIAL PROGRAM $1.00

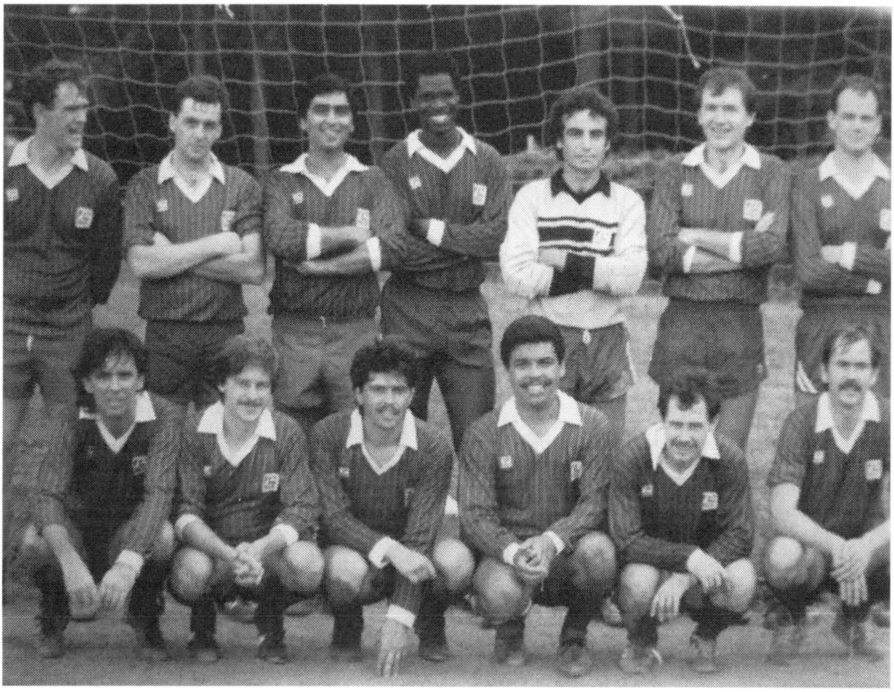

TART OF MIDLOTHIAN

VS

HIBERNATING HIBS

OFFISHUL PROGRAM

COMING TO AMERICA 233

234   FITBA DAFT

COMING TO AMERICA 235

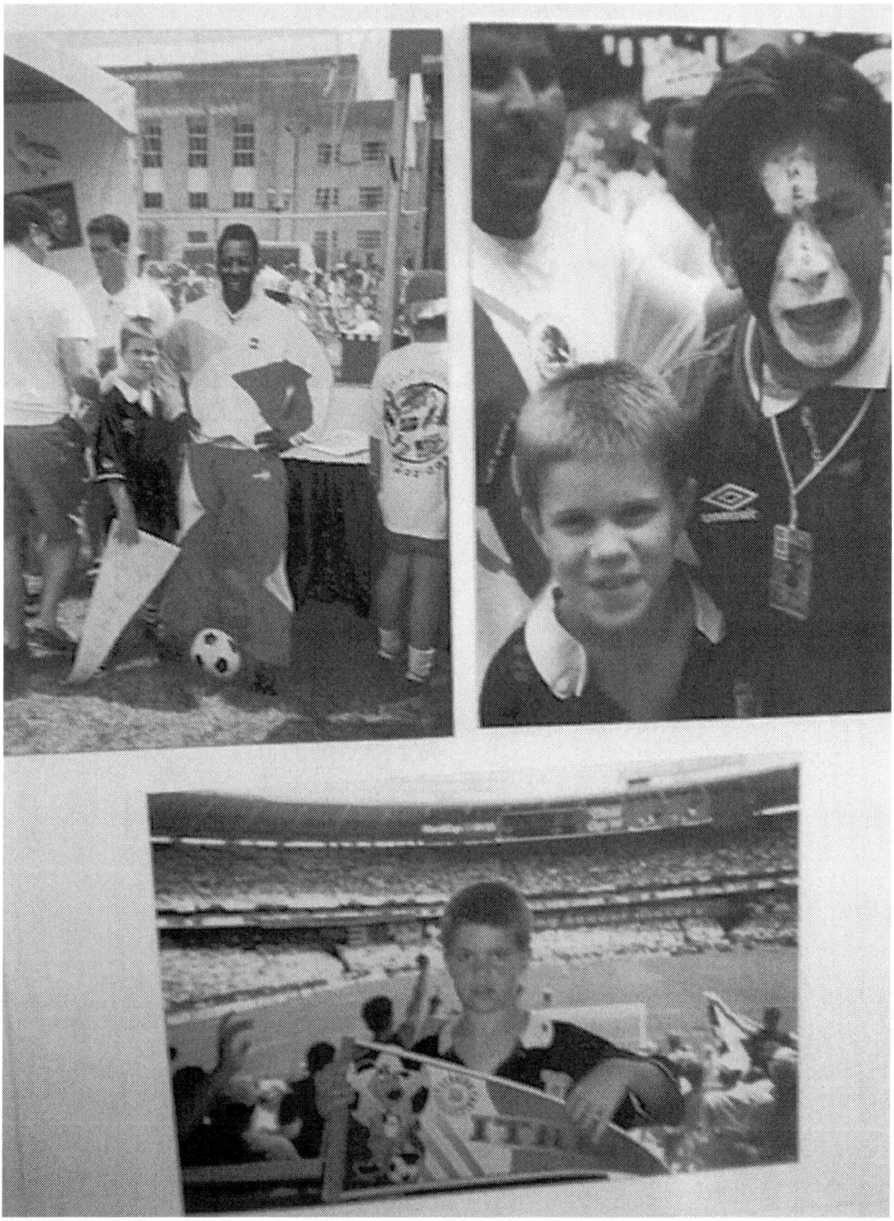

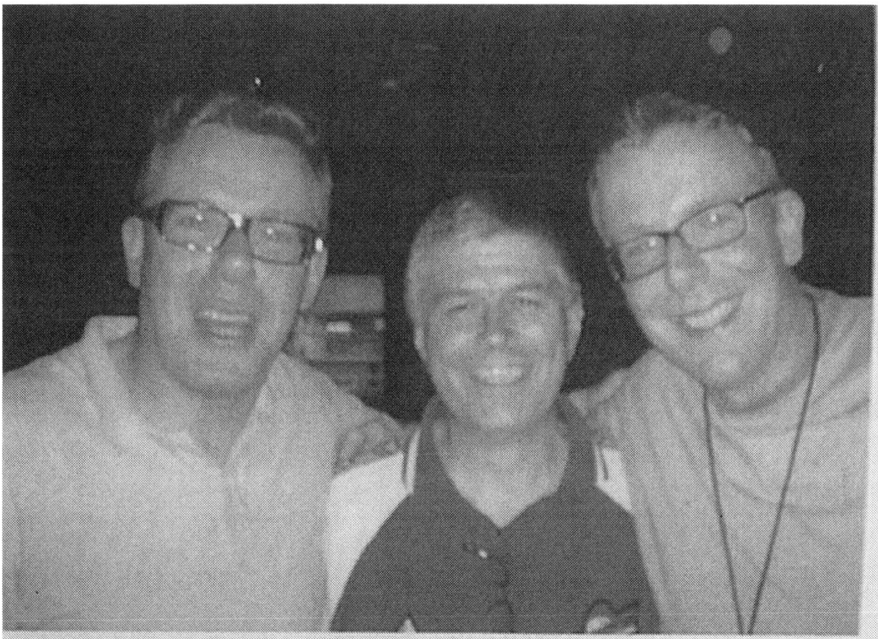

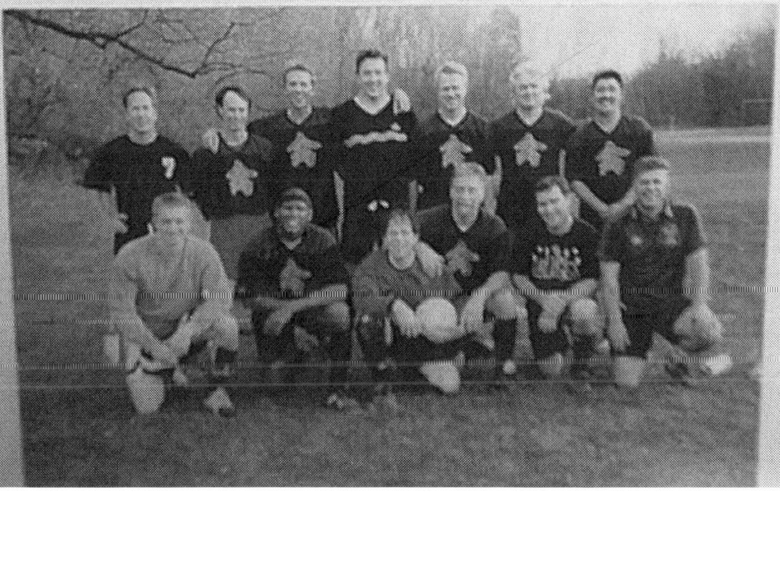

238 FITBA DAFT

COMING TO AMERICA 239

30

DIXIE LIQUER AND TURKEY RUN

And so we leave our beloved Scotland with varied emotions ranging from nervous at one end, to relief in the middle (at finally getting our chance at something different) to the unabated excitement which comes from venturing into the mostly unknown in ones early twenties. We've already had a taste of the economical potential with a few generous advanced allowances for clothing and the likes enabling me to get a Bunty a little gold Seiko watch she'd always admired in Ratner's Jewelers window. It's for her birthday and something I never previously managed to round up the cash for.

I have to spend a couple of days in London for briefings on the way out so we decide to take a full week with Bunty's older sister; Senga. Her husband Brian is still in the military and they are living in quarters at Mill Hill which we recognize as the centre of the universe for all things forces mail. It's been an IRA target from time to time but that's not a big deal to us as we've both been constantly around military establishments since we started working. It's actually a good strategy as we need space to unwind after the fairly intense preparations and a whirlwind of farewells which included a disco at the Junior Ranks' club at Craigiehall and our ten pin bowling night at The Carousel in Leith. It's a funny thought that the contents of our lovely Dalry flat are now sitting in mothballs in Jenner's' Depository (such a posh organization couldn't just call it a store or warehouse) next to the Carricknowe Golf Course where I won the second of my two lifetime golfing trophies; Waverly Star Football Club Golf Championship. Confusing title, isn't it?

After a relatively relaxing week we head back Northwest via Paddington Station British Rail to Swindon. Then on by coach to Brize Norton from where we will be flying Royal Air Force (RAF) to Washington. We get a night in the neat little forces hotel there, a place we'll come to know quite well.

On the morning of Friday 15th August 1980 we board the RAF VC10 in pelting rain. At less than three years old Dale has little clue what's going on but she's taking the constant travel in her stride and enquires "What's that?" several hundred times along the way. Other than sitting back to front, the RAF flight isn't too much different than a commercial flight and we touch down safely at Washington Dulles in the mid-afternoon. There are these strange looking buses on stilts buzzing around all over the tarmac. We've never seen their likes before and they make me think of Sci-Fi movie insects; some deviant forms of mechanized giant ants, as they always look "busy". We soon learn that these are the normal mode of transferring arriving international passengers directly from the planes to the buzzing Immigration hall. They surround us, rear up on their cantilever hind legs and move in for the kill. With hindsight, Dulles was a relatively quiet airport at the time with the main terminal only half its current size and no significant "Midfield" terminals (notice that, almost four paragraphs before a vague fitba reference). Unfortunately all of the international flights seemed to arrive within the 3-5 p.m. window so it's packed for a few hours then dead again! We're very proud of our old style hard cover navy blue passports with the gold lettering and fancy diplomatic stamps in them. These get us in a faster "Blue Lane" alongside the airline staff.

Quickly and smoothly through Immigration then and onto the Customs hall where we are intercepted by a young man who looks like some kind of official with a bunch of overlapping badges/passes clipped to his neat navy blazer with the smooth, shiny brass buttons. He's smiling warmly at us and seems to know who we are. About ages with me I guess, slightly curly dark hair, tall and well built.

"You Jim Meikle?" he asks in a clearly Scottish accent but with strong American undertones.

"That's right, you Pete?" I ask as I've been told the guy I'm replacing is Pete Gilbert and he'll be there to see us into town.

He shakes his head; "No, I'm Alex … Alex MacAdam" and he thrusts out his right hand for an obviously sincere handshake"

"Nice to meet you Alex, this is my wife Bunty and my daughter Dale"

He also shakes Bunty's hand and nods and smiles down to Dale at the same time.

He explains. "Pete's waiting outside for you. I'm embassy liaison here at the airport and just wanted to say hello—I heard you were Scottish and play football?"

"A bit, yeh."

"My Mom and Dad have been here for years but we're originally from Ayr, what about yourselves?"

"Both Edinburgh."

"So are you Hibs or Hearts?"

"Diehard Hibee. Yerself?"

"Ayr United of course."

Then he changes direction to politely include Bunty in the loop too.

"So Bunty was everything alright at Brize and on the flight?"

"Lovely, thanks" she says.

Despite the limited conversation we know already that he is in fact talking to us because we are *Scottish*. He's definitely Scottish as opposed to "Scarrish" and the real question he's probing us with is; are we Scottish-Scottish and I later understand why. It's because he meets lots of Scottish people who have worked and lived down South (i.e. London) for years, some affected by it, others not.

It's already becoming clear to him that we are likesay, SCOTTISH! Dale confirms this to him when her Mom asks her; "Dale, remember yer manners and say hello to Alex."

"Hi-ya Al-ik" she says in that wonderful wee brogue which will ultimately be totally lost in Kindergarten. Pretty good start though. Only in the country a few minutes and we've met someone who we can tell might be a good pal. He enhances his own Scottishness by explaining that he's a piper in the "City of Alexandria Pipes and Drums" and invites us to stop by "Irelands Own" pub in old town Alexandria (Virginia) any Thursday night to listen to them practice and have a few pints. We will do so many, many times.

He sees us through customs where he obviously knows them all well and hands us over to the waiting Pete and his girlfriend, Chris and they're both in shorts. Frankly, other than for playing fitba and gym class, I hadn't been in shorts since primary school. They're also about ages with us, English midlands I'd guess. As we exit the main terminal we get our first distinct blast of a fundamental difference from home. The heat and humidity are overwhelming and Pete explains that they are amidst the longest run of consecutive one hundred-plus degree/one hundred percent humidity days that they have had in one hundred years. The lower parts of our backs are already soaked with sweat before we even get to the car. They blast the air conditioning until its freezing but they seem used to it so we say nothing until Dale innocently blurts out; "Am cauld mammy" and they laugh and turn it down a couple of notches.

We head in on the dedicated Dulles airport road and they start imparting general local information in the way we have since done hundreds of times to arriving visitors. We take the George Washington Parkway and are amazed how green everything is. By now I've seen photos of Washington city centre so I should know what to expect but my mind is firmly locked into anticipating a towering silhouette of skyscrapers a la American TV shows. Ironically, this proves to be accurate in every other major US city except Washington with Manhattan of course the daddy of them all.

"Almost there" says Pete after tracking alongside what he explains is the Virginia side of the Potomac River for about fifteen minutes. We see Key Bridge for the first time and Georgetown University perched atop the hill across the other side. We loop under and upwards to the right to get on the Bridge and head into Washington DC (District of Columbia) for the very first time. Ironically I find my skyline but on the wrong (Virginia) side of the river. Pete explains that there are rules about not building above the height of the Capitol dome in Washington and that's why its buildings are so low compared to elsewhere. He also tells us the skyline which is now behind us as we cross the bridge is Rosslyn where many companies who want high rises but can't have them in Washington are sticking them in the nearest possible spot. Apparently there's a similar enclave called Crystal City a bit further down the river.

In amongst all of this the one thing I remember most vividly of my entry to Washington is … Dixie Liquor. As we make a right turn off Key Bridge and into Georgetown proper the multiple neon signs of the liquor store caught my eye as something which finally met my expectation levels in my mind's TV stereotyped American imagery. Hooray. Pete gives us a quick run down of American booze lingo. Hard Liquor is their collective term for what we refer to as "Spirits". Wine and beer are typically available in any grocery store but there are dedicated Liquor stores for the hard stuff. In Virginia the Liquor sales are run by the State via a series of "ABC" stores. (Alcohol Beverage Control) I'll get to know my ABC's quite well. Apparently booze rules vary greatly from State to State and even from county to county when you get a little further South into the "Bible Belt" (Carolinas, Kentucky, Tennessee etc)

We head along M street then left up Wisconsin Avenue. About a mile or so up we emerge from the pub/restaurant/boutique stretch of Georgetown into a slightly more residential looking section. I know I must sound like an Alchie but the next building which really strikes my eye is another liquor store; Pearsons (it's just that for me the signage is so fundamentally American). Twenty five years later a thousand businesses have come and gone in Georgetown but the neon signs at both Pearsons and Dixie are still shining brightly. What does that tell us?

We pull into the small parking lot in front of the Wellington Hotel at the corner of Wisconsin and Calvert, right opposite the massive Soviet Embassy complex. The Wellington has gone through several name changes but is still there, currently as the Savoy Suites. We have an "Efficiency". It's the first time we've heard the term but it's essentially a typical hotel suite but with a full kitchen included. It'll be our home for the next two to three weeks. Peter makes sure we're all set and tells us he'll be back Saturday to take us shopping and then to a barbecue at the apartment block where he and Chris live in Landmark, Virginia—wherever that is!

We should be tired but the adrenalin is still pumping. The Wellington has a small pool and we are quickly changed and down to it. Nobody else there and Dale loves having her own private swimming pool. Bunty likes it too as she loves swimming but not in crowded situations. The heat is overpowering so we can't stay out very long. We get changed and take a walk down the street. There's a stretch of restaurants (and of course Pearson's Liquor). Pearsons also have a very traditional drugstore on the corner. This really meets our pre-conceived imagery with a prescriptions counter at one end and coffee/Soda fountain counter at the other. Opposite is the Guy Mason park where beaming floodlights illuminate a baseball field. A few dozen spectators are scattered around the bleachers (American for tiered, bench seating). We buy a takeaway fish and chips from a place called Arthur Treacher's and join the crowd. We have little clue what's going on in the game but it seems like a big fuss for a few middle aged men in very tight pants mostly with serious stomach overhang! Seems very like what we called "Rounder's" as kids but the surrounds look, sound and smell so different there's enough to hold our interest for a while. Then it's back to the hotel and Dale goes out like a light. We are then fascinated watching the TV which is also initially so different to us.

Peter and Chris show up late morning Saturday and we head over to Virginia, this time via Rock Creek Parkway so we get our first glimpse of Watergate and the Kennedy Centre and the main monuments; Lincoln, Washington and Jefferson. The stone is strikingly white and pristine. Everything looks a little surreal and larger than life as many things do the very first time. We cross via Memorial Bridge so also get a glimpse of Arlington cemetery and the Pentagon before heading onto 395 South for a few miles to Landmark. We make our first stop at a Giant food store. Again everything seems … well … big. They have a lovely apartment in a nice building with a pool, tennis courts and a picnic area where we have our first American barbecue including my first Budweiser (I'm already forgetting my German but this must mean fizzy water in English). They show us a very nice afternoon with a bit more background on everything to expect then drop us back at the Wellington early evening.

I last a bit longer than Bunts and Dale and end up channel hopping and guess what I end up watching? Shocker; soccer! There's a game between Vancouver and Tampa Bay on from the West Coast which is three hours behind time-wise. Peter Lorimer (Leeds and Scotland) is playing for the Vancouver Whitecaps and Rodney Marsh (Various English teams) for the Tampa Bay Rowdies. There are various other mainly aging European veterans in the game. The commentators are really bad referring to the penalty area as the "Hotbox" and every foul as a penalty kick! Just looking at the pitch makes me a bit uncomfortable. It's some kind of "Astro" turf and the ball seems to run far too fast and bounce too high! It also has multiple markings all overlapping each other with the soccer lines marked in Red! The players seem oblivious so they're obviously used to it.

Early Sunday morning the phone rings in the room. We look at each other quizzically and I pick it up.

"Hello, Jim?" in a distinctly North East English (Sunderland as it transpired) twang.

"Yes?"

"Jim. WO I Edwards here; Malcolm … Mal. I'm from the embassy. I play for the first team; the British Lions."

"Oh, eh, hi Malcolm."

"Well see, we have a game today. It's pre-season for us and I wondered if you wanted a run out? I could swing by and pick you up about 11:30 if that's okay?" By now you know me well enough to know what the answer is but I 'm trying to be seen to be considerate.

"Can you hold for a sec please Malcolm?" and I cup my hand over the mouthpiece.

"Bunts, chance of a game of fitba—what d'you think?"

I'm delighted and relieved when she just shrugs and says fine and that maybe she and Dale will come too—give us a chance to see a bit more of the surrounding area. I'm thinking, Whoosh.

We get ourselves ready and I have my customary visit to the room with the little white throne. Malcolm pulls into the Wellington parking lot right on time. We're headed to a place called "Turkey Run" which he explains is about twenty minutes away. We're crossing the Potomac River again, this time via Chain Bridge and we get a spectacular view to the West as we cross. I think to myself; Native American Indians and deer wouldn't look a bit out of place here and I later learn that the former were once here in abundance (Powhattans) and the latter still are and all within a spit of busy Washington DC. As we reach the other side we see the large "Welcome to Virginia" sign with the red bird and white flowers. Malcolm clarifies:

"Cardinal—state bird of Virginia, Dogwood—state Flower". We turn right and I see from the green and white sign (my favorite combination) that we're headed South on route 123 towards exotic destinations like "McLean" and "Vienna".

Malcolm's quite the tour guide and as we take the first hill he points out a large gated estate on the right which is the Washington area headquarters of the Kennedy family. A couple of miles along and we pass the Central Intelligence Agency (CIA). Now we really know we're in America. We veer right onto route 193 and then immediately right again into a small hard mud car park. We've made it to the venue; "Turkey Run". I can see a few people limbering up through a small hedge row. The field is big though very parched, the grass looking much more like straw. It has a fairly pronounced slope end to end. A couple of guys are busy at the lower end near the car park putting up a net. No changing rooms to be seen. Malcolm explains that this is the norm for all the local leagues. You arrive mostly kitted out and leave sweaty! Each team has a net and two corner flags and takes them from game to game. I immediately think; what a great and simple idea. All those fights we had at the netless Gyle back in Edinburgh arguing if a shot went in or not. I remember one in particular of my own which referee Davie Patrick ruled over the bar costing Waverly Star a win against Carricknowe. I'll bet Davie's got pretty thick specs by now.

There's even good courtesy between the teams where you often just give your net to the team you are playing after and keep theirs up to save double-handling. Very civilized.

Malcolm introduces the Player/Manager; Tommy Kaufman. He's a big burly American with an awkward, labored looking stride. I learn that he manages more than he plays now due to deteriorating knees. I meet a few of the players and am delighted to find the team dominated by Scots. There are the Muir brothers; Len and John. Len's accent is a bit suspect by now but we do eventually claim him for "International" duty. John still has a charming Northern lilt in his brogue. The Scottish contingent also includes Peter Campbell, Jimmy Smith, Norrie Barker(RAF) and last but not least Johnnie Kerr. Everyone you meet in the States at that time has supposedly played pro somewhere but Johnnie Kerr is the real deal. He's played back in Scotland for St Mirren and Partick Thistle, he's played on the Cosmos in New York, he's played in Washington for the Darts and the Diplomats and, being Glasgow tough as well as a great player, he's even survived a season in the Mexican Pro league. No surprise that Johnnie is now a stalwart on the Professional Players' Association.

The goalie is big Peter Thomas, a rugged Welshman with hands like shovels and shocks of fair hair falling over his brow. He's built like a tank and forwards tend to steer clear of him when he comes lumbering out in his favored green goalie top with the turned up black collar. He always says rugby is his number one game and that makes absolutely perfect sense! There are a couple of other RAF lads ; both Dave's—Smith and Hardinge. The player closest to my age is a young Latin looking guy called Eddie Koebke. Transpires he's American but off Guatemalan immigrant parents. He's a recent graduate of the University of Maryland, part of its growing soccer programme which will ultimately reach sustained national prominence.

Tommy then introduces me to the coach of our opponents, yet another Scot; Ken Jones. He's also the President of the Northern Virginia Soccer League (NVSL) in which we'll compete. He's a diehard bluenose and it's no surprise to hear that his team is called Iron Skillet Rangers—a combination of his favorite restaurant and you know who. He works at the World Bank in Washington. Ken tells me how they play two separate seasons; "FALL" from September thru' December and "SPRING" from March thru' June.

"When d'you arrive?" asks Ken.

"Friday afternoon" I reply.

I'm given the number 14 jersey which is about to become very big in Washington. More on that shortly. The kit is smart enough; White tops, Blue Shorts, Red socks but just a bit too "England" for me. We'll have to do something about that but all in good time. I start in right midfield and am playing quite well and even get an early goal in what would be a 4-1 win. However I'm shocked when after about twenty minutes Tommy pulls me off. He can tell by my reaction that I'm not amused but just laughs and says; "Get some water, you'll be back on in five". And so I learn about unlimited substitutions for the first time and not just for friendly games (which they call exhibitions). This is their norm. Most teams are sensible about it but you do occasionally encounter a team who send on six or eight new players at once which we come to know as the "Charge of the Light Brigade" substitution. Bunty and Dale are starting to cook a bit on the sideline and there's no shade to be had so I find some water for them. It's a reasonable start and Tommy asks me to get him a couple of passport photos soonest so that he can get me a player pass. All players have one and must carry them to games so it all but eliminates the use of ringers. This is yet another simple but great idea. It would've saved countless arguments back home. Especially cup games in country villages where I played against some very mature looking 14-16 year olds.

Malcolm actually lives nearby at Tyson's Corner so to save a double trip Dave Smith kindly volunteers to drop us back at the Wellington en route to Rockville. Dave's married with young kids so he gives us a bit more background on what to expect. He also gives me the background on the British Embassy Soccer Club. It's been around for over thirty years and has claimed one National title; the US Amateur Cup, in 1971. Malcolm was a very young player in that side. There are currently two teams; Lions in NVSL Division One and Tigers in NVSL Division Two. The Lions see it as a first team, second team situation but I will soon learn that the Tigers don't necessarily agree!

We get back to the fabulous air conditioned cool of the hotel and are already learning why the Americans are so obsessed with ice in their drinks. Aaaahhhhh … and that's only a coke.

And so, less than forty eight hours after touching down in the states and before I've even seen where I'll be working, I've made my "Soccer" debut at Turkey Run and am signed up for the British Lions.

31

A GRAND HOUSE AND … A BOAT

Monday morning I take the short walk from the Wellington Hotel down Calvert Street and around the North side of the US Naval Observatory.

The Observatory is a sprawling, lush, green circular complex over a half mile in diameter with a few small office buildings and large residences sprinkled around sparingly. It fills the entire wedge of space between Wisconsin and Massachusetts (Mass) Avenues in North West Washington DC (District of Columbia—it is not a state). DC is set out in a basic grid system of East-West; North-South numbered and alphabetized streets. It's divided into four quadrants; North West, South West, North East, South East. Simple eh? Ah but … the original planners add a couple of creative twists. There are a series of diagonal Avenues, named for various states, intersecting the grid and all pointing towards the central mall area. In very simple terms, think of a dart board with the US Capitol, Washington Monument and White house clustered around the bulls-eye. (How ironic is that analogy nowadays?) The edge of the dartboard is approximately defined by what they call "The Capitol Beltway"; the city ring route. There are also quite a few small parks where streets just disappear and although they mostly emerge again at the other side, it's a nightmare for the uninitiated navigator. DC is approximately square less most of what would be the SW quadrant which is cut off by the curve of the Potomac River. NW is clearly the "Posh" part. This is where most host government, commercial interests and the multitudes of embassy and other multi-national (World Bank, International Monetary Fund, and Organization of American States to name but a few) are located. A couple of people have suggested that SE is the opposite side of the tracks. I've heard nothing of NE.

As well as some of the world's most powerful telescopes and some quarters for naval brass, the Observatory is the site of the official residence of the Vice President, currently occupied by George (Daddy) Bush as Ronald Reagan's number two. This explains the high chain link fence with barbed wire top and constant presence of uniformed Secret Service. (*Though with 20/20 hindsight over twenty years later, the Security then was very low key compared to the "Fortress" it has become—a sad sign of the times*)

I make the right turn onto Mass Ave, the Observatory fence now separated from the sidewalk (American for pavement) by a twenty foot wide strip of grass. Past the Norwegian and Vatican missions. In a few minutes I reach the seven-storey, red brick "New Chancery" which has served as the British Embassy since being built in the late 1950's. It's straight out of "British Government Architecture 101" of that era and reminiscent of all things General Post Office. The Rotunda on the front corner at least softens the otherwise bland squareness. This is a much maligned feature but I think it's one of those things which will find its way back into vogue if it survives long enough to be called "Retro".

By stark contrast it is flanked on the other side by the famous (Sir Edwin) Lutyens building which served as the Embassy and Residence from 1928 until the "Telephone exchange" took over. Prior to the 1920's the entire British mission to the US was housed in a modest mansion at Connecticut and 18th Street downtown. The original office part on the front is called "Old Chancery" and is used for overflow office space and accommodation for on-site staff. The Ambassadors' Residence part to the rear still serves that function very well. It's a spectacular house with grandly decorated, oversized reception rooms which remains a magnet to the Washington upper set—a true asset in the world of international diplomacy and politics. Given the desired ear, the key seasoned British diplomats are as effective as any of the army of overpaid lobbyists on Capitol Hill.

I reach the reception desk and offer my passport as ID. I'm expected and a temporary pass is waiting for me. I'm directed to a room on one of the upper floors which house chunks of British Defence Staff (BDS) the Ministry of Defence contingent within the embassy. I'm introduced to my immediate colleagues a mixture of Royal Navy, Army, RAF and some civilians like myself. I'll be replacing Pete and working with Les. Our boss is Watty; a retired Squadron Leader. He explains that they'll take a very liberal view of my attendance and hours until I get the family settled into a house and acquire some "Wheels". Les is a diehard cockney Chelsea shed boy (Na't a meen?). tall with dark features and tightly curled black hair and beard. He mentions that he's heard I play a bit of football and asks if I'll be joining the embassy soccer club. He's shocked to hear I've already played a game and signed for the Lions.

"Dint 'ang abat mate, didya?"

I tell him about Malcolm getting me at the hotel and he bursts into a smile, blinks his eyes and nods knowingly.

"Old Mallie beats the Tigers to the ball again" he says and goes on to explain that although the Lions and Tigers form one club, they are in constant competition for players. Of course that snippet was left conveniently vague on Sunday.

Various other staff and spouses take Bunty, Dale and I on a whirlwind tour of potential apartment and houses. Most are strong advocates for the areas that they have chosen themselves. We see some stunning high rise apartments in the Friendship Heights and Bethesda areas just a few miles North of the embassy with incredible views of the city. Convenient and tempting but we really fancy a house with a garden. I still haven't gotten over my dismal attempts at growing my own tatties in our corner of the backgreen at Dalry Road. I'd like another go at that.

A lot of my military colleagues have settled in a place called "Yale Village" in Rockville. It's a townhouse (Terrace/Row house in our terms) complex with its own swing park, picnic/barbecue area and a swimming pool. The houses are modern, light, spacious and well equipped and within my allowance range. There would be easy car pooling and company for Bunty and Dale until we get fully settled. Hmmm?

We see one house, two, three, and four. All nice but all more or less next doors to each other. Interesting that these guys are normally allocated fixed quarters on military camps with little or no choice so stuck next doors to their colleagues for better or worse and yet, finally, having some freedom of choice they elect to stay in such close proximity to each other. It's a forces thing. We conclude that whilst this would be great initially, it might wear a bit thin eventually. Still, Yale Village is high on our short list.

Malcolm takes us to "The Commons" in McLean where he lives. Same route as we took to the game at Turkey Run but keep straight instead of turning at the CIA. These are "Garden Apartments" (as opposed to high rise) six in a block, really just a tarted-up version of our stairs back in Pilton but with balconies, great communal facilities and in a prime location. On one side is the quaint "Evans farm" (a working farm but with up-market country shop and restaurant included as well as a duck pond and tiny millhouse/waterwheel). On the other side is the fast developing Tyson's Corner with its state-of-the-art Shopping Mall already in place. Very tempting. It makes our short list.

On the third day of looking Les' wife Marilyn suggests we try some family houses on the Virginia side. She explains that there is a "Myth" around Washington that crossing the bridges equals a disastrous commute but that it is mostly a fallacy and that Chain Bridge is generally a well kept secret. She adds that the public schools in North Arlington and McLean are as good as any in the country. So it's over Chain Bridge for a third time and the view is still breathtaking. This time we bear left and stay on route 123; Glebe Road (the address makes me think of "The Broons" classic Scottish cartoon strip). After about a mile we make a right on Williamsburg Boulevard and two blocks to a left onto North 35TH St. 4941 is the one right on the corner with Williamsburg, it's the one with the lovely Pine Tree defining the front corner of a decent sized garden. A two-storey Colonial with a full unfinished basement under it with laundry facilities included. No garage but a small driveway up one side.

The street is generously wide and there is a kid's tricycle sat unattended on the opposite sidewalk. We haven't even been inside and I can feel the vibes. I can sense them from Bunty too. The Landlord gives us a quick tour, Living Room with brick fireplace and screened porch off to one side. Dining room to seat eight, Kitchen (with Dishwasher) little barbecue patio at back. Upstairs three decent sized bedrooms and bathroom. It also has a full basement with tremendous playroom/game room potential. It's about $100 over my monthly allowance but much like me taking a game of fitba when it's available it's never really in doubt.

The landlord swithers (hesitates) a bit over the standard diplomatic "Get out" clause but he gets over it quickly with the thought of 3-4 years of respectable tenants and steady checks. Within twenty minutes the lease is signed. Well move in on September first.

The journey back to the hotel emphasizes how close we are. Just two minutes to reach Chain Bridge and another fifteen to the embassy. That's a fabulous commute by Washington standards.

Now that we know where we'll be living I need a driving license; a Virginia driving license. Back at the hotel I skim the Yellow pages and find "EZMethod" listed as DC, Maryland and Virginia compliant. I get through first time and within minutes have a special "Introductory" lesson set for the following morning. "Miguel" shows up in what he describes as a compact Buick. He's Mexican but his English is fine with a bit of an accent (much like me). Compact is small in American terms yet this thing is as big as David's Micky/Goofy stickered car and that was one of the bigger models at home.

He asks if I've driven before and I tell him I have lots of experience but with gears. He explains that in America this is called "Stick shift" and it is the exception by far. I have driven an automatic once before. My auntie Mary suffered childhood polio. Sadly this was quite common in 1930's Scotland and all for the lack of a small, laced sugar cube. She had to wear calipers all her life. Still does at the ripe old age of … better not say. She used to always be provided with one of those little light Blue three-wheeler jobs. However when they switched the system to "Mobility" allowances, she could choose her own. My dad found this little White Morris 1100 automatic and converted it to hand controls for her. I had a shot (turn, go) once, besides I've been on the dodgems at the shows (the Fair) plenty times and that's about the same complexity level.

Miguel invites me to take the drivers seat. He points out the controls and suggests we head down towards Georgetown. We're off. After about two hundred yards he laughs and says I'm ready to sit my test. I think he's joking but he's not. He asks if I can spare an extra hour, afford the extra cost and have ID and money.

Yes to all of the above. I pat my right pocket to confirm my passport is in it.

We swap seats again and he hands me the "Virginia DMV Learner Driver" booklet.

"Study zee chapters five and six. Zey have zee stopping deestance, zee alcohol laws and such. Zee rest eetz easy for you. You do zee eye test and zee wreeten test today. In zee morning you do zee driving, yes?"

I say "Yes" which I seenk is zee correct response.

It takes about twenty minutes but I see little of our route as my nose is buried in this little booklet and I'm peppering Miguel with questions. We're headed to the Virginia Department of Motor Vehicles (DMV) in a place called Bailey's Crossroads.

We get there and it's a pretty busy place. I take a number and a clipboard with a pen chained to it. I pick up a couple of forms and start scrawling. After about half an hour (used to continue my studies) I am summoned to a counter. Not having a Social Security number (I will subsequently learn that in America your "Social" number runs your life) slows the process a little but the lady has seen plenty diplomatic customers and allocates me a "Control" number in lieu. The eye test is right there at the counter on a machine which looks like an elongated pair of binoculars. I ace line six on my first attempt. The lady puts a couple of stamps on my form and directs me to the far end of the building.

There I find a little cordoned-off area marked "Written tests". As I cross the threshold Miguel reminds me;

"Remember, here you can turn right on zee Red if no sign".

I'm handed a multiple choice form with twenty five questions (including lots of diagram/picture stuff) and instructed that there is a tolerance of six wrong. The pressure is on. Except that it really is as basic as advertised. To demonstrate how so here is a question more or less verbatim:

"You wish to make a right turn, you:

a.   Turn on your right flasher. (Indicator)

b.   Turn on your left flasher.

c.   Flash you lights.

d.   Toot your horn loud."

Pretty sure I got that one correct. As predicted the signage ones were common sense and there was of course the "Turn on Red" one (a staple I guess). I was done within five minutes. I took my paper back to the counter where an elderly gent in a plaid shirt and sleeveless sweater pulled a pencil from behind his ear and hummed away to himself as he marked it.

"Your good, sir" he proclaimed and invited me to take a seat in front of a blue cloth for a side on shot with a Polaroid camera atop a square black suitcase. I'd used one of these machines myself many times back in Scotland. One of my tasks there had been going around MOD establishments making passes for people. As well as the camera, the kit had a built in developer and laminator. After waiting about five more minutes I'm handed a still warm plastic pouch containing my Virginia Learners permit. This will entitle me to sit my road test the next again day (amazing service as the waiting period for a road test at home at that time was over six months). Bunty is a bit anxious that I've taken so long but pleased when she hears about the progress I've made.

Next day Miguel is back and this time I get to drive to Bailey's for practice. When we get there we wait for a specific space which Miguel wants me to get and he instructs me to back in. He explains this will give me the easiest possible take-off for my test.

After another form and long wait a lady with a clipboard in her hand calls for; "My-kill, James My-kill".

She smiles as I identify myself and we head for the parking lot. By now Miguel and I have had the inevitable Scottish/Mexican share our love of soccer conversation and are good buddies. He gives me the pursed lips with the thumb and forefinger together forming a circle which means it'll be a breeze. My only previous road test was at home a few months before we left. Attempting to strengthen my posting options, I scraped together enough for a couple of refresher lessons prior to taking it. I failed for (I think) not using my mirrors enough a bad habit I'd developed in driving so long without my license. I was bitterly disappointed and that memory was keeping me on my toes right now. I remember my British test taking about forty five minutes.

My Virginia test took less than five! I pulled out of the prime space Miguel had picked and made a right onto what I think was Seminary Road. I followed it back around to the right onto a quiet slip road which ran alongside the busy route seven (Leesburg Pike). I made another right at the light by a TOYS R US (turning on red after a complete stop of course) then yet another right back onto Seminary and a fourth right back into the DMV car park. No hill start, no reversing around a corner, no three-point turn, no emergency stop with the slap on the dashboard and not a single left turn. The lady just said "fine" and got out of the car. I can't contain myself and blurt out;

"So, ma'am, I passed?"

"Fine" she repeated and looks at me like I'm daft (likesay not fitba daft just regular daft). She exchanges a word with Miguel as she passes him. He confirms the good news:

"What I tell you jeem, no problema mi amigo".

This time I get my photo taken straight on and shortly thereafter I have a warm Virginia driving license. What amazes me is that it does not have an "Automatic only" stipulation so without any other test you could now get in a stick shift and take your chances! Relatively few here do.

I return to the hotel triumphant and quickly phone Scotland to tell my parents the good news. My joy is short lived as my Uncle Charlie answers the phone at my Ma's and explains without pre-amble that he's there because my grannie Meikle has died. We just visited her in the Eastern General Hospital the week before we left. She seemed to be doing okay and we were even allowed to bring her a miniature of dark Rum as a wee farewell treat. She did predict that would be the last time we'd see her but she was quite calm and unperturbed about it. She said that when she was very young a few of her pals took off for America never to return. A few years later we'd find one of them! Having just barely arrived it'll be difficult for us to go back for the funeral and my dad advises against even trying, reminding us that "Nelly" was well into her eighties and had a pretty good kick at the ba'. Small waves of sadness hover in the back of my mind over the next few days but I'm young and busy, three thousand miles removed and (quite frankly) somewhat selfish with the ability to push undesirable bits of thought towards the back part of the mind most of the time.

I go to my first embassy soccer club training session on the Wednesday. It's at 23rd and N streets and I'm surprised to find a full sized field squished into the mass of buildings downtown. There's not much actual training in the sense I'm used to. In fact they call it practice rather than training. It just becomes a "Scrimmage" (informal practice match in American terms) between the Tigers and Lions. Even here I get my first sense of the rivalry and adopt the view that the Lions are much the stronger team but the Tigers have at least two players who belong in that stronger team. I file the names away for future reference—Donnie Kraft and Abby Jama. Practice is followed by a few pints at the embassy social club where the intra squad rivalry continues via table tennis, darts and elbow bending. The barman is a Scot, John Mulraney, late 50's I'd say, graying gracefully. Without saying a lot he gives the impression of knowing a lot. He's old school Celtic and I enjoy a good beer exaggeration induced exchange with him on my favorite subject.

I decide I'd like to get a car for the weekend so Bunty, Dale and I can start exploring a bit on our own. The embassy has a "Welfare" car for hire but it's well spoken for. A lady in the office; Sheila Condie, mentions that she and her husband hired from "Rent-a-Wreck" when they first arrived and that it was cheap and practical. It's at Duke Street on the Virginia side and she volunteers her husband Jimmie to drop us there on their way home to Alexandria.

Jimmie picks Sheila and me up at the embassy around 4 p.m. and stops by the hotel to get Bunty and Dale. We now get to see what a serious commute would be like as he picks his way through town and onto 395, the main route south. It's bumper to bumper most of the way to the Duke Street exit where he drops us at the strip mall which houses; "Rent-a-Wreck". I have a reservation but at $9 dollars per day including insurance, I'm dying to see what we'll get! I go into the pokey little office which is clearly in keeping with the low budget approach. We have a seat on some sad chairs which have chunks of yellowed foam showing through holes in the coffee-stained, heavy weave cloth.

"Mr Meeclay?" says the man behind the counter.

"Meeclay, that's me" I respond already giving up hope of ever getting Americans to pronounce my name properly.

We quickly take care of the paperwork and I have to leave a cash deposit of fifty bucks (see, I'm picking up the lingo already) as I don't yet have a credit card. I'm thinking what can the cars be like if they only take fifty bucks to secure them? My question is answered quickly as he points to a monster sized Station Wagon (Estate) and hands me the key for it without offering any basic instruction. It's a horrible mossy green color with a thick black rubber trim around the edge. This remind me of the tires they place around small boats to cushion them against bumping the harbor wall, quite an appropriate anomaly as this thing looks more like a boat than a car to me. It's a late 60's model Oldsmobile. I open the door which weighs a ton. Bunty asks if I'm sure I can even drive it and I know she's not joking. It has three rows of seats which were once leather though there's not too much of it left now. We pile in and Dale complains that the shredded dried out leather is jagging her bum. I find all the basic controls and start it up. It sounds and feels like a tank. Seat belts on and we're headed to Interstate 395, one of Americas busiest roads. Still, at least we are going against the rush hour.

We slide down the northbound entry ramp from Duke Street and I'm immediately getting tooted like crazy for going too slow and barely managing to keep the boat in my own lane! It has AC but it stinks so I turn it off and we get baked instead. Bunty manages to get a window down a little but all that does is make the noise from outside even more intense. I'm drenched with sweat all down my lower back. We see an exit sign for route 120 Glebe Road and although I'm pretty sure we're away at the wrong end of it, it sounds a better option until I get a bit more comfortable in the boat.

We are both relieved as we take the exit ramp and see the distinct Pizza Hut sign across their typical chalet style building. We agree on an early dinner. This gives me a chance to re-gather my frazzled nerves and I allow myself one Michelob to help the cause. We eat our fill then take Glebe Road (North) having little clue where we actually are but fairly confident it will eventually get us back to Chain Bridge. Half an hour and several dozen lights later it does just that and whilst slow and laborious, it is much less stressful than the 395. En-route we get our first look at the big green monster which is the front of Parkington Hecht's (now Ballston Common) and we take the brief detour just before Chain Bridge to have another look at our house to be. By the time we get back to the hotel I'm reasonably comfortable with the controls and the width of the boat and Bunty has stopped digging her fingernails into what's left of the seats. However navigating through the hotels tight underground car park full of pillars is a real challenge. I eventually find a space where it almost fits. I badly need a shower and something much stronger than a Michelob!

As we get out the wee voice chips in; "My big car dad?"

"No darlin', we're just borrowing it for a few days."

32

MEIKLE AGAINST CRUYFF ... NOT QUITE

Last couple of pieces of domestic business to take care of are a real car and some furniture for the house.

Whilst driving the boat out of the underground parking lot for the last time I've caught the rubber trim on a pillar and stripped a section off. I'm sweating over this as I'm convinced that, despite the shoddy state of the vehicle, they're bound to use this as a reason to keep my $50 deposit. I get some glue and stick the trim back on just before we reach the strip mall at Duke Street. Fortunately the guy is not going to leave the comfort of his countertop fan and venture out into the heat to check the clunker—he signs me off and I make a swift exit in search of a cab. Two days later he calls me and asks if I had any trouble with the trim;

"Not at all" say I, fingers crossed tightly behind my back. I'm an honest man but, c'mon, if you'd seen this car you'd know that the already negligible value would hardy be hurt by a missing section of rubber trim. I get a small wave of mild fleeting Catholic guilt but it subsides quickly.

Anyway I'm quickly focused on my quest for a proper car. Les and a couple of others have started a "Convertible" club and bought typical American convertibles on the basis that we are only here for three years and might as well have as much fun as possible. No argument from me on that. Les has a cardinal red early 1970's Impala. Ron has a Green Mustang about the same age and Graham has a monster White Cadillac complete with White leather seats. Les has put me in touch with Major Davies who has just the car for me on sale at a mere $2500 dollars. We had a system where you could get an advance for car purchase and pay it back over your tour so this is easily manageable. Plus we're getting $2.60 to the pound at the time.

Major Davies suggests I take the car for a spin at lunchtime. Good idea. He walks me out and shows me it. A 1974 Chevy Caprice Classic gleaming mid-blue with Black Leather seats and oversized whitewall tires. He pops two small handles where the roof meets the front windscreen and flicks a switch. The roof disappears smoothly into a cavity behind the rear seat. I'm sold already though trying not to be too gushing so as to preserve some bargaining power. He leaves me to it and I head off to the hotel to pick up Bunty and Dale for lunch. It takes all of two minutes for us to agree that we want it. We'd been back on buses the last couple years since the demise of the Anglia so this is quite a step up. Besides looking "Cool" it really is a dream to drive. With the top down, peripheral vision and consciousness of other traffic is vastly superior than in a regular car. I offer the Major $2100, he counters and we settle on $2300. Sold.

The last big chore is furniture. We're directed to a place called Scherr's in Rockville, Maryland where they specialize in furniture rental to the thousands of foreigners who staff up the diplomatic missions, World Bank and International Monetary Fund. The main guy there, Dean has it down to a fine art. Bunty gets to go around and more or less choose what she likes, mostly new but some respectable used for kitchen and 2nd/3rd bedrooms. The house has one constraint that she's not mad on; fitted "Shag" carpets in a sort of Mustard tone but she'll work around that. We find that Americans seem to love shag pile! Having always had to furniture shop cautiously, one piece at a time out of necessity, she quite enjoys this exercise. Dean pretends to hit a few buttons on his calculator and surprise, surprise; the monthly rental amount is spot on our allowance. It will all be delivered on September first.

And so it is we get settled into 4941 North 35th Street, Arlington, Virginia, USA.

I've been at "Soccer practice" a couple times now and already concluded that I need to take the team over and start some proper training. I've also made my league debut in the NVSL. It was at a place called Virginia Highlands so I develop a picture in my head of something which might remind me of home. Not so. The "Highlands" are tucked in between a very busy section of 395 and the concrete jungle around Crystal city. There will be even more encroachment later with the addition of Pentagon City Mall.

We are playing a team called "Calico Regents" they're in all red. The pitch is flat and even. It's more hard packed, dried out mud than actual grass. It makes for a fast pace and I'm pleasantly surprised by how well our team flows in the game than as opposed to practice. The difference is the presence of the two veterans John's; Kerr and Muir who hadn't been at the practices. At this level, their quality is enough to push us from okay to very good. I get two goals in a 4-1 victory. A good start. Of course I've already opened my mental file on signings for next season when I take over. I pencil in one from the Regents team; the guy who scored the goal; Kevin Scannel—nice ball skills and never stops running. I hear his dad's the coach so there might be some loyalty issues there.

Next week it's back to Turkey Run to face The World Bank. I get to meet Jim Cowley who is our number one supporter. He's one of a ton of "Scousers" who have come to the area in support of the McAteer Brothers' thriving construction and electrical interests. He's always followed whichever has been the top "British" team in the area and he confirms that, in his view, the Lions are that for now. He's an ex-comedian, naturally hilarious and finds it hard to go thirty seconds without telling you a joke. And of course, he loves his football.

"The Bank" is not a bad side but we get really flowing down the slope in the second half and run out 5-2 winners. I get a goal but more importantly I have my best game so far within a smoothly flowing midfield. Johnnie Kerr gives a real roasting to their left back, Bill Cartwright who would later become one of the better known youth referees in the area. The Bank has a player who immediately goes to the top of my recruiting list. An Irishman; Eddie Crossan. I learn that he played goalie for Derry City when they won the Irish Cup. So he breaks the mould—a goalie who really is a superb forward. He's one of those "One move" dribblers with a classic hesitation stutter step. You can see it twenty times and know its coming but you just can't ignore the body language which always gets you leaning the wrong way and … whoosh … he's gone. He also has a shot like a cannon. Yep, I'll definitely need him.

The following Sunday I get my first glimpse at our "Arch-rivals" Athletic Attic (A sports shop) who are based in Manassas, Virginia. Their Captain is Alan Ross who I come to admire greatly as a player but hate intensely as an opponent! Isn't that what good rivalries are made of? They also have John Velesz; a burly striker who is a handful to defend. His dad Frank goes around all the amateur and youth soccer gathering data and clips it altogether in a Newsletter. This pre-dates computers and so it's literally pasting and photocopying dozens of snippets. However when I look back at one that I saved it preserves a wealth of historic football information. I'll come back to it in detail later. It is clear that I'd waste my time trying to recruit Attic players for the Lions. We take great satisfaction from a 1-1 draw which keeps us comfortably ahead as they've tied (drawn) another and even lost one.

Next we meet Soccer Supplies (also named for a sports gear shop) and although we beat them 4-2 they play some exquisite one touch passing stuff. In fact they seem more intent on quality passing than scoring and end up relegated that season. They'll be right back up. The players I covet for my master plan are the Milone brothers (Paul and Greg) but they run the team and the business which sponsors it so not much hope.

We get a bit complacent in the second last game of the season and lose a 0-1 squeaker to Bolivia. What I see in Bolivia (and Arriba Peru) reminds of the Peruvian national team in the 1978 World Cup. They have some brilliant ball skills and have a fairly simple system where they overload the midfield to one side or the other after a feeling out period to decide which is more vulnerable. They play on waves of momentum and often overpass around the penalty box which costs them many good scoring chances. Of course when one of their elaborate moves comes off it really does come off! You can also kill them off with early goals and they lose interest. However on this day they score early and stay very interested and we fail to break them down.

This puts us into our last game against Ken Jones' Iron Skillet Rangers needing a win to clinch the title. After a cautious, pedestrian first half we're down 0-1. We give up a penalty and a great character called "Lefty" (Greek I think) beats Peter Thomas with a cheeky flick of his left foot crossing behind his right! As always we flow better down the Turkey Run slope and dominate the second half for a 4-1 margin. Tommy Kaufman proudly collects the trophy from Ken Jones and I have my first American medal. But wait it's not a medal. It's a bright yellow patch, about four inches diameter and embroidered with circular red writing:

"Northern Virginia Soccer League Champions Fall 1980".

It has adhesive on the back so that it can be sewn and/or stuck on a bag or Jacket. Mine is still in a drawer somewhere.

Most of the team ends up in my basement for an impromptu tourney on my recently acquired pool table. Despite half a case of Budweiser Norrie Barker shows some deft touches with the cue. Skills no doubt acquired in Leith bars. The Rockville mob leave late and they're feeling no pain.

I also get a representative shirt that season as I'm selected to the Northern Virginia Select Team which gets to play against the Washington Diplomats of the NASL. About mid-season I get a phone call from Ken Jones to tell me I'm on the select team. I have to be at Robert F Kennedy Stadium (RFK) Auxiliary field at 3 p.m. Wednesday. RFK is the stadium used at the time by the Diplomats (NASL) and the Redskins (National Football League) and formerly by the Senators (Baseball) before they left for Texas (Now the Rangers) in 1971. Washington is lobbying for a replacement pro-baseball team. They'll have to wait a very long time!

Morph to present day—The Washington Nationals have started play back at RFK and will move to a new state-of-the-art ballpark in 2008.

I don't actually know where RFK is at this stage. I ask around and Sgt Dave Smith volunteers to take me as he'd like to see the game and meet the Diplomats' players if possible as he's a regular fan at their games.

We head down Mass Avenue. The furthest I've been so far is Union Station but we carry on beyond and I get my first proper look at South East DC. There are some fairly dodgy looking spots and an abundance of corner stores with neon booze advertisements in windows protected by wire mesh. Mind you that particular feature is not so much different to some spots in the schemes of Edinburgh and Glasgow nowadays. I can't help notice that the people on the streets are almost exclusively Black and Dave confirms that the demographics in S.E. are so much different than N.W. where we spend most of our time. He says it's a similar situation around most of the major US cities. It emphasizes to this naïve newcomer that real integration has still got a long way to go.

We finally reach the Stadium and circle around the right side to a small parking lot by the Auxiliary field. The "Dips" use it for practice and it certainly looks by far the best surface I've seen thus far stateside. The Dips are going through training (real training from what I can see) at the far end. Ken is standing at his car with the obligatory ciggie hanging from the right side of his mouth a bunch of shirts draped over his left shoulder. He is missing several players and thinks they may have lost their way which would be no surprise for someone headed here for the first time.

He recognizes Dave from the Lions.

"Got boots with you?"

"Probably 'av in the car yeah."

"Then you need to get them on, you've just been drafted into the team!"

Now Dave would never mind me saying he was a steady, reliable fullback and that the Lions appeared to be the pinnacle of his fitba playing ambition. Yet here he was suddenly thrown into a game (albeit a friendly) against the guys he's been watching all season from the terracing (well actually the seats as RFK is all-seated). I can tell he's both chuffed and a nervous wreck simultaneously.

Ken throws us a jersey each (yellow with red sleeves and collar) and tells us to help ourselves to (blue) shorts and (white) socks from a cardboard box sitting by his car. The bold mix of colors seems appropriate. The few pictures I'd seen of soccer in US always seemed to have over elaborate color and style combinations. There is a proper badge on the shirt showing us as representing NVSL select and apparently we get to keep them. I don't know their players yet except for that new guy they've signed; Johan Whatsisname? Oh … used to play for Ajax … Barcelona … Holland? Lithe frame and wispy long hair. Cruyff, that's him. Knew it'd come to me! Imagine. Even if he plays for a few minutes Dave and I have a great story to tell. I may even put it in a book someday. Alas, he's nowhere to be seen. Probably too valuable an investment to risk in this format.

Even without him the Dips have us heavily outmanned. Dave has the arduous task of trying to cover Bobby Stokes (who got the winning goal for Southampton when they upset Manchester United in the classic 1976 FA Cup final). Bobby gets bored by half time having already scored a hat-trick and takes himself out. They're also taking the chance of giving some of their younger players a run and of course they are going full pelt to try to prove they're ready for first team play. I end up mostly trying to cover Billy Steele (ex Rangers/Dundee) which forces me into a very deep (non-creative) defensive role. How can someone known for his voluminous intake (and subsequent party antics) in the bars of Georgetown run around this much? They thrash us 9-0 and that's taking their foot of the pedal for the last fifteen minutes. Frank Schoon (Soccer World F.C.) has our only serious shot on goal. With hindsight, had our full squad made it (seven selected players did not) we could have given them a decent workout. Another time perhaps.

Still it was fun being involved despite having little chance to make any impression on the Dips' coaches. They even lay on a few beers. Dave enjoyed rubbing shoulders with the pros and became good pals with "Stokesy" and "Steely" who subsequently attended our soccer club socials quite frequently. When Dave dropped me home Bunty took our photo in the very American strip and I presented him with a framed enlargement as his farewell gift when he got posted.

So I played on the RFK practice field and saw the RFK stadium but what I really wanted was to play inside in a real game in front of a real crowd. Time to get down to business.

33

THE STUFF OF DREAMS

Our first Christmas in Washington is fantastic. There's so much to see and do. The Americans go mad with lights outside their houses. The house one block up from us on Williamsburg Boulevard has an incredible display including a life size Nativity scene and life size choir boys on a balcony complete with piped music. Twenty four years later it's still there. Incredible. A simple slow drive around the neighborhood keeps Dale totally amused.

We've got to know some neighbors by now. Immediately next door we have "The Frenchies" an older couple who are, you've guessed it; French. I told you how we are with nicknames. They're real keen outdoors folk and have a cabin in the mountains. They like to go there on weekends. Monday morning Dale comes out of the house ahead of me. She shouts;

"Dad, Dad, Rudolph's sleepin' in Frenchie car."

I say "Sure darlin'—he's probably tired from pulling that big sleigh around"

As I get to our car and walk by theirs I see what she means. There is a fully grown buck lying in the back of the Frenchies' jeep (hadn't started calling them SUV's yet). It's so cold outside and of course in the car too, they've deliberately left their hunting prize in this makeshift freezer overnight!

"He's so cute" (she's already picking up the lingo).

"So he is pal" and so dead, I'm thinking. Bloody shame.

The Frenchies also have two cats which spend as much time around our garden as they do theirs. I'm sure they have French names but they become Lion and Caithness to us. Lion is grey and fluffy and tends to keep his distance. Caithness is Ginger and White patches and very sociable. Caithness goes AWOL for a couple days and we eventually hear meowing from Dale's bedroom. Turns out that Dale has decided to keep him and so she's tucked him in her bottom dresser drawer! We explain that she can't do that!

Caithness also spooks me one time as he just "appears" in my car's rear view mirror as I'm speeding along the beltway. What a fright. Transpires he had taken a nap in the space where the convertible roof retracts.

Opposite us are Lane and Paul. Lane fits our stereotypical mental picture of the young American Mom; tall and slim with fair hair, smiling with a few freckles on her upper cheeks. Paul's a budding Lawyer. They have a son Paul junior. He's ages with Dale and they've already become playmates. They're all amused by our quick adoption of Big Paul, Wee Paul to differentiate. Next to them is Mr Lymer, an old retired government staffer who passed through Scotland as a GI en-route to fight in Europe. The Celtic scent stuck in his nostrils and he's still interested in all things Scottish. He always has a bundle of questions most of which I can answer.

We also have Alan and Judy who are much more off-beat. Judy does a lot of (Catholic) church stuff and Alan is a (no longer practicing as far as I could tell) Jew from Brooklyn. Alan was a childhood Brooklyn Dodgers fan. Sadly when they moved the team to California he was so upset that he mostly lost interest in the sport. When he talks of Ebbit's Field you can sense real passion. Through his stories I feel some parallels between my fitba and his baseball. Also, based on Alan's vivid depictions of his early youth, running around Brooklyn and New York City as an eight year old doesn't sound nearly as different to Pilton as you'd imagine. Over the years I meet many old true "Dodger" fans who have forsaken the game for life. Just can't imagine how I'd have felt if Hibs did a runner to another City.

Further along there are Mark and Kathie, New Zealanders who are with the World Bank. Their daughter Sarah and Dale will become great pals.

Next door to them is Jerry "The Colonel" who still runs hard every day despite being retired from his beloved Marine Corps. I make an immediate connection with him through the fitba. The marines are headquartered at Quantico and they have a team in the NVSL. Of course they are fit as fiddles and give us a good run but we generally beat them on ball skills. However they have some useful players the best being their player/coach a guy called Bob Johnson. Bob is off Scots hence his self confessed soccer addiction. He's always good for pre-season matches as they have their own nice fields at Fort Belvoir, about half way between Washington and Quantico. He was posted away and we lost touch.

Next time I hear of him is in an article in the Scottish Sunday post where he is organizing fitba matches in Kuwait during the first Gulf war. They've picked up the Scottish/fitba connection and of course the fact that he's now a General adds some extra spice! Only downside was the article mentioned his family affinity for the Hearts! You've all heard of "Rambo" but I bet you didn't know there was also a real "Jambo". Jerry remembers Bob well from their early USMC days.

So we're well settled in and being much better off than we ever have before, we make a trip to Toys R Us and buy a ridiculous amount of stuff for Dale on Santa's behalf.

New Year is very different than in Scotland. There's a big build up towards midnight but then things tail off very quickly. Bunty saves me from embarrassing myself as too much "Bell's" has me proposing to do a once round all the neighbors at about 2 a.m. Graham of the White convertible is English but was good pals with a Scot and he stops by on New Years Day with a lump of coal for which he receives several large Scotches (which is what the Americans call our Whisky). I decide that we'll need to get something a bit more traditional organized for next Hogmany.

The British Embassy Soccer Club holds its "winter" meeting early in the New Year. The agenda is packed and I've already started stirring things up. Tommy Kaufman has agreed to let me become Co-Coach of the Lions. He'll do the administrative stuff and I'll take training and pick the team. I've managed to sign my number one target; Eddie Crossan. I've also got "Branco"; ex-Red Star Belgrade and a former Yugoslavian international. He's a good age now but stays in shape and can still play a solid squad role in this unlimited subs situation. I try hard for Bruce Craig but he's loyal to his very strong Takoma Wolves squad. I've met Billy Duff another Edinburgh guy who I remember as a decent keeper. His old man used to play for the Jambos but more on him later. Billy is carrying extra weight but he's still pretty mobile. I sign him as back up for Peter Thomas who's charging style leaves him prone to injury.(Though not as much as it does his opponents!)

I've still got my eye on the two Tigers but try a different approach. I table an item on the meeting agenda which would certify that the Lions/Tigers formally adopt a First team/Second team system with movement between the teams. I open the discussion bluntly by saying that as we are first division and they are second it makes perfect sense. Athletic Attic, our arch rivals do it. This sets of a firestorm led by Tony Bell and Karl Horsham the Tigers' leading lights. It'll take them both many years to forgive me! Even some of the Lions are uneasy about it as they used to be Tigers. There is clearly not enough support for my proposal and it gets rejected in a show of hands. We then have to endure Eddie Koebke's impassioned pleas for reduced club dues for "Students" and he's our only one. It passes unanimously as we're all frightened he has a follow-up speech.

A guy called Mike Scully who is better known for rugby in the area has tabled a motion for us to adopt his NVSL third division side "George Washington Exiles" as a "Pub" team. I suspect he's mainly after access to the Social club bar but at least it will provide a game for guys who can't make the Lions/Tigers or just want a slightly more relaxed approach. This one passes easily and Scully buys drinks all around.

My gloves are off and I immediately get to work on Donnie Kraft and Abby Jama over a beer telling them they're far too good to play in the second division. Donnie's another graduate of the Maryland University team. His work rate is incredible and he's extremely competitive, even in practice. Abby's from a soccer background too. (African extraction) I can tell they both want to make the move but are struggling with loyalty issues and Karl and Tony are selfishly playing that card hard. Loyalty is something I value greatly so I do have some empathy but these two players clearly belong in the top flight.

I feel them wavering and throw in my ace.

"Look lads training starts next week and I mean real training. I have one main objective for this season. The NVSL cup final is being played in a double-header with a Diplomats game at RFK in June. I intend for the Lions to be in that match. I fancy our chances for the NVSL "Double" (League and Cup) too. We might also be a threat in the State (Virginia) and nationals but that may take another year or two. Now if Karl or Tony were good enough what d'you think they'd do?"

Abby's a very proud man and asks; "you've signed Crossan so where would I play?'

"Both wings. I see you both switching back and forth shredding most of the fullbacks I've seen so far" (except perhaps Kip Germain of Annandale, he looked pretty useful).

"You put a decent cross over and you know that John Muir will put it away. Besides by June it'll be so hot we'll need depth well beyond our starting eleven."

Selfishly, I think subbing in and out isn't for me personally but that doesn't mean I won't take advantage of it.

"Think about it. Let me know. I'll give you a week 'cause if you don't come over some other lucky guy will be playing at RFK in June instead of you."

Sarge Dave Smith moves in. Dave knows my agenda and his more relaxed approach might help the case. Before they leave the bar, Donnie's name's in the book. Abby is still thinking it over. Abby calls next day. He's in. Good lad, thought he'd come around.

I've decided that with the short season, getting a few games prior will make all the difference. The marines will be good for a game but then Tommy tells me that the "German Military"; a second division team, are having a pre-season tournament at their GM school field, perfect. Rock on Tommy (if you know it, you'll get it) put us in.

I also need to do something to shed us of the "Inglan" kit. I approach British Airways for sponsorship but they drag the process out for ages. A poor advert for their marketing at the time. Pan Am hear we're looking for new kit and contact me, offering full funding of a light Blue kit if we'll put the Pan Am badge on it. I have no problem with this. We end up with Man City gear and taking this sponsorship causes a good deal of correspondence within "The Wash"; the embassy monthly magazine of that time. All I have to say on that is B.A. had first shot. If they had existed at the time, I venture that Mr Branson would have had us plastered in Virgin symbols in any colors we wanted within days.

Tommy and I appear in "Washington Travel Magazine" summer 1981 edition. He with the Pan Am Sales Rep (Dolores Welling) who cut the deal (we got nice kit bags too) and me holding the previous season's league championship trophy. The distinctive Pan Am badge is deliberately featured. Now there was a time when anyone from Europe landing in America who had ever kicked a ball was presumed to be a great player. I met many who made little effort to refute this often flattering mantra. However "Scouts honor" (And you know how dedicated a boy scout I was) I honestly did not encourage the skewed caption which accompanied my photo. It finished "Meikle, who played professionally for Edinburg in Scotland, has made the British team the number one amateur club in the Washington area." By the way the spelling of Edinburgh in the quote is not a typo. Americans tend to drop the H off most European cities and refer to them as "Burg" rather than "Burra". Anyway if you give the quote a selective read you can rationalize it. I did play for Edinburgh (Thistle) and I did play for big money as you know from my heady West Calder days. The "Number one" thing is a little premature but I'm also about to make that true too.

I land one more bonus before the season starts. Word is getting around that the Lions have a new Scottish coach and are pushing to be the top amateur team in the area. I get a call from Casey Bahr. Casey is a graduate of the Naval Academy. He's very persuasive and articulate and from good fitba stock. His dad Walter was a key member of the USA team which shocked the mighty English in the 1950 World Cup (they just made a movie about it). That alone has me sold! He also has two brothers who are kicking in the NFL; Chris for the Oakland Raiders and Matt for the Cleveland Browns. They'll be well known to anybody who follows American football. I go with my gut. Before I even see Casey practice he's on the team. Boy was that a good decision.

So I have my squad in place and we head to the German Military School for a pre-season tourney. We're in a section with Dempsey's (their Player/coach Mario has a restaurant in McLean) and a new team; Korea. We get two 1-0 win's and top our group. I can feel us starting to come together. We meet a decent team from Baltimore (the Kickers) in the semi's and this confirms to me that the plan is sound. They are a top grade amateur team and we beat them 3-1 with Eddie Crossan in a pivotal role.

In the final we get the Korean's again. This time we've found rhythm and take them comfortably 4-0 with two goals apiece from John Muir and Malcolm Edwards. It's quite nostalgic as they both played on the Lions together as far back as that 1969 national amateur championship team. So a pre-season trophy is in the bag. A good start then which helps everyone bond and buy into the forward plan.

We open the season well again with three victories and all the new men amongst the goals. Soccer World, fresh up from the second Division give us a real run in the second game but we get by them 2-1. Our only slip is a draw against lowly United Virginia Bank. The Tigers start with three straight losses with no goals for and ten against. Donnie, Abby—likesay; you can thank me later. Even the Exiles are doing better. They have three draws courtesy the acrobatics of Syd Boyne in goal. The indominitable Mister Scully even gets on the score sheet salvaging them a late draw against White House Realty. God knows how many pints he chugged to celebrate that goal.

The Lions are going well but will still need some tweaking for broader competition. We go down 1-2 to Espana in the State Cup at Turkey Run. They are by far the best team I've seen since coming to the states. They'll be the benchmark for our progress.

We get to the last league game and predictably it's between us and Attic for the title. It's at their Ben Lomond Park in Manassas. We need the win, a draw will do them. The heat is oppressive. We play one of our best games but cannot break through against Alan Ross' stubborn defense and when we do get past that the attic goalie; Tony Antefermo, pulls off some spectacular saves including a Gordon Banks-like backward stretching tip over which I am sure is already in! The best goalless game I've ever played in. So Attic has the league but my master (Cup) plan is still alive. Stoked by a few cold ones, Eddie Koebke, Billy Duff and I still manage a hearty sing song in the convertible on the ride back in route sixty six; an appropriate road on which to "Get our Kicks".

In the cup quest we've already dismissed Woodbridge and Puma with ease then labored by Bolivia in the quarters. I get our first goal but take a Red card following a skirmish with a Bolivian midfielder. They often deliberately bait key opposition players and on this occasion I bite like a sucker and they happily trade red cards to get me out of the game. More critically; this also gets me an automatic ban for the semi's. We play Alexandria at Turkey Run and I feel helpless as we lose two soft early goals and trail well into the second half. Abby Jama has been inconsistent to this point but he takes this game over in the final twenty minutes, laying on goals for John Muir and Eddie Crossan and adding two of his own, including a spectacular solo effort. Mission accomplished. Soccer World await us in the final at RFK.

There's even more good news from home. Hibs have strolled to the First Division Championship and will be straight back into the Scottish Premier League. Even sweeter; they will pass the Jambos on the way as they have finished rock bottom of the SPL and are going down. The English Premier hasn't quite started yet but Aston Villa take the English First (Top at that time—no Premiership yet) Division title ahead of Ipswich Town and West Bromwich Albion. West Ham United is also headed back to the top flight where they belong having won the second division by a mile.

So to 24th June 1981 at RFK Stadium, Washington DC. You know the dream where you're always scoring the winning goal in a cup final seconds from the final whistle? It would finally come true for me.

The Dips game is at 7 p.m. so we are scheduled for a 5 p.m. start to get the crowd warmed up. I'm still a bit iffy about directions so Dave Smith agrees to let me follow him down there directly from the embassy. This means no opportunity to pick up Bunty and Dale a little disappointing for such a big occasion. We are there nice and early show our ID's and are directed to the old baseball dugouts which we have to use as changing rooms.

With it being such a big occasion and with such a full squad I've removed the mystery at training and announced my starting line up as well as laying out some initial strategy. This will be subject to in game review as always but the main message is that we'll use everyone as it will be over 100 degrees in the tight confines of the stadium. I'm also giving up a forward to start an extra midfielder. Soccer World has a kid called Matt Addington and he gave us fits in the first game as a deep lying forward. I'd like to quiet him down early. This means Abby starting on the bench despite his semi-final heroics. He calls me and informs me that if he isn't starting he won't come. I explain that I'll do what's best for the team on a given day and that he'll still get as much playing time as he can handle but ultimately it's his call. He never shows! Pity.

In the two weeks since our last league games Soccer World have rested up and we have trained hard. I met Frank Schoon and he smiled and said; "This one will be about emotion more than anything, Jim." Whilst I agree emotion will be key I also want my entire squad as fit as possible as we know how hot it will be.

After just five minutes Frank's prediction is looking good. Soccer World come out flying but relaxed and we are collectively tentative. Sarge Smith is so nervous he pukes up on the sideline. Eddie Koebke, slots right into his place. Jimmy Gavargis is bubbling in the middle and crosses for Addington to score on a diving header. Jamal Hadad adds another two minutes later. Then Peter Thomas makes a great stop on a potential third and you can see the ripple effect on our team. We calm down, start knocking passes around and taking control of midfield. Casey Bahr gets one back with a tremendous long range rocket shot and John Muir ties it on a feed from Johnnie Kerr. I then get us ahead 3-2 on another long range shot which takes a kind bounce off their sweeper on the way in to fool Mike Dempsey, their excellent young keeper. The half ends with us in control. A couple thousand watch the start of our game but by the start of the second half the main Dips crowd is flowing in.

The second half flows and Soccer World even things up after about an hour on a great run by Junior Philips. Addington again plays a role. Normal time ends with us deadlocked 3-3 so it's on to extra time; 15 minutes each way. By now we have over seventeen thousand in the crowd and they are into our game. The Dips and Jacksonville Teamen (ex Boston hence name!) are dotted around the edge of the pitch waiting to get on. Legs are starting to wilt in the heat and there are good chances at either end. At half time of extra time I have to stay off to get a cramp treated. Branco spells me. After about five minutes of massage from Tommy I'm good to go. As I come back in Johnnie Kerr catches my eye and says; "Right Jim, stay up front." He's got the experience so I take his advice and wave Eddie Crossan into midfield.

With less than a minute to go Johnnie makes a mazy run across the penalty spot and back heels the ball into my path. He has everybody leaning the wrong way and I take it in stride, slotting a hard right foot shot into the low left corner. It barely gets by Dempsey's stretched fingertips. The crowd reacts and it's total exhilaration as I collapse in joy a la Charlie George for Arsenal in an early 1970's FA Cup Final. Soccer World barely has time to kick-off before the final whistle sounds. I push Tommy forward for the trophy presentation as an acknowledgement of his great unselfish season where he did all the hard work and played sparingly.

The press is all over us and there are reports and photos in all the local papers. For a fitba daft laddie it doesn't get any better than this.

I have great difficulty finding my way back to Virginia and run out of petrol (gas) on Spout Run. I'm rescued by a passer by. I'm still too wound up to sleep and anyway I don't need to, likesay, I've already had my dream and it's come true.

34

THE OLD GUY WITH HIS NOTE PAD

I mentioned the Frank Velesz newsletter. It deserves more coverage. I'm guessing it's typed on a creaky old manual typewriter amongst piles of paper on a well worn desk. It's typed in columns which are then manually pasted together onto 8 ½" x 11" sheets approximately three columns across. Cuttings and photographs are then pasted into every available gap. There are also a few logos and adverts dotted around which perhaps get Frank a few dollars to help defray his expenses. It typically ends up as four pages photocopied back to back on extra large paper then folded in half to pamphlet form. It looks extremely "Home made" a bit like the "Clipped" notes a modern movie serial killer might send to tease the police and press without revealing handwriting. However what you realize years later is that the content is so much more important than the presentation. In just trying to confirm a couple of facts for my book I realize just how valuable a historical soccer reference it is. Just taking me as an example; it's loaded with all sorts of connections to my fitba interests, past, present and future, Virginia, America, even Scotland and England. Let's just broadly assess one edition so that I can better illustrate my point.

The one I saved is "Metropolitan Washington SOCCER BULLETIN number 21 of July 10th 1981." It has a passport sized snapshot of Frank identifying him as the "Publisher". It hasn't copied very clearly but his trademark "Harry Worth" glasses over the graying thinning locks leave no doubt who it is. It shows rates of 35 cents per copy or a $10 annual subscription for 26 issues. This one's a bumper issue with two supplementary pages. I saved it mainly because the leading photo (credited to John Defreitas) is of Tommy Kaufman, Dave Smith and Billy Duff holding the NVSL Cup which we had recently won (well Billy is actually holding a bottle of champagne—shocker). I'm sure Tommy didn't mind being referred to in the caption as one of the "Happy Britons".

PAGE ONE CONNECTIONS …

On the front page I find a team picture of Annandale Rovers who have just finished third in the nationals (McGuire Cup) at Under19 level. I recognize the coach; Pete Johnson who produces a string of outstanding youth teams ably assisted by John (West 'am) Lamb who now works at the embassy. John is heavily into the coaching and Annandale is a national leader in bringing the latest developmental techniques from Europe, especially Holland which always produces a disproportionate (versus population) stream of top players. The feeling is that the secret is in their early (8/9/10 year old) handling of talent. John and I have some great debates over the merits of modern technique versus those of poverty induced street training! Pete ends up as one of the leading referees in the area. He and I get on much better off the field than we do on it.

Before and between the two main Amercan Pro-soccer leagues of our times; First NASL(1970s/Early 80's) and now Major League Soccer (MLS—Mid 1990's to date), a plethora of regional semi-pro leagues always kept a high level of play (if not income) available to the top tier players emerging from college. The newsletter reminds us of one of these; The American Soccer League which boasts teams from Carolina, Detroit, Rochester and Cleveland in the "Freedom" conference and teams from Pennsylvania, New England and two from New York (United and Eagles) in the "Liberty" conference. Pennsylvania is clearly the dominant team at the time with eleven wins and only one loss.

Summer coaching visits are prevalent and we're informed that Jake Gallaher (Irish) and Peter Hein (English) both FIFA rated coaches are hosting clinics in Annandale and Fairfax. The Dips have upcoming fixtures against Toronto, Montreal and Minnesota. We also get the French Cup semi final results; Bastia 2 Lens 0 and Saint Etienne 2 Strasbourg … blank? A typo? Quick Strasbourg fans get on the phone to home. Besides this there are a slew of details from various youth tournaments.

PAGE TWO CONNECTIONS …

This is priceless. We get a detailed listing of NASL leading goal scorers and goalkeepers. It reminds us of the difference between NASL and MLS. The former was heavily dependant on imported players, mostly in the twilight of their careers whereas the latter has strict limits on foreign players forcing the development of their own US talent. It's working, I can assure you. Anyway back to these lists which are likely to tickle you're nostalgia buds. No surprise who the leading scorer is. The one and only Giorgio Chinaglia of New York Cosmos fame. He's now the gruffest, deepest commentary voice you'll ever have trouble understanding. He actually makes great points during games but only the very experienced fitba listeners are likely to fully understand and appreciate them. He's the prototype of Italian American male. If he wasn't a football player he would have made a great mobster or at least played one on TV had the "Sopranos" been going at the time. He's well ahead with 20 goals and 9 assists. In second spot is Brian Kidd, Atlanta, with 14 goals and 3 assists. Fifth; Teofilo Cubillas, (Scotland's nemesis in 1978) Fort Lauderdale, 10, 6. Sixth; Gordon Hill, Montreal 9, 6. Seventh; Duncan McKenzie, Tulsa 8, 8. Twelfth; Peter Lorimer, Vancouver 5, 10 (notice the assists. Stop passing, start shooting Peter—hardest shot I ever saw, then, now forever!) Fourteenth; Steve Daley, Seattle, 8, 3. Fifteenth; Francois Vand der Elst, (the great Belgian) New York, 5, 9 and twenty second; George Best, San Jose, 6, 6. The Goalies are topped by Barrie Siddall, Vancouver and include Kevin Keelan, Tampa Bay, Keith Macrae, Portland and Phil Parkes, Chicago (see what I mean about twilighters?).

I mentioned that Tony Kornheiser of the Washington Post is my favorite sports columnist. His "Alter-ego" at the post nowadays is Michael Wilbon, a displaced Chicagoan from Northwest University who I also love to read. They even have a national TV show together on ESPN called PTI—Pardon the Interruption in which they argue over the hot sports stories of the day. Wilbon is Black and not afraid of some of the more delicate racial issues that still transpose sports (more coaching than playing issues at this point). I would have excluded soccer from the controversial category nowadays but a recent incident in Spain (where England's' Black players were brutally berated by the crowd) throw us back into the mix. Of course I would not have cared a hoot if the Spaniards had berated them over just being English rather than Black! Anyway here in this obscure newsletter I find a reference to Michael Wilbon (Who could have only just got here to Washington) and a colleague, Joe Ritchie, counting votes on behalf of the Professional Soccer Reporters Association. Perhaps Wilbon is a secret soccer fan?

There's also a story explaining that some local boys have made it on to the US Under 17 ½ Eastern Region Select; a big honor. One is Matt Addington (Bishop O'Connell High School, Arlington, Va) who just gave us fits at RFK. Another is Todd Hitt (the Virginia building family) from our local high school, Yorktown which my kids will attend in due course. I've watched a few of their games and singled him out already as a potential star. He's very much in the Strachan mould and even has the red hair and serious on-field grimace. He goes on to play for the University of Virginia. I end up having a couple of games alongside him in my own "Twilight" stages. I hear he's heavily into the coaching side now and I suspect he'll surface at the top levels eventually.

The same page also covers the national success of a Maryland based team; Montgomery United Ponies U16. They're coached by our own Johnnie Kerr and another Scot, Gordon Murray the Pro Golfer at the Bretton Woods Country Club on River Road. Both have sons who are stars on that team; John Kerr Junior and Bruce Murray. More on these two later.

Pete Mehert also gets a mention. He's the soccer Coach at American University and I get to know him well. He keeps the nucleus of his squad together in the off-season in an indoor league at Northwest High School in DC. I play along with them serving as a mentor to some of his younger guys. He brings a slew of great players through the AU programme including Mike Brady and Richie Burke. He eventually gets his team to the National Championship (NCAA) game at the Kingdome in Seattle against UCLA (University of the City of Los Angelos). I'm frustrated as the game is live on television but we have to leave for the Ambassadors' annual Christmas party. We have a good time and detour to Lums for some grub on the way home so I'm surprised to find the game is still on. At first I assume it's a re-run but then I realize it's still live. They don't have penalty kick tie breakers at the time and they go seven or eight "Overtimes" before losing a heartbreaker in a game that spans several hours! Possibly the longest of all time?

SUPPLEMENT PAGE CONNECTIONS …

The supplementary pages are filled mostly with results from a massive summer tournament called the "Robbie". To put it in perspective there are one hundred and seventy results listed and that's just "Some" according to the heading! There's coverage of a controversy over one team; McLean Stingers trying to field … a girl on a boys' team—Allegra Millholland. The committee let Allegra play and her team get a 3-3 tie with Wheaton. For reasons not given they do not allow a fifteen year old Danish girl to play? It won't be too long until American girls make their mark on soccer. Denmark is one of loads of countries represented. Canada, USA, Mexico, Australia, Sweden, Scotland, England, Northern Ireland, Eire to mention but a few. I pan down the list and smile to see two teams from my own youth; Hutchison (Hutchy) Vale and Tyncastle (Tynie) Boys Club. This is likely the equivalent of the tourney Mark Curtis and Jim's Boys Club used to come for in the early seventies.

There's also "All regional" team selections with the name of John Stollymeyer (Jefferson High School) jumping out at me. He was a great player whom I got to play with and against much later following his very successful college career at Indiana. His sister is mentioned on the all girls team—a soccer family I guess.

There is also a fascinating summary of the refereeing arrangement in the NASL at the time. They are all "Part time" at this stage (i.e. it's a secondary job). The referees get $150 dollars per game, Senior Linesman $90, Linesmen $75 and fourth official $50. They also have guest referees over from Europe. They get $180 per game. I remember that Ken Jones is good pals with David Syme, one of Scotland's top refs at the time. David always does a couple of NASL games when he comes to visit Ken. It mentions that officials who do play-off games also get a "Souvenir" but this is not qualified?

Gene Mishalow, who played in the futile game against the Dips for NVSL, also gets a mention for the success of his Under 12 Virginia Cardinals who inexplicably are listed as wearing White—surely it should've been Red! Talking of colors, no connection but I have to mention one of the more creative names of one of the girls teams listed; The Bowie Lemon Frogs! I guess it's safe to assume they wore yellow?

PAGE THREE …

Has a harsh critique of how little impact Cruyff is having for the Diplomats. It also has an advert for "Soccer Bowl '81" which is to be played at Exhibition Stadium (Toronto) on September 26th and one for a Girls' soccer camp at Pine Lake in the Pennsylvania Pocono's. There are pen pictures of a few Toronto Blizzard players and they include Jimmy Greenhoff another ex-Manchester United star.

PAGE FOUR …

The back page has all the subscription info as well as recent action shots from local youth games. It has local results which remind us of the variety of leagues;

MC CO-ED LEAGUE (Strikers, Monolyth).

NATIONAL SOCCER LEAGUE (Takoma Wolves, Iran, Laos, LaBergerie, Intipuca)

MID-MARYLAND SOCCER ASSOC. (Americans, Olympiads).

GUATEMALA LEAGUE (Guatemala, FAS, Aguilas, Mayas, Quetzal, Aucas).

TAKOMA PARK SOCCER ASSOC. (Everton, Takoma Park, Sligo Creek, Hyattsville).

These are just a few local examples from dozens of leagues which existed.

Local soccer enthusiasts would know all this but readers from Britain might be surprised to hear of the shear volume of fitba played and this is before the real explosion leading to the expression "Soccer Mom" where almost every youngster plays in some form of league by age five and Mom predominantly does the shuttling around, typically in minivan carpools. The ultimate playing pool both male and female will be tens of millions (no shock that the US national team have recently broken into the top twenty in FIFA world rankings).

So thanks Frank for all the times you hung around at the end of our games to gather details of scorers and sorry for the unreliable data provided by the likes of Messrs Winney and McHale who often told scoring fibs (lies) just to get their names in "The Bulletin".

35

A TRIP TO THE BEACH

Big news on the home front is the Royal wedding between Prince Charles and Lady Di. Just prior Charles makes a visit to the embassy and we are invited to drinks at the Residence. I'm told the best way to meet a celebrity at a do like that is to try hard not to! There are people constantly planting themselves in his path as he wanders around the room. I observe carefully and conclude that he breaks the boredom by consciously avoiding the stalkers. We stay on the terrace as it's a lovely night and sure enough he wanders out and makes a bee line to us. He shakes our hands, asks our names and then with his classic move separates his overlapping hands and waves his right approximately back and forth at us and asks:

"So, are you two married?"

"Yes, sir. Almost six years now."

"And so do you have any advice for me Jim?"

"Well sir … just don't let it interfere with your sports."

He smiles and says; "Thanks, I'll keep that in mind."

Of course I don't think he was much for fitba, more of a Polo man as I recall. He moved on to another group who were making no effort to stalk him.

The fall football season was always going to be a let down after such an exciting Spring/Summer but there are compensations. We make our first trip to Florida to take Dale to Disney World. She's at a great age for it and it's absolutely everything it's cracked up to be. We have as great a time as her except for when I misunderstand what "Space Mountain" is and end up riding it with her (I'm terrified of roller coasters). We would go back many times over the years with our other kids and always have a good time but that first visit really was magical.

I fulfill two more ambitions by driving the convertible on Daytona Beach (Bunty and her sister Carol also take a turn of this) and by attending a genuine drive-in movie theatre. There's none of these left in Washington area but we find one in North Florida and decide to go regardless of the fact that the only movie playing is "The Texas Chain Saw Massacre". The sound comes through on our radio via an AM station number. It's very cool, just like in the original Grease movie. Of course I can't get chummy with Bunts with Carol and Dale in the back. Unfortunately we have to put the car top up as we are besieged by Florida's version of Midgies and have no bug spray. We also visit the Kennedy Space Center and then have a few days at a beachfront hotel called Fantasy Island. They have "Boogie" boards there and Bunty I get a bit carried away "Surfing" in the ocean and both end up sunburned. Of course it's only later at night under the bright electric lights of "Gilligan's" restaurant that we really see how bad it is. We both have that embarrassing shiny red glow on our cheeks, nose and forehead which says to everyone; haven't heard of SPF 30 yet. A few Pina Coladas dull the pain. We even get to see the fantastic spectacle of the space shuttle taking off whilst my kids are nonchalantly making sand pies on the beach.

I do get to make another appearance for the Northern Virginia Soccer League Select this time as Captain against the touring Royal Air Force—Strike Command team. We play them to a 2-2 tie at the 23rd Street Park in downtown Washington. They are a high quality side and we are also loaded. The game deserved a much better field. Alan Ross, Gene Mishalow, Greg Milone, Ken Krueger, Eddie Crossan, Mike Demsey and Kevin Scannel are some of the faces I recognize from that team picture.

The embassy has a Halloween fancy dress dance and I have this brilliant unique idea for a costume—I'm going to be Rubik's cube which is at the height of its popularity. I get one of the 30" square heavy duty cardboard boxes which carried some of our personal baggage here. I buy the appropriate colored card from the drugstore and get to work. Using shiny electrical tape to define the seams I'm very proud of the result. I have one square cut out in the top for my head to fit through and the centre cube on either side "Hinged" so I can open them and stick out my hands for food and drinks and dancing. I'm convinced I have the "Most original Costume" prize wrapped up. We decide to drive in through Georgetown which is typically wild and fascinating, especially when Halloween falls on the weekend. I'm totally devastated when two other "Cubes" overtake me on the GW Parkway (bastards). Still, as it transpires I'm the only cube at the embassy party so I must be a lock right? But no; the judges bypass me for an Egyptian, a Jester and a f**kin Fairy. Can you believe it? After several Brandy/Cokes I am convinced the judges are all fairies too but Bunts manages to persuade me not to share this view with them. I get over it quickly and end up doing a pretty respectable "Twist" in my cube. One of my squares gets severely torn by an over enthusiastic pirate in the inevitable last Conga line. This was just before "New York, New York" supplanted the Conga and "Auld Lang Syne" as the ultimate party ender. As usual we stop off at Mario's on Wilson Boulevard in Arlington on the way home for some of their classic booze absorbing subs. It's one of the few places serving grub past midnight at the time.

The Lions' season is predictably disjointed with several players (including yours truly) missing chunks of it via injury and/or travel/holiday ("Vacation" here) commitments. The results reflect this and there is no silverware to add to the trophy case. Before the season's even done I'm plotting a few more adjustments to go hard after the State Cup which is the Championship of Maryland, Virginia and DC combined. To get passed the likes of Espagna we'll have to make a few harsh, mercenary moves.

I suggest to Tommy that he becomes non-playing Manager but he is not interested and resigns and signs to play for the Tigers in the spring. Peter Thomas, yet another closet centre forward of a goalie also moves to the Tigers who are willing to let him play up front which I refuse to do. This poses a problem as Billy Duff, despite his extra weight, is still very good but has a penchant for some very heavy Saturday nights which make him a bit unreliable for 9 or 10 a.m. Sunday kick offs. We draft in Jim Cowley's boy Neil and hit the jackpot as he is first class.

Dave Smith has been posted and Branco has moved into a "Veterans" league. Terry Bell has gone to the Bulldogs where he'll play a bit more under Scully's new Manager; Alex McAdam. Things start to look up when we get Mike Dillon in return.

No offence to Terry but this is one hell of a deal for us. Of course we won't lose touch with him as a stream of us will make regular visit his salon in Georgetown (ILO, one of the best in Washington, he co-owns it with Gary Walker, another Embra man) for discounted haircuts. Mike Dillon is ex-Tottenham Hotspur. He's came over to play in the pros here but recurring knee problems have cut that short. However, at our level he is still one hell of a player. He also gets the coaching job at Georgetown University and asks me to take over when he eventually moves to Texas. Unfortunately my work schedule can't accommodate early afternoon practices so I have to take a pass. Keith Tabaznick takes the job in my place and he's still there! I also get Nigel (Noig) Ellacott from the Bulldogs (ex Luton Town). He's got a sort of Elton John (hair departing early doors and the perfectly round glasses) look but it's deceptive as he's a fast, skilled midfielder and is as "'appy ti put it abatabit" on the field as he is with the ladies too.

I get another great break when, out of the blue, I get a call from Mark Brennard who's just arrived in the area and is looking for a game. Turns out he's also former English league (Northampton Town) and still relatively young and in great shape. A serious upgrade.

My biggest disappointment is at not being able to pry young Stevie Winney away from the Tigers. He's an aggressive, ambitious, dynamic young striker, tall and slight with a cascading wave of red hair. He pulls it out of his eyes every few seconds and it immediately falls back over them. Imagine how good he'll be if he ever gets a haircut. He's still got a couple of freckles on each cheek which accentuates his youthfulness. He really should be attracting college soccer scholarship attention. He's certainly selling himself short in the second division. He seems to appreciate all of this in my persistent talks with him but still won't move. I've even failed in my back door bid to get his parents, Trevor and Freda to nudge him our way. Pity. He coulda, shoulda, woulda been a Lion.

I have one more go for Bruce Craig but he bleeds Takoma Wolves and they have they're own plans for the State Cup. They have a contingent of Jamaicans some of whom have played pro so they are indeed a force to be reckoned with.

To round off the master plan Johnnie Kerr suggests that we sign his and Gordon's boys for State Cup play only. They'll have turned seventeen making them eligible. Johnnie thinks it'll do them good to get a bit of "Blooding" against the men as they prepare for college and we will get the benefit of pure youthful blinding speed. A fair trade then—done. As it transpires they both go on to tremendous college careers; John Junior at Duke and Bruce at Clemson where they win the Herman Award (National college player of the year) in consecutive seasons. Both also go on to become seasoned pros and regulars in the US national team. (A bit more on this later too)

So we're set and when we put out our top line up on the field we should be a formidable force. Unfortunately travel and injuries prevent us doing so in league play and we lose twice which is enough to kill our league hopes in such a short season. Likewise in the NVSL cup where we lose another squeaker to Attic.

We do manage to get our "A" team out for State Cup play and charge to the Semi Finals without a serious threat. We draw Stihl Chain Saw of Norfolk away. I'm a bit miffed as I think the semi should be on neutral turf but Ken Jones explains there is some kind of rotating system for balancing home advantage between regions. We did get to host Richmond and a Virginia Beach teams in previous rounds. Likesay, fair enough then.

So we have to travel to somewhere around Hampton Roads, close to Virginia Beach to the appointed pitch. This is a three to four hour trip, depending on traffic. We decide to hire a mini-bus and I have the usual fight with the Tigers' Committee members over us having the Lions' (no pun intended) share of club funds (can I help it if they never progress far enough for a road game?). Noig volunteers to drive and we meet at the embassy for pick-up. A couple of stragglers get us off to a late start. Despite this we have a good laugh on the journey down and a few dollars exchange hands at cards.

We do indeed have a much shorter than ideal loosen up after what turns out to be about three and a half hours in the cramped minibus. Stihl live up to their reputation as a strong classy side and have an outstanding young Scottish striker who's apparently from one of the local college teams. He's put two goals in before we find any rhythm and Stihl are far too good a side to spot a lead. We play very well in the second half and get a boost from the two youngsters off the bench but we still end up going down 1-3. I'm still convinced we take them if the travel role is reversed.

It's a hot day and someone has the bright idea that we should pop over to Virginia Beach "Just down the road" for a quick conciliatory dip in the ocean. Sounds fine except that it actually turns out to be about another forty five minutes away. We make the briefest beach visit ever, load up the minivan with beer and start the long trip back. By the time we hit Washington most of us are feeling little pain and card games and grossly exaggerated tales of fitba glory are flowing freely. Not a bad day, even in defeat.

Despite a disappointing fitba season I do manage to add a bit of silver to my collection. Anyone for tennis? One of my farewell gifts on leaving HQ Scotland was a Slazenger tennis racquet (the other was a Scotland strip) and it's now getting regular use. The ambassador has a court and allows staff to use it during lunch break. I've become quite keen and quite competent or at least I'm starting to think so. The embassy has annual championships and I get through a couple of rounds in men's singles. Then I meet Wing Commander Stokes. He's supposed to be pretty good but explains that he's been having chronic back trouble. So we delay our match until the absolute deadline.

I'm thinking he'll just concede but he insists on playing. We knock a few practice balls back and forth and he looks as if he's hurting. I feel a bit awkward about playing at such an advantage. So he wins the toss and elects to serve. He proceeds to dink a little underhand serve over the net and it has lots of spin and kicks off to the side. I make no attempt to even play it. What the f**k was that; I'm thinking, though this is not the place for such expressions. I ask;

"What was that Peter?"

"Why that was a serve old chap. Underhand. Quite legal you know. Fifteen love" and he swaggers over to the let court with a smirk.

I'm thinking "underhand" alright. Right, that's it. No more Mr Rosewall politeness to respect the cripple. From now on it's all mercenary McEnroe, Stokesie-my-boy.

Problem was, even with his chronic back, he was brilliant. Had me running all over the court whilst he stood effortlessly in one spot looking almost bored. I didn't even manage to win one game; game, set and match to the justifiably smug bastard on the other side of the net; 6-0, 6-0. "All you need is love" right? Except in tennis. Another serious lesson in humility then. I felt slightly better when someone explained he was a former tennis and squash champion of the entire Royal Air Force. No doubt what he spent his Wednesday afternoons doing.

Anyway I was lucky enough to get Pat the telephonist as my partner in the mixed doubles. She didn't exactly look the athlete and was in her fifties by now but its one of those sports where high skill and experience allow you to play on years after you might have to quit other sports. She is a good balance to my constant running/chasing and we manage a runner-up finish for which I get a little silver bowl. Cool.

36

IN SEARCH OF A GOOD SIGNAL

Remember what it was like before likesay; Summer's in Arlington and Flanagan's in Bethesda existed? Sure, in the twenty first century I can meet Russell Barclay and old George from Leith for a pint at breakfast time and see almost any Hibs game against the Old Firm. Not so long ago it was oh, so different.

We are all a bit starved for soccer coverage from home in the early eighties. This is true whether you're from Europe, South America or Africa (the latter is just starting to emerge on the world scene as a serious international football threat, they've come a very long way from Zaire in 1974). The mass migration of players to wherever the big money is has not really started. Most players still play within their own countries and certainly their own continents. There is no Internet yet.

Even just getting relatively fresh results from home is difficult. I subscribe to the Washington Post (its current rival Washington Times doesn't even exist yet and another potential rival The Washington Star has a very brief run before going bust). At the time my reading of the Post consists of a quick squint at the front page headlines. Short of war or major catastrophe I bypass this to the "World News" and scan the "World in Brief—Europe section" for British/Scottish snippets then it's quickly onto the serious business of sports. Not that I lack an interest in politics but I find a read of the British segments of the Economist magazine which circulates at work a much more "Economical" way to keep up to speed on such things.

For overseas fitba news the Post is completely random. It sometimes has a "Sports abroad" column segment within the main results page of the sports section. Frustratingly this always starts with the English top division scores. It even occasionally prints the English Second and Third division scores running out of ink space before it gets to the Scottish Premier results. I send several complaints about this and speak to others Scots who do the same. Maybe this is why they generally change over to always publishing the top division from each country before anything else. Of course the top English division stays first. Still at least they usually have Scottish Premier next, above the Spanish, French, German and Italians.

Usually inside the front page of the Sports section there is also a small piece called "Sports in Brief". This tends to mop-up items which don't merit full and proper coverage and which are often just picked off wire services (i.e. Reuters, AP). Occasionally this will have a paragraph or two with a few details from the top European games of the previous day and once in a great while a photograph almost always featuring Manchester United or Real Madrid. The only time a Scottish game ever makes this photo call is when Celtic play Rangers. Impatience for a key result almost always means a quick call home to family in Edinburgh.

We do get British Newspapers at work but even these are typically days or even weeks late by the time they make it around a very large and slow circulation route. So for printed press, early eighties, good old Frank Velesz newsletters are just as likely to keep you up to date as anything.

TV wasn't much better at the time so on the few occasions where there is genuine live soccer or even tape delayed coverage available it draws attention. Video tape exchange is also prevalent though there are constraints with regional systems. For example a tape from UK cannot be played on a standard US VCR. This means slow and expensive conversion is required and the games are well out of date by the time you see them. Other than watching your own team play great, retrospective watching can never match the excitement of a live match. A few options emerge.

THE MULTI-SYSTEM

There is a small "Specialist" electronics shop in Wisconsin Avenue called Murrells. The guy there claims he has a new "Multi-system" VCR which can be simply "Switched" back and forth to play video tapes from all around the world. They are extremely expensive (at around $800—more than four times the price of a normal US VCR) but a couple of people still get them. One is Len Muir who is then besieged by requests from new found friends to come visit him with their UK tapes.

SOCCER SATURDAY

The Canadians had a weekly soccer show which ran about two full hours on a Saturday morning and would end with live coverage of the days actual results.

IN SEARCH OF A GOOD SIGNAL   287

Surprise, surprise it was hosted by a Scot; Graham Legget. I can't say I remember him as a player but apparently he was a winger for Aberdeen. The show was a comprehensive wrap of the previous weekend's action around Europe. It would go around country by country showing highlights and goals and end with extended highlights of one top English game. The good news was that the Canadian VCR was US compatible. I made a contact in the mail room in the High Commission in Ottawa and sent him a box of blank tapes. He would tape the weekly show and send it down early in the week. It was a great treat to receive it and it would be passed around a load of people.

CABLE TV

The cable boom is still fairly new. ESPN is just getting started and using the obvious established US sports (American football, Baseball, Basketball) to cement its place in the industry so soccer gets very little exposure, especially with NASL folding around the same time. Fox Sports World isn't even a blip on the horizon. The best bet for soccer coverage at the time is the "Spanish" channel. There are several now but at that time "Univision" was it. You'd get a few live international games, mainly from South America. You'd get league games from Mexico, Peru, Chile, Argentine and Brazil. You might even get the European Cup final once in a while. The fact that you could barely follow the commentary mattered little. In fact even now I admit to occasionally watching a game with Spanish commentary which is also available with English as the Spanish commentators exude so much more raw passion which transcends the language barrier. Their guy Andres Cantor who does the "Gooooooooooaaaaaaaaaal" call was around way back then but has been made world famous by the vastly broader soccer coverage here in recent years. There was also a weekly show called "Soccer made in Germany" featuring a "Bundeslega" (top German Division) match from the previous week shown on the PBS (Public Television) station. You could get this with a decent UHF Loop antenna but the reception through cable was always better. Some of the games were excellent but the commentary must have been dubbed in later. It was a guy called Toby Charles and he had a very dull monotone voice. Once in a while he'd get a split second ahead of the play and announce a goal before the shot was even taken!

POOR ROBERTS PUB

Satellite coverage is barely started. There's a bar called "Poor Roberts" on Connecticut Avenue in a little strip mall just north of the Washington Zoo main entrance. It shows the FA Cup Final live and ends up packed to the gills regardless of which teams are participating. "Summers" in Arlington, Virginia will ultimately take this concept to the limit with multiple soccer games showing in various segments of the place and fans happily handing over twenty dollars a pop to watch their teams on TV. In some cases it's more than a ticket to the actual game would cost.

SOCCER BRIGADOON

The only way to see a Scottish game live is to make the five or six hour drive to Kearny, New Jersey. Kearny is "Scotland" in America. Just west of the New Jersey turnpike approximately level with Manhattan you find this odd little enclave which has traditional Scottish Butcher and Bakery shops dotted along its main street. You can get a mince pie or Bridie which is as good as any you used to get in Crawford's or Martin's in Edinburgh (though something called Greggs seems to have taken over nowadays). You can even get real sausages and bacon which is distinctly different and vastly superior to the American versions thereof. And of course the Scottish Sunday Post and Mail newspapers. The demand from ex-pats for all this stuff is so high that "Wee Charlie the Sausage Man" as he is affectionately known, makes the trek to Washington from Kearny once a month with a van filled with meat and pastry. He also loads up with a ton of chocolate bars as you could not get the British sweeties over here at that time. He does brisk business at the back door of the embassy despite the hefty prices. Kearny also has two social clubs; the Scottish and Irish American clubs respectively which show Celtic and Rangers games via satellite. No prizes for guessing which is which though the guys who make the trek up say they are well received in either or both. My first personal look at Kearny comes years later when Johnnie Kerr makes a detour enroute back from a semi-pro tourney at Great Neck to buy pies! We eventually make a family stop there as a side trip from New York and see the "Brigadoon" main street in full flow. The butchers and bakers are exactly as advertised but neither club is open that day.

Even beyond the narrow selfish confines of Scottish football coverage both the print and TV Medias in America are relatively colloquial or at best national. For example, though cable has now changed things considerably, "Local" news is still incredibly narrow with very little outside the beltway making it onto a full hour of nightly coverage by channels 4(NBC), 5(FOX), 7(ABC) and 9(CBS). The Posts world news coverage is slightly better now but still far from extensive on most stories. Likewise it's new rival the Washington Times. So what is the best option for keeping up to speed with things from home pre-internet availability/affordability to the public at large? … Good old radio—of the short wave variety.

The BBC World Service, though I say it with admitted bias, gives you more of what of genuine importance is happening around the world in a thirty minute brief than the entire above do in a day. Even better you get football results and a brief summary of the bigger games at least a couple of times a day. On Saturday morning you get a two hour sports show with live coverage of a key game and constant updates from the various football grounds (and other sports in season) around Britain. To the BBC's credit, Scotland gets a reasonably proportionate share of coverage. Just one moan. They have strictly allotted "Airtime" slots and once in a while the first run of "Classified" (i.e. Final) results occasionally gets cut-off. Because they use the traditional English divisions 1,2,3,4 then Scottish Premier, 1,2 … format it means that they sometimes get cut off before getting to Scotland's Premier scores and I have to wait a further forty five minutes for a reprise which they run on one of the Caribbean frequencies! You might think I'm over sensitive on this but it doesn't seem right that I've listened for two hours and know that Colchester have beat Northampton (no offence to either) but still don't know if Hibs have held onto their lead against Aberdeen!

However in these early days a decent short wave radio is an expensive proposition and I don't yet own one. They are also still relatively big, bulky (maybe 15" x 12" x 4") and have heavy square handles and manual (as opposed to digital) tuning. Actually few individuals own them but we have a couple in our Press Office which are available on loan for the weekend if you're well in with Len Muir or Neil Matthews. I am and this no doubt explains to a few readers why Len sustains a starting spot on the Lions through my managerial tenure! Anyway, once in a while I borrow one of the shortwaves for a big match. It's an early 1980's England versus Scotland, one of the last before a Maggie Thatcher ban put a stop to the oldest (and arguably most exciting) rivalry in international soccer. Can't say the exact year. Suppose I should look it up—no doubt what real authors do (or what research assistants do for the established ones) but since I'm just writing for fun here I'll settle for early eighties.

So Len's let me borrow the radio to keep his starting spot and explained what the multiple dials are for. He's also given me a few frequency options as you can pick up the North American transmission on various different ones. They are very odd, exacting numbers like 15300 point something. I have them scribbled on a piece of paper for ease of reference which is a civil service cliché for too thick to remember stuff of more than four digits/letters.

It's Saturday morning around 8:45 am and I fire up the radio by way of a trial run. I twiddle around the various oversized dials and they make high pitched whirring sounds as I get near, and then pass the perfect reception point. Apparently "Stewpot" (aka Ed Stewart former serious disc jockey) should be on with his now global version of his Saturday morning kids' requests show. I smile thinking that was a programme David and I sometimes listened to when I was younger just to hear radge songs like "Granddad" by Clive Dunn (of Dad's Army fame) and "My Bruvver" by Terry Scott (of Terry and June fame) David could manage a pretty good goofy rendition of that one. It's a delicate process to hit the frequency just right. Len has advised me that I may have to move around and tip it up and down (and do the hokie kokie and twirl around) to get the right signal. It reminds me once again of the good old days in Scotland when my dad or father in law might get stuck in a kung fu pose with the antenna so that the rest of us could see the game on a decent picture.

"That's it. Stop. Keep it right there dad. Don't move."

"Do I look like a bloody contortionist?"

I end up moving outside the house on my front doorstep listening to a reasonably clear "Hello murra, hello farra" dedicated to a guy called M'buto from Kenya (amazing how quality music transcends cultural divides). Of course this is another personal favorite of mine and I hum along. I even know what poison ivy is now that I've lived in Virginia for a while. This is definitely the spot for the game broadcast. I go back inside and put on my Scotland shirt on and start to get myself wound up (psyched as they call it here).

At kick-off time I pitch myself on the lower front step and have the shortwave cocked and locked on the previously successful frequency, cold Lowenbrau in hand. Alas I now have a serious crackle and can barely hear. I shuffle forward towards the street and it clears again right as I reach the edge of the sidewalk. I plant myself on the curb. The commentary breaks up for about ten seconds out of each minute but its good enough to follow what seems like an even flowing game.

Suddenly Alan Schulman appears from his house diagonally opposite. He's not you're your conventional North Arlingtonian. He does wear the shorts but for some reason always with big tackety boots and hiking socks. He's spotted what he recognizes as a fairly serious short wave radio and wants (no, needs—radios to him are like fitba to me) to have a look. He explains that he's an amateur "Ham" and loves all things radio communication.

"Zadda shart wave Jim?"

"Yep, I'm trying to follow a football ... eh soccer game from home, BBC radio; World Service"

"Cool. I listen to their news sometimes. It's priddy good. Who's playin then?" and he sits on the curb.

"England, Scotland; Oldest international fixture in the world" and I offer him the background from my totally biased perspective. This is pre-Braveheart. Now the one thing we have to thank Mel for is his film saves us a ton of 'splainin the auld enemy stuff to the average American.

"So you call Soccer football right. It's like … trying to kick a ball in a big net right?"

Likesay; "Yep"

"Never tried it myself, more of a stickball/baseball man" and he continues;

"This kinda reminds me of Brooklyn days. Used to sit on the street with a little transistor listening to Dodgers broadcasts from the mid and far west on balmy summer nights."

That's it he's got me. Brooklyn Dodgers. Don't know too much about baseball yet but I do know a little Brooklyn Dodgers. They're sports history and folklore. They're fitba's Leith Athletic, St Bernard's, Third Lanark, Accrington Stanley and the likes all wrapped up together in a bundle. Baseball relates to our fitba in the sense that it's rickety old stadiums with specific smells and peculiarities around them and arguments over the merits of players from different eras and the odd cheating scandal. It's pure nostalgia and I love it.

This is as much conversation as I've had with him and we're both enjoying it so the next question's obvious.

"Fancy a beer Al?" (See; the fact that I've shortened his name reflects respect and warmth already).

"Sounds good" and he pulls up his sleeves a little like he's ready for a serious drink.

And I'm thinking. Wow. The previously guarded Al's gonna have a beer with me—sitting on the street curb too. So we have a displaced Jew from Brooklyn and a homesick Scot from Edinburgh united over a beer and sports. Is this a great country or what? Al soon takes over as chief tuner. He's fiddling with a vengeance and suggests we move about ten yards to the left to upgrade reception. We shuffle past the Frenchies and the radio is floating out and in with disjointed commentary.

The game progresses and we hear little of it. Before half time we're on beer three and much more interested in exchanging nostalgic youthful stories than the game itself. Al's explained to me how at seven years old he can take the subway into Manhattan on his own, sneak around Macy's toy department and be back for dinner. This sounds much more like my own upbringing than anything I've heard from the Americans I've met thus far. He even tells me how he and his mates swam in the Hudson River, jumping in off the pier without the luxury of lifeguards to keep an eye on them. I explain about Cramond, the Almond, leaches and all. More bonding.

Around the one hour mark Scotland get a penalty and John Robertson is taking it. He steps up and … we lose reception. Five minutes later we end up across the other side of the street and finally the commentator confirms the good news;

"Scotland still leading 1-0 on the Robertson penalty kick"

"Yehhhhhhhhhhh" shouts Alan with a clenched fist. He's as loud as me! Little Katie Baird keeps her tricycle a safe distance away from these two dads acting strangely.

I should clarify that this is not our family Robertson. It is JR the elder and he's a bit chubbier. One of Brian Clough's Nottingham Forest gems. A deep lying left winger who has one simple "Stop-Stare-Start" move which mesmerizes defenders. Then he whizzes down the left wing at a speed you would think him incapable of and whips over deadly out swinging crosses. An old buddy of Martin O'Neil he's now Martin's assistant at Parkhead.

Alan and I interrupt Brooklyn/Pilton life comparison conversation to throw in the occasional cheer as we shunt our way up and down North 35th street in search of decent reception. By noon we have a 1-0 Scotland victory and Alan is in no doubt of what this means to me and the average Scotsman. Soon thereafter I'll help Alan string a serious wire antenna over his entire roof so that we don't ever have to struggle for reception again!

To emphasize the TV coverage futility—I see a rerun of the game advertised on an obscure early cable station a few days later. I watch. Scotland is awarded the penalty just as they go to commercial break. When they come back Scotland are up 1-0 and I never will see the damn goal. They still haven't quite got it.

Still against England; a win is a win is a win!

And Ally's army which has finally passed into the hands of The Big Man; Jock Stein, has added a very unlikely Brooklyn Jew to its fan base!

37

YET ANOTHER GALLANT FAILURE

In the fall of 1981 Scotland strings together an excellent run of results to become one of twenty four finalists (from an original field of 105 teams) for the 1982 World Cup Finals in Spain. The mascot is a football playing Orange called Naranjito! We come out of a section which includes Sweden, Portugal, Northern Ireland and Israel. Even better, N. Ireland also make it through with us. That other lot just south of us is also through for the first time in a while.

It is a reflection of the strength of British Football at the time. This comes on the end of an incredible run of six consecutive European Champions cups going to an English team. (1977 and 1978 Liverpool, 1979 and 1980 Nottingham Forest, 1981 Liverpool and 1982 Aston Villa) This "English" dominance chokes me much less than you'd imagine because all of these championship sides are a broad mixture of English, Scots, Irish and Welsh players, managers and coaches but before the invasion of the continentals! When they played against anyone other than rival British sides, these teams enjoyed very broad support across the whole of the United Kingdom. We'll come back to how that works on the international front a bit later on. Suffice to say it is somewhat different, at least in respect of Scotland.

We do actually find live coverage of the 1981 European Cup final on one of the Spanish cable channels. It's a dream match up with Liverpool in their prime against Real Madrid who are fast returning to the dominant echelons of European Club football. My basement is packed out with the Kerrs and Cowleys, Duff, Winney and McHale amongst others for a 1-0 Liverpool win on a most unlikely late solo goal by "Barney Rubble" a.k.a. full back Alan Kennedy.

The same channel is showing the World Cup Games so my basement is also well booked for those. In the first round who do we draw? Surprise, surprise; Brazil again. This time along with a dogged, stuffy Russian team and the first timers from New Zealand, at least a couple of who are ex-pat journeymen from home. The Kiwis even have an old Jambo on the Staff; Jimmy Cant. Of course we Hibees always added the word "Play" on the end of his name!

Brazil takes Russia 2-1 in the first game after trailing at the half. They have all their flair back but seem to take long rests between waves of sheer brilliance. We do what's expected against New Zealand easing to a 3-0 lead before getting a bit complacent in the second half and giving up two soft ones. So it's a 5-2 win but a bit worrying as we already know our world cup goal difference woes.

We have Brazil next and my basement is bursting at the seams. Who can forget the dream start for Scotland? When David Narey of Dundee United turns Brazilian for a split second and strokes a tremendous bending shot into the top corner early on my neighbors must be wondering what the hell is going on based on the volume of the jubilant screams. However scoring just serves to awaken the Brazilians from their slumber and they start a soccer samba. Amazingly we keep it at 1-1 until half time but they come out even looser in the second half and dance around us for three more wonderfully crafted goals with poor Alan Rough again rooted to the spot watching balls bend passed him in a ridiculous manner. We're a very decent side but they're simply in a class of their own that day. Final 1-4. Despite the result the kilted masses party all night with the yellow shirted dancers producing some of the most colorful photo opportunities a fan photographer could ever wish for.

Still we're well in the hunt. Russia have also taken care of New Zealand 3-0 and we assume Brazil will do the same in their third game (they do 4-0) so it's down to ourselves. If we beat Russia we're through. Another disaster which you couldn't script if you tried. We play well and lead but end up in a 2-2 tie thanks to one of the ugliest defensive blunders you'll ever see at this level. Alan Hansen (Liverpool) the prototype smooth, composed sweeper clunks into a fellow defender with little imminent danger and they both stumble clumsily to the ground leaving the ball free behind them. The Russian striker nips in to convert the gift with a clinical finish. For the third consecutive World Cup we're undone by goal difference and so it's an early "Adios" from us to Naranjito. Mind you one thing we have plenty of at home is wee Orangemen.

Both N. Ireland and Thingummy make it through to the second group stage the latter eliminated from a deadly group with Germany which also extinguishes the high hopes of host; Spain. N. Ireland can't get passed Belgium and Poland. France are probably the second best team in the competition and look set for the final until the Germans add yet another last ditch comeback to their long repertoire and sneak past the deflated French on penalties.

The Brazilians are definitely the most talented team but young Paulo Rossi gives them a clinical lesson in smash and grab finishing as Italy eliminate them 3-2 and go on to beat the omnipresent Germans 3-1 in a very exciting final. The lasting memory is of the eyetie sub; Something..elli or etti or iggi with no teeth, wild hair and berserk eyes and the most ungainly stride, taking papal-like acclaim with his twirling palms after sliding home the clinching third goal.

Towards the end of the year we have yet another revamp of the British Embassy Soccer Club and this time I've conceded that work and family commitments will prevent me from continuing as player/coach. With Tommy gone and other potential leading lights moving on, the Lions will fold for the time being. The Tigers cash in on this demise with a few of our players moving over to them but I don't get an invite which is really no surprise.

I'll just wait until spring and see who needs a player.

38

JINGLE BELLS, JINGLE BELLS …

With Hibs and Hearts bouncing between divisions, proper local derby matches have been few and far between. They try to fill the void with "East of Scotland Shield" matches and the fans try their best to care but I suspect most get little satisfaction from these. When we do eventually get a proper one there is little or no chance that we'll find it available on TV anywhere in America.

The embassy Hibs' contingent is at an all time high with four genuine (i.e. Regular boyhood attendees) supporters all overlapping for about a year. Ron Gilchrist is an RAF sergeant who's turned to golf now but he's still a loyal Hibee.

Big Tam Cullen is even more diehard than me and I have to step between him and Billy Duff to prevent a good old fashioned pagger (an Edinburgh word for fight) at a party as the banter gets a wee bit too serious following too many pints!

The other Hibee is Charlie Carr and Charlie provides me with yet another wonderful small world moment. I'm introduced to him at a "Pub Lunch" social in the "Crown and Eagle"; the old embassy bar and we get to chatting. Right off the bat he asks;

"So it's Jim Meikle right M-E-I-K-L-E?"

"Aye, that's right Charlie."

"And you're Edinburgh right?"

"Aye, originally Albert Street but I was raised mostly in West Pilton"

"So before you say anything else let me guess something".

I'm intrigued and purse my lips and nod "Sure."

"Your dad is John Meikle, 27 Ferry Road Avenue."

I'm really taken aback.

"How'd ye know that?"

"Because son; I used to be your postman."

"Yer kidding me, right?"

"I'm not. I remember that name and address, clear as a bell—top flat right hand side—opposite the old Pennywell School. The blind man Mr Fraser was right opposite you; he used to get some brail mail".

"Surely ye cannae remember every address you delivered mail to Charlie?"

"No but some stand out."

"So how come my dad did?"

"Simple. I was fitba daft tae and I delivered postcards your dad got from Dunfermline Athletic Football Club each week telling him where to report for pick up on Saturday. Mostly Waterloo Place from what I remember. I always wanted to knick one but it was more than my job was worth."

This is amazing. I squint my eyes and imagine away the graying temples and the Mexican mouser he now sports and sure enough there's our old Postie fae Pilton—Wow.

I also loved those postcards a few of which are still in a drawer in my dad's. I used to take them out and show off to my pals should any of them doubt my story that my dad was a professional. They were proper printed things about 3" x 5" with the official D.A.F.C badge and all. The format was also printed but with blank spaces for the vital time and places to be written in biro.

And so it transpires that Charlie, like quite a few other Scottish guys from the old General Post Office (GPO) were recruited to various government communications departments down South.

I remember his favorite Hibs story. He lived on Bothwell Street just outside the ground and he and his pals managed to sneak in one time through an inadvertently unlocked gate (the old invalid car entrance). The nets were actually up and they managed to get in about five minutes of "shooting in" before a disgruntled grounds man chased them all for their lives.

"Mind, I've scored at Easter Road". He'd always say with a really hearty laugh which made his shoulders bob up and down. He also managed to represent his country once which we'll come back to in a wee while.

So there are four of us and we're ganging up on Billy Duff (the lone Jambo at the time) at every opportunity. I have to keep reminding Billy to check his temper but he's desperate for some payback and we find a civilized alternative; subbuteo.

We've had a night out at "The Bottom Line" at 17th and "I" Street and Billy's ended up on my basement sofa. He awakes to Dale hauling toys out of a box including one of my subbuteo goals.

"Subbuteo?" says Billy immediately.

"Daddy's game" replies Dale immediately.

"D'ye play subbuteo Jimmy?" says Billy as I clump down the basement stairs with a coffee.

"Aye. Huvnae fir a while though"

"I'm brilliant at subbuteo" says he in his usual totally confident manner. I'm thinking; anything you're not brilliant at Billy?

And so it is that we develop the concept of holding a proper New Years Edinburgh derby match right here in Arlington, Virginia, US of A!

We'll hold it on January 1st 1983, traditional three o'clock kick-off and invite any football fans who show the vaguest interest and designate them to support one or the other. Of course we know Hibs will have at least a few real fans!

We recruit Ron Twigg as commentator and John May as referee. We do have one of the little plastic referees but he'd have no chance when Billy and I get at it! The invites go out and we split the preparations. Billy will do the programmes and I will get the teams ready. Subbuteo hasn't reached the States yet so I'll have to make do with what's left in my box. I do have a respectable basic red and white team so I'll convert them to jambo maroon with some "Airfix" model paint and the tiniest brush I can find. My Hibs are a bit broken and depleted but fortunately I've had two lots over the years so I can pull together a respectable eleven and give them all a fresh coat of paint too!

I get to work and if I say so myself I do an excellent job. The players are fresh and shiny in Emerald Green/white and Maroon/white respectively and I've even given them proper numbers on the back of their shirts. The pitch is spread immaculately (not a single crease) on my pool table with corner flags and my best set of nets. The pool table light makes perfect floodlights.

Of course Billy has taken the opportunity to vent via the programme which he has no doubt printed at the IMF (International Monetary Fund) without permission. They're obviously not keeping him busy enough either. I'll give you an overview, corny though it is.

It's a basic legal size sheet folded to form four pages. The front cover has "Tart of Midlothian" facing "Hibernating Hibs" and is of course marked "Offishul". I'm not sure if this last one is a joke or just his genuinely crap spelling? There's space for a picture but that will have to be inserted later.

Inside the cover are a few "Adverts" including one for Brattisanis "Lovely Fush and Chups". This page also has a quiz section which he's called "Is it True?" featuring the following:

… Hibs supporters think Sheffield Wednesday is a holiday …

… George Best doesn't drink … (Mercenary Billy, mercenary) …

… Hibs bought 500 hot water bottles from Boots the Chemist to use as an underground heating system for the pitch …

It finishes with; "A word from Bobby Parker—Hello" (A man who says little apparently)

The opposite inside cover has the teams (Set out on an old 2-3-5) and he's given me no say in the selection, leaving out Stanton just to torment me. Here's what I end up with:

FIBS green

NAEBODY,
ANYBODY, SOMEBODY,
CORMACK, MEIKLE, LITEMACK,
BEST, WORST, HOOEVER TURNSUP, B.R.OTHER, A.N.OTHER

Of course he's been much kinder to himself and the Jambos:

FARTS maroon

DUFF (Not sure if that's himself or his dad who really did play for them—more on that later too)
CLUNIE, SHEVLANE (who eventually saw the light and crossed over the city)
MACKAY, (Dave not Gary for sure!) ANDERSON, CUMMING,
YOUNG, CONN, BAULD, WARDHAUGH, HAMILTON (Not sure which?)

He's even given himself subs:

CRUIKIE (JIM CRUIKSHANK THE GOALIE)
BATTLES
THOMSON (Eddie)
MOLLER (Mop haired Scandinavian)
WALKER

I can't believe he passed on Donald Ford. Probably because he knows I actually like him.

The back cover is a big T (ennants lager) advert with a final jab at me via another advert for "JIMMYS TOOL WORKS … but who cares".

Several beers and even a few whiskies have already been consumed before kick-off. The fans crowd around the table and Ron does his best John Motson. Despite my rust and Billy's prior bravado I am clearly a much more seasoned subbuteo player and Hibs cruise into a comfortable three goal lead courtesy Stanton, Best and, of course; Meikle (c'mon indulge a man and his fantasy please).

Billy recognizes he's on a loser so adjusts his strategy to try to have the game abandoned by kidnapping Jim Meikle, flicking Peter Cormack into the top left pocket and snapping poor Georgie Best's legs at the knees with a cruel vindictive press of his big spongy thumb.

He's quickly given a red card and the result is declared final; Hearts 0 Hibs 3.

Ron presents me with a tiny plastic trophy which we've acquired for the occasion. I do a lap of honor and one verse of the customary New Year derby song, both fists pumping;

"Ohhhhhhhh … Jingle Bells, Jingle Bells, jingle all the way,
Oh what fun it is to f**k the Hearts on New Years day … ay".

Whilst the game stops, the beer continues to flow generously into the evening and a good time is had by all. There are no fights in the crowd. We still have all the photos to prove this game actually took place, precisely as described.

39

FINDING GED

We get a couple of really big snowfalls and I enjoy the novelty of digging out. The system is very simple and civic. Each occupant is responsible for clearing the section of sidewalk around your house. Everyone seems to do this very conscientiously and those too old and frail pay local teenagers a decent rate to do theirs. The end result is clear walk ability throughout the neighborhood. Another Americanism which exactly matches the imagination version is the big yellow school bus. There are millions of them. Of course as it turns out, you only get the bus if you live a certain distance away from the school. In fact most elementary school kids walk. The numbers of kids bussing it increases at Middle and High schools as catchment areas spread out a bit farther. Point is then that keeping the sidewalks clear is important so that the kids can make it to school safely.

The snow is a great consistency for shaping and sculpting. Dale and I get busy making an igloo in the garden. She's enjoying it but it's a bit like summer at Ocean City where having her there enables me to test my building and engineering skills in the sand without getting too embarrassed. Before too long we have a structure big enough for her and her pal; Sarah, to comfortably sit inside!

We head for the local sledding hill; in our case the side of Jamestown elementary. Again Dale is a great excuse for her big bairn of a dad to have some fun.

"We'll go much faster if I come on with you hon, the extra weight will make us go much faster."

"Yeh, sure dad."

See. What happened to "Aye, okay daddy"? Accent gone.

I think back to our sledding hill in Pilton; the one which split the upper and lower halves of the big field, Pennywell school at the top side Craigmuir school at the bottom. The main difference here is that many parents are here along with their kids and that almost everybody has some kind of sled, mostly the injection mould plastic jobs from Toys R Us. At Pilton we tended to have just a few sleds between dozens of kids. A good sled was a bit like a good football. It could drastically increase your popularity albeit temporarily until it broke. Breakage was almost inevitable as we would always end up seeing how many people we could balance on a single sled and one of the runners would collapse under the collective weight!

The temperatures here are generally lower than winter in lowland Scotland but it's somehow more bearable. My amateur, unscientific conclusion is that it is to do with damp! You can hap up here with the right gear and stay outside for long periods reasonably comfortably. In Scotland the cold was always somehow "Damper". The damp penetrated your bones in a way that it does not here. Now go a bit further north to New York or Boston or Buffalo and you might get a different comparison. You certainly would in Canada. Scott Porter and I worked in Montreal a couple times during mid-Winter and had to go inside buildings every few seconds just to keep our breath! I guess it's all relative. For example, in Scotland I can't remember ever getting a day off school or work because of snow or any other severe weather (though I recall Bunty always teasing me about her local Catholic primary; St Ninian's, getting a half day in severe rain and being cruelly referred to as the "Water babies" by their jealous proddie neighbors). Interesting also that a couple of inches of snow can put Washington DC in turmoil yet a couple feet barely causes a hiccup in Canadian cities.

We're starting to realize that the climate is actually one of the things we like about living in Northern Virginia. We get four very well defined seasons and rarely see the extremes which regularly cause havoc in other parts of the country. For example California has its mudslides, Florida its Hurricanes, Kansas its Tornadoes. Our actual temperature patterns are pretty predictable too. I guess the worst thing we have to deal with is humidity in August. That really gets you the first couple of years but you eventually get used to that too. So you are just about getting fed up with one phase when things move on to another. It's a bit like when, as a kid you're calendar might have well had a series of events rather than months listed. This would change a little with age but an early comparison might look something like this:

(JANUARY)	NEW YEAR GAME, 5 NATIONS RUGBY, EARLY CUP ROUNDS
(FEBRUARY)	PANCAKE DAY & VALENTINES CARDS
(MARCH)	GRAND NATIONAL HORSE RACE & BOBAJOB
(APRIL)	ALL FOOLS AND EASTER EGGS
(MAY)	HOME CHAMPIONSHIP & CUP FINALS (Scot, FA, Euro et al)

(JUNE)	MUSEUMS, ZOO, BEACHES & SCOUT TOURNIE
(JULY)	BRITISH OPEN AND WIMBLEDON
(AUGUST)	WICK WONDERLAND
(SEPTEMBER)	NEW SCHOOL BLAZER, LEAGUE CUP SECTION PLAY
(OCTOBER)	CONKERS & GUISIN (Trick or treating!)
(NOVEMBER)	FIREWORKS & BONFIRE
(DECEMBER)	CHRISTMAS PRESENTS & GOOD FILMS ON TELLY

Likewise for days within a week too though that was often driven more specifically by the telly:

(MONDAY)	(Early years) BLUE PETER	(Later) MASTERMIND
(TUESDAY)	VISION ON	TOMMORROW'S WORLD
(WEDNESDAY)	SPORTSNIGHT	SPORTSNIGHT
(THURSDAY)	TALES OF EUROPE TOP OF THE POPS	MAN FROM UNCLE TOP OF THE POPS
(FRIDAY)	CRACKERJACK	DALLAS
(SATURDAY)	DR WHO	KOJAK
(SUNDAY)	BIG FILM SONGS OF PRAISE	ROOTS SONGS OF PRAISE

Yes. Seriously. We did used to watch Songs of Praise every Sunday as it was one of the few telly things my ma liked. We would have just had a bath and hair washed with the powerfully stinking Suleo medicated shampoo. As my ma sang along with her favorite hymns she would be scraping our skull with the dreaded bone comb checking for nits! Apparently all worth the effort as you'll recall I never got a Brown Envelope. It was poor form to admit in front of anybody but I actually quite liked Songs of Praise and would sometimes sing along heartily and smile to suck up to my ma, especially when it was David's turn for the bone comb. John hardly seemed to know the words and often made faces at it behind my ma's back to make us laugh. Laughing at Songs of Praise was a serious crime punishable by it as in "You're gonna get it". Not good. John would be desperate to sneak away to the room and listen to Radio Luxembourg on his wee tranny with the cool ivory colored earplug.

See where a mention of snow can lead?

So we're settled and enjoying Arlington and I've eased off the heavy commitment of Player/Manager of the Lions for the casual weekly game with the Bulldogs in NVSL Division three. Problem is the competitive edge is embedded deep in our fitba instincts. Reinforced with a few former Lions' team the Bulldogs are suddenly in the hunt for promotion starting the season with three wins in a row! With that the "Turn up when you can" mantra quickly reverts to "You've all gotta be there".

Towards the end of the season we have a game against the "Fifth Street Players" yet another classic team name. The game is at the new "Front" field at Turkey Run. The original field has been lost to a local historical project for "Claude Moore Colonial Farm" which will be used as an educational tool for local school kids, Scout troops and the likes. There are two new fields. The front one which even has a proper car park next to it and the "Back" one which is buried deep in the woods next to the CIA perimeter fence. The walk down to it is a sufficient warm up in itself!

The front field is a good size sloping end to end (but nothing as pronounced as the slope on the original field). It does not take water well and there has been a fair amount of rain. On game day it rains again and is even a bit misty, something we don't see a lot of here. Fifth Street wears some kind of Maroon strip with light blue trim. Bulldogs are in Chelsea Blue kit with white socks. The tops are quite trendy with an understated white criss-cross diamond background. Fifth Street has a couple of decent players. Wee Dougie Painter an Ex-Tiger with the motorized arm running style is perpetual energy and difficult to escape from. Ron Bianchi holds things together at the back with the help of John Trutko and John Finch. Again good fitness partly compensating for finite natural footballing ability. Ron is an Argintinean/American hence his great love of soccer and I find out he's also rugby daft and that quite a few of these guys are rugby players first (which explains a lot).

We handle them pretty comfortably in what gradually turns into a quagmire field. In the second half I become conscious of occasional screaming outbursts of instruction from the opposite sideline. Hard to see the face because of the murky conditions and the fact that it's barely visible under a very tightly pulled navy blue hooded tracksuit top. But wait. The accent is clear. Scottish, possibly "Embra" even. My view is that Scottish accents are first divided into four main sub-categories; East, West, North, Islands, but that in itself is a little misleading as it's not as neatly geographical as it sounds. For those already tuned in through living in Scotland or even having had an extended holiday visit the easiest one to pick up is west.

For West read Glasgow. However it's not just Glasgow but a large circle taken from the Glasgow city centre and reaching southwest down the cost and eastwards half way over to Edinburgh. Most people would pick this all up as a Glasgow accent. Weedgies don't like to hear it of course but as it moves closer to Edinburgh the accent mellows out and is generally a bit less guttural. Many Americans tell me that they understand me a bit easier than the average Weedgie. Edinburgh's accent is more localized. It does spread a little down to the South and East but even in nearby Mussleburgh, Dalkeith, West Linton, Penicuik and Bonnyrigg, it's thickening up quite noticeably.

For North I think much more of everything North and East of Stirling including Fife and the East Coast; Dundee, Arbroath, Montrose, Peterhead. A gentle "Lilt" creeps in around Perth and gradually thickens as you move North East towards Aberdeen. There is the odd little "Accent Oasis" of Inverness, possibly the result of that burghs tendency to keep a relatively neutral, commercially-protective position through some of our historically turbulent times. More English influence retained in the accent but mixed with a Scottish brogue for which many people say is the purest "English" in Britain.

Immediately North East of Inverness the general thickening picks up speed again, culminating in Wick and Thurso. Generally people communicate comfortably with those in bordering accent zones. It's only when you skip a few zones there's a serious problem. For example the Wick accent is so thick and includes such narrow colloquial terminology that many of my Edinburgh pals, hearing her speak, ask if my Grannie Miller is French!

I keep saying North and East and that's because beyond the major Scottish towns, there is very little to the North West. A lot of rugged beauty of course but very sparsely populated. The Island accent incorporates these areas as well as everything from Skye up to the Outer Hebrides and around the North coast to the Orkneys.

Reasons for the lack of a South category are twofold. First, there is very little by way of populated area between the Edinburgh/Glasgow corridor and the borders region, just a big gap really. Then the borders, at the other side, are like a little sub-culture with their own distinct farm-based character and traditions. A couple of examples come to mind. Unlike Scotland generally, Rugby probably outranks fitba as the top sport and in politics, Liberals are often elected ahead of Scotland's overwhelmingly dominant Labour party candidates (something to do with the land rights and farming aspects I suspect).

Being so near the border they are often unfairly looked on by us as potential English collaborators much the same way as many Perth and Stirling natives would see us in Edinburgh as Sassenachs (anglicized lowlanders).

So the accent coming from the Fifth Street Players' sideline could well be Embra. With the game well in hand (6-2 I think) I focus in on the screaming from under the hood. Yes. Embra—no doubt. As the final whistle goes I make my way over to investigate. I get within a few feet of the tall dripping figure and prepare to introduce myself. I always prided myself on great retention and recollection (at least until I started to attempt to write this book directly from my head) and I know who this is before he even pulls down the hood or says a word.

"Gerrard Corrigan" I say.

He's flabbergasted. "How d'yae ... who are you?"

Another huge dent in my ego. I've been running around, controlling the flow of the game and he doesn't even know who I am. Despite my injury invoked fall from fame after the first year of Secondary school football, I always thought myself high enough profile via football, card-sharking, pitch 'n toss and assorted general troublemaking to be instantly recognizable. In fact I would have bet good money on anyone from school at least knowing my name even ten years down the road.

"James Meikle, St Oggie's, B's—you were left or right back right?"

"Aye, sortie recognize the name right enough."

"A wiz left wing. Marinello, Cubby, Sam Lynch, Stevie Torrance—remember?"

"Definitely remember them, aye."

"You were in 1G or 2T or 3U right?"

"Think so, cannae really mind."

"You hung aboot wi' the crowd that played wi' a tennis ba' in front o' the science block right? Big Ben (Benignus—how'd you get named that in Scotland?) Conway 'n that."

"Aye, were you in that game?"

"Not usually, too busy smoking 'roond the back of the gym"

And so we make a ton of immediate connections by the end of which Ged says he thinks he has me placed but just vaguely (whoopee). I soothe myself with the explanation that he actually went to "Prep" at St Andrews. Prep was for those with slightly earlier birth dates who left and had a few months waiting for the rest of us to leave in the summer before forming that years' class. Oggie's (St Augustine's) was a combination of St Andrew's and Holy Cross. So he had most of his pals established and would admit that he tended to stick with his own crew and all things associated with his beloved Celtic. Neither was he into school trips (Ben More) or extra curricular theatrical activities (Pirates of Penzance) or other things (smoking, gambling, and general troublemaker) through which I thought I had achieved a degree of infamy.

Still it was fun to make the connection and we pledged to get together socially soonest with families. We did so and made plenty other connections between Ged and his wife; Janet, Bunty and I. They were also a "Mixed" (Catholic/Protestant) marriage so we had a good laugh at some parallel issues and experiences though some of Ged's views and bias were clearly a bit more pronounced and extreme than mine.

It transpired that his sister Maureen had married a US Serviceman (Harvey) who had been stationed at Kirknewton near Edinburgh. They were now based at Andrews Air Force base in Maryland. They were able to sponsor Ged and Janet for a Green card. Ged was a time served joiner (carpenter here) with Miller builders and since arriving stateside had been working mostly on new housing sites but with much less permanent tenure than in the "British" system. Janet had been a clerkess at the Bank of Scotland (a lucrative job at home) so was quickly employable in the vast array of U.S. banks. They came about the same time as us and were now living nearby us at Malcolm's old enclave; "The Commons" of McLean. It would be the start of a long friendship.

40

CARPENTER UNDERCOVER

About this time I met another Scot at the embassy. Benny Lynch is a driver for the Hong Kong Office which at the time was still part of the embassy with Hong Kong under British Governorship. He was the younger brother of Joe who worked with Alex at the Dulles airport detachment. Benny had come over on a few visits to Joe and eventually come over to take his own chances stateside with wife Margaret and daughter Pamela. Like many of us, his ticket to stay here was via an embassy job and accompanying indefinite A type visa. I didn't know him that well but had chewed the fitba with him a few times in passing. He was Catholic and Celtic and named for the famous Scottish boxing champion, a hero of his dad's. He had apparently been a decent player at youth level and tried out with and against a few future senior stars. He couldn't have been totally addicted though because he'd mostly given it up and seemed at ease with that.

Benny got into a good old fashioned "Auld Enemy" argument with Dave Ramm an England diehard who worked on the gardening staff and also played left wing for the Tigers. This culminated in a bold challenge between the two to have a Scotland versus England match right here in Washington to settle the score.

So Benny comes to visit me in my office and opens;

"So Jimmy. You know a' the fitba players aroond this place right?"

"Well, aye, think so Ben"

"Know that Ramm boy on the gairdners? Big English mooth on um"

"Aye, played against him—nothing special"

"Well. We—have—got—a—challenge—going"; Benny would sometimes talk exactly like that. With a pause between each word, kind of like he was making a pronouncement.

He continues. "Scotland, England fitba match, local like."

I doubt at this early stage Benny even knows how strongly this appeals to my base fitba nationalism. What an opportunity.

"Know quite a few Scottish boys in the area Ben, some decent players. Mind you know a few decent English players too."

"See that's the thing Jimmy. We've set some ground rules a'ready—embassy connected players only."

"Mmmmmm. Likesay that might be a wee bit tougher Ben."

"Bit we cannae go back oan the challenge noo, right?"

"Naw, coarse no Ben. Jist needs a wee bit thinkin' aboot."

And so it was that I suddenly become co-manager of the Scottish national squad for the first time. I immediately pencil myself in at central midfield and debate with myself if I'll wear number 10 or number 7.

I'm not so worried about having a great team. Just one that I'm sure can beat whatever the English can pull together. The buzz is around the embassy. Dave Ramm has engaged a co-coaching team of Peter Morrison; chain smoking scouser (Evertonian) building works supervisor with whom Bunty now works and quiet, pleasant driver; Tommy Harrison whom we know from the corner stool; Friday nights at the Social Club.

The obvious starting choices are the players from the embassy teams but that only constitutes about half a team each. The balance will have to be carefully crafted. As we get to work on it what is patently clear is that the English will have a distinctive age advantage from the players made to make up the rest of the teams. They have a bunch of youngsters who, whilst not regular fitba players nowadays, are relatively physically fit. On the other hand, we have diehard Scots who once played in their dim and distant past.

Through regular chats with the young messengers who constitute a few of the English squad I am able to carefully monitor the progress of their squad.

We ink in Peter Campbell and Jimmy Smith (used to work at embassy—possibly eligible) which means we already have a quality central defense. We have me and Benny to anchor midfield and the Muirs' up front so we need to pad around that with whatever we can. As you read earlier; Charlie Carr our old postie once hit the net at Easter Road so he's in. He suggests we also bring in his son Kevin who is Scotland daft despite his broad "SKABORO" accent! Done.

Two slightly older gentlemen have heard about the game and aggressively pursue me to solicit involvement:

NUMBER ONE DIE HARD:

Mr Colin Hollomby (Sgt, British Army)

"Hello, you Jim Meikle?"

"Good. Sarn't Colin Hollomby. Used to play serious. Still play in old boys' league here. If we're playing England I'm in. Don't you f**ckin dare have that game without me"

"What d'you play Colin?"

"Against England. Anywhere you f**ckin want me to"

"Struggling for a 'keeper Colin"

"If it gits me a game against England, that'll be jist fine"

"Pencil ye in then Colin"

"Good"

NUMBER TWO DIE HARD:

"Hi, Jim?"

"Tam Cullen here. Work upstairs. Hear there's a game against England?"

"Aye, that's right Tam. D'ye play then?"

"No fir a while bit a'll be makin' a comeback"

"Where d'ye play?"

"Anywhere pal, jist gies five minutes" Once again, I sense Embra.

"Where ye from Tam?"

"Leith". See and that tells you all you need to know. Not Edinburgh and wait for you to ask where in Edinburgh. "Leith," right off the bat.

"What school d'ye go to?"

"St Mary's York Lane, Holy Cross, die hard Hibby by the way" and I'm thinking; how the hell could I not have met this boy yet?

"Yer in the squad Tam—I'll be in touch."

"Yer f**ckin right I am."

And I wonder what would have happened if I'd suggested otherwise. Mind you somebody who's a genuine Leith, hibee and that Scotland daft can't possibly be bad.

So I've added two more players but without the courage to ask their ages. Middle aged at least I'd guess.

We also add wee Jimmy Marshall from Security but I'm now reduced to looking at parentage. I steal two players from the English squad. First big Knoxie (Ian Knox) a gentle giant chef who decides to take his ancestry over his immediate national ties and Nigel Woolett from the mail room who shocks me with the revelation that his mother is Scottish and he'd rather play for us. He might be the only Nigel (this is pre Quazie) to ever be capped for Scotland and at least he's young and fit.

I then find yet another Hibee in the woodwork. Ron Gilchrist, Sgt RAF has just arrived and although golf is now his passion he'll put on his old fitba boots for Scotland. That makes four cabbages in the Scotland squad; possibly a modern record?

So the squad is pretty much set and I've seen the final English squad and done my football arithmetic. It's a close call. Experience versus youth. I immediately get to work on the psychology with the young English guys.

"You guys will be so fast, you'll overrun us" and I can tell they're biting the overconfidence bit and feeding it back to their coaches.

Benny and I get together to study the final squads. We're in okay shape. We've agreed to let them play big Peter Thomas in goal in return for us using Jimmy Smith both of whom are also former embassy staff. I try to work a similar deal for us to play Billy Duff but to no avail so Colin and Jimmy Marshall will share goalie duty.

As I study their squad I reckon one more real fitba player would likely be enough to push us over the edge; in particular; Ged. Then I find out the Muirs' are doubtful because of another commitment. That seals the deal. I need Ged.

But he has bugger all to do with the embassy and that's a problem. On the other hand, nobody there has met him yet. Hmmmmmmmmmmm. I have a plan. We have people dotted around US Government establishments in the area.

So as we exchange the final-final squads with the English Managers all's well. Except that they immediately ask who this "G. CORRIGAN" guy?

"Oh, eh, works up the road in Columbia, Maryland. Embassy staff but not embassy staff if you know what I mean, nudge, nudge, wink, wink?"

"Fair enough" says Morrison, well used to such scenarios. "Never thought of looking there for players".

"Aye, well you have plenty Peter but we were stretching for a squad. Even just drafted in Bill Firsby (Residence footman) who hasn't seen a football in years" and I can tell by his expression he's bought our underdog ploy; hook, line and sinker.

And so it was set. Thursday 23rd June 1983 at Lewinsville Park in McLean, Virginia there would be an auld enemy home away from home international.

To set the scene a well preserved copy of the Olivetti typed-circular to members of the Scottish squad marked "Scots-in-Confidence" is rounded off with the following paragraph;

"Some of the opposition have been suggesting that this match is as important as a full international match … Rubbish! This is much more important!!"

I've instructed Ged to answer any questions about his employment details as simply "Up the road" with a wink and a finger pointing North. I haven't even told any of my teammates that this is a complete lie so as to vest their sincerity in the façade.

So we come into the game with a perfect traditional scenario, Scotland; aging team—heavy underdog.

Jimmy Marshall even brings a wee radio cassette player and a tape of "Scotland the Brave" and blasts it out as we proudly take the field. Please don't underestimate how seriously we take this game. Scotland versus England at tiddlywinks would still have us wound up. The game is even better than any scenario I can imagine. We really dominate play and run out 4-0 winners. Benny got one, I got one, Ged got one when he literally walked around the advancing Peter Thomas after coolly selling him a fake move the other way. Ged has an incredibly deft touch for such a big man. None of us can remember the other scorer but it was definitely four.

There are so many highlights and all typically Scottish. Colin starts in goal and then eventually yields to Jimmy Marshall so that he can come out and mix it up a bit with anyone who's interested. No takers so after about ten minutes he retreats to the bench for a cold Heineken. Wee Jimmy rubs in salt, dribbling to halfway in his tartan bunnet with the loose bobble swinging all over the place. He's challenging anybody to come and get the ball off him, arms all over the place, Ricki Fultonesque smirk on his face. He gets too excited and loses control and has to go sprinting back to his penalty area.

Tam Cullen has had several beers and is constantly screaming "C'moan Scotlin". He catches me near the sideline. We don't need him at this point but he's begging;

"C'moan Jim, av goatae say a played in this".

He's got a pair of boots reminiscent of the ones from my own "Billy's boots" story. In fact the studs are even longer. They might even be rugby boots.

"Awright, on ye come Tam" and he spells big Knoxie who's starting to feel the pace.

He walks on and simply kicks the first innocent Englishman to come within reach of him—young Jonathan Whitetree who's genuinely shocked. Danny Brogan the neutral "Irish" referee has no choice but to immediately red card him. Tam is over the moon and quickly retreats back to the sideline full of national pride. Billy Duff hands him another cold one.

Towards the end I just can't resist. I dribble the ball to the corner and feign sitting on the ball ala Baxter. Luton Noig takes this very personally and comes storming over to have a kick at me. Good to see an Englishman who feels just as strongly as we do about this. Of course before he reaches me I'm up from my squat and have made a long side foot pass to nobody in particular.

And so Scotland get off to a great start in what will become a series of challenge matches though the English will never be suckered in this way again.

The aftermath is surprisingly good natured as most of the players from both teams and friends and families completely take over the Pizza Hut in McLean and the pitchers flow generously. My original plan is to admit Ged's "Ringer" status right there and then after the game but we are riding our victory so hard we can't possibly risk a protest so he remains mysterious and clandestine throughout the party.

My last memory of the happy drunken haze was Danny Brogan asking Billy Duff if he could split a twenty dollar bill. Billy takes it and without hesitation tears it in half and throws it back at Danny.

"Bastard" says Danny through uncontrollable giggles as he goes in search of cello tape.

Peter Thomas, the Welshman who just played in goal for England leads a hearty chorus of "Flower o' Scotland" to round things off.

A few days later Bunty was lucky enough to be in earshot for an interesting exchange. Sir John Kerr (Future Permanent Under Secretary—Head of the Foreign and Commonwealth Office) stops by the maintenance office. He's a bit less formal than the typical senior FCO official of the time and occasionally takes a wander around the embassy unannounced and asks how people are doing. A simple touch which makes him immensely popular amongst the support level staff. The maintenance team senses his down-to-earthness and can't do enough for him. They are very motivated in keeping his grand but challenging official residence in good repair. He has a fairly "Neutral" public school accent and has been away from home for many years so what's not immediately obvious is that he's a borders area Scot.

Peter Morrison is unaware of this fact.

"Good morning Peter, how are things in the works group today?" says Sir John as he lights a cigarette and invites Peter to join him.

"Thanks sir, I'll have one of these" says Peter pulling a pack from his left shirt pocket. He likes his own particular brand. "Things are good, keeping busy, no complaints sir."

"Heard something about a football match? You were involved?"

"Well, a bit passed playing sir, we had an England versus Scotland match and I did a little coaching" pushing his sliding glasses back up his nose as he did every few seconds.

"So how did it go?"

"Afraid we lost sir" clearly including Sir John in the 'WE' part.

"Oh, what was the score then?"

"Four nil to Scotland"

"Excellent. WE actually won Peter, I'm Scottish!"

Peter flushes easily and this one gets him good as he quickly flashes red from the neck upwards.

Poor Peter has another shock in store a couple of weeks later. He has a vacancy for a carpenter on the maintenance squad. He looks at me quizzically when I hand him a completed application from one "G. Corrigan".

"What the fu … Ged's the big lad who works up the road right?" and he taps the side of his nose a couple times with his right index finger.

"Well, actually Peter, I've been meanin' to tell you. He's actually a Joiner, time served, would be a great fit for your group"

"You dirty bastards, you cheated us"

"Likesay. Just leveled the playin' field a bit Peter"

"Bastards," he repeats, pushing his top teeth against his bottom lip in a rye smile and shaking his head slowly and pulling out a smoke.

Anyway, he obviously got over it because he gave Ged the job!

41

A GAME OF DIPLOMACY

I also manage to persuade Ged to transfer from Fifth Street to the Bulldogs for the Fall season of 1983. Young Kevin Carr, who as it transpires is a pretty decent player also joins. The Bulldogs have become a very well balanced side and easily win the third division. We always get good trophies of course as this is one of Scully's many "Sidelines" (I still have a very unusual one which is a "Pen pot" with an engraved metal plate mounted on the front).

We won the league with a victory over Virginia United at a very strange field in an Elementary school off the old Route 1 behind the Dairy Queen ice cream stand. "Strange" because many US soccer fields have baseball diamonds encroaching onto them but this one is the most extreme I ever experienced. There is no transition from the grass to the baseball infield—about a six inch drop! So you make a run up the wing, almost have to stop and chip the ball up then step up and continue your run. This game is also famous for a major defensive blunder argument between Alex and Ged which carried on well after the final whistle. In fact the proof is in the championship team photo taken a few minutes after the game ended where Ged can still be seen clearly scowling towards Alex as they take their positions on opposite ends of the back row. Eddie Koebke and I are front and centre as usual.

That summer the National Bank of Washington (NBW), recognizing just how prevalent soccer had become in the area, decided to sponsor an international tournament as the central piece to a publicity campaign. Riggs Bank seems to have most of the embassy business tied up at the time and perhaps this was NBW's attempt at challenging for a bigger share. Regardless they spared no expense. They somehow got permission from the National Parks Department (no easy feat) to set up two soccer fields right on the main mall. They were immaculate with spanking new goals, nets and corner flags, freshly marked lines.

NBW wrote directly to the Ambassador of every embassy and the Heads of all the international organizations inviting participation.

This was finally an opportunity to get all the embassy players onto one team and the result was quite respectable. With official embassy backing we were provided amenities funding for a new (Roy of the) Melchester Rovers kit. Yellow shirt with red pin stripe and red vee neck, Red Shorts, Yellow socks with two red stripes. We played it pretty straight the first year with no "Ringers" and put up a decent showing losing to Chile in the quarter finals. We got our revenge the following year in the final when we beat them 1-0 in front of a frantic, festive crowd on the mall. I got our goal from the penalty spot and I confess it's by far the most nervous I recall ever being whilst taking a penalty kick. It was just one of those very tight games where you felt a single goal would probably win it. A miss from the spot would certainly have sent momentum in the opposite direction.

Peter Morrison and Steve Shear were running the team and installed Ged as captain in my place when I missed a game taking visitors to Florida. I confess that would have been a serious petted lip job from me if it had been anyone else but Ged.

By the second year the town really got into this tournament with a more liberal registration process allowing teams to draft in any nationals who happened to be in the area. By the third year some teams were even bringing professionals in as it became an immense source of national pride for ex-pat communities. I recall Jamaica, Haiti, Trinidad and Nigeria ending up dominating play, all under suspicion of importing pro's.

This tournament also provided us with a complex "Diplomatic" situation. Britain had been at war with Argentine over the Falklands (Malvinas) and whilst hostilities had ended we had not yet restored full and normal diplomatic relations. We were drawn against Argentine in the quarter finals. I was all for not even asking the question; "Can we play?" for fear that the answer would be "No". However it had to be asked.

Peter Morrison asked the guy in charge of Management.

"Interesting question" says he.

He asked the Minister.

"Interesting question" says he.

The ambassador had to get involved and rumor has it that it went all the way back via telegram to the Foreign Office in London and maybe even to number ten Downing Street!

We were ultimately relieved to be given the message to just get on with the game. "Keep it clean and sporting and for goodness sake, make sure you win" is how it was relayed to us.

The war had created some minor tension and related incidents around Washington DC. A few scratched cars for displaying Union Jacks or Argentine decals. A couple of minor arguments in local bars. Fairly low key stuff.

However the significance was not lost on the local media and they swarmed to the game as did a fairly large crowd. We were warned to be on our guard against hungry reporters looking for naïve and incendiary sound bites.

In the end it was a very good game which we won 3-1 with the blazing speed of youngsters Steve Winney and Mark Shear tipping the balance our way. There was definitely an extra edge with all the publicity surrounding it but I'm guessing the "Argies" were also well briefed to keep it good natured. Even the referee seemed to make great efforts to avoid any controversy. He flashed the Yellow card a couple times but the Red stayed safely tucked in his top pocket. We joined them in a beer afterwards and hopefully made a small indirect contribution to the eventual normalization of relations.

42

SEIZE THE PEN AND THE MOMENT

Despite dropping down to the Bulldogs I've managed to retain a spot on the NVSL select squad and we get a very special opportunity. The NASL is clearly floundering and the demise of the "Dips" has been a major blow to the collective ambitions of US soccer enthusiasts but they are not ready to give up. They put together what they call "Team America" which is essentially the national team in permanent training. They'll play in what's left of the NASL and will also play a series of "Community" games in recognized soccer hotbeds against local all-star teams.

Following the determined efforts of Everett Germain (President of Annandale Boys Club) Ken Jones (President NVSL) Bob Storin (Team America staffer) and Gordon Bradley, the first of these Community fixtures is scheduled for Annandale High school in Virginia.

Gordon has been (still is) a key figure in the development of soccer in the US. He's coached various professional teams and ends up with a long run at George Mason University in Fairfax, Virginia, bringing that team from relative obscurity to national (NCAA) tournament prominence. He later doubles as a commentator on just about any TV soccer coverage we get in the area.

The Annandale club deserves this. Since starting up in 1962, they've put together some excellent youth teams thanks to a stream of tireless volunteer soccer enthusiasts and already collected three national championships. They've been innovative with a men's soccer team scholarship program partnership with The College of William and Mary and broad promotion of Women's' collegiate soccer in Virginia. They've even helped get a soccer program started at the Lorton Jail. Their latest introduction is the "Annandale apprentices" program which it's hoped will offer a few more players a second bite at the big time.

The co-operation of the Team America coach is also vital for this game but he has no hesitation in supporting it. Alex Panagoulias is a naturalized Greek who has also been in the thick of sustaining soccer in the U.S. waiting patiently for the right long term professional league plan to get established. He's coached top Greek pro clubs (most recently Olympiakos to the Greek title) as well as the Greek national team. He's also had great success stateside with the Greek American Soccer Club in the late 1960's and the New York Greeks in the early 1970's.

Annandale High School stadium sells out the 3,000 advance tickets for the game and several hundred more find their way in through the understandably "Porous" security of a location not accustomed to handling such volume. The concession stands are hopping and a professionally printed game programme, featuring a red, white and blue cover, is on sale at a dollar a pop. I never heard the final numbers but the Lions' share of the not insignificant total proceeds will go to the further development of youth soccer in the area.

Now in my mid-twenties, I'm still very excited about the programme. I've always desperately wanted my name in a proper programme. We never had such things, even for high level youth games or in my brief Junior pro career at West Calder. It has a word from Ken Jones and Everett Germain and Gordon Bradley and Coach Panagoulias. What do these four men have in common with me? Simple—regardless of what level they are currently dealing with they are all likesay; fitba daft. The programme also had a brief history of the NVSL and my winner at RFK got a mention as an all time highlight. Ego city. Of course I still dreamed of my name in a Hibs or Scotland programme but hey, this was not chopped liver! In the centre pages with the two staples peeking through; Northern Virginia Soccer League Select on the left, Team America on the right.

The great thing was for the NVSL team it even listed "Country" (rumor has it that Billy Duff had a hand in the programme production and this may be borne out by the fact that he is listed as one of the NVSL goalkeepers even though he was on injured reserve at the time). I confess I bought several copies and sent them home to Scotland and yes, of course I still have one.

The NVSL team was as follows and I replicate the lay-out.

POSITION	NAME	CLUB TEAM	COUNTRY
G	Bill Duff	British Lions	Scotland
G	Kurt Kuykendall	Reston United	US
G	Mike Raffael	Quantico Marines	US

D	Casey Bahr	British Lions	US
D	David Dodge	Annandale Apprentices	US
D	Kip Germain	Annandale Apprentices	US
D	Greg Milone	Soccer Supplies of No. Va.	US
D	Alan Ross	Athletic Attic	US
D	Scott Schiffert	Athletic Attic	US
D	Jeff Smith	Vienna Shannon & Luchs	US
M	Adolfo Alvarez	Reston United	US
M	Richie Burke	Annandale Apprentices	England
M	Mike Gribben	Soccer Supplies of No. Va.	US
M	Colin Kerr	Reston United	Canada
M	Mark LeMair	Reston United	US
M	Jim Meikle	British Bulldogs	Scotland
M	Paul Milone	Soccer Supplies of No. Va	US
M	Alan Spavin	Annandale Apprentices	England
F	Terry Fontenelle	British Lions	US
F	Ken Krieger	Athletic Attic	US
F	Gene Mishalow	Soccer Supplies of No. Va	US
F	Bruce Strassburg	Murphy's FC	US

We were coached by Adolph "Butch" Bucci and Ken Jones refereed with M. Pyszka and Mike Burke on the lines and Jose de Lorenzo in the newly introduced "4th Official" role.

Whilst some of the NVSL names might be familiar around Virginia, the US national team line-up featured some names which will be recognized by a much wider fitba audience. Again, presentation exactly as in programme:

1	Arnold Mausser	Goalkeeper
2	Bruce Savage	Defender
3	Tony Bellinger	Midfielder

4	Jeff Durgan	Defender (Captain)
5	Dan Canter	Defender
6	Alan Merrick	Midfielder
9	Andrew Parkinson	Forward
7	Perry Van Der Beck	Midfielder
8	Boris Bandov	Defender
10	Rudy Glenn	Defender
11	Sonny Askew	Midfielder
12	Rob Olson	Midfielder
13	Tony Crescitelli	Forward
14	Chico Borja	Forward
16	Pedro DeBrito	Midfielder
17	Hayden Knight	Defender
20	Greg Villa	Forward
28	Alan Green	Forward
99	Paul Hammond	Goalkeeper

Their trainer was Eddie Rodger and their kit man was Brian Byrne.

There was great local interest in 23 year old Rob Olson a product of Fairfax, Virginia. He'd played at William and Mary then in the lower level "American Soccer League" with the Georgia Generals before being promoted to NASL with San Diego. Now he was turning out for his country; a shining role model of the potential soccer success available to the hundreds of local youths in the carnival atmosphere crowd.

Time warp to 2005 old farts' indoor league Monday night final. Chez Marc just lost to a team which included a still respectably fit Rob Olson! … and back …

Team Americas warm-up consisted a short game against a team of Annandale 12-year olds. The kids pledged to sell two hundred Team America season tickets in return—talk about a good PR/Marketing combo?

The match was respectably competitive though my own contribution was limited by a deep ankle bruise but no way was I sharing that particular injury report with the coach. Also, playing against players at that higher fitness level tends to force you to look after defensive responsibilities first (never my strong suit) hampering opportunities for creativity. I was a little late on a tackle on Chico Borja and got a mouthful from their trainer as he helped him off. I resented his condescending inference that we didn't belong on the same field as our opponents and suggested that if he was any good himself he'd be playing too rather than rubbing other men's legs! There were a few niggling moments like that where some of our guys who hadn't quite "made it" found it hard to disguise base envy of our opponents' success—especially when beaten by a confident, arrogant opponent. For example; a very young Sonny Askew who I got to play alongside some years later. In terms of instinctive skills Sonny is still one of the best Americans I've seen to date and boy, could he piss off an opponent. His soccer body language was Baxteresque and he couldn't help smirking when he sent a defender sliding hopelessly in the wrong direction. Funny how we can love and hate exactly the same thing. Sonny in a Scotland shirt—creative, fun loving genius. Same Sonny in an England shirt—arrogant bastard—target for the HATCHET man. This is the term we use for an enforcer who's job it is to eliminate the opposition playmaker. He is typically the opposite end of the skill spectrum but mercenary and always willing to take a card for the team. A bit like the ice hockey goon baiting Wayne Gretzky.

Tony Crescitelli was the main difference in the game, scoring two then adding a measured cross for Andrew Parkinson to give them a three goal lead. Gene Mishalow got a consolation for us on an angled drive from the left wing. So final score 1-3 but smiles all around at the end of a very healthy night of soccer.

We even got a half column report and large action photo of our US Marine goalie; Mike Raffael pulling in a cross, in the Washington Post Sports section. My randomly shaped cuttings (more tear outs really) reveals other hot sports stories of the day as including the start of the demise of Dan Fouts as the Chargers quarterback, a view from Ken Denlinger on a traditional "Gentlemen's" approach to tennis at Wimbledon with Kevin Curren and Tim Mayotte earning kudos, Steve Howe of the L.A. Dodgers in trouble for substance abuse and "The Alexandria Dukes" minor league baseball team about to be relocated.

What I especially enjoyed was the dozens of enthusiastic kids thrusting programmes at me for an autograph, finally justifying my years of practicing a fast and squiggly signature. Another dream fulfilled albeit at Annandale High School. Mind you, it's a curt reminder to savor the moment because I haven't been asked for my autograph again since!

43

A SPARTAN EXISTENCE

It was getting close to decision time for me and Bunts. Besides all my selfish fitba stuff we really had a great time in our allocated three year tour here in the US. Thinking we had such limited time we really did make the most of it. We had started with the usual trips to Florida; Disneyworld, Seaworld, the beaches, the everglades, all the usual suspects. Of course this was prior to EPCOT, MGM, UNIVERSAL and the many other new mega-theme parks to follow. It also preceded the cheap transatlantic holiday packages and the subsequent second British invasion (Beatles, Stones et al being the first) which filled the Orlando area with more milky white legs, freckles and tight, short, shorts than it had ever seen. We'd also been to New York many times as the hotels there had cheap visitor packages on weekends for Friday/Saturday rooms which are likely brimming over with business people during the workweek but in less demand on the weekend.

We'd also had our "Supertrip" around the entire country via a combination of trains and hire cars where I gained the nickname of "Vacation Nazi" because I was constantly chasing Bunty, Dale and Carol (Bunt's sister) to keep up with my very structured itinerary which I had spent months planning. We essentially did a giant loop from Washington to Chicago then all the way cross country to San Francisco, drove around California, Mexico, Nevada, Arizona and New Mexico before re-boarding a train in El Paso, Texas and looping back to Washington via New Orleans, Louisiana and Atlanta, Georgia. Over seven thousand miles as I recall. Some highlights were the gangster stuff in Chicago, the sheer vastness of the prairie across the mid West, Alcatraz prison, Yosemite National Park, Hoover dam, Las Vegas and of course we had to spend several days in Hollywood as Bunty is a major classic movie buff. For a wee fitba daft laddie from Pilton and a cute girl from Craigentinney seeing these places for the first time had that certain mystical magic about it.

Besides my great experience with soccer here I'd also got quite keen on American sports in general. Tim Mulligan, my most reliable conduit to getting below the surface of American sports, tried desperately to get me on board with the Baltimore Colts. He bought me a Blue "Bert Jones" (number seven) Colt's shirt and spoon fed me Johnny Unitas trivia and lore. He even took me to the old Memorial Stadium to see them play Dan Fouts' San Diego Chargers—I've still never seen a more glamorous sports uniform than the Chargers' lightning bolts. Despite all his best efforts I was now a die-hard Washington Redskins fan. It was the original coming (He's just come back for a second go around) of Joe Gibbs. A relatively unknown assistant under Don (Air) Coryell, coach of the above-mentioned Chargers and one of the gridiron games great innovators. My addiction was already set, even in the final days of Jack Pardee's fading reign I learned to love the 'Skins and hate the (Dallas) Cowboys. Boy did Gibbs consolidate my Redskins' addiction. He took the place by storm with a domineering offensive line (The Hogs) and a very special running back called Riggins (The Diesel) and had the Redskins a perennial Super bowl contender for the next decade. I was on the "Bandwagon" (Tony Kornheiser's factitious super bowl bound vehicle) early and never got off since, even though it ran out of petrol many years ago but with Coach Joe back, who knows? Time for a tune up Tony?

So we're luvin' life here. We've eked out an extension on some marginal US/UK education transition issues concerning Dale but it's now time to go home. Problem is, if I have any desires on a decent Ministry of Defence career at that time, a posting to London is inevitable. Now don't take me wrong. London is a fascinating place to visit and has a million things to do but I have never had the slightest inclination to work and live there. Besides even if I did take a job there I wouldn't actually be able to live anywhere near the city. Most of my mates with families who've been posted there recently can't afford to stay anywhere near the place. So they're commuting from places like Milton Keynes, spending great chunks of their lives on trains and buses. There's also some gut feelings at play which reasonably or not see taking a job there as some kind of disloyalty factor. I know many Scots who have gone there for a "Year or two" and never made it back North. In short then; London's not for me and Bunts and I are in total harmony on this.

What we really want to do then is stay on here for at least a bit longer. But how? I was doing well at my fitba and got one more game for Virginia against the national team, a 3-0 defeat in a crowd less RFK stadium. Shortly thereafter the outdoor professional league collapsed into liquidation and besides some semi-pro regional leagues which could offer neither a living wage nor the prized "Green" card, the only other alternative was Major Indoor Soccer League. (MISL)

To purists this was glorified five-a-sides. The top players made a decent living but I always got the impression that the fringe players barely got enough to make ends meet. It wasn't an option for me as there were limits on foreign players and the few foreign "Allocations" (i.e. work permits) per team were certainly going to be saved for well established pros.

Yet MISL thrived for a while and even got some TV coverage. The action was constant and at a breakneck pace and the relatively small indoor arenas would be blazing with lights and music and all sorts of peripheral activity. It was probably much easier for the average non-fitba daft American to take an interest in as the scoring was much higher than the real thing. It also got a brief boost from the demise of the outdoor game with name players looking for jobs and some of the most desperate die hard fans just keen to support anything which might keep U.S. pro-soccer ticking until the real game got another chance (which it would in due course).

Existing MISL teams were as follows:

Baltimore Blast
St Louis Steamers
Pittsburgh Spirit
Cleveland Force
Las Vegas Americans
Kansas Comets
Wichita Wings
Tacoma Stars

They were joined overnight by the remnants of NASL in the form of:

San Diego Sockers
Chicago Sting
Minnesota Strikers
New York Cosmos

Having watched the game a fair amount both in person in Baltimore (Bob Storin used to sell us discounted group tickets to lure us up from Washington) and on TV my conclusion was that it was fitba, but a very specialized form thereof. Certain types of players thrived in it, others, including some well known outdoor stars, failed miserably at it. New York Cosmos folded after just a few games of it. Ironically some superstars evolved who will always be identified only with the indoor game.

A new team, the Dallas Sidekicks joined the league and built a successful run around a chubby little Brazilian who had calves like tree trunks. He was known simply as "Tatu".

Baltimore had Stan (The Man) Stamencovic who scored from all sorts of ridiculous angles. They also had a goalie called Scott Manning who made some spectacular point blank stops. Goalies seemed to make the transition much better than outfield players.

I do remember the one season I followed closely had an epic play-off final series between Baltimore and San Diego which the Sockers won four games to one. 5-4, 7-3, 6-10, 14-2 (Ouch) 5-3. That's 59 goals in the cup final—must be a record! A guy who likely got a bundle of these goals was MISL's biggest star; Steve Zungul. He just seemed tailor made for that particular version of fitba. He's probably still playing in some gym in an old farts league!

So MISL had its run but still offered no hope of employment to yours truly.

The obvious choices were to take a "Local" job in an embassy or other international organization which could get you some kind of related visa to stay here indefinitely. World Bank and International Monetary Fund were everyone's first choice as they had generous benefit packages (i.e. annual trips home) included. However competition there was tough and turnover low as who wants to leave such a good thing?

Bunty heard of a potential job and introduced me to Pat Foley. Pat was Edinburgh (Leith) and looking for an assistant to help him set up a new regional procurement operation based in Washington. We hit it off. I pass the interview and I'm offered the job. Of course this means me resigning from the Ministry of Defence and giving up the cotton wool protection that still came with civil service employment in those days.

We had several nights of serious debate on the stay/go scenarios. Pat had a pressing agenda but knowing the dilemma we were in, gave me a week to decide. One night I'd be all for making the bold move and Bunty against it. The next night the roles would be reversed. Of course the situation was all the more complex because Bunty was expecting our second child within a matter of days! Medical arrangements for local staff were much less comprehensive than for those on a tour so that was a big concern. As it transpired our son Kyle was born a few days before my resignation took effect so we were able to get him home from the hospital without getting the credit card out!

Warp speed to present. He turned twenty one last week and is petitioning to sponsor his old mom 'n dad for the elusive Green card! Back … whoosh.

So we've made the big decision and we're here to stay for a while longer. We'll see how it goes. Nowadays they have something called SUPL—Special Unpaid Leave whereby you can take a few years off and rejoin the Civil Service without penalty on your seniority. If only they had that then. Then again, a soft option would have given me an easy out and I might have taken it in the early days when I suddenly had to pay my own rent and medical premiums. Still, working for Pat will certainly make it a little easier. He's very good to me. Transpires his mother now stays in Drylaw just a few hundred yards from my own folks.

That summer I'm a free agent again. Call it arrogance but I think I'm too good to bow-tow to the likes of Peter Morrison (Bulldogs Manager) or Tony Bell (Tigers Manager). They both have old scores to settle with me. I decide I'll have a time-out from playing but as usual it lasts about five minutes.

I'm in summers, the new name for Lums in Clarendon. The new owner (Joe) is committed to try to make it a regional soccer bar and he's having some early success. I can't even remember the game I'm there for. I'm guessing Rangers or Man U in Europe. I meet John Kerr (Senior) for the first time in a while. He's with George Lidster (long time Coach at George Washington University) and Gabor (long time Hungarian advocate and patriot). They can all still play.

"How's it gaun Jimmy?" As a Glaswegian I wonder how many times he's asked that question in his lifetime.

"Awright John, Yerself?"

"Fine. So who ye playin' for?"

"Nobody at the moment. Taking a break."

"What age are you now?"

"Twenty-seven."

"Too young to be taking a break. Why don't you come and play with us."

"Who are us now, John?"

"Spartans. Good side. Won the Eastern (U.S. Open) region this year. Hoping to go one better (i.e. National championship) next season."

"Sounds interesting, what's your practice schedule like?"

"Heavy. Two tae three nights a week, minimum."

"Might struggle with that. Really busy wi' bairns and I'm in a new job wi' lots of travel."

"Dae whit ye can. Try to run twenty minutes at three-quarters speed every couple days. That's enough to keep you in touch." Now that sounds like a ridiculously simple regimen but amazingly, mixed in with at least one serious training session and a game a week, it works pretty well.

"Worth a shot."

"Monday night, Kenmore Middle School, Arlington. That's near you, eight O'clock."

"Right, see you there."

And just like that, in a chance conversation, I've gone from semi-retired to semi-pro. Spartans play in NVSL but I know that's just for practice. Their goal is "Ethnic" tournaments and national championships. No big bucks of course but a few dollars here and there and a very high quality of play.

The first practice says it all. The squad is the most loaded I've played on since that exceptional under-16 Edinburgh Thistle team. They also practice at 11 P.M.—Friday nights at the "Corner Kick" a newly opened indoor soccer place in Gaithersburg, Maryland. Alan Spavin runs it along with, Alan Kelly, a former pro-goalkeeper. The latter's son later plays full back for Leeds United.

It's a double edged sword. Great to be on a really serious team again. Crap to be just another player amongst a squad of twenty some really good ones with the prospect of spending time on the bench watching. Besides Gabor and Georgie we have Andy Harris, Martin Conklin, Geoff Lurie, Terry English and Julian (Jules); a very competent young English sweeper. The real stars are Sonny Askew, Dougie Davis (UVA), Mike Reynolds (GMU—Canadian international) and Freddie Thompson (GMU—Jamaican international). Mike Reynolds is a gem of a guy and I pick him up as a training partner most times I'm there. He later dies of some previously unsuspected rare heart condition at a very young age. Tragic.

There's also the obligatory other Scotsman. This time it's Scott Snyder. He and Alan Ferguson (the wee man) have come over on a visit and stayed and stayed! Alan plays for the Bulldogs and has doubled Ayr United's fan base in Washington area! Scott is a silky striker who should really be playing at a senior level.

John Kerr Junior and Bruce Murray appear for the odd game. With no pro league both are looking towards Europe for their future. This results in a couple of really absurd scenarios. In May 1985 Spartans play a midweek NVSL league game under the lights at Nottoway (public) Park in Vienna, Virginia. Subs outnumber spectators. Young John Kerr is at striker. We win comfortably. John junior leaves directly from there for Dulles Airport to catch a flight to join the US national team for a World Cup qualifier in Costa Rica! He scores that weekend in a 1-1 tie. This emphasizes how well the U.S. team was doing just to hold things together through the mid-eighties without a real league (i.e. main player base) of their own. Young John's persistence pays off. He eventually ends up at Portsmouth via Linfield (Northern Ireland). John senior describes with great pride going to take his complimentary seat in the stand to watch Portsmouth play Liverpool at Anfield in the new English Premiership. Bruce heads off to Lucerne in Switzerland to develop his craft.

I pick up my first "Pay" after we beat Espagna in a challenge match at RFK auxiliary field. After the game John walks around the players congratulating us each with an individual handshake. I open my palm to find fifty bucks stuck to it. The best fitba pay day of my life. We had Greek restaurant "Team owners" and I'm guessing they won a decent sized side bet from their Spanish counterparts.

To balance this I have to endure warming the bench against all my old team-mates when Spartans play the Bulldogs at South Run Park. They actually give us the toughest game we had in NVSL but we still win. I'm too proud to beg John to put me in so I have to put up with those looks from my old mates which say "Well THEY beat us but YOU didnae even play."

John has strong connections and we put several hundred people in the stands at Yorktown High School (where my kids will eventually go) for an exhibition against a semi-pro team from New York. Their coach is affectionately known as "The Professor" and apparently well known in New York soccer circles. Again, I spend too much of the game on the bench and when I do get on the field it's to help out New York who are thin on subs! Frustration is setting in. Despite my personal angst the importance of these Semi-pro teams all over the country must never be underestimated. Along with the improving college soccer scene it was just enough to keep the pot boiling. By now we were almost certain America would get to host a World Cup Finals in the near future and that was seen as the perfect springboard for a new national full time professional league.

My addiction to playing a lot rather than being a "Bit" player on a great side comes to a head when we travel to Great Neck, New York for a tourney. I have to leave home at 5 a.m. and get back at 10 p.m. having played all of ten minutes in the two shortened games we manage to get in before torrential rain causes the tourney is abandoned.

My preference is just to go back to the Bulldogs but my pride won't let me do that yet. Instead I call Tony Bell and ask him if the Tigers need any players. Under pressure from a couple of his stalwarts who know me well, he brings me on board.

I play a handful of games for them with some success but am inexplicably benched in the big "Derby" match against the Bulldogs which convinces me that Tony and Karl Horsham still haven't fully forgiven me for establishing the Tigers as the "Second" team of the Embassy Soccer Club. I'm on the move again. This time I eat my pride and its back to the Bulldogs. They've changed a lot now with some decent new blood in the team including the Irish pair of Davie Butler and

Mick Reardon. Andy Harris and Martin Conquest have also got fed up bench warming for Spartans and joined the Bulldogs. Ged and Gary Quinn are still there and they've even signed a few college boys including Gary Walker an excellent young Scottish striker from George Washington University. Steve Winney and Bernie McHale also finally make the move over from the Tigers so it's a very strong squad by NVSL standards.

Training and practice is still not quite at Spartans level but with this much talent together the Bulldogs ultimately make the State Cup Final, essentially the Maryland, Virginia, DC soccer championship at RFK stadium. Unfortunately my third and final appearance in the stadium is in front of an almost empty stadium as there is still no professional team to tie into at the time. We beat yet another Greek-sponsored team; Knossos, 2-1 in the final on the strength of a deceptive low bouncing shot by Gary Quinn and Mick Reardon's powerful sweeping follow-up in a goalmouth scramble. I play an effective but fairly low key role, trying to disguise a heavily bruised right ankle by staying a little deeper than I would normally. It doesn't have anything like the buzz of our 1981 NVSL Cup visit here with the Lions and is further marred by an ugly fist fight at the end. Ironic that their greatest success is the beginning of the end for the Bulldogs.

So the Lions have gone, the Bulldogs have gone, my bridges are burned with the Tigers and I have no desire to warm the bench for Spartans. So it's time for my latest retirement. It lasts all of two weeks.

Murphys FC, named for the old town, Alexandria, Virginia pub, are the only club I know which have been around since I got here until present day. Amazingly even today they still have a player we faced regularly as far back as 1980; Roy Pepper. This means he's been on the same team for at least twenty seven years and it's not like he has eased into a coaching role. He's still an active player and will moan seriously if he doesn't get enough playing time. Clearly he's just as much of an addict as me and he must be doing something right to keep himself in the shape he's in. I know all this because we play indoors together but we'll come to that much further on.

For now Murphy's are run by Tommy McGovern and he needs me! He calls me and explains why. He's trying to get use of Yorktown High School so that Murphy's can have indoor practices. They practice outdoor at McLean High School but can't get inside facilities there for reasons unknown to me. He swings a deal where he has permission to use the Yorktown gym but this is conditional on him having at least nine Arlington County residents on the roster. He knows where I live so I agree to pretend to be a Murphy's player in return for indoor fitba once a week just a few blocks from my house. Through this connection I've always kept in touch with Tommy so when he hears I'm available he's right on the phone. I'm signed on the promise of a pint of guiness. I'm back in the game. Of course Roy is there and Bruce Niles; also from the early 80's team. Big Lee Schwartz is still a fixture too. Eddie Crossan's there and Syd Boyne, though Syd has shoulder issues so he's playing outfield (who just cheered?). They also have a very promising youngster called Marc Hill. I really enjoy my season with Murphy's and not just because they play in Green and White. However it ends abruptly with a serious injury. We're playing White House Realty at Fort Belvoir (Army) fields and with just a few minutes left I block an attempted shot by a massive guy who plays midfield for them. The ball actually gets jammed between our respective feet and mines gives and bends in a direction it's not supposed to. I'm carried off behind the goal and left to fend for myself. I hobble to the car and end up having to drive home using my left foot as the pain is rapidly increasing. By the next morning my foot's the size of a balloon and I'm headed to the emergency room at the Arlington Hospital. My ligaments are a mess and I won't be kicking a ba' for, likesay, ages.

44

NEGATIVE JOLLIES AND THE MISSING MVP TROPHY

It's hard to be exacting on timelines with so many fitba memories intersecting but somewhere in between Spartans and Murphy's I picked up some peripheral silverware.

From the early sixties (Kilmarnock) to the mid-eighties only Aberdeen and Dundee United had broken the Old Firm (Celtic/Rangers) dominance of the Scottish League title. Nothing has happened since to reverse that trend in fact if anything the economic gap between the old Firm has increased even more with them being the only Scottish participants in the lucrative group stages of the new European Champions League. Take as an example last season 2004/5 where Hibs had their best season in years to finish third. They were still more than twenty points behind the big boys come May. What happened? Rangers immediately nicked our outstanding young Scotland Under twenty one captain; Ian Murray.

The last serious threat to an Old Firm title happened in May of 1986. I had mixed feelings about this occurrence as the team which, coulda, shoulda won it was the dreaded Jambos.

Hearts had a fantastic season with a bunch of veterans at their peak making it through mostly injury free and Bunty's young cousin John Robertson banging in goals good style, especially in all the big games. They reached the last weekend of league play with what seemed like a fairly simple task compared to what they had managed to that point. All they needed to do was beat or draw at Dundee. Celtic were close behind but needed Hearts to lose whilst they beat St Mirren by a lop sided score.

I confess I was in a real dilemma. I loved the general encouragement the rest of Scottish Football would get from breaking the mold but could I stomach the thought of Hearts fans pontificating over my fellow Hibees back in Edinburgh? I also kinda, sorta had a yen for young JR to get a league championship. But in the end I admit it didn't bother me how things transpired.

Hearts lost 0-2 at Dundee to a couple of goals by a previously relatively anonymous player called Albert Kidd. Still even that poor result meant Celtic needed a three goal margin in Paisley. Guess what? St Mirren 1 Celtic 5 and so you have the poor Hearts players strewn around Dens Park in tears, their fans in the same state on the terracing.

I think of all the die-hard Jambos (especially John Falconer and his Stratty's mates) and the despair they must have felt that night. I feel some fleeting guilt for not pulling for them but then I think—what would they be doing if the situation was reversed? Grinning from ear to ear I suspect, so I'm likesay, quickly over my guilt.

When I eventually see the highlights of these games on that weeks tape from "Soccer Saturday" from Canada it features one of the most amazing goals I've ever seen. Not so much for the actual finish but for the cumulative quality of the build up. I think the goalie rolled the ball to Danny McGrain as I remember him having the ball first. From him it went through several short passes ending up in the St Mirren net without any of their players having even touched the ball. Hearts even had a chance for some solace the following week in the Scottish Cup Final but they fell to Celtic in that too. Hibs were very poor and barely escaped relegation just ahead of Motherwell and Dumbarton. However it's a season which will always be remembered for what Hearts did not do.

The Jambo fans had the World Cup coming along quickly to help take their minds off that horrible week. This was still when hosting of the tournament flipped between Europe and South America and it was the latter's turn. It was supposed to be in Uruguay But they were having trouble meeting FIFA's increasingly strict stadium criteria and so at fairly short notice it was switched to Mexico.

Scotland was in but as usual got off to a poor start losing to a decent Denmark team 0-1. Next up was Germany. A promising start got even more exciting when Gordon Strachan worked a great one two on the right side of the penalty box and slotted in a clean finish after just seventeen minutes. As usual for us in the World Cup finals we're not allowed too much pleasure as Rudi Vohler equalizes just five minutes later and Germany inevitably get a second from Allofs for a 2-1 win. Despite two losses we still have a distant mathematical hope as some third place section teams will make it to a knockout (what the Americans refer to as single elimination) round of sixteen. Our first two games were at a place called Queretaro which is a tough one for a Scottish accent to get around. Our third game is at

Netzahualcoyotl. Even Archie MacPherson struggled with that one after several days' of practice. We need to hammer Uruguay but can't even beat them despite them having a player sent-off and us having a man advantage for a good portion of the game. 0-0. They go through. We go bye-byes again.

England are in too and get off to an equally bad start losing to Portugal 0-1 and scraping a scoreless draw with Morocco but Gary Lineker comes to life in their third game and his hatrick against Poland for a 3-0 win puts them through. Lineker stays hot with another two in their second consecutive 3-0, this time against Paraguay in the round of sixteen. So they're looking good and have a hot striker and Jimmy Hill is becoming unbearable! Then along comes Diego Maradona. They draw Argentina for the glamour quarter final tie in Mexico City. The stocky young Argentinean would grab copa mundial 1986 within a five minute span and make it all his own. He used this tournament to take that special mantle which, for at least a brief period makes you unequivocally; the best player in the world. Pele was the first and Cruyff and Platini (who also is here with a seriously contending France) also tasted it though perhaps not as fully. This is not something that we need polls or votes or anything like that for. It's a fitba thing which unifies the world in a way almost nothing else can. At a certain moment like right after the 1986 World Cup you could go just about anywhere you like on the planet and ask the question;

"Who's the best soccer player in the world?" and you'd get a consistent answer; MARADONA. His solo run against England was one of the special footballing moments of all time. It was like one of my old daydreamer stickmen doodle drawings where you go from halfway, elegantly strutting past several opposing players who are all left hopelessly sprawling in wrong directions, then finish with an arrogant tap in. This time it was done for real by a genius on the world's biggest stage. To rub in salt he added the infamous "Hand of God" goal where he clearly got his fist, not his head, to the ball to score another. Lineker completed his excellent tournament with another goal but it's too little too late. England is coming home to join us. Likesay, phew.

Maradona scores two more to put Argentina past a very organized (hard-to-beat) Belgium and into the final. Guess who's awaiting them? Germany again. They've squeaked by what we all saw as a more talented French squad who have to settle for third place by beating Belgium on penalties. Argentina takes the final 3-2 and the only surprise is that the world's latest greatest player isn't on the score sheet.

So Hearts lost the league and cup and England got stuffed by young Diego. Now Hibs done pretty poor and so did Scotland so it raises the age old question;

isn't it sad when you get your jollies (kicks, thrills) from other teams' failures rather than your own team's success? Well sometimes that's all there is! We'd all prefer our own team to win everything but supporting Hibs, Scotland, Washington Redskins, Capitals (Ice Hockey) and Bullets (Basketball—now called the Wizards) that's not going to happen often so the next best thing is your arch rival not winning either. Sad but likesay; true.

Never mind. Something very positive is on the horizon. We are awaiting the arrival of our own little surprise package. We kinda, sorta had looked for bairns number one and two but this one was a genuine surprise. By now we know how it happens of course and we know who's to blame. Jack Frost of course and his freezing winter nights! No complaints though. We're not raving religious zealots but do think God's in charge of that stuff. So we're to be blessed with a third child. I confess I really want a third child. Why? I've talked to too many people who, like us, were lucky enough to get a boy and a girl in their first two and decided in very clinical fashion that that's enough. Good for them. No criticism intended but that's just too organized and conventional for me. For example I would never have wanted to know what sex my kids were before they were born. I know. There are a hundred good logical/practical/financial (Ugh) reasons to know the sex. Now, don't get me wrong. I think it's great that they could tell if there were health issues to deal with in advance of a baby arriving but … the sex? To me that's one of life's fabulous moments—finding out;

a. You've got a baby and it's just fine.

b. It's a boy or it's a girl.

So we're expecting number three and we're pretty cool with it. Bunty is working right up to the last minute. Her boss is a guy called Malcolm Hall. He's a family man so he's been there. He's very considerate and sends her home early at the slightest sign of action but she doesn't want to sit about waiting so she's right back the next day.

In the meantime fitba goes on. As a spin-off from the National Bank of Washington tourney we've established an "Annual" challenge cup with the Australian embassy. We should be able to dominate them but they've adopted quite a few Brits culminating with recruiting Richie Bùrke and Duncan Reynard who I'd played against a couple times in Spartans/Espagna games. Any team with these two players in it is going to be very competitive at embassy level.

We also get to play this challenge match at Bretton Woods which is still the best field in the area and it usually draws a decent crowd too. The game is on Saturday 8th November and I'm really looking forward to it.

Then, on Friday 7th November the kicking in Bunty's womb starts going again in earnest. Malcolm gives me a shout and we're headed to Fairfax hospital with Carol taking care of our other two. They think she's not quite ready so we get told to wander around for a while to help things along. I guess you've all seen couples in this situation—wandering around the hospital cafeteria with what looks like no particular direction or purpose. Before the day is out we get a great result. Bairn number three; Brooke Miller Meikle and via her middle name we keep the Wick connection alive for another generation. I am so excited as I head back to the house early Saturday to call around the world with the good news and collect Dale and Kyle to come and meet their wee sister. Of course last night I promised myself that my participation in the Australia game was a non-starter and I resolved to just put it right out of my thoughts.

But guess what. Somewhere in the back corner of my brain the wee fitba numskull has started up with his seductive whisper;

"Jamesie boy, Jamsie boy, have you seen the time? Think about it, work with me here. Traffic willing you could get to Fairfax with the bairns, have a respectable visit with your wife and new born girl and still make it to Bretton Woods for kick-off."

"No chance numskull. I've made a decision and I'm sticking to it. So F*** off."

"Language, language Jamsie boy. S'up to you of course and the right thing to do, the nice thing to do is not to even mention it and just let it pass. Mind you though. Great day for a game. Crisp sunny day. Wee bit rain overnight. Lovely give in that beautiful Bretton woods turf. Just perfect for a touch player like yourself. Hear they're even having a new man-of-the-match award with a smart little shiny trophy."

"Bastard, go away."

Now my stomach's churning a little. Definitely not going. Love to go. Definitely not going. Love to go.

So we arrive at the hospital and I manage to switch off the numskull whilst Dale and Kyle get swept up in the excitement of seeing Brooke for the first time. As the initial euphoria subsides he's back.

"This is truly lovely Jamsie boy. Truly lovely. What a nice family you have. Lovely wife, three lovely bairns what a happy moment and yet … it's you that let me in here. You're an addict and you know I'm not going anywhere until it is absolutely, unequivocally impossible for you to make the game. Look at the clock on the wall Jamsie boy. You could still make it."

So in spite of my promises to myself, the words just tumble clumsily out of my gob;

"Eh. Would you mind if I, eh, went to the game the day? Probably not play much likesay but just to make an appearance. I think we're tight for numbers."

What I really mean is we're tight for quality player numbers. Decent starting eleven but not much real depth on the bench.

"What game?" says Bunty innocently.

"Mind (remember) doll, we have that challenge match against the Australians. Not that bothered but wouldn't mind a wee bit fresh air"

"Not bothered. Not bothered. Tut-tut Jamsie boy. Why don't you just be honest and tell her that if you don't get to play yer wee daft game you'll cry and beat yourself across the head with a big stick?"

Thing is. Bunty knows the numskull too. She's seen him many times. Empty words saying it doesn't matter but eyes and body language writhing in contradiction.

"Go if you want." She says probably hoping I don't actually do it but never wanting to devalue my chivalry by having to tell me not to go.

"That was a yes Jamsie boy. A definite yes. Bury the guilt deep. You can worry about that later. There's a ripe, juicy apple of a game waiting. You can taste it. Can't you?"

He's right. I can. So, even knowing how Bunty would be really impressed if I didn't go. I've grabbed the bottle, unscrewed the top and am taking a swig. I grab Kyle by one hand and Dale by the other for re-delivery to Carol if she doesn't mind which she doesn't. I've kissed my wife and new daughter and … whoosh … I'm on my way.

Bretton Woods is a fair drive. Around the beltway, over the Cabin John/American Legion bridge and into Maryland. Off on River Road then that endless run to Bretton Woods which seems to get further and further, especially when I'm racing time and wrestling guilt. I make it there with the game about twenty minutes in and evenly balanced.

Big Ian Knox has been covering my spot with his usual enthusiasm and dedication. Knoxie totally contradicts my Pilton stereotyping theory about chefs! He has some nice touches for such a big lad. However even Peter Morrison has no hesitation throwing me in as soon as I tell him I'm ready. The numskull was right about the pitch. It's perfect. The harder somebody tries to tackle in those conditions the easier it is for a good dribbler to send them sliding by. I'm quickly into the flow and we start to dominate. I'm in my favorite central attacking midfield role and with Ged playing a mainly deeper defensive position most of the play is coming through me. I score a couple and lay on the other in a 3-1 win. I also get an old fashioned but valued compliment from the embassy Management Counselor who has come to watch. He's a good supporter of all the embassy sporting activities and a decent golfer. He calls me a tanner ba' player; a reference to skill levels developed in street football when the ball was often a small, cheap (a tanner was sixpence) thing which you had to work even harder to master. We have the victory and I have wrapped up the MVP. A bairn, a cup and an MVP trophy and called a tanner ba' player all in twenty four hours. Total exhausted satisfaction.

The guilt pangs start up again as the adrenalin calms on the drive back to collect the kids from Carol and make a second visit to see Brooke.

"How'd the fitba go then?" says Bunty.

"Aye awright, played well, won three-one. Presentation the night but I'll not be going of course." And there I go again. I promised myself not to even mention it but I have.

We always had a joint social with the Aussies the night of the game. Usually a good night with food, open bar and a disco. However my addiction is to play. Not watch or talk or any related social stuff. Of course I enjoy all of those but I'm not really bothered except that there will be a presentation and I'll get my MVP. A moment in the fitba spotlight. How many more of those will there be for me? Not getting any younger. So my ego would like to be there just for that one moment but that's all.

Much easier to pass on this one without the numskull on my case. I take the bairns to McDonalds and we go for a video rental. I do my own little double (Brooke/MVP) celebration over several Asbach 'n cokes and fall asleep half way through whatever film we got. Slept like a baby.

I find out Monday that Steve Winney graciously accepted the MVP trophy on my behalf and as far as I know the wee bastard's still got it! Just co-incidence then that Brookie is the one who inherited by far the most fitba instincts from me? Couldn't have anything to do with how that weekend unfolded, I'm sure.

"Likesay; how sure Jamsie Boy?"

45

GOING DUTCH & TAKING OVER THE TOLLIE

In the summer of 1988 we managed our first trip home to Scotland with all five of us. A chance to introduce Kyle (almost four) and Brooke (almost two) and re-introduce Dale (almost eleven) to their hundreds of relatives in and around Edinburgh. We're all very excited about the trip.

Only disappointment for me is that Scotland has failed to qualify for the 1988 European Championships in Germany which will be heavily covered on television whilst we are home. No need to scramble around various Washington area pubs for the odd game or to watch Univision at one in the morning hoping for a re-run of a top game. Between the zillion pubs and dozens of relatives' houses, wherever we go in Edinburgh in June of 1988, a quality game is never far away. Luxury.

Not much domestic football buzz to speak off that year. Hibs are a distant seventh in the SPL and Hearts are also sliding back a bit after their close calls of the past couple of seasons. The Jambos do still manage to split Celtic (1st) and Rangers (3rd) by finishing runners up in the league. This is just fine by Hibs fans. We all like to see nibbles at the Old Firm dominance but this doesn't come with the type of bragging rights which accompanies actually winning something. Celtic also gets the Scottish Cup again with Davie Provan and Frank McGarvey bringing them back for a 2-1 victory over that outstanding Dundee United side.

Despite Scotland's absence we aren't completely without a vested interest in Euro88. As always we have England to pull against but this time we also have (Republic of) Ireland to pull for with all sorts of sub-plots and connections in motion. As a bonus, they've both been drawn in the same section. This is just before the mega-commercialization of every big tournament so it's still only eight teams in the finals which means just qualifying is incredibly tough.

We had been in the same section as Ireland and ended up actually pushing them through. We started well by drawing in Ireland but then lost to them at Hampden which put an irreparable hole in our campaign. Meanwhile they did enough to stay top except that Bulgaria only needed to tie us in the final qualifying match to overtake them. Gary Mackay (another old Jambo) poked in the only goal of that game and so it was that someone interrupted Jackie Charlton's salmon fishing trip to pass him the good news! Herein lays the first twist. Most of you will remember Jackie Charlton. The big lanky brother of Bobby who "stole" the Fairs Cup game from Hibs in a much earlier chapter. He was also in the thingummy side which won the thingummy cup in nineteen sixty wotsit.

He had started with a reputation as a very dour Manager. I think it was Middlesborough who he had made into one of those not-so-great but hard, dour, stuffy and a bastard to try to beat teams. A bit reminiscent of the East Fife side developed by the old Hibee, Paddy (The Mighty) Quinn. Nobody wanted to play these teams because beating them on paper was so much easier than getting an actual result on the field. So you imagine such an approach would go with a really dour personality and that was always my impression from a great distance. However big Jack had become something of a mellow guru, at least his public face had. I can't imagine he wasn't still as pushy and aggressive as ever out of the spotlight but he seemed to take great delight in acting Mister Nonchalant in front of the TV cameras. The fact that he went fishing when the most important match (Scotland/Bulgaria) in his team's history to that point was taking place gave emphasis to the image (though I'd be surprised if he didn't have a little tranny—transistor radio—handy).

He also had been quite critical of the England team performances and selections a few times which endeared him to both the Irish and the Scots somewhat. His early days as a Manager had shown he could squeeze the most out of limited resources and in his current Irish squad he had a good bit more than average tools to work with. They had taken full advantage of the new more liberal rules on International playing qualifications scouring the public records for obscure grandparental connections of players not yet committed to their prime countries (i.e. uncapped at full international level). As a result they had several players on their team who had less than Irish twang. For example Ray Houghton who will become a big part of the story was broad "Glesga". Likewise Mick McCarthy's northern English brogue. With players like Stapleton (Man Utd), Quinn (Arsenal) and Aldridge(Liverpool) they also have unusual depth of quality strikers which means they will be a threat to score in every match.

They had to overcome the loss of their most talented player (in my humble opinion at least) Liam Brady due to a late season injury. There was also a clear indication that it wasn't always total harmony behind the scenes when a serious rift occurred between big Jack and David O'Leary one of his most experienced players.

On arrival home in Edinburgh we had both been reminded by our respective mothers (as always) how we would offend any of our aging relatives if we didn't visit them all at least one time. Pressure on. We resolved to try to have some kind of family gathering at a central location where we'd invite everyone so that they could come to see us and ease our visit load. As well as the tons of relatives we had lots of pals we wanted to see too. We started exploring a suitable venue for this event.

Sunday 12th June 1988 was a beautiful, exceptionally warm, sunny day in Edinburgh and we were spending it visiting Linda (next sister up from Bunts) and Nigel and yes, he's English. They had a lovely bungalow at Craiglockhart at the time. Everyone had their windows wide open and the well kept gardens were full of people enjoying the tropical heat wave. The visit was timed to enable Nigel and I to watch the England versus Ireland game together. Whilst he strongly supports England, he is much less biased than me and will pull for any of the other home countries, including Scotland against all other opposition. He's well aware of my pre-disposition and knows I'll be a fervent Ireland supporter this day. We crack open a couple of cans of beer and settle down on the sofa.

This first game is pretty vital because they also have Russia and Holland on the slate and the latter are clearly the cream of European football at the time.

Big Jack has taken all of this talent and blended it well with his "Stuffy" style with natural forwards also working their backsides off in support of their defense. Much more so than with any of his club sides he's also got some real flair in this mix which means a few inspirational moments per game can bag a win against just about any team. Less than ten minutes into the England game, Houghton, the aforementioned Glaswegian Irishman pounces on a bouncing ball in the penalty area whilst all others hesitate and deposits it high in the English net.

Nigel shakes his head and smiles with irony as he hears the cheers cascading across the entire neighborhood and keep in mind this is about as conservative a neighborhood as there is in Edinburgh.

Even though it's very early in the game Big Jack sends out the stranglehold instruction and Ireland proceed to sit on this goal for the rest of the game for an historic victory. The only thing I might concede in terms of any type of sympathy for English players is the ridiculous stick they get from their own press. I guess it's another sign of their arrogance that they expect to win every single game. This means they have post-mortems which drag on for days. Big Jack's comments at various times have fueled this even more and of course the 20/20 vision fans are already asking why Jack isn't in charge of England. They've only got a couple of days to chew this one over as Holland awaits them on Wednesday.

It transpires that friends we knew from Washington were also back visiting their families in London at the same time as us. It's really the wives that are pals—Sue is a girl who works beside Bunty. I've met her husband Rick a couple of times. He's a top notch Chef at the ultra-posh Hay Adams Hotel in Washington DC. He seems a nice enough lad but I don't really know him well and I've never really talked fitba with him. Anyway, Sue had called Bunty and asked if we might meet in Edinburgh for a day. They were keen to see the city and thought it might be easier to get much more value from a whistle stop tour courtesy of our local knowledge. I knew this was hovering in the background somewhere but didn't really pay attention until Bunty confirmed the day—Wednesday.

"Bit Bunts, that's when the England/Holland game's on".

"Don't think Rick's much into the fitba and they're only up for the day anyway".

Oh Falkirk I'm thinking. Don't tell me I'm going to miss such an appealing game to be a bloody tour guide.

So by the time they arrive at Waverly Station midday Wednesday I am briefed to be on my best manners, give our guests total priority and … oh yes … don't mention the game!

We start at the Holyrood Palace and work our way up the Royal Mile ending up at Edinburgh Castle. That's a serious uphill hike. Their bairns are even younger than ours and they are starting to wane but the spectacle of the castle gives them new momentum and interest. Damn! It's within an hour of the game starting—a late afternoon kick-off as I recall—somewhere around 4pm. I'm smiling and pointing out "Mons Meg" the giant cannon, the dog cemetery, my Uncle Andrews name in the memorial hall logs and St Margaret's chapel but inside I'm feeling sick.

Of course the fitba *playing* numskull is a regular in my brain but the fitba *watching* numskull is a much less frequent or intense visitor. He's here today though and he's peaking about now.

"Jamsie boy, Jamsie boy. What the f**k are you doing? Humping bairns and English tourists around the bloody castle when you could be sitting in a comfy seat in a nice house or pub supping on eighty shilling ale and watching the game. Talk to Ricky boy. Tell him the truth. Tell him where you'd really rather be right now."

Mmmmmmmmmmmmmmmmmmmmmmmmmmmmm. Nope. I promised.

Then I get a gift from Heaven when Rick suddenly blurts out.

"Eh Jim. You's a footbawl fan intya?"

Quick eye contact with Bunts to confirm I never started it but I'm in like a rocket.

"Of course Rick."

"Y'na we av a big game today against 'ollind?"

"Well yes but it's okay. No problem taking you guys around."

The numskull's peeing himself laughing at me now *"What a crapper Jamsie boy."*

Rick's getting a bit of a look from his wife but he pushes on anyway.

"Wouldn't mind seeing it meself y'na."

That's it. Gloves off.

"Well I'd love to take you to see it if you want."

The wives are both laughing at how long our good manners held and Bunt says simply.

"Go on then, see you later."

Likesay … Whoosh (up yours numskull).

We're headed down the mound quickly in search of a bar where the game will be showing which is just about every one. As we chat about football for the first time he explains he's West 'am, keen but not fanatical. I select the Queens Arms, George Robertson's old local which has its own pub team and which I know always draws a decent fitba crowd.

We get a nice wee table in a good spot for the main large telly which is mounted on a black swivel stand protruding from the ceiling. Pint of Eighty, pint of Lager, two bags of cheese 'n onion crisps and we're in great shape. The pub is filling up rapidly with people sneaking off work just a little earlier than usual.

Then Rick asks the sixty four thousand dollar question.

"So wots it lak here Jim. D'you lot support us in these games? Loik in moi village we get be'ind whichever 'ome country is playing."

And I'm thinking absolutely no sense in patronizing him because he's going to find out first hand shortly.

"Well not really Rick. It's kind of the opposite. We generally pull against England—always have."

"Wot serious? Even against the loiks of the Krauts and Argies?"

"Basically against anybody on the planet."

And I'm a wee bit embarrassed as it's evident that he's genuinely surprised, maybe even a wee bit hurt and disappointed. I'm thinking, oh dear; wait 'til the place really fills up.

By kick-off the place is standing room only and the pints are flowing fast. Rick starts to get some sense of the reality of the situation when even the English members of the pre-game talking heads panel get a fair amount of abuse from the punters with Jimmy Hill always singled out for special attention.

Can't remember quite how far in the game was when Holland scored but the place erupted. Nothing I said could have fully prepared Rick for this. It was like he was in slow motion. His head slowly rotated, taking in the scene with that forlorn gaping open mouth and glazed look in the eyes.

"Can't believe it moit, can't believe it."

Then Van Basten hits a rocket volley from an impossible angle and it steams into the far corner of the England net. This time it's absolute bedlam.

Rick's eyes are even wider and as the roar finally subsides he turns and says.

"Unbelievable Jim, am oi in Enbra or Amsterdam?"

"What can I say Rick? Now you know."

I've been very well behaved myself subduing my own natural inclination to jump off my chair, especially when the volley went in!

Pretty sure it ended up 3-1 Holland and we depart a party atmosphere at the Queens Arms. Generally very happy campers are streaming out of various pubs.

All the way back up the Mound Rick continues to express his shock at experiencing Holland playing a "Home" game. We meet up with Bunts, Sue and the bairns and he gives them the short version.

As soon as we see them off at Waverley Bunts asks me.

"Was it bad then?"

"Ohhhhh yeah. You should have seen his face."

We both burst out in the giggles.

Really though. Getting whacked by Holland was hardly a disgrace as they finally fulfilled their true potential at this tournament. Ireland gave them a typical stuffy game in the last sectional match but still lost 0-1. I don't quite put it at Scotland/England level but if Holland has an arch rival it's Germany. Dutchmen I know explain that the intensity comes from the Second World War when their major cities were occupied by Nazi troops. Holland have had constant brilliant teams over the past ten years but they always seem to stumble in the major tournaments with the determined Germans often blocking their path. They get over that particular hump 2-1 in the semi's and handle the Russians comfortably in the final, 2-0. There's a big orange glow around Europe.

In between all the games we manage to get the party room above the Tolbooth Bar in the High Street booked for our "Family and friends" get together on the Saturday night. Anyone who ever visited Edinburgh would have passed the "Tollie" with its convex curiosity shoppe window. It's right under the famous Tolbooth clock and right next to the Cannongate Kirk, two must sees on the tourist rounds. It's also directly opposite Bunt's folks stair which is entered by the door sandwiched between Benny's chippie and the posh Whisky shop.

Handy for a pint then and it's currently got an added attraction for me. It's run by Pat Stanton and his wife and they are in there serving in person quite often. He's actually poured me a couple of pints during this visit. I have very mixed feelings about it. On the one hand it's really cool to talk fitba with him in person and he senses my depth of Hibsness and says he'll bring me a real Hibs shirt to take back to America. On the other hand he is my all time hero and it just doesn't seem right that he's pulling me a pint of beer. Part of me wants him to stay on the surreal, untouchable pedestal where he's always belonged. It's also ironic that most of Bunty's relatives are Jambos and they seem to form the core of Pat's regular customers.

Mrs Stanton agrees to organize a spread of Sandwiches, Sausage Rolls, dessert and Coffee at what seems like a really fair price. We also put a couple of rounds' worth of cash behind the bar to get the night started.

We get a great turn-out, especially from Bunty's "Robertson" strain who mostly live local. I'm really chuffed that Paul Ferguson and his wife Anne make it. With so many relatives to see, we never seem to get around to visiting all our pals. The great thing with Paul and I is that we have long gaps (years) without actually seeing each other but it doesn't matter. Remember—we went to Wick together and seen Hibs win the Dryburgh Cup. We did lots of other great stuff there too but I'll save all that for the Wick book. We don't miss a beat. I've only seen him a few times (Funerals—sadly) in the past twenty five years yet genuinely still consider him my best pal for life. Mongo and I were really tight. Harry Owen and I were really tight. Mark Curtis and I were really tight. But Paul is the constant pal of my lifetime. All we really do now is exchange Xmas cards but I bet if I called him tomorrow needing something he'd give it if he possibly could.

We also have a "Celebrity" appearance. John Robertson has recently been transferred to Newcastle United but is up for the weekend and makes the effort to come along. He still offers no reasonable explanation as to where my missing subbutteo teams are. It's funny to see how the family all interact with him. No matter how high his star rises he's still the "wee brar" to a powerful group of big sisters who keep his feet firmly planted on the ground. My workmate Steve Shear is "Geordie" die hard and John writes him a lovely personalized note and autograph with which Steve is really chuffed. No outward sign that night he was struggling a bit to get properly settled down South and ultimately headed back to the Jambos to torment my Hibees for several years more.

We're over the moon when the night takes a very traditional turn with a good old fashioned sing song. Round the crowd and I'm really impressed as Paul takes a turn despite being amongst relative strangers. Mind you no shortage of singers in both our families so a great time was had by all. What we also loved, which was somewhat reminiscent of both our own upbringings, was that it was all kid friendly. Loads of little ones there and no panic that they might go beyond their assigned bed times. Brooke ended up kissed by one of the Robertson Clan boys dressed in a wee sailor suit. Pretty sure he was called "Rob" but can't remember which sister he belonged to.

Everyone's favorite uncle; Jimmy Dolbear even does an abbreviated version of his infamous "Hitler" impersonation for yet another generation who find it amusing without any real appreciation of the war to which it refers.

Despite Mrs Stanton's lovely spread, Benny's chippie is invaded by the masses around 11 p.m. and sold out of fish and mince pies within seconds! As usual, Benny is delighted. If you need to find out what's going on up and down the Cannongate just ask at Benny's. He relays to me how he's already heard the story of how my Dale and her adventurous cousin Kelly Robertson have done several rounds of the city on the Guide Friday tourist bus without ever paying. This will earn Dale a stiff lecture from her gags (Grannie).

The singing cascades into several houses down the Cannongate (including ourselves at Kenny and Jeanette's latest pad) and a great old fashioned family night was had by all.

Not quite fitba of course but likesay bloody good stuff.

46

MAMMY'S AWAY & THE YANKS ARE COMING

At the start of the nineteen nineties the civil service is going through yet more changes to its infrastructure and even the FCO isn't exempt. This resulted in me having to go back to London to try to secure a position for myself which could keep me in Washington for at least a few more years.

Aberdeen is giving the old firm a decent run again and finish runner-up to Rangers in the League. The Dons win both cups beating Celtic 9-8 on penalties for the Scottish and Rangers 2-1 for the league cup. Hibs are mired in mediocrity and financial difficulty and Hearts chairman Wallace Mercer is smelling blood. The world cup finals will be in Italy. Scotland, Ireland and England are all in again as are a young United States team. But first there is some harsh real life to face up to. It was really sad when my grannies and granddads died but with cold hindsight I was lucky to know all of them well. I even knew a couple of my great grandparents quite well. That was lucky too.

These were all sad occurrences and little bits of the experiences stick. The first to go was my granddad Meikle who used to give us a row for kicking the wee swirly rainbow colored plastic ball too near my grannie and Auntie Mary's collection of ceramic ornaments (mostly leaping fish from the "Gift" shop in the Cope Road in Wick as I recall). These are neatly displayed on a big white alcove shelf in the lobby. He'd banish us to the garden then we'd get another row for using the side of my auntie Mary's disabled car shed as a goal, thumping it continuously. He was a heavy smoker and the lung cancer got him. What I remember most is him calmly saying that his (already dead) brother was coming to "Collect him".

My other gramps would follow soon. I vividly remember studying my dad's face as he emerged from a phone box somewhere around Inverness and absolutely knowing he was about to tell my mom that her dad had died. We were on our way to our holidays in Wick and were to be joined by my grannie and granddad later as he had taken a "wee turn" (Scottish for anything the kids aren't supposed to know about but usually actually do) whilst visiting his sister in Newcastle. I also remember my Aunt Cissie insisting I kiss my grannie Miller "goodbye" when she was laid out for "viewing" on her own bed prior to burial. I didn't want to but was frightened not to. What do I honestly remember? Her face was ice cold and her mouth didn't look right.

Mind you they were mostly into their seventies and had led generally healthy lives for the eras. Ironically death too was often couched in fitba terms;

"Hud no a bad kick it the ba'.

All sad then but nothing like as deep and intense as now.

My Mom's health had been failing for the last few years. She never really properly recovered from a stroke and that was followed by a constant string of setbacks. The last of these was when she was diagnosed with Cancer. It was hard to get specifics from my dad but by what was not said the situation sounded ominous. I eventually got to talk to a doctor at the Western General Hospital cancer centre. I explained that I was three thousand miles away and having difficulty getting chapter and verse on my Mom's condition and prognosis. I asked him if he could just give me the word straight and after going through some cursory checks of my identity to satisfy patient confidentiality protocol he let me have what I wanted and expected. She was not going to recover and it was likely to end sooner (weeks) rather than later.

I re-organized my London itinerary to allow me to go straight up to Scotland for a few days first. By now my mom was confined to bed and worn out beyond even feigned resistance to her fate. She didn't actually speak directly to the situation but her eyes said it all. It was just so uncomfortable sitting waiting for the inevitable to happen. She would talk for a few minutes then take a tiny sip of water and go back to sleep. I think she maybe even feigned the sleeping to give me an excuse to leave. I'm ashamed to admit but even after just a few days of this I would use any excuse to get out of the house for a few hours. Not sure how my dad coped with it for almost three years. We all like to think we'll be brave and inspirational in that situation but the reality is so different and our human instincts are mostly selfish survival. She had seen all the other members of our family recently so my romantic take is that she was only hanging on to say goodbye in person. Maybe.

I was getting a ride to the airport with my Aunt Dorothy very early on the Tuesday morning as she happened to be flying out on the same shuttle. I went into my Mom's room and she was fully with it. It was even sort of uncomfortable to cuddle her as I could feel her sharp bones through sagging skin. I confess to thinking what a contrast to that lovely warm, spongy, secure feeling she provided with her cuddles when I was a wee laddie. Can't remember what was specifically said that morning except her last phrase as I stood to walk out.

Her mouth said "Be a good laddie, Chames." Her eyes said "Bye son." She seemed more tired than scared.

Even in death fitba still squeezes into the mix. My dad and I had watched a thrilling 3-3 draw between Crystal Palace and Manchester United in the FA cup final at the weekend. Ian Wright is Palace's young new striking phenom. He scores two. A wee bit of temporary solace from the depressing reality of the situation at home. Fitba and other sports undoubtedly have some value in this respect. Anything which can take ones mind of something so sad, even for a few minutes, is okay by me. Later that Tuesday I find myself in Croydon, South of London, which is staunch Crystal Palace territory. The streets are bedecked in sky blue, burgundy and white. It sort of reminds me of pictures of the end of war celebrations with strings of little flags strung across entire streets and alleys.

I'm staying back up in town at the Union Jack Club. I call home Wednesday—no surprise—no change. For some reason the FA Cup final replay is Thursday rather than Wednesday. I take a stroll around the Waterloo area and scope a few pubs looking for one which has a decent crowd and atmosphere in which to take in the game. I pick one out, find a corner seat and nestle in with a pint of Lager and a double Grouse.

The big talk is of a controversial goalkeeping change for Manchester United with Jim Leighton being dropped in favor of journeyman Les Sealy. In a game which is much less stirring for the neutral, Manchester United squeaks a 1-0 victory. Interesting that except for a few obvious Man U fans the crowd is overwhelmingly pulling for the underdog. A local volunteers to me that Man U are generally hated by all except Man U fans. I guess I heard that but I really didn't appreciate it until now.

I walk back to the Union Jack picking up a battered sausage supper at a chippie en-route to soak up the booze. When I get to my room on the twenty second floor I find a folded note tucked under my room door. Before I even pick it up I know what it is. I unfold it and sure enough it simply says, "Call your father." No phones in the UJ rooms at that time so I have to traipse down to the lobby and wait in line for the pay phone which is always busy with soldiers phoning home to say how much they're missing their wives prior to heading out on the tiles for birds!

I finally get my turn and slot in a fifty pence. My brother John picks up the phone.

"Hi John, was out at the game, pretty poor. What's up?" Like I need to ask.

No hesitation from John. "Mammy's away pal."

He puts my dad on and he's composed. "Was time." Is all I can remember him say and we all know he was right about that.

I wind up my business in London and head back up to Scotland Friday afternoon with permission from my boss to take as long as I need. Bunty and Dale fly over from Washington and join me for the funeral. Service at St Paul's in Muirhouse followed by burial at Seafield cemetery then a traditional wake at the Merith House hotel overlooking Leith Links.

A couple of weeks later we're back in Washington and the whole experience feels like one of those out of body things. You know it all happened yet you still wonder if it did.

Still. I'll no doubt find some diversion in the World Cup finals.

Just before that gets started there is another flurry of this Mercer takeover stuff where he wants to subsume Hibs into Hearts! In steps Tom Farmer a local Hibs boy made good via his car repair empire; "Quick Fit". He buys enough shares to put paid to Mercers plans. I even have a "small world" connection with Tom Farmer. Apparently he goes through tons of designer label suits and periodically donates them to charity. Can't remember the exact route but someone in the custody chain skims a few of these suits off each batch and my dad ends up getting one through a friend of a friend. It's up market gear. Something like an "Aquascutum", Navy with sharp pinstripes and is not quite a fit for my dad so I get it for just a fiver. To quote an old favorite beer TV advert of mine; "Gid lad Tam." Saved Hibs and got me a decent suit for David's wedding to Mina at Star of the Sea behind the Kirkgate. I thought it looked pretty cool 'til I saw the photos years later. Mr Farmer definitely must have had shorter legs than me so the trousers where what we used to call; "cat's died" (too short).

And so to the World Cup of Italia 1990 where there should be more scoring courtesy the new offside law which means "Even" is on! We've got a decent veteran squad and Andy Roxburgh, who is much better known as a youth coach is getting decent production out of them. Unfortunately we draw Brazil again as well as an always respectable Sweden. Still we've got an easy one to start with; Costa Rica. Except nobody has explained to Costa Rica how easy they are and they proceed to add to our chapters of world cup finals misery by beating us 1-0. We claw our way back in with a great win over Sweden on goals by McCall and (Mojo) Johnson. Our last game is against Brazil and we put in yet another brave failure losing 1-0 to a late goal by Muller (shouldn't he have been playing for

Germany?). Costa Rica proves they're no fluke by also beating Sweden and advancing along with Brazil. Yet again we fail to make the second round.

The Costa Rican coach is a swaggering young Yugoslavian called Bora Mulitinovic. This will be the first of several teams which he takes to respectability in the world cup finals. He makes it there so often the world will come to know him simply as; Bora.

My adopted next choice team, USA, is starting to be taken very seriously on the world soccer stage despite the lack of a serious domestic league of their own at this point. They take a strong squad captained by their effervescent goalie, Tony Meola and coached by the cannie (wise) Bob Gansler. It includes the likes of Harkes, Ramos, Balboa, Wynalda, Caliguiri and Henderson. It also includes three players who I've had the pleasure of playing alongside; Des Armstrong, John Stollymeyer and young Bruce Murray who by now has matured into a respectable top level striker.

Unfortunately their first game is a total disaster. They face a tough Czech side and are completely overpowered when Wynalda loses the rag and gets sent off early second half. Despite a good effort by Caliguiri and a penalty save by the heroic Meola they still go down 1-5.

In the second game they face host Italy in Rome. They bring in John Doyle to shore up the defense and he has a decent impact as they restore their credibility in a 1-0 loss. In the third game it's the Americans' turn to play a man up as Austria have Artner sent off early. However they can't take advantage. Bruce Murray gets a late goal but they still go down 1-2. Still, the world is definitely starting to take them seriously.

So it's back to the usual. Pulling against you know who.

England, Ireland and Holland are getting sick of the sight of each other. For the second consecutive major tournament they're all drawn together in the same group. They all draw with each other and all three somehow advance. The Dutch are dumped by their old nemesis Germany.

Ireland wins a classic on penalties (5-4) against Romania before narrowly losing to the hosts (Italy 0-1) in the quarters to a lone Schillaci strike.

England are playing really well (swallow hard) and even might be a threat to win the whole thing! They take care of Belgium after extra time on a David Platt goal. They then survive a mammoth quarter final against everyone's adopted favorite; Cameroon. This team reminds us of early Brazilian teams. There is a natural flow and exuberance to their play and defense is clearly a secondary consideration. They lead the English twice before going down in extra time, Platt and Lineker doing all the damage. The English have even got a player I really like (though please don't tell anyone). Paul Gascoigne is a young Geordie who has that rare magic flair. I've seen him on documentary, tears in his eyes, talking about dribbling his ball down the street as a bairn. I adore that stuff. There are some early signs that, as so often happens, the genius is mixed in with a fatal flaw and moments of madness let him down.

He plays superbly in this tournament and is sat on the grass shattered in tears when England lose on penalties to the Germans in the semi's with Chris Waddle claiming the infamy of the critical missed shot (for which, yes, I jumped off my chair. Sorry Rick). More evidence for my theory of stars blowing it in penalties in big games.

The Argentineans take the title against the Germans with England losing the anti-climatic third place game to the hosts.

So how come the American national team has now reached the World Cup finals a couple of times and their world ranking is steadily rising? This is probably surprising to most people outside America but not to those of us who know a little about the game and have had a long steady insight into their developing soccer infrastructure. Despite the lack of a true national professional league since the early eighties the youth, adult and college game is constantly growing and improving. Besides this, a sprinkling of their best players are now good enough to compete in professional leagues in Europe and the experience they are returning with is invaluable. Mix in lots of American born kids of immigrant families (mainly South and Central American at this point) many of whom have second and third generation soccer instincts and the picture starts to form. I have no doubt that within thirty years they will be a serious threat to win the world cup.

I mentioned earlier that all my kids were able to play in organized games and that's really where it all starts. Take Arlington as a typical American suburb. In my immediate area of North West Arlington, Virginia, the local soccer club is called Potomac Kiwanis (PK for short). It is what the Americans generally call a "House" club which means that there is absolutely no qualifying minimum in terms of physical fitness or skill level. You sign up and you play. And millions do. They start at "Kindergarten" which is around 5 years old.

They play with small teams on mini fields gradually increasing the size and scope to where, by 7 or 8 year old they are playing real full matches on full sized fields.

At this stage loads of shy or sensitive non-athletic kids who might not try baseball or softball because it forces that moment in the spotlight (i.e. at bat, fly ball opportunity) will happily join a soccer team. Except for the goalies, who tend to be the larger than life characters even at the very early ages, kids can cruise through a soccer game mostly unnoticed in the moving scrums which typify the early play. They still are part of a team and enjoy the social element. You'll catch quite a few of them picking daisies or even their noses during the game!

The parents turn out faithfully for every practice and game and mostly have very limited appreciation or understanding for what they're actually watching. In my early time here any type of European accent automatically makes you a soccer expert. Just opening my mouth after a service at St Peter's Episcopal church got me the job of coaching the PK boys U7 (seven and under) team. Father Tim captures me and asks me oh so politely to help out. How do I say no to a priest (albeit a "Pisky" one)? You might ask what a good catholic boy like me was doing at an Episcopal service anyway. Well Bunty is a Pisky and some of our neighbors invited her. I went along to prove my non-bigot approach to religion. Actually the service wasn't too much different to what I was used to.

They're all delighted to get a "Scarrish" coach and expect me to immediately make a silk purse out of whatever kids they throw at me. As it happens they do have one boy; Michael Bird, who is streets ahead of the rest. He can be a big time player if he stays with it. However he also turns out to be a very serious golfer and goes in that direction by high school. That's another key factor. There are so many competing interests and good athletes are generally good athletes and because of practice regimes, they will ultimately have to focus in on just one or two major sport interests.

So you have PK house teams. I'm guessing one or two teams at each age group U7—U13 though if enough people sign up they'll simply create more teams. Times that all by two as boys and girls are generally on separate teams after the first couple years. However if you feel strongly enough about it they'll let your kid on any team, regardless of sex. A conservative estimate would mean around twenty PK teams at any given point. Now in the same catchment area you also have Northwest Lions, Civitans, Tanzmans Tornadoes and Hurts Hammers, all similar sized clubs with multiple teams. So it's no stretch to guess there at least a hundred teams combined and that each has, say 16 players on their roster. That means you have 1500–2000 kids playing soccer regularly in Arlington County alone. There are literally hundreds of such zones in the Washington metropolitan area and it's a similar story at most other major U.S. cities. Therefore millions of American kids are constantly playing and practicing and just the basic law of averages means they will find enough gems to put together a consistently powerful national team.

Each area then has at least one "Travel" (select) soccer club. The name is derived from the fact that these teams "Travel" outwith their own immediate areas to compete in leagues and tournaments. "Arlington Travel Soccer" subsequently combs through all the house teams and invite the stronger players to join. Even within travel soccer there are multiple divisions and levels. Again taking our own area as an example there is a Travel league called ODSL (Old Dominion Soccer League). A winning team in the top division for their age group in ODSL might then progress to WAGS (Washington Area Girls Soccer) which is recognized as the strongest such league in this area (and the whole country I would think from the few WAGS division one games I've seen). Arlington even has a fall back situation for players who just want to show up and play without the heavy practice/travel commitment of select level play. It's called Teen Soccer Arlington and reverts to the principal that all who want to can indeed play.

It's a very subtle approach starting with "everybody who wants to plays" to careful and systematic sifting to help the soccer cream work it's way to the top. Most travel/select players would also be competing for places on their high school teams and you'll typically find clusters of players on the same high school and travel teams. Players at this level also become the focus of attention for college soccer programmed scouts and the very best players can land scholarships worth tens of thousands of dollars.

The college game deserves a lot of credit for helping keep the soccer momentum flowing, especially during the absences of a national professional league. I think the U.S. women's teams are prophetic of what's ahead. It's reality rather than sexist to say that women's professional soccer around the world is a relatively recent phenomenon on any kind of broad scale. So the Americans are not a generation or few behind in the women's' game as they are in the men's. In fact they have an edge in the women's' game. Why? College soccer. Lots of travel/select women's players have been making it to college for many years now. The top twenty or thirty (and always increasing) women's' college programmers are serious stuff. They practice/train daily and have a good level of regular competition creating a very strong selection pool for the national team. From what I have seen of women's' international soccer recently this has also had a spin-off for many other countries with some of their top female players having the opportunity to play on scholarships at U.S. colleges. In recent matches both Mexican and Canadian national female teams were loaded with U.S. college attendees. No surprise at all then that the US women have been dominant at International level for the past ten years and already have a World Cup win to their name. In terms of depth only China will offer them sustained competition and although not all "Professional" in the monetary sense you sense that the Chinese squad is pretty much a year round outfit with no constraints on resources!

Men's college soccer also gives the opportunity for thousands of male players to continue at a high level of play and practice typically from age 18–22. The best of these will make professional rosters, especially when the new national pro league is formed in the mid nineties (more on that later).

I mentioned that my own kids all played without being particularly talented at soccer. Dale, my eldest girl was pretty indifferent about it, though she really liked her Gold (Shirt) Blue (Short) Gold (Socks) PK uniform and getting to choose any number she wanted. I confess I may have swayed her towards seven in honor of Kenny D. She ended up finding her own niche in Softball and starred at "Shortsop" (one of the glamour positions of that game) throughout High School play and on the softball equivalent of a high level "Travel" team called "The Diamond Masters" (even though they were actually all Misses). She even won the batting championship her senior year. More often happens I think her Mom and Dad were more chuffed with that than she was herself. I still proudly display her plaque on my desk whilst my own trophies are gathering dust in basement storage.

My boy Kyle also played on PK from age 5 thru' 13 and I had the fun of coaching most of those teams. Despite it only being house level I had lots of good players through those teams. Some were travel players who just loved to play all the time (you were allowed to keep 2-3 per house team) as well as many who moved on to travel/select play in a variety of other sports (baseball, basketball, swimming, diving et al) but continued on the house soccer team as well. Kyle scored one goal in his eight years of play with a wind assisted shot curving past a fairly hapless goalie at about two miles per hour. He will become a fan when we eventually have a Washington team to support.

My co-coach is another immigrant European; Greg Idziak. Greg is Polish and he is one of the few people I've met who shares my absolute passion for kicking a ball at the slightest possible excuse. We had several outstanding players come through those PK teams who ultimately came very close to taking Yorktown High to a State title.

Anyway Kyle continuing to play enabled me to spend lots of extra time with him and ultimately afforded me an opportunity of a lifetime. He would be around eleven at the time and PK had a game against Civitans at Virginia Highlands. My Dad was visiting from Scotland at the time and would be close to seventy years old at the time but a lifetime of walking kept him in good shape. There was some other major activity going on in the county schools that week and a lot of players were missing from both teams. The ref suggested that since he was there, the field was freshly marked out and the nets up we might as well play though the game wouldn't count in the standings. We had eight players so Greg, I and my dad made us up to eleven. Likewise Civitans where the Coach his assistant and two older brothers who had came to watch made them up from seven to eleven.

And so it was that three generations of Meikles got to play in an actual match. My dad was sweeper, Kyle left back and I was in midfield and we did manage to string a few passes to each other during play. Inevitably my dad pulled a hamstring near the end whilst obeying his fitba instincts above his brain trying to intercept a full speed teenager. It was a nice change for someone rather than me to go limping into the house and get the "Shake o' the heid" accompanied by the famous phrase from Bunts,

"You should have more sense at your age."

I think he enjoyed that too, probably reminded him of how many times my ma had said exactly that to him.

Think of it. How many people can say they played in an actual match with their dad and granddad on their team? Priceless stuff.

My youngest girl Brooke can play. She is a very physical player and aggression offers a big edge at the very early stages. She's equally competent in defense and midfield and confident and brave enough to play goalie. This makes her a very desirable commodity on any squad. She definitely has some fitba instincts in her genes as she make some passes which come from beyond anything which can be taught in practice. She also quickly recognizes key playmakers on opposing teams and will take it upon herself to neutralize them, almost always by fair means though she is not averse to a wee nudge here and there.

She will afford me a deep insight into travel and tournament soccer as we spend many hours in the car together. She gets the benefit of playing for a very purist young coach; Tim Andrews. They practice lots and he works very hard on physical conditioning and teaching his girls a fundamental passing game. He has a very gentle, passive style of coaching and I'm frequently frustrated that he is not screaming in a player's face (or even the referee's face for that matter). I occasionally volunteer to do that for him. However it needs to be said that after a couple of years with the same core group of girls his persistence pays real dividends and once in a while they produce some really quality soccer, especially when they get a truly flat, even playing surface. With so much competition now it's unlikely that any of this group is top scholarship material so if he only teaches them the beautiful part of the beautiful game that is a worthy achievement.

I love the great debates which Brooke and I have in the car on the very long rides home. Of course we're both second guessing just about every move Tim has made and picking apart the play of just about everyone on the team. Without prompting from me she will often recognize and bring out points which typically require a much more experienced fitba mind. Definitely some instincts involved.

Meantime yours truly is on the move again. I try out for a new version of the British Tigers which is playing in a Washington international league. My first game is at Bretton Woods and I suffer a rare sending off after head butting a far too big opponent who rewards me with a stiff right to the ear. It stings for days. Still. I've had a decent game, scored early and bonded with my new teammates. I'm in.

Bunty and I are finally resolved to trying to stay stateside indefinitely so we buy a small "Rambler" (US term for a single level detached house) within the neighborhood where we've always lived. It's a stretch to afford it but we're determined that we want the kids to stay at the same schools and to preserve our fabulously short commute. We somehow squeak through the closing process and whilst Bunts is packing up the old place, Dale and I are furiously painting the new place so that we can move in at Thanksgiving. It's a cozy thanksgiving in front of a roaring wood fire at our very "own" place; the American dream.

47

KICKIN' AROUND

I should mention there is another major stadium back in Edinburgh besides Easter Road and Tyncastle. It's the one used for that other ball game which I mostly could care less about. As our old high school P.E. teacher Donald Cohr used to say and as Stevie Torrance used to impersonate very effectively, "Rugby boys?" Murrayfield is a spectacular stadium and home to the Scottish Rugby Union. Many tourists will have passed it on the train and mistaken it for a major soccer ground as you get a great look at it when leaving Haymarket Station. I mentioned how I had once been press-ganged onto my high school rugby team and was totally humiliated but this is not the reason for my general disinterest. It's actually a social thing.

When I was growing up you would never see a rugby ball around our streets or playgrounds. It was a predominantly "Public" schools sport though some regular (State funded) high schools played it, mostly the "Grammar" schools which were the recognized "Academic" stream prior to the comprehensive system. The terminology is a bit confusing to Americans because the system and definitions are completely different here. So here's a mini thesaurus of the basics for reference:

SCOTLAND	=	UNITED STATES
Nursery School		Pre-School
Primary School		Public Elementary School
		Public Middle School
Grammar School/Secondary School (Later all "Comprehensive")		Public High School
Public School (i.e. Fee paying)		Private School (i.e. Fee paying)

Another thing which confuses most Americans is when I tell them I went to Catholic School. They immediately assume I therefore went to private school and are quite amazed to hear that no, in fact we actually had Catholic Schools within our normal state funded school system.

"Then did you have other religious options within the state funded system?" is always their immediate next question. "No just Catholic or Protestant." And because I attended both types I can also confirm to them that we prayed every day at either type. They are amazed. They have major basic constitutional issues separating church and state so you won't even see a Christmas tree in a (US) Public school and everything has been changed to the politically correct term "Happy Holidays."

Sad thing is if they'd asked me that same question at nine years old I would have most likely answered, "What, there's other religions besides papes, proddies and the Americans in the dark suits selling their (Watchtower) magazines." The latter (No pun intended) being the Mormon missionaries to Scotland. Now there's what I call a devoted religious zealot; an American in a suit and tie banging on doors around Pilton and Niddrie trying to convert men in string vests who are right in the middle of eating.

As usual I digress.

Point is whether we like it or not Rugby was mainly an upper crust sport and likely still is for the most part. The vast majority of the international players were (our) Public schoolboys and played for amateur clubs, typically alumni teams with very traditional names such as "Old Thingummyonians". I understand that has all changed drastically now with real professionalism in Rugby too.

So as a rule rugby was of little interest to most of the people I knew except that, even us fitba fans would take some interest in the "Five Nations" (Scotland, England, Ireland, Wales, France—since added Italy and renamed "Six Nations") championship. We all knew Bill Mclaren's voice well and even in rugby supported anybody but you know who. Of course we would take a special interest in the Calcutta Cup which was the annual match between us and them! The other great thing about the rugby was the visiting fans, especially the Welsh and the French who would turn all of central Edinburgh in to one giant party zone every other year, regardless of the results.

Scotland opened the nineties with a very rare rugby "Grand Slam" (i.e. Beat everyone and absolutely nothing to do with Denny's breakfast specials) which automatically meant they also won the "Triple Crown" (i.e. beat the other three home countries). Sweetest of all, it also meant they won the Calcutta Cup in the final and clinching game against England in front of a capacity crowd (sad to admit but by this time Murrayfield held more than Hibs and Hearts grounds combined).

Being abroad and amongst so many English on a daily basis many of whom are big "Rugga" fans I suddenly become a passionate rugby boy myself for a few weeks. Knowing my psyche well, my mother-in-law sends me a "Grand Slam" tie which I wear regularly to work for several weeks thereafter. The blunt truth is, when I was growing up you could draw a crowd for tiddlywinks if it was Scotland against England.

The other lot who play with that funny shaped ball this side of the pond were also getting the nineties off to a fabulous start for me. The Washington Redskins picking up their third Superbowl with a thrashing of the Buffalo Bills in the Metrodome in Minneapolis.

Meanwhile Hibs were under the cosh. The receivers were hovering and so was the evil Wallace Mercer of Hearts. He sounded very serious about to trying to take over Hibs and merge them with the Jambos. So started the "Hands off Hibs" campaign with a massive petition signed by in excess of 50,000 supporters, including many Jambos who found the thought of a "Joint" Edinburgh team just as repulsive as the Hibees. Funny how they suddenly are all united against the prospect of being united! Mercer even had his house spray painted with abusive graffiti and several bricks through his windows. Not clear if it was done by Hibees or Jambos, probably some of each.

As previously mentioned Tom Farmer swoops in to save the day with the help of anyone of note who had ever played for or supported the Hibs. Of course my buddies-to-be (story much later); the Proclaimers are right in the middle of the mix.

And so in good traditional Scottish/Hibs fashion when their backs are firmly against the wall what does an otherwise fairly mediocre side do? It's obvious. They win a major trophy for the first time in almost twenty years! The League Cup is now called the Skol Cup. It's renamed frequently as the sponsors change—one of the "Joys" of the modern game. Mind you I used to like a pint of Skol (Lager) and that name actually sounds quite modest compared to its latest commercial re-christening as the CIS Insurance Cup. As mentioned elsewhere we play Rangers in the semi's and they totally dominate play but we somehow get by them 1-0. Many people see it as fate engineered by the fitba gods.

One of the big frustrations of this time was that although quite a few pubs had good satellite facilities by now, a Scottish game (even a cup final) which did not include either Celtic or Rangers was unlikely to be shown. This was so for our Skol Cup Final against Dunfermline Athletic and I couldn't even get shortwave radio coverage so I was reduced to calling home for periodic updates. A boy called Tommy McIntyre who I know almost nothing about scores a penalty just after half time and big Keith Wright gets a second on a breakaway near the end to seal it 2-0. There are only a few players I clearly remember from that team. Pat McGinlay, a died in the wool Hibee who eventually is nicked by Celtic (some things never change) but returns later for a second productive spell. Murdo McLeod who I still think of more as a Celtic man, despite his obvious total commitment to Hibs during his time there. We also had this English goalie John Burridge (nicknamed "Budgie") who was a bit of a nomad and known for his clowning to the crowd. One of the very few Englishmen to win the hearts of the Hibs fans (that phrase's got a certain ring to it—don't you think?).

With a cup in hand and the evil Darth Mercer defeated there was only one thing to do in the early nineties … make a video. And so it was that "The team that would not die" was produced and a copy quickly shipped to Hibs' most loyal fan in America. Only thing is it was only made in UK (PAL) tape mode so I had to beg a shot of the embassy press room to watch it over lunch time and have yet to have it converted. I'm sure it will be much better with a few nippie sweeties accompanying it though I doubt it can hold a candle to "Turnbull's Tornadoes".

My main thought about this is—did it cement yet another generation of fans? I'm thinking if I just happened to be born in say 1977 rather than 1957. By the time I'm old enough to start getting into it properly I'm say 5 or 6 years old and it's early eighties and there's not a lot to get excited about after the genius George Best goes AWOL on the booze again. Yet true fans are made of very basic loyalty. They go each week and hope for something good. They take small blessings in lean times. An odd upset win against the old firm, a win in a local derby, a decent cup run, an occasional appearance in Europe. There must still be some teams who have never won anything yet they still have some loyal fans, right?

My thoughts stray for a second to the famous "Ripping Yarns" (translates as great stories) episode where Eric Idle (Ex Monty Python) brilliantly spoofs the extreme soccer fan who is clinging to his team (Barnstonworth United) former glories. He has his son reciting old line ups over breakfast and clips his car for any mistakes made. His family hears on the radio about Barnstonworth's latest lopsided loss and quickly start hiding anything breakable before he gets home. He comes stomping up the street in a temper and puts a half brick through his own living room window! He then proceeds back to the club social hall and trashes the place. The reaction from his few remaining Barnestonworth die hards? "Aye, no ow yu feel lad." A classic response—well worth a look by the true soccer fans who'll empathize with the spirit.

It must be easier to support a team which is a perennial challenger/winner of titles but even that comes with a down side. Many of them become totally spoiled. Loads of Rangers, Celtic and Man united fans I know see it as a failed season if they have no silverware to show for it.

So when Hibs win the Skol Cup in 1991 are there a few thousand 5-10 years olds who can suddenly believe their dad's (or Mom's nowadays) promise, "It's only a matter of time, son (Or even hen nowadays) until we return to our former glory." My view is still that a great Manager is more likely to take you there than a few great players. Nowadays though even my base theory is in jeopardy because teams who have come into big money have been able to buy some success (I'm thinking Blackburn Rovers, Chelsea and dare I say it, the Heart of Midlithuania). Although none of this has happened without a fairly respectable Manager being bought in too.

I think regardless of how the game evolves Dad's (and Mom's) will always be telling sons and daughters that the current players will never reach the standards of the players of their own generation. That's just fine. It's how things are and how they should be.

My national concentration is off Rugby and back on fitba as Scotland win a very tough qualifying group which contains Romania, Switzerland and Bulgaria to qualify for yet another major finals; EURO 1992, which will be held in Sweden. We are drawn in a monster group with Holland, Germany and Russia (CIS). We put up stuffy respectable resistance in losses to Holland (0-1) and Germany (0-2) prior to a sterling performance against the Russians where goals by the three Macs; McStay, McClair and McAllister give us a comfortable 3-0 win but as always it's too little too late.

England are in the other group which is not much softer with host Sweden as well as a still brilliant French side and Denmark who had sneaked in the back door at the last minute due to the deteriorating political situation in Yugoslavia who had to withdraw. In the final round of games Sweden dumped the English 2-1 whilst the Danes were upsetting the fancied French by the same score.

Germany then beat the hosts in the Semi's 3-2 and Denmark squeaked by the Dutch on penalties. The Danes then upset the Germans in the final 2-0. And so it was that a team that hadn't even qualified was the European champions. This rekindled all our Scottish fantasies because if Denmark could win it, surely we could one day too.

I'm plodding away with the Tigers but there's something missing with this team. They have good players but never seem to quite merge the sum of their parts and I endure several seasons without any kind of championships or even play-offs. Father time is also starting to catch up to me and I've slid back to sweeper, something I promised would never do! I do enjoy playing alongside big

Neil Owen and Mark Harper who both kick lumps out of most forwards, slowing them down before they reach the old guy at the back. The long drive out to the pretty crappie field called "Clopper Road" is also starting to wear thin.

I'm also traveling a lot with my work now so have trouble getting any real continuity in my play with the Tigers. The travel eventually becomes very wearing but one great spin off is that I do get to see lots of famous stadiums and get to see and feel first hand the environments which spawned the likes of Pele, Maradona and Cubillas.

Of course in North America it's not so much football as just famous old sports stadiums but I love these and find that especially the older baseball stadiums have a lot in common with our aging fitba grounds as I remember them in my youth. I don't know baseball that well but have followed the (Baltimore) Orioles after initial prodding by Tim Mulligan. My kids know the game well enough to enjoy it. They adopt the Orioles too as they all love Cal Ripken Junior. Cal will ultimately eclipse the consecutive games record previously held by Lou Gehrig—even Scottish sports fans will know him.

In baseball it's really the parks I want to see and I take any opportunity to do so on my frequent trips. I get to games at Yankee Stadium (New York Yankees) and Shea Stadium (New York Mets—though I also know the Beatles played one of their first U.S. shows there) in New York. The Old Comiskey park (White Sox) and Wrigley Field (Cubs) in Chicago. These have lots of exposed metal "I" beams painted dark green but flaking drastically and the look, smell and feel is very reminiscent of our older fitba grounds in Scotland. They just reek of nostalgia. I also get to games at parks on the other end of the spectrum; the Astrodome (Houston Astros) and later the new Skydome in Toronto (Blue Jays).

On route to a family holiday to Cape Cod I also get to see Fenway Park, Boston. I just love the feel of that park. It has little symmetry and has had to fit the available space rather than the reverse and so has all these oddities like a great wall (the "Green monster" as it's known) along one part of the outfield and a very manual scoreboard which reminds me of the one at the old Albion Road end at Easter Road. Being a Hibs fan I also empathize with the Boston Red Sox fans who are always suffering in the shadow of the evil Yankees. This is even put down to a curse stemming from them trading Babe Ruth away all those years ago. This also has a baseball lore name; "The curse of the Bambino". I guess the Yankees are to Boston what Celtic and Rangers are to Hibs and Hearts—the team with all the money which steals all your good players!

Talking of Rangers it is thanks to a true "Bluenose" that I get to see Fenway. Bunty's Mom's distant cousin Billy Hepburn lives just south of Boston in a blue collar town called Brockton. Though Billy's been out of Glasgow for most of his adult life you'd never know it by talking to him and surveying his tattoos. He's still broad Weedgie and proud of it. He's old mates with the likesay Jimmy Boyle so you don't want to go messing wi' oor Billy. And yet he's got a heart of corn, insists on putting us up at short notice and spoils our bairns rotten. Anyway Billy manages to get us tickets for a Red Sox game and he and Kyle and I get to inhale a sports legend experience.

There is one small price to pay as Billy makes me sleep in a bed with Glasgow Rangers insignia all over the pillows and blankets and serves me a cup of tea in an "Aye ready" mug! He's still in constant touch with Ibrox and has all the up to the minute news all the time. I'm only surprised he hasn't started a supporters' branch called the "Brockton Derry".

Baseball officialdom and fans alike tend to embrace tradition and nostalgia in the same way we do fitba. Even when they start building their second generation of stadiums with more modern conveniences they go to great lengths to incorporate some traditional features into the design concept. Baltimore starts this trend with the new Oriole Park at Camden Yards which replaces the old rickety Memorial stadium. Various other cities will follow suit. However, in my humble opinion they will never be able to replace Fenway Park or Wrigley Field.

I even make the effort to visit a few of their minor league (Baseball has about four professional levels which players generally work their way up through) stadiums. My favorite of these is in Durham, North Carolina. This is the one made famous by the Kevin Costner movie, "Bull Durham" and I drag Scott Porter sixty miles off our designated route just to make a game there. The giant Bull with the smoking nostrils really does exist. How cool is it to have seen that. The weather is cool too and Scott has to buy a sweatshirt as he's freezing his ass off. You can thank me later Scott.

As I travel further South to Mexico, Central and South America and the Caribbean it does nothing but confirm to me that fitba/football/futbol/soccer is an international language in its own right.

In Brazil I fulfill a boyhood fantasy by seeing the Maracana stadium. Our own Hampden was always amongst the biggest with pushing 150,000 in it a few times. However the Maracana in its heyday can take 200,000. Amazing. I don't see a game there but a driver readily takes a detour from our assigned route to make sure I get a look at it. Because he speaks little English and I speak no Portuguese you'd think we'd have a pretty boring journey right? No chance. Using broken bits of Spanish and English along with hand gestures we are fitba soul mates within a few minutes. He quickly senses my true love of fitba. What I learn is that in terms of football the Brazilians love Scotland as much as we love them which is great to know. I listen to Scottish football results on a short wave whilst sitting on the famous (girl from) Ipanema Beach in Rio with Andy; a young FCO protégé as my tour guide. I also get to sit sipping cocktails and watching the human traffic flowing into the "Help" night club on the Copa Cabana though I'm too much of a coward to actually venture into the place.

I see the national stadiums in Argentina and Ecuador and Bolivia and Peru and Uruguay and Paraguay and have similarly quick bonding with the local drivers at all these places because they are all, without exception, futbol loco.

In Cuba I spend Saturday morning listening to Hibs and Aberdeen on the BBC world service with an ardent Aberdeen fan at a house once frequented by Frank Sinatra (how cool is that). A draw too so no hard feelings. Havana must have been some place in its heyday. Even though it's crumbling a bit when you see it you can just feel what it once was.

I also have the privilege of being in Bogota, Colombia on the night when one of their own teams, Nacional, win the Copa Libertadores which is the South American equivalent of the European Cup (now the Champions League) Yet another diehard Bluenose (is there anywhere in the world where Rangers FC are not represented?). Gerry Evans is my host. We gather in his apartment and sink a few beers whilst watching the game live. Nacional run riot scoring four or five goals but certainly enough to win the title! Gerry dumps me back at my hotel which is on one of the main drags in Bogota. It's wild. There is a constant parade of cars up and down the road. Guns are being shot in the air like in a good old Wild West film and horns are being honked worse than Manhattan at three o'clock on a Friday afternoon. An impromptu bar is set up outside just to watch the proceedings. I guess it's mildly dangerous but it's also impressive to see the absolute ecstasy fitba can bring to a nation, even one mired in some pretty serious drug issues. Until I leave Colombia every TV station is showing the goals accompanied by a quickly composed song which as far as I could discern was "Nacional, nacional, nacional etc" in a constant loop. It's even on every screen at the airport as I wait for my flight out.

I have a Saturday lay over in La Paz where the American bound flight doesn't leave until late evening. I'd love to go see a fitba game there but am daft enough to tell the ambassador there that I play golf (though I forget to mention the frequency—maybe once or twice a year at the time—somewhat out of practice—too late). He's old school FCO and says well you can join me for a match Saturday morning. He picks me up at my hotel in his old beat up Subaru. I'm impressed that he's not using his official driver on overtime! We head up a very steep, narrow, dusty road into what look like some pretty serious mountains. I'm very impressed again as he stops to pick up three local men who appear to be hitch hiking. He explains that they are caddies at the Golf Club. They pile into the back seat all smiling with significant tooth gaps and clearly very grateful for the ride. He smiles back and says to me with no attempt to disguise his words and flicking his right hand across the tip of his nose a couple times;

"Nice chaps Jim though you'll find them a bit smelly. Might want to crack your window open a touch." And they are indeed pungent but continue to smile and nod as if in total agreement with his assessment! I guess if I lived in a tin shack in the mountains I might not be showering that regularly either. From being completely engulfed in harsh grey rock we suddenly emerge into a virtual oasis of green which I'm told is the highest altitude golf course in the world. Our three Bolivian pals get out and join about another forty who are milling about the car park looking for assignments. The ambassador pulls a decent looking spare set of clubs out of his trunk, hands them to me and directs with a casual wave of his right palm; "Pick a caddie, Jim."

I'm immediately surrounded by about a dozen smiling faces and up stretched hands. I feel a bit like Miss Westlake choosing someone to answer a question in primary school class. I just thrust the bag forward and one of them gets control of it. We head into the very plush club house for coffee and I get to meet our opponents, a local banker and his son. When we emerge to the first tee a cart is waiting with clubs, balls, scorecards, soft drinks and smiling caddie in place.

I'm relieved to get a "safe" four iron off the first tee without embarrassing myself in fact the ball carries well in the very thin air. I can tell within their first couple shots though that all three of my playing partners are likely in the low teen handicap bracket so it's going to be a long round for me. My caddie tries very politely and tactfully to help me though he's probably thinking to himself, what's a turkey like him doing playing on a decent course like this? I end up losing about twenty dollars to our opponents who hardly seem like they need it. I do get a great feeling when I pay my caddie his ten dollars which I'm told will feed his entire family for a week. No wonder there's such competition for assignments. At least I can honestly say I've played golf at the very highest level.

I do a fair amount of work in the islands of the Caribbean too. Even in places like Trinidad and Jamaica where I expect cricket to trump all comers, fitba still has a very prominent place. In Port of Spain I can bond quickly by just mentioning Dwight Yorke (and later Russell Latapy) Likewise in Kingston where it's big news to the locals that I've played with Freddie Thomson one of their own international players. I'm once put up at the house of former Beatle Manager, George

Martin on the tiny island of Montserrat and have free reign in and around "Air Studios". They have a mini "Hollywood" set up in the garden with hand and footprints in cement and carvings and graffiti by some of the world's best known musicians; Beatles, Stones, Bob Dylan, James Taylor … you name the pop star and they've probably spent time at this place. I confess I didn't see anybody playing football on Montserrat. Mind you I didn't see anywhere flat enough to make a pitch.

Lastly I get around Central America and finally understand what I later see at DC United matches mainly via the Salvadorian fans. The Guatemalans, Hondurans, Costa Ricans and Salvadorians are fanatical and so nationalistic that they will support any team that has a star from their own country in it. I also get to see the Panama Canal. Not a stadium of course but another boyhood fantasy inspired by our big maroon Collier's gazetteer.

So the message is simple but clear. It's just a game for daft laddies like me but millions all over the world genuinely love and treasure it.

Getting to travel this region extensively is an eye opener. There is some serious poverty in and around most of the major cities and towns. Many have vast sprawling shanty towns with no running water, electricity or proper sewer/sanitary systems. It helps me understand better why for example a Bolivian or Peruvian family might be delighted to have a small garden apartment in Seven Corners, Arlington and a second hand Toyota Corolla. Clearly, most of the wealth in their own countries still resides with the top few percent of the population and it appears very difficult for the average citizen to progress up the economic chain. This is obviously why many of them still see America as the land of milk and honey. Sad but true is the fact that they hear from relatives here that there are indeed true educational and economical opportunities beyond what they can typically aspire to in their homelands. This is no doubt why the Hispanic population in America continues to grow at unprecedented rates and of course they all bring their love of fitba with them.

I'm still not quite content playing sweeper for the Tigers so I fill the void by playing indoors with John Kerr, George Lidster, Karl Minor, Gabor and company at a new indoor sports centre in Manassas, Virginia. The place is called Sports Network and its founder is one of the more accomplished youth coaches of the time, John Ellis. John's a supplanted Englishman but can't be all bad because he lived in Edinburgh for a while. The Astroturf soccer field is longer and wider than any of the previous ones, a superb facility. We play in men's over 30 division and I see lot's of old familiar faces there. It's a tanner ba' players dream and on the odd occasion when John Kerr pulls together all his buddies we play some really nice stuff. It's also a superb fitness work out as the ball is almost never out of play so you can run really hard for a few minutes at a time then get off for a blow. We get our stiffest competition from a team called "Café 28" which also has a few familiar old faces in it, including the Muir brothers, Keith Proudfoot, Bruce and Roy from Murphy's and good old Syd Boyne. They even go for a pint together afterwards. Hmmm.

We also get an occasional ad-hoc indoor game at St Alban's school gym, just up the road from the embassy. It emphasizes how soccer is spreading when I tell you that this is where the U.S. SECRET SERVICE SOCCER CLUB practices at the time. They even host a five-a-side tournament annually as a fund raiser for the local D.A.R.E effort (Drug Abuse Resistance Education) a program to keep local youth headed in the right direction. We put in a very competent, confident embassy team only to have our backsides kicked by a bunch of cops! Our John still wears the tee shirt!

In desperation for extra fitba we even go through a phase where a bunch of us have an ad-hoc embassy lunchtime game. Back in the sixties in Scotland the lunch time quickie game is quite a common thing. You'd often see the factory workers from Ferranti's on the Crewe Toll field around twelve with jackets down as goalposts. My dad was usually amongst them! Our embassy lunchtime game is initially at the U.S. Naval observatory. There's a small running track which the Observatory guards kindly allow us to use. There are various patches of grass around so we find a suitable space and start to play daily. The lunchtime game gets so popular we outgrow the first space and move to a larger one. We then start cutting up the grass so much we are moved to a third spot before politely being asked to find another venue. It's reminiscent of the old Pilton days with the cops chasing us from field to field!

We move the venue around to Guy Mason Park on Wisconsin Avenue but as this is a bit further away and people have limited lunch breaks we reduce the frequency to just Friday's. Fitba word spreads quickly and we end up with various non-embassy players turning up to join in, most notably, Desson Thomson the main movie reviewer for the Washington Post who just happens to be … you've guessed it … likesay, fitba daft! Kyle's so impressed I know Dess. Kyle does reviews at High School (Yorktown Sentry) and College of William and Mary (Flat Hat) and he loves Dess' reviews in the Washington Post Weekend section each Friday. Dess is keen Man Utd and I also meet him occasionally at Summer's.

We eventually gets the boot from Guy Mason too as we're tearing up the baseball outfield and so endeth the embassy lunchtime game which made stars of the previously football disinclined such as Geoff Pierce and Terry Thomas. A shame. Maybe we could resume it on the Ambassadors lovely big lawn? Naaaaaah.

48

THROUGH KALIEDISCOPE EYES

So let's review Scotland's World Cup record since that heady day at Hampden twenty years ago when Joe Jordan bulleted us to that first world cup finals appearance of my lifetime:

GERMANY 1974—IN

ARGENTINA 1978—IN

SPAIN 1982—IN

MEXICO 1986—IN

ITALY 1990—IN

And guess what? America is finally getting to host the tournament. It's so exciting to think I'll actually get to see Scotland play in a real World Cup Finals match. Possibly even take my kids. Don't care where in America, we'll be there in full tartan regalia. Then there's even better news. RFK stadium in Washington will be one of the host sites. Could we be lucky enough to see Scotland play in the World Cup at RFK?

But here comes the qualifying draw; MALTA (Yummy) ESTONIA (Yummy) SWITZERLAND (Hmm, take it) PORTUGAL (Uh, oh) ITALY (Falkirk!)

Our defense starts out playing like their cheese as we go down 3-1 in Switzerland. This is followed by two scoreless home draws against Italy and Portugal and we're already in a deep hole. We beat Malta 3-0 at home then have a total meltdown in Portugal 0-5. The rest is academic really. Two expected consecutive wins against Estonia then we fail to even beat the Swiss at home, 1-1. Italy predictably finishes us off 3-1 at their place. We beat Malta 2-0 in the final game at home. Whoopee doop. End result.

USA 1994—SCOTLAND OUT

This will always be one of the great disappointments of my fitba life. I had several dreams where we beat Brazil, Germany and Holland at RFK. Not sure how but I managed to score the winner in each of those games. An early and slightly different version of fantasy football I guess. So much for dreams. Don't even have the auld enemy to pull against as they're not coming either. This is a double-edged sword for me but on balance I like it because if they're not in it they can't possibly win it. I imagine the various British Consular offices around the States are secretly relieved. World Cup finals tend to create lots of extra business for them in the host country. Something to do with Lager I believe.

Of course I'll enthusiastically support the U.S. team but I can't pretend that, regardless of how long I live here, my level of passion for them will quite reach up to the Scotland notch on my heart. I'll also pull for Ireland as they have made it once again and Big Jack's team is at the height of maturity and still very tough to beat. Besides that I'll just pull for a great tournament, tons of glamour, excitement and goals as it's hoped that this will be the springboard for finally launching a new professional U.S. soccer league. Could I finally be discovered at thirty seven years old? Doubtful based on how fast twenty year old opposing players were making me eat their dust lately.

The one thing Americans do as well as anyone is marketing. Besides the old creaky parks which I love, they have large, modern stadiums in quantities which simply don't exist anywhere else in the world. They even have college stadiums in places like Ohio and Michigan which hold around 100,000. The competition just to host world cup games has been intense. RFK has good soccer pedigree since the Diplomats played there and once brought in over 50,000 for a game against the New York Cosmos. It's also hosted many international exhibition (friendly) matches with great success. It configures quickly and easily from the Redskins' American Football to soccer. It also configures to baseball as it was originally built for the Washington Senators (now the Texas Rangers) and it still hosts a couple of pre-season exhibition baseball games there each year as part of the effort to attract a Major League Baseball franchise back to the city. There are several adequate stadiums with much higher capacity but it's hoped that Washington will become one of the bedrock teams in the projected new domestic soccer league so I'm sure that's a clinching factor.

By the time the finals roll around I'm over the worst of my Scotland-less tournament depression and at least looking forward to finally attending a world cup finals game in person. I had been to an Olympic soccer game involving Canada at the Naval Academy Stadium in Annapolis some years earlier and it was fun but I expect the world cup to be on its own magical atmospheric level.

The tickets are expensive and only available in "Packages" per location, part of the aforesaid marketing strategy which will enable this finals to break all previous attendance and receipts records by miles. Can't remember the exact pricing but it worked out somewhere around $60 per individual ticket. A group of us club together and buy two packages for the five games which will be played at RFK Stadium in Washington DC. I manage to raise enough for two "shares" in each package. We make a random drawing and I luck out getting arguably the best, at least on paper, two games of the five. Mexico versus Norway and Mexico versus Italy. The other matches involve Holland, Belgium and Saudi Arabia but not the first two against each other which would have been a plum. Who to take with me is the next question?

Tradition dictates that the holders open the tournament so the first game is between Germany and Bolivia in Chicago's "Soldier Field" home of "Da Bears" that would be the Chicago Bears of the National Football League. Whilst in Chicago on business, Scott Porter and I had actually got to see an exhibition between the Germans and USA so I knew it was set up well for soccer. The only oddity about it was the way they cut the grass. I always loved how Hampden and Wembley looked when the grass was freshly cut in a sort of criss-cross lattice pattern. As always the Yanks do love to add their own twist. So Soldier field was cut in an ever growing circle from the center spot. For a purist like me this was a little distracting so I put a small asterisk against an otherwise perfect setting. Scott and I tested the single malt rack at the Swiss hotel bar starting with the Laguvulin. We both slept well.

Even from just watching on TV the atmosphere seemed great. Of course the Germans are always well supported wherever they play but there was added color to this one as there is a massive Bolivian ex-Pat community in the states and a decent concentration of them in Chicago area. The Germans eked out a 1-0 win on a goal by Klinsman their latest prototype blonde striker who looked like he spent as much time in the hairdresser and tanning salon as he did in practice. One of those players with an extremely deceptive gait which lures defenders into thinking they have a step on him then all of a sudden he's past them. A very emotional Bolivian player loses the plot in the last couple of minutes and is ejected (sent-off). His name is Marco Etcheverry. A youngster named Jaime Moreno also makes a brief appearance as a substitute in that game. I'll get to see a lot of these two players in the not too distant future.

The USA's first game is against Switzerland in Detroit. The stadium there is "The Silverdome" and it's completely indoors with Astroturf. So how come it's able to host a real world cup game when any kind of artificial surface is completely taboo? Easy, just bring in a whole grass pitch when needed. Absurd as it sounds, that's exactly what they did. I don't have the exact technical specifications but in simple terms they wheeled in loads of pallets of lovely fresh turf and joined them all up to create an instant World Cup quality field. After the game, they took them back outside to keep the grass healthy until the next game. Only in America. Despite it being indoors the stadium has 73,000 in it creating a fantastic atmosphere. Eric Wynalda gets the USA goal in a 1-1 tie.(draw) To emphasize a point I made earlier, you may have noticed that's three more language oddities in this chapter alone; exhibition/friendly—ejected/sent-off—tie/draw … pi-tate-oh, po-tah-toh, ti-mate-oh, toh-mat-oh, let's call the whole thing off; always room for a wee bit Francis Albert, even in a fitba book.

The American's second game is at the Rose Bowl in Pasadena, California. This time the crowd is 93,000 and the opposition is Columbia. The Americans won the game despite the presence of Carlos Valderamma in the opposition. He is another of those players who shows early glimpses of genius and toys with the notion of reaching Pele, Cruyff, Maradona type status. But despite a respectable career he never quite got there. I talked before about my first hand experience in Bogota of how fanatical the Columbians are about their soccer. This World Cup elevated that to a new level. A player named Escobar scored an own goal in the 2-1 U.S. win. When he got back to Columbia a fan shot him dead. Now I've been pissed off at a few full backs over the years but that's a wee bit likesay O.T.T.

Meantime there are exciting games going on in front of massive crowds all over the country. If you've ever been to New York you'll know that the easiest two things to find there are an Italian restaurant and an Irish pub. Both nationalities have massive ethnic populations who retain very strong ties to their homelands. So guess who's playing a World Cup game at "Giants" stadium in East Rutherford, New Jersey in front of a capacity crowd of over 70,000? Ray Houghton the weedgie Irishman does it again. An early goal and Ireland cling to it throughout for a famous 1-0 victory. I'm delighted for them but I'm also jealous as hell. Shoulda been Scotland! There's also a local Washington area soccer connection to this game as Alan Kelly is one of the assistant (Goalkeeping) coaches and he used to help run the "Corner Kick" in Gaithersburg where we all played regularly. His son Gary is in the Ireland squad. Ireland uncharacteristically stutter against Mexico 1-2 before recovering with a 1-1 draw against Norway. Big Jack is banned from the bench for that game after questioning the parentage of the officials in the loss to Mexico. Still, it's enough to take them through to the knockout stages once again.

Of course this is the group which I have tickets to watch at RFK. The first of my two games is Norway versus Mexico. Bunty's folks are visiting at the time so despite multiple bids from several of my pals I'm taking my father-in-law and fellow Hibee, Tommy Barnes to this one. The stadium is set up for 52,000 and every seat is sold. Tommy can't believe they consider this stadium outdated. He thinks it's a great venue. Only drawback is the beer. Watery Bud is not much good to a long term Scottish & Newcastle Brewery employee. Our seats are down near a corner flag but not bad considering they were in the cheapest price bracket. A colorful atmosphere with face-painted Mexicans heavily outnumbering Norsemen many of whom are sporting full sets of horns. Not a great game. Mexico are by far the better team and the Norwegians are happy to let them stroke around their "Ole" passes all day as long as it's in the middle of the field. The Mexicans pay the typical price for lack of directness when the Norwegian, Rekdal sneaks home a goal in the dying minutes. So it was fun and colorful and entertaining and Tommy and I were pleased to have finally attended a World Cup finals match live. However, with 20/20 hindsight it was only a dress rehearsal.

On 28th June 1994 I got to take my son to a World Cup match. Though his own fitba interest is still pretty marginal he loved the spectacle of large scale events. The whole Mexico/Italy experience was by far the most colorful sporting event I have ever attended. I can't imagine it being rivaled. Well maybe by one fixture … do I hear bagpipes and samba drums?

Looking from a distance (i.e. on the telly) Scotland/Brazil World Cup finals matches always looked brilliantly colorful. Something just felt and looked right about the contrast between their elegant Yellow/Green, Blue(shorts) with white socks and our strong Navy, White (shorts) and Red(Socks). Even the small splash of contrast from the national badges played a vital role. Our yellow and red rampant lion and their white cross, both real badges. None of this screen-printed crap. Properly thick three dimensional hand sewn-on badges which occasionally pulled a visible resulting crease or two in the shirt around it.

Their mainly Black, sleek, muscular, athletic players with the odd contrasting tall, long blond haired player who still somehow had the exact same rhythmic, flowing stride. Us always with a few small milky white skinned players with signature Scottish ginger(red) hair and even a few freckles on the younger ones(think Bremner, Strachan, McCall). We also had a few tall long blond haired players of our own but the difference in gait was reflective of the general concept here. For example think of Gordon McQueen and Falcao jogging alongside each other. A greyhound and an Alsatian (German Shepherd—see even the dogs in USA have different names) come to mind both with their merits but one clearly more elegant than the other.

Not that we didn't have our own share of brilliant elegant players. I always imagined Kenny Dalglish with his incredible blend of speed, grace and balance stuck in a prototype perpetually flowing Brazilian team would have been spectacular. We just didn't (Nobody else did) have these type players in every position as well as several respectable spares always lined up on the bench awaiting their chance.

The essence of the match-up though was always our strength, resolve, determination-despite-underdog-status versus their footballing ballerina's. Throw all of that described onto a plush, freshly cut green field; a fabulous sight.

Move to the terracing and areas surrounding the ground and you have all the elements mentioned as well as swirling kilts of every tartan hew and wailing bagpipes blending with bouncing (often including many individually bouncing attributes in too small tee shirts) yellow conga lines and never ending samba drum rhythms. The most fascinating thing though was that although both sets of fans fervently want their teams to win, there isn't the underlying sense that violence might erupt from it. As opposed to say when hordes of German, Dutch and English fans cause very frayed nerves to the local constabulary. It genuinely looks like the Scots and Brazilians are all having likesay … a ball!

Just like it was at RFK Stadium in Washington DC on 28th June 1994. I thought just maybe if my son sees and feels first hand the true passion that is soccer, it may rub off and take his thus far lukewarm interest to new and sustainable heights.

We decided (well I did and Kyle was happy to play along) to force a little bit of Scotland to the World Cup despite their agonizing absence. I had the very summery Yellow, white and Navy hooped top with navy button down collar, Kyle the traditional navy one with white collar and open vee neck. Parking will be impossible so we take the Orange metro from East Falls Church to the Stadium/Armory stop. The nearer we get the more the train gets packed with an ever growing mixture of fans, both Mexican and Italian. We have gone extra early to fully savor the atmosphere in and around the ground.

Kyle had already had his picture taken with the US mascot, a large "Dog" named Striker, when we attended a preceding event, a youth "Soccer fest" on the mall in the shadows of all Washington's famous monuments.

My Geordie brother-in-law (Sheona's man) was on a brief business trip in Philadelphia and tacked on a weekend to come visit us. He's not a bad lad considering he's English and his name is Trevor. When we Scots think of the prototype English fan it's always either Trevor or Nigel. Something about Geordies though which somehow softens their Englishness to us. Some Newcastle United fans have told me they'd take a Newcastle FA Cup win over an English World Cup win. Much as I adore Hibs I would always put a Scottish World Cup win top of my dream list. We (Embassy ad-hoc team) were amidst a fairly disjointed version of The Embassy Cup and playing the French in the quarter final at the small tight field at the French International School in Maryland. Trevor came to watch and ended up with the referees whistle in his hand!

What I remember from that game is that Kyle came with us but disappeared from view briefly and I had to sub myself out of the game to find out where he'd gone. It transpired he and another kid had spotted a swing park just out of sight of the field. Most of the wives of total fitba addicts like myself have been watching bairns for years whilst their biggest bairn runs away to play and watch games at every opportunity. As we get older we can soften the impact of this and feel less selfish by taking one or two of the bairns with me, right? This is always with the parting instruction to keep them in plain view at all times which we sincerely agree to do, right? All the time knowing that's virtually impossible to do properly because for at least a few brief seconds at various points you instinctively get totally wrapped in the flow of a game. Now you might think it absurd to sub out of a game to find your kid but my more recent observations suggest I'm not unique in that respect. My own family is big enough now where this is no longer an issue for me but I've watched carefully as some of my younger teammates have tried to play with one eye on the field and the other on the sideline trying to track the movements of their effervescent kids.

So I found Kyle quickly and we cruised to a 5-2 win over the French without giving the "volunteer" referee too much abuse though I do recall him politely telling a couple of frogs to stop whinging. Funnily enough that tournament seemed to just sputter out as I don't recall finishing it. The French were in the forefront organizing so perhaps they just lost interest when we cuffed them. Trevor's fair skin had taken a medium rare roasting in the eighty-plus degree heat and we were now headed to the Mall for Soccer fest to get him to the well done stage. Fortunately there was an odd tent in which to shelter which is where we ran into Striker. Immediately after the Kyle/Striker pose we withdrew to the wonderful air conditioning of the Air and Space Museum.

I don't recall many World Cup Mascots and I hate the fact that the one that I remember most vividly was a furry lion who was (gulp) ... English. This may cause some concern as to my own sexual stability but I could never get "World Cup Willie" out of my head. He was mascot for either the 1966 or 1970 England team and I was just so jealous that Scotland didn't have one. Mascot that is as opposed to Willie! We had tons of those, most famously "Oor Wullie, your Wullie, a'bodys Wullie" and of course that Wallace boy. Besides, we each had our own individual one too with which, especially in our early teens, we were regularly intimate. But we never had a world cup Willie because we couldn't make it to the finals back then and the highly publicized mascot was yet another painful constant reminder of this fact. Ironically, by the time we did make it through to major finals on a regular basis, Scottish Wullies were being supplanted by "CU Jimmy's" and their one piece tartan bonnet/fuzzy ginger wigs.

So back to the spectacle at hand—the World Cup at RFK. The activities outside the ground did hold one magnet for Kyle. Souvenir stands, lots of them. If there was one thing which would sway Kyle to attend a major sporting (or any other for that matter) event with me it was the prospect of buying a souvenir. I suppose we were the same as kids but of course our expectation level was different. We were usually at the event on our own and never had the money for souvenirs. So like most of my slightly weaker, less disciplined generation of parents, I've promised Kyle in advance that he can pick anything he wants as his world cup match day souvenir. Funny how we hold a kids hand and "guide" them alongside us until they see something they desperately want and the balance of power suddenly shifts. And so it is that Kyle quickly hones in on a small white tent and despite his slight stature, hauls me there in a determined straight line and makes a quick and decisive selection; an "Italia" pennant. No complaints from me though as I get off with a $6 item when they have plenty bits and bobs in the $50-$100 range—phew!

Next we have a few more photo ops which raises another question. Is it better now that we all have cameras and videos and other assorted technology coming out of our ears and can record everything from our children's first fart? Or was it better in the "Old" days when we got our photo taken at school once a year and perhaps a few snapshots on our summer holidays at the beach? Are memories better and richer in our own mind? Are they enhanced or diluted by having four hundred pictures to look through? Who knows? My own early fond memories are so vivid that I'm easily able to touch them by closing my eyes and concentrating. Yet I find this more difficult doing so in respect of much more recent memories so I guess some aide memoirs can be useful. The latter probably also allow us to give our kids more insight than words alone can into our own evolution. My motivation for starting this entire scrawl was because I thought that normal conversation, even accompanied by some photos or video would never be enough to explain to them how I became the normal dysfunctional person I am. Conversely, one of the most exciting (for me at least) things I ever showed my kids was the one 8mm movie I had of my mom in her prime, sitting around our backgreen in sunny Drylaw on a multi—colored striped deck chair in just her bra, drinking vodka and lemonade. On Bunty's side, everyone's favorite uncle; Jimmy Dolbear, also had a cine camera and took clips of all the family weddings. Chris Robertson managed to get these converted and strung together on a video and was kind enough to send us a copy. It has about thirty seconds from our wedding which was also a great thing to show our kids.

Is it even possible that just knowing everything is recorded makes this generation somehow sub-consciously retain memories less intensely? That's a bit like the perpetual debate on comparing great players of all sports from different eras. You'll simply never be able to know for sure unless perhaps they have era-neutral games in heaven. Then again with many of the great players having such severe character flaws, a lot of those required to stage a conclusive test would likely be missing in that other burny place.

Regardless we proceed to the MasterCard tent and stand in line to pose with Pele for a picture. Unfortunately it's not the real Pele but a cardboard cut-out. However there are cardboard cut-outs and then there are cardboard cut-outs. This is a really high quality one. A bit like the Presidential ones in front of the White House where the photographer is always getting pissed off with people trying to take a freebie with their own cameras (C'mon, admit it, you've tried it). Anyway this is a cracking cardboard Pele. Of course he's in a MasterCard track suit rather than the beautiful Yellow Jersey we prefer but we'll take it. Kyle slides in alongside him in his Scotland shirt, click! I think how I would have felt at nine years old getting to pose with Pele, even cardboard Pele. Put something like this on the big field at Pilton and the queue (line) would have stretched for miles.

The atmosphere is pure carnival and many fans have had the same notion as us wearing their own national shirts in honor of absent friends. There are lots of Italian flags and "Azzuri" blue shirts but by far the most predominant single feature is the Green Mexico shirts. The latest one has a kind of Aztec pattern in a slightly darker contrasting green as background with the umbro logo subtly worked through it. The Mexican face painting is also superb.

I find one perfect example of all of the above combined. This guy has an elaborate paint job. The left side of his face is green, the right is red. No half measures either the paint is thick and coverage is comprehensive. Down the centre of his forehead and over his nose, mouth and chin is an equally thick white strip. It forms the shape of a bowling pin with his dark piercing eyes either side of the pin neck, one on a green background, the other on red. The letters M-E-X starts vertically down his forehead in green and continue I-C-O in red down his nose. His lips look vivid pink and his teeth yellow against the pure white paint. He has two great swathes of raven black hair parted in the center. He has the new umbro shirt. I ask him to pose with Kyle for a photo and he readily agrees and grabs Kyle tightly around the right shoulder. He is both friendly and menacing at the same time. The photo comes out great and although Kyle is smiling you can trace just a touch of trepidation in his eyes and the dimples around his mouth.

We move inside the stadium and it's even better. The pitch looks so perfect it's hard to believe it's real grass. Hard to imagine simple white lines could look "good" but they do; not a single blotch or blemish anywhere. The nets are very deep and also a simple white. They don't even look tacked down. They just have some slack at the back simply nestling neatly on the turf like folds on a trailing wedding gown. The dug-outs are Perspex. The corner flags are red on yellow poles. The perimeter is lined with low multi colored boards displaying all the main sponsors. My photo shows Snickers, JVC, Canon, Philips, MasterCard and Chevrolet. The sum reminds me of Kenny Manson's perfectly laid out totally undisturbed, fully accessorized subbuteo pitch. There is intense passion in the air but it somehow feels friendly as opposed to aggressive/hostile passion. I talked about this recently to my longest running teammate Eddie Koebke. He took his Guatemalan immigrant dad to that game and says they both got exactly the same vibes.

The pageantry rolls on as the players parade onto the field in perfect formation. The Italians have their normal blue shirts, white shorts, blue socks but I'm surprised to see Mexico in a change kit consisting White tops with some red flashing around the shoulders (a bit Bay City Rollerish looking actually) red shorts, white socks. I guess there is still a significant portion of fans in third world situations watching in black and white. At least that's the only reason I could think of for the switch. Both national anthems are belted out with serious devotion. As always, all the fans seem to know the words well but some of the players look like they're padding when you get to a second verse.

The Italians have a few superstars in the team. I especially like Maldini, Signori and Baggio. We get a very close up look at Baggio with his signature pony tail as he takes a corner just a few yards from where we are seated. The superstar of the Mexicans is their goalie Jorge Campos. He is famed for his elaborate Goalie shirts and boy has he outdone himself for the world cup. Tough to do it any justice with words but here goes. The shirt and shorts sort of merge into each other to form what looks like an Aztec smock! The base is canary yellow but there are green and black striped segments on the groin and forearm arm areas, black triangles which look a bit like arrow points up the chest and zig-zagging red flashings on the sides of the shorts and shoulders. Even the referee and linesmen contribute to the pallet, forsaking their traditional all black garb for trendy gold colored tops.

In the end it was always unlikely the game itself could do justice to the setting and build-up. A fairly tame stuffy affair though the Mexicans did manage a couple more of their signature short passing routines to resounding "Oles" from the crowd. There were even a couple of successful contemporary "waves" which made it around the entire stadium. Bernal got the Mexican goal, Massaro the Italian one for a 1-1 tie, just about right.

As a rule I couldn't care less what the surrounds and atmosphere is like, I just want to see a decent game. However this was a rare exception. Many purists like me left that game knowing they'd seen a mediocre fitba match yet fully satisfied they had witnessed a very special spectacular celebration of the joy of the world's greatest game. Ironically, the least anticipated RFK game; Belgium versus Saudi Arabia, was apparently by far the most entertaining of the five played there.

Massive sold out crowds continued throughout the tournament. Ireland fell to Holland and the hosts to Brazil. In that 1-0 game, Bebeto scored the Brazilian goal and introduced his signature "Rock the cradle" celebration to the entire world. Baggio carried Italy all the way to the final with a slew of goals against Nigeria, Spain and Bulgaria in successive knockout rounds. In the semi's the Italians got by the upstart Bulgarians who had become the darlings of the tournament with a massive upset of the Germans along the way. Their star was a chunky attacking midfielder called Stoikov who's shot belongs in the hardest ever category alongside Peter Lorimer of Scotland and Roberto Carlos of Brazil.

The Brazilians got past Holland 3-2 in an old fashioned barnstormer of a game then eked past Sweden 1-0 to join the Italians in a much anticipated final. Another 93,000 packed into the Rose Bowl in Pasadena, California for this one but they were mostly disappointed by the lack of a goal through ninety minutes plus extra time. And so it was down to a penalty shoot out for the championship of the entire universe. I suppose this had a plus to it in that Americans generally hate ties and have tie-breaking formulas in all their major sports. This might make up for the lack of goals, especially as it's being watched by a much larger than usual U.S. TV soccer audience. Hopefully we can hook a few of the marginal fans.

A fairly common occurrence in these shoot-outs is for a usually supremely confident superstar to wilt under the extreme pressure of the moment. Baggio made a basic schoolboy error by leaning too far back and blasting his shot well over the crossbar and Brazil had won the world cup once again.

More importantly the tournament had been an incredible economical success and definitely, as always hoped, set the table for the re-introduction of a fully fledged American soccer league.

Kyle really enjoyed it too but as far as being the pivotal moment in clinching his belated soccer addiction? I asked him recently what he remembered about that experience.

"Not much" he mumbled without even lifting his head away from his laptop.

"Sorry?" I said hoping to solicit a slightly more encouraging response.

Again; "Not much."

Yet I know if you asked him to describe the lead singers' outfit from a random Weezer concert he could write up a decent paragraph about it in seconds. Case closed then. My mission is now crystal clear. Likesay, just write on and explain how I became a fitba loony rather than try to help him become one.

49

BACK IN THE LIMELIGHT

After the glow of a very successful American World Cup subsided it was back to the important business of getting ready in case one of the new pro teams might need an "Auld heid" to help them get started. This meant staying in playing shape and so to a pre-season friendly in early Fall of 1994 which would persuade me that it was finally time to revert to playing with (older) boys my own age again. I'm still playing with the Tigers but I'm all the way back to sweeper and that's just far too far away from the opposing goal for me. I'm aching to get back into midfield yet, to be fair to big Mark Harper who's now running the Tigers; the pace in the "Open" (i.e. no age constraints) league makes it a stretch for me to play a whole game in midfield anymore.

We are playing the friendly against the (thirty five and over) "UK Raiders" a name clearly influenced by the long since retired Steve Shear—ardent Oakland Raiders fan just because he found their colors to be the closest he could to Newcastle United within the NFL palette. He's even an Orca whale freak because they're black and white. The current Player/Manager is Danny Brogan better known as one of the leading lights the British Embassy Players who put on plays and concerts. I know Danny well as I've done a lot of art work for his stage sets over the years. He uses every opportunity to practice his singing/dancing/acting skills and his football manager role is no exception. Apparently he gives some of the more interesting half time talks you could ever hear. I look forward to hearing some of these in due course. He also plays a good referee and that's his role today. He tends to be extremely generous to his own team and will give a penalty for the slightest contact with his forwards in our box. He uses the ensuing protest to hone his acting skills, scrunching up his nose indignantly, biting on the whistle clenched in the left corner of his teeth and waving both hands outwards. He's reminiscent of "Tiny" Wharton in his heyday except he smiles a lot more and has been known to attempt to defuse an on-field controversy with a joke or a line from a Harry Lauder song!

The team is about fifty percent embassy staff and alumni and fifty percent Danny's wide and wonderful world of random contacts. They give us a decent test and seem very motivated to prove they can still play with the youngsters. Ironically, several of Danny's "Old" boys are clearly younger than yours truly. Because of the more forgiving pace, I'm able to forage forward into my more customary attacking midfield role and I really enjoy it.

We have a beer afterwards and Danny get's to work on me the way I have on many players myself over the years. He acts the daft laddie but he's noticed I hated being subbed out a couple times. Even in a low key friendly my petted lip is still automatic and obvious despite my best attempts to hide it. He's clearly sniffed an addict in need of a more substantial fix. He suggests I turn out for them the following week. No cash signing bonus available but otherwise very attractive terms. I can be Captain, pick my position, play all ninety minutes, wear whatever jersey number I like (7, no hesitation, Kenny Dalglish—I'm not worthy) and I can even take all free kicks, penalties and corners if I so choose. This lends great emphasis to how irrelevant money ultimately is to true fitba addicts. It's also great ego-therapy—reminds me of being the first Tick-Tack pick in boyhood games in Pilton and Drylaw. It's also by far the richest offer I've had in many, many moons and as the Tigers have no game the subsequent week, it's certainly worth a wee taste.

I turn up at the Saul Road fields, just off Rock Creek Park in Kensington, Maryland and am introduced to Danny's Boys. Most give me a warm welcome though wee Eddie, their current Captain and star, is a little cool and withdrawn. He's clearly a wee bit threatened which is exactly how I'll be when Danny eventually but inevitably recruits my successor. I get the impression that Danny's been open about the super-sweet deal he's offered me. It's a common theme in fitba that most players don't give a damn about your personality traits if you can deliver on the field without totally imploding the rest of the team.

We're playing a friendly against Bethesda and I'm in the central midfield with wee Eddie who's a very useful player. I'm old enough now to read and compromise so I give him his place make an extra effort to play a lot of stuff through him and still enjoy my own game immensely. The rest of the team seems to appreciate me and I get lots of warm congratulations after a couple of well taken goals in a 4-1 win. Yep. This makes me feel good. It's for me. I break the news to big Mark and the Tigers who seem to cope with it just fine. I may have just saved myself from one of those awkward conversations where you're given the chance to politely resign rather than taking it between the eyes.

My league debut for the UK Raiders is on a blustery September Sunday back at Saul Road number one. Reasonably even surface though not much grass in the center areas on a slight slope end to end. Well lined, posts, nets and corner flags in place. Only pain is a hill immediately to one side where everything slopes off to a road which in turn slopes off towards Rock Creek Park. Retrieving can take several minutes which is no bad thing for a couple of the much older players who seem to appreciate the breather. It reminds me of the Drumbrae in Edinburgh where we could lose several minutes retrieving balls which got started down Clerry hill. Mind you in those days you didn't change the match ball except in really dire circumstances. Nowadays you can switch the ball as often as you like. Perhaps it's not co-incidence then that the old farts teams tend to only have one decent ball available per match.

There is an actual bench at Saul Road number one but that's literally what it is; a well worn, paint flaking, hunter green wooden, standard six foot long park bench complete with splinters to be shared by the entire squad and any spectators who are brave enough to show up. We congregate around it on Danny's command for which he lifts both arms high and waves like an auctioneer beckoning bidders in for a closer look;

"Alright, bring it in here for a minute boys" (I make no attempt to sound out the phonetics for Danny's accent as he has several and they're all pretty good).

Funny how the term boys is still used for a bunch of thirty to fifty five year olds (I'm guessing that's the age of our oldest player; Richard Beaman but he can still contribute a lot at this level). And yes I did mean thirty. It transpires most teams in the league will have a "ringer" or two a little under the age limit, but as long as they're not totally dominant type players everyone seems to ignore it and protests are very rare. There is a sign-in system and "Official" registered roster. So each week, at the start of the game, we are all told who is using which registered name for that particular week. There are cursory attempts by teammates to remember and use these but they tend to be overtaken by instincts by half time.

Anyway it's my first insight into Danny's legendary team talks. We're playing a team called "The Ratcatchers" who are apparently the cat's whiskers in this division. I already recognize a few faces including one of my old nemesis; Tony Bell, manager of the original Tigers. They are in smart white kit and certainly look the part in warm ups. We are in a variety of shorts and socks with dark blue tee shirts. Danny is also known for a wonderful variety of strips which he treats more like a costume wardrobe but I'll get into that in more detail later.

As always with my first real game for any team my nerves have been jingling since the previous day and I've spent a good half hour in the wee throne room prior to leaving today. Saul Road is an easy thirty minute drive for me. Five minutes on the Route 66/Dulles/Toll Rd link, twenty minutes around the (495) beltway and five more up Connecticut Avenue, right on Saul, over the little hump back bridge and we're there. I say "we" because Bunty's dad is visiting again and has come with me. This is good news for me. Over the years Tommy's been a lucky charm for me. I've never failed to score in a match he's attended. I'm not really his type of player, a bit too cocky and arrogant on the field. He tends to admire the big, strong hard working midfielders which make me think that's exactly what type player he was himself. He ends up being commandeered to run the line for the first twenty minutes as the second official (they use one in each half at this level) is late in arriving. Interesting to see a linesman with a flag in one hand and a fag in the other.

And so to Danny's opening words of wisdom.

"Now we know this lot won the league last season and they're used to dominating the play so let's shock 'em. We have some new blood ourselves. They have a couple of old blokes at the back so let's test 'em early".

So far so good. All sounds reasonable although I think in relative terms we're almost all "old blokes" (I'm thinking; blokes? I guess this must be Danny's Aussie accent).

"For today big Guy will be Dave Ritchie and "Trickie" will be Dan Weiss (two regulars who are away that day) and try to remember that because we're gonna take them today and we don't want them protesting".

The good news is that they have at least a couple of questionable aged looking players so I suspect that issue will be null and void.

Big Guy is a 6'6" Weedgie die-hard blue nose. He's gangly and has a tangle of long light brown hair. He even still has a few boyish plukes (sorry big man). He reminds me of the boy who starred in "Gregory's Girl" and then played the drummer in the ceilidh band in "Local Hero"; two classic John Forsyth efforts. Can't be more than twenty nine? Trickie (Dickie-Richard Siarey) must be near but not quite at the requisite thirty five years.

"Right, the line up." And this is always fascinating with Danny as he never uses the same sequence. One week he'll start with the goalie and defense, next with the center forward. Sometimes he'll even start with the midfield and work his way around from that. He often will name a formation consisting ten or twelve players and we just have to agree amongst ourselves who gets added or dumped. We tend to sort the actual formation once we actually get on the field. He does great with the subbing pattern when we have three or four spare but struggles a bit with the inevitable moans over playing time when we have a full turn out of eighteen players.

We go downhill first and as per Danny's instructions we storm the Ratcatchers right off the bat. Eddie and I are complimenting rather than competing with each other and the net result is we have an edge in the midfield. It works out well as we lead twice in the first half 1-0, then 2-1 on goals by yours truly which were not spectacular but well earned by being in the right spot following sustained goal-mouth scrambles. They are a decent, well balanced team and make a couple of adjustments and have righted the ship by half time. I think we'll have our work cut out to hold onto our goal lead.

Big Ron Richards, not the most skilled but certainly the most enthusiastic American soccer player I've ever met, pulls out a bag of oranges cut in quarters. Danny is big on tradition and Ronnie's half time oranges are apparently a Raiders staple. After two orange quarters then splitting a smoke with ex Spurs' big Bill Fear (RIP—we miss you Bill), Danny is ready to impart his pearls of wisdom;

"Got 'em exactly where we want 'em. Look at their faces. They're shocked. They haven't had a challenge like this for the last couple of seasons. Keep it going. Now, eh, Eddie for strategy." This is another Danny custom where he just gives the general overview and hands over to one of his veterans for specifics.

"If they keep pushing up to play the off (sides) let's have a go at the old c*nt at the back. He's fine sweeping with plenty space but we'll take him in a foot race".

I'm thinking, spot on Eddie. Couldn't have put it better myself. Though it does sound eerily like what some opposing coach was likely saying about me recently in the Tigers games! I see a couple of obvious flaws in our full back alignment as they have a really fast winger who keeps switching sides to milk the weakness but I decide to hold my powder until Eddie gets a bit more used to having two naturally dominant players on the team.

Art Wilson and big Erik Pages, both accomplished players also often chip in a few specific pointers.

I get Tommy a couple of the extra orange bits and hand them to him.

"No bad half" he says "Looks like ye'll huv yer hands full now though."

The one thing which needs to be said is that although it's age group stuff it's no less competitive. Ratcatchers come out flying and equalize about half way through the half and are pressing for a winner. We're holding on courtesy a few good bounces and Eddie, Trickie, Guy and I all spending a lot of time deeper than we'd like.

With around ten minutes left I get an opportunity to test Eddie's half time theory. They play a very square offside trap close to halfway and catch two of our slow reacting forwards by several yards each. I'm enjoying, for the first time in a long time, being one of the faster, fitter players on the field rather than the reverse. There's a small gap between their centre half and sweeper so I just pop it through between them and take off full pelt. I'm moving uphill so keeping the ball reasonably close is easy enough. I hear multiple hoof prints at my back but duly ignore them thinking the worst I'm going to get is a direct free kick in decent position, maybe even a penalty if I can reach the box. To my slight surprise I manage to stay ahead of the pack and draw the goalie who's taking a decent central route out. I feign left and he bites hard leaving me a gentle side foot roller in the opposite corner. It's a finish even Kenny himself would be proud of.

We end up camped in our own box for the last five minutes under constant pressure and trying our best to get the ball headed towards Rock Creek Park as often as possible. We make it to the final whistle and the team seems genuinely elated to have beaten the arrogant Ratcatchers for the first time in many seasons. My teammates are all over me and Danny gets them to give me one of his patented traditional three cheers routines which I learn are only for very special occasions. Of course it peters out by the third cheer but I'll take it.

"ip, ip"—"hooray"
"ip, ip"—"ray"
"ip"—"ray"

It's a long time since I scored a hatrick and played such a prominent role in a meaningful fixture so I'm feeling that deep down total satisfaction which only comes around once in a great while now. I'm going to be really sore later but what a great sore it'll be.

Maybe there's something to this playing with boys my own age after all.

50

A LEAGUE OF THEIR OWN

The next major soccer tournament on the horizon is Euro 1996 and there is no doubt that you-know-who are going to be in it because it's being held in … England. We have tried to get a chance at this hosting thing but with no joy thus far. Surely if Sweden can host a major tournament we could too. We're known for our strong aggressive approach to playing but perhaps our self-marketing in respect of fitba has a long way to go to catch up with, say, our whisky trade. I recall a "Chewin' the fat" or "Only a game" type parody of Craig Brown in a kilt and Scotland shirt, standing in a heilan' glen waving a Scottish flag and begging EUFA in his poshest brogue; "EUFA, please gie us Euro 2008." A reference I guess to the failed low budget campaign.

I always thought that it'd be a cinch if Britain bid as a whole for either a Euro or a World Cup but I guess either the suits that run the associations are too snooty to co-operate for the good of the common fan or maybe UEFA/FIFA couldn't envisage pre-qualifying four countries as hosts?

Must be great to know you don't have to claw your way through the rapidly growing number of countries. Used to be hard enough trying to get past Russia when it was just one big USSR. It reminds me of the scene from Jason and the Argonauts where you smash one of the skeletons and each little piece of bone becomes a new nuisance in its own right.

I joked once before about trying to keep track of the changing names of all the African countries. At least their shapes generally stayed the same and most of them were good sized chunks. The former Soviet Union has all sorts of little fragments of land appearing as new countries and crowding the qualifying process. The only plus so far is that I finally understand who Frank Sinatra is on about in the song "Let's do it, let's fall in love"—Lithuanians and Lats being some of the many types who apparently "do it." Until the break-up, in asking about this song a common response would be; "What the f**k's a Lithuanian?"(Stop press: nowadays just ask a Jambo).

In addition to this raft of new teams, the former pushovers are almost non-existent now. Not too long ago you'd get an Iceland or a Cyprus or a Malta drawn in your qualifying group and immediately chalk up some points and a positive goal differential. Just can't do it anymore. Europe (indeed the world) has shrunk and the cross fertilization of players continues with potential talent being dug up anywhere it can be found and imported to where the big money is. The net result is more and more players from all these small, new, previously obscure countries getting a much higher level of training, practice and play which ultimately brings significant improvement to their national sides.

I don't suggest we interfere with this as it's democracy and capitalism working together, supply and demand, equal opportunities and all that good stuff. It's had some good spin-off if you think of the fuss not that long ago over the first few black players (thanks Mark Walters) yet now, save for a few loonies (and unfortunately there will always be a few of these,) racial issues have mostly disappeared from the soccer radar. Even the pape/proddie, Celtic/Rangers stuff seems seriously dissipated if not eliminated.

Do the Chelsea fans care that foreign cash enabled them to finally get past Manchester United and Arsenal? Will the Jambos give a toss who bankrolls them if they can get past Rangers and Celtic? And yet, I still see some short-termism in all of this. You just can't convince me that it isn't somehow retarding the progress of much of our home grown talent. They can only develop so far with reserve football and the odd few first team minutes off the bench. So here's the bottom line. We appear to be generally regressing as others progress which means appearances in major finals will be harder and harder to achieve.

Still. It is fitba and in the magical world of fitba there is always hope. I still think of the St Mirren side of the early seventies. Very young and totally home grown with a promising and innovative young manager (that Ferguson boy, still doing okay for himself) and kept intact until it had a chance to at least prove the basic concept. Likewise Dundee United of the Eighties under Jim Mclean. Some bright football spark is going to do this again but they will need a sharp business mind alongside them to try to prevent the start of the cherry picking before the whole product matures.

Belated insert, long after draft—warp speed to present. Are Hibs on the verge of proving my theory? Can they keep Rangers and the English vultures away from Mowbray and Cardiff City (who'd've thunk they'd ever be rich raiders?) away from Reardon? Beam me back Scottie.

So here is our qualifying round draw for a place in Euro 1996 in England.

RUSSIA—Or at least what's left of it—could've been worse. (Italy, Germany, Holland).

FINLAND—Used to be for long distance runners but some useful players now.

GREECE—Not bad. Great players but don't always gel and don't travel well.

FAROE ISLANDS—What, they have a fitba team? Brrrrrrrr.

SAN MARINO—Good bottle of Merlot as I recall.

For us this is a damn good draw. If there are anything close to minnows left in the Europond we have just netted two of them. We have an experienced squad who don't give up many goals but unfortunately don't score many either. However that style might be well suited to this mix of opponents and although we're unlikely to rack up goals against the Faroes and Marinos the current Scottish side are also unlikely to be upset by them.

Meantime I'm really enjoying my own game again. I'm quickly over my snobbish shame for moving out of the open age divisions and love being a significant weekly contributor to the ever improving UK Raiders. I'm even scoring much more than I have in years though I'm at that crossroads where making a perfect "Assist" is almost as satisfying as rippling the net myself.

Hibs seem stuck in perpetual mediocrity. They appear to be content just to survive in the top division. Are they becoming Pat Quinn's East Fife or Bertie Auld's Partick Thistle? You might think so if I remind you they go through a two month stretch where they draw eight of nine games. To compound the "Blaah" that streak is broken only by a loss to Hearts. They do get their revenge with a now rare, genuine first-of-January, New Year's Derby win (2-1) at Easter Road. An admirable result considering just a couple of days earlier Rangers mauled them 7-0!

The U.S. soccer authorities have reached a very difficult but ultimately sensible decision to delay the launch of their new pro soccer league for one more year. Despite the commercial success of the World Cup they just don't have all their ducks lined up properly and the last thing they need to do is rush. They've done that with all previous attempts at establishing a pro league and the impatience has always backfired. This time they are determined to set it up on a basis which will be realistically sustainable in the long term. Though many fans such as me are disappointed, we fully understand the cautious approach. We've waited since 1984, another year won't hurt. Besides, my move to the oldies is a final acceptance that I will not be one of the inaugural players of whatever they decide to call the Washington D.C. team! Mind you, maybe they'll need coaching help?

I continue to travel extensively around North, South and Central America and the Caribbean and this does nothing but constantly reinforce my strongly held view that fitba is its own universal language.

So it's down to serious qualifying business for Scotland and we get off to a flier with a somewhat unexpected 2-0 away win in Finland. Despite my skepticism we then put a 5-1 drubbing on the Faroes at Hampden. Being the worry wart I am, I still manage some pessimism. I've already decided that the Faroes' away goal is the one that will probably put us out. Next up Russia at Hampden—a 1-1 draw, not a disaster as they are favored to win the group. We then squeak a 1-0 home win over Greece. Unable to break them down for seventy minutes we send on the oldies striking tandem of John Robertson and Ally McCoist and within two minutes "Super Ally" earns his supper with the vital goal. We enter the Winter break from qualifying games in really good shape.

In the spring we pick up a real bonus point getting a goalless draw in Russia. Now we can seriously think about winning the section rather than just making a play-off as a best runner-up. We get two consecutive efficient away wins against the minnows. The Greeks spoil our unbeaten run with a 1-0 at their place. We get by an improving Finland 1-0 in a nail biter at Hampden then crush the Marinos 5-0 in our final home game. I make that seven wins, two draws and one loss with 19 goals for and only 4 against in the ten games. That last statistic is the key one which can make us competitive against anybody. If only we had a couple of serious international strikers at this time to compliment the fortress of a defense. Alas, Robertson and McCoist are past prime and the likes of Darren Jackson and Scott Booth are solid workers but there's nothing vaguely approaching a Dalglish or Jordan available. We do have a Shearer (Duncan) but I have to admit that my least favorite team has the Shearer (Alan) who matters most.

No complaints though. It's been as efficient a qualifying campaign as we've ever had and we're headed into auld enemy territory in the summer of 1996. England has a really strong squad at the time and when we get drawn in the same section with them some of my fellow ex-pat Scots are openly concerned. If I felt the same as them it's certainly something I'd never admit in public! But I honestly don't. Tommy Tucker, the ultimate England fan (because he is just like us—except in the exact opposite sense) asks me, "Well Jimmy-me-boy, what d'ya fink?"

Stiff upper lip (to steal one of their phrases,) "Delighted Tommy-my-boy, over the moon. What could be sweeter than to kick your arse in your own tourney at your own ground?" And I'm dead sincere. Not so much in terms of being confident of beating them but just pleased that we'll have the opportunity. Think about it. How often are we likely to play each other in a major tournament at a stadium where we've had our greatest international moments? It's likely a once in a lifetime thing. Win that game and we'll likely have bragging rights for a long time. Of course the reverse is true too and they'll be favored but you can't grasp glory without exposing yourselves to failure and you know how we love being a heavy underdog. Anyway, both sets of fans will have several months of banter to enjoy prior to the start of tourney and often the build-up is more fun and less stressful than the eventual games. Holland and Switzerland are the other teams drawn in our group.

Before we get to that tournament we are finally getting pro-soccer restarted in America. Major League Soccer (MLS) is the name and it'll open with ten teams:

Dallas Burn
Los Angeles Galaxy
Kansas City Wizards
San Jose Earthquakes (California)
Chicago Fire
Columbus (Ohio) Crew
New England Revolution (Boston)
Tampa Bay Mutiny
New York/New Jersey Metrostars
… and our very own (Washington) D.C. United.

It was really exciting to think we'd finally have a local team to support. Maybe there's still time to get at least one of my kids truly hooked. We get a bright young General Manager (GM) called Kevin Payne. Our colors will be black, white and red. For Coach Payne recruits Bruce Arena from the University of Virginia where he had one of the most constantly successful men's' college soccer programs in the country. I'd played with tons of UVA alumni soccer players over the years and they were all very useful. However I was a little cynical initially, thinking it would be such a big leap from years of handling 18-22 year olds to a professional setting. Many soccer veterans here said they shared my concerns. We hear the same concern quite often here relating to American football and Basketball coaching. Some coaches make an easy transition from college to pros, other supposed shoe-ins fail miserably. As it transpired all of us in the "Doubting Thomas" lobby would ultimately be proven dramatically wrong about Bruce Arena.

A key difference here with their sports versus Europe is the draft system and soccer is no exception. The draft is designed to try to develop a level playing field so that the clubs with the richer owners/fattest bank accounts can't simply buy up all the top players. The way Celtic and Rangers have done in Scotland, Manchester United, Liverpool and more recently Chelsea and Arsenal in England, Real Madrid and Barcelona in Spain and Juventus and the two Milans (AC and Inter) in Italy. It obviously works when you consider that the above mentioned group of teams has won well over half of all European Cups (now called Champions League) between them.

The American draft is usually accompanied by some type of "Salary cap" which puts a limit on how much each club can spend. However there are a lot of clever corporate executives who find ways to twist and manipulate the salary cap, diluting its impact via deferred payments and/or fat bonuses "spread" over many years for salary purposes.

The draft entails the worst team from the previous season having the first pick from the pool of new incoming players (mostly graduating college players) for the new season. This runs worst to best with the top team picking last. There are several rounds of this running in the same order until the pool of new players is all used up. Combined with the salary cap this system has worked to varying degrees in the different sports. It is most successful in achieving the desired parity in the National Football League where formerly dominant teams with deep pocketed owners (say Jack Kent Cooke of the Washington Redskins or Jerry Jones of the Dallas Cowboys) now tend to go through constant transitions like every other team. It also seems to work reasonably well in Basketball and Ice Hockey and produces a decent variety of champions.

It's had least impact in Baseball where the Yankees and their controversial fat cat owner, George Steinbrenner still somehow manage to scoop up all the top players and dominate play. Baseball is constantly introducing additional rules (i.e. some sort of scaled "Luxury" tax which is beyond my comprehension) to try to balance things but big George and his accountants always seem to find a loophole.

As there is no "Best" and "Worst" yet because MLS is just starting up, they use some kind of initial lottery to determine the picking order (not Tick-Tack as far as I'm aware) and they make sure already established pro's (returning from play abroad) are sprinkled fairly. Likewise with the foreign players who are looking to play in MLS though they are sensibly limiting this to four players per team to make sure they still leave room to properly develop their own young talent (how ironic is that considering the direction this particular aspect is headed in Scotland and throughout Europe). There does seem to be at least a small degree of marketing manipulation with key players ending up in locations with specific ethnic interest. A high profile pole—Peter Novak—to Chicago, a high profile Mexican—Jorge Campos—to Los Angeles, a high profile Bolivian—Marco Etcheverry to Washington.

D.C. United fair very well in this process. Far from being a foreign has-been (a clear problem with the failed NASL) Etcheverry is still in his prime and transpires to be a magician of a player with some of the sweetest touches you could ever see. He is exceptional at the long, angled, switch pass and can drop a ball on a dime (tanner in our terms) from fifty yards away, reminiscent of Alex Edwards of Hibs. He is also brilliant from dead ball situations, especially corners where his accuracy bring D.C.U. a ton of goals. He earns the nickname "El Diablo" (Devil) for his intense piercing stare and trailing hair which looks like a jet black shiny version of an old judge's wig. He also carries his arms unusually high when running and looks like he's about to start sparring with someone. The fans love him and no surprise that he is adored by the local, not inconsiderably sized Bolivian ex-pat community. He returns the love by participating in lots of community based events. D.C. United does a great job of this and you always feel like Kevin Payne is skillfully pulling the off-field strings.

We get another marketing coup with the addition of Raul Diaz Arce, a Salvadorian striker who is revered by that, also massive, ex-pat community. He is an old fashioned fast and direct striker who converts a decent percentage of his quality chances. Just "El Diablo" and Diaz-Arce between them will put close to 10,000 fans in RFK each week and that's before we even start tapping the vibrant youth and amateur soccer community. The squad also has a sprinkling of UVA alumni who will be well used to Arena's soccer methodology. This includes John Harkes (Harksie) who has gathered valuable pro-experience playing in England. He'll be Captain. I initially think this might be a bit awkward with Etcheverry and him crowding each others' obvious leadership instincts in midfield. However they end up complimenting each other well with Harkes the physical leader and Etcheverry the creative spark.

D.C.U. play in the first ever MLS game on 6th April 1996 at San Jose. Though they lose 1-0 but the vital statistic from that game is the crowd of 31,683 a very encouraging start. After another road loss (0-4) at Columbus they return for their first game at RFK on 20th April. Dale, Kyle and I are there amongst over 35,000 enthusiasts who see a disappointing loss (1-2) to the L.A. Galaxy. It's still great fun as I meet dozens of old soccer buddies. It's almost like a re-union. After yet another loss in a shoot-out tie-breaker to New England DCU finally get their first MLS win on May 1[st.] A 3-1 win against Dallas in a rare midweek game. The crowd is much sparser but still above 10,000.

I've made a special effort because young John Kerr is on the Dallas Burn and I'm keen to see how he's doing. He's gained some initial exposure during his "study abroad" in England playing for Harrow Borough in the "Non-league" (second tier of pro's—mostly part timers combining soccer with other careers) and manages to secure a trial at Portsmouth, a team very much on the rise in England. John makes a big impression in a reserve (youth/second team) outing and is signed on the spot. John senior is bursting with pride as he describes the experience of watching his son play at the top level over there including a visit to the legendary Anfield. Young John gets a few first team games but doesn't really stick. He then confirms his own soccer addiction by traveling far and wide in relentless pursuit of his fitba dream. This includes stops back in Washington (Stars), England (Wycombe Wanderers) France (Boulogne-Sur-Mer), Ireland (Linfield) and Canada (Hamilton Steers). Even as a teenager, John's fitba pedigree, combined with his dedication, smarts and work rate pointed towards ultimately coaching. He got a serious coaching start at his alma mater, Duke and took to it well. This is where his future lay. But first one last serious playing fling in England with Millwall another traditionally lower division team on the rise, before his inevitable return to be part of the historic start of MLS. And so to today.

We catch a break when, following warm-ups, he heads for a tunnel at the corner where we're seated. I catch his attention and he stops by the wall to say hello and signs Kyle's programme. He and Dale are quite impressed that their old man really knows a pro. They've heard all about my boring connections with famous Scottish players whom they've never heard of but because they can touch this one first hand it means more to them, especially one in glamorous uniform sporting a fire breathing stallion! I'm guessing John senior and a slew of other pals and relatives are sipping cocktails in one of the plush sections on the mezzanine level.

It's an exciting and satisfying occasion for me. It's the fruition of a lot of dreams for a whole generation of American players who finally have a real opportunity at a proper full time football career without having to go "Nomad" like young John had to. He also endears himself to me through a quote I get from an interview he did for a 2001 New England Soccer magazine article. It reads as follows:

"It's a disease you know. It's something that I can't get out of my life. Sometimes it's frustrating to my wife that my relaxation time is spent watching an MLS game or watching Champion's League on a Wednesday. Sometimes it gets in the way of other family things, but it's in my blood and in my heart and it's something that will never go away."

Likesay, couldn't have put it any better myself son.

No real surprise that he'll end up as Head coach at Harvard.

So MLS is off to a healthy start but our focus switches back to England during the summer. Scotland once again managed to miss qualifying for the knock-out stages via the most frustrating count-back whisker. An honorable goalless draw against the Dutch at Villa Park (Birmingham) is a good start. Then The Game goes way off my dream script with Paul Gascoigne in the wrong shirt scoring my fantasy goal at the wrong end of Wembley stadium. He even cheekily "chips" big Colin Hendry in the process. Oh no, we'll have to endure it on replay a million times. We recover for a 1-0 victory over Switzerland back in less glamorous Birmingham and are in the awkward and unusual position of having to pull for England to score a barrow load against Holland. They oblige with a stunning 4-1 win. So we end up tied with Holland on points and goal difference but they've scored more goals. The Dutch have had a lot of in-fighting within their squad and although they're loaded with talent they are just not as joined up as usual in this tournament. Of course even with all that disruption they've pipped us at the post. We're out early once again. The Tartan Army are headed back North and with no regular Auld Enemy match nowadays, god only knows when we'll have a chance at redemption.

Gascoigne shines brightly in this tournament and along with Shearer's clinical finishing the two propel England to the semi's and our worst fears of a host victory are in real danger of materializing as all the other heirs apparent are conveniently knocking each other off. Thank god for the dogged Gerries who once again manage to oust der Englanders on penalties, 6-5. Perhaps life in America is softening me? I confess that I felt sorry for Gascoigne sitting in tears again … but only for a split second until I came back to my biased senses. If he'd been Scottish we'd have adored him. In fact, a certain segment of the weedgies did for a while whilst he wore Rangers' blue.

The Czech Republic, who are stealthily working their way up the world rankings, meet the Germans in the final but are squeezed out 1-2 in extra time.

We had MLS to keep our minds off yet another disappointment and it was starting to take shape in terms of who might take the initial title. Los Angeles and Tampa Bay were looking good with the diminutive Salvadorian midfielder, Mauricio Cienfuegos outstanding for LA and Roy Lassiter of Tampa setting the initial MLS goal scoring pace. D.C.U. had also steadied after their poor start. Arena's playing philosophy was starting to become evident to any experienced observer and he showed a Midas touch with substitutions almost always getting a significant yield from his in game adjustments. They stroked the ball about really nicely. This was a very entertaining team to watch by any fitba standard.

United make the play-offs and open against New York. We have the home field advantage which means we play the first game in New York the second at RFK and a third, if necessary again at RFK. We lose up there in a shoot-out but recover with two consecutive home wins (1-0 and 2-1) to advance. Through luck rather than planning a visit from my dad coincides with our home game against Tampa in the semis. He and I are amongst the close to 24,000 crowd which watches D.C.U. dismantle the Mutiny 4-1. It's by far our most complete performance so far. My dad is amused when I explain that RFK is considered an outdated venue. He thinks it's superb. MLS will have to work very hard for international credibility overseas and especially from a cynical European audience. I'm one of the early advocates telling anyone who'll listen, mostly my dad via telephone, that the standard is very respectable. After seeing it in person he concurs, suggesting that this D.C. team could certainly give Hibs a decent game and compete respectably with the lower segment of the English Premier League. So now D.C.U. will have their first PR man in Edinburgh. He'll start with Drylaw then cascade the word towards Leith.

To show it's no fluke D.C. travel to Tampa and get a hard fought 2-1 victory to book their place in the first ever MLS cup. It's being held in Foxboro, New England and the Western play-offs have gone to form with L.A. winning through. D.C. United and L.A. Galaxy end up playing through a torrential downpour. I suspect, under any other circumstances, the game would be abandoned but the weather has come in suddenly and thousands of fans from D.C. and L.A. are already there. Besides, it's scheduled for live coverage during prime sports Sunday national television time, a rare major coup for MLS. A shame in many ways that the first real "MLS showcase" game should be in such dreadful conditions with two very attractive crisp passing sides unable to display anything like their normal fluidity. Still, it's back and forth splashingly entertaining and we get a made-for-TV dramatic ending with Eddie Pope heading a "Golden goal" winner in overtime and body surfing the massive puddles in celebration.

A few days later D.C.U. complete the first modern American soccer "Double" by beating the wonderfully named Rochester Rhinos 3-0 in the US open cup final. Rochester (up state New York near Buffalo) plays in what's now called the "A" league, which will be a place for fringe MLS players to stay sharp. Some of these teams will also be hopeful of an "Expansion" shot at MLS in the future.

MLS has consolidated its promising start, especially in respect of the numbers that matter the most. A crowd of 35,000 watch the final despite the horrendous conditions. L.A. is the best supported team with an average 28,000. D.C.U. ends up with over 15,000 home average. They also get a strong kids' supporters club "The Screamin' Eagles" established. Kyle's in for that as it comes with all sorts of souvenirs and autograph sessions. We also have an instant tradition with what's called the "Bara Brava" section directly opposite the team benches taking great pride in standing for the entire game, rocking the stadium in a way which only the Redskins' fans had previously managed. MLS league wide average is over 17,000, also slightly ahead of their best projections. These are all great numbers for a fledgling venture in a country where the likesay Baseball, Basketball and American Football have a firm stranglehold.

From a personal standpoint it's also worked out well. I've really enjoyed following D.C.U. and Dale and Kyle are keen if not quite addicted yet. Dale likes "Harksie" and Kyle likes one of the goalies, Jeff Causey, because he was very patient with him at an autograph signing session. Me? I'm pretty stuck on El Diablo's dramatic body fakes and magical weighted passes and precision set plays.

51

A JAMBO-ROBBO DILEMMA

From a playing perspective the late 1990's are great to me. Wee Eddie's moved on and I have the playmaker role all to myself on a variety of Danny teams including such precious names as the Royals and the Crusaders. I've also met Syd Boyne the original Bulldogs' goalie in a bar and he's invited me to play in a mid-week thirty-plus indoor league at the Sports Network in Manassas, Virginia. Indoor soccer is massive now. It all started with Alan Spavin and Alan Kelly opening the Corner Kick in Rockville but now, everywhere you look there's an indoor facility.

The previously mentioned Sports Network is another of the early ones. Started by the highly respected youth coach, John Ellis, it's different in that he has settled for the one large field rather than multiple small ones. It allows for lots of space in which to get creative. By contrast there's a newer indoor place in Springfield where I played a few times but they've squeezed in so many fields they're just too small for adults to enjoy the game properly. The result is like being inside a human pinball machine. The surfaces have also improved dramatically from the original rock hard Astroturf to a more forgiving cushioned version which is much gentler on old knees.

I had played at Sports-Network the odd time when John Kerr senior would round up the usual suspects of me, Karl Minor, Sonny Askew, Andy Harris, Gabor (the Hungarian stud) and Bolivian Willie for a game. As also mentioned we played against Café 28. It was named after a bar on route 28, the main drag into Manassas and that would serve as the after match watering hole though higher drink/drive awareness had tempered that activity considerably.

Café 28 became a French Restaurant called Chez Marc (after owner Marc Fusilier) and the team followed suit. At one point the team roster got so crowded they had to start a second team which they named Chez Fais for the owner wife. By the time I join it's just Chez Marc and it's loaded with Murphy's FC (NVSL) alumni as well as my old buddy Eddie Koebke. There is a noticeable difference in the pace from the over 35's outdoors to the over 30's indoors. Of course indoor is always faster but there are many players right on that thirty year old cusp and they all seem as fast as Whippits. (Small sleek racing dogs) None of them are on our team which likely has by far the oldest average age but with lots of skill to compensate, a large bench (lots of subs) and always a decent keeper. In indoor a real keeper is worth his weight in gold. With unlimited substitutions on the fly I use this as training, running really hard for five to ten minutes then grabbing a breather. The benefits to my outdoor game are obvious as I find my legs able to deliver much more of what my mind dictates. This separation of mind from legs is always the key sign of soccer aging. You see it all the time in the old boys' leagues where the intent of a great play is obvious but it's smooth execution is encumbered by a belly or a bandage or a brace!

So I have indoor Wednesday and outdoor Sunday and I love them both all the more for the relative fitness this combination brings. Once again I think back to the message from wee Bobbie the professional scout at Saughton Park all those years ago. "Ye huv tae be fit tae enjoy yir game properly son". Likesay, spot on Bobbie.

I get a great bonus when my Dad visits. He's now past the seventy mark but still enjoys very good general health via his walking regime. Not smoking or drinking also helps his fitness as well as how far his pension goes no doubt. We have a game at Gloxena Park at Tuckerman Lane, Maryland. It's not in great shape but still one of my favorites as it has a slope which reminds me of the Seagulls' Hill at Ainslie Park., Inverleith number five and of course Easter Road. We play Bethesda United and Danny agrees to bring on my Dad for ten minutes or so towards the end. We figure the chances of a protest against a seventy year old unregistered player are pretty slim. With about fifteen minutes left Paddy, our consummate Irish striker with the curly grey locks and rosy cheeks, needs to get off for a fag. "On ye go John". My dad has no fitba shorts so he just rolls up his trouser legs, sticks on the shirt (one of Danny's more respectable efforts—real football shirts with a small black and white diamond pattern giving the overall effect of grey—of course he has to have something bright so the number is vivid yellow). Dad jogs into a very wide right position. He's fed the ball close to his feet several times gathering it neatly and making clean return passes. One of these one-twos is with yours truly and leads to a nice clean finish after faking the keeper the wrong way. So my dad and I have played in a real game together when he's in his seventies. That is real treasure. Though I know there is at least one older than him who still plays weekly in our league. His name's Murray Grant but we'll get to him later.

On the fan front there are the usual highs and lows. DC United repeat as the MLS Champions and this time the final is at our very own RFK Stadium. Over 57,000 are packed into the stadium and it's by far the most enthusiasm I've seen from my own kids Dale and Kyle over anything fitba related. We now have a second Bolivian player, Jaime Moreno who has top level experience in England. He has silky control and a very deceptive long first step which leaves defenders flat and gets him into great crossing and scoring positions. He scores one. The other goal is from big Tony Sanneh. He's a tall hunched shouldered, lumbering player who can look fantastic one minute and awful the next. As always, Bruce Arena seems to find a way to get the most out of him.

So we're strolling along at 2-0 and suddenly Colorado Rapids pull one back on a cracking shot. There's a little finger nail biting during the closing minutes but we hold on for our second consecutive MLS Cup in yet another driving rainstorm. I make Dale and Kyle hike up three levels so that I can buy a celebratory (and warming) double brandy.

Another bright spot are Scotland who have recovered from an opening qualifying loss to Sweden to get past Austria, Latvia, Estonia and Belarus and book their place in the 1998 world cup finals in France. The section illustrates the growing and changing face of European qualifying competition with three teams which didn't even exist for most of my lifetime.

Hibs balance my euphoria by having their worst season in years and ending up relegated to the first division. The only highlight is an April derby win but this is small solace as the Jambos have reached the Scottish cup final against Rangers. The Jambos have been knocking on the door for years but with no actual silverware to show for it Hibs fans always had the last word courtesy our two league cups. We were now in danger of a serious double-whammie (yet another Scottishism for not good) of a Jambo cup win and the loss of the last word in every embra fitba argument. I confess to a tiny bit of mixed sentiment creeping into my thoughts. John Robertson's had a great career and came so close so many times and a part of me thinks of that wee laddie I played subbuteo with and his passion for the game and what a Scottish cup winners badge would mean to him. We're all fed up with Rangers and Celtic picking up almost all of the major honors. On the other hand it is Hearts we're talking about and JR did steal some of my subbuteo players and has scored more crucial goals against Hibs than I care to remember. No. To hell with sentiment I just can't pull for the Jambos regardless of the ramifications for dozens of Bunty's cousins as well as her ma.

I certainly can't stomach a visit to Summer's bar to watch the game. Regardless of the outcome I'll likely have to face a jubilant Jambo or a bubbly bluenose.

I decide to do the garden instead. However I will have the BBC world service commentary playing on my pocket sized Radio Shack digital wide band sat upon the front steps. I chuckle again when I think of it compared to the large clunky box with all the monster dials borrowed from the embassy in an earlier chapter. Reception is loud and clear and when Hearts' Adam adds a second goal to Colin Cameron's first half penalty a Jambo cup win looks a serious possibility. My feelings are still wavering back and forth and I'm starting to curse Jim Jeffries, the Hearts manager who still has JR sitting on the bench. Meanwhile JR's Rangers counterpart "Super" Ally McCoist pulls back a goal with about ten minutes left. I've now dumped the garden tools and am fully ensconced in the game. Bunty has came out to join me. I think of all the Jambos I knew growing up. They'll all be at Hampden, knowing the magic is within their grasp but expecting the worst to happen as it almost always has/does against the old firm. Though few I knew were church goers they'll be praying like crazy right now. Many won't even be able to watch the field anymore. Head down, eyes shut, pursed lips, pained expression. Something along the lines of:

"Please god. Jist nine mair minutes. Nae mair goals, ken. Jist leave things is they ir eh? Ul dae any hing. A mean it. Any hing. Please. Jist this once."

My own resolution was that I'd accept a Jambo win but with a condition. If I was going to be that open minded then Jeffries has to at least put JR on the field for the last minute and make my moral compromise worthwhile. I know all the arguments for professionalism and understand that McCoist's goal made things more tight and complex but surely you put one of your team's all time greats into the most significant game in over thirty years. You can even waste a few valuable seconds in the process. The Jambo prayers are answered and the ref blows the final whistle on their 2-1 win. At that moment, the ultimate Embra bragging rights (i.e. only the last major trophy counts) moved from Leith to Gorgie for the first time in my consciousness.

Don't get me wrong. JR would no doubt be over the moon at Hearts' cup win but as an individual player not getting on the field would matter greatly to him. I still love Willie Ormond for taking Denis Law to the 1974 world cup in Germany on what I still say was predominantly a lifetime achievement acknowledgement.

So. In a heartbeat (no pun intended) I've changed my mind again. I want Hearts to lose. I want Rangers to beat them. I don't want to hear about a big maroon parade around Gorgie. I want my Embra lifetime bragging rights back … but it's too late.

It's down to Scotland to cheer me up again. Not a bad first round draw really. Okay we've got Brazil again but this usually brings great PR to Scotland as the fan interaction is so colorful and friendly. Besides, we usually do okay against them in the first round, so long as we don't get them all riled up by having the cheek to score early. Norway is stuffy but beatable and we're still not too sure what to expect from the African teams though they are clearly all on a fastrack upwards.

My daughter Dale is on study abroad that spring semester at St Andrews in Scotland. She calls me when she arrives and tells me she has a lovely view of the beach and the ocean from her Macintosh dormitory window. There's also a golf course but it looks a bit run down and people are traversing it walking dogs and even pushing a couple of large prams over it. *Oh I should explain that prams are perambulators—the bulky predecessors of the modern day buggy which many young moms—and occasionally dads too—would have to lug up and down several flights of narrow old Edinburgh tenement stairs. I guess it all started with Mothercare's sexy quick fold version in the seventies and I'm sure by now there's an ultra-super-new-improved version which you can fold up and carry in your back pocket.* I remind Dale that it's actually quite a well known course, even in America. In the summer she ends her study abroad with the obligatory backpacking trip around Europe.

She spends a lot of time in France right amidst the world cup and says the atmosphere is great. On a students budget she can't make a live game but she does get me the obligatory world cup tee shirt which I still wear despite its stained and shrunken state. She is sensible enough to wait many years before telling her Mom about how she and her buddies got hopelessly lost in Corsica or Sardinia by boarding a train in the wrong direction. Fortunately they were rescued by a lovely old lady whose description sounded very similar to our own Mrs Boyle back in Pilton.

Next summer we're all headed back to Scotland for a family holiday together. An exciting prospect except for the fact that all my Jambo pals will be telling me how great it was on the day they won the cup. Unless of course Hibs can manage to pick up a major trophy before I get there.

52

CRAZY BUS

We reach the summer of 1999 and it's time to visit bonnie Scotland. We're on a bit of a mission this time. Besides the usual family stuff we're committed to filling the afore-mentioned High School history curriculum void by visiting some of the key highland sites. We're joining up with Bunty's sister Linda, husband Nigel and daughter Tomma and hiring our very own mini-bus in which to do our Highland touring. Unfortunately Dale can't join us because she has begun her own career with Price Waterhouse Coopers in the Ivory towers of downtown Washington DC. Nigel has managed to get us a great deal on a big suite at one of the main hotels in Inverness which we will use as our highland HQ for the week. Something goes amiss with our van hire booking so we end up doing a quick phone around for an alternate.

Clark's in Leith sound like the best option so my dad runs me up there to take a look. By co-incidence the rental lot is right by Easter Road. It's nestled under the famous Bothwell street bridge which has been traversed by many millions of fitba daft fans over the years. The stadium is undergoing yet another round of renovation including the removal of our beloved slope. I've been watching progress via a webcam. When the angle is right I enjoy seeing the silhouette of Arthur's Seat and the old town in the background. It sometimes makes me a little homesick. Anyway, I'll now have a chance to view it all first hand but that'll have to wait until later in the trip.

We're looking for something to accommodate seven people and luggage comfortably and they come up with a Renault Van. It's a big black thing with the typical high Renault roof. Think it was called an Executive. Each time I go home I have to get re-acquainted with gears (stick shift) which always seems like extremely hard work, especially on hill starts in the busier than ever city centre. I have great difficulty maneuvering the thing out of the narrow car park and back up onto the main Easter Road stalling twice in the process. When I check my rear view mirror I see my dad smiling broadly. I get through a bustling Junction Street and even driving through I count three toots and two waves from my dad to people he still knows there. Ferry Road seems bliss by comparison except for my stuttering negotiation of the ever busy Crewe Toll roundabout. By the time we reach Drylaw my lower back and upper arse is covered by one of those embarrassing large wet patches. I have to park with one side mounting the curb to leave enough space for other cars to get past. The thing is leaning so much I'm worried it might keel over like a wounded elephant. Don't want any bumps or scratches as I've been a cheapskate and waived the exorbitant daily collision option. The guy has given me that ominous look, tut and headshake you always get when you initial that wee box.

My hope of Hibs quickly recovering the city bragging rights expired very early with the mighty St Johnstone trouncing us 4-0 in the League Cup and that perennial juggernaut; Stirling Albion dumping us out of the Scottish; 2-1 after we could only manage a draw with them at home. Of course we can't win the other major honor as we are not even in the Premier League! As expected we do romp away with the first division title so we will be back up to the premier next season but we are resigned to a year of Jambo jibes.

I get my first taste of the new Jambodom as we go to the Cannongate to meet up with Linda, Nigel and Tomma for our highland departure. I nip into the Tolbooth (Tavern) for a quick pint and run into Jim Robertson. The conversation inevitably turns to fitba and in turn the cup win and Jim describes how special the day was. On a purely one-off, individual basis I'm sort of pleased for him. He confirms that a lot of the family shared my disappointment that they didn't get young (it's all relative in both senses of the word) John into the game. He gives me a straw to grasp when he tells me he thinks Hibs have turned the corner and will be a growing force next season under their dynamic young Manager; Alex (Big Eck) McLeish as he has good "Eurocred" and might be able to talk a few big names to wear the emerald green. He even suggests that all the Easter Road stadium renovations will be well justified as Hibs will likely be back in European competition very soon. Let me see. That's a dedicated lifetime Jambo telling me he expects us to win a cup or finish near the top of the SPL (the latest trendy abbreviated handle for the top Scottish league) in our first season back! If only I could be so objective in reverse. A lovely pint of Eighty Shilling by the way. Though I'm not a big beer hand that first one in a long while always tastes special. I've not got the bottle (nerve) to try to park the van right on the Cannongate so I've left it on the ultra wide New Street just a block away.

Time to satisfy the wander lust and head up to the heilans. We all pile into the Renault and claim our places. I'm up front with Nigel who's running over the directions. Bunty and Linda are ensconced in serious conversation in the second row. Tomma and Brooke are quick soul mates in row three and are constantly whispering and giggling. Kyle is tucked in back with his nose in a book but he takes an occasional break to attempt to tease and torment the girls.

Our itinerary includes Loch Ness and as we head towards the Forth Road Bridge I randomly think about an old TV show called the Crazy Bus where a bunch of characters traipsed around the country in a converted double-decker. The only name I recall was Una Mclean but I do remember there was an episode involving a weird visit to Loch Ness. The theme tune even runs in my head.

"Crazy bus you will be taking us away,

Crazy bus I wonder where we'll go today" or words to that effect.

I know. This is supposed to be a fitba book. So as we turn off the motorway into Inverness I get a clear look at the smart new stadium where Caley-Thistle plays against all the top teams regularly nowadays. Funny to think back to childhood when we passed the little stand on Telford Street on our way to Wick back when all the Inverness teams were stuck in the Highland league. We arrive at the Thistle hotel and have all been a bit nervous with Nigel explaining the special deal is based on saving up Weetabix breakfast cereal box tops. We soon owe him a major thank-you as we are indeed led to a lovely spacious suite with a little room off with bunk beds which the girls enthusiastically claim.

It transpires to be a perfect base for our daytrips to Culloden, Glencoe, Ben Nevis (Highest Scottish mountain) Skye and various other places of interest. We even manage a ride on an old steam train to Mallaig on the West coast which takes us by additional important historical points including the (17) '45 (Jacobite uprising) monument. The weather is also very kind to us with the rain stopping several times during the week.

We include a full circuit of Loch Ness and I confess that we are all highly amused, maybe even a wee bit embarrassed by the extreme commercialization of our famous Scottish dinosauras aquaticus. There are large tacky model depictions at various stops and more stuffed toys than you'll find at a low budget fun fair. Of course the kids love all that stuff but they do admit to finding the loch quite eerie especially at the more remote points when mist rolls over. I finally prove to myself that the village of Drumnadrochit really does exist and we have a super pub lunch there. We've always taken a lot of stick for our Scottish cuisine or lack thereof but some of the pub grub nowadays is very respectable. And of course everything tastes better when you're on your holidays.

It would be interesting to find out how many Scots have never actually been to Loch Ness. I suspect true nationals might even be outnumbered by tourists in the visit stats. By contrast, in conversation with Scots about Nessie you'll always find someone who knows someone who saw something at sometime! I'm no exception. My mom had a good friend whose dad became caretaker of one of the old castles dotted around the shores of Loch Ness. There was no inside plumbing and her pal always swore blind she saw a massive head and neck rise from the loch whilst visiting the outhouse in the early hours of a frosty winter morning.

On a deliberately long, round route home we manage to pass through the charming village of Plockton which had been popularized by the TV series, Hamish MacBeth. It starred Robert Carlyle as a no-si-daft highland bobbie (policeman—this nickname originates from Robert Peel the original London cop and made it all the way up to Scotland—unusual). We even managed to follow this show in America through PBS (public television). Everybody thought it was hilarious when our crazy bus got stuck trying to get past Highland coos (cows) on the small country road leading out of Plockton. They were right off a heilan postcard or the McGowan's toffee wrapper. All I could think of was their sharp horns and that bloody insurance waiver.

We skirted the bonnie, bonnie banks of Loch Lomond and ended up cutting through Glasgow. I'm sure some of the road works around that city were the same ones we got stuck at trying to get to Hampden for the Czechoslovakia game in 1973. That's the speed of Corpie contracts for you!

Back in Edinburgh it's too early even for any kind of pre-season Hibs games so I settle for a stop at Leith Links on my way back from visiting my ma at the Seafield cemetery.

She's probably laughing up there saying I only came to see her hoping there'd be a game on. Thing about the Links is there's almost always a game on. Mostly boy's leagues and usually quite young. I'm guessing these kids are nine or ten. They're fairly getting stuck in to each other and as always, even in a ten or fifteen minute look you always see one or two and say 'Aye, he knows what he's daein'. Some of the modern pro's have a lot to answer for as the laddies always follow their leads and they've obviously been watching some of the ridiculously elaborate goal scoring celebrations. It was a nice shot son but it hardly merited you doing the Charleston with the corner flag.

Brooke is quite into fitba at this time and decides to chum (accompany) me down to Easter Road for a look at the place. She also knows I'll be in the club shop and she'll have no qualms about playing to my weakness and extracting a Hibs flavored piece of gear or souvenir from me. I park at the cemetery wall opposite the club shop but unfortunately the shop isn't open on that day at that time. We walk along towards the old Strangs School corner and there's a small gap in the corrugated iron builders fence. That's handy, hop in—and we do. We wander around what we knew as the shed end which is now filled by the smart Famous Five stand. The place is totally silent and deserted except for one old guy working on a wall at the far end and two pigeons pecking at the halfway line. Both men and bird seem totally disinterested in our intrusion so we just carry on.

The stand at what we knew as the old Dunbar/scoreboard end looks very smart with its green seats, white aisles and sky lighted cantilever roof. It kind of reminds me of one of the fancy subbuteo stands which I could never afford. The old original stand is looking its age and somehow looks uncomfortable with the contrasting modern floodlights perched on its roof. These definitely look like elements from different eras which simply don't belong together. The same floodlights look fine on the opposite side on the long basic shed with modern looking columns and a much flatter roof. I explain to Brooke how the main terracing on that side used to almost reach up into the clouds when we were wee.

We wander on the pitch and luckily Brooke carries a camera with her so we take each others picture which we still have. If I knew we would have this much license to roam I would have worn my full strip and brought a ball and got some action shots. If the shop was open I'd have bought a kit and ball and changed right there and then. Really, those close to me know I would've. At least Brooke has a football shirt on though it's the red Kansas City Wizards one.

The pitch was now flat though I couldn't really tell if they'd dug out the top of the slope or topped up the bottom. I relayed a little of the folklore of Hibs' famous second half downhill charges to her. I also explained how at one time we could run on the pitch for a few seconds after a goal without fear of any serious repercussions. She was respectfully interested but still a bit sick the shop was shut. Anyway I'm not sure it's possible to transmit the true joy of such moments to offspring except perhaps to liken it to something they have done where you have sensed their own similar elation. She did seem genuinely amused when, on the way out, I explained how they used to heavily grease all the telegraph poles around the ground so desperate fans couldn't climb up them.

The photos would convince anyone that I must be well connected at Easter Road to have such free access. I'll save that for a rainy day when I'm trying to convince some skeptic that I was once great.

Funny thing about the photo of me is the slope still looks like it's there.

Dooroodooroo … dooroodrooroo.

53

HIBS WIN THE LEAGUE

So now, just like that, we're definitely in the twenty first century. Definitely in the twenty first century, definitely in the twenty first century; to steal the style from another of my favorite movie characters; Rain Man (a.k.a. Dustin Hoffman). Who doesn't know where he gets his underwear? K Mart, K Mart in Cincinnati—but I digress, sorry. I find it hard not to write about things I really like.

Anyway I emphasize the DEFINITELY part because even some of the world's top scientists have disagreements over when the Millennium (i.e. Change of Century) actually occurs. Like the world at large, we celebrated Happy New Century on 1 January 2000. We even had some tooters, hats and fireworks and even our bairns, who have never experienced New Year the way we did growing up, get quite into the spirit of things.

However there are some respected scholars who argue that the REAL millennium is actually on 1 January 2001. So regardless of who's right, in Spring 2001 we are definitely in the twenty first century!

I think back to primary school in the mid 1960's. How many times did teachers make us talk, write or draw about what it would be like in the "Twenty first century"? Such an exciting subject and so untouchably far, far, away. And yet, we blinked, we're here.

A couple of my more basic forecasts came out sort of right, I just wasn't bold enough in how far things would go. Left hand flat on desk, Right arm stretching as high as possible, bum bouncing on chair;

"Please, Miss Westlake."

She points her big spongy right index finger in my general direction and in her "Mrs Doubtfire" tone, responds;

"Yes, James?"

First name. Wow. Must be in a really good mood today. More often "James Meikle" or even just "Meikle" on a bad day. I quickly double check behind me.

James (Jimmy) Watt and James (Jamsie) Craig are in the same general direction as me but neither have their hand up.

"Well James?" she chases, frustrated by my hesitation.

"Eh … Well Miss … I think in the next century there will be TV's and phones in every house … and even in cars"

(Very big thick) Puckered lips and nodding;

"Probably right James." though with hindsight she was hardly impressed by the predictability of my response. I'm only about eight mind. I've got in there and said something and not been slagged or scolded for my response so I'm feeling pretty good.

"Sheila?"

Big, tall Sheila MacDonald's next.

"Well Miss. By the next century we won't be buying Black Babies any more 'cause there'll be no starving children in the world"

"Black Babies" was a way the schools collected money for charities in Africa at the time. They had little cards about three inches (Pre-metric) square with a picture of an African baby on. You gave a penny (Pre-metric) and you chose a card with the idea that your money went to help feed that particular baby. Sticking your money in the plate at church was always a bit vague but this was very specific and gave you a feeling of getting a result. So it worked.

"Oh I really hope your right" said old Wessie who, for all her faults with us, seemed like a very charitable person in that respect. Pretty sure she eventually donated her very big posh family house in Ferry Road as a laity centre.

"David?" she then goes onto one of the two budding boffins (our nickname for boys who were good at science) in our primary class; David (Davie) Butler. The other was Christopher (Chris) Mulligan. Not to be confused with Andy Mulligan (our own goofy class clown).

"Thank-you Miss Westlake. I think that by the millennium," (what the F's that most of us are thinking) "most people will have computers, remotes and robots to help them in their daily lives."

"Very good, David" she says to her best mannered, best behaved student.

And we're all sitting thinking. Sure. Computers, robots. Remotes—what's that? Aye 'n they'll probably have a plane thit kin fly tae America in a couple ae 'oors.

Now that we're here let's have a quick review of the results.

Of course I was right except that the tellys and phones are also in most cars as well as houses!

The real irony is that whilst all David's technological stuff has come to fruition to an even greater extent than his adventurous young scientific mind could have imagined, we still can't get Sheila's bit right. There are still thousands of Black babies dying in Africa. Why is that?

There I go again on my soap box.

So it's definitely the twenty first century and one other prediction has been fulfilled. This one made by many a cocky Hearts fan over the past ninety-eight years since Hibs last won the Scottish Cup. "Lucky if yaes'll win the cup again this century." And we did not. We haven't won a league championship since the mid 1950's but the new century is going to get off to a great start in that respect.

Hibs *WILL* win the league in 2001 and I *WILL* be in the team. I guarantee it. But wait a minute James, if I remember correctly Hibs finished well down the Scottish Premier League that year and bordered on bankruptcy. Ah … but … as my old grannie used to say "Thirs many wiys tae skin a cat."

Remember I'm now starring in the Montgomery County Department of Recreation, Men's 35+ Soccer League—Central Division. Danny Brogan is our rotund and effervescent Player/Manager. Known more for his comedic/acting/singing dancing skills as a stalwart member of The British Embassy Players. His shirt generally can't make it all the way over his belly, leaving a smile of pale flesh above his shorts. Mind you his limited mobility belies some deft touches and scorching shots from set pieces. He uses the role of Player/Manager to enhance his acting skills, giving some of the most entertaining and optimistic half time pep talks you will ever hear. He incorporates some very respectable impersonations of some of the true characters who have played for the various teams of the British Embassy Soccer Club over the years.

For example. One time we're down 3-0 at the half time to an admittedly poor side, who, besides their starting eleven, has eight substitutes on the touchline. Tommy Tucker's been sent off which is not entirely unusual. He's a great sweeper and still really fast for our age group but he has a habit of suddenly losing the plot which may have something to do with a lifetime supporting Havant and Waterlooville. Danny fires Tommy at least once a year and I play peacemaker as we need his speed in the play-offs. Tommy's as *English* as I am *Scottish* and I love the fact that he never pretends otherwise (wee Sam his boy will settle him down in due course). Our goalie, Mike has had a tremendous first half. It's eighty five degrees and we'll be shooting up a steep slope in the second half at Gloxena number 1 at Tuckerman Lane, Maryland. It's not quite Inverleith but a significant slope nevertheless. Paddy's limped off and several cigarettes appear to be doing nothing for his recovery. So we're in deep trouble, right?

Not according to Danny. In fact it's quite the reverse. Besides bringing himself on as Supersub he has the following inspirational advice;

"Listen up. Right boys, we're playing really well. Got 'em just where we want 'em (his favorite phrase) and they know it. They are scared of us and they realize how unlucky we are to be down by a couple". Danny has no qualms about dropping the odd goal off the score sheet to add to his positivism.

"We'll take 'em easy this half. Now over to Jimmy for some strategy."

What I really want to say is sign a few more players who have two working legs and actually show up every week but of course I couldn't do that to Danny. He puts in all the time and effort to organize things and so we're still able to play fitba rather than semi-retire to the Gowf.

"Eh (I spot Erik giggling at the back) … well done Mike, kept us in it. Let's just pump a few long balls for Mo and Trickie to chase. Their two central defenders are not very mobile and the ba'll hold up better going up the hill. Take a wee bit pressure off our defense, too."

Miraculously they have little clue how to exploit their extra numbers, we get a few favorable "Guilty" calls from the ref who's also carded Irish Liam, Marco the Great and scouse Gordon Leslie and we manage to draw 4-4! Does Danny know his stuff or what?

To the main point of this chapter. Danny has a tradition that the top goal scorer from the previous season gets to choose the team name for the ensuing season. I score lots of goals at this level, even from midfield but I also lay on tons of "assists" for a series of very effective pure strikers. As a result we play under a great variety of names:

UK Raiders, West Ham, Crusaders, Arsenal, Royals, Rangers (Cough) and Crystal Palace to name but a few.

Last season I've managed to go injury free (a rarity for any of us nowadays) whereas our strikers have been in and out the team. As a result my eleven goals qualify me as top scorer. At last it's my turn. No prizes for guessing what our team will be for Spring season 2001.

So here is the full official printed list for the MCDR MEN 35+ Central Division—team, coach, colours:

VOB (Very Old Boys—my guess) SOCCER CLUB—
David Milligan—WHITE
FURY—Eric Mania—ORANGE
IKAROS—Fotis Martinos—WHITE
HIBS FC—Danny Brogan—GREEN/WHITE

WHAT 4? (Why? Don't know)—Bernie Shapiro—GRAY (Hair and strips)
CHEVY CHASE CHARGERS—William Hocknell—WHITE
BETHESDA—Chip Gerfan—GREEN
ARARAT—Murat Haulacoglu—BLUE

Whilst Danny was very generous with the team name changes we didn't always have the budget to adjust the strips. Which is why West Ham played one season in Black and Grey diamonds! A sponsor would occasionally pitch in to help and we did have real fancy Arsenal strips provided by a BMW dealer (Leon had an in) when he was launching the new Mini Cooper. We never quite knew where some of these "strips" came from and they ranged from basic tee shirts with numbers on to quality soccer shirts. We suspect he got end-of-line job lots from sports wholesalers. The most absurd set he came up with (which we all became quite attached to somehow) were meshy American football jerseys in the Baltimore Ravens colours (black and purple) with a large yellow Chinese symbol on the front. Even now when I quiz him on it, Danny refuses to divulge the origins.

For our Hibs season I'm relieved he comes up with a fairly respectable solution. The shirts are actually Green and Yellow (but by now Hibs have had a couple of yellow away jerseys so that's OK) with white shorts and Green and Yellow socks. As it transpires I get away with wearing my own real Hibs tops several times that season as its close enough to ours and different enough from most opponents.

It's my most inspired season for years and Hibs sail to the title on the strength of our dominating midfield play where I'm joined by the still lethal passing and shooting of Phil Matthews.

One drawback is having to listen to Mo (Moses; he can part an old fart defence like the Red sea) encouraging us on in his extremely high pitched cockney squeal.

"C'mon 'ibs, c'mon 'ibs, gimme d' bawl."

Phil and Erik and I have put him through a zillion times and he's converted enough to take the top scoring title by a mile (although in baseball terms he's probably still only batting less than .200). God only knows what we'll be called next season!

So finally Hibs have won the league. Not only that but I've played a major role in it.

Even at age forty four. Feels likesay great.

54

SUNSHINE ON LEITH

Mid to late eighties we start hearing little snippets about a new Scottish band. They're starting to get some notice for singing songs with a fairly wide appeal but without any accent adjustment. Other than for traditional "Heedirumho" (Scottish term for very traditional highland singing) stuff or Scottish folk music we all tended to sing with an American accent. I don't really understand why but loads of people with the broadest Scottish accents suddenly go yank when they switch from speech to most forms of popular song! I'm pretty sure we first hear this one particular song on a Scottish mix sent on a cassette tape from Bunty's mom. However I guess we had company and were talking a lot at the time we initially played it because I never really took it in properly.

Soon after we're visiting Scott and Shirley Porter at their house in McLean, Virginia. You just can't go anywhere in Virginia or indeed the entire Appalachian chain, without encountering Scottish names. Scott's another Ministry of Defence guy who falls in love with the States and decides to stay by taking a "Local" job at the embassy. He's even followed the same career path as me having been posted from good old Army HQ at Craigiehall. He knows quite a few of the same people we knew there though most of the real old timers have retired or passed on. Scott's Celtic and has been a very regular attendee at their games both home and away just prior to coming Stateside. Another of the frequent family supporting oddities because his Dad is traditional Hibs and one of his brothers is diehard Rangers. Still, at least he's Jambo free.

He plays a little fitba and has a brief run with the Bulldogs in NVSL. He's keen and fit but really just a fringe player at their current level and spends far too much time on the bench to justify keeping it up. This nudges him back to his first love in sports; The Gowf. (Golf) He and I are also both former champions of the ECSGS MOD (A) BRANCH. That is the Edinburgh Civil Service Golfing Society, Ministry of Defence, Army Branch, club championship. An appropriately government long winded title for a very minor golf tournament. I won it in

1977 at Longniddry but the real highlight of that day for me was I got to meet the great "Famous Five" Hibee; Lawrie Reilly in the clubhouse. The tournament was full handicap based over two rounds and my 20 at the time was a shade generous. I recall I beat out a retired Colonel Bob Graham on a countback of the afternoon back nine. However to put me on a Gowfing par with Scott would be very misleading. I'm mostly a hacker but I hit a decent mid-iron fairly straight which means I scrape an odd par. Scott on the other hand is superb natural swinger and is quickly down to "Scratch" when he devotes his full attention to it. He even manages to play in a pucka (real) qualifying round of the US open.

We end up working together when Scott goes "local" and often share a few drinks on a Saturday night and on this particular occasion he's also received a tape of this Scottish group and gives it some extended play where I really take it in. We listen to a track called "Letter from America" several times over. I ask him:

"What they like then? Have you seen a photo o' them?"

"Aye" says Scott "Should see thum. Two big, tall specky boys wi' ginger hair."

You might have noticed the "Big, tall" and thought that was a mistake or typo. It's not. That's exactly what he said. It's another local language thing. We all would say "Big, tall" or even "Big, huge" or "Big, giant" for someone really tall.

Now I can see why you'd think we only need one or the other as they are both the same but it's an emphasis thing for us. We'd also describe somebody at the opposite end of the size spectrum as "Wee, short" or "Wee, tiny". We always use this emphasis. There's "millions" of everything! It's second nature to us.

The sound and flow of the song has distinct discernible characteristics of other Scottish music but is somehow also distinctly original. It's very strong and guttural. It quickly appeals to my primal Scottish patriotism which surfaces anytime my nationality is insulted or when we play England at fitba. I trust my gut. Always have, always will. It's never wrong about telling me something's wrong and always right about telling me something's right.

I'm paying close attention to the words now and able to fully appreciate their meaning thanks to my (better) late (than never) blooming interest in the history of my beloved Scotland. I once again thank my pal, US National Archives Historian, Tim Mulligan for introducing me to John Prebble and starting me off remedying my previous embarrassingly limited knowledge of this particular subject area. This again causes me to question my less than comprehensive "Comprehensive" high school history curriculum. I certainly am one of the millions of "Coulda, shoulda, woulda" been a better academic performer at school but I actually loved History and even got a respectable pass in my "O" level in it. As I recall this was mostly due to Second World War stuff which I absorbed enthusiastically and steadily even after Math and Science became an interference to my daily smoking and card school needs. I was able to retain key dates, names and places the same way I could anything at all to do with fitba. I barely recall getting anything of depth on Scottish history yet I somehow remember that the Battle of Hastings was in 1066, depicted on the Bayeux tapestry with King Harold getting a French arrow right in the eye (with which I had no problem by the way).

So with my fairly sound grasp of the Jacobites, Culloden and the ensuing Highland Clearances, my own recent decision to make my home here and several Grouses (Scotch Whisky) already down my throat, I'm relating very strongly to the words of the song. It's a very clever blend of two separate eras in Scottish history which shared a similar fate but through different means. The Highlander "Share croppers" were cleared out of their famous glens to make way for the more profitable sheep, hence the line;

"Lochaber no more, Sutherland no more, Lewis no more, Skye no more"

Then in the modern era (1960/70's) Scotland's industrial central belt lost it's oomph and hundreds of thousands of jobs as heavy industry/manufacturing took a beating. (Shipbuilding, Coal, Steel and ultimately the Car industry). This inspired the alternative symbolic line to the same tune and rythym;

"Bathgate no more, Linwood no more, Methil no more, Irvine no more"

The song hits the mark so me and *THE PROCLAIMERS*, we're off to a great start. Then I find out that the Specky, gingers; Craig and Charlie Reid, not only make a great sound but are serious Hibs fans and even mention Hibs in a couple of their songs! I'm hooked. I want to hear all of their stuff but this is pre-internet so you can't just click, buy and download stuff from anywhere in the world. I manage to get a cassette tape copy of the album "This is the story" sent over.

"Throw the R away" tells the story of them being asked to soften their accents by one of their early London based record producers. Thank God they steadfastly refused to compromise! "Misty Blue" and "Make my Heart Fly" make me feel like I'm at one of the good old "Hoose pairties" (impromptu family gatherings) where all my uncles and aunties would sing their favourite song and of course they all sung with an American accent and nobody minded that. Just don't ask them to Anglify! "Letter from America" is also on it and they finish with "The Joyful Kilmarnock Blues" which is still one of the most rousing songs you could ever see performed live. Of course the "Hibernian" reference makes it extra special for me but I even know a Scouser (Big Ant'ony WinterT) who goes just as mad as me for that one.

It's also a perfect time for this type music as the Scottish National Party (SNP) is on a steep rise. The Second World War generation was always much less inclined to go for total separation for Scotland but the youngsters are less influenced by that bit of British unifying history in which Jocks (Scots), Taffs (Welsh) Micks (Irish) fought alongside the English to see off Herr Hitler and his cronies (pals, buddies). The New Labor party revival has also peaked and the Nationalists are steadily gaining in the new Scottish Parliament at Holyrood in Edinburgh. The SNP are even officially represented in America and one of our oldest, dearest friends; Alison Duncan leads the movement stateside. We attend various related functions and even get to meet the guy who will soon be Scotland's First Minister; Alex Salmond. Likesay, no a bad lad for a Jambo.

With its own new Parliament Scotland will also get some additional official representation overseas. This is a mixed blessing for me as for many years I've been the informal point of contact for Scottish-specific enquiries to the embassy in Washington. The front desk and telephonists are always putting calls through to me with questions about things like Haggis and Tartans. This reaches a high point when I'm interviewed by National Public Radio when the movie *Braveheart* spawns a fresh wave of interest in all things Scottish. So there'll be a new "Scottish Executive" representative planted in the British Embassy, Washington D.C. The first "First Secretary" appointed is Susan Stewart who turns out to be a great advocate for our country. This also spawns some privileged opportunities for me to meet some famous Scots including Jack McConnell whose kilt length comes under great scrutiny during a visit to the world's leading political city. My favorite though was Ian Rankin. I was lucky enough to be at a very small book signing function and had the opportunity to talk with him for more than just polite formalities. He was so down to earth as was his co-celebrity that day; Val McDermid. I love that he writes about locations that I know well. It gives his already well crafted stories so much extra meaning and interest for me. Yet many Americans are buying his books too which proves his content has such quality in its own right. I even got to see a couple of TV versions and loved the "Bible John" connection which was so big when I was a teenager. He signs a copy of his latest; *THE FALLS* for us as well as personalizing a greeting in Kyle's paperback copy of *KNOTS AND CROSSES* (thank you Mr Rankin).

With SNP's progress the office will evolve to the less ambiguous name "Scottish Government Office". I expect this will ultimately provoke a move outside the embassy but we'll see. Is this just another step towards independence and a proper Scottish Embassy? After all, the Stone of Destiny is now back from London and in its rightful place though many might even argue that the real one never left home! Is there any doubt which way I'd vote if I still lived at home?

See the kind of emotions and thoughts the Proclaimer's music instigates? That means their songs are important.

So not long afterwards I go back on a business trip to London and manage to get up to Edinburgh for the weekend. Hibs are at home to Dundee. Can't even remember the score but I do remember the day. By now my dad's got a season ticket for the North Stand at Easter Road and going pretty regular. Sounds quite posh but actually it's just an eighteen inch segment of wooden bench painted green with a white number stenciled on it. That's the bit where his arse has exclusivity when he deems to show up. I pay in and sit on his right which he knows is not an "owned" bum space. A couple more spaces to my Dad's left I see who I think is one of the Proclaimers. I'm cautious mind you because I do have a habit of false sightings of celebrities for which Bunty gives me plenty stick. (Though I still swear blind that Martin Sheen once sat beside me at St Agnes RC Church in Arlington, Virginia) At this early stage in my fandom I honestly can't tell Craig and Charlie apart. He catches me doing a double-take but just smiles politely and focuses back on the players who are warming up.

Nobody else seems interested so I whisper in my Dad's ear;

"Dad. See that boy on the other side o' you. D'ye know who it is?"

"Aye. One o' they singer laddies. Dae Scottish stuff. Apparently they're no bad. No heard them masel yet mind. That's the auld man next to him. Dead ordinary, blethers away."

"D'they get peace?"

"A've seen the odd younger laddie come up and speak to them but mostly oldies up here nowadays so naebady really bothers them."

So at half time my Dad goes away to pick up the obligatory pie and Bovril for me. He prefers the coffee now himself and even has a Cigar with it just like the big knobs (VIPs) in the Directors' box! Dad Reid also goes away. Probably hard to believe after reading all this but I'm a bit shy the few times I've been around real celebs, especially when fully sober. All I've had is two pints of lager at Robbies, opposite The Shrub on Leith Walk. and it's mostly worn off by now. It's just me and a Proclaimer, a few yards apart and we eventually make eye contact and nod. We spend a few minutes exchanging views on a fairly boring first half display by Hibs without me even acknowledging that I know who he is (well I know now either likesay Craig or Charlie). The Dad's return and we go back to our own conversations. A couple people nod to him as they go by but he does indeed get relative peace to watch the game. Another wee friendly nod as we're leaving along with a mostly disgruntled crowd and that's it. I'm sort of pleased I resisted my impulse to blurt out;

"I live in America and I love your song."

Time for a fish supper. My dad will pass several other chippies to wait patiently in the long line which snakes around the perimeter of the distinct green tiled walls and floor of Demarco's, next to the Anchor Inn at Granton. Bert the owner still makes everything fresh:

"Well worth the detour" my Dad always says, "Better than the dried up crap you get fae the Drylaw chippie" (sorry Joe). I think there's also a bit of base loyalty in this too as my Grannie Meikle's house is just a hundred yards away at the foot of Royston Mains Road.

Sunday is nine-thirty mass at St Pauls Muirhouse. The crowd seems to get sparser each time you go back. It somehow reminds me of the scene from the Disney animated version of "Robin Hood" when the greedy bastard Sheriff of Nottingham steals the last penny out of the poor box in the mostly empty old church. My Dad delights in telling his cronies;

"This's ma youngest laddie James fae America, back for the weekend." As always there are a few familiar faces, all looking much older and worn (I'm sure they're all thinking the exact same about me). Slightly retarded but always contented Joseph grudgingly shakes my hand as I'm stealing a wee bit of his weekly thunder by supplanting him from the front passenger ("shotgun" stateside) seat. He and his lovely folks squeeze in the back to get a ride back up the road with us to the paper and roll shop at the Doo'cot, now run by several young Pakistani gentlemen with broad Drylaw accents. A quick run through Leith to the Seafield cemetery to visit my Ma then its back for a very serious fry-up with to die for "Well fired" (Burnt) rolls plastered in Danish Lurpak butter. Before I know it Monday's here and I'm on BA 216 headed back to Dulles.

My wife's sister Carol has a pal called Heather. She's a big girl in every sense of the word not least of which her heart. She is a nanny for the kids of some ITV reporter who is doing a stint in Washington at the time. Nannying is a way for many girls to get their Green card (Permanent Resident status) as there is some kind of clever lawyer justification for just having to have a "Scarrish" or "Inglish" nanny. Heather's from Aberfeldy where, we always remind her, the train never stops! She likes a wee vodka (Well several actually) and is always up for a laugh and a sing-song. The ex-pat nannies of Chevy Chase (one of Washington's poshest suburbs) often take over the singing on Thursday nights at "Irelands four Provinces" (known locally as the"4P's) on Connecticut Avenue with Heather always very difficult to separate from the microphone once she gets her hands on it. She's a bit of a karaoke queen and prides herself in knowing the words to every song ever written. She does have an encyclopedic knowledge of a vast variety of music. She's a human iPod before they were even invented. One of her party tricks is to stick the front of her tee shirt over an unsuspecting males head and smother them with her not inconsiderable Scottish mountains. She did it to my son Kyle when he was about ten. He protested violently but seemed to have a glazed smile on his chops for a good hour afterwards.

Of course Heather knows all about the Proclaimers. This includes such crucial detail as one of them once being married to a midget. She let's us know that they will be doing a show in the Washington area and suggests we all go. It'll be at a place called U Street theatre which she warns us is not in the poshest part of town. We get tickets and make our way there. There are some signs of redevelopment a few blocks to the east but when we reach U Street Theatre it looks more like a disused warehouse with a wholesale plumbing supplies shop along the side complete with metal grilles, shutters and graffiti. When we get inside it is indeed very Spartan with lots of exposed brick and mortar. However it has a certain harsh, raw charm about it which well matches the powerful rasping tone of what turns out to be a brilliant Proclaimers set. "Letter from America" was to be the showstopper and whilst it was great to hear it performed live with a decent sprinkling of ex-pat Scots in the crowd, it was outdone by (at least five hundred) miles by an exhausting performance of "Oh Jean". This ended with both Craig and Charlie flat on their backs on the bare concrete stage, girating like two Elvi and flailing wildly at guitars with large globs of sweat splashing in all directions; absolutely brilliant. Besides the ex-pats the crowd included hordes of teenagers who had clearly met the Proclaimers via a single song in a movie.

I don't know how things evolved but some director took a shine to their very aggressive love song "I'm gonna be" (500 miles) and used it as the theme to what became a very popular American teen cult love flick; "Benni and Joon". Fairly or otherwise, such exposure can be the leg-up which gets a group separated from the thousands of potentially great ones out there.

After the show we hung around the back alley behind the theatre where a large bus waited to whisk them off to another town. Taking full advantage of their clearly genuine Scottish accents, Heather, Carol, Caroline and Bunty managed to convince a tough but naïve bouncer that they're distant cousins of Craig and Charlie. He let them up the alley to stand by the bus door leaving it up to the boys whether or not they wanted to say Hello on their way out. They did indeed. They were very amused by the "cousin" thing and I consolidated their interest in us by driving my infamous Renault five into the mouth of the alley where they could clearly see my Virginia license plate which reads "HIBS FC". It got their immediate interest. Feeling slightly groupie-ish I jumped out wearing a classic shiny Emerald pre-sponsorship Hibs jersey and the conversation was up and running. Despite being knackered from a very physical performance they chatted away to us and even posed patiently for photographs. That was and still is what I find so compelling about them. I believe they're still genuinely ordinary. They remind me of the fitba players of my childhood who were just boys from the neighborhood and totally accessible after games as opposed to some of the egotistical primadonna's of today who slink out side doors into Limo's.

I next see them in a video in the early 1990's when they get directly involved in the campaign to save Hibs from financial ruin. The video is called "The team that would not die" and it depicts Hibs winning the League Cup when the business side of the club was collapsing around their ears. They took Dunfermline 2-0 in the final with big Keith Wright starring but that cup was really won in the semi final against Rangers when they were bombarded for the entire game and somehow came away with a 1-0 victory. After a mere twenty year wait the open deck bus was back in Princess Street heading towards Leith Walk.

The Proclaimers hit the jackpot when Mike Myers decides to use their song "I'm on my way." Myers; yet another Canadian comedian from the "Saturday Night Live" stream had shown strong connections with Scots and Scottish humor in his earlier film; "So I married an axe murderer" (a must see if you haven't already). By now he was a superstar in his own right and the film concerned; "Shrek" became a family blockbuster. And so the Proclaimers suddenly had a new audience consisting millions of little kids. This was very evident at the next concert we attended.

It was at The Birchmere in Alexandria, Virginia. It's a small compact venue well suited to the Proclaimers and they have just about sold out there every year or so since. There were lots of very young kids in the front few rows all there for one song only and noticeably bored by chunks of the rest of the set but over the moon when their song was played. It came quite early and a few of them left and were likely tucked in bed before the show was finished.

The other great thing about the Birchmere is that there is a bar area where you can meet the bands after the show and this often extends to a very informal format after an initial CD signing session. This is certainly the case with the Proclaimers as we've got to know both Craig, Charlie and their keyboard man; Stevie Christie (another diehard Hibee) reasonably well. They seem to notice Bunty and I at the same corner table and I confess I'm hardly low profile wearing a selection of Hibs tops to the shows! Likewise big Billy Young now of Yorktown, Virginia who is always at the next table and this time he's in his Hibs number 50 jersey having just passed that milestone. The first year Stevie saw my strip and started giving me the 7-0 (New Years day 1973) sign with his fingers during "Cap in hand". At the most recent show launching their latest album; Restless Soul, it was Stevie who gave me the wonderful results from that day whilst tuning up his keyboard before they started (League Cup—we beat Ayr United and Hearts lost to Livingstone—the Jambos only loss of the season thus far and they're still unbeaten in the league—scary).

The rawness of the first show at U Street Theatre (now tarted up as THE NINE THIRTY CLUB; one of DC's hottest concert spots) will always be special for me and we also had a great laugh at the 2003 Birchmere show with my older Brother John and his wife Julie. However I had most fun at the show on St Paddy's Day 2004 at the Birchmere with the help of a considerable quantity of Captain Morgan's spiced rum. The only time I've ever had the stuff. The waitress brought me the first one by accident so I tried it and it slid down easily. So I just kept 'em coming in double doses. Stevie let me have the set sheet for that one and I still have it, complete with autographs:

Born Innocent
Hate My Love
5 o'clock World
Over & Done Wi'
I'm on my Way
Unguarded Moments (yet another Hoose pairtie flavored song)
Cap in Hand
You meant It Then
Let's get Married
Scotland's Story
Letter from America
Sean
Role Model
Throw the R Away
Sunshine on Leith
Shouldv'e Been Loved
I'm Gonna Be (500 miles)
Hate my Love (Scored through—a mistake repeat)
There's a Touch
No Witness/No Doubt
I Met you/Doodle Song/Blood on Your (hands)
Joyful Kilmarnock Blues (Almost blew the roof off the place!)

One hell of a show that was.

Finally, getting back to the fitba context, sorry. To my favorite Proclaimers song for all time. One which has taken on almost Hymnal-like status. At first I liked "Sunshine on Leith". Then I really liked it. Then I loved it. Now I adore it. Part of this is because my dad's family is all auld Leith. He still can't walk five yards along Great Junction Street without somebody saying "Hiya John, how ye doin?" He played for Leith Athletic, I played for Leith Schools and I already explained how Leith is distinguishable from Edinburgh at large. I remember hanging around my auntie Mary McGinty's in Buchanan Street with Great Grandad Kelly (well into his 90's) sat in striped pajamas in his bed in an alcove in the main room, a wee drink in hand (dark rum would be my guess). My first house was at number 7 Albert Street.

Lots of my own fondest memories are pure Leith. Besides the obvious Hibs stuff there's Dockie Bell's baths where most of us learned to swim with the school and the public "Vickie" (Queen Victoria) baths (what we called swimming pools because they used to also have lots of little individual cubicles with bath tubs. They were built at a time when few people had baths/showers in their own flats so they came here for a decent wash). The toffee doddle shop, Thomson's Sports where many of us got our first real strip and fitba boots. The State picture house, The Eldorado wrestling, Pilrig Park, the kilt and bike shops in Jane street, the Craig and Rose kids Christmas party (my great uncle Andy McGinty's work). Anne; the lady Barber in Constitution Street, The Viking and Tiffin cafés, Woolies and the Kirkgate to mention but a few things. It's where I still go to visit my ma. In Seafield cemetery at the end of Leith Links.

I wonder how many million meetings have been set for simply "The fit ae the Walk". The bottom part (slopes downward—although its actually the North end in geographical terms) of Leith Walk, the main street linking Edinburgh's central district (Queen Street, George Street, Princess Street) to auld Leith.

How did we end my Dale's wedding (to John Harris III of Roanoke at the famous Wren Chapel) in Williamsburg, Virginia? With our families and Scottish friends blasting out "Sunshine on Leith" to an appreciative group of Southern Virginia Clan Harris. John wore his grandfather's kilt to the wedding whilst I wore a hired outfit with Bufford, Tim and others. Alex finally came good on his promise of almost thirty years earlier to play at her wedding. His lovely daughter Melanie and wife Mindy got to see our tradition and passion first hand as they sat at a table named for "Leith" which also included Alison and daughter, Alyth, Rose and Douglas and Tim and Bonnie.

I had heard how Hibs fans had adopted the song but I didn't fully appreciate this until experiencing it first hand relatively recently. I'm back again in London to do with work and squeeze yet another whistle stop weekend trip up to Edinburgh. By sheer lucky timing we have Hearts at home. I've spent Friday night at Burntisland (in Fife, just the other side of the Firth of Forth) with my brother John. He's moved there from Clerry to a charming duplex stone cottage (Bendameer) to lead a quieter lifestyle. Not sure it's worked as Clerry seems to visit him frequently in the form of Gordon Burden; one of the funniest men on the planet. He may be Clerry now but they really only have him on long term loan because, as he will proudly tell you;

"Ye kin take the man oot ae Niddrie, bit ye'll never take Niddrie oot the man."

We take the train over to town Saturday morning so that he can have a pint or two. It's fun coming over the Forth Train Bridge for the first time in many years. It's a very quick trip as we whiz by Aberdour, Inverkeithing, N. Queensferry, Dalmeny, South Gyle (a new station to me,) Haymarket and Waverley before you know it. We grab a cab at the Princess Street side and head for "The Gates" (Golden Gates pub) at Meadowbank where Big Dode (George) Hunter quickly fires in the pints and passes over precious enclosure tickets.

HIBERNIAN Football Club

Bank of Scotland

SCOTTISH PREMIER LEAGUE

HIBERNIAN

V HEART OF MIDLOTHIAN
SUN 21-OCT-01   3PM

WEST STAND   LOWER

ROW   G   SEAT   73

TO BE RETAINED (which I have obeyed).

I get a great unexpected bonus when Kenny McCallum an old teammate from Under 16 Edinburgh Thistle strolls in with his daughter both draped in green scarves of course. He now lives just around the corner from the Gates. We have a fabulous time reminiscing and, as always, the beer makes the stories even warmer and sweeter. A few pints later and another taxi, this time straight to Easter Road. There's a great buzz around the ground and I'm relieved to feel some of the old pre-derby excitement/butterflies kick in. Can't help thinking ahead how good it will feel if they win, how crap if they lose. What I knew as the Dunbar end with the old manual scoreboard now has a fancy new stand and is usually reserved for away support. Hearts have it all today but it's almost empty. John explains there's some kind of weird Jambo protest boycott going because Hibs have put the price of "Derby" tickets up. We're actually in what I knew as the enclosure (below the main stand) and that's also been converted to seating. Very smart and comfortable I might add.

Both Hibs and Hearts are generally mediocre at the time but Hibs do have Frank Sauzee a Frenchman who toys briefly with Stanton-esque status at Easter Road. He's aging but still well worth the price of admission. Only small reservation I have about him is he sometimes wears gloves whilst playing; a pet peeve of mine since Antony Perry did so at Oggies. Goalies are exceptions of course. Alex McLeish has good international contacts and credibility which enables him to lure Sauzee and a couple of other special players who may not have otherwise come to Easter Road or Scotland for that matter. Another of these is a young Ecuadorian; Oscar De la Cruz who puts the place in bedlam by scoring an exquisite curling shot in the first two minutes. He follows up with a tap in to put Hibs two up and they stroll to half time in total control.

I get another pleasant surprise at half time. I've noticed the guy behind me doing a couple of double-takes when we were celebrating the goals and he does look familiar. At half time he taps my shoulder. As I turn to face him he asks:

"You James Meikle?" The James bit immediately reveals the connection is pre or early teen.

"Aye" I say and the penny's dropping slowly ... yep, gotcha.

"Winker Watson" a confident statement, not a question.

"Aye, wisnae sure ye'd remember me like"

Winker (Robert) was a Royston boy, played on all Mr McGauran's teams as well as Leith Schools Select on my second go round with them. Very energetic player was my immediate thought from memory.

"What you up tae nowadays James?"

"Eh. Live in America, been there a while now. Work for the Government."

"Still playing?"

"Aye, likesay auld fart's league. Yersel?"

"Odd five a sides but no much." He rocks his left thumb towards a kid and woman beside him without looking at them and continues.

"We're hoping to go to America soon oursels, San Fransisco. Um serious intae the guitar and have a chance at something ower there. Where are you?"

"Oh. This side, likesay East coast, Washington DC … well actually I live in Virginia"

"Ye obviously like it then?"

"Been very good tae us Winker, nae complaints."

Then he abruptly turns to his kid (I'm guessing) points his right index finger right in the centre of my chest, grits his teeth for emphasis and says;

"See this man … James Meikle … best fitba player I ever played with."

Now, we can all pretend we're suitably modest but if we're being totally honest flattery like that does absolutely no harm to the ego as one approaches serious middle age. So I feign embarrassment but inside I'm chuffed to monkeys (Scottish for very pleased). I always thought Winker saw me as a wee bit conceited. He probably did but as I've said before fitba appreciation is often personality flaw tolerant. Anyway I can tell his compliment is completely sincere and I'll take it.

We settle in for a more mundane second half. Hearts steal a scrappy goal towards the end and the pocketful of their fans that've ignored the boycott have a brief flurry of hope which fizzies out without any serious further threat. So my first derby in twenty years is a clear victory and I'm really lucky because there haven't been that many in that period. The real highlight comes at the end when the entire crowd stands up together and blast out "Sunshine on Leith" with all the scarves raised up a la Kop "Walk-On". The song is perfect for that style. The decibel level is off the charts. I'm sure they can hear us across the water in Burntilsland. It's a fantastic experience. We've just beat Hearts comfortably, I'm in one of my most special settings in the world sharing my favorite song by my favorite group with over ten thousand equally passionate fans. We head back to the "Gates" for a celebratory pint.

It just can't get any better … or can it?

55

VIVA LAS VEGAS

In the fall of 2005 I'm being strongly recruited by Eddie Koebke and Bruce Niles from my Chez Marc indoor team for the annual Friendship cup soccer tournament in Las Vegas. This is where hundreds of very old soccer players converge over the Martin Luther King holiday weekend (mid-January) for yet another "final" shot at glory. Eddie and Bruce have been going for years and always return with very positive reports. As well as participating in a few matches it sounds like a fair amount of beer is drunk and significant dollars are lost in the casinos and strip joints. One guy even lost the coat off his back but I'll leave him to write that story himself one day.

There's a slight twist this year. Their teams have always gone as Murphy's FC from the old Northern Virginia Soccer League though they typically borrow a few appropriately aging players from other Washington area teams. They generally focus on the 40-plus division but this year there's also a 48-plus division and they have several relatively fit players just reaching eligibility for that age group, including yours truly. They've decided to make a push to put together a serious contender for the title rather than the competitive but mainly social approach they've taken in the past. Lee Schwartz is the man at the helm and with help from Eddie and Bruce he's assembling a squad that should match up well with just about any group their own age. Lee's also cast the recruiting net much wider than usual signing up what we are assured are quality old farts from as far afield as New Jersey, Ohio and even an old pro veteran of the Scottish and English leagues.

Playing regularly indoors and out and walking extensively, I'm keeping myself in fairly good physical shape now notwithstanding popping a few pills daily for high blood pressure and the odd one for a decent sleep and of course a steady supply of Advil and Ben Gay for general maintenance. I'm now used to being one of the older guys on the field, especially at indoor, so the thought of playing only against guys my age or older is very appealing. Maybe I can be a star again for a couple of days. Bunty and I have been to Vegas a few times over the years besides which I had a work related convention excuse to be there on expenses once in a while. However neither of us had been for a while and the timing is attractive. The kids will be headed back to college after their exceptionally long (about six weeks) Winter break. Now we adore our kids but after that long they're usually ready to head back to their nocturnal college existence and we're usually ready to let them go!

So, after splitting a bottle of Sutter Home Merlot one Friday evening which puts us in very mellow and positive form, Bunty and I get on line just to "explore" Vegas possibilities and before you know it, voila, we're travelocited into four nights at the Flamingo complete with return flights on United, which sounds like the appropriate airline on which to travel to a fitba tournament, right?

I get a feel for how serious Murphy's are about this venture when I arrive at the first Vegas-dedicated training session on the new artificial turf field at Virginia Highlands in the shadows of Pentagon City mall. Over thirty players show up. They are also sending a 40-plus division team and this is supposed to be a joint session for the two squads. However there are several players whizzing around at a pace which indicates they are nowhere near qualifying for either team. As it transpires some players from the regular open age Murphy's team were along for some extra practice. The new surface is great. Nothing like the original brick hard, hundred-mile-per-hour Astroturf but rather a softer forgiving version, still a tiny bit faster than natural grass but the ball goes exactly where you put it so no blaming tuffets for poor passing. It's a fast, crisp scrimmage though very hard to get a handle on who's who. I enjoy the work-out and withdraw gracefully a little before the end just to make sure I don't stretch or pull anything significant.

We have a couple more similar sessions and I'm starting to recognize a few names and faces besides the two or three I already knew. I'm usually playing alongside Eddie Koebke which is cool as he and I played together as very "young lads" for the British Lions my very first weekend in America and we've never lost touch since; including him selling Bunts and I some dodgy insurance policies. Mind you, as he reminds me frequently, these policies did enable me to fund a nice deck for my house when John Hancock went public!

As always I'm packing at the very last minute and resolved to my usual one hand luggage bag maximum. I know I have a suitable little black hold-all (tote bag in American terms) tucked down in the basement storage area. It even has a separated compartment for my pungent fitba boots and shin guards. I'm too lazy to plug in the proper lamp so I fumble around the dimly lit back corner and grab the bag I need. Except when I get back upstairs and start to throw my gear in it transpires that this bag is in fact navy blue with the powder blue letters YHS (Yorktown High School) on one side and the full legend Yorktown Dance Team on the reverse complete with an ever so sweet little pair of intertwined dance slippers. On the top flap is the name Brooke. However the size is perfect and I just can't be bothered starting over. Anyway, maybe taking my daughter's bag with me to Vegas will bring me some luck. Not that I'm likesay, superstitious.

My awareness of Las Vegas goes way back to when I first started work at the good old Army Headquarters Scotland. Billy the GD (general duty) man and part time Elvis look-alike, at least in his opinion, would stop by the archives (where Bunty and I were supposed to be weeding old files) once a day and collect the trash. He would tell us tales of his pilgrimages to Vegas for Elvis conventions and go on at length about the amazing lights along the strip.

I later put Bunty and I in serious debt for a few weeks to buy a cine camera kit from a military officer who worked on camp beside me. He "sold" me on it by showing me a film he'd taken of the lights along the Las Vegas strip and this blew me away at the time. I just had to have it. Still do though it hasn't been used for many years. My X generation kids think it came out of Noah's Ark. To me it's still a thing of beauty, lovely heavy silver/black model 5X SANKYO SEIKI MFG CO LTD, TOKYO, JAPAN. Real state-of-the-art in its day with various filters, telephoto zoom and all operable on 4 x AAA batteries. It even has a compact sized hard black leather case and carrying strap. With hindsight, though youthfully impulsive this proves one of the great purchases of my life as I have a couple of now priceless family movies. My most precious is the one I mentioned which features my healthy, happy, well endowed and scantily clad mom sipping vodka-lemonade-on-ice in a striped deck chair in blazing sunshine in our back garden in Drylaw. By sheer luck almost the entire family make cameo appearances within the brief four minute reel though you do have to watch carefully to see my dad washing the dishes behind the kitchen window as David retrieves a tennis ball after my smooth passing shot. We're playing scaled down "Lawn" tennis between the washing poles! Our blue jeans/shirtless combos are not quite Wimbeldon standard but this is before either of us have any significant flab folds to hide. It even has our family dog Bonnie stealing the ball and taking it behind the deck chair for her customary possessive growl. Still, saved David from another defeat I suppose. Another film shows our wee darlin' Dale being discharged from Simpson's Memorial Pavilion in Edinburgh at about one week old. She looks like a tiny baby Snowhite in the safe, soft hands of a bubbly black nurse. All convertible to video nowadays and no doubt CD's shortly. Such camera equipment was likely commonplace stateside in the sixties/seventies but not so in Pilton or Drylaw or Leith.

Our own first trip to Vegas was back in 1982. Thinking we'd only be in America for three years we decided to make the most of it and did a significant amount of touring in those early years. We had a meticulously planned West coast trip for which I earned the nickname "Vacation Nazi" for pushing to keep us on our exacting schedule to maximize the number of vital attractions we saw and had our photos taken at for proof. That trip was mostly economy class with an odd special night thrown in (i.e. the old gracious El Tovar hotel on the very edge of the Grand Canyon). The Vegas part was strictly economy class. We stayed at a Motel 6 which has somehow survived to this day between the towering new MGM Grand and the Tropicana. Less than $30 per night for a room for four, including use of the hot tub. How can you beat that? Food was also mostly economy grade. Our favorite casino that first trip was Circus, Circus where you could significantly increase your ass size at just one sitting of the $3.95 all-you-can-possibly-eat-and-stuff-in-your-pockets-for-later buffet dinner. Well worth the jockeying for good early position as the potential feeders were herded into a long narrow corridor awaiting the opening of the barn door.

Even the first time I went on business (and took Bunts) we stayed at "The Circus" and our room was so far from the main tower we had to take a tram there. I eventually realized that "reasonable actuals" even on government budgets could stretch to Bally's or the Tropicana.

In the very early hours of Friday 13th January 2006 we board United 891 from Washington Dulles to LAX (Los Angeles). Being a glass half-full person I figured that traveling to a gambling Mecca on Friday the 13th was likely to be very lucky rather than the reverse. Not that I'm likesay, superstitious.

As reading material for the long flight, this being a fitba flavored trip, I've selected "How Soccer Explains the World" by Franklin Foer (Harper Perennial) a great choice as it transpires. I especially enjoy his jaunt into the world of Celtic/Rangers and find some of the other chapters extremely educational as well as entertaining for even the marginal fitba fan.

Before leaving I've asked each of my kids plus my wee niece Libby to choose a number on which I can have a little gambling flutter on their behalf. Though three thousand miles apart at the time (Dale working in Luxembourg and Brooke in Harrisonburg, Virginia at James Madison University) both my daughters pick red nineteen. As I've said I'm not, likesay, superstitious but when we board the plane and are seated in row nineteen our magic number for Vegas is established beyond any doubt. Libby chooses ninety nine and I show my roulette naiveté by accepting it without question. I end up substituting the green double zero on her behalf but to no avail. Kyle goes for black twenty and his girlfriend Mary Ann weighs in with black thirteen. The latter comes up several times but never when I've got my big two dollar-fifty bet riding on it.

We arrive at the Flamingo via airport shuttle service around noon. Of course this is not the real Flamingo but rather a massive modern version with thousands of rooms. It still pays some respect and homage to the style of Bugsy Siegel's seventy-seven room original via the art-deco pool, bathhouse and cabanas and the signature main door multi-flamingo light signage.

The place is absolutely heaving as one might expect on a holiday weekend. We know we're in Vegas when the receptionist asks if Bunty and I share the same surname. She also asks if we want two Queen beds or one King and despite Bunty's slight hesitation. Okay, I admit it; I'm a sweater, a slight snorer and occasional producer of other strange odors under the covers. We end up with the King, enhancing my aim to mix at least a little romance into the mainly fitba focused trip. Lee's pre-trip correspondence and instruction was extensive and comprehensive but I'm pleased to say he had not adopted the rule of some recent professional coaches who choose to ban sexual relations on the eve of big matches. Fat chance of enforcing that anyway with the likes of "Don Juan" Koebke in the squad. We are quickly settled into our sumptuous suite on the seventeenth floor overlooking the menagerie of Flamingos, Penguins (who'd have thunk it in Las Vegas?) and an assortment of other exotic birds and fish which forms the back garden of the hotel.

The only team thing slated for the Friday night is an informal invitation to meet at a pub called the Crown and Anchor but myself and many others don't make it beyond the main strip as a half hour late afternoon walk turns into an exhausting four hour slog. We finally conclude that all Vegas strip walking routes are designed to guide you into every casino and make it extremely difficult to find your way back out without a trail of breadcrumbs. We're back in the room around eight and snoozing comfortably by nine. So, at least for the first night, we won't have to worry too much about adopting the latest tourism catchphrase; "What happens in Vegas stays in Vegas".

I have made what I later realize is a tactical error by not hiring a car. Lou (Luis) Robles who's also on my indoor team is staying at the Flamingo and has a car but he's on the 40-plus squad and their game times don't merge well with ours. I'm subsequently in a van pool with Bruce and Lee and some others who are staying at the Tropicana. Like everything in Vegas the Tropicana looks reasonably close by … until you actually start walking towards it. I head for the Tropicana around ten in the morning. Our first game's not until twelve-fifteen but the drive out to the Spring Valley area takes about twenty minutes and we have to go through a registration process on the first day.

The walk turns out to be a brisk fifteen minutes and includes several sets of stairs and escalators. I'm always careful to keep the more decorative side of my dance bag tucked in against my hip. The walk actually serves quite well as a loosening up process for my old muscles. I notice over a period of three days that all the down and in (to the casinos) escalators are working perfectly whilst several of the up and out ones are "Out of order" and there are no signs of repair crews. At the Tropicana the alternative egress is a very steep manual staircase. All purely coincidental I'm sure though I confess I spotted several very old folks take a look, shake their heads and turn back into the Casino to lose more of their hard earned retirement funds.

I go to a receptionist and ask for the room number for Bruce Niles. Her computer draws a blank. I ask her to try Lee Schwartz. Bingo. Room 5254 which she explains is in a separate wing and she pulls out a map of the casino and draws me directions. She also asks me to relay a message to Lee that he needs to call his mom. I guess I must look like a page boy in my Hibs tracksuit? I make my way past Java, Java, the cashiers Office with the always shiny brass bars on it and the Havana Hideaway and along a long narrow corridor to staircase number five. Up one flight right, left, left again and I find room 5254. Bruce answers my knock and suggests we'll be leaving when Lee gets back from recovery therapy at the Spa. Lee's got some old college (Bucknell boys) buddies in town and stayed out a tad later than planned. As soon as he appears I dutifully relay the message about Mom which is apparently about the tenth time he's had it.

I always thought of myself as very dedicated to the cause of continuing to play my favorite sport through nagging injuries and malaise but as Lee gets ready I see how this can be taken to an extreme level. For starters he's been to the doc the previous Wednesday for a cortisone shot. He carries a wide selection of knee and ankle braces which he wears at various times of the day and night. His immediate and pressing issue today is a problem with the arch of his left foot. Bruce gets to work on a tape job, experimenting with several different sizes and grades of tape before they both give up on getting any serious adhesion to the particularly awkward problem spot along the sole of his foot. Instead he chooses a pre-formed cushion held on by a stretchy strap. For good measure he puts one on the other foot too. Several more layers of socks and tape and shin guards and he's good to go. He explains that he has several other issues going on further up his legs which we just don't need to know about. We all agree with that. Mark Hill, Keith Barraclough and Mario Lopez-Gomes also show up and we're ready to go.

We pile into the plush maroon hired minivan with the sliding doors on either side. Bruce will drive and Lee takes shotgun. Lee is a real tough cookie but he shows a softer side by phoning an elderly relative in a nursing home in Florida to talk bets with him. He explains that this is a weekly call which serves to give the aging, ailing man a little bit of variety and interest in his otherwise fairly mundane twilight years. I'm impressed by the compassion.

I already know Mark (another Chez Marc regular) but also manage to make a couple of local football connections with Keith and Mario during the journey. We reach the fields which are more sand than grass but reasonably flat. They're on a very large open plain and you just know that if the wind gets up it's going to be a dominating factor. We hand over our driving licenses to be checked in and get a quick look at the scorer tent area where there are a slew of boards showing all the teams and fixtures. By my count there are over 40 teams just in our age group. I estimate that in all there are close to one hundred teams averaging around twenty players and guests. That's an influx of an extra two thousand tourists for three to four days. I assume the organizers get a suitable back-hander from the Vegas Chamber of Commerce.

I get to meet our entire squad for the first time and our French Coach, Philippe Moisa is handing out a guide sheet on possible line ups. It has lime green circles, ovals and squares with names in red letters showing groupings of potential players for each position in a four-four-two formation. Some players have asterisks to indicate they are listed for two positions. I'm delighted to see myself listed in central midfield without an asterisk. Philippe lists himself in the squad but only for emergency use. He recently lost sight in one eye in a freak heading accident on the field, the only such one I've ever heard about in all my years connected to the sport.

No debates on the goalie as we only have one. I see the name Bob Wilson and think to myself; surely not the old English accented Scotsman with the tight curly hair that ended up hosting the Saturday lunch time preview? No. A much younger specimen and one I've played against in the Maryland old farts league. He made a spectacular save on one of my best shots of the previous season so I know he's good.

As well as Eddie and Bruce we have Tim Cooney, Juan Ballve, Doug Lindholm and Tony Bell to rotate at the full back spots. Matt Lowe is the Jersey boy Lee has recruited to play sweeper and after a few minutes of game one it's obvious why. Lee will play stopper in front of him. In central midfield we'll have me and the strapping and instantly lovable Frenchman; Pierre-Yves Robin. I also recognize him from the old boy's league in Maryland and recall him scoring the goal of the season for the Rangers against us. As well as a rocket shot he has an immense work rate and some really deft touches. It's obvious he's played at a very high level and we're instantly bonded and delighted to both be in the same uniform. Wide-mids are the two Daves (Modi and Lauer) and a German called Uwe who is built not to be messed with physically. We also have Tim Sansbury a fast, fit left sided player, who's joined us all the way from Cincinnati, Ohio. Ageless Roy "Pep" is here too.

Up front we have an outstanding Scottish tandem. Mark Cabrelli is still a greyhound in his late forties and will feed off the deft flicks and headers of Ian Smith. Ian is formerly of Hearts, Birmingham, Leicester and many more teams. He is now a family practitioner in the English midlands, clearly in great shape for his age and we'll quickly see that he has retained considerable skills and agility. I vaguely recall seeing him in the Jambo maroon in the curly permed hair era of Scottish football and he confirms this as correct by telling me that his mate and Hibees rival of the time was big Tony Higgins who I always recall constantly sweeping said permed hair off his face during games (I still think that hairdo and or his equally garish moustache caused him to miss the sitter against Leeds). Ian is still brimming over with boyish enthusiasm for the game and is happy to spread this particular infection throughout the squad.

Whilst waiting around I got a glimpse of a few of our perceived rivals and within just a few minutes of the start of our first game I knew we were a genuine contender. The games were all very short halves (25 minutes) and so the first goal is often the winner. Despite giving up an early, scrappy goal to "Fresno 48" (it would be the only goal from normal play we gave up the entire tournament) we had no panic and steadily clawed our way back in. Ian got us level just before the half and our constant pressure finally paid off when he put in a second with a firm back post header off a corner kick.

With our confidence established we then strolled to a 3-0 win over "Simi Valley United" in the second game with Mark getting a neat finish and yours truly getting a brace, one neat chip and the other somewhat assisted by the wayward punch of one of the many "non-regular" goalies on duty. Ending day one with only Scotsman on the score sheet would provide a fun theme for our after match discussions. The venue was a little too far to go back to town between games so our holding hang-out of choice was Brewsky's, a sports bar conveniently adjacent to the fields. There, Ian and I converted the entire squad to our Scottish between match regimen. The barmaid really thought he was joking when Ian ordered; "ten hot teas with honey and lemon honey!"

This is when I realized that a hire car was essential for proper mobility. Most of the guys were there stag and so very difficult to move from the comfort of Brewsky's when play was done for the day, especially with play-off American football in progress, including the Redskins at Seattle Seahhawks. Being in Vegas I had put twenty dollars on the Redskins as over 3-1 underdogs, a large bet by my own quarter-slot-machine standards. Bunty and I were supposed to be meeting up with some friends of hers who were also there for the weekend so I decided to venture outside for a cab. I then learned that once you get this far off the strip even empty cabs will not stop for you! It took me close to an hour to reach this conclusion so I ended up back at Brewsky's scrounging a ride. Lou was kind enough to rescue me but we then got stuck in horrendous traffic and so our night out got off to an extremely late start. We just managed to catch Bunty's friend for a drink or two and ended up singing Irish songs in a bar in New York, New York with a lovely couple from Dublin. We ate far too late at Mon Ami Gabi but, hey, that's Vegas.

The second day's weather made me think I was back in Edinburgh. We had blazing sunshine, rain, gale force winds, giant hailstones and snow all within the course of a few hours. We started the day sluggishly but eked out a 1-0 win over "IESL San Bernardino" on another goal by yours truly. Game two was interrupted by the giant hailstones and we all tucked under a very small overhanging roof of the tiny toilet pavilion where we stayed warm and amused by the sight of Pierre's colorful pajama trousers. "NEOTHSL 55" had been so demoralized by our four goal outburst in the first half they did not come back out on the field when the weather finally subsided sufficiently. The game again featured nice goals (one each) from the usual trio before Dave Modi finally broke the exclusive Scottish scoring streak with a nice downwards header(from a Scottish cross of course). Pierre had so desperately wanted to be the one to break the Scottish scoring monopoly he burst the ball trying—really.

I was better organized Sunday with a lift back from Mark Cabrelli who was also accompanied by his better half. We talked about dining options on the ride home and by sheer coincidence ended up eating at the same restaurant in the Venetian several hours later. The Miss America pageant was imminent and the contestants were taking Gondola rides on the Venetian's canal which was causing great interest. Most of them looked amazingly young to us.

The good news was that we had easily made the quarter finals, the bad news that our game was at eight o'clock Monday morning against the "Dirty Dozen" (fortunately, Marvin, Bronson, Sutherland and Savalas couldn't play as they were all dead). A couple of our guys hadn't counted on us getting this far so they had flights that precluded them staying for this game. The forty plus team had just failed to advance but to their great credit Mark Hill and Keith Barraclough turn up at the Lee/Bruce room at 7 a.m. to support their older brethren. By now the team van had a perpetual smell of Ben Gay. As usual the ride out was very smooth with Bruce at the wheel. He cruised into the parking lot and picked out one of his favored corner spots, backing in with meticulous accuracy.

Despite being a couple players down we were still by far the better team but the strong winds (so strong that they had to chain down the goalposts on one field) were a great leveler and we ended up 0-0 and subsequently in a penalty shoot-out. Conversions by me, Mark, Matt and Pierre, coupled with Bob's goalkeeping exploits put us through without Ian even having to take our fifth kick.

By now Ian's pre-match and half time talks had taken on a legendary quality. They included some genuinely shrewd observations mixed in with a generous helping of traditional inspirational fitba clichés all delivered with tremendous verve and gusto. Unfortunately, in one such speech he lauded Eddie Koebke so much that Eddie pledged to be a Hearts fan for life (it cost me two Hibs' shirts to get him back on the straight and narrow). Still at least I know how Eddie always gets a full game in Vegas. Turns out that Cousin Thomas who lives locally allows him to wash the uniforms at his house! He's always ably assisted by our number one fan and adopted mascot, nephew; "little Thomas" who is already taller than a few of us and seems to get all the dirty jokes at our team banquet!

So we reach the semi-final and after a half hour break we are matched up with the elegantly named Old Wankers from Denver, Colorado. They are certainly not wankers in football playing terms and by far the best team we've seen or played against thus far. We have been further depleted by departing players but assume most teams face this problem. It will definitely be a game of two halves with a gale howling fiercely and directly towards one end on a field appropriately nicknamed the windbowl. We win the toss and take the wind. We fail to score though are most unlucky to see Ian's tremendous looping header come back off a post.

Even against the wind the Wankers create some decent chances and on reaching half time goalless most of us (even Ian I suspect) are thinking we'll be pushed to keep them out in the second half. After being barraged for about fifteen minutes without loss we sense that survival is possible and play some respectable possession stuff to reach our second consecutive penalty shoot-out. Though I'm not likesay superstitious I do insist on going first again. I'm not overjoyed that we're shooting with the wind at our backs as I much prefer the reverse. The field markings are poor so the ref steps out the twelve yards and places the ball. As I get up there it seems far too far out. I'm immediately in a dilemma. I'm a finesse penalty taker, always with the same approach, stride, stride, shimmy, stare at right corner, and stroke it just inside left post almost always sending the goalie clean the wrong way. This has worked flawlessly. It's over twenty years since I've missed a penalty of any significance and I've taken plenty. However do I protest the placement which perhaps will show their goalie a lack of confidence on my part? See I'm thinking and that in itself is bad. I don't normally do that until I'm trotting back to halfway with my right fist clenched upwards.

I have another look, lift and re-spot the ball in exactly the same place. It still doesn't look or feel quite right but I decide that it doesn't matter. I go through my usual routine and it all works perfectly with the goalie throwing himself hopelessly towards the wrong post. My first thought is goal but I watch the ball veer just a fraction more to the left than usual. If it's a putt it lips in but this ain't golf. The ball catches the inside of the post just enough to force it barely outwards away from the line. So close but a miss is a miss is a miss. Without me even protesting the other ref has decided they check the spot anyway. They do so and agree it's fourteen yards out! However rather than have me re-kick they decide to just make everyone else kick from the same spot. Mark and Matt convert just fine but Pierre meets a similar fate to mine with the opposite post and Murphy's old boys are done for the day! We wind up third as the wankers go on to win the final.

I still feel bad about it but my therapist assures me every week that had I taken the same exact kick from twelve yards it definitely would have gone in.

Jersey Matt kindly gives me a ride back to town so the upside is that at least Bunty and I have a full evening to enjoy together. We go up the Eiffel tower then watch the spectacular Bellagio water show before feasting on their buffet dinner which is the absolute opposite of our typical early Vegas Casino bun fights with a superb array of cuisine, beautifully presented in a well decorated, subtly lit, soothing dining room atmosphere.

All in all we had a really good time and the fitba was great fun and very satisfying. I've got a feeling we'll be back next year.

56

FROM HELL TO HEAVEN

To use an old Hollywood term; Bunty has become quite the "IT" girl (but referring in this case to Information Technology) since she splurged her tax refund on the creamy white Apple Mac Notebook laptop. Up to this point we both tended to learn only whatever computer stuff was necessary for work purposes and neither of us ever had a problem doing that. Yet the gulf between our IT abilities and those of our children seems so vast and ever growing. They are constantly laughing when we ask for help with something they consider so basic and automatic. They will offer help but cannot seem to slow down sufficiently from their routine warp speed for us to be able to properly absorb whatever it is they are showing us.

 Anyway Bunts is perched on a Shaker style stool in medium Cherry with the red/white interlaced weave seat. She's addressing her laptop which is in its now customary spot on the end of the kitchen counter. She doesn't like clutter on her countertops but is making a generous exception for herself. She's squinting at the small screen through her art deco vintage glasses. They give her that sophisticated look of a typecast office secretary from a black and white Cary Grant film. She has become quite adept at *saving money* by buying lots of stuff on E Bay and other assorted internet sites. Bunts has even got us a little Webcam and has managed to get it working so that we can have trans-Atlantic "Virtual" drinks with John and Julie in Burntisland, Scotland on the odd Friday night.

 What the hell's all this computer crap got to do with fitba you're thinking?
 Likesay, just bear with me a minute.

 In the mail we get what looks like an invitation postmarked Edinburgh. First thought is; who do we know that's getting married, engaged maybe? Nothing comes to mind. I clumsily thumb it open and it is indeed an invite. It's to the 50th birthday party of Mark and Margaret, the Curtis twins who've had a mention or two many chapters ago. It'll be in March 2007. Though we couldn't possibly make it this spurs a phone call or two and revived contact. Like our own kids, Mark's daughter Becka is an IT whiz and before you know it they are on our virtual contacts list and we are meeting them on the webcam for a blether. Just like old times—none of us have changed a bit, right. Well at least they're in Black and White which is a bit more forgiving than color, especially on the graying locks. Mark drives private taxis now and has exchanged his player/coach responsibilities for a whistle and small notebook. Why am I not surprised to hear that he hands out yellow and red cards like Halloween candy.

"I jist don't take any crap" is his concise description of his refereeing style. I bet he disnae! So anyway here's the fitba bit.

Hibs are having a really great season. John Collins is our latest prodigal son Manager and has us passing the ball like a vintage (Bill) Nicholson Spurs. We reach the League Cup (now called CIS Insurance Cup) semi's and draw St Johnstone. This competition has had a tradition of major upsets and not just in the early rounds. When Celtic had their great late 1960's/early 1970's spell they were still losing League Cup Finals to the likes of St Johnstone and Partick (I think we Hibs fans have it hard but think of all those Thistle devotees who are still living of the fumes of their 1971 skelping of Celtic). Anyway this season is a dandy for upsets and it's all working in our favor.

See, here's the thinking for a Hibs fan when the cup draws are made. Avoid Celtic, Rangers, Aberdeen and Hearts in the early going and hope that they knock lumps out of each other. This CIS they don't have to. The mighty Queens Park dump Aberdeen, Falkirk take out Celtic at Parkhead and Rangers lose at home to St Johnstone—you could've got a million to one on that treble from Ladbrokes. Courtesy of very forgiving opposition in the first couple rounds the Jambos and us have strolled to the quarters where we're drawn together. We've got the home field and take advantage of it with one of those 1-0's which should have been a lot more. So let's see who's left in with us? Kilmarnock, St Johnstone and Falkirk. Likesay we're now the favorites. Oh, no. Remember what happened the last time we were in this position a couple years ago? Livingstone in the final. A dawdle right? They skelped our tentative arses. But first there's St Johnstone. No gimme. We barely squeak by them after extra time. Still we're on our way to the new Hampden and just so-so (Kipling?) Killie await.

The final is scheduled for March 19th. Dale and John are at us for Christmas. We're due to visit them in Luxembourg in March. What date was that party we couldn't possibly go to? Kyle's in Edinburgh doing his Masters in English. I know his mammie's missing him. Bunts ma and my dad ain't getting any younger. The wee Hibee numskull's starting to do the math for me!

So when, on one of her surfing expeditions through Travelocity or Expedia, Bunts pulls up cheap fares between Edinburgh and Frankfurt, she says;

"Is that Frankfurt no quite near you Dale?"

"Is it Frankfurt or Frankfurt Hahn?" asks Dale.

"Oh, eh, yeh, here it is; Frankfurt Hahn."

"That's only about an hour's drive from us—it's easy".

Perfect answer and Bunt's hits the buy-it-now button.

So we'll be in Scotland for just three days but should manage to squeeze in the big "Pairty" as well as the CIS Cup Final. Likesay, magic.

I then discover one small snag. Because of where I am in my "Green Card" process (on a temporary work permit pending a final-final approval) I have to carry what's called a "parole" document to get me back in should I travel outside the US borders. I got one of these with my initial application as a contingency for family emergencies. Fortunately I've not had to use it but it suddenly strikes me that there's an expiration to it. I whiz down to my desk in the basement and extract our "Immigration" file which is now thicker than the heal (I think our Glesga brethren call it an 'ootsider') of a plain Billsland loaf. I finally locate my Parole document and sure enough it has just expired. My stomach heaves when I read the fine print and discover that there is three months' notice recommended for renewal applications. I'm supposed to leave in about six weeks. Falkirking Shugar. (another avoid real sweary-word words expression)

Now unless you've had some direct experience dealing with the US Immigration and Naturalization Service (INS) you'd likely think—no matter—this is 21st century—America—you can no doubt pop-in to the local office, explain the oversight, make your apologies, pay a few extra bucks for accelerated expediting and you're on your way, right? Think again. The INS is a massive immovable bureaucracy which makes our old British Tax Office seem like a McDonalds drive thru' window. People get lost in their 'customer-friendly' phone system for longer than Robinson Crusoe was stranded on his desert island. But I still have to try because I'm desperate to make the party and see my laddie and eh, oh, aye … there's that fitba thing too.

So begins my latest nightmare that is the INS phone system abyss. They really do need to add an option along the lines of;

"Please press ninety nine if you are now crying like a baby or spitting green stuff like the possessed girl in the Exorcist and wish you had selected option twenty seven, fourteen menus ago. Please don't hang-up or you know what'll happen—back to the back of the line. We thank you for your patience and are recording your reactions for quality assurance purposes".

Of course pressing ninety nine would not solve your problem but it would play you forty five minutes of Vivaldi's Four Seasons so that you could get refreshed and calm for the next round of bitter frustration.

After multiple restarts and transfers and "brief" periods of holding I finally talk to someone who at least seems to understand my dilemma. I'm advised to go on line and make a "Speed pass" appointment at my local INS office in Merrifield, Virginia. I get the very encouraging steer that the process I need can be expedited within twenty four hours of that so no need to sweat. Hmm, sounds great but not very IRS-ish (as opposed to Irish who it seems can get US green cards within a week by filling in a simple one page form in pencil at the local newsagent in any small village in County Cork). I follow instructions and the computer offers me the first available Speed pass appointment which is only about two weeks from our proposed departure date. However there is no negotiation available with the INS computer. If you think Hal was a bit dictatorial in the first Alien movie you should try this guy. Hesitate for even a few seconds and you fall back another million places in line. So I hit the accept button and get a reference number with my very specific date and time and a list of a hundred things I could screw up on to instantly disqualify myself. But if I'm a very good boy I'll finally get to talk to a real human being in person. I'm good with people face to face. I've handled some very senior diplomats so I'm sure I can finesse a customs agent. I'll be just fine now.

The appointed day comes and I put on my best suit and tie and even polish my shoes. We were raised with the notion that, all other things being equal, respectful attire (or at least an obvious sincere attempt thereat) may provide a needed edge when competing with fellow customers for sympathy and approval, especially in dealing with battle-hardened civil service frontline counter staff. Complimented with appropriate pleases and thank-you's, I have found this parental guidance to be a generally reliable rule of thumb. Unfortunately, some of the INS staff I encountered over the years seemed to see me as no more than a big grey *foreign* blob of matter with a Social Security number (ironic as many of them were immigrants who, judging by their own limited spoken English skills, had lived here for a fraction of the time I had). On this critical day I've promised myself that I will remain calm at all times.

Having quadruple-checked my letter en route from the car park I get in line for Security check at the entrance to the Merrifield Office of the INS. I'm impressed with the initial impact of my Speed pass letter as, on reviewing it, the Guard directs me to the much smaller of two lines approaching a reception counter. I'm summoned forward within five minutes, show my letter, am given a ticket with a number and letter (C7) and am directed to a large waiting room which is not terribly busy. Along one side is a row of numbered counter booths. It's reminiscent of the newer Virginia Department of Motor Vehicles Offices with a sultry sounding female making announcements likesay;

"Now serving … customer D44 … at window number 10."

As always I'm immediately observing and over-evaluating every detail of what's going on and what influence it might have on the outcome of my own case. Which counter server do I want to get? The man on number 8 already looks pissed-off plus he's a baldy and they usually hate me because I've got lots of thick hair left. Definitely don't want him. Middle aged white woman on 5 just spotted me studying her and didn't like it all. Don't want her either. Older Black lady on 12 looks best bet. Hope I can't get her and follow some really nasty bastard so I can seem nice and polite and shake my head at how those people just treated her. "Tut-tut, terrible that ma'am—how're you doin' today" with my nicest smile.

Also see there are some A and B and D prefixed numbers. Why am I a "C"? Do they know I'm a Catholic? Was that on any of the forms? Now seven is usually a good number for me. It's my fitba number of choice since Kenny Dalglish supplanted Denis Law (10) as my idol. Of course neither of these will ever have Pat Stanton status but Paddy wore four and that's just too defensive a number for me!

Inevitably I get none of the above servers. I get a middle aged guy but thank Falkirk he's got plenty hair. He even greets me with a smile and correctly identifies my Scottish brogue after my first phrase which, based on my advanced strategy must not be;

"Geez ma fuckin green card now ye IRS git".

So I'm off to a good start. I ask him how much longer he thinks my green card proper might take and he taps on his keyboard for a few seconds then suddenly turns into the Little Britain transvestite Travel Agent;

"Computah says … don't know, can't give any more details, sowwy".

That's disappointing but the secondary issue at the moment. I keep on smilin' and ask what it takes to renew my Parole document. He says;

"No problem. Just get a form blah, blah, blah from the receptionist, go get a couple of passport photos and bring it all back to me later today and I'll put it in the system.

"They'll let me back in here okay?"

"Sure, just keep your speed pass letter handy and tell them you have a same day follow-up with me, Officer Blank, at counter number thirteen, here let me just write it on there." Yep, thirteen, I sorta skimmed passed that didn't I? Always despised that number. In fitba it meant second reserve, get your arse on the bench son, ugh. So I know what you're thinking—INS and thirteen—fogetabatit!

Back I tappy-lap (walk with no particular urgency—this is a Geordie (Newcastle) one which I picked up from Steve Shear and have always liked) to the receptionist. She asks what I'm after. I explain and she tells me in very authoritative and convincing fashion that I'll get my parole document much quicker if I go straight home and do it on line as they'll use my existing photo from their system. Excellent. I rush home and do just that. It all seems to go very smoothly. Problem is, a few days later I get my acknowledgement saying that I'll receive my parole document within ninety days! I immediately get back on line and make another Speed pass appointment and this time I get one less than a week before we're due to leave. Based on some further telephone advice I also express mail a letter explaining my problem to one of the many INS addresses, this one's somewhere in New Hampshire. Day before my next speed pass appointment my letter comes back telling me I should have sent it to Merrifield, Virginia. When I eventually get to this appointment and explain all I've been through the guy tells me I should have come in much sooner even WITHOUT an appointment. This is something which totally contradicts everything I'd been told about the system to that point. Major migraine.

I'm offered the option of paying extra to have my parole document expedited urgently. Why the hell didn't somebody offer me that option previously? Of course I do so but the guy says it may still take three days to arrive at my house. And I only have two. And so it is that we two pathetic souls are sat on our packed suitcases all ready to travel watching the street for a Fed-ex or UPS truck. We're like two kids looking at the sky for Santa and when he doesn't show we act just about the same as two kids would in those circumstances, the only difference being that we then proceed to get seriously sloshed on Californian merlot.

We cancel our flights and rebook at extortionate extra cost. As a precaution we allow three extra days for the magic envelope's arrival. Our trip is now going to be as condensed as a tin of Campbell's cream of tomato.

I decide to make another pilgrimage to INS Mecca. I've decided to just try begging and weeping openly at the INS counter and see if it might have any impact. I get through security and am second in line for the receptionist when my cell phone rings. It's supposed to be off but I manage a quick exchange with Bunts before I get the dirty look and lecture from the guard. She's just yelling "It's here, it's here".

So just one day saved in amongst all the above crap and we would have been OK. I need a holiday.

So it's finally set that I'll be heading out on Sunday, March 11th 2007, to Hampden Park to see my beloved Hibees. Of course the game's not until the next again Sunday but due to having to grab whatever we could I now have to go to Glasgow via Washington, Dulles—Chicago, O'Hare—Paris, Charles de Gaule—Metro to Paris, Guard de Nord, Rail France to Luxembourg—Dale's Car to Frankfurt—Ryan Air to Prestwick—Hertz rent-a-car to Edinburgh … then back to Glasgow. If that's not dedication to ones fitba team what is? Oh, and by the way—I don't even have a ticket for the match!

Short version on that. Brother John offered to buy tickets early doors but as I was never absolutely sure about my bloody parole situation I'd told him to hold off. Anyway I had faith that one of my many good old fitba contacts would get us tickets. How was I to know that 40,000 Hibees would be chasing tickets. Where are all these people when we're playing St Mirren in the pissing rain in a November league game?

So all my obvious ticket avenues have closed; except for one.

They're selling off a batch of "returns" via the Hibs club ticket office in person, via internet and by special phone line all on a first come first served basis at 9 a.m. on a specified Sunday morning in early March. Rumors of the quantity available range from 1200 to 6000 tickets. Though I still don't have Parole at that point I've decided just to buy a couple of tickets and take my chances. Of course that is 9 a.m. in Scotland which is 4 a.m. for me in Arlington, Virginia. I've set my alarm for an ungodly 3:30 rise and am set up at my computer already in the Hibs web site by 3:45 a.m. I also have a phone stuck between my hunched left shoulder and ear. As a contingency, I have my son and his girlfriend sat by their cell phones in Edinburgh. One will constantly call the hotline and the other will keep me informed of progress. I have on my lucky, silky, shiny emerald home top. The last one before the sponsors' logos took over our breasts!

At about 4:01a.m. I hit the button to enter the "virtual" waiting line to buy tickets. I have one of those horrible blue bars at the foot of the screen which show how you're doing. It's typically excruciatingly slow and makes me feel a bit constipated. But it is moving and after about ten minutes I am given access to the oracle. All I have to do is place my order—they don't like my AMEX card but that's okay, I've got Bunty's VISA handy too. I tap in all the necessary detail then it asks me to confirm my Hibs Account Number …

What the F …? What account number? A've no goat a F**kin account number. Oh no.

But wait, there's an option to set one up. Quick dae it. But as I go to that screen and confirm my new account number I'm bumped back into the line with the F**kin blue bar again. Home Alone style aaaaaaaaaaaah!

Call son's girlfriend, Mary-Ann.

"How you doin' hen?"

"Struggling to get through Mr Meikle—obviously very busy." Notice she still calls me Mister Meikle—I like that. Good manners those Southern Virginia girls have. By the way, she lives right next to the real Walton's Mountain, gen-up (another Scottishism for true).

"Listen hen, if he gets through just tell him to buy any tickets they've got. I was in but needed an account number so I'm back in blue bar purgatory."

I finally get back in after about another fifteen minute wait. Try every category, try for even a single ticket but now everything showing simply; "Not available". Aaaaaaaaaaaaaaaaaaaaaaahagain.

Phone Mary-Ann back and it's more bad news. Kyle's getting a recorded message to say all tickets sold.

That's it. Around half an hour and it's all over. No ticket for Jimmy.

And that was the short version. Gen-up.

Our now very squished trip was indeed at a hectic pace but we managed to hit our main Paris objectives including the successful search for the graves of Jim Morrison, Edith Piaf and Oscar Wilde in a sprawling cemetery somewhere in Paris. This probably sounds a bit weird but they really do have some very 'cool' tombs there. Also made the Musee d'orsay with perhaps the finest collection of impressionist paintings in the world. Pure dead brilliant to steal yet another very Glesga expression of approval.

We get the whistle stop tour of Luxembourg and I'm even brave enough to drive Dale's Left Hand drive stick shift Audi to Germany to visit the fabulous ancient little town of Trier. Other than coming out of a parking lot via the entry ramp and acting like an alien trying to work out the procedure at a German petrol station, I do damn well with this car.

We're not even attempting to do the family visiting thing though I do manage a quick stop at my Auntie Mary's in the Westfield flats. My dad's like the rain on the plain. He's in Spain again. Loves it there though he avoids the plain and sticks to the Costa-del-various-cheap-packages. All something to do with the sun coming out more often than it does in Drylaw apparently.

Alexander McCall-Smith's the latest Scots author to make it stateside and his books are going around the school where Bunts works so we do a once-around the Edinburgh new town to get a few snaps to show her pals. This includes a (very nice) pint at the Cumberland Bar, a lunch at Valvona and Crolla at 19 Elm Row and a photo of the last stair in Scotland street, number 44, to prove that number 44 ½ is indeed the fictitious invention of the aforementioned Mr McCall.

Friday afternoon Kyle and I take a quick run down to Easter Road to visit Stuart Crowther, Hibs' Media Director. I've been corresponding with him and he's agreed to take a browse at my manuscript and see if he might be able to point me towards a suitable Scottish publisher. We go to the ticket office counter and are directed upstairs to the Media offices. Stuart gives us a warm welcome despite clearly being up to his ears in CIS cup final stuff. He's a Pilton boy too and we wax lyrical and nostalgic over some old Pilton Sporting Club memories. Turns out the lad I got in trouble with as a kid at Pennywell is one of his in-laws! I present him one of my HIBS FC genuine Virginia DMV license plates and he places it on a shelf beside some other precious club memorabilia. I salvaged the plates when one of my car's was written off in a crash. Gordon Burden has the other in return for a framed, signed first team strip he won in an auction and sent over to me. Of course I did get a replacement pair for my latest car.

I thank him for his time and head for the club shop. I'm proud that I resist the temptation to beg for a cup final ticket—that would just be too forward. I pick up a bunch of CIS cup final tee shirts (including one for Eddie K of course) and a 1979 vintage cup final shirt. I'm very embarrassed when the boy at the counter explains they don't take Amex! For once Kyle has to bail me out with his Visa card. Talk about role reversal.

That evening Mark and Margaret's 50th works out great. It's at the Wester Hailes Community Centre function rooms. The Trainspotting-famed area's still a bit dodgy but we get a taxi right to the door so don't have to worry about car tires disappearing. We cut through the bar and snooker room en-route to the party room and I take considerable stick from the locals for my "Cowboy" hat. I'm so used to it now I forget such attire may be a bit unusual in the Edinburgh schemes.

We get a special introduction as "all the way from America" and Mark and Margaret seem genuinely surprised and touched to see us. We have brief celebrity status but you have to be cautious with that stuff and get the balance just right. The dreaded drink can change perceptions rapidly and so, some local might start the night along the very friendly lines of;

"You fae America, that's barry. What's it really like thair? A'd love tae go"

The exact same Scotsman, six pints and two Grouse nips later;

"You the c**t fae America. Aye think yer f**kin barry, ae? Better watch yersel".

So we mingle with suitable modesty and put emphasis on the fact that we've not lost our accents and we manage to avoid the steamin' local boy bi-polar syndrome.

They've got a good old fashioned Disco going and the place is hopping. One odd but very consistent thing I've found about the DJ's in Scotland versus those in America is that the Scots ones were much better at maintaining momentum once they'd got it. Most disco's I've been to over here the DJ's silence the hall by sticking rigidly to their pre-arranged play list or via ego's which make them think they know best. How difficult is it to work out that a well inebriated crowd who have just totally enjoyed making complete fools of themselves to successive "Twists" (The … and Let's … again) do not want a piece of rap crap, albeit the very latest, to kill the buzz?

About an hour into the party, four semi-gatecrashers (we had mentioned this possibility to Mark's wife and she was cool with it) show up in the form of Brother John and Julie and Gordon and Aggie Burdens (ex Mr & Mrs Niddrie—now Clerry socialites). We don't have enough time to do a Clerry or Burntisland social detour so they've stopped in to say a quick "hiya". Before you know it Aggie and Julie are bouncing around the dance floor, Gordon's got a sausage roll in one hand and a salmon paste sandwich in the other (traditional Scottish self-catering party fare) using them as props to tell his latest joke and John is settled with his left elbow on the bar beckoning me towards him and grinning like a Cheshire cat. In his weird Marty Feldman-in-a-tight-elf-costume voice;

"Guess what a've goat in ma poa … kit?"

Of course I think I know but is it? Is it? Could it be?

Yes. From a friend of a friend of Rab Haldane (thanks so much Rab) John has scored me a ticket to the match and at mere face value (I had set no limit on what I would be paying a scalper at the ground had that become necessary).

YESSSSSSSSSS! Yaaa beauty.

I'm running around telling anybody who'll listen. I remind myself of wee Charlie boy when he snagged the last Wonka ticket. This only enhances the joy of what was a very special night out. Happy 50th Mark and Mags.

Sunday morning is Mothers' Day and I'm up early and headed down to Seafield Cemetry to visit my own Ma. I go down Easter Road and the crowds are already gathering in little pockets of Green and White outside the pubs, awaiting their Hampden bound transports. The number of women and bairns is really noticeable if I compare it to 1968 or 1972. I stop off at the Florist opposite what I knew as Leith Academy and pick up a nice bunch of flowers. As I drive along the side of a deserted Leith Links, a couple of ghostly fitba highlights run through my head. I can see and hear everything vividly. Firstly an embarrassing sending off (for a stupid, futile, mouthing off) by Blair Welsh in front of a really decent summer cup final crowd against Salvesen. Second, releasing Joe Morgan with a perfectly weighted, defense splitting pass for him to crush a winner in a Sunday Churches Cup final against the dreaded Carrick Knowe. I try to quell the first one and savor the latter. The numskulls co-operate and I even turn to glance the other way and see Joe's house where we celebrated after the match.

When I snap back to consciousness I wonder how the hell I didn't crash whilst I was so deeply engulfed in my imagination yet operating a moving vehicle. You must have done that sometime? Especially when you're driving alone, cruising a relatively quiet stretch of motorway (interstate). You know how you just finish a vivid thought and then wonder who was steering the car whilst you were away.

I reach the grand and decorative Victorian black wrought iron gates with the customary pointy bits at the top. They're chained shut. I give a thought to a climb-over. Back in the Pilton day I'd have hopped over (or even through) these in a jiffy but suddenly it's forty years on and my fifty year old ass isn't quite as spry! The sign confirms the gates won't open until noon but I need to be on my way to Hampden long before then. The guilts are back but then I think what would my ma say?

"Away tae the game pal, might even stop by Hampden masel tae see how your doin'—I know the thought was there and that's what counts"

Selfless reaction. Just like when she pretended to be over the moon when I got her the People's Friend annual for her Christmas.

And so my mother-in-law gets double flowers for Mothers day.

Kyle and Mary-Ann are coming through to Glasgow with us as they know the centre well and will act as Bunty's guide for some shopping and tea and scones at one of the old/new shoppes popularized and tourist-exploited by the Charles Rennie Macintosh connections. The journey starts to set the tone. As we hit the Maybury area, the fitba traffic is incredible with a constant convoy of busses and cars decked out in Green and White. Scarfs, secured by tightly shut windows, are flapping hard in the air stream like the flags on a windy day at the old course in St Andrews. Excited, expectant, hopeful faces leave smudgy nose and smiley lip marks on steamy windows. Horns are blaring and thumbs are being raised all around. It's a Wagon Train West except it's in search of Silver rather than Gold.

We park off Sauchiehall Street and I'm quickly headed to Glasgow Central. I get my ticket to Mount Florida and have plenty time to nip into the station bar for a quick beer. After being queue-skipped by many people and subsequently reminded at how pathetic I am at Scottish pub ordering assertiveness, I go for the

Caffrey's. Since I am so bad at the ordering part I get a pint and a half to save me fighting through the crowd a second time. Mostly Killie in here and in fairly optimistic mood themselves judging from the banter. I get snug in a corner by the window and absorb all the usual pre-final verbage and statistics from the newspapers. The beer is great and the crisps (one packet each; salt'n'vinegar and prawn cocktail) are the perfect compliment. A pint and a half is just right for giving me that comfortable warm fuzzy feeling which can enhance the intake of my surrounds without impairing the experience.

As I walk across the station to board the train the balance of power has shifted considerably and there is much more Hibby green than Killie Blue roaming the Hampden bound platform. My early memories of Hampden Park are of trekking through endless streets lined with very small houses with very small gardens, always uphill and always heading towards the floodlights. The immediate surrounds seem very different this time. I'm sure it's all improved with much more paving and much less mushy reddish brown mud and yet there's something a little disappointing and antiseptic about it! I'm constantly struck by the number of female fans. Inside the stadium is also so different from the one I remember. Everything is clean and organized and compact but it just strikes me as small compared to that behemoth which rocked 134,000 plus.

I first pick out the wrong spot and get embarrassed when someone arrives and points out that an extra letter on my ticket pushes me much further down the terracing! I settle in my correct spot just a few rows from the field and am barely undercover and we'd see rain, sleet and snow before the day was out. Within five minutes I remember why we liked the pies and Bovril so much. Despite all my reservations over all the changes, when the end I'm in fills completely with green and white and this spreads around approximately two-thirds of the entire ground the atmosphere is intense. The seating is superfluous today—nobody will be sitting down. I'm feeling the kind of hair-up-on-the-back-of-the-neck excitement which is quite a rarity nowadays.

On a very rare occasion a fitba script might go exactly the way you dream it the night before. This is that day. Following fairly even skirmishes at both ends big Rob Jones climbs above the crowd to head home a corner and once in the lead, even always-find-some-daft-wee-thing-to-fret-about me, feels a confidence that it's definitely going to be okay. The second half reminds me of one of those fabulous old European nights down our slope. No slope here of course but we go through one of those rampant flurries where it seems everything we touch goes right. Result: Kilmarnock 1 Hibernian 5. I celebrated each goal enthusiastically, spontaneously squealing, bouncing like a pogo stick and hugging guys I'd never met before and would likely never see again.

I honestly thought that the "Sunshine on Leith" chorus at the end of my last derby game could never be topped but it was unequivocally outdone here with somewhere in the region of 35,000 blasting out several consecutive Proclaimers' hits as Hibs hoisted the trophy then dived and slid around the wet field like a bunch of playful otters as we savored every silly moment. Eutopia? Not quite but that would follow shortly.

As I went to leave the ground I got stuck in several people jams and so diverted sporadically several times exiting at a totally random part of the main concourse. Just as I went to walk out the gate some movement to my left caught my eye. The last few people from the wheelchair area were getting ready to leave. One wheelchair with occupant, an adult and two kids, just silhouettes against the grey sky from the angle I was looking. As they swiveled I thought I recognized the profile of the face of the man in the chair but it couldn't possibly be. He was far too sick to even think of being here. I took a few steps towards the group and immediately recognized the distinctive round smile of the man pushing the chair; my cousin Bruce Miller. And in the chair: my Uncle James, a stroke victim whom I didn't think in a million years would or even could be here.

I probably hurt him as I hugged him so hard and unhesitatingly kissed him on the head several times but he didn't complain and, though he couldn't say it in words his eyes clearly told me that the feeling was absolutely mutual. Through uncontrollable dripping tears I blurted out to his grandson; Kyle and friend how this was the man who took me to my first game (Barcelona—chapter?) and who gave me the forty some year old scarf I had wrapped around my neck. A truly magical moment which I will never forget and the wonders of modern technology via his nifty cell phone enabled Bruce to capture it in a picture. I was still shaking with adrenalin as I left them and thought again of how my day had begun. My uncle James looks just like my ma and I couldn't help but wonder if she had a wee role in the alignment of the stars that particular day.

Leaving the ground I passed another face in the crowd which I felt sure I knew. (Did I mention I once sat beside Martin Sheen in church?) So many times that happens and so as not to risk a redder we say nothing then later regret never finding out if it was really whom we thought! I'm on a roll today so I just shout "Kevin". The immediate reaction tells me I'm right. Yesssss, another win. It was indeed Kevin McColl, a former schoolmate and teammate I hadn't seen in over thirty years. He was searching for his own dad who had become separated in the crush but we still found a few precious minutes to catch-up. I was so glad I spoke up. Cheers Kevin, great to see you, hope you found your old man.

The voices were all starting to croak a bit as we were herded into a long line awaiting re-entry to Mount Florida (why Florida I wonder?) station. To their credit Glasgow's finest were well on top of things and the line moved quickly courtesy of several well timed extra trains. As I made the walk back from Central to Queen Street I recalled doing this many times at what now seems far too young an age. Myself, Mongo, Deek and Big Tam—a bunch of raw eight to ten year olds, turning up in Glasgow with little cash, no pre-set plan or directions. Parkhead, Hampden and Ibrox were always easy—just follow the crowds—but we also somehow managed to navigate back and forth to the likes of Shawfield (which Clyde FC shared with the greyhound racing) and Firhill (home of the Jags better known universally as Partick Thistle). I recall a terrifying experience we had returning from a Scottish cup tie against Partick whilst waiting at one of the Glasgow stations. Through unfortunate timing we ended up on the same platform as an incoming train from Falkirk where Rangers also had just played a cup tie. The "Brickton Derry" announced their arrival in song and were immediately surprised to see a bunch of green clad youngsters. As the howling, scowling Blue mass approached we managed to lock ourselves inside one of those fully glazed waiting rooms. I still don't know how the glass held up to the thumping fists as they passed on both sides, mostly in threatening jest I think but I'm glad we didn't have to find out.

I've to meet Bunty, Kyle and Mary Ann in a pub called Waxy O'Connor's. Not that easy as it's a weird multi-leveled maze-like lay out and reminds of the scene at the end of one of the Star Wars movies where all the Ewoks are partying on roped bridges! When I finally find them we resolve to have one quick celebratory drink before we head to Prestwick Airport and they catch the train back to Edinburgh. The tears once again drip involuntarily as I recount my meeting with Uncle James.

Prestwick transpires to be further than I thought and we end up racing time for our Ryan flight back to Frankfurt Hahn. We then learn why they're so cheap. Two minutes over the projected closing time and the hard hearted man at the counter simply says sorry—tough luck! I'm sure the bastard was a disgruntled Killie fan who saw my scarf. We eventually find a young "Ryan" lady who's much more sympathetic and helps us rebook a flight to Paris early next morning. Well it's sort of Paris (Le Sticks might be the appropriate term) and takes a very long ride in a coach to actually get to the city. Still we recover our original itinerary and the only side effects are an aborted drive to Hahn (sorry John) and us leaving a few of our clothes and souvenirs behind in Luxembourg for a while.

And so it was that I finally got to be there to see my team lift a cup again at Hampden. A mere thirty five years after the glorious Stanton game. Well worth the wait and well worth all the hassle which preceded and permeated through the trip.

POSTSCRIPT 2008

So finally I start getting ready to try to publish this thing blissfully unaware that self-editing is a long and grueling process; much less fun than writing down the story in the first place (must be great for real authors who get all that done for them). In fact it took me so long to edit that I already have quite a few updates for you.

See I had really hoped to finish the book with a second trip back to see my beloved Hibs finally break the hundred-plus year hoodoo in the Scottish Cup. All we had to do was beat a game but very pedestrian Dunfermline side. A racing certainty. Then it's Celtic in the final. Another dawdle (easy). Collins has got us playing Celtic and Rangers with a confidence we haven't seen since Turnbull's Tornadoes. We're beating both of them more often than not, even in Glasgow! So what happened? Oh, eh, lost 0-1 to a late Dunfermline penalty in a midweek replay in front of a few thousand die hards. I figure tens of thousands more were saving their cash for the final or still skint from the first game; a 0-0 draw which, of course, we should have won comfortably. Who won the final? Who cares!

Scotland will surely make me feel better. They've beaten France twice. The second win in Paris is relayed to me by Dale on my mobile as I chauffeur Bunty to her Jazz singing gig in Annapolis. Dale sticks the phone out her wee Montmartre attic flat window to let us hear the Tartan Army celebrating outside the Moulin Rouge. God only knows what all those men in kilts might do there later that night (I'm thinking; Full Monty can, can?). So we're getting psyched for EURO 2008 in Austria/Switzerland who beat us out to host it (I'll need to wax my skis, borrow John Harris III's Disneyworld lederhosen and buy a packet of Ricola's). But wait. We lose to Georgia (the country not the state) 0-2. How can we beat France twice then lose to F**kin Georgia? Because we are Scotland. We'll forgive them by game one of the next campaign. That's a sure thing.

On the playing front there's bad news, good news, more good news and a wee bit more bad news.

The bad news is that Danny's team (now called Royal Mile after a pub in Wheaton, Maryland) has folded. The normally sensible schedulers have inexplicably given us (remember; over forty five year olds) back-to-back fixtures on Sunday afternoon and Monday night. Most of us are too old to cope with that so it ends up on the Monday night with Danny cobbling together a team including some really flagrant ringers (twenty year old Peruvian kids do tend to stand out on a "British" old farts' team). We're playing "Old Red" who are mostly Jamaicans and in the running for the title but our youngsters enable us to upset them 3-2. They are incensed and for the first time in the overage stuff we face a formal protest. The league finds in Old Red's favor and we end up with much less than a full squad after we have several guys banned for the rest of the season. The league makes us take people from their "waiting list". Yes, they really do have a list of over forty five year old players waiting to join any team who'll tak'em (only in America as the saying goes).

They are all keen as mustard. Problem is they are mostly hapless. Two have reached this age without ever having kicked a ball! I've always prided myself as having much more patience and tolerance as I got older myself but this is extreme. I'm thinking what home truths Ged might be screaming to these guys. He was never famous for patience with inept teammates. Every team is running up cricket scores on us.

It reaches critical mass when we fall about nine goals behind Murray Grant's Rangers. Even at his very sedentary pace, Murray's left one of our novices in his wake! Eddie Koebke and Bournemouth Nick Grimes are so embarrassed they're continually apologizing to me during play. Pierre even gives me the up stretched palms, pursed lips shoulder shrug after hitting a cracking goal from about forty yards. He's saying, likesay; quelle qui c'est Jacques d'ecosse (I love that nickname) I'm zuppose to stop tryeeng? I storm off before the end in a very juvenile tantrum. Yeh, I know; big bloody bairn. Danny's pretty pissed off himself and so Royal Mile is put in mothballs for a season. Pity as there were a couple of really decent players left including Robin; a very accomplished sweeper despite being a diplomat and a Clyde supporter (now there's a rare combo). I'd miss playing with him. I'd also miss playing with big Erik (Pages) the Dane, a tireless player, ex-Dickinson College, Pennsylvania. As he approaches his own half-century he still goes back annually to play for the alumni against each year's new side, even scored a goal against the kids this year. Probably stems from his European genes but Erik really *gets* the game. If we need a goal, he urges me to stay forward and more often than not delivers me the ball I need tight to my feet.

The good news is that Danny will have Royal Mile back up and running shortly and they'll even win their division play-offs sans big bairn. Well done Danny.

The more good news is that I've just clinched another piece of silverware at the fabulous field number 24 of the Germantown Soccerplex in Maryland. This is the first division (there's no "Premier" at over forty five—thank god you're thinking) and we've outlasted arch rival Saints in the final. I've got my bottle (testicles) so I've gone first and this penalty spot's at the proper twelve yard distance so my usual process has worked perfectly with the goalie chucking himself to his left as my smooth side footer sneaks just inside the opposite post. Oor Bob Wilson's made a couple of great saves so Eddie clinches it with a cool top right corner blast. Pierre doesn't even have to take the fifth kick though we know he'd have scored. He only misses in Vegas!

I need this new trophy as my collection has taken a beating recently. My niece Libby Sheehan who lives a block away comes over daily as she's fascinated by my new half size snooker table. She's competitive and proposes she chooses one of my trophies each time she beats me. She's motivated and well co-ordinated and is beating me enough to clear my hardware shelf! She is using the trophies to fill the void left in her room when Harry-Fred her Russian tortoise done a runner into the wilds of Virginia and his monster sized enclosure was relegated to the carport.

So what's the wee bit more bad news Jamsie boy? Well haven't you guessed who I play for now? Yup … Rangers! I know. Me, Colin Stein, Kenny Miller, Ian Murray all traitors (still at least me and Colin started regularly). Stop peeing yourself in your comfy villa in Cyprus Uncle David. C'mon, give me a break, please. I still need to play. Anywhere, anytime. Fitba daft at five years old and still fitba daft at fifty. Lucky man.

So I ask our Murray; American born and raised Doctor, still playing a few minutes at eighty years old—that's special; "Why Rangers Murray?"

He blinks and hesitates a couple times, as he often does now;

"Simple Jim, when I got interested in soccer, Glasgow Rangers was the best team in the world." Can you believe a good pape (catholic) boy is admitting this? See; still not a bigot. I think Murray's headed for that Guinness book of thingies.

By the way, tough though it is for me I do have to give the dreaded INS some credit. Each time I visit they become a little more human, a little more thoughtful on how their system impacts the masses. Like me, they are still imperfect and in need of improvement but seem headed the right way. I'll just keep going to Perpetual Adoration (church on whatever terms you choose) and hopefully the IRS will pay attention to feedback, even from those who already speak English.

It's early Tuesday night and I'm just about to get off the computer, I think I've finally finished this thing. Hooray. The phone rings in the empty nest (which we both love but please don't tell our kids).

"Sure hold on please" says Bunts, "Bruce for you."

"Hi Bruce, what's up?"

"Eleven thirty wow. Okay I'll try to stay awake."

Put the phone down.

"Eh Bunt's, Bruce is struggling for a team for their game at Dulles indoor the night."

"Nae wonder, auld men playin' fitba at that ridiculous time of night. Well? Are you going?"

Likesay; whoosh.

978-0-595-49612-9
0-595-49612-1

Printed in Great Britain
by Amazon